# THE ENGLISH COUNTIES

*Illustrated*

FINCHINGFIELD, ESSEX

# THE ENGLISH COUNTIES

## *Illustrated*

ADVISORY EDITOR: C. E. M. JOAD

*NEW EDITION*

REVISED BY B. WEBSTER SMITH

*With nearly three hundred half tone illustrations and more than one hundred specially prepared maps and drawings*

W. W. NORTON & COMPANY, INC. · NEW YORK

# CONTENTS

## MIDLAND COUNTIES *cont.*

## NORTHERN COUNTIES

*The head and tail piece illustrations have been specially drawn for this book by Lindley Searle, E. Wigglesworth and W. Savage. The Pictorial County maps have been prepared by F. D. Blake.*

In the Lake District: a view across Ullswater.

# INTRODUCTION

THIS IS a book about both the people and the counties of England, since it is designed to present the people in the setting of their counties. Hence, county by county, it touches on the ways of life, the industries, the occupations and pleasures of the men and women who dwell therein. Hence, too, though it is primarily concerned with geography, with mountains and rivers and fields and woods, it has in it something also of geology and history, makes its bow to anthropology and does not disdain economics. For it is about the towns that men have made no less than about nature and their love of it. (Even so, this must be but a partial Introduction, for I do not like towns and have little to say about them. I can never wholly rid myself of the belief that as our countryside is the loveliest in the world, so our towns—that is to say our post-industrial-revolution towns—are the ugliest.)

Inevitably, this is a book of patriotism and praise; for who that writes of the English counties can refrain from praising them and expressing his pride in what he praises? In this particular department there is little enough left for the introducer, who when he sets out to praise England finds that the authors have done his job for him with a far greater particularity of loving knowledge than he could have brought to the task. Indeed, the keenness of the partisanship which the various counties evoke is one of the most remarkable features of the work of those who have contributed to this volume. Oxfordshire farmers are unusually intelligent and up to date and diffuse a "sense of serene well-being"; Hampshire men are extolled; nobody, we are assured, commits crimes in Rutlandshire; the Lakeland dalesmen are proud and strong and have a rough speech; the purest English is spoken in Lichfield; while Yorkshiremen, inevitably, are the finest of the lot.

It is rarely that a writer permits himself a word of criticism, as when J. Wentworth Day comments on the "excessively ugly cottages and small farmhouses . . . square, grim

boxes, with their square windows, whose draped lace curtains hide unbelievable aspidistras and dreadful, shiny 'suites'," in which live the rich farmers of the Lincolnshire fens, and even permits himself to avow that the Lincolnshire people are "uncompromising, dour in parts," "ugly in patches," while Gillian Price, writing of Staffordshire, concedes herself the indulgence of the masterly understatement that the Black Country "is not a pleasant place to live in." But such passages are rare.

Not to present his county as a thing of beauty and a source of pride, would, indeed, seem to argue a certain disloyalty in the writer. All this, no doubt, is very much as it should be; but it is hard on the introducer who finds all the winds of praise taken out of his sails. What new thing, then, am I to find to say about the counties of England?

I can remind you of the extreme variety of the English scene, a variety which is exhibited not only by the country as a whole, but by nearly every county in it. Rutlandshire is uniform "pastoral scenery," to quote J. Wentworth Day, of "hill and vale, of great woodlands and broad shining valleys," and so, within its limits, is Bedfordshire. But, apart from these, there is scarcely a county which does not exhibit startling changes of scene, of people and of occupation, from Buckinghamshire with its four parts (so carefully distinguished by Martin Halliwell) of the Thames Valley, the Chiltern Hills, the plain of Aylesbury and the valley of the Ouse, through Devon with its three parts, the high and comparatively infertile north, the rich, fat, red-earthed south and the forest of Dartmoor, to Yorkshire, with its three Ridings, each so different from the other two.

Or I can write of the changes that have come to these same counties in the last half-century; of the invasion of the Thames Valley in Buckinghamshire by commuters and light industries, of the tourist industry in Devon which, spreading first along the south and then along the north coasts, now

A view of Colne, Lancashire. Here was once a country lane barred by a squeeze gate. This picture conveys more clearly than words what 19th century industrialism did to the English countryside.

sends its chars-à-banc and plants its guest houses in Dartmoor and has, Jack Simmons tells us, within the last half century been "putting the county's economy on a new basis." And though, to read Sidney Dark, you would still think us living in the hearty London of Sam Weller and Mr. Micawber, I could speak of the changes that have come to the county of London itself, and tell, in particular, how the last war turned London into a nerve-racked, irritable city. Yet even here generalization is unsafe, for Rutlandshire, we are told, has been affected to a remarkably small extent by a series of revolutions which, during the last one hundred and fifty years, have changed the English scene more rapidly and more radically than those of the preceding two thousand; so, too, S. B. P. Mais tells us, have the villages of the Oxfordshire Chilterns; and so, if we are to believe Sir William Beach Thomas—I put it thus because of how few of us, to our shame, can it be said that we know that delectable county?—has Huntingdonshire.

Or I could develop a private division of my own, the division that runs between the England east of a diagonal line drawn from Newcastle to Portsmouth and the England that lies west of it. To the east is the England that braces. It stands in the intellectual sphere, for theological heresy and moral controversy, for mathematics and metaphysical poetry and for physical science; in the political, for radicalism, reformism and sturdy individualism; in the æsthetic, for clear, pale blue skies, the sky here being often the main feature. It is lit with a bright gay light and pretty well all the great landscape painters who have celebrated the beauty of England from Constable to Cotman and Crome are from the east of the line. In matters of the body, this half of England stands for dry skins, bright eyes and great gales of physical energy; the general attitude of its people is common sense, realistic and matter-of-fact; they stand no nonsense, and, in particular, no snobbish nonsense, about kings, priests, nobles and what not.

When Adam delved and Eve span
Who was then a gentleman?

The question would not have occurred to Englishmen living west of the line.

# INTRODUCTION

Metaphysically, the Easterners tend to the view—and this in spite of their admirable metaphysical poetry—that there is only one order of reality, the natural order, and as a matter of common prudence they hold that we had better make the best and the most of it, and not go a-whoring after mystical will-o'-the-wisps. It will be seen that Cambridge falls very clearly on the eastern side of the line.

On the west is mysticism. The world is not all of a piece nor is there only one level of reality; what is more, unseen things lie very near to the surface of the familiar world. Here are pomp and pageantry and colour, a care for externals and a feeling for rank. It is no accident, by the way, that the Oxford Movement with its contemporary progeny, Anglo-Catholicism, should have come from the west. In spite of the painters, there is in the west, a greater feeling for beauty, especially natural beauty—our nature poetry, though, comes pretty equally from both—and above all, for music. West of the line are idling, day-dreaming, brooding and mooning; the passions are disposed to sultriness; at least they are as sultry as they ever manage to be among the English. *Accidie*, the noonday demon, which attacks us about three o'clock in the afternoon, especially after a good lunch, and takes all the colour and savour out of things, whispering into our ears that nothing is worth doing or trying or saying or thinking—*accidie* lurks mostly west of the line. The only ways of dealing with the demon are to take exercise or go to sleep. This has long been known at Oxford. Here are softness of scene and water, with, as a result, a quick and abundant lather, and a general relaxation and loosening of the fibres. Nothing is taut, trim, flat, obvious, but there are overtones and undertones, half lights and hidden depths. Here are Anglicanism, port-lovers, woman-haters, royalists and Jacobites.

The colours of the eastern half of England are light—light browns and pale blues

**In contrast with Colne is Ashwell, Hertfordshire, unchanged by the passing years. Its old cottages, built by village craftsmen from local materials, are an essential part of the English country scene.**

and greens (one thinks of the colour of the old carriages and engines of the Great Northern and Great Eastern Railways). In the western half, the characteristic colours are darker, purples and yellows and deep velvety browns. And if you tell me that you do not know what I am talking about, I challenge the Londoner who takes a train from Paddington or Waterloo on a Saturday afternoon and arrives in the evening in Surrey or Sussex or Wiltshire or Dorset or Devon or Cornwall—above all in Devon or Cornwall—to deny that in the evening he finds himself a different person, lazier, stupider, sleepier, but also kindlier and more serene. And did I hear you say that Surrey and Sussex are to the east of the line and that I contradict myself? Well, then, as Walt Whitman said, I contradict myself; you cannot, after all, expect all generalizations about England to be watertight.

### Four Layers

But perhaps you would prefer to be led to a safer and more familiar territory, by a division of the counties of England into layers. Of these there are four; the country England; the England of the pre-industrial-revolution towns; the England of the towns of the post-industrial-revolution, and the England which was brought into being about the beginning of this century by the second industrial revolution, the revolution in transport, the England, in fact, of the Great West Road, lined by its industries, of the dormitory towns and the great spreading suburbs. Now the history of the English counties this last hundred years or so has been the history of the encroachment of the third and fourth Englands, and especially the fourth, upon the first and second. The effects of this encroachment—they are well described by I. O. Evans in his chapter on the coming of mining to Monmouthshire—are an ever-spreading ugliness which no familiarity can stale and to which the photograph I reproduce on page eight bears melancholy witness.

### Geographical Grouping

Before I say any more about these four Englands, I should warn you that the foregoing is strictly irrelevant; for I have not used those four divisions or any variant of them as a basis for grouping the articles on the individual counties. For this purpose I have used five simple and geographical groupings. What these are can be seen from the contents page and from the admirable map of England divided into its counties, on the opposite page. Having said so much in acknowledgment to myself of my capacity of editor, I propose to continue to develop my concept of the four Englands.

The first England has been often described. We English have had, I think, a greater love for it than any other people has had for its countryside, and it has evoked the loveliest and most abundant nature poetry of any countryside in the world. Who, then, am I that I should praise with my thin and donnish pen what a long line of superb nature writers stretching from Richard Jefferies to W. H. Hudson and from Gilbert White through Cobbett to Thomas Hardy, have so lovingly and so nobly celebrated? Let me, then, content myself with a bald enumeration of those characteristics traditionally associated with the English countryside, of softness of atmosphere, haziness of outline, gentleness of contour, thatched cottages, deep meadows and slow streams, the whole in miniature, so that every quarter of a mile yields a fresh outlook and a new view.

### Melancholy Reflections

To the threat which to-day hangs over this England many of the writers in the present book pay melancholy testimony. Here, for example, is Wentworth Day, ascribing it as a merit to Rutland that "there are no factory chimneys to stain the bright air and . . . only three great main roads . . . to bring the stink of petrol and the unholy haste of motor-cars into this county which has lived for centuries to the sound of the galloping feet of horses and the slow tread of fat cattle." Or consider the implication of Jack Simmons's surprised comment on the village of Newton St. Cyres in Devonshire, that it "has somehow managed to keep its pink cob-walled cottages, even though it lies all along the main road." It is, indeed, a melancholy reflection that when in discussing our holiday plans we

This map shows the English Counties in outline. The heavy black lines show the groupings of counties adopted in this book. These groupings correspond with the sections headed Southern, Eastern, Western, Midland and Northern Counties. The Lakes, which have a separate chapter, and Furness, which though part of Lancashire is dealt with under Cumberland, are indicated.

11

praise one to another the virtues of some unspoilt village, what we mean is a village *not yet spoilt by us*, a point well brought out by S. B. P. Mais in his admirable account of the villages of northern and western Oxfordshire. This country England is a heritage of noble beauty which our ancestors bequeathed to us in trust for posterity, to hand on to our descendants the beauty we inherited and not a sprawling suburb threaded by rushing highways and studded with preserved beauty spots.

The England of the small country towns is no less lovely, constituting one of the happiest blends of the works of nature and man that man has yet contrived. To them, too, our authors pay fine tribute. Read, for example, John Cherrill on Chichester and Midhurst and Alfriston in Sussex—and how lovely they are—or Robert Bryan on the no less lovely towns of the Cotswolds, Chipping Campden, Burford and Cirencester or Wentworth Day's fine description of the glories of Boston.

Of these towns I would say three things. First, each was in a very real sense the centre and focus of a whole countryside, as Barnstaple is to-day in North Devon, or Long Melford in Suffolk or—supreme example of the type—Ludlow in Shropshire. Go to one

of distinguishable squalor and undistinguished ugliness. Oxford, for example, is ringed first with the products of nineteenth century England, the gas-works, the coal wharves and the slums of St. Ebbes, and then with an outer twentieth century ring consisting of the far-spreading northern suburbs and the motor-works at Cowley. (It is a sobering reflection that when the inhabitants of an English country town propose to take a visitor to see the sights, wishing to show him something which is lovely and celebrated, which has won their affection and evokes their pride, he can safely prophesy that nine times out of ten it will be two hundred years old.) Often these outgrowths link one proliferating conurbation to its no less proliferating neighbour, as though our towns were octopuses ever stretching out their arms like tentacles to clasp yet another new stretch of country, until, in the process, they meet and link themselves to the tentacles of the octopus next door.

In this way pretty well the whole stretch of the Sussex coast, from Hastings to Selsey Bill, has now been ringed, as John Cherrill points out, by a scurf of towns linked by scattered and untidy buildings.

### Democracy's Visiting Card.

Some of the writers blame the holiday-maker for the slow destruction of the first two Englands. This, I think, is a mistake. We all know the deplorable effects that attend the townsman's invasion of the countryside, the open gates, the broken glass, the uprooted bluebells, the cigarette cartons and the beer bottles. Yet what, after all, do you expect? You cannot bring up the generations in the slums of London or Liverpool and then expect their descendants to accommodate themselves easily and naturally to the uses of nature. Indeed, it was in the nature of things that democracy, when it first went to call upon the country, should leave its visiting card in the shape of orange peel and all kinds of litter.

But what then? Is that a reason for excluding democracy? Even if it were, the

of these towns on its market day and you will have the sense of a community with a soul and a speech of its own which come down to us from the traditional England.

Secondly, the influence and importance of these towns are diminishing. Jack Simmons tells us how in recent years the population of the north Devon towns, Lynton and Ilfracombe and, I might add, of Bideford, or in Somerset, Dulverton, has declined, the decline being part of the "steady drift away from the countryside to the large centres of population."

Thirdly, most of them consist of a lovely central core surrounded by concentric rings

exclusion could not be enforced. But apart from the consideration of fact, there is also the consideration of right. Englishmen have a birthright in the beauty of their country-side and there is no reason why they should continue to be disinherited merely because centuries of disinheritance in the past have rendered some of them unfit to enjoy, without maiming, the thing that they love. For how, one may ask, are they to be taught the right use of natural beauty except by habituation of user? And so, since the flood must come, since, too, it is right that it should come, it is the part of wisdom to make plans for its reception.

### Preservation of the Countryside

We come here to the proposals for the future use and protection of the English counties, which are made explicitly or by implication in the following pages. Here, for example, is a lovely old mill at God-manchester in Huntingdonshire; Sir William Beach Thomas tells us that it has perforce been pulled down by the local authorities. Here is another, Houghton Mill at Houghton, in the same county; it is old, beautiful and of great architectural interest. This has been turned into a Youth Hostel where young people, coming perhaps for the first time to the country, may learn to habituate themselves to beauty and to take easily and naturally to nature. The first is destructive the second constructive.

Here is a lovely old house in a great park —you can see pictures of many such in the pages that follow. Is it to be allowed to fall into decay, its park cut up and sold in parcels to the speculative builder? Or is it to be taken over by the National Trust and preserved in perpetuity for the nation, with perhaps the proviso that the owner's family shall continue to live there as tenants, exempted from disabling estate and death duties and from payment of rates and taxes? That this can be arranged is proved by the negotiations between Lord Sackville and the National Trust over Knole House which the Trust acquired in 1946.

Here is the Lake District, indisputably the loveliest track of country in England, threatened, as Sir Norman Birkett warns us, by a host of influences which bid fair to destroy its beauty. The Army monopolizes the hills round Ullswater, industry raises the level of Ennerdale Lake, hydroplanes roar across the waters of Windermere, the hills of Eskdale and Duddondale are blanketed by line after line of regimented conifers, valleys are submerged to make reservoirs; pink, perky villages appear in the dale heads, or try to, roads are driven over the passes or are clamoured for, while on the lake sides beach pyjamas are agitated by the legs of those who gyrate to gramophones under the shade of gaudy umbrellas. The preservation of wildness, of solitude, of beauty, ought, as Sir Norman Birkett says, "to be one of the nation's primary concerns." And, indeed, it is true that their survival to-day depends upon the acceptance of the view that such areas as the Lake District are a trust which concerns the nation as a whole. If they are to continue to be wild and solitary and beautiful, they must come under the care of some body endowed with sufficient powers to protect them from chars-à-banc, speedboats, bungalows, tea huts, shacks, shanties, concrete, barbed wire, gramophones, beach pyjamas and whatever else in the way of progress there may be. In short, to quote Sir Norman Birkett, there is "an imperative and urgent need for the Lake District to be made forthwith a National Park."* And not only the Lake District, but whatsoever other areas the reader likes to include according to taste.

### Not All Loss

But, I remind myself, that it is not a list of recommendations that I am required to make, but of writers to introduce, and I cease here from complaints, apologizing to the reader for the length of my complainings. Besides, I do not wish only to complain or to pretend that the effects of the encroachment of the third and fourth Englands upon the first and second are all on the debit side.

On the credit side, I would put the new mobility which the private car and the public bus have brought to the countryside, the breaking down of old barriers of iso-

---

* *The Lake District, Exmoor Forest and the Peak District are now National Parks.*

lation and remoteness and a new vitality born of better wages, better conditions and a new facility for getting about and keeping in touch which expresses itself in Women's Institutes and Young Farmers' Clubs. Nor are these new expressions of the life of the country a mere reflection of the life of the towns; as the reader will learn from David Peck in his admirable article on Wiltshire— I say "admirable" because it represents most closely my own view and expresses my own feelings—or, with more lamentations and reservations, from H. J. Massingham in his learned article on Dorset—they bear strongly upon them the impress of the region. They are, indeed, one of the signs of the coming of new life to the English countryside, a life which—let us be fair—has been made possible by the development of transport and the machine.

I cannot resist the temptation to conclude by adding a word in answer to a question which may well be running through the reader's mind. "Why," he may ask, "all this fuss? What, after all, is the importance of the English countryside as we have known

it in the past, of its tradition, its way of life; what, above all, is the exaggerated value which you seem to attach to beauty?" Since the praises which the writers of this book bestow upon their counties and the love which they palpably feel for them, implicitly assume the importance both of the beauty and the tradition, the answer of the question is, I submit, strictly relevant to the purpose of this book. And here at the outset one is struck by something odd and strange.

### The Losing Battle

The English spirit has not in the past shown itself particularly sensitive to the beauty of art—not, at least, since the great days of Shakespeare and Purcell. It is not in painting, in sculpture or in music that we have taken the prize and swept the board. But always in the past we have shown ourselves responsive to natural beauty. In the present time these feelings seem to have left us or to be in abeyance. Those of us who, as members of such bodies as the Council for the Preservation of Rural

**Described by S. P. B Mais as an "enchanting hamlet," Minster Lovell on the Windrush in Oxfordshire grew up "when men had a feeling for style and harmony" that seems to be dying.**

# INTRODUCTION

England, the National Trust, the Sussex Downsmen or the Friends of the Lake District, have tried to do our part in preserving the beauty of England have too often found that, as Sir Norman Birkett puts it, our appeals "fall in this modern age on deaf ears."

The destruction of England's beauty has for many years been one of my stock themes; in season and out I have hammered away at it with wearisome reiteration. Here is a book of description and of praise; many distinguished men have contributed to its writing and between them they have produced an informed and comprehensive volume, consisting of a number of gay and vigorous dissertations in which delight is mingled with instruction. The book is also magnificently produced. Here, then, is a book which will at least be bought and read; a book which will reveal to a host of readers exactly what is at stake. That is why in this introduction I have seized the chance to sound once again my note of warning and lament. I am delighted to notice how many of the contributors strike in their chapters the very note that I have here sounded, so I shall incur no charge of mounting a *solitary* hobby horse.

I should add a final point that the writers of these articles have been free to express their own opinions on the subjects on which they have written. Neither I nor the publishers always agree with the opinions expressed. On the other hand, I should add that the writers were not responsible for the selection of the illustrations used throughout the book.

C. E. M. JOAD.

## FOREWORD TO NEW EDITION

This book first appeared under the editorship of the late C. E. M. Joad, himself an ardent lover of the English countryside and a staunch advocate of its preservation. A new edition having been called for, it has devolved upon me to take his place, however, imperfectly, in bringing the volume up-to-date; my excuse for which must be that for many years I have spent my leisure in walking over most of the English counties.

Since the war the face of England has changed a great deal. Many hideous scars due to bombing have been removed, though many, alas, still remain; and against the rusty girders, the piles of rubbish, the willow herbs and rank grass must be set many a tall and not unhandsome building. New towns have sprung up, agricultural land has been lost for ever, lines of transmission towers have spread across the fields and hillsides, huge power stations have begun to darken the sky, and factories large and small (often of bizarre exterior) have appeared where only a few years ago rabbits played and foxes watched. A vast and ever-growing stream of heavy motor traffic clutters every main road throughout the day. The horse has become a natural curiosity, except on "old-fashioned" farms and in the hunting districts. Because it pays farmers better to breed cattle, sheep have become comparatively scarce. Even in towns the independent retailer—the little man, who formerly was so much identified with the very character of the place—is finding it harder and harder to exist against the threat from the multiple store. Fresh eggs are fresh no more, milk is retailed by the Milk Marketing Board. The Welfare State has come to life and is rapidly altering the outlook of the English nation.

Under such conditions things of beauty, whether natural, architectural or artistic, are bound to suffer. We are in a period of transition, when the old no longer satisfies, whereas we are not yet accustomed to the new. Utility is being shouted from the house-tops; nothing else matters, and the urgent summons by Dr Joad to all lovers of beauty therefore calls for more attention than ever at the present time. A reading of this book, with its many fascinating articles on different aspects of English life, will it is hoped, act as a corrective to this modernising tendency, though it is too much to expect that it will check it.

For the reasons mentioned above, a considerable number of minor changes have been necessitated to the text. Opportunity has also been taken to correct a few factual errors, some of which are almost inevitable in a book of this scope.

B. WEBSTER SMITH.

*Waterloo Bridge from the Embankment*

# LONDON

### By SIDNEY DARK

LONDON is the most higgledy-piggledy of all the world's great cities. Thomas Burke says it is "as unknowable as the man on the bus." The truth is that London is as knowable as the man on the bus. There is little that is secretive about either.

The difficulty is to decide exactly what is meant by London, for there are in fact several Londons for different purposes, and none is exactly the same as the other.

First in order of size there is the great, sprawling mass of bricks and mortar known as Greater London. As such it has no official status. It is the vast collection of streets, factories and houses along both banks of the Thames, with a centre at Charing Cross, and reaching out in every direction over a radius of at least fifteen miles. Greater London, as defined by the Registrar General, covers an area of 721 square miles and has a population (1954) of eight and a quarter million souls.

This vast area is coincident with the Metropolitan Police District, and the writ of the

*Arms of L.C.C.*

Metropolitan Police runs throughout it. But, and here is one of the many London oddities, there is an exception, for that writ does not run within the bounds of the City of London, which is a law unto itself. Nor is there one common authority for the administration of Greater London, for the area includes not only the whole of Middlesex, but also large parts of Surrey, Herts, Essex and Kent. In fact, it embraces not only London as a working centre, but also the dormitories of its workers. Even this statement is not quite true, for, with the development of fast electric trains over a growing network of suburban lines, of the motor-car and the Green Line coach, London's dormitories now reach to the south coast, from Eastbourne to Worthing.

Apart from these suburban lines, London has its own vast transport system operated by the London Transport Executive. The system includes all the Underground lines (and these, with their above-ground extensions, run from Southend to Uxbridge and from Morden to remote Wendover and Aylesbury), heirs to the now defunct tramways, and the red monster of London's street, the bus proper. Inside this Greater London is the administrative County of London, the area with which I

17

Cheyne Walk, one of Chelsea's best known streets, containing a palace for the Bishops of Winchester up to the year 1824. Chelsea has been famous since the eighteenth century as the haunt of great figures of the literary and artistic worlds. Rossetti, Whistler, Swift and Carlyle lived there.

am concerned in this article. There is considerable ignorance (even in the minds of London policemen) as to where this administrative County begins and ends.

It covers an area of 74,850 acres, stretching from Poplar in the east to Hammersmith in the west—from the northern heights of Hampstead to the southern heights of Sydenham, topped by the ghost of the Crystal Palace. It houses a population of about three and a half million people and embraces twenty-nine separate administrative entities, consisting of two cities— London and Westminster—and twenty-seven boroughs—namely: Hammersmith, Fulham, Kensington, Chelsea, Paddington, Marylebone, Hampstead, St. Pancras, Holborn, Finsbury, Islington, Stoke Newington, Shoreditch, Stepney, Bethnal Green, Hackney, Poplar, Woolwich, Greenwich, Lewisham, Deptford, Bermondsey, Southwark, Camberwell, Lambeth, Battersea and Wandsworth.

Each of these boroughs, as well as the two cities, has its own mayor (a Lord Mayor in the case of the City of London) and municipal council, and each of them is represented on London's governing body —the London County Council—the offices of which are situated in Lambeth and

almost face the Houses of Parliament across the Thames at Westminster Bridge.

The historic square mile of the City of London stands on the north bank of the Thames. It was originally a walled city, and traces of the old Roman wall can still be seen, particularly at the Tower. The memory of its ancient gates is perpetuated in the names of such streets as Moorgate, Ludgate and Bishopsgate.

The City is the capital of commerce and finance. Here is the Bank of England; here are the City Guilds, the Livery Companies, whose members are freemen of the City, have complete self-government and appoint their own ruler in the person of the Lord Mayor. Even the King may not enter the City without the Lord Mayor's permission, and when he does cross the boundary from Westminster at Temple Bar, he is to this day handed the keys of the City, although the old gates no longer remain, and is received as the City's honoured guest.

Looking down on the City of London from the top of Ludgate Hill is St. Paul's Cathedral, Christopher Wren's masterpiece. Go up to the Stone Gallery and look out across the ancient city! Below is the winding ribbon of the Thames, crossed by Blackfriars, Southwark, London and the

Tower Bridges, and the railway bridges from Cannon Street and Blackfriars stations. Between London and Tower Bridges is the Pool of London, with its docks and cranes. This is the highest point up river that can be reached by large ocean going steamers. Down the river, as far as the eye can see, stretch mile after mile of docks; for London, as well as being the world's greatest city, is also the world's greatest port.

Just where Tower Bridge crosses the river is the Tower of London, a grim grey sentinel, embodying almost nine hundred years of London's history, while scattered throughout the City you can see the graceful spires of Wren's churches. Many of these, though damaged in the bombings and fires of the Second World War, have now been or are being skilfully restored, notably St. Lawrence Jewry and the Church of Bow Bells. The same may be said of the Guildhall and the Old Bailey, both of which have quite regained their pre-War aspect. The great cathedral of St. Paul's, though still surrounded by many a gaping bomb-site, has acquired a fringe of new and not un-handsome office blocks, besides an attractive new public garden on the east.

Adjoining the City to the west is part of Westminster, the richest of the London boroughs, created a city by Royal charter as recently as 1900. Within it are the Houses of Parliament, the Abbey, the Law Courts, Buckingham Palace, and most of the older finest buildings in London. Whitehall houses the departments of state.

The boundaries of the County of London have been arbitrarily settled without apparent rhyme or reason. Why, for example, should semi-countrified Hampstead be in London and grim, squalid, entirely, and often hideously, urban Tottenham and Willesden be outside? But London is a planless city, ever growing, without sense or reason, an octopus of bricks and mortar, steel and concrete.

The centre of an Empire, the character of which is drastically changing, and of a Commonwealth that still retains a tremendous influence in the shaping of human destinies, and for a century the financial hub of the world, London has accepted its

**Hampstead was developed as a spa during the eighteenth century and became a fashionable residential area. Many of the Georgian streets survive, as in Church Row, seen below. The parish church dates from 1735, and contains a bust of the poet Keats, who lived in Wentworth Place.**

# LONDON

**HOUSES OF PARLIAMENT**

**TOWER OF LONDON**

**THE CENOTAPH**

**BUCKINGHAM PALACE**

The Archway, Highgate

St. Paul's School, Hammersmith

Kenwood House
Hampstead Heath

Charles Lamb's House

Arsenal, F.C.

STOKE NEWINGTON

HAMPSTEAD

ST. PANCRAS

ISLINGTON

SHORE

MIDDLESEX

The Zoo

Lords.

St. Pancras  Kings X

FINSBURY

MARYLEBONE

Euston

Regents Park

PADDINGTON

Marylebone

HOLBORN

THE CITY

HAMMERSMITH

Blackfriars

Paddington

Peter Pan's Statue

HYDE PARK

MARBLE ARCH

OXFORD CIRC.

WESTMINSTER

Cannon St.

14  15  16  17  18

19

Fenc.

KENSINGTON

PICCADILLY CIRC.

TRAF. SQ.

WORMWOOD SCRUBS

KENSINGTON GNS.

HYDE PK. COR.

Charing X

13

Waterloo

London Bdg.

SOUTHWARK

Victoria

12

11

The Oval

10

CAMBERWELL GREEN

Fulham Ch.

CHELSEA

7  8  9

Fulham F.C.

Chelsea F.C.

6

Battersea Pk.

FULHAM

5

BATTERSEA

LAMBETH

2

3  4

The Boat Race

The Plough
Clapham

CLAPHAM COMMON

WANDSWORTH

PUTNEY HEATH

Flats at
Streatham

SURREY

## Miles

0   1   2   3   4

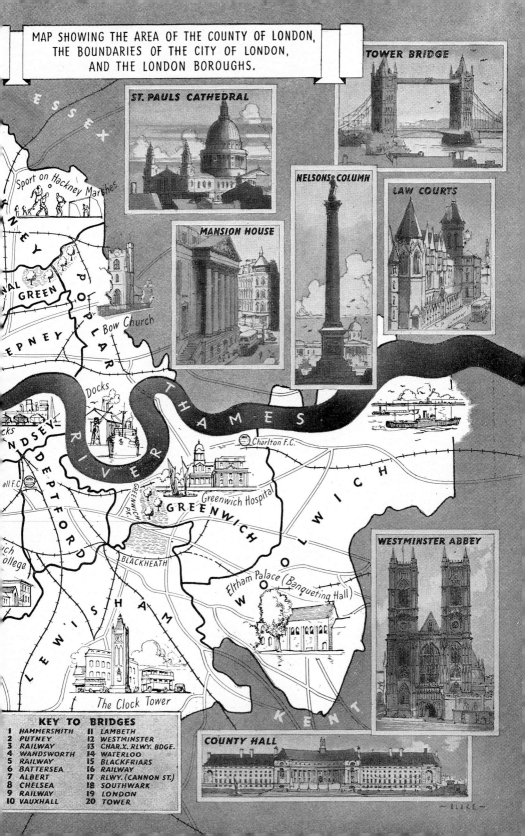

MAP SHOWING THE AREA OF THE COUNTY OF LONDON,
THE BOUNDARIES OF THE CITY OF LONDON,
AND THE LONDON BOROUGHS.

TOWER BRIDGE

ST. PAULS CATHEDRAL

NELSONS COLUMN

LAW COURTS

MANSION HOUSE

Sport on Hackney Marshes

GREEN

POPLAR

Bow Church

EPNEY

ESSEX

Docks

THAMES

RIVER

Charlton F.C.

GREENWICH

Greenwich Hospital

DEPTFORD

BLACKHEATH

WOOLWICH

LEWISHAM

Eltham Palace (Banqueting Hall)

WESTMINSTER ABBEY

The Clock Tower

KENT

COUNTY HALL

### KEY TO BRIDGES

| | | | |
|---|---|---|---|
| 1 | HAMMERSMITH | 11 | LAMBETH |
| 2 | PUTNEY | 12 | WESTMINSTER |
| 3 | RAILWAY | 13 | CHAR.X. RLWY. BDGE. |
| 4 | WANDSWORTH | 14 | WATERLOO |
| 5 | RAILWAY | 15 | BLACKFRIARS |
| 6 | BATTERSEA | 16 | RAILWAY |
| 7 | ALBERT | 17 | RLWY. (CANNON ST.) |
| 8 | CHELSEA | 18 | SOUTHWARK |
| 9 | RAILWAY | 19 | LONDON |
| 10 | VAUXHALL | 20 | TOWER |

—BLAKE—

Adelphi House, on the site of the famous terrace built by the Adam brothers in the eighteenth century, overlooks the Savoy Gardens and the Embankment.

*Arms of City of London*

high destiny with little more than amused indifference. Its historical possessions are for the most part unappreciated. It permits " improvers " to destroy its beauties with a ruthlessness almost equal to that of the German bombers. Londoners made no effective protests when the Adams' Adelphi and Nash's Regent Street became the victims of the housebreakers' picks, and during the war Londoners regretted the destruction of some of its finest buildings—and these were sadly numerous—far less than they mourned the loss of the cramped little houses in the mean little streets.

London lacks imagination and the historic sense. Its people admire Bush House because it is large, but leave American tourists to admire St. James's Palace. Westminster Abbey, a supremely beautiful possession and the burial-place of the nation's heroes, is to London not a monument of loveliness bequeathed to us by the ages of faith, but a sort of Madame Tussaud's. It is not the West front that interests Londoners, but what William Morris called "the beastly monuments to fools and knaves."

To the poet Henley on an October day

Trafalgar square
(The fountains volleying golden glaze)
Gleams like an angel-market.

To the Londoner, Trafalgar Square is the place where the children feed the pigeons and trade unionists demonstrate on Sunday afternoons. Wordsworth, standing on Westminster Bridge in the morning exclaimed:

Earth has not anything to show more fair:
Dull would he be of soul who could pass by
A sight so touching in its majesty.

But the Londoner who crosses the bridge twice every day on his way to and from work is wholly unaware of the beauty that Wordsworth felt so keenly.

The City and Westminster were the cradles of political liberty. But London has little pride in the fact. It is possible that more great men have walked in its streets than in

*Arms of City of Westminster*

the streets of any other city except Paris. Paris names its streets after its great men, but there is no Shakespeare Street in the City, no Chaucer Street, no Milton Street, no Dickens Street, though there are a Goldsmith Building in the Temple and a Johnson Court off Fleet Street. There is a Browning Road outside the City area.

The Thames is the repository of London's history. It is, too, in a diminishing degree, its playground. King Edward the Confessor dedicated the Abbey Church of Westminster to St. Peter because of the legend that the saint appeared on the river bank at Westminster and there, as a reward for the fisherman who ferried him across, he ordained that the man should catch "a plentiful supply of fish of which the greater part should be salmon."

It is pleasant also to remember that the great hospital at Lambeth just across the river preserves the name of St. Thomas of London who was murdered in Canterbury Cathedral and who was loved and trusted by the poor. So was Archbishop Laud, who, centuries after St. Thomas died, was taken down the river from Lambeth to die in the Tower, and, as he passed, the people lined the river-bank and wept. Kings have passed up and down the river in picturesque pageantry, cheerful pleasure-seekers like Mr. Pepys have gone by river to boisterous evenings at Vauxhall. For centuries ships have passed up and down our oldest road, carrying, in H. M. Tomlinson's words, "those unknown folk whose mind created London out of reeds and mere." The Thames, he adds, is "the main thoroughfare from Kensington to Valparaiso."

As a man has many moods, so has London. It can be dignified and undignified. It can be kind and cruel. It can be tragically foolish and acutely wise.

In his book *A Texan in England*, Frank Dobie calls London "the supreme world receiver." This suggests that London is cosmopolitan, but this is only partially true. London is less of a world city than Paris, and is much less

The Foreign Office and Commonwealth Relations buildings seen from St. James's Park.

cosmopolitan than New York. True there are many foreigners within its gates, but they are in it, not of it. The colony of German Jews in Hampstead, for example, remains definitely, often uncomfortably, German, spiritually as the poles asunder from the assimilated English Jews. The Italians in Soho and Saffron Hill were never Londoners. Unlike their compatriots in New York, few of them sought naturalization.

It is said, I do not know whether accurately or not, that it is rare to discover a Londoner of more than the fourth generation. The suggestion is that the population is constantly being recruited by immigrants from villages and other British towns and cities. But the newcomers soon lose all the distinctive qualities of the places from which they came. When they arrive, they nearly always hate London. It is as strange and uncomfortable to the man from a back street in a Lancashire town, as it is to a man from a Wiltshire village. But London is a melting-pot for the folk whom it receives. It remoulds them in its own likeness: in less than a generation they become Cockneys, and a Cockney is far more unlike the rest of the people of this island than the Parisian is unlike the rest of the people of France. London is, indeed, the Londoner's own city, and it is impossible to determine whether the Londoner has made London or London has made the Londoner.

Thomas Burke, whose writings have proved his deep love for London, a Charles Lamb-like love, has written: "When you can perceive the spiritual difference between the squares of Bloomsbury and the squares of Bayswater, between the sadness of the Caledonian Road and the melancholy of the Ball's Pond Road you are beginning to know London." But, it seems to me these alleged differences are either superficial or imaginary. The Bloomsbury and Bayswater squares have much the same history, and no one can explain why Bayswater now houses the working respectable middle class in its boarding-houses, while Bloomsbury has become the home of the student and the intelligentzia, as no one can explain why

24

This panorama, looking down river, shows the sweep of the Victoria Embankment on either side of Waterloo Bridge. From left to right can be seen Shell Mex House, the Savoy Hotel and

London's few painters moved first from St. John's Wood to Chelsea, and now from Chelsea to Camden Town and Hampstead, as the Paris Bohemians have moved from the heights of Montmartre across the river to Montparnasse. Incidentally, is it safe to say that Dickens would now find the Caledonian Road wholly sad or the Ball's Pond Road entirely melancholy? He would have heard laughter in them both.

### The Londoner's Character

Frank Dobie notes that there are more birds in London than in any other great city, and he suggests that this is indicative of the character of its people. Possibly, possibly not. Londoners must be kindly folk, Dobie thinks, or they would snare the pigeons for food. But, I am told, frugal Italian restaurant-keepers have proved by experiment that even the deftest cooking cannot make London pigeon edible.

However, it is true that the Londoner is as essentially kindly as he is cosy, and the kindness is most apparent in the districts where the streets are mean and the means scanty. The most valuable communal qualities seem to be most highly developed amongst those whose lives are limited by economic circumstances. The poor are affected by their environment because they rarely escape from that environment. To discover the real Londoner, therefore, it is necessary to avoid the Dorchester Hotel and turn into the Pig and Whistle, and to journey from the West End to Islington and Pentonville, striking south to Bethnal Green, then, carefully skirting the City, making one's way to what the Germans have left of Stepney and Poplar (more genuinely London than their cosmopolitan neighbour Whitechapel), then across the Tower Bridge to Rotherhithe and Bermondsey and westward to Southwark and Lambeth. Or another journey of discovery might be from the West End to the streets between Lisson Grove and the Edgware Road, going westward to the slums of Paddington—some of the worst slums left in London—and so to the mean streets of Royal Kensington, that are little better.

There are, again superficially, many Londons—rich London and poor London, literary London and artistic London, virtuous London and raffish London and

26

Brettenham House (behind Cleopatra's Needle). Somerset House rises above the last northern arch of the bridge. Beyond are the spires of the City churches and the dome of St. Paul's Cathedral.

suburban London. Most of them are real London, though some of them are practically foreign colonies, the people of which would be happier elsewhere. But it is in struggling London that the genuine Londoner is to be found, and, when he is found and understood, he will be recognized as a kindly, easy-going, indifferent man. The majority of the folk who sleep as well as work within the County borders belong to the working class. The rich, who are nowadays selling their mansions to commercial firms, have been for generations only sojourners in London, and rarely there from Fridays to Mondays. The middle classes, from the poorly paid clerks to the heads of businesses, are constantly trekking farther and farther from the City's centre to its outskirts and over its borders, and the greater their resources the longer is the trek.

The Londoner is the purposeless amateur of life, and his City has been thrown together by purposeless amateurs. "Here is a church . . .," said Mr. Wemmick, "let's have a wedding." "Here is an open space," says the Londoner, "let's build a house." It does not matter what sort of a house, or in what style it is built. Indeed, the Londoner prefers that it shall have no style. The result ought to be, and almost always is, repellent ugliness and heartbreaking discomfort. But—and this is the marvel of London—with all the misuse and lazy indifference, even with the horror of the new suburbs built after the First World War, London has to a London-loving Londoner like myself an appealing and attractive cosiness, hardly to be found anywhere else.

### Helping Hands

There are pessimists who declare that the London kindliness that Dickens dramatically describes over and over again has been destroyed by the hard trials of the wars. I do not agree. It was magnificently apparent in every blitz, but the kindliness of the Londoner does not need unusual peril to bring it into existence. It is evident, again I add at least to me, in the ordinary traffic of everyday life. "It's the pore that 'elps the pore" is a London truism. No hard-luck story ever fails to find a helping hand. There is no kindlier place on earth than the London of the mean street, even if there are few noisier places than Oxford Street in the

27

rush hours. "What I miss 'ere," said a Bermondsey woman, a war village evacuee, "is my neighbours." I suggested that she must have found many new neighbours. "Yes," she said, "but they're not the same: they're not so matey."

The familiar little knots of women, gossiping outside the little houses or on the balconies of the tenements, are regarded by the censorious as examples of slatternly laziness. Yet they stand for London's mateyness—little knots of sympathetic and understanding friends sharing their troubles and laughing at their misfortunes. That is the Londoner's distinguishing quality. He can laugh at almost everything. He finds occasion for laughter when other men would weep. He agrees with Dibdin, "What argifies snivelling and piping your eye?" In the mean streets is commonly heard the remark, "I didn't arf laugh," when some unforeseen misfortune has occurred. London enjoys the incongruous and half welcomes the unexpected, even when it is misfortune. It is a "bit of a change." The Londoner is the laughing stoic. "It might have been worse," is the

Best known as the centre of the newspaper industry, Fleet Street is one of London's main thoroughfares joining Ludgate Circus—near which stood an old city gate—with the Strand.

summary of his philosophy. Experience has taught him to expect very little. He is not surprised when he receives nothing.

The essential kindness of the Londoner is accompanied with fickleness and lack of firmness of purpose. He can never be interested for very long in the things that matter. He will kick hard against economic grievances, but Derby Day or a football tie will drive serious concerns from his mind. Consequently none of the popular social movements that led to the Labour Party triumph in 1945 began in London, though London has always been sympathetic.

### Playing the Fool

The Londoner is apt to be frivolous-minded. Unlike St. Paul, he never puts away childish things. He is never really happy except when he is playing the fool. Frank Dobie says that "the English belong to the realm of naturalness." The Londoner is natural only when he is free to give himself to the frivolous—darts and football pools and the cultivation of a back garden.

The tiny suburban gardens and the flower-pots on the tenement window-sills suggest the Londoner's love of flowers. His parks, too, are beautiful, even though the military had their way with them in the war. This seems to contradict my assertion that the Londoner has small care for beauty. But the parks have been imposed on the City by authority in a past age, and the Londoner's interest in the often gorgeous flower-beds is perfunctory and in the trees disastrous. His own patch or his own flower-pots supply the means of growing something under difficulties; for they are a gamble, and appeal to the Londoner's sporting instinct.

The Londoner is tolerant, not given to harsh judgments of his neighbours. If one of them is arrested by the police he is commonly described as "being in trouble." The miserable sinner is a "pore feller" to be pitied. Max Beerbohm once said that he always pitied the wrong-doer, since he generally has a bad time. The public bar agrees with him. The respect for the law with which the Londoner is often credited is, in fact, vastly exaggerated. He detests

"Orator's Corner," at the north-east corner of Hyde Park and opposite the Marble Arch, always attracts the crowds. Here the Londoner speaks to Londoners with complete freedom on all matters.

being "ordered about," and, in so far as he obeys laws and regulations without more than humorous protest, he does so from that consideration for others that is the Londoner's virtue—from, that is, his mateyness. On the whole, the Londoner is more courteous than the Parisian, the New Yorker or the man of Manchester and Leeds.

The Londoner, says Thomas Burke, is "vital and gusty," he is also knowing and kindly. But one thing he cannot abide; he agrees with the theologians in regarding pride as the first of the deadly sins. He has no use for the man who "chucks his weight about." This human and, I would venture to add, Christian dislike was expressed by the late Gus Elen in his song:

Since Jack Jones come into a little bit
    o' splosh,
    'E dunno where 'e are.

The Londoner is naturally lazy. How comparatively lazy he is I discovered when I took to living among the industrious people of a small agricultural village. He is the born loafer forced by hard necessity to labour, and there has never been a song

more certain of the Londoner's applause than the ditty of which the chorus ran:

Standing at the corner watching other
    fellers work,
    That'll never upset me.

The Londoner works to live; to live to work would seem to him sheer idiocy. That is why Scotsmen and Irishmen and migrants from the outer English marches have most of the good London jobs. No true Londoner was ever a disciple of Dr. Smiles.

This instinctive revolt against "the daily round," the weary task, derives from the fact that the Londoner is sufficiently interested in the trivial to resent being compelled to spend his time with the serious.

Yet—so contrary a creature is man—the Londoner hates change. Where he is, there he wants to remain. Novelty has no attraction for him. Most of the people who were removed from overcrowded Stepney to the model streets of Dagenham sadly missed the familiar "local," the old neighbours, even the insanitary home. The villager after a time settles more or less happily in London. The Londoner is miserable in the country after a few days. I met scores of evacuees during the war; I did not meet one (except perhaps the very young children) who was not aching for the trams and the shops, the cinemas and the noise of his London.

Superficially, London has changed immensely since Dickens described the stinking slums, where Oliver Twist was caught in Fagin's web, and the humorously endured poverty of the Cratchits and the Kenwigs. It is cleaner, healthier and more comely. It has changed, indeed, in my lifetime. Many good new things have been added to the City's life, some good things have been lost.

One of the most grievous losses is the music-hall, the shrine and the preserver of genuine Cockney humour. Dan Leno, pathetically puzzled because his audience didn't "know Mrs. Kelly," the "vital and gusty" Marie Lloyd, that genius of friendly, high-spirited naughtiness, the stout, genial Herbert Campbell, the philosophic Alec Hurley advising

Never introduce your donah to a pal,
For the odds is ten to one he'll sneak
    your gal

—these and their comrades were the authentic voices of the London of fifty years ago. Their songs were banal, their humour was robustly coarse, they were natural. "All, all are gone the old familiar faces," and their places have been taken by insufferable crooners, babbling fake plantation ditties about "Kentucky babbies."

The coming of the cinema and the Hollywood film has revolutionized London's language. The obedient Cockney child now replies, "O.K., chief," to every instruction. The Cockney now says, "yeah" and not the old-time "yuss." The accent not only of the Wellers, but also of the Londoner of forty years ago, has almost disappeared. This is due to better schools, the radio and the cinema. But, in spite of all these changes the Londoner is as he has always been. His soul is more stubborn than his streets.

After the last war there was an opportunity to rebuild London such as had not occurred since the Great Fire of 1666. However, all the efforts to make the City more accessible, from Sir Patrick Abercrombie's fine schemes to the humblest local redesigning of streets, met with the same fate as Wren's plans of three centuries ago; and London has continued to grow mainly along the old lines. Some few improvements there have been; others will never in our time be anything but dreams. But, however that may be, I do not doubt that the Londoner of to-morrow will be the close kin of the Londoner of yesterday. With, alas, small devotion to or regard for religion, and still with negligible appreciation of the things of the mind and the imagination; his life is lived in obedience to the great command, "Judge not, that ye be not judged!"

*Piccadilly Circus*

*Much Hadham, near Ware*

# HERTFORDSHIRE

## By SIR WILLIAM BEACH THOMAS

A FOND and charming annalist once emphasized a quality of Hertfordshire which time is not likely to destroy, though some new rural factories may one day affect it. Thomas Fuller, travelling through the county on the conclusion of the Civil War, after expressing his joy at the singing of the birds and the sweetness of the flowers, added, "It is the garden of England" (a phrase appropriated by Kent), "for delight and men commonly say that such who buy a house in Hertfordshire pay two years' purchase for the aire thereof." And, indeed, the air flows freely, for the valleys, made by rivers trickling down from Chiltern ridges, are open and gentle; and the uplands, though seldom more than some four hundred feet, are higher than the surrounding levels of Essex, Cambridge, Bedford, if not of Buckinghamshire and Middlesex.

A more widely known tribute was written some one hundred and fifty years later. It might have been expected, so strong and affection-

*Arms of Hertfordshire*

ate is county patriotism throughout England, that constant epithets would have been attached, say, to Sussex, Yorkshire, Lancashire, Devon and the rest; yet Hertfordshire remains conspicuous for possessing at least two, bound to it by the strong chain of alliteration. It is impossible to write of the shire without reference to Charles Lamb's epithets, evoked by his famous visit, accompanied by his sister, to Mackery End and Wheathampstead. His "hearty, homely, loving Hertfordshire" "staid put," at least as to the first two, as the farmhouse he visited and the lovely Elizabethan country house beside it have "staid put." The first adjective is doubtless one of Lamb's favourite puns, and "homely" is the more appropriate. It is in a particular sense a county of homes. No other county of a like acreage (Hertfordshire covers only six hundred and thirty-two square miles) contains anything like so many old and lovely country houses, from such palaces as

31

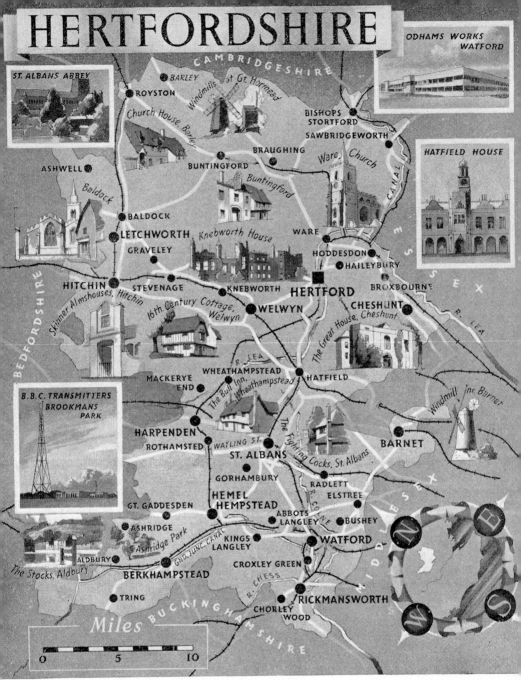

# HERTFORDSHIRE

ODHAMS WORKS
WATFORD

ST. ALBANS ABBEY

CAMBRIDGESHIRE

BARLEY

ROYSTON

Windmills at Gt. Hormead

Church House, Barley

BISHOPS
STORTFORD

SAWBRIDGEWORTH

BRAUGHING

ASHWELL

BUNTINGFORD

Buntingford

Ware

Church

CANAL

HATFIELD HOUSE

Baldock

BALDOCK

LETCHWORTH

GRAVELEY

Knebworth House

WARE

HODDESDON

HAILEYBURY

E  S  S  E  X

HITCHIN

STEVENAGE

16th Century Cottage, Welwyn

KNEBWORTH

HERTFORD

BROXBOURNE

Skinner Almshouses, Hitchin

WELWYN

CHESHUNT

The Great House, Cheshunt

BEDFORDSHIRE

R. LEA

MACKERYE
END

WHEATHAMPSTEAD

The Bull Inn, Wheathampstead

HATFIELD

R. LEA

Windmill, nr. Barnet

B.B.C. TRANSMITTERS
BROOKMANS
PARK

HARPENDEN

ROTHAMSTED

WATLING ST.

The Fighting Cocks, St. Albans

BARNET

ST. ALBANS

GORHAMBURY

RADLETT

GT. GADDESDEN

HEMEL
HEMPSTEAD

ELSTREE

ASHRIDGE

Ashridge Park

ABBOTS
LANGLEY

BUSHEY

M
I
D
D
L
E
S
E
X

KINGS
LANGLEY

GND. JUNC. CANAL

WATFORD

ALDBURY

CROXLEY GREEN

The Stocks, Aldbury

BERKHAMPSTEAD

R. CHESS

TRING

CHORLEY
WOOD

RICKMANSWORTH

Miles

BUCKINGHAMSHIRE

0          5          10

Hatfield, to the manor house and the
smaller historic homes, like Lilley Hoo or
Lamer. The greater ones begin to lose
their original purpose. Cassiobury is the
municipal park of Watford, the biggest
urban concentration in the county.
Kimpton Hoo, where Viscount Hampden lived, was bought by the Nuffield
Trust, and became for a while a railway
headquarters; one large and lovely house

32

became a preparatory school; Rye House is a grossly neglected ruin; the Letchworth Garden City has converted a glorious Jacobean manor house (once owned by the most freakish of Hertfordshire worthies, so called, the Reverend but unrevered Alington) into a hotel and its farmland into a golf-links. Tewin Water House, now owned by the City Council, has become a special school for deaf children.

### Houses Great and Small

Such changes multiply; but almost all the smaller houses remain, and indeed increase, especially along the Buckinghamshire and Bedfordshire borders, though Water End by Ayot is a good example of restored glory. We may hope, too, that the very greatest and most pleasing will survive. Hatfield House is supreme on any account. It has remained in one family since the days of the first Lord Salisbury, son of Queen Elizabeth's chief minister, who was induced by James I to exchange it for Theobalds, which he preferred. The Jacobean house which he planned has no architectural rival of the period; and the old hall and buildings beside it are relics of the very finest Tudor architecture. Nor can a successful rival be found to its internal decorations and gallery of pictures. Those who attend the yearly agricultural show in the vast park have to walk very few yards to see the oak under which Queen Elizabeth was found, so the story goes, when the news was brought of her succession to the throne. Again Panshanger—of which Lord Desborough was peculiarly fond—has a park in some ways more pictorial than Hatfield Park, and within the house are the priceless pictures are a memorial to the great day of the English country house, where, as a much-travelled Dutchman said, the highest point in civilization was reached. To give one more example, the descendants of Bulwer Lytton still inhabit Knebworth; and time has added virtue to the intricate flamboyance of the too-imaginative architecture of the house.

Is it too much to hope that the remnants will survive death duties and modern planning? To-morrow has a question mark printed particularly large in Hertfordshire.

A curious example is on record. A signpost once stood at the corner of a Hertfordshire lane leading to Hatfield, and one arm bore the legend "The Way to Yesterday"—so Lord Salisbury told me, and he went bail for the historic truth of the fact. It was alleged later that the post bore a second arm pointing north to Welwyn Garden City, and on this was written "The Way to Hell." No one has gone bail for the historic truth of this gloss. Anyway, to make the antithesis quite crisp as well as true, that northern arm ought to have given the direction "The Way to To-morrow," for To-morrow was the first and whole title of Ebenezer Howard's epoch-making book, later called *Garden Cities of To-morrow*, which created the Garden City movement. Yesterday and to-morrow may be said to have coalesced when Howard founded Letchworth in 1903; the change was confirmed when the owners of Hatfield sold—for a very moderate sum—the site near Welwyn of a second Garden City to a group, again inspired and represented by Sir Ebenezer Howard.

In no shire in England does to-morrow so obviously threaten to-day. At Stevenage, between the two garden cities, and not far from either a satellite town of thirty thousand inhabitants has been built; Hatfield and Boreham Wood have also grown enormously.

### Peace Undisturbed

The rural calm of Hertfordshire has persisted for centuries in spite of the neighbourhood of London, in spite of the passage of the Great Northern and Midland railways, in spite of the Great North Road in its centre and Watling Street on the west. One carries a signpost "To the North" and the other "To Holyhead," and the through-faring leaves Hertfordshire's peace almost undisturbed: indeed, less disturbed than when Dick Turpin frequented Ermine Street, especially at its approach to Royston. Only over a narrow strip on the south, by Barnet and Watford, has London conquered and the built-up area superseded the farm. But even Watford has a core of antiquity and a lovely park, and Barnet still celebrates its fair with much of the old gusto. The unhappy prospect is that the

The River Mimram, a tributary of the Lea, at Tewin, near Hertford.

34

green belt, of which an arc crosses the county to the south of these, will be no more than a temptation for new towns to leapfrog over it. Nevertheless let it be put on record that until after the Second World War not only its villages, but its dainty little towns—Hertford itself, with Ware, Hitchin, Buntingford (which still seems a village); indeed, in some aspects St. Albans savoured of the deep country. Will the new towns or the enlarged villages such as Harpenden, where the famous Rothamsted Research Station was founded by Gilbert and Lawes, acquire as pleasing a savour? It may be said that all the towns, except those on the Middlesex border, still retain a sort of rural flavour, like the hundreds of villages and hamlets which remain "wrapt from the world."

**Past and Present**

It is likely to remain a true verdict that there are few shires where past and present jostle one another in so friendly and palpable a manner. The county town itself, though many of the streets are urban in the ordinary sense, gives a good example. The old castle of Hertford, where King Arthur checked the invasion by the Danes by manipulating the navigable waters of the Lea, to-day provides some charming municipal offices, and its surroundings are as pleasant a public playground as can be found anywhere in the Southern Counties. Again, St. Albans has suffered a number of new additions that are not of the loveliest, if we except the architecture of the new post office; but you slip out of the main street straight into the precincts of the cathedral—famous for its possession of the longest nave in England—and at its side the yet older gateway, which is now part of St. Albans School; and this claims to be older, even by several hundred years, than the oldest of our public schools. It was a happy idea of the restorers of the magnificent screen in the cathedral to include the figure of Nicholas Breakspear, the only English Pope, who took the title of Adrian IV. He was a Hertfordshire man, born at Abbots Langley; his family name is perpetuated in Breakspear Farm. When you leave the cathedral and wander down the green slope

towards the River Ver, you presently pass the Fighting Cocks, perhaps the oldest house used as an inn in England; and over the river you are in Verulamium proper, with its eloquent relics of

Old, unhappy, far-off things
And battles long ago.

Battles in and about St. Albans have been many and fierce ever since the days of Queen Boadicea and Cassivelaunus. In the centuries that followed the Roman victories successive invasions by northern and western tribes seem almost to have wiped out the imported civilization. Verulamium itself was utterly destroyed, probably by the Angles round A.D. 500. A more or less peaceful period succeeded in which King Offa, as the tale goes, found the bones of the Christian martyr, St. Alban. His cathedral was partly built of the stones and the tiles of Roman Verulamium, whose destruction was thus completed. Battles were resumed at the Norman Conquest (when peace was made at Berkhampstead), and then was a pause until the Wars of the Roses, when the opening battle was fought at St. Albans, and yet a bloodier battle six years later on the way to Harpenden, after which Queen Margaret's borderers were said to have ravaged the city, including the Abbey. The war finished as it began in Hertfordshire, at the Battle of Barnet in 1471. The chief victor of the earlier battle was the Earl of Warwick, and the tomb of unnamed members of his family is to be found in Flamstead Church, where the medieval wall paintings are of particular interest.

**Ancient Remains**

Since those Civil Wars Hertfordshire has not only cultivated the arts of peace, but restored evidence of the Roman civilization. Almost where Boadicea and Cassivelaunus and the British tribes fought bloody battles with the Romans is now shown the beautifully preserved outline of a Roman theatre, which is unique in England, and the museum near by is an archaeologist's feast. A little to the east, ivied ruins recall that famous lady, Juliana Berners of the Sopwell nunnery, who wrote the earliest of our books of sport and anticipated Izaak Walton as an authority on fishing by several hundred years. However, before turning east to the nunnery, those who take such a walk should have visited the old and beautiful church of St. Michael, built at the very centre of the Roman Verulamium. Apart from the many architectural charms of the church, an unusually artistic monument stands over the tomb of Francis Bacon, whose views on gardening, given in a charming essay, were acquired at his home of Gorhambury, close by.

It is difficult to imagine a change more pleasantly abrupt than the passage from the busy street under the shadow of the spreading cedar by the east end of the cathedral. A pleasant throw-back to a later antiquity is to be found in the yet busier and broader part of the street to the north. Here an old barn from Waterend House (favourite home of the Duke of Marlborough) has been re-erected as a modern restaurant. "Great is juxtaposition," and there are few of the little towns that do not acknowledge some such obvious and agreeable touch with a distant past. Berkhampstead, a market and residential town, will seem to the motorists one interminably long stretch of no very particular charm except perhaps for an odd house or two.

### Castle and Common

The castle where the Black Prince lived and played the beneficent lord of the manor is a much less conspicuous object than the railway station beside it, but on the north side you find yourself almost instantly on a glorious common, famous for the fight for its preservation between Mr. Smith and Lord Bridgwater. Alongside it is Ashridge, one of several places in the shire owned by the National Trust. The vista of the fine avenue excels even the chestnut avenue at Hertford. Behind are such gems as the two Gaddesdens and Nettleden, and a little to the west spread out a view only less spacious than those from Telegraph Hill, near Lilley Hoo, or the northerly view from the bare downs above Royston, where James I loved to hunt, when he was not hunting at Theobalds (or "Tibbies"). On the whole the shires of Bedford and Buckingham give rather wider and richer views than Cambridgeshire and Essex.

Just one town in the shire is associated with a comic past. Cowper, who was at school for a while at Berkhampstead, made Ware the bourne of the most facetious of holiday rides; and long before John Gilpin's expedition, the Great Bed of Ware, some eleven feet square and seven feet high, built of carved oak, became a popular jest, used by Shakespeare in *Twelfth Night*. It is a deprivation that after several migrations from inn to inn it has been removed to South Kensington. Ware should be appreciated for other than comic reasons.

### Ware's Malt Houses

The waterways, increased by Sir Hugh Myddelton's canals, cut for the sake of London's water supply, make the lower part of the town a sort of Venice. Navigation is busy, and one line of dwelling-houses on the waterside makes a delightfully unexpected picture. Behind the most attractive of its hotels rise malt houses which here, as at Bishops Stortford, indicate an important county industry, still in being after a long and flourishing past; and their presence truly suggests that the farms round about produce as good barley as Norfolk itself. Malting has played, and still plays, a very large part of the industry of a wide area, especially along a line from the Bedfordshire boundary near Hitchin to the Essex border near Bishops Stortford.

No modern additions, though some are very unlovely, have actually destroyed the spirit of these little, merry Hertfordshire towns, in spite of such a "cautionary guide" as a preserver of modern England wrote of St. Albans. Many of the villages are unhurt. Charles Lamb could still fulfil his final ambition. "I had thought," he wrote in 1822, "in a green old age (O green thought) to have retired to Ponders End, emblematic name, how beautiful! in the Ware Road, toddling about it and Cheshunt, anon stretching on some fine Izaak Walton morning, to Hoddesdon or Amwell, careless beggar; but walking, walking ever, till I fairly walked myself off my legs, dying walking." Of all these places Amwell at any rate still remains a walker's paradise, and there the source of the New River still makes a neat and unspoilt picture under the little old church and the famous memorial stones. While such villages as Westmill, Aldbury, Ayot, and Gaddesden are still in being, homeliness refuses to be ejected.

If you do not believe, go visit Ayot St. Lawrence where George Bernard Shaw sought serenity, or Aspenden or Nettleden. The old type of labourer is found in these hamlets as well as the craftsmen; but the craftsmen have changed, not their nature, but their methods. For example, in a village near the little gem of Ayot lives a blacksmith whose forbears have worked at the same trade for some two hundred years. He and other blacksmiths, at Hatfield and elsewhere, have of late years become experts of such artwork as fire irons and iron gates, and have had the eagerly accepted chance of studying traditional patterns at South Kensington. While engaged in such work the financial return hardly enters this smith's head. He will work for continuous hours well into the night; and is so conscientious an artist that nothing in the world would persuade him to use a file instead of a hammer. I once saw him fall into a passion when he detected marks of a file on a piece of iron-work sent for exhibition at the County Agricultural Show. To correct bad hammer work with a file was in his eyes high treason against true art.

### Valley of Glass

The shire has, in part, protected itself against urbanization behind the defences of the River Lea, especially towards the east along the reaches which Izaak Walton made famous. Few counties have enjoyed a more persuasive tribute than the opening pages of *The Compleat Angler*, when Piscator joined the otter hunt and foretasted the cheer at The Thatched House—now, alas, no more—in Hoddesdon. That defensive barrier changed its nature abruptly from the beginning of the century. Glasshouses began to spring up, and presently many miles of waterway between Cheshunt and Hoddesdon helped to create a veritable valley of glass. Within a few years the transformation of the scene became scarcely credible. Quick fortunes were made, employment multiplied, the kings of Covent Garden set up headquarters on the riverbanks—almost at the spot where the Rye House Plot against James I was hatched. It has been plausibly alleged that the value of the produce under glass now at least equals the value of the open-field output within the county, though the farms still retain their old reputation for barley and wheat. The example became infectious as well as contagious, and many isolated glasshouses sprang up.

### Village Industry

A more pictorial industry flourishes by several villages higher up the valley. Agreeable springs bubble up in many places near the river, and these were found to give ideal conditions for the growth of water-cress. Its culture is singularly attractive. The first January harvesting may be a chilly performance, but an expert craftsman of my acquaintance could excel at his work of cutting the cress, as well as rolling and planting it. It is a village industry to be encouraged. Much more than a village industry is the manufacture of high grades of paper, carried out at Hemel Hempstead, at Apsley, and at Croxley Green, near Watford. Poultry keeping on a large scale is practised at King's Langley.

Within the memory of living people Hertfordshire has lost a village industry, straw plaiting, that brought some wealth and much occupation to great numbers of poor people. For example, soon after the world-famous Rothamsted Research Station was started at the edge of the hamlet of Harpenden in 1843, a small boy of ten years old—the usual age at which boys went out to work in those days—was employed on the farm. In the course of years he rose to be farm manager and, on his retirement, under the wise encouragement of Sir John Russell, the director, he put together a book of reminiscences, which gives a most engaging picture of village life just before the railway came. He preserves a number of racy words and phrases now half or wholly forgotten, the old beliefs or superstitions, and, what are most important, the old ways of thought and habits of life. The village folk were poor and worked very hard. The boys often

Founded as a Benedictine monastery in 792, St. Albans Abbey has the longest nave in England. In spite of alterations it remains one of the finest examples of Norman architecture in the country. The Abbey became the Cathedral of a diocese in 1875.

began work at 4 a.m., and were boarded out on the farms for a good part of the week, taking a three or four days' supply of food with them. Wages were miserably low, but poverty was relieved to some extent by payment in kind, by the keeping of pigs and general cheapness.

Throughout the account of such things as remembered most faithfully by Mr. Gray, the author of the reminiscences, straw plait runs like a thread. The women plaited straw almost continuously, the tiny babes learnt and practised the simpler patterns, and continual journeys to St. Albans, largely by Shanks, his mare, were concerned with the selling of the plait as well as the purchase of goods. This cottage industry, destroyed in part by the beginning of the twentieth century by cheap imports from Japan, was a godsend: and nothing has been found to take its place.

It is difficult in more expensive days to realize how cheaply life could be lived. Perhaps the most pleasing of all the smaller golf courses within the county was made towards the end of the nineteenth century and the bill for its construction is in being. Its burden is this: "To making golf course £8 16s. 0d.," and it was credibly reported to

me by the first secretary that the maker apologized for the size of the bill on the ground that he had been forced to hire a horse and cart! One of the earliest golfers was the son of a commoner, who fashioned a club for himself out of holly that he cut on the common. He rose to the distinction of a plus handicap and made a notable appearance as an amateur in the Open Championship. He used to say that everyone who played on this course ought to become a plus golfer, for it is so enclosed in ling and gorse, not to mention thorn and juniper and raspberry, that only the straightest hitter can survive. He might have added that at certain seasons your concentration is liable to be disturbed by the song of larks and nightingales!

In the earliest account of Hertfordshire, Michael Drayton, in his *Polyolbion*, concerns himself chiefly with the rivers and woods; and then Epping or Waltham Forest extended into Hertfordshire. To-day the villages and little towns are of more concern than woods and rivers, but the rivers, especially the Lea ("Which oft doth lose its way"), remain important. Most of them have their source in the Chilterns, those lovely chalk ridges that begin to lose altitude, but to gain in richness of clothing, as they enter the western side of the shire. One of the few that has nothing to do with the Chilterns has its most attractive source in the old and famous village of Ashwell. Here, as elsewhere, the villages were first built along the valleys, sometimes for the sake of the mills. For example: the mill in Wheathampstead is in Domesday, and the old beams within are old enough to show the holes made for the reception of the iron spikes of the candlesticks, necessary for lighting its dark interior. It is a hopeful sign for the return of some measure of self-sufficiency that after lying idle for some years, the old mill wheel revolves again for the grinding of chicken food from local grain. Most of the mills, which were once numerous, have ceased to be, but what is of more vital importance is that the rivers themselves are in danger of extinction. There was a large and famous mill on the Mimram by Codicote, which was turned into a singularly attractive country house. One owner, Lord Hampden, the Lord

Lieutenant of the county, made a pleasant swimming-pool beside the house. Then, with small warning, the weight of water diminished, and in a few weeks you could walk dryshod across an ex-fishpond and the swimming-pool.

The failure of the water was due in part to London's greed. Ever since Sir Hugh Myddelton in the seventeenth century doubled the water-courses of the Lea from Amwell southwards to fill an Islington reservoir, the demand for more and more water has grown, till it begins to exceed the supply. Loss of water is not the only threat to the rivers. Hertfordshire, as I have already said, is dotted from east to west with great country houses. A fine flourish has been set on a number of them, such as Luton Hoo, Tewin, Wormleybury and Brocket, by the formation of a wide lake made by holding up the streams; and these lakes have greatly added to the bird population of the county. When the war came it was felt that they were a guide-post to the German airmen, so the barriers were removed,

Aldenham, near Elstree, is typical of those villages where "the rural calm of Hertfordshire has persisted for centuries in spite of the neighbourhood of London." The "Hertfordshire Spike" on the church tower is typical of many village churches in the county.

The Maltings at Ware on the Lea. The town is famous for the Great Bed of Ware, formerly kept in the Saracen's Head inn, but now in the Victoria and Albert Museum in South Kensington.

and the rubbish accumulated over centuries in these lakes was decanted into the bed of the stream. Contamination ensued; and for various reasons effluents of a poisonous sort were caught up. On the upper reaches of the Lea the trout, with which the river was well stocked, died first; but not even the coarse fish could resist for long. Even the fresh-water cray-fish (for which London hotels used to compete) at last perished. A robust fight for the purity of our streams should be joined by all dwellers in Hertfordshire.

Hertfordshire is as many "fathoms deep" in history as Pevensey itself. When, for example, Mr. Kindersley, then Member for Hitchin, decided to have a tennis-court by his Welwyn house, a workman struck into a nest of Roman relics. The Samian ware looked as good as new, and bore the maker's mark, giving the precise date. Many of the buried urns were quite unharmed, so was one beautiful green glass decanter, and so would have been its pair, but for the too eager pickaxe of a reverend excavator. Most of these relics are to be seen at Letchworth—the first fruit of "To-morrow"; and to-morrow has become of overwhelming present interest within the county.

The first of the satellite towns organized by the planners of the New England, with

**Welwyn Garden City was the second satellite town built in Hertfordshire. It was planned in 1920, seventeen years after the foundation of Letchworth. The town is a centre of the film industry.**

Hemel Hempstead as second, was ordered by the Government to be built around the old village of Stevenage, hitherto distinguished mainly by its grammar school, four centuries old, and by a row of ancient Danish barrows.

As the first of the new towns which were to absorb some of London's teeming millions, the development of Stevenage became at once a cockpit of opposing interests. It was designed to take a population of sixty thousand, to be self-supporting, to have its own community centre, modern schools, libraries and cultural services; and at the same time was to attract such light industries as would provide work for its

mortar. Nevertheless the growth of Stevenage went ahead. The town can now muster about 25,000 inhabitants and it has, besides, fifteen or sixteen factories, which are in by no means unsightly surroundings; but the town centre has yet to be erected. Hemel Hempstead, in fact, has far outstripped it, though of course it was originally much larger, and now numbers some 45,000 people.

It was a rather surprising fact that in the more westerly part of the shire two existing centres of population, St. Albans, a considerable town, and Harpenden, still desirable as a village, suggested through their representative that they should each

**Knebworth House, near Stevenage, home of the Earl of Lytton, was built in the last century on the site of a Tudor Mansion, part of which, including the banqueting hall, was retained.**

people without upsetting the semi-rural amenities. On the other hand, these changes necessarily involved the uprooting of much that was old and cherished among the existing inhabitants. Land had to be compulsorily acquired, sometimes at prices which to the vendors seemed utterly unjust. Unsightly mounds of earth, rows of drainage trenches, unmade roads, all the flotsam and litter of streets of "council houses" in the making, disfigured the landscape. There were many protests and public meetings; and farmers especially complained that land which they had brought to a high pitch of fertility was now being wasted on bricks and

be increased by another ten thousand or so, in preference to the proposal that a brand-new satellite town should be built near Redbourn. Apart from such considerations, it has been the general feeling in Hertfordshire that its nearness to London has been wrongly exploited. The new towns, instead of freeing London from factories have partially served to house London workers. Why should the bulk of satellite towns and the first experiments be tried out so near London, against which the county has fought so valiant and successful a fight for centuries?

Yet, in spite of the threats of the new

planners and the necessities of so-called development, the native scenery of the county holds out. Rupert Brooke might still take pleasure in

The Roman Road to Wendover
By Tring and Lilley Hoo.

From the charming manor house at Lilley Hoo over one little reach of the Icknield Way (which is pre-Roman) to Telegraph Hill, you may still lose yourself, and find no one who can put you on your way.

Village cricket flourishes both at No-man's Land and in fields by country houses. Were those Lamb epithets of hearty and homely ever more pleasantly illustrated than at St. Paul's Walden in the days when our Queen Elizabeth as a girl helped her sister to score, while her father upset the wickets of the team of the neighbouring village with his slow, leg-breaking deliveries? The cricket, at which most of the family of Bowes Lyon excelled, keeps its zest and simplicity in the same villages; and country house and cottage, to the satisfaction of both, enjoy a mutual and most English relation. At the yearly ploughing matches one-furrow horse-drawn ploughs compete in the company of five-furrow ploughs drawn by tractors; and on such occasions I have heard street-arabs on holiday from London express their desire to be ploughers—a rare omen.

A large number of local words survive, though many are dead. When the time comes for hedging and ditching, the labourers still make their own "mollies" (mallets) out of hedge timber, preferably hornbeam. The villagers express their dislike, in true Shakespearean idiom, for the "hugger-mugger" work. When we see great changes—factories in village, schools in country houses, satellite towns, green but urban belts, ribbon developments and over-mechanized farms—we may still have good grounds for nursing the hope that the more it changes, the more it remains the same thing. Since only a few bits of the county belong to the National Trust, and so are saved "in perpetuity," the rest must be preserved by native watch-dogs, who will not allow the rivers to be polluted, or the commons invaded, or the half-year land forgotten, or the hedges destroyed, or the spirit of the village to be contaminated and its cottages made ugly or left insanitary. To-morrow, however different, may keep the essential quality of yesterday throughout the length and breadth, while it grows in comfort and vitality. The glory of the old village was its local self-sufficiency, and to this ideal we see some signs of return in the Village Produce Guild (which has its headquarters in Hertfordshire), the activity of Women's Institutes, where flourish greatly the revival of spinning, as of the Country and Agricultural Societies and, above all, the pride of Hertfordshire, its craftsmen.

*Model Farm, near Codicote*

*Parish Church, Ruislip*

# MIDDLESEX

### By SIDNEY DARK

WITH the creation of the administrative County of London, Middlesex lost nearly all its wealth, its history and its interest. It still retains the shadow of its ancient possession of London by continuing its local government from the beautiful Middlesex Guildhall in Westminster. But it has become, after Rutland, the smallest of the English counties in area, and it has very little of the natural beauty that is still Surrey's despite suburbanization. It is certain that few Londoners know where London ends and Middlesex begins.

On the south-east the county starts on the Thames just below Chiswick, and continues upwards to Staines, where the Colne flows into the Thames. The Colne is the county's boundary with Buckinghamshire, from Staines to Harefield. From there Middlesex borders Hertfordshire eastward by way of Pinner and Mill Hill, where the boundary makes a sharp switch north to South Mimms and then east again to the Lea, which divides Middlesex from Essex. Middlesex continues down the Lea to Stoke

Newington. From there it touches London westward to Golders Green, and then southward along the borders of Hampstead, Paddington and Hammersmith to the Thames.

Large and typically London districts have been left within the county, and hundreds of thousands of the inhabitants of Tottenham, Willesden, Acton and Ealing would be surprised, and possibly annoyed, if they were told they are not citizens of that anything but mean city. Middlesex is London's poor relation.

It has an area of 148,691 acres and a population of over $2\frac{1}{4}$ millions, which means that almost the whole area of the county is taken up in providing living and working space (for those who do not work in London) for its overmany inhabitants. Between the wars, the population increased by approximately eight hundred thousand, and in consequence the few remaining villages became completely urbanized. For example, Kenton, near Harrow, had a population of about two hundred in 1914. In 1938, its population was twenty-five thousand. Greenford, east of Uxbridge, with a tiny church that could barely hold two hundred persons, has increased in population from one thousand to fifty thousand. There is practically no "real country," to use Beach

*Arms of Middlesex*

# MIDDLESEX

CHISWICK MALL

SOUTH MIMMS

POTTERS

Sth. Mimms Church

Gate of Honour, Mill Hill School

MILL HILL

Airfield

STANMORE

EDGWARE

HENDON

HORN

NORTHWOOD

PINNER

HAREFIELD

Sport in the Stadium

RESERVOIR

Welsh Harp

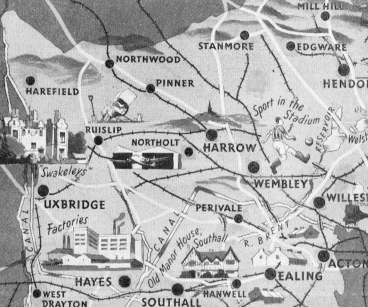

RUISLIP

NORTHOLT

HARROW

WEMBLEY

WILLESDEN

"Swakeleys"

UXBRIDGE

PERIVALE

R. BRENT

ACTON

Factories

Old Manor House, Southall

CANAL

R. BRENT

EALING

Middlesex Guild Westminster

HAYES

WEST DRAYTON

SOUTHALL

HANWELL

BRENTFORD

CHISWICK

HESTON

ISLEWORTH

HOUNSLOW

RIVER THAMES

R. COLNE

HEATHROW

R. CRANE

Rugby

London Airport

RESERVOIR

STAINES

FELTHAM

TWICKENHAM

TEDDINGTON

SYON HOUSE, BRENTFORD

Kempton Park

HAMPTON

RESERVOIR

SUNBURY

SHEPPERTON

PALACE

On the River

Hampton Court Palace

BUCKINGHAMSHIRE

Thomas's phrase, left in Middlesex except in the areas round Harefield in the north-west and round Stanwell farther south. The increase in population has been due to some extent to the general tendency of the Londoner to trek from the city for his home. Finchley, Hendon, Edgware, Harrow, Pinner and Ealing are residential suburbs, the refuges of the season-ticket holders. But Middlesex has been industrialized more than suburbanized. Tottenham is a factory town. Acton is the home of London's laundries. Hanwell has motor works. Southall is a railway town with many factories. The railway at Hayes, which twenty years ago was bordered by an orchard, is now bordered by an ugly gramophone works. Even West Drayton, at the extreme west of the county, which until very recent years was still a country town, is an industrial centre. The consequence is that, unlike Surrey, Middlesex mainly owes its increased population to the growing local demand for labour, and this means that it has a far smaller number of the leisured, the well-to-do and the retired.

### Hampstead Garden Suburb

The most interesting of the well-to-do settlements in Middlesex is the Hampstead garden suburb in the Hendon area. The suburb has been enthusiastically described as "a delightful rural town of twenty thousand people." It has none of the cheap ugliness of the jerry-built dormitory towns that were allowed to disfigure the metropolitan outskirts after the First World War. Its houses and its churches were designed by distinguished architects. It is comely and spacious, with gardens and lawns and avenues of trees, "trimmed like hatboxes." But it is not a rural town or any other sort of town; for a town is a place where men work as well as rest, and where men of many avocations mix and act together. In the perfect garden city the well-to-do are segregated in depressingly symmetrical prosperity. For all its superficial charm, the garden suburb is a warning for the planners. What is needed are community centres not class colonies.

Exploring Middlesex west from Chiswick, the little village of Strand-on-the-Green, at

Strand-on-the-Green, in the borough of Brentford and Chiswick, still retains the atmosphere of a Thames-side village, in spite of being only two miles from the London county boundary.

the foot of Kew Bridge, once a settlement of Thames fishermen, is interesting, since it has somehow contrived to keep its detached character. Up the river is Twickenham, where Pope lived in a villa, bought with the money that he received for his translation of Homer, where Horace Walpole lived on Strawberry Hill, where Fielding wrote *Tom Jones* and Dickens wrote *Oliver Twist*. From Twickenham and its neighbour Hampton the view of Richmond Hill across the river is perhaps the loveliest in Middlesex.

Hampton Court is the county's chief historic possession. Built by Cardinal Wolsey, who spent there his few years of ostentatious power, it became the favourite residence of Henry VIII, and the birthplace of Edward VI. Mary Tudor spent her honeymoon with the dreary-souled, plotting Philip of Spain at Hampton Court. Here Shakespeare acted before Scottish Jamie. Dutch William commissioned Christopher Wren to add Fountain Court to the Tudor building. This is one of the very few good things that this country owes to the imported sovereign, who introduced the English

people to gin and stabilized the power of money in the national economy by sponsoring the Bank of England. Hampton Court contains interesting pictures and matchless tapestries, with its maze for the amusement of the general public, its great vine and its gorgeous herbaceous border which, backed by a Wren wall, is perhaps the most beautiful of all English flowerbeds. Still following the Thames, one remembers that Thomas Love Peacock, the novelist, Shelley's friend and executor and the father-in-law of George Meredith, lived at Shepperton, and Matthew Arnold was born and was buried at Laleham. The broad Laleham Reach is the Thames at its Middlesex best.

The Romans built four of the main roads that run from London, west, north-west and north across Middlesex. The most southerly of the Roman roads passes by way of Chiswick, Brentford and Hounslow to cross the Thames at Staines. At Hounslow there is a loop which leads to Slough in Buckinghamshire to cross the river at Maidenhead. Brentford, with a hideous great gasometer and a mean and narrow

High Street, was a ghastly traffic bottle-neck before the construction of the Great West Road. This road, one of the first by-passes, is lined by modern factories, many of which prove that a factory need not be an eyesore.

Hounslow Heath, once famous for its highwaymen, is now market gardens and chemical and soap factories. Near Hounslow is Stanwell, which, as I have said, is one of Middlesex's two remaining villages.

A second road runs through Willesden, Harrow and Pinner. Gladstone Park on Dollis Hill at Willesden has its name from the fact that the Liberal statesman spent his quiet week-ends as the guest of Lord Aberdeen at Dollis Hill House long before Chequers became the Prime Ministers' retreat. Crowds of Londoners used to flock to watch Gladstone on a Sunday morning going to and from St. Mary's Church, Neasden Lane, where he always read the lessons at Mattins whenever he was at Dollis Hill. This evidence of popularity, which seriously disturbed his devotions, caused Gladstone considerable annoyance. Mark Twain was another occasional visitor.

Harrow is now a great suburban district which has absorbed a dozen villages, and has a population of two hundred thousand. But the view of Windsor and of the high ground of Surrey and Kent from the top of Harrow Hill, where the spire of St. Mary's is four hundred feet above the sea, remains. The noble record of Harrow School is a great county possession, and the old town itself has kept a good deal of what has been called its "cloistered air." St. Mary's was consecrated in 1094, and a small part of the Norman foundation remains.

Harrow School was founded in the reign of Elizabeth by John Lyon, a yeoman, who left lands to a corporation "for a free grammar school for the poor, for poor scholars at the universities, and the repairing highways." As has happened with many other of England's miscalled "public schools," the intention of the founder has been largely ignored, and Harrow has become famous as the school for the sons of the prosperous and the privileged. It has been the school of six of England's Prime Ministers—of Percival, Aberdeen, Robert Peel, whom Queen Victoria first disliked and

**Stanmore Common is a well-wooded, delightful tract of country within easy access of London. Strangely, however, it seems little known and attracts far fewer visitors than might be expected.**

An aerial view of Wembley Stadium where the Football Association Cup Finals have been played since 1923. The stadium, which will hold a hundred thousand spectators, and other buildings, some of which are seen in the background, were built for the British Empire Exhibition of 1924–25.

Hampton Court Palace was built by Cardinal Wolsey in 1515 and given up to Henry VIII eleven years later. Partly rebuilt by Christopher Wren for William III, it remained a royal residence until the reign of George III. The gardens, famous for their vine and maze, were first laid out for Charles II.

afterwards came to trust, of "Old Pam" (Lord Palmerston, whom she always detested. Stanley Baldwin and Winston Churchill; of Sheridan the dramatist and Shaftesbury the philanthropist, and of Manning, the great churchman, who was the ally of the London dockers when they struck in the eighties for "a tanner an hour," who is Harrow's one Cardinal.

There are portraits and busts of its worthies in comely halls and rooms in the school. But Harrow is properly proudest of

famous as the librettist of the Savoy operas and the writer of lyrics, as Maurice Baring contended, comparable to those of Herrick. The one most often in my mind, as I grow old, is:—

Is life a boon?
If so, it must befall
That death. whene'er he call,
Must call too soon!

The Edgware Road from Hendon to Edgware, up the steep Brockley Hill near Stanmore, is the Roman Watling Street.

Hampton Church seen from the Surrey bank of the Thames at Molesey. The river side and nearby Hampton Court and Bushey Park, famous for its magnificent avenue of chestnut trees, attract many visitors during the summer months.

Byron, who wrote the earliest of his poems sitting on John Peachey's tombstone at St. Mary's.

Byron lazy, lazily lay
Hid from lessons and game away;
Dreaming poetry all alone
Up-in-top of the Peachy Stone.

W. S. Gilbert lived and died at Grim's Dyke, Harrow Weald, a quarrelsome man,

There is a legend, almost certainly unfounded, that Handel was moved to write "The Harmonious Blacksmith" after sheltering from a storm in a forge at Edgware. The Prince Regent, the Tsar of Russia, the King of Prussia and Louis XVIII of France met to discuss the future of Europe at Bentley Priory at Stanmore when it was believed that Napoleon was safely tucked away in the island of Elba. During the war Bentley was the headquarters of Fighter Command of the R.A.F.

Highgate Hill, where Whittington turned again to be Lord Mayor of London, is the most famous of the northern heights. Here are buried in strange post-mortem neighbourliness Herbert Spencer, the philosopher of individualism, who might have married George Eliot had she been better looking, and Karl Marx, the philosopher of revolutionary Socialism. George Morland painted many of his pictures at the Bull Inn at Highgate, and at Highgate lived Leigh Hunt, whom Dickens lampooned in *Bleak House*. Shortly before their deaths, Coleridge, a man of nearly fifty, had his one meeting with Keats, then twenty-six, "a loose slack not well-dressed youth," at Highgate Hill, and nearly two hundred years before, two other poets, Milton and Andrew Marvell, often met there.

In the extreme east of the county, Enfield, one of the last places in England where there was a yearly fair for the engagement of farm servants, carters, to indicate their craft, coming with their whips, labourers with a spade and woodmen with a bill, and Edmonton, where John Gilpin finished his famous ride, are associated with Charles Lamb, "the most lovable Londoner of them all."

He went to live in Enfield with his sister Mary, when he retired from the East India Office and became a superannuated man. He was visited by Leigh Hunt and Tom Hood, by Coleridge and Wordsworth. But the super-Cockney hated the country. He wrote to Wordsworth: "Let no native Londoner imagine that health and rest and occupation, interchange of converse and recreative study can make the country anything better than altogether odious and detestable." In 1833 the Lambs moved to Edmonton, and there a year later the gentle Elia died.

Middlesex, the mother of London, has come to be its unconsidered dependant. As is common with most poor relations, it has little character of its own. No one dreams of saying of a man that he has distinctive Middlesex qualities, as we say that a man is "very Yorkshire." Middlesex has lost most of its wealth and most of its beauty. But, here and there in tucked-away corners, some of the beauty is still to be found, and the Little Home County has rich memories of great events for which it provided the scene, and of great men who lived and died within its borders.

*East Bedfont Church*

*Unloading Hops at a Kentish Oast House*

# KENT

### By RICHARD CHURCH

THERE is no way of dodging the old tag about Kent being "the garden of England." So let us agree at once that it is so. The label is right enough, so far as it goes. But the trouble is that it gives a false impression to people who do not know the county, or rather the ancient Kingdom of Kent. Only recently a North Country dalesman referred to Kent as "suburban." He must surely have once been down to Beckenham!

It is really a matter for wonder that this county, which penetrates into the heart of London, the county through which every traveller to and from the Continent sooner or later must pass, should yet remain so untouched by such proximity and such traffic. All along the Weald, the great stretch of what was once the forest land of Anderida, between Sevenoaks and Ashford, sleeps on from year to year, century to century, with its natives still wholly rural in their way of life, their culture, and their tempo. There is no sign of suburbanity along the Weald.

*Arms of Kent*

Nor will it be found along the mid-Kent Ridge, amongst the rich "dene" villages that marked the first subjugations of the primeval forest, and the rise of England's two principal industries, wool and iron. And certainly the other large division of Kent, the marshland of Romney, shows no sign of villa-dom. That contemptuous critic of the county may perhaps have been also to Margate; but Margate is in Thanet— the small nose that sticks out towards the Goodwin Sands. A slight disfigurement of the nose is not necessarily evidence that the whole person is corrupted.

The faults of Kent are certainly not of an urban kind. On the contrary, the weakness both of the Men of Kent east of the Medway, and the Kentish Men west of that important river, is that they are so wholly rural in their lives, and so proud and prosperous in that rurality, that they have no time for cultural activities, or for a proper appreciation of the vast historical wealth of the land out of which they make their substantial fortunes.

On the historical side especially, this is a pity, for in the history of Kent there lies the explanation of why these farmers are somewhat

51

different in their methods, and their land tenures, from their fellows in the rest of England. Their singularity, of course, is affected by many factors; the geology and climate, for example; but principally the farmers of Kent are what they are because of their special origins, and the form which the drama of history took in its passage over their fields and hop-gardens.

Let us look at the structure of the county, its position in relation to the rest of the island of Britain, and the geographical differences which have divided it up into its distinctive parts. This view will partly explain why the present-day inhabitants of Kent are what they are, and do what they do. Geography, in fact, has been of immense significance in the county's history.

### Link with Europe

To begin with, Kent is the nearest part of England to the mainland of Europe. It is the prow of the ship. Practically everything that has come to England during the last several thousands of years, including the latest diabolical Teutonic inventions, has come to Kent first, either to be intercepted or passed thence to the rest of the country.

One invasion Kent did escape. During the last great Ice Age it was one of the few parts of England left unsubmerged beneath the ice cap that crept down from the frozen north. It escaped only by reason of the width of the Thames estuary, but that was enough to make it one, during the long hibernation, with the rest of Europe. It is no fanciful idea to believe that this has given Kent an ethnological venerability, a quality of time-wisdom that tinges everything in the county. Julius Cæsar, when he came to Britain, noted in his Commentary that the inhabitants of Kent were as civilized as those of Gaul. One can believe that they were disciplined by a racial memory, as well as by the fact, noted a thousand years after Cæsar by William the Conqueror's historian, William of Poitiers, who wrote that "Kent is situated nearer to France, wherefore it is inhabited by less ferocious men than the rest of England."

That still holds good to-day. The most noticeable characteristic of the Kentish folk is their tolerant kindness. To live in Kent is to be constantly aware of the European tradition, and of its root in the Roman Empire. One might equally well be living in Normandy, where the scenery, the domestic architecture and the nature of the people are comparable. All that is different now is the language—and the lamentable fact that grapes for the making of wine are no longer grown in Kent. But even that loss has its substitute in the culture of the hop, round which the economic life of a great part of the county turns. It is a rougher, paler substitute, but it involves much the same ritual and customs as does the cultivation of the grape-vine. The leaf is the same, and has the classical shape sacred to Dionysus. We shall see in a moment how this similarity affects the natures of the people engaged in its cultivation.

Other odd little survivals due to these geological and historical facts crop up again and again. For instance, the fauna of the county is remarkably rich and various; Kent has sixteen different kinds of ants, and is the wealthiest of all the English counties in beetles and immigrant butterflies; while the great white snail, introduced by the Romans and cultivated in the grounds of their villas, is still found throughout the county, especially along the northern side of the Downs above the shores of the Thames, where the Roman civil servants lived two thousand years ago.

### The Weald

Present-day life and economics in Kent are governed by certain elementary geographical facts. In the vast distance of geological time, a ridge of chalk heights, alpine in nature, ran east-west along the counties south of the Thames. Rivers therefore flowed from that watershed north and south, either to the Thames and its estuary, or to the Channel. They still do so, though the ridge has been eroded, decaying like a molar and leaving an inland plain now called the Weald which stretches from the Hampshire border through parts of Surrey and Sussex and on into Kent. In Kent this plain is contracted by the greensand hills to the south-west of the county.

Looking across Romney Marsh, the stretch of flat land between Hythe and Dungeness.

The North Downs run on through Kent, turning south-east to end at the "white cliffs of Albion" by Dover and Folkestone. The Weald proper is heavy clay, but it is fertile. Here the hop is cultivated, in the district east of Tonbridge running as far as Ashford, with the heart of the culture round about East Peckham and along the valley of the Medway approaching Maidstone. Many of the great brewing firms have their

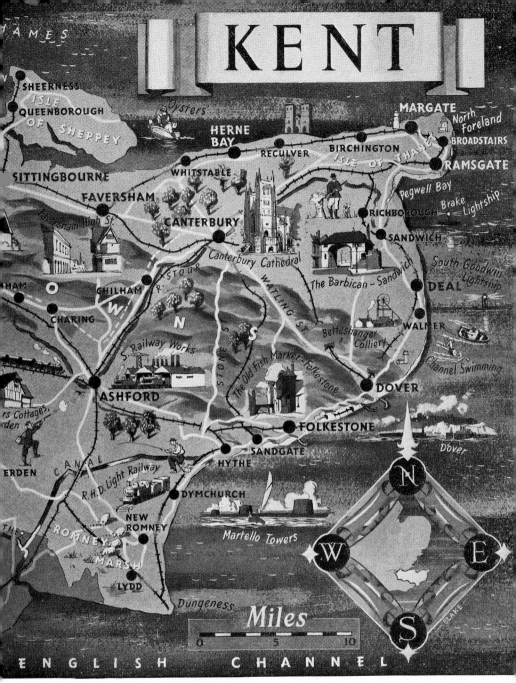

own hop-gardens in this district, run in a scientific way by horticultural experts engaged in constant research towards a disease-proof hop-vine. The seasonal processes of the culture are intricate and costly.

A hop-garden is an expensive undertaking. But it is also a profitable one. Not only the men, but their families, too, are caught up in the work. At three periods of the year—first, for the stringing of the hop

Oast houses amidst fruit blossom are a characteristic feature of the Kentish scene. This view was taken near Sittingbourne. Hops and fruit are the chief staples of the county's agricultural produce.

gardens, second for "twiddling" or training the young shoots on the strings, and third for the picking—the country women have to join their menfolk in the gardens.

In March they go out to do the stringing. The men precede the women, some on long stilts, tie the strings to the top wires which are stretched permanently on the high poles: others lace the strings at lower levels. The women follow, pegging down the strings to the ground, and looping four strings with a band about four feet from the ground. The result is a funnel-shaped design, running away in diminishing perspective, with a geometrical precision that is wonderful to see. How do the women, who work quickly and apparently without measuring, achieve this precision? In the same way, probably, as the local builders who put up the circular oast-houses: by rule of thumb—it is the thumb of a racial genius! It costs about a hundred pounds to-day to string a four-acre hop garden.

Then in May and June the women are out again, for weeks on end, "twiddling."

Twiddling is training the young vine shoots, anti-clockwise, up the base of the strings. It is a tedious job, but it occurs in the glory of the year, and the women appear to enjoy it, for it brings them together and they live a sort of community life during this period, going home in the evening sun-burned, to get the evening meal for the family. The young children of Kent learn early in life to help with the household chores and the cooking, for their mothers play a large part in the out-door work. If they did not, harvesting the hops would be much delayed.

Picking, the final labour, is the one best known to the outside world. It begins at the end of August, and often goes on until the first week of October. It is a seasonal work which wrings the county dry, breaking into its ordered way of life with a bacchic fury. Man, woman and child are swept into the rout, which has a Keats-like abandonment about it. I have seen these sober, English countrymen working in the gardens with crowns of the hop-vine foliage tied round their heads. The reason is not a ritualistic

56

or religious one. It is because they find such a headdress cooler than a hat, and one, too, which keeps the flies away. But the effect is completely Theocritan.

The number of local folk is, however, quite inadequate to the needs of the moment at hop-picking time. As a result there takes place an annual invasion from the East End of London, supplemented by pseudo gypsies from their winter quarters at Mitcham, Maidstone and elsewhere. There are usually over forty thousand of these invaders, for whom special camping arrangements are made in the hop-fields, and whatever the local folk think of their behaviour, they know that the work they do is essential. The invaders combine a camping holiday in the country, for the whole family from the very old to the very young, with remuneration for hard work.

The growing of the hop, with all the activities that it entails, is well mirrored in our English literature; but I know of no more vivid picture of it than in C. Henry Warren's *A Boy in Kent*, or in the poems of Edmund Blunden, whose birth and particular genius make him Kent's Laureate. His bucolic poems spring from the same soil as the main tributaries of the Medway; those meandering streams, the Beult and the Teise, which wind their way through hop-gardens, luxuriant meadows and iron-stone outcroppings. They pass water-mills, feed ponds where huge pike lurk, drop down weirs against which trout and roach dash themselves madly every spring. They shelter the kingfisher, the nightingale and the smaller wildfowl. All these things, so characteristic of the Weald in the flats and foothills below Maidstone, are embalmed for ever in Blunden's verse, which has the static quality of the countryside it celebrates.

All this district, however, was once part of the vast forest that stretched for a hundred and twenty miles east to west from behind Folkestone right through the country into Sussex and Hampshire, while from south to north it was about thirty miles wide. Domesday Book has practically no records of settlements in this forest. It was primeval, consisting mainly of gigantic oakwood, under which fed the wild boar and deer. Even as late as Henry VIII's time—the sixteenth century—a traveller

**Some of Kent's "invaders" from London at hop-picking time, which lasts five weeks. Workers with long poles pull the hop vines down from the strings on which they were trained in May and June.**

from the south of the county had to come to London via Canterbury, a journey that took two days. There were no roads through the forest until the time came in the days of Elizabeth when it was discovered that the soil under that forest was rich in iron ore. For the following three centuries that part of England was its Black Country; but a sweet-smelling black —for the smelting of the iron was done by charcoal, produced from the seemingly inexhaustible supplies of wood in the forest. Seemingly, but not so in fact, for very soon we find that Parliament was passing laws regulating the consumption and replacing of timber. Even so, the depredation went on rapidly, until by the eighteenth century most of the forest had disappeared. Bits of it survive to-day, notably around Goudhurst and Cranbrook. Along the ridge-road from these two handsome villages to Tenterden, one may see, stretching along gentle valleys east and west as far as the eye can reach, a sort of ghost-survival of that mighty forest. The people, too, have a sylvan character, in their ways of life and their homes. The soil is magical still, and

the cherries and apples grown in that district are the best in the world.

All along this inland ridge that divides the Weald proper from the Romney Marsh and the sea there now run orchards, set above the frost line, and in the early spring this part of the county is a fairyland of blossom—cherry, plum, apple and pear. After, or often during, hay-making the local folk are doubly put to it to get the fruit in. They are helped again by visitors, usually the caravanners who come later in the year for the hop-picking. All are paid piece-work—for so much a bushel—and the Covent Garden lorries keep up a shuttle traffic during those busy weeks, running the fruit direct from farm to market.

All this side of Kent farm life was formerly done by rote and superstition based on folk methods. To-day it grows more and more scientific. The Fruit Research station at East Malling, with experimental orchards, is at the service of the farmers, sending out experts to advise them on methods of pruning, grafting, disease control, manuring and spacing. During the war, when fruit was fetching

**Dover has long been England's chief port for travel to and from Europe. Its white chalk cliffs surmounted by a Norman castle have become symbolic of England's independence.**

**From the "Devil's Kneading Trough" at the south-eastern end of the North Downs between Ashford and Hythe, a wide view opens over the fertile land of the Weald of Kent.**

such good, Government-controlled prices, the farmers were able to undertake big-scale experiments. Most of the Kent orchards were thinned, every other tree being taken out, many orchards cut down to the trunk and the trees re-grafted with more profitable, better-grade fruit. New orchards were set as soon as the compulsory growing of corn was relaxed. The result of this revolution in horticultural method is a reduction in the picturesqueness of much of the fruit-growing country. The old, leaning and mossy trunks have disappeared. So, too, has much of the disease with them. In time this will mean larger and better supplies of fruit.

These fruit- and hop-farmers of the Weald and the central ridge are specialists, but many of them to-day insure themselves against big losses (mainly by frost, the bug-

bear of this particular kind of farming) by doing a little general farming, in arable and stock. During the war, of course, the arable became the major activity, and the face of Kent was transformed. The first crop of wheat, grown on fields many of which had been pasture-land for a century, was too light-rooted to maintain so abundant and full an ear as that battle-year of 1940 yielded, and much damage was done by wind. Indeed, this wonderful soil can be an embarrassment, for it produces more harvests, both of fruit and corn, than the farmer can find labour to gather in. This odd economic problem is repeated in the north of the county, on the rich soil between the chalk downs and the Thames Estuary.

That strip of country seen by travellers and mariners coming and going between

London and the sea, so easily accessible by water, and removed from the dangers of the southern forest, became the residential quarter of the Romans during the four centuries of their highly civilized and even sophisticated occupation of England. It breaks through the hills at three gaps, by Ashford, Maidstone and Dartford; and it opens out over Thanet to include the rich lands where Richborough and Canterbury (Rutupiae and Durovernum were settled as the military and administrative headquarters of the colony. All this stretch of country is a paradise for achælogists. Neolithic, Roman, Saxon and Medieval relics are eloquent of a continuous story of human settlement. The Roman officials built their villas on these northern slopes, whence they trafficked between the two centres already mentioned, and Reculver (Regulbium and London (Londinium), along Watling Street, the first great Roman road. The Thames shore off Reculver has receded a mile inland since then, for tesselated pavements, cisterns and arched vaults have been found as far out as Black Rock, on the bed of the estuary, while coins and domestic fragments from the period of Julius Cæsar to that of Honorius are constantly being washed up by the tides. All this, the story of the past, is so abundant that it needs not a chapter, but a volume to itself.

### A Famous Shrine

So, too, does the record of Canterbury—for three hundred years one of the most famous shrines in Europe. It is difficult to see in that quiet cathedral city of to-day one of the greatest centres of Christian ritual and ceremony, approached throughout the Middle Ages by a traffic of worshippers. Between the thirteenth and the sixteenth centuries its streets and hostels were filled with a concourse of pilgrims and the tradesmen who battened on them. Every nationality and social grade were represented. By the time Geoffrey Chaucer pictured the scene, it was becoming decadent and over-blown. Abuses had crept in—abuses which a little later Erasmus and his friend Colet contemplated with such disgust. The genuine worship at the shrine

of Becket had degenerated into a perennial fairing totally commercial in both practice and purpose.

I have not space enough to write of Canterbury here. There is so much to say of this sacred place where the seed of Christianity was first organized in Britain in the sixth century. Nor could I attempt to describe the architectural glories of this city, as beautiful as any in Europe, without trying to keep a balance by writing of the Castle and Cathedral of Rochester, and of such parish churches as that of Cranbrook, "the cathedral of the Weald," or the little chapel of Stone-cum-Ebony, which contains an ancient Roman altar originally dedicated to the worship of the Bull, that grim forerunner of the Ram, or Lamb of God.

### Great Houses

And again there is the secular architecture: the great palaces such as Knole at Sevenoaks, with its three hundred and sixty-five rooms and fifty-two staircases; or the smaller Penshurst, where Sir Philip Sidney the poet and hero was born; or Leeds Castle, which still stands in its moat near Charing, the pretty village where once the Archbishops of Canterbury had a palace (amongst many in the county). Sir Winston Churchill's home at Chartwell Manor has been purchased for the National Trust.

This Kentish architecture, the pride of town, village and country mansion, has been conditioned by the nature of the materials, all of local origin. Kentish ragstone and Bethersden marble were used for the churches and many of the big houses. Red tiles and rose-coloured bricks were frequently made from clay near the sites of the cottages and oasts. Medieval building was lavishly timbered with oak beams, but these diminished in size and quantity as the price of wood rose during and after the seventeenth century. Conspicuous features of Kentish domestic architecture are the tile-hung or weatherboarded upper storeys of houses. Brenchley, one of the most beautiful villages in the county, has samples of both. Chiddingstone (now National Trust property), Eynsford, Hollingbourne, Goudhurst, Cobham with its palace,

**The county cricket matches at Canterbury attract many spectators to this delightful ground. The Kent Club has won the county championship four times and has numbered many distinguished players among its members. There are other county grounds at Blackheath and Maidstone.**

Biddenden with its row of shops and seven-gabled weaver's house, Igtham with its moated mansion, Tenterden with its broad High Street—these are only the more famous of Kent's inland villages. Outside the villages, the open country is dotted with manors and farmhouses of every period of English architecture from the fourteenth to the nineteenth centuries. Yet another unique feature of the county is the weather-boarded seaside building (dwelling, warehouse, fishing-shed) found in the villages round the coast, from Gravesend to Romney, with a few surviving Martello Towers to serve as memorials of Napoleon's threat of invasion.

The mention of Cranbrook again reminds us that this was the place from which the national economy of medieval Eng-land was so successfully augmented by Edward III, when he had the bright idea of more than doubling our national income by exporting not the raw wool (hitherto our principal commodity), but the manufactured cloth. For this purpose he brought to Cranbrook expert Flemish weavers, who speedily affected the local life and culture with their greater wealth and civilized manners. For example, they at once re-built Cranbrook Church. There are still some half-dozen "weavers' halls" in and around the village. These halls, or houses, are typical of many scattered throughout the county. All of them are spacious, nobly planned works of Renaissance domestic architecture. They survive to-day, as strong as when they were built some four to five hundred years ago, as reminders

Leeds Castle, dating from the fourteenth century, was built on an island in a branch of the Medway near Maidstone. Although largely restored, it is a classic example of a medieval moated fortress.

of the first emergence of England as a great economic force in the comity of Europe.

Alongside these houses are a few that were built by the ironmasters of the Weald, though the centre of this great and now vanished industry was just over the border of Kent, in East Sussex. But Lamberhurst had one of the biggest foundries, from which the original railings round St. Paul's Cathedral were forged at the end of the seventeenth century. All that remains to-day of those rich activities is an indicative place-name here and there: Hammer Pond, Colliers' Green, Forge Pond. By the end of the eighteenth century a trade that had existed for a very long time in Kent had come to an end. The spirit of the King's Forest has overlaid the memories of that great industry, making them no more than "a green thought in a green shade." Both weavers and ironmasters have disappeared, as the fulcrum of the wool and iron trades has shifted nearer to the new supplies of fuel and power in the north of England.

The surviving industries of Kent are the coal-pits in the extreme south-east of the county, and the cement works, ship-building and engineering that flourish alongside the prosperous market-gardening

in north Kent, which feeds Covent Garden market daily. The coal-pits have mostly been developed since the 1914-18 war, inland behind Deal. The product is a soft coal used for industrial purposes, and the mining is done through modern pits that neither disfigure nor soil the countryside. For example, Lord Northbourne's model estate near Deal carries on experimental agriculture within sight of the pit-heads. Round the pits are clustered garden villages to house the workers, whose labour brings a new source of wealth to the county.

### Shipbuilding Industry

The building of seaplanes at the mouth of the Medway (an industry which has recently been transferred to Belfast) maintained the tradition of the naval ship-building which has been carried on at Chatham and Rochester since the Middle Ages. Lambarde, the historian, writing in the sixteenth century, at the time when Henry VIII was co-ordinating and strengthening the naval force of the nation, said of Chatham and its fleet that "it presenteth itself, a thing of all other the most worthie the first place, whether you respect the richesse, beautie of benefite of the same; nor shipping any where els in the whole world to be founde, either more artificially moulded under the water, or more gorgeously decked above.'' It was at Chatham that Pepys, as Secretary of the Admiralty, carried on his good work of clearing up the muddle and peculation which had so reduced our naval strength that the Dutch fleet was able to penetrate as far as the Medway during the war with the Netherlands, causing havoc among the shipping there and panic in London.

At Maidstone, the capital of Kent, and in the coast towns north of it (Dartford, Gravesend, Greenhithe and Northfleet), the major part of England's paper-making is done. Here, too, are large cement works. It is odd to see round the factories and installations acre after acre of market-gardens. This horticulture is so closely organized as to be more in the nature of a mechanical industry than a rural occupation. So, too, is the oyster dredging and culture carried on off the coast of Whitstable. This activity is in the hands of a Royal Corporation, administered by officers whose authority still has a medieval sanction about it. The famous "native"— the oyster of oysters—is not necessarily

born there. Cultures—the young bivalves— are brought to the Whitstable beds from various parts of Europe, notably Portugal and Brittany, a special fleet of boats being maintained solely for that traffic. But the nature of the waters off the coast of North Kent, fed by iron and other salts brought down by the many small streams running from the Downs, fosters these foreigners along with the natives, and gives them the unique flavour that satisfies the gourmet. No, not satisfies, for the oyster is like love or music, re-creating the appetite which it appeases.

### Cinque Ports

The other marine industry of Kent is the general sea-fishing carried on round the coast since history began. Along this coast grew up a medieval confederacy for self-protection, which eventually became the Cinque Ports—Romney, Hythe, Dover and Sandwich in Kent, with Hastings in Sussex; to these were subsequently attached the ancient towns of Rye and Winchelsea, besides a good many other places. The Royal Charters granted to this first of our trade

**Betteshanger Colliery near Deal is an up-to-date pit. Though coal has been mined in considerable quantities in Kent since 1894, the real development of the coalfield only began after the First World War.**

organizations date back to the reign of Edward I, and they stipulate that the ports shall provide men and ships, in the King's need, to support the Royal Navy. To this day the Lord Warden of the Cinque Ports acts as Governor of Dover Castle, and resides officially at Walmer Castle.

Dover, with its great Norman castle, its naval and military position, its famous (and expensive) harbour, its towering Shakespeare Cliff, is world-famous. Kent is the gateway to England. Dover is the lock to that gate. Ramsgate, Deal and Dover are the principal fishing ports of Kent, and their boatmen provide the skill and courage to combat the dangers of the Straits and the Goodwin Sands. These mariners, who man the lifeboats, are celebrated in the annals of heroism.

### Coast Town Life

Finally, there is the rest of the coast-town life, with the pleasure resorts that attract ozone-seekers from all over England. From Herne Bay on the Thames estuary to Dymchurch on the Sussex border, holiday towns lie right round the coast of Kent. They are maintained by a population of caterers, hoteliers, lodging-house keepers, staffs of convalescent homes and hospitals, who provide food and service for millions of visitors every year, with an industry that adds vastly to the wealth of the county.

Folkestone is the gem of these resorts. It is worthy of a bluer sea than the Channel. I should call it the Antibes of the North, with its gay cliff gardens, its warm temperatures, its wonderful air. And there is Broadstairs, a village still, with recollections of Dickens, that genius whose childhood was spent principally at Rochester. Pegwell Bay, just below Broadstairs, is the place where Julius Cæsar probably, and St. Augustine certainly, landed.

Dickens's tales are coloured with the personality of Kent. But he is only one of many writers whose art was suckled by this queen of the English counties. I think of Kit Marlowe, son of a Canterbury shop-keeper; of Richard Barham, who laid the scene of many of his Ingoldsby Legends in the village where he was born, and from which his family took its name; of Geoffrey Chaucer, greatest of them all; and, amongst present-day writers, V. Sackville-West and Edmund Blunden, both poets who, when they sing of Kent, add greater depth, greater tenderness and reverence to their music, because of all that they recognize in the beauty, of past and present, in the county that has nurtured them.

*Aylesford from the Medway*

*The Pagoda, Kew Gardens*

# SURREY

### By SIDNEY DARK

AN AMERICAN writer recently said that people no longer live in states, but in metropolitan areas, and it is certainly true that the people in what is left of Middlesex, in the larger part of Surrey and in parts of Essex and Kent no longer live in counties, but in London suburbs. The development of the London suburb has had three stages. Often less than a generation ago it was rural. Then it became urban. Now it is metropolitan, not administratively of London, but spiritually in it.

The suburb is the place where men sleep. It is the retreat from the workaday world, where the harassed can "get away from things." The richer a man becomes, the farther he contrives to get away. That is evident as one travels through Surrey southward from the London border. First, for example, at Mitcham, once famous for its lavender, sold in the London streets at three bunches a penny, are the rather ugly little homes of the poorer workers. Farther south at Purley are the more modern and

*Arms of Surrey*

more expensive homes of the better paid. Finally, at Haslemere, almost in Hampshire, are the large houses with large gardens of the comfortably retired and the captains of industry, whose cars are stacked in the railway station yard from morning to evening.

The populations of these varying districts—they are typical of many others—disperse between eight and nine and converge again between six and seven. They live two lives. When they go to the station in the morning, in the fullest sense, they leave their homes and families behind. When they catch their evening trains they leave their work behind. The result is that the majority of the season ticket population "cannot be bothered" with the community affairs of what are for them dormitories and week-end rest houses.

At diocesan conferences the clergy are constantly bemoaning the fact that there is no civic spirit in the dormitory parishes. This is, I think, not altogether true. Nearly everywhere there are clubs of all sorts, but the suburb reeks with classism. It resents newcomers. The suburban home is a castle where the drawbridge is seldom let down. It is so valued because it is exclusive.

65 (E.N.C.)

Looking down Guildford High Street towards the bridge over the River Wey.

66

# SURREY

An American writer has said: "Something treacherous is created in the emotions and attitudes of a man who escapes after work to irresponsibility. In his leisure hours, when his most creative thoughts are born, he is beguiled by the lethargy of his surroundings. Suburbanitis is a sort of sleeping-sickness which infests the shaded avenues of suburbia as malaria hangs about Southern swamps." And the conclusion is that "it is dangerous to separate the most fortunate people geographically from their work and morally from the world."

### Retreats from the City

The suburb segregates. In it there are no sympathetic, intimate contacts between people of different economic circumstances and different backgrounds. The suburbs are retreats from the city, but they are also its parasites. They sap communal life, for a true human community is not a place where men only sleep together and on rare occasions may pray together, but where they work together, sharing common interests and ministering to common needs.

The trek from the city is said to be due to the instinctive longing for trees and open spaces and quiet. But I have suggested in the chapter on London that the true Londoner detests quiet, and only has an occasional longing for the fields and the hills. When he lives far away from his work it is because he cannot find a house near his work. Then the suburbanite, despite himself, only finds the quiet tolerable on Sundays because of the familiar rattle on the other six days. The influence of the housewife, who is suburbanite all the week, perforce and often against her will, gradually but surely urbanizes her new home town. Croydon, where Purley shops, is as London in all essentials as Streatham. The certainty that the encroachment of poorer settlers inevitably means urbanization—the cinema is always hard on the heels of the immigrants—is the reason why the richer districts strive, and generally unsuccessfully, to surround themselves with barbed wire.

Forty-five years ago it was regretted that Surrey had become a mere playground for London! To-day it is much more a dormitory than a playground, though Epsom Downs in Derby week is still the Cockney's favourite holiday resort. Mr. Pepys spent a happy Sunday at Epsom with his wife and a friend, taking with him "some bottles of wine and beer and some cold fowl in the coach," and finding the country "very fine, only the way very dusty." Mr. Pepys was a pioneer of the week-end habit, for on returning home on that Sunday evening he resolved "not to have a country house, but to keep a coach, and with my wife on the Saturday to go sometimes for a day to this place, and then quit to another place."

There are in Surrey four other race-courses and countless golf-courses. The county, too, is happy in the possession of many commons, which is one of the reasons why it rivals Hampshire and Kent in the number of its cricket worthies. The County Club, now a London possession, was founded at Dorking in 1844. Some of the commons—Clapham, Tooting, Streatham and Putney—have been filched by London. Richmond Park, the home of many sovereigns from Edward II to the girlhood of Queen Mary, and Kew, associated with the Georges, though geographically belonging to Surrey, actually belong to London. But Surrey still has many commons of its own.

### County Boundaries

Surrey extends southward from the County of London, on the east touching Kent from a few miles east of Croydon to a few miles east of East Grinstead and Ashdown Forest. Its southern Sussex border-line goes westward to a few miles west of Haslemere. There it touches Hampshire in an irregular line running north-west to a few miles west of Camberley, where it turns north-east to the Thames. Two principal roads run through the county from London to the coast; the Portsmouth Road by way of Kingston, Guildford and Hindhead, and the Brighton Road by way of Croydon and Reigate. Its principal river is the Wey, which flows through Godalming and Guildford to enter the Thames at Weybridge.

While Surrey, and particularly North Surrey, is metropolitanized—this began in the years between 1780 and 1830, when the smallholdings were bought up in large

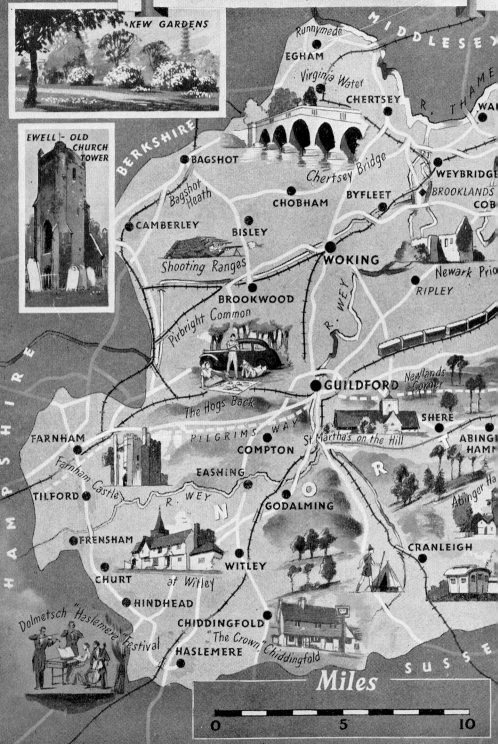

# SURREY

KEW GARDENS

EWELL - OLD CHURCH TOWER

BERKSHIRE

MIDDLESEX

Runnymede

EGHAM

Virginia Water

CHERTSEY

R. THAMES

WA

BAGSHOT

Chertsey Bridge

WEYBRIDGE

Bagshot Heath

CHOBHAM

BYFLEET

BROOKLANDS

COB

CAMBERLEY

BISLEY

Shooting Ranges

WOKING

Newark Prio

RIPLEY

BROOKWOOD

Pirbright Common

R. WEY

HAMPSHIRE

GUILDFORD

Newlands Corner

SHERE

ABING HAM

The Hogs Back

PILGRIMS WAY

St Martha's on the Hill

FARNHAM

Farnham Castle

COMPTON

N

Abinger Ha

TILFORD

EASHING

R. WEY

O

GODALMING

CRANLEIGH

FRENSHAM

at Witley

WITLEY

CHURT

HINDHEAD

Dolmetsch "Haslemere" Festival

CHIDDINGFOLD

"The Crown" Chiddingfold

HASLEMERE

SUSSE

## Miles

0          5          10

FROM REIGATE PARK

SHERE CHURCH

KEW
MOND
TERSHAM
HAM
KINGSTON
WIMBLEDON
BARNES
MERTON
MITCHAM
SURBITON
MORDEN
R. WANDLE
MALDEN
SUTTON
CARSHALTON
CROYDON
Airport
ESHER
EWELL
emont House
"The Derby"
PURLEY
EPSOM
ASHTEAD
LEATHERHEAD
CATERHAM
D O W N S
K E N T
PILGRIMS WAY
REIGATE
REDHILL
GODSTONE
Crowhurst Place
DORKING
R. MOLE
Reigate Market
CROWHURST
Mills at Outwood
LINGFIELD
GATWICK
Gatwick Airport
The 'Cage': Lingfield
PYRFORD MILL,
Nr. RIPLEY

N
W
E
S

numbers and farms became country houses —the county retains a wealth of natural beauty and historic associations. In the long-drawn-out battle between Nature and iconoclastic beauty-decrying man, Nature is not always beaten. For example, as is suggested by its place-names, Surrey is the fertile home of the oak, the ash, the beech and the box, and it is still for its size the best-wooded county of England. Its roads are often lovely, and so is its countryside, and even in the towns where the jerry-builder has been most active there are relics of the picturesque past.

I have written that Croydon is now practically London, but its Whitgift School is the reminder that it possessed one of the many palaces of the Archbishops of Canterbury. That unhappy and much-maligned lady, the Tudor Queen Mary, lived there. She regularly visited the poor with her maids and "enquired into their circumstances, relieved their wants, spoke in their favour to her officers and often, when the family was numerous, apprenticed at her own expense such of the children as were of promising disposition." During his Archiepiscopate Whitgift himself, described by Izaak Walton as "prudent and affable and gentle by nature," entertained Elizabeth at Croydon, and did her very well.

Kingston, the county town (and once the first stage out of London on the Portsmouth Road, but now avoided by a by-pass), has a market-place, and retains thereby its suggestion of a county town. The near-by Thames Ditton is no longer, as Richard Steele described it at the beginning of the eighteenth century, "an elegant solitude"; Chertsey, higher up the river, where there was one of the three great Thames-side Benedictine houses, is now given up to the week-ender. Edward Gibbon went to school at Kingston, and it is amusing to remember that the future great historian had a future notorious highwayman, Jerry Abershawe, as a schoolfellow.

Following the Portsmouth Road from Kingston, Esher, another suburbanized village, is chiefly remarkable for the posses-

**Richmond, only eight miles from central London, is the nearest riverside resort to the capital. Every summer it is visited by thousands of Londoners, attracted by the boating, gardens and park.**

Farnham, birthplace of William Cobbett, retains many old and still unspoilt buildings in its streets. Over it towers the castle, founded in the eleventh century, but much of it rebuilt in the seventeenth.

sion of Sandown Park Race Course, but history persists in obtruding. Claremont House was rebuilt by Clive—Macaulay says that "the Surrey peasantry whispered that the great wicked lord ordered the walls to be made so thick to keep out the devil"— and sheltered King Louis Philippe when he was exiled from France in 1848.

After it has passed through Cobham, where Matthew Arnold lived, the Portsmouth Road escapes from the suburbs, and there is a lovely stretch of pines and open common to Ripley, and so to Guildford, with the steepest High Street in England. Cobbett wrote of Guildford: "I who have seen so many many towns think it is the prettiest, and taken altogether the most agreeable and most happy looking that I ever saw in my life." Guildford was crammed with evacuees during the war; it has largely become a dormitory, and even the Abbot's Hospital and the remains of a medieval castle have not saved it from the metropolitan taint. But south of Guildford there is still country in Surrey which for unspoiled natural beauty is as good as anything to be found in southern England. Godalming is a real county town with an

attractive narrow High Street from which motors are happily diverted by a by-pass road. Godalming was the birthplace of General Oglethorpe, one of the forgotten worthies whom it is interesting to recall. He was one of the earliest prison reformers, was the first Governor of Georgia and prohibited slavery in the State, and he was a crony of Dr. Johnson. It was to him that Johnson made the somewhat unexpected remark for so good a Tory that "luxury, so far as it reaches the poor, will do good to the race; it will strengthen and multiply them."

Leaving the Portsmouth Road, and going eastward, the traveller comes to Dorking, pre-eminent among the Surrey towns for the beauty of its setting and the interest of its associations, though the town itself has little of the old-world charm of Farnham and Godalming. John Evelyn, the diarist, who lived and died and was buried at Wotton, three miles west of Dorking, wrote: "I will say nothing of the air because the pre-eminence is universally given to Surrey the soil being dry and sandy." Whether or not this is due to the soil, many great writers have found their inspiration in

A view at sunset on the Pilgrims' Way, near Guildford. This ancient track from Winchester to Canterbury follows the top of the North Downs from Farnham across the county to Godstone.

Dorking since the days of Evelyn, who in the irreligious time of the second Charles was the pious penitent of Jeremy Taylor. Defoe lived in Dorking; Sheridan had a house there; Keats wrote *Endymion* in an inn at Burford Bridge at the foot of Box Hill, north of the town, which Matthew Arnold called "the most enchanting country in England"; Disraeli wrote *Coningsby* at Deepdene, for generations one of England's stately homes, which later became an hotel and is now used by the Southern Region Railway. George Meredith lived for years at Box Hill, enduring, sometimes impatiently, the visits of "literary pilgrims" from London and America. Vaughan Williams, the eminent music composer, has encouraged not only Dorking but other Surrey towns in their musical festivals.

But perhaps for most of us Dorking is most clearly associated with Tony and Sam Weller, who, though they may never have lived in the flesh, are more real for us than two-thirds of the historic characters buried in Westminster Abbey. It will be remembered that the elder Weller was the landlord of the Marquis of Granby in Dorking, which, so it is said, Dickens founded on the Old King's Head, which stood on the site of the present post office. It was at the Marquis of Granby that Sam visited his father after the death of his stepmother and assisted at the ducking of Mr. Stiggins.

From Godalming to Hindhead the Portsmouth Road runs through romantic and almost desolate country. On or near the road are attractive villages, one of them Eashing, with a bridge across the Wey, said (probably quite untruly) to have been built in the reign of King John. The countryside is wild moorland from Milford Common until the road skirts the Devil's Punchbowl, where a granite cross on what is the second highest point in Surrey (Leith Hill being the highest), marks the spot where three murderers were hanged in chains in 1786. It is one of life's pleasant oddities that men often take pains to record events that are of small consequence, and quite forget the things that matter. Well into last century Hindhead was infested with law-breaking gangs, and highway robberies were a commonplace. All are forgotten except this "very shocking and barbourous murther" by "three abandoned villains" of a seafaring man journeying from Godalming to Portsmouth. Nicholas Nickelby and

72

Smike went the same journey, and "Smike listened with greedy interest as Nicholas read the inscription upon the stone, which, reared upon that wild spot, tells of a foul and treacherous crime."

Cobbett called Hindhead "the most villainous spot that God ever made," but Cobbett was prejudiced by the fact that the soil was so poor that even turnips would not grow on it. In fact, the miles of bracken and gorse, with their pine-crowned ridges, make Hindhead perhaps Surrey's most precious beauty spot, and it was no wonder that fifty years ago it became the home of artists and writers. Tyndall lived and died there. So did Grant Allen, the novelist who popularized scepticism. Near by, at Grayshott, Tennyson lived for a while, and at Shottermill, George Eliot lived with George Henry Lewes, the oddest middle-aged pair who ever lived together without the blessing of the Church or the consent of the State. George Eliot wrote *Middlemarch* at Shottermill, and she recorded that after the day's work she and Lewes filled "our evenings with physics, chemistry or other wisdom if our heads are at par; if not we take to folly in the shape of Alfred de Musset's poems."

Haslemere, down the hill, is an ugly little town with again a distinctive culture stimulated by the concerts of the Dolmetsch family, the erudite performers of ancient music. The "literary gents" have now abandoned Hindhead, and the height is covered with opulent villas, hotels and boarding-houses, the homes of the retired.

The Pilgrims' Way crosses the county from Hampshire to Kent by way of Farnham, Guildford, Dorking and Godstone. The highway was along the chalk downs, not the sandy track at their base. The North Downs, "the surging hills of Surrey," as Arnold called them, beginning with the Hog's Back, west of Guildford, and widening as they go eastward, supplied the only possible travellers' road when south Surrey was all forest. From Leith Hill the Channel can be seen through the Shoreham gap, and on a clear day, Highgate Hill.

John Bunyan took refuge in the Surrey Hills when he was threatened by arrest as an unlicensed preacher, and they are said to be the Delectable Mountains of the *Pilgrim's Progress*, while the Shalford swamp, south of Guildford, may have suggested the Slough of Despond to Bunyan, and the nearby Vale of Albury the Valley of Humiliation.

Farnham, with the most fascinating High Street that I know, is towered over by the castle, where in more prosperous days the

**Looking across the Devil's Punchbowl from the London–Portsmouth Road at Hindhead, a well-known beauty spot. Sandy, gorse and heather-covered soil is characteristic of western Surrey.**

Bishops of Winchester lived, and a small part of which is now the home of the Bishop of Guildford. To a considerable extent Farnham has contrived to keep its character. It is the home of what has been called "well-heeled old age" rather than of busy season-ticket-holding maturity, a refuge of the retired. But it has a community spirit demonstrated in its enterprising and well-supported repertory theatre.

Swift lived at Moor Park, outside Farnham, as secretary to Sir William Temple, for a wage of twenty pounds a year and his board, and Stella was a maid in the house. Again it is fun to remember that Swift and Cobbett have often walked up the High Street, dropping in, may be, at the Bush Inn, the embittered Irishman and the stubborn Englishman, bursting with righteous anger.

In Cobbett's day, Surrey was mainly if not entirely an agricultural county, then and much later growing a considerable quantity of hops, particularly in the Farnham district, where there are still a few hop gardens. There remains a considerable agricultural industry in this part of Surrey where Earl Lloyd George had his farm at Churt. Elsewhere in the county there are old-time villages, away from the railroads, with an unurbanized population in farmhouses and cottages, and where the townsman will find himself in an unfamiliar world.

For example, in Chiddingfold, six miles east of Hindhead, with the oldest inn in England, once a Cistercian Guest House; in West Horsley, between Guildford and Leatherhead, where, it is said, Walter Raleigh's head was buried after his execution; in the Vale of Mickleham, between Leatherhead and Dorking; in Chilworth, between Guildford and Dorking.

Cobbett described Chilworth as "one of the choicest retreats of man which seems formed for a scene of innocence and happiness, so perverted as to make it instrumental in effecting two of the most damnable of purposes, the making of gunpowder and bank-notes."

Surrey once had many flourishing industries. There were blast furnaces for the iron stone found in many districts. Evelyn says that there were jet-pits in Wotton, and at Wotton were built the first mills in England for casting and wiring brass. Guildford was once a flourishing cloth centre, and the two woolpacks in the town's coat of arms are the reminder of a flourishing industry which, according to Aubrey, was killed by the avarice of the merchants. At Farnham pottery-making still continues.

Nowadays it may be said that Surrey generally has escaped the machine while supplying a resting place for the machine slaves who toil outside its borders.

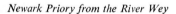

*Newark Priory from the River Wey*

*View from Sidlesham Church near Chichester*

# SUSSEX

### By JOHN CHERRILL

IT has been said that property-buyers are the only green things Sussex folk see to-day. Fortunately there is more cynicism than truth in this statement, but it does aptly illustrate to what extent Sussex is being overrun by bricks and mortar.

In the north, from Crowborough through to Haslemere (which is just in Surrey, but takes its tone from Sussex), are a succession of small towns increasingly exploited as residential centres by London's middle class. Along the southern coast, from Selsey to Hastings, lie another fringe of towns that are not only the holiday playground of teeming thousands of Londoners, but also the dormitories for a growing number of London's clerical population. Three-fifths of the county's population lives in this coastal belt. Sussex is by no means a small county; its coastline measures over ninety miles, and it has a maximum north to south depth of nearly thirty miles. Yet, because of fast electric trains, the motor-car and steadily "improved" roads fanning out southwards from the Surrey borders, the

county is in danger of being completely over-run.

It was not always so. Once upon a time *Suo Seaxe*, the ancient kingdom of the South Saxons, was more isolated than any other southern county. The causes of this isolation profoundly influenced the county's development. First, along its coastline there are no good, natural harbours. Small ports, fishing villages and "invasion beaches," yes; but, despite its rivers, no large, sheltered anchorage. Secondly, at either end, west and east, were formidable natural barriers. In the east was once a great morass extending over Pevensey Marsh and the basin of the River Rother, an area impenetrable except by little-known tracks. In the west was a similar barrier—Chichester Harbour, extending inland, up to the wooded Downs. And thirdly, in the north, the great forest of Anderida, which at one time covered the whole of the Sussex Weald and stretched far into Kent, hemmed in the county. Not only did its tangled undergrowth and great trees make almost impassable barriers to travel, but its mixture of clay and sandy soil provided the poorest foundation for roads.

Historically, therefore, early Sussex lived a life of somewhat

*Arms of East Sussex*

75

Watchbell Street, Rye, on the River Rother, one of the Cinque Ports. Because of the silting up of its harbour, Rye, like its neighbour, Winchelsea, has lost its medieval importance.

unsplendid isolation. It was fairly widely colonized by the Romans; but it long resisted the Danes, and was one of the last of the English counties to acknowledge the over-lordship of William the Conqueror, despite the fact that he landed at Pevensey. When he did at last conquer its wild and independent people, he did it very thoroughly. Sussex lay on his communications with Normandy, and he saw to it that not only was the administration well organized and in strong hands, but also that the county was adequately garrisoned and defended. To that fact we chiefly owe the large number of surviving Norman castles. From it also Sussex derives its division into six rapes. A rape is an administrative area of a kind found nowhere else in the kingdom.

### Medieval Defence

Of course, roads have, from time immemorial, run east and west across the county; a number of tracks also ran north and south, for nothing could alter the fact that it lay, geographically, between the Thames Valley and the sea. But the chief way into the county has normally been from the south via the river-mouths. Because of this fact the coastal landing-places and the fords or bridges across the rivers were defended during the Middle Ages by castles such as Bodiam on the Rother, Hastings and Pevensey in the eastern gap, Lewes on the Ouse, Bramber and Knapp on the Adur, and Arundel and Amberley on the Arun. The fourth river, the Cuckmere, was always, it seems, too shallow, and too blocked by sandbanks and the bar at its mouth to provide an easy means of ingress for the invader—although its haven was later a godsend to smugglers!

None the less, the main north and south roads do not keep to the river valleys, because all these valleys are very subject to flooding, and, generally speaking, provide a route only for a short distance into the interior. The lines of the roads as we know them to-day are based fundamentally on Roman survivals, and stride boldly over the Downs.

The invasion which changed the face of Sussex did not come from

*Arms of West Sussex*

the sea, but from the north. It really began with the Prince Regent towards the close of the eighteenth century, when, attracted by its medicinal waters, its relative closeness to London and its equable climate, he turned the little fishing village of Brighthelmstone into a fashionable resort.

First turnpike roads, then railways, gave easy access to the coast. Once Londoners discovered how pleasant it was to spend the summer in the warmth of newly christened Brighton, and how easy it was to get there, exploration went on at ever-increasing speed. One coastal fishing village after another was invaded; new towns grew up; each threw out its tentacles, not only along the coast, but often inland as well, until to-day, except where the Downs tumble into the sea between Eastbourne and Seaford, there is not an unspoilt stretch of coastline between Hastings and Selsey.

The early development of the county had been accelerated by the fact that Sussex possessed two important raw materials. The first was iron, found in great quantities beneath the trees covering the Weald; the second was timber. The oak tree was so common as to earn for itself the name of the "Sussex weed." (The pine, so typical, alas, of modern Sussex, was introduced later.)

### Industry of the Past

The chestnut tree made excellent charcoal, which, until the exploitation of coal, was the only fuel available for the smelting of iron. The "red rust" of many Wealden streams and the numerous hammer ponds are present reminders of the iron ore that was once the raw material of a great industry. A rough and hardy population of charcoal-burners and iron-miners lived a wild life in the central and northern part of the land. Between them they did much to clear the forest and open up the Sussex landscape. The forest, and particularly the Sussex oak, played a large part not only in determining the style of Sussex half-timbered architecture, but also in founding Britain's naval supremacy; for from it was built a high proportion of those lordly sailing-ships on which Britain relied for her pro-

CRAWLEY

St. Leonard's Forest

HORSHAM

HAYWAR
HEA

Old Granary - Cowdray

East St.

Christ's Hospital

MIDHURST

R. ROTHER

PETWORTH

PULBOROUGH

Grammar School

W

E

S

Wild
Brooks Chan Chanbury Ring

AMBERLEY

STEYNING

Ditch
Bea

S

U

T

D

O

The Market
Cross

Goodwood Racecourse

ARUNDEL

HOVE

CHICHESTER

R. ARUN Arundel Castle

SHOREHAM

BRIGH

BOGNOR REGIS

LITTLEHAMPTON

WORTHING

SELSEY

Selsey Bill

E N G L I S H

tection and her trade. It was also exported as timber in great quantities to the Continent. So much, indeed, was exported, burned or used for house- or ship-building, that to-day only minor relics of it remain, and such modern "forests" as Ashdown, St. Leonards and Worth are ghosts of a forgotten past.

In terms of numbers of workers directly or indirectly employed, the major industry of modern Sussex is the tourist trade. The grim, hard and dour race of charcoal-burners and iron-workers has given way to a grim, hard and dour race of hoteliers and boarding-house keepers. This race, recruited from all over the land, is alien to native Sussex. Yet it is ubiquitous. Scarcely one of the beautiful towns or larger villages in the county but has its "guest-house" or "Ye Olde Tea Shoppe," frequently run by

78

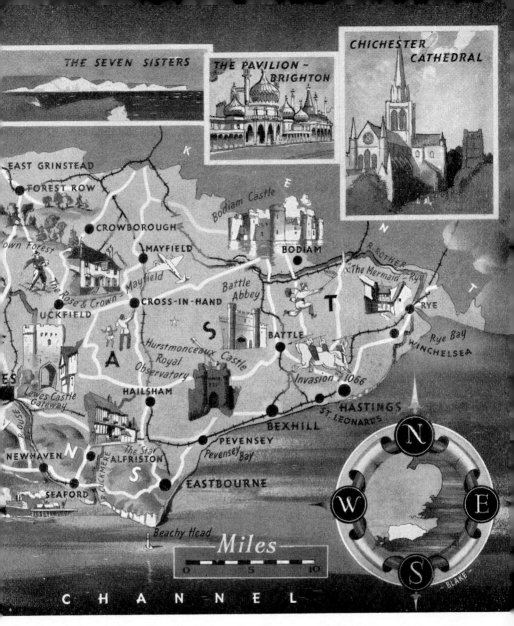

THE SEVEN SISTERS

THE PAVILION - BRIGHTON

CHICHESTER CATHEDRAL

EAST GRINSTEAD

FOREST ROW

CROWBOROUGH

MAYFIELD

BODIAM

Bodiam Castle

"The Mermaid" Rye

R. ROTHER

RYE

CROSS-IN-HAND

Battle Abbey

Rye Bay

WINCHELSEA

UCKFIELD

Mayfield

The Rose & Crown

BATTLE

Hurstmonceaux Castle

Royal Observatory

Invasion 1066

HAILSHAM

HASTINGS

ST. LEONARDS

Lewes Castle Gateway

BEXHILL

NEWHAVEN

ALFRISTON

PEVENSEY

Pevensey Bay

The Star

SEAFORD

EASTBOURNE

R. CUCKMERE

Beachy Head

Miles

0     5     10

N

W     E

S

BLAKE

CHANNEL

emigrant ladies from London. Others keep riding stables and let out hacks to holiday-makers and week-enders—for the pro-visioning of modern horse-riding has become largely a feminine industry.

In clearing so much of the land, the iron- and wood-workers made possible the northward extension in the county of a type of agriculture that is surpassed by few counties. To-day agriculture, if not the largest, is still the staple industry of Sussex, and to its service the traditional Sussex man and woman, with their slow, slurred, mellifluous dialect, their staunch individual-ism, their lazy vigour and their homely kindliness, are dedicated.

Somehow—and it is a miracle for which we should be grateful—the modern invasion has largely passed them by. That invasion is typified in summer by the strained-looking

79

travellers in the noisy motor-cars and coaches that jostle, nose to tail, along the main roads; by the rich and by the poor visitors thronging the palatial and not-so-palatial hotels, the ugly, large, and the dingy, small boarding-houses along the coast, or the guest-houses in the villages. These people, their vehicles and their temporary homes, are alien to the real Sussex; here is a country where it is still natural to travel in a creaking wain behind two plodding horses along the quiet of a

and local tradesmen's motor-vans, electric light, bathrooms in the squalid, mournfully out-of-place rows of Council cottages that to-day erupt redly on the fringes of many an old village—despite all these and the other manifold signs of modernity, to the real Sussex man and woman the summer invaders belong to a world of noisy foreigners. With that world they mix politely, but with it they have little in common.

Yet even if suburbia has invaded the northern fringe of the county, and the

The origins of the "Long Man" cut out in the chalk at Wilmington, near Eastbourne, are in dispute, but he possibly dates from Roman or even pre-Roman times.

winding lane; to live in inconvenient, half-timbered, thatched dwellings sheltering under groups of noble oaks and elms.

The Sussex farmer, of course, has his motor-car and his refrigerator. The farm labourer travels by modern bus to the cinema in the local town; but despite the radio set that blares from almost every dwelling-house, the tractor-pulled plough

season-ticket holder and the holiday-maker have taken the south coast for their own, there remains an area of the country between these two that those who know and love it think one of the loveliest, not only in England, but in the whole world. To stand on the top of Windover Hill on a fine day in high summer, breathing in the scent of the scabious flowers and the gorse bloom carried on the faint south-west breeze, listening to the murmur of bees and the song of a rising lark; to glimpse the distant, silver sparkle of the sea beyond the Cuckmere; to look down on Alfriston nestling in the river meads, across to the majestic sweep of the South Downs stretching from Firle Beacon westward as far as the eye can see, and northward over the chequered pattern of the Weald rolling on to merge in the distant misty blueness of the North Downs—to stand there in the midst of all these revelations of beauty is to experience an uplifting of spirit, as though one has been touched by the finger of God.

## The Sussex Weald

Laterally, Sussex is divided into four distinct strips. First, in the north lies the Weald, a broad belt of mixed patches of clay and sandy soil. It is here that to-day are found those areas of open heathland known as Worth, St. Leonards and Ashdown Forest; they are a land of lonely pine-trees and heather. Villages are few, and towns fewer still. Agriculture is at a discount. The land is rough and high-lying, reaching in Crowborough Beacon to seven hundred and ninety-two feet.

This area was once a lovely land over which to walk and to ride. The country round Forest Row compared with any in Sussex; but the area became a military training-ground during the war, and tank-tracks have reduced large parts to seas of bog in wet, or scarred clay in dry weather. Crowborough itself is the centre of a scattered residential area, as, too, are East Grinstead and Crawley. The largest town in this northern strip is Horsham, which possesses a Carfax, a distinction that only Oxford shares. Shelley was born in neighbouring Warnham, and spent much of his boyhood in the town. Since 1902 the famous Christ's Hospital, or Blue Coat School, has been situated at West Horsham.

The second of the lateral strips lies to the south of this belt. Sheltering under the northern faces of the South Downs, it is a country of hazel, elm and oak, of meadowland and small streams, of fields under a variety of crops, of dusty, hedge-girt lanes which wander, apparently aimlessly, round

one corner to the next; of ancient, mellowed buildings, clustering into occasional villages or farmsteads.

It is the real heart of Sussex. On its northern edges are the relatively dull towns, Haywards Heath and Uckfield (the latter celebrated by reason of the fact that nearby was found the Piltdown skull, a now discredited relic of our sub-human ancestors; but along the southern fringe, clustering under the shelter of the Downs, is a string of villages and small market towns, that for old-world charm is still one of the glories of England. From Wilmington to Harting they stretch, like architectural spangles in a cloth of green pastures.

Alfriston, with its famous market cross (so stupidly damaged by the Canadians in the First World War , its fourteenth-century Clergy House, its picturesque Smugglers Inn and Star Inn, both of them celebrated in smuggling history, and its ancient church, whose spire lifts above the Cuckmere meads like a miniature Salisbury above the Avon, is claimed by many as the most beautiful village in England. But that claim is made for many of these villages. One has only to mention such places as Keymer, Poynings, Thakeham, Amberley, Graffham, Oving, Singleton, Wilmington, Midhurst and Harting, to realize how formidable is Sussex's claim to the possession of more of England's most beautiful villages than any other county.

## Midhurst and Cowdray

Midhurst is distinguished for more than its beauty, for it is an ancient town, and was a full borough as early as the fourteenth century under Edward II. Here was the great castle and manor, destroyed by fire and now a ruined shell, of the once mighty family of the Bohuns. The surrounding Cowdray Park is one of the most noble parks of England. Midhurst lies on the road from Horsham to Chichester, and its historic coaching inn, the Spread Eagle, dates back to the fourteenth century.

Amberley is, in my view, the loveliest of all these villages. It was built near a ford on the River Arun, on one of the most ancient trackways in this kingdom. Where it crossed the river a castle was built, and

Southdown sheep, now fast disappearing, on the slopes of the Downs at Bignor, near Petworth.

under the shadow of this castle grew up Amberley, though a settlement existed long before. This castle was, as were so many in Sussex, a secondary defence to a primary fortress, Arundel Castle itself. Unassailable from the west, it was protected on the north by the Wild Brooks, a stretch of flat land (always marshy and, in winter, flooded by the river) extending as far as Pulborough. From the low escarpment on which Amberley village stands there is a striking view across the Wild Brooks, cut up with innumerable dykes, and still the home of grazing sheep. The village itself is small, but rich in thatched, half-timbered cottages, many of them bowered in roses during high summer.

Other centres in this western area are Pulborough and Petworth. Pulborough, an ugly, straggling town, lies in the midst of delightful country on the edge of Amberley Wild Brooks. Petworth stands on a little hill barely two hundred feet high, but high enough, in this relatively flat country, to make of its church steeple a landmark for miles around. Petworth is a lovely old country town. Nearby is Petworth House, standing in its vast and noble park. Parts of the house date back to the days of the great family of the Percys. Indeed, twenty generations of that family lived there until, in 1682, Elizabeth, daughter of the eleventh Earl of Northumberland, and the greatest heiress in England, married the sixth Duke of Somerset. It was he who built most of the present house and hung her portrait in it. To-day its picture and sculpture gallery, where are to be found some of Turner's best works (which he painted there), and its wonderful reception rooms, particularly the carved room, designed and decorated by Grinling Gibbons, make it one of the most magnificent country houses in England.

The chief town in this belt of the southern Weald country is, however, Lewes, at the eastern end. It is the capital of the county and the administrative centre of East Sussex. (The county is divided, for administration purposes, into East and West Sussex.) Before the Normans, the ancient Britons, Romans and Saxons all had settlements there. To the Normans we owe the castle, to-day used largely as a museum.

Lewes figures significantly in our early constitutional history, for just outside it, in 1264, was fought the battle between Henry III and the Barons, led by Simon de

Montfort. The Royalists were defeated, and the subsequent treaty, known as the Mise of Lewes, is still one of the most important of our great national charters in the evolution of constitutional government.

East of Lewes, Sussex stretches away in a belt of flat land terminating in the sandhills of Pevensey Bay. Much of this area was once a bleak morass. Pevensey, the ancient Anderida, gave its name to all the forest stretching through to Worth, and was so named by the Romans. Parts of the Roman wall that surrounded the town still exist, and upon Roman and Saxon foundations the Normans built their castle, only the ruins of which survive. Pevensey, which

Bosham, on an arm of Chichester Harbour, was once an important seaport. Today it is no more than a quiet village on the only remaining unspoilt stretch of Sussex coast.

once stood on the sea, shared the liberties of the Cinque Ports, and was a corporate town from 1066 to 1883; but as the sea went back and its harbour silted up, its importance declined.

The whole of this area is haunted by history in stone. Battle Abbey, founded and largely built by William in thanksgiving for his victory at Senlac over Saxon Harold and his valiant house-carles, was once an enormous affair, being perhaps the richest monastery in England. Hilaire Belloc estimates that in its prime its revenues amounted to the equivalent in modern money of £25,000 annually. It suffered, as did so many others, at the Dissolution.

Midway between Pevensey and Battle lies the castle of Hurstmonceux, which now houses the equipment of the Royal Observatory. In some ways it is more beautiful than Leeds (Kent) or Bodiam. It is moated, but, unlike the Norman structures, is built of brick, and represents the half-way stage between the stone castles of the Middle Ages and the manor houses of the Tudor period. Most of the present structure dates from about the middle of

the fifteenth century, though it was very largely restored in 1910 and in 1933. Its battlemented gateway is possibly the finest example in the country of this type of brick structure.

Bodiam Castle, an almost perfect survival of a moated fortress, lies among lovely meadows near the Kent border. As a fortress it dates from the fourteenth century, and, as did so many of these uncomfortable dwellings, fell into disrepair when more peaceful times in England allowed comfort to oust security as the primary consideration for a dwelling-house. Its present appearance we owe almost entirely to the loving care with which the late Lord Curzon rebuilt its ancient shell.

Rye and Winchelsea were once prosperous ports, although to-day Winchelsea lies some distance from the sea; and Rye's harbour, on the Rother, is of no commercial use. Both of them were Cinque Ports, and both were once of august importance as medieval towns. Parts of the old town walls of Rye survive, chiefly in the celebrated Land Gate and Ypres Tower; but visitors tend to be better acquainted with the interior of the famous Tudor inn, the Mermaid. Winchelsea, dominated by the church of St. Thomas à Becket, founded by Edward I, and a masterly example of early town planning, fills me with a slight melancholy. Its modern population, engaged in the commerce of agriculture, seems to jostle with the ghosts of sailors and stevedores who once thronged the now desolate quays and docks that in their days fronted the English Channel.

Before leaving this area, I must mention the sub-Riviera stretching along the low-lying coast (broken only by a scarp of low cliffs at the back of Hastings). Here are a succession of typical seaside towns—Hastings, St. Leonards, Bexhill and Eastbourne. They are pleasant enough, and perhaps not quite so consciously commercial as their counterparts from Brighton westwards; but there is little more than that to record of any of them.

The third of the lateral strips into which Sussex can be divided is composed of the South Downs. In all the world there is no range of hills like them. They are the backbone of Sussex, indeed of south-east England, and are unique both in their uniformity and in their individuality.

Yet while they are the essence of Sussex, they are not of it at all, for in all their seventy miles and more of length there is (and let us be thankful for it) scarcely a human habitation to break their marvellous skyline. In their western reaches they are often well wooded; in their eastern reaches, particularly between Lewes and Eastbourne, they are practically barren of any vegetation other than straggling clumps of gorse. East of Seaford they break off into white cliffs over the sea. From the Cuckmere mouth the cliffs climb over the saddles of the Seven Sisters to reach their highest point, five hundred and thirty-three feet, in Beachy Head. To those who know them intimately, the Downs enfold some of the loveliest scenery that can be found in the length and breadth of England. Despite motor-cars and electric trains, they still enjoy in long stretches a loneliness that is not to be found anywhere within comparable distance of London.

They owe both their relative freedom from human habitation and their strikingly distinctive contours to the chalk of which they are formed. How exactly they were formed, geologists are still not agreed; but everyone can understand how this vast

**Amberley, on the River Arun, with its thatched and half-timbered cottages has claims to be the loveliest of the villages sheltering under the northern face of the South Downs.**

mass of chalk, pushed up long ages ago, has weathered into contours that, particularly from the north, offer such a unique spectacle. Moreover, chalk will not store water, and in the Downs water can be found only by digging wells to great depths. This fact has saved them from exploitation at the hands of man. Another feature of chalk which has influenced the story of the Downs is the fact that it carries only a thin top soil, except in the valleys, chiefly on the southern slopes, where rain has washed down silt into deeper layers. This thin top soil is useless for agricultural purposes, although it will produce a turf on which sheep have grazed for centuries in fat contentment.

Since, then, man can neither live on the Downs for want of water nor till them for want of soil, he has, on the whole, been content to leave them to the shepherd with his flocks of Southdown sheep and to whomsoever wished to walk over them. To-day, for reasons connected chiefly with the development of Britain's national economy, the flocks of sheep that once roamed so widely and in such numbers across these Downs are fast disappearing.

Their remote descendants are to be found in ever-increasing numbers on the vaster downlands of New Zealand.

The Downs have dominated the history of Sussex as much as they still dominate its scenery. They are an archæologists' paradise, for they abound in relics of prehistoric times as much as they offer visual evidence of their close association with the life of the county ever since man kept records of his activities. Apart from the fossils that can be dug out of the cliff faces or found in the numberless man-made quarries, there are flint arrow-heads still to be kicked out of the exposed chalk and picked up by any quick-eyed walker, along their whole length. Indeed, at Cissbury—that place that was old long before recorded things—was found a complete workshop of flint instruments with a store of products both finished and half finished, and cores, the raw material, lying to hand. Chalk has a queer habit of "sweating out" the flint within it. It is, therefore, by no means odd that a number of the houses in old Brighton and elsewhere were built from flint.

The Romans cut their own roads through the Downs from north to south.

**Regency buildings, such as these at Hove, emphasize how Brighton and Hove changed from fishing villages to fashionable resorts. Their dignity is in marked contrast with the modern attractions.**

We know of four such Roman roads to-day, the most clearly traced of them being Stane Street, which, from Chichester, crosses the Downs near Bury Hill on its way to Pulborough. The Romans also built their villas in the foothills. A remarkable survival of these is to be found at Bignor by Bury, where is preserved the remains of a house built in the first century A.D. by some wealthy Civil Servant of those days.

### Treasures from the Past

The Downs are stores of more than Roman history. Dotted along their ridges are tumuli, ancient burial-places. Some are of Saxon chiefs ; they have yielded a treasure of skilfully wrought bronze ornaments and weapons. Many are far earlier. It is probable also that the often vast earthworks (to be seen at their best on Mount Caburn, Chanctonbury Ring, Cissbury, the Devil's Dyke or the Trundle, where the relics are possibly four thousand years old) were Celtic, though there is evidence that they were, for some reason, exploited later.

But perhaps the most interesting of all the ancient survivals in the length of the Downs is also the most visibly striking, the great figure cut in the chalk and known as "the Long Man of Wilmington." This figure, similar to the giant at Cerne Abbas, except that he holds a staff in each hand, overlooks the village of Wilmington and fronts the Weald. He is a sizeable chap (his staves are two hundred and thirty-five feet and two hundred and thirty feet respectively in length), but when he was fashioned, and why are questions the answers to which are still disputed ; it is enough for us to-day to see him there, striding across the velvety turf below Windover Hill, preserving by his presence our link with an older England.

Before the Second World War the Downs were being increasingly used by walkers, not always in harmony with the spirit of the places they invaded. Lewes was a convenient centre, easily accessible from London, from which to start an exploration of the Downs ; and it followed that the eastern reaches of those majestic, rolling, inviting spaces of turf supported hundreds of variously garbed, noisy people at each of our summer festive holidays. Those who

sought the quieter places of the Downs were therefore driven perpetually westwards, and to-day it is only in those wooded stretches, such as are found round Linch Hill and Bow Hill, that the reverent seeker can find the solitude of nature undefiled, that once was the heritage of the whole range of the Sussex Downs.

During the war a more dreadful invasion happened ; in defence of freedom, these sacred places were given up to the military, and in pitifully numerous areas that lush turf, that age-long face of mother earth, was thrashed and scarred by the tracks of tanks, by hutments, by latrine trenches—in short, by the squalor that a vigorous and triumphant military always brings in its train.

The fourth and last of the lateral belts of the county is the coastal plain which, from a broad, flat stretch fronting Chichester Harbour, narrows eastward until it is thrust into the sea east of Brighton. Here is buried the wealth of modern Sussex, not only in its coastal resorts from Brighton through to Bognor, but also in the prosperous market gardens that reach from Selsey Bill up into the lower valleys of the Downs. It is an ancient, smiling land, fanned by the south-west breezes and warmed by a kindly sun. Its soil will grow almost anything, and its climate will do much to ameliorate most human ailments. But to me it is not Sussex—except in its westernmost fringe, from Chichester round the Harbour, past Bosham and Dell Quay, down to the coast at West Wittering, a small segment of ancient perfection in an area of modern mediocrity.

### Lingering Charm

Most of the plain is the home of the "commuter", the seaside landlady and the tomato-grower. Here is to be found Sussex's largest town, Brighton, with a population of some one hundred and fifty thousand and a history, as a town, barely one hundred and fifty years old. In parts of old Brighton and Hove the charm that the exponents of Regency architecture brought to ex-fishing villages still lingers. But most of Brighton's sprawling shops and villas, its efficient buses and its man-

Looking south-west from the lofty promontory of Blackdown, West Sussex. This famous viewpoint, which rises to a height of over nine hundred feet, gives an extensive panorama of the Sussex Weald.

made concrete sea-front (despite the Regency houses that line it), belong to an age that seems to have little thought for beauty and less care for its preservation. Brighton is the nearest genuine seaside resort to London, and on the highdays and holidays of summer its beaches are as dark with people as are those of Margate or Blackpool. One can forgive its sprawling along the foreshore, but one can forgive less easily its proliferation into the hinterland of the Downs. Before the war suburbadom was running rife, and year after year new acres of ageless downland turf were being destroyed by the red excrescences known to our age as desirable villas. The protection which recent legislation affords to the Downs is not enough; an absolute veto is needed on any further "developments" in the Downland or its occupation by the Services.

What uncontrolled development can do may be seen at Peacehaven, not far from Brighton. Once it was a gentle valley running southward to the sea from the higher levels of the Downs; to-day it is a pigsty of hideously coloured bungalows, shacks and even tents, set down, without rhyme or reason, in a fair, green land, over which still lingers in some pathetic way the spirit of the Sussex downland, rather as a betrayed maiden clings to the seducer who has ruined her.

It is not fair to omit to mention that places like Brighton, Hove, Littlehampton, Angmering, and, even to-day, Bognor, give great pleasure to multitudes of Londoners starved both of sunshine and of fresh air. It would be churlish to deny the social importance of such towns or to decry the efforts they are making to improve their amenities and to cater more exuberantly than ever for pleasure seekers. But those who love Sussex will wish success to their efforts less, I believe, through philanthropic motives than for selfish ones. These towns and the attractions they hold act on Londoners in the height of summer as do fly-papers on flies; and the more flies on the Sussex fly-papers the fewer are to be found in the cooler and pleasanter places of the county.

How different is Chichester, capital of West Sussex, and the county's cathedral city! Although five miles from the sea, it possesses a "harbour," for an arm of the sea (though of little use for navigation) runs round the west side of Selsey Bill up to the city itself. The Romans named Chichester Regnum, on discovering it was the capital

SUSSEX

city of the ancient British race, the Regnii. It was later renamed after Cissa, the first King of the South Saxons.

With their passion for town-planning the Romans divided the new town by two main streets, running north and south and east and west. These streets still survive, living memorials of two thousand years of history. Most of the cathedral belongs to the period between 1200 and 1350. Christopher Wren built the upper portion of the spire, which collapsed and crashed into the church in 1861. The reconstruction of the present steeple was finished in 1867.

At the junction of the main streets is the celebrated Market Cross, the finest example of this type of building in England. Built very early in the sixteenth century, it was designed as a shelter for the country folk selling their wares in Chichester's busy centre. Little survives of the old Norman castle, but the old posting inns, the chief of them the "White Horse" in South Street, and the "Angel and Dolphin" under the shadow of the cathedral, still flourish. To-day Chichester is a thriving agricultural centre that also supports brewing and tanning industries.

### Engulfed by the Sea

South of Chichester lies Selsey Bill at the tip of a flat, triangular sweep of land. Round the Bill itself the sea is encroaching on Sussex, and indeed old Selsey's church now lies buried a mile out to sea. On the east the invasion of modernity is nearly complete, for the little seaside resort of Bognor leapt into prominence when King George V spent his convalescence there in 1929. From Bognor Regis it is but a stone's throw to Pagham Harbour, which is also now nearly engulfed, and Selsey itself is a mass of villas and bungalows. On the west, however, through West Wittering and up round the Harbour to Dell Quay and Bosham there exists an unspoiled stretch of the Sussex coast, comprising the Harbour and its surrounding villages, so well known to dinghy sailors. Chichester Harbour is protected by the local authorities. Quay Meadow, at Bosham, from which King Harold set sail for Normandy in 1064, is owned by the National Trust. Thanks to

the public spirit of the citizens of Chichester, the sand dunes at West Wittering have been purchased so as to ensure the preservation of this stretch. Behind these dunes the plovers and the sea birds are also protected by a special order of the County Council.

### World's Loveliest Race-Course

From Chichester the Roman Stane Street (on which a large stretch of the modern road is founded) crosses the plain to strike up into the Downs by Boxgrove, where is the famous Priory. Farther on is Goodwood, the beautiful estate of the Duke of Richmond, with its noble house and the loveliest race-course in the world. In Goodwood Park stand some celebrated cedars of Lebanon, but to me the Goodwood estate is most impressive for its noble beeches, for its stretches of open turfland and for the great views of the distant sea across the coastal lowland.

Through the middle of this coastal plain the River Arun makes its leisurely way under the walls of Arundel Castle down to the sea at Littlehampton. In the days of Norman William, Roger de Montgomery was appointed Overlord of the Rape of Arundel, and at a strategic point on the river raised up a great castle on and around fortifications dating from the time of the Saxon King Alfred. (The great keep of the castle, for example, is pre-Norman.) It later passed to the FitzAlans, and from them to Howard of Norfolk, the premier peer of the realm and Earl Marshal of England. Cromwell's Ironsides destroyed most of the original castle, but extensive restorations were begun at the end of the eighteenth century, and were continued on and off up till 1890. They followed the style of the original castle closely, and to-day the pile is the most imposing of the inhabited private castles in England.

### Modern Industries

Sussex supports a number of miscellaneous small industries. There are, for example, brickworks to be found extensively in the clay soil of the coastal plain and the south and central Weald, and one of them, despite protests from all over the country, has recently invaded, and will probably spoil forever, the peace of Midhurst Common. There are cement and lime works, some vast, such as those cut into the chalk hill at the back of Lewes, whose chimneys and noisy operations, affronts to ear and eye alike, cover acres of the surrounding country with a fine white dust. Quarrying has diminished the comeliness of the Downs, and in some places the disused quarries are dangerous to walkers. Paper-making is also a local industry, and here again, as for example in the case of the mills at Tarring-Neville in the Ouse Valley, there is a danger of industry spoiling the landscape. Of the other industries, brewing and tanning, pottery and even glass-making—this last chiefly at the back of Hastings, where is found a particularly valuable form of fine sand—are prominent. And although Sussex has never bred a race of seamen, as has Devon or Cornwall, it has a thriving local fishing industry, particularly for shell-fish, and, in Newhaven, one of England's principal gateways to the Continent.

Fundamentally, however, Sussex life is based on agriculture, and although the great days of sheep-rearing are over, sheep are still important. The Bat and Ball Sheep Fair at Chiddingly, the fairs at Lingfield and Findon and, largest of all, at Lewes, are annual events of great moment in Sussex life. Dairy-farming is on the increase, and so are root crops and grain crops, particularly in West Sussex. In many ways the economics of Sussex farming were considerably aided by the incidence of war.

The modern age has shown a lamentable tendency to overrun large areas of Sussex and to turn many beauties into "beauty spots"; but there is still a hard core of resistance to spoliation, and it still embraces by far the loveliest scenery to be found anywhere within comparable distance of London, or, as some people like myself think, anywhere in England. It has inspired innumerable poets and writers, both native-born and foreign, to passionate, lyrical praise, and I wish I had space in which to tell of some of Sussex's famous literary sons. Since I have not I must be content to quote from one poem by Hilaire Belloc, for whom no other country on earth compares with Sussex :

If ever I become a rich man
Or if ever I grow to be old,
I will build a house with a deep thatch
To shelter me from the cold,
And there shall the Sussex songs be sung
And the story of Sussex told.

I will hold my house in a high wood
Within a walk of the sea,
And the men that were boys when I was a
  boy
Shall sit and drink with me.

*Alfriston, near Lewes*

*The Rufus Stone, New Forest*

# HAMPSHIRE

### By SIDNEY DARK

IN SIZE the seventh of the English counties, Hampshire is packed with history. Romans, Saxons, Danes and Normans landed there. Winchester was the first capital of a united England, and for a short period the capital, too, of a Scandinavian Empire. Many battles have been fought within its borders, and in the Puritan victory in Cheriton Wood which, so Clarendon recorded, "broke all the measures and altered the whole scheme of the king's counsels," the Civil War came to its end.

Hampshire to-day is a county of many characters. In particular, the Services have marked it for their own. Portsmouth, for centuries the first of British naval ports, gives the county a naval flavour, especially as retired naval officers solace their leisure by taking part in its local government. What Portsmouth is to the navy in south Hampshire, Aldershot, a modern and particularly ugly town, is to the army in north Hampshire.

*Badge of Hampshire*

Southampton is the most important of England's Atlantic ports, and it was from here in 1944 that the Mulberries were towed across the Channel for the invasion of Normandy, and from here that many American and British soldiers embarked. At Eastleigh, near Southampton, the Southern Railway has one of its major maintenance centres, and in this area also are aerodromes and aeroplane factories. At Basingstoke are engineering works. At Laverstock, the paper for Bank of England banknotes is manufactured by the Portals, the descendants of a Huguenot who escaped from France to Southampton after the Revocation of the Edict of Nantes. In Bournemouth, Hampshire has an exclusive and formerly "select" English sea-side town, a favourite refuge of the aged well-to-do with, in consequence, a larger proportion of church-goers than any other English town. The Isle of Wight and the ugly Hayling Island are among Londoners' popular playgrounds.

But the greater part of Hampshire is, mercifully, neither naval, military nor industrial. It remains one of the most rural of the counties near London. Its distinctive charms are found in the little market towns, each full of distinctive character; in its villages, where there are still to be met people who have never been to London; and in the fascinating variety of its natural beauty; parts of the county reveal England at her loveliest. Though the scene of her book *Our Village* is set in Berkshire, Mary Russell Mitford was born in Hampshire at Alresford, and she wrote that Hampshire's "prevailing and pervading charm is not the woods or streams or villages or even the sparkling ocean, but the exquisite arrangement and combination of the whole."

The east of Hampshire shares the character of West Sussex. The South Downs invade the county at Petersfield and throw out a spur of high land, covered with wooded hangers, north-westwards towards Alton. In mid-Hampshire the deep-cut lanes, leading south-westwards from Selborne towards Alresford and Winchester, are comparable with those of Devonshire. In the south-west the New Forest strikes a distinctive note, having no resemblance to the rest of the county.

Hampshire is a great county for trees. There are beeches and yews—the "Hamp-shire weeds"—on the chalk hills, the Selborne yew being the most famous; there are Scotch firs and oaks in the New Forest, and juniper abounds. There are over one thousand species of wild flowers in Hampshire, many of which are not found in the adjacent counties. Among them are several varieties of wild orchid.

As is natural in a hilly, wooded county bordering the sea, Hampshire is rich in bird life. Fallow deer still live with the half-wild ponies in the New Forest, and both the Hampshire rivers, the Test and the Itchen, are famous trout streams.

### Travel Difficulties

Two branches of the Southern Railway, converging at Woking in Surrey, cross the county. The eastern branch crosses the border south of Haslemere and passes through Liphook, Liss and Petersfield to Portsmouth. The western branch goes by way of Farnborough to Basingstoke, turns southwards to Winchester and Southampton and thence westwards to Bournemouth. The difficulty of communication from east to west has so far precluded really democratic local government. It is a Sabbath

**The wild ponies which roam freely over the New Forest are rounded up once a year, after which many of them are auctioned at sales, of which the one below is typical.**

Freefolk, in the upper Test valley, is a model village. Before the war it was largely rebuilt, by the owner of the manor, Lord Portal of Laverstoke, without spoiling its charm.

day's journey for a man without a car living in Liss or Petersfield to get to Winchester, where the county is administered.

The eastern railway runs for most of its way parallel with the London-Portsmouth road, which itself runs close to the boundary between Hampshire and Sussex. Both road and rail pass through country which as late as the seventeenth century was wild forest, Mr. Pepys recording that on one of his official journeys for the Admiralty to Portsmouth, he had to secure a local guide. Liphook, the first station in Hampshire, is a large, characterless village on the edge of the military country that stretches northward to Aldershot It has the distinction of possessing, in the Anchor, an old English inn which was once a famous posting station. Nelson often stayed there; and Queen Victoria slept there once when a young girl, before her accession to the throne. Four miles away stands Liss, equally characterless and even uglier, being in effect the modern emanation of the neighbouring camps of Bordon and Longmoor. North of the village, Liss Forest, so-called, although in fact there are few trees

left, has a semi-suburban charm. To the west on the way to Alton, is Selborne, reached by a typically deep-sunk Hampshire road, with its lovely beech-covered hanger and its memories of Gilbert White, author of *The Natural History of Selborne*— a book which has been described as still "the best book of natural history in the language." It was first published in 1789. Here the well-to-do parson-naturalist lived his quiet, sheltered life, "tranquil and serene with scarcely any other vicissitudes than those of the seasons."

### Selborne's Giant Yew

Selborne to-day is the centre of one of the hop-and-fruit-growing districts of Hampshire. The beauty of the village has been marred by some shockingly ugly and comparatively modern cottages, but White's giant yew with its "thousand years of gloom" is still to be seen in the churchyard, and some of the village retains its quaint loveliness.

Within what has come to be known as "the Gilbert White country" are Woolmer Forest, still largely uncultivated; the spick and span village of East Tisted, the tiny

# HAMPSHIRE

IN THE NEW FOREST

H.M.S. VICTORY
PORTSMOUTH

BERKSHIRE

Medieval Ch. Kingsclere
SILCHESTER
KINGSCLERE
BASINGST
LAVERSTOKE
FREEFOLK
WHITCHURCH
STEVENTON
Paper for the Bank of England
ANDOVER
WHERWELL
MICHELDEVER
Wherwell
Cottages at
STOCKBRIDGE
R. TEST
WINCHESTER
ALRESFOR
TICHBORNE
R. ITCHEN
ROMSEY
HURSLEY
Winchester Cathedral
Romsey Abbey
BROADLANDS
EASTLEIGH
MARTIN
WILTSHIRE
FORDINGBRIDGE
SOUTHAMPTON
HAMBL
BOTLEY
NETLEY
DORSET
NEW
LYNDHURST
Cloister Doorway
FAREHAM
R. HAMBLE
Southampton Water
R. MEON
FOREST
BEAULIEU
Abbey
PORTSM
RINGWOOD
Christchurch Priory
BROCKENHURST
BEAULIEU R.
EXBURY
GOSPORT
R. AVON
LYMINGTON R.
Spithead
LYMINGTON
SPITHEAD
CHRISTCHURCH
The 'Queen Mary'
THE SOLENT
COWES
BOURNEMOUTH
Hengisbury Hd.
CARISBROOKE
RYDE
FRESHWATER
NEWPORT
BEMBRIDGE
Grammar School
ISLE OF
SANDOWN
GODSHILL
The Needles
Carisbrooke Castle
SHANKLIN
VENTNOR
WIGHT

WINCHESTER COLLEGE

GODSHILL, I. o W

Miles

0      5      10

village of Empshott, with its gem of a church, and Hawkley, which is distinguished by another typical Hampshire hanger. Hawkley was the home of Harry Roberts, the writer and doctor, known to so many of London's East-enders. Cobbett once rode from Hambledon down the precipitous Hawkley hanger, where I have more than once nearly broken my neck, and complained bitterly of the state of the road.

Hambledon, outside the Gilbert White country, was the nursery of English cricket, though the game was played by Ken at Winchester School in the seventeenth century. The Hambledon Club, under the leadership of the famous Richard Nyren, the landlord of the Bat and Ball Inn, flourished from 1750 to 1790, and during those years it played and defeated an All England XI twenty-nine times. One match was for a stake of a thousand guineas, and on another occasion the prize was "eleven pairs of white corded dimity breeches and eleven handsome striped pink waistcoats." For thirty years the Hambledon Club dominated the English cricket scene, successfully challenging all comers. Their greatest victory was in 1777 when they defeated a representative England side by an innings and 168 runs. The club played its last match in 1790.

### Charming Petersfield

On the eastern border of the county is Petersfield, where Pepys stayed for a night "in the room which the King lately lay in at his visiting here," a comparatively unspoiled market town of uncommon charm. Gibbon's father was M.P. for Petersfield, and the historian found "much trash" in the parental library when he went to live at his father's house at Buriton, just south of the town, after he returned to England from Switzerland in 1758.

From Petersfield fine views are to be had of the South Downs and of the more modest Hampshire hangers on the west. It is a curious fact that although the Downs are the chief glory of Sussex, they reach their highest point, eight hundred and sixty-eight feet, in Butser Hill just south of Petersfield in Hampshire. The town's Norman church overlooks the market square, with its statue of William III,

The Hursley Hunt, moving off from a meet at Romsey. An old market town on the River Test, it held a prominent place in the wool trade during the Middle Ages.

where the Wednesday cattle market is still held, though with less distinction than before the war. In Petersfield are a number of picturesque old houses, mostly tucked away in odd corners, and one of the best equipped bookshops in the county; near by is the flourishing school of Bedales, the first co-educational institution in England. It is, in fact, due to the influence of the masters and mistresses of this school that there is a considerable cultural life in the town. Its symphony orchestra is good enough to attract Sir Adrian Boult regularly as conductor at its annual festival.

### Cockles and Mussels

After leaving Petersfield the road to Portsmouth passes beneath the shadow of Butser Hill and then traverses comparatively featureless country. Havant, at the junction of the roads from Portsmouth to London and to Brighton, is a town without distinction. A mile or two from the town is Langston Harbour, famous for its mussels and cockles, and from Havant there is a branch railway line to Hayling Island, a sprawling mud-flat, centre of mysterious

activity during the war, which offers little to attract anyone in normal times, but is rarely lacking in visitors.

Portsmouth suffered only less badly than Hull and Plymouth during the war, and the devastation in Fratton, its northern suburb, reminds one of London's East End; the centre of the city was practically destroyed. The front at Southsea was also badly hit. But the bombing also destroyed much slum property; and a newer and more handsome Portsmouth has arisen from the ruins.

The protected waters of Spithead and the Solent have made Southampton England's leading civil port, and Portsmouth, with its appanage of Gosport, Britain's most important naval station. A local historian has said that "Portsmouth is naval first, with everything else too far after to be worth consideration." Even more attractive to visitors than the grey warships in the harbour, the famous old *Victory* in her dry dock symbolizes English history.

The first dockyard was built at the beginning of the sixteenth century and, from Henry VIII onwards, English sovereigns have regularly visted Portsmouth;

96

# HAMPSHIRE

Charles II married Catherine of Braganza (whom that amorous king found "not so exact as to be called a beauty") in the Presence Chamber at Government House. The murder of Buckingham by the fanatic Felton, so graphically described by Dumas in *The Three Musketeers*, took place at the Spotted Dog Inn in Portsmouth. Dickens was born in Portsmouth, and it was at the Portsmouth Theatre that Nicholas Nickleby and Smike acted with the Crummles family.

Let us now turn to the north and enter the county by the Western Region Railway from Berkshire; here on the border, a few miles to the west of the railway is Silchester, nowadays a village with a population of fewer than five hundred souls, but once the Roman fortified town of Calleva Attrebatum. The remains of a considerable number of Roman buildings have been unearthed, and the antiquities recovered are among the most valuable relics of Roman Britain. A Roman road ran from Silchester south-west to Winchester and another west to Salisbury.

This stretch of country in the north and north-west of the county remains aloof from the hurly-burly of modern times; here are to be found all the distinctive Hampshire characteristics—chalk, deep lanes, fine timber and a wealth of wild flowers. At Kingsclere, once a royal manor, there is a strong suggestion of modernity about the racing stable (the horses are trained on the north Hampshire downs), but, in general, the county is bordered in the north by a stretch of quiet, untouched country where unspoiled villages with ancient churches and old (and insanitary) cottages convey an atmosphere of the long ago.

### Jane Austen Country

Basingstoke, the largest town in the north of the county, with its railway works and engineering establishments and a population of many thousands is, as an antiquarian laments, "singularly lacking in evidence of the past." Jane Austen was born and lived the first sixteen years of her placid life at Steventon, south-west of Basingstoke, where her father was rector. Hampshire is indeed the county that should be most held in honour by her admirers. Jane lived at Chawton, near Alton, from a time soon

**Southampton is now England's leading transatlantic port. The liner *Queen Elizabeth* seen at the landing stage in this aerial view of the town's extensive docks.**

after her family left Steventon until the year of her death in 1817.

Alton, south-east of Basingstoke, is one of Hampshire's attractive "small towns," and the centre of the county's main hop-growing district. Lying to the south-west, on the Basingstoke–Winchester road, is Alresford, another pleasant little town watered by a tributary of the Itchen.

Immediately south of Alresford lies the country of the Meon River which, rising in the chalk hills, is still little more than a trickle when it reaches the sea. Lovely and remote is this country where centuries ago the sporting bishops of Winchester hunted the deer. At West Meon there is another Hampshire link with cricket. Thomas Lord, who made Lord's Cricket Ground, is buried there. He sold Lord's to my great-great-uncle James Henry Dark, who in his turn sold it to the Marylebone Club. Botley at the extreme south-west corner of the Meon Valley is the centre of the strawberry district.

### England's First Capital

Volumes have been written on the city of Winchester. It was the first considerable Roman settlement in Britain after the landing of A.D. 43 when the legions marched up the Itchen, and from it radiated England's first Roman roads. It was the first capital of united Saxon England; the city of Alfred the Great and the favourite city of William the Conqueror. A fifteenth-century writer called it "that Joly Cite," and four hundred years later Matthew Arnold was moved to rare enthusiasm by a city "so venerable, so lovely, so unravaged by the intellectual life of our century, so serene."

### St. Swithin's Cathedral

The Venerable Bede related the story of the building of the original Saxon cathedral, practically nothing of which remains to-day, and of the establishment of the Saxon See in the seventh century. Saint Swithin, to whom the existing cathedral is dedicated and who is remembered not for his saintliness but for his legendary connexion with the weather, was bishop in the ninth century, and Alfred, the greatest of the Saxon kings, reigned in Winchester, which, under Canute, was the capital, not only of England, but of a Scandinavian Empire.

Winchester retained its importance for centuries after the coming of the Normans, and in the fourteenth century the Hampshire-born William of Wykeham, prelate, statesman and architect, used the considerable sums he had accumulated in his many secular and ecclesiastical appointments to add lovely chantry chapels to the cathedral and to found Winchester College and New College, Oxford. The present cathedral was begun by the first Norman bishop, the choir and the nave dating from

**Luccombe Beach, near Shanklin, in the Isle of Wight, is typical of the coastal scenery of this island. Its sands and climate attract hundreds of visitors every summer.**

the fourteenth century. It owes not a little of its glory to the clearing of the chantry chapels, a few years ago, by Dean Hutton. William of Wykeham's Winchester College was the earliest of the mis-called English "public schools"—it supplied Eton with its first headmaster. It was established for the benefit of the poor and needy scholars "studying and becoming proficient in the grammaticals and the art and science of grammar."

After the loss of Normandy by the English crown, Winchester lost its earlier commercial importance (since its trade had been made up chiefly of imports and exports to France), and its political importance gradually passed to London. But it continued to enjoy royal favour. Charles II had a great affection for Winchester and began to build a royal residence there. The building forms part of the Deanery which, with its lovely garden, is one of the two most desirable residences that I know, the other being the Provost's Lodge at Eton. When Bishop Ken, the hymn writer, was a canon of Winchester—he spent most of his clerical life in Hampshire—he piously declined to put up Nell Gwynn in his house in the Close when she visited Winchester; Charles, who never lost his sense of humour and was incapable of feeling deep resentment, soon afterwards appointed "the good little man that refused his lodging to poor Nell," to the see of Bath and Wells.

Winchester has preserved some of its ancient glory, notably the Cathedral, the Deanery and the Close, St. Cross, the College and the old West Gate at the end of the High Street. Its streets and odd corners harbour many memories—Jewry Street, for example, being the reminder that Winchester was one of the few English cities that ever had a ghetto and one where, it is a relief to note, the Jews were treated with unusual consideration.

### Literary Associations

It is not surprising that Winchester has also many literary associations; Izaak Walton lived his last years there, and Keats, who also spent in Winchester some of the "last good days of his life." confessed himself enchanted by the city's "maiden-like

**Richard Nyren, famous eighteenth-century captain of the Hambledon Cricket Club, was landlord of this inn, the Bat and Ball. The cricket memorial stone can be seen in front of the inn.**

gentility." Pope went to school in the neighbouring village of Twyford, where Benjamin Franklin wrote his autobiography. Charlotte Yonge, the Anglo-Catholic novelist, was born at Otterbourne, and Keble wrote *The Christian Year* at Horsley, both neighbouring villages. There are references to Winchester in Thackeray's *Esmond* and *Vanity Fair*.

### From Romance to Commerce

And now from Winchester to Southampton, that is to say, from the romantic to the bustlingly commercial. West of the main road, on the banks of the Test, which, with the Itchen, runs into Southampton Water, lies Romsey with its magnificent Norman abbey, almost untouched during the succeeding centuries but now surrounded by mean and modern streets.

Southampton, which to-day has a population approaching two hundred thousand, laid the foundations of its modern prosperity when it became the home port of the P. and O. steamship line. Its importance was immensely increased when it also became the principal passenger port for the United States. It was almost as badly mauled as Portsmouth during the blitz, and it is difficult for one to realize, when looking at the city to-day, that in Tudor times Southampton was counted among the fairest of English towns, and that so late as the end of the eighteenth century, when Jane Austen lived there, it was a fashionable watering-place. It is pleasant to recall that at a spot near the quay, where the giant *Queen Mary* or *Queen Elizabeth* may be berthed, Canute, so the story goes, took post on the shore and bade the sea come no farther; and when it continued to roll on, exclaimed: "Let all the inhabitants of the world know how weak and frivolous is the power of princes."

### In the New Forest

The 145 square miles of the New Forest stretch from Southampton Water to the Wiltshire border. Every schoolboy knows that the New Forest was enclosed by that lover of the chase, William the Conqueror, and that in it William Rufus, the inept son of a gifted father, was killed, perhaps accidentally, perhaps by design, by an arrow shot by Walter Tyrrell, a contemporary chronicler recording, "No bell was tolled, no prayer was said, no alms were given for the soul of the one baptized and appointed ruler, whose eternal damnation was taken for granted by all men as a thing of which there could be no doubt." There are few deer left to-day and little of any other game in the Forest, which is Crown property, but it is still the sanctuary for birds, many of them rare in England, and its trees, its birds and quiet solitude make it a "beauty spot" of a kind hardly to be found anywhere else in England. At least they did so once; but vast tracts of the Forest have been ravished by the Services.

On the south of the Forest is Bournemouth, a modern town without a history, now almost contiguous with Poole in Dorset, prosperous, decorous, elderly, religious, neat and ugly. During the war it was brought pleasantly and sometimes riotously to life by the presence of swarms of British, Dominion and American airmen.

### The Isle of Wight

Until the end of the thirteenth century the Isle of Wight was an independent unit under the authority of its own feudal lord. Then it became incorporated into the county of Hampshire, but, by the Act of 1888, it recovered administrative independence with its own County Council, the Hampshire of

the mainland becoming thereafter officially known as the "County of Southampton."

The island is reached across Spithead from Portsmouth to Ryde, across the Solent from Southampton to Cowes, and from Lymington to Yarmouth. The Elizabethan poet Michael Drayton wrote of the Isle of Wight:

Of all the southern isles she holds the highest place,
And ever more hath been the greatest in Britain's grace.

The Isle of Wight lives fundamentally on its holiday traffic, though inland agriculture is a considerable industry. The shipbuilding yards at Cowes, which built ships for the navy in the days of wooden walls, are still renowned for their yacht building. Unhappily many of the once-flourishing island industries have disappeared, among them the quarrying of a local stone, held in high esteem by that judicious builder, William of Wykeham. The inflow of summer visitors has increased immensely in modern times, particularly into the south-eastern and southern coast towns, with the consequent growth of a permanent urban population to cater for them.

### Growth of Population

When, in 1756, the novelist Fielding visited Ryde (which now has a population of over twenty thousand) there was not even an inn there, and when John Wilkes had a country retreat at Sandown, where he "amused himself with his bantams, peacocks, Chinese pigs and the solemn gallantries of his guinea fowls," his "villakin" was one of the few fishermen's cottages. Now Sandown has a population of over eight thousand. At an even later date, Ventnor consisted of a few thatched huts, and there were only twenty houses in Shanklin.

From Ryde, where a wise guide-book says "no discriminating tourist will linger," there is a short railway journey to the island's capital, Newport, which lies almost under the shadow of Carisbrooke Castle standing on a hill just outside the town. A Norman Castle was built on the site soon after the Conquest, but the older parts of

100

Start of a race at Cowes. The yachts in the foreground, spinnakers set, are coming up to the starting line. Cowes, headquarters of the Royal Yacht Squadron, is the Mecca of British Yachtsmen.

the castle, as it is to-day, date from the fourteenth century. Its defences were strengthened at the time of the Armada, and Charles I was imprisoned there for a year after his capture in 1647.

Arms of Isle of Wight

Tennyson lived at Freshwater, on the west of the island a few miles east of the Needles, where the cliffs rise to a height of five hundred feet. He went there in 1853, three years after Queen Victoria had appointed him Poet Laureate, and Edmund Gosse says that the place "ringed round with ilexes and cedars, entered into his life and coloured it with its delicate enchantment."

### Queen Victoria's Favourite House

Cowes, at the mouth of the River Medina, enjoys a world-wide fame for its yachting regatta. It is the home of the élite of all yachting clubs, the Royal Yacht Squadron, the only yachting club permitted to fly the White Ensign. At Whippingham, just outside Cowes, the Prince Consort designed and built Osborne House, which became Queen Victoria's favourite

home in her widowhood; it was here that she died in 1901.

The beauty of the Isle of Wight is all its own. Particularly notable are the coloured cliffs at Alum Bay; the six miles of the Undercliff west of Ventnor, "a rugged wall, stained with a thousand hues and draped with luxuriant foliage" and the chines, wooded ravines, at Shanklin and Blackgang.

Everyone who has felt the fascination of Hampshire will have his own peculiar and personal memories. As I write I recall the road from Petersfield to Alton which, before reaching Froxfield, passes, on a fine October day when the leaves are turning, through a brilliant scarlet tunnel; the view that varies from season to season from Oakshott hanger, and the old world charm of Alresford. When I think of the Isle of Wight I recall the dead grey autumn day when, as a young reporter, I watched the destroyer carrying the body of Queen Victoria through the lines of saluting battleships from Cowes across Spithead to Portsmouth Harbour.

*The Needles, Isle of Wight*

*Windsor Castle from the Thames*

# BERKSHIRE

### By JOHN BETJEMAN

BERKSHIRE is like a tattered old shoe, kicking out eastwards from Gloucestershire. Bits of the old shoe turn up in most unexpected places, because the whole northern boundary of the county runs for one hundred and ten miles along the south bank of the Thames from Old Windsor, which is next door to Egham, by many convolutions through Henley, Reading, Wallingford and Oxford right up to Buscot, which is by Lechlade in Gloucestershire. The south boundary of the county, and the sole of the shoe, stretches for the most part along the northern edge of Hampshire. And the uppers make a western border for the county on the Wiltshire downs. As for the toe, at the eastern end, that is Windsor Great Park.

Such a geographical introduction is necessary because it helps to explain Berkshire, which is far less of a self-contained county than is, let us say, Oxfordshire or Shropshire. There is no way of generalizing about Berkshire.

*Badge of Berkshire*

You cannot say of a town or village or river "that is typical Berkshire" because various parts of the county, socially and scenically, take their flavour from the neighbouring counties.

Berkshire has been a border county for centuries. In the sixth century A.D., it became part of the kingdom of Wessex and the scene of continual warfare with the heathen kingdom of Mercia on the opposite bank of the Thames. Then Wessex was attacked from the east by the Danes and became a stronghold of King Alfred, who was born at Wantage in 849 (his Victorian statue, dwarfed by four lamp-posts, may be seen in the middle of the market-place of that town). Berkshire had more than its share of battles between barons and kings, and between barons and barons, from Norman times until the end of the Wars of the Roses. Wallingford and Windsor Castles were always regarded as strong defence positions. William the Conqueror saw the strategic value of the chalk cliff above the Thames at Windsor and built himself a castle there. At Wallingford Castle Henry, son of Matilda, concluded a treaty with King Stephen in 1153 by which he

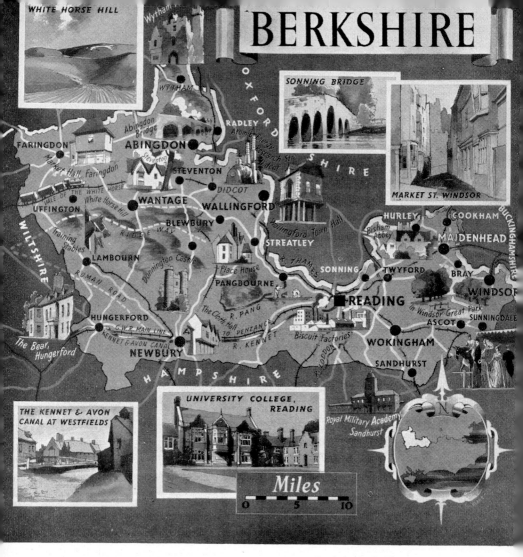

# BERKSHIRE

WHITE HORSE HILL

SONNING BRIDGE

MARKET ST. WINDSOR

THE KENNET & AVON CANAL AT WESTFIELDS

UNIVERSITY COLLEGE, READING

Royal Military Academy Sandhurst

Miles

0    5    10

eventually came to the throne as Henry II, first of the Plantagenet kings.

Because Berkshire lies around the meeting points of the chief roads from the West Country to the south Midlands and London, it became the most important battleground in the Civil Wars. Charles I and Parliament skirmished all over it, and at Newbury, two big battles were fought. Most county histories and guides written in the last and the present centuries regard the end of the Civil Wars, or at any rate the end of the eighteenth century, as the beginning of "progress" and "peace." Every-

thing gets better and better, poor law institutions are opened, towns are paved and lighted with gas, public libraries dispense their culture, and sewage farms deodorize the unhygienic. Now in the middle of an accelerating century, we are beginning to think otherwise, and only too clearly we can see that Berkshire is once more a border county and the scene of skirmish. This time the invasion is again from the east, not by the Danes, but by the industrial peoples of London. They have captured the east of the county. Their leaders, company inflators, have established themselves domestically among the pinewoods of the Bagshot beds in the Sunningdale area where electric light of an evening falls on bridge parties in modern mansions built in the Tudor style. The richer have percolated as far west as Newbury, where main roads and good trains have brought them into a remoter acreage of their beloved pines and rhododendrons. For a long while they occupied Maidenhead.

Motor transport, which has changed the face of England, has naturally very much changed the face of Berkshire. The chief main road to the west, the old Bath road of lumbering eighteenth-century coaches and handsome posting inns, runs into the county from London at Maidenhead and goes through Reading and Newbury and out into Wiltshire from Hungerford. So the south of the county is pocked with light industry and with whatever factories can be served by lorries. From Maidenhead to Newbury their brick sheds have sprung up, and so have the villas for their workers. Industrial people, under the generalship of

Lord Nuffield, have also established themselves in the north of the county. There are now no "lone homesteads in the Cumnor Hills" such as were known to Matthew Arnold and Arthur Hugh Clough. The neighbourhood of the Berkshire villages, called the Hinkseys, is not the same. Like Cumnor, it is a suburb of industrial Oxford. Abingdon is now almost a suburb of that city which makes motor-cars.

Reading, too, is almost a suburb of London, thanks to the Great Western main line and the Great West Road. Its two chief industries, seeds and biscuits, are relics of the time when Reading was the only industrial town in an agricultural county. Great allies of the industrial people are the mechanized sorties of the Army and Royal Air Force. Sandhurst Royal Military Academy is in Berkshire and so is Bagshot Heath. In this sandy, coniferous district most areas which have not been acquired already by public institutions, such as Broadmoor Criminal Lunatic Asylum, attracted in the first place by the poor quality

A view of the Berkshire Downs, "stronghold of the old agricultural Berkshire." Much of the Downs was ploughed up during the war, but some sheep breeding remains.

of the land and consequent low rental—all these districts are the scenes of manœuvres and camps of Nissen huts. And not even agricultural land has escaped. On the flat fruit-growing land between Didcot and Milton is the biggest ordnance depot in England. At Aldermaston are vast sheds and wire for use in connection with B.O.A.C.

The west of the county, on the chalk downs and in the fertile Vale of the White Horse, remains the stronghold of the old agricultural Berkshire. In recent years the downs have been ploughed up, so that there are very few of them left. And, if the present ploughing-up policy were ever relaxed, it would still be a century before the downs regained their smooth and springy, flower-bright turf. Sheep-breeding, for which the county was famous, is consequently dying out as the tractor drags a plough along the slopes. The August sheep fairs at East Ilsley, within living memory the largest in England, have died out. This little downland town, which maintained more than a dozen inns on the strength of the fair, now has only four. Old grass tracks along the tops of the great downs, *e.g.* the

prehistoric Ridgeway, were, even before the war, becoming muddy and worn thin under the tyres of tourists who were too lazy to get out of their motor-cars and walk, but who preferred shutting themselves up in their cars on a hill-top with the Sunday paper and the wireless crooning them to sleep. Now these same tracks are still grassless, but from the imprint of tractor wheels. Only around Lambourn, where trainers have managed to keep a few gallops and where hills are too uneven to plough, do the downs remain.

### Atomic Research

Lately, Berkshire, this battle-ground of the centuries, has been chosen for the latest plan of industrialization. Atomic energy has descended, as it were, by parachute, right into the agricultural stronghold. Harwell, at the foot of the downs, has been selected as a research station for this latest blessing of science. The neighbouring undeveloped industrial sprawl at Didcot has been ignored by the developers and will remain neither village nor town. But the old market town of Wantage has been industrialized for half

A harvest scene near Didcot which lies between the foot of the Downs and the Thames. Nearby, at Harwell, the atomic research station was established in 1946.

The Thames at Basildon, a Berkshire hamlet near Pangbourne, where the river runs between the Berkshire Downs and the foothills of the Chilterns in Oxfordshire.

the Harwell workers, and some of the rest are housed in the crowded and ancient town of Abingdon.

So in the latest battle, that between the old agricultural way of life and the new industrial one still in its beginnings, Berkshire is, as usual, a prominent seat of war. Those on the industrial side have every reason to expect victory for their modern cinemas, chain stores and community canteens. And the conquerors are bringing their undoubted benefits of internal water and drainage and of power and light to the villages. But as the pipes tunnel slowly under the fields and as the pylons stride even more slowly over the hills and disperse into forests of poles and wire among the old cottage clusters, so the buses draw more workers off the land to the factories and the depots in the towns and along the main roads and railway lines. To-day there is hardly a village in Berkshire so inaccessible that, in the evening, the majority of its few remaining inhabitants are not away from home at the nearest cinema.

But local patriotism and local associations in England die hard. Something you can call Berkshire, physically and historically subdivided into separate districts, may

still be found under the levelling and the centralization of the industrial age. Though Reading is its seat of local government, and though the town mentality of that industrial borough imposes its wishes, as far as housing is concerned, on the western and agricultural half of the county, still east and west Berkshire retain their distinct individuality.

### Difference Between East and West

One expression of the difference is in the circulation of local papers. East Berkshire takes in the *Reading Mercury* (one of the oldest provincial news-sheets, founded in 1723), north-west Berkshire takes in the *North Wilts Herald*, which is edited in Swindon, Wiltshire, and south-west Berkshire has its newspapers from Newbury. A further subdivision of distinctive parts of Berkshire is made by the parliamentary constituencies which are Reading and Windsor for east Berkshire, Newbury and Abingdon for west Berkshire. The last-named constituency is overbalanced because it contains thousands of industrial voters who work for the Nuffield organizations and whose centre is Oxford. Industrialized people in the South of England have

A curious gate leading to the tiny downland hamlet of Compton Beauchamp.

not yet had time to develop those local constituencies—if they ever will develop them—which we associate with the farming age. For this reason you will only find people who may really be labelled "Berkshire" on the western farming districts of the county up in the downland villages and in the Kennet Valley and the Vale of the White Horse.

In these parts local dialect survives. A specimen of it, quoted by Thomas Hughes in *The Scouring of the White Horse* (1859), holds good for to-day. This is part of a description, told by a pig, of its capture at Kingston Lisle by Uffington youths, who carried it off to White Horse Hill, for the sports which were to be held on its grassy top when the chalk horse was to be cleaned by local inhabitants. At these sports backsword fights occurred, cheeses were rolled down the great bowl of down, known as the Manger, from the hill-top. The last scouring was in the 1850s.

Berkshire men, vrom Hill and Vale
All as ever hears this tale,
If to spwoort you be inclined,
Plaze to bear this here in mind—
Pegs beant made no race to win
Be zhart o' wind and tight o' skin;
Dwont'ee hunt 'em, but instead
At backswyrd break each others yead—
Cheezes down the manger rowl—
Or try and clim the greasy powl.
Pegs! in stubble yerd and stye,
May you be nevir zard like I,
Nor druv wi' greasy ears and tail,
By men and bwoys down White Horse
Vale.

Thomas Hughes, who quotes this, was born at Uffington, and opens his more famous book *Tom Brown's Schooldays* with a lyrically beautiful description of Berkshire village life of the Vale before the Great Western main line to Bristol ran through it. In some of the remoter downland villages of west Berkshire, between Newbury and Wantage, there are children of ten years old who have never seen a train, let alone travelled in one, though they have been to cinemas and travelled by bus to the local town. In these quiet parts, too, country crafts survive. Excellent straw thatching of cottages and ricks continues. In the Vale you may still see circular ricks with little straw figures on each apex. There are smiths and wheelwrights. Shortage of petrol during the war brought many of the grand old Berkshire wagons into use again. These wagons, with their small front wheels and large rear ones protected by a wide curved hoop, are like the Wiltshire type, particularly splendid when painted with red, blue and yellow devices. Here there are local industries. Snow-ploughs are made at Ashbury, a straw-thatched, chalk and sarsen village on the Wiltshire border. Whiting was, until lately, made from chalk at Kintbury, near Hungerford. Bell-founding and cloth-making, for which Berkshire was famous, have died out. So have nearly all the local brickfields. Since most of Berkshire is on chalk and sand and clay, it lacks stone.

### Building in Brick

There is no cathedral in the county. St. George's Chapel, Windsor, is easily the finest medieval building, and the parish churches of Uffington, Lambourn, Abingdon, Aldworth and North Moreton are the next most notable. Berkshire architecture only becomes remarkable with the introduction of brick in Tudor times. And in brick Berkshire architects and builders excelled. Wantage, Abingdon, Wallingford, Hungerford, Newbury and Reading are all brick towns. You will easily date houses from their bricks. The earliest dark brownish-red Tudor bricks are very small. Then come the dark red bricks of the seventeenth century which are slightly larger. Often they are shaped into moulded curves for cornices. One of the most charming examples of this use of brick is to be seen on the main street of Newbury above a ruthlessly modern and inharmonious shopfront. In Georgian times most of the farms and medium-sized houses of towns and villages seem to have been rebuilt with brick. Plain surfaces were diversified with glazed bricks. A usual west Berkshire trick of this time was to have a border of red bricks round the sash window (where woodwork ought to be painted white), a brick or plaster projecting cornice below the brick parapet and, between the windows, an upright oblong extent of bricks, glazed bluish-black. Wantage, Hungerford and Newbury have notable examples. In Reading plainer brick was used.

Few towns are less prepossessing at first glance than Reading, seen from the windows of a Great Western train from London, as it slows into the station by that castellated gaol where Oscar Wilde languished. But few towns better repay exploration, for in the London Street area and near the university (which has wisely preserved some rows of Georgian houses) are brick mansions of the late eighteenth century designed by that great architect, Sir John Soane, a local man. In these, brick is used to perfection. Surfaces are rendered noble not by glazed or moulded bricks, as they were earlier in the century, but by relation of window-pane to window and window to wall space and wall space to size and texture of individual brick. Sir John designed the stately Obelisk in the market-place at Reading which is disfigured with tin signs and dishonoured by municipal accretions beside it. Another town of lovely brickwork is Abingdon, which abounds in almshouses. But its finest building, the town hall (wrongly ascribed to Inigo Jones or Wren, but every bit as handsome as their work), is of stone.

### Variety of Cottages

As for the cottages of Berkshire villages, their buildings vary in structure as do all old cottages of England; they are made from the nearest building materials available. None is earlier than the seventeenth century, most are of the eighteenth and nineteenth centuries. In the widest area, that is to say, the chalk, they are usually of flint and brick combined, with thatched roofs. At the foot of the northern slope of the downs, that is to say, on the south side of the Vale of the White Horse, the cottages are often built of clunch, which is a hardened form of chalk. Timber-framed cottages survive throughout the county; the earlier ones have spaces between the timbers filled in with wattle and daub, the later with brick. On the Wiltshire border are some tile-hung cottages and houses.

No one travelling in Berkshire can fail to be appalled by the council houses which mutilate almost every village and which were put up in the 1920s and 1930s. In the Wantage and Faringdon areas, where were once some of the loveliest villages in England, the council houses are generally considered to be amongst the most ill-sited, disproportioned, inharmonious and badly built houses in England; and with some justification, for they provide a glaring contrast with their surroundings. Only two old Berkshire villages survive untouched in these areas: Woolstone, sited amidst elms below the great grassy height of White Horse Hill, and its neighbour Knighton (Compton Beauchamp). Both of these are scheduled for almost complete destruction, unless the new spirit of the Ministry of Town and Country Planning makes itself felt in this neglected district.

### Local Preference

So far as local sincere feeling is concerned (as opposed to that whipped up by local careerists), an old cottage enlarged to contain plumbing and sanitation and light is preferred to a new council house, for the former has its worked and well-stocked garden and its thick walls for shutting out the cold of winter and the heat of summer. All it lacks is space and modern facilities.

I have left to the last the most satisfying feature of Berkshire—its variety of natural scenery. And in the descriptions which follow mention must be made of artificially created landscape in the form of planting and house building and use of the soil. For instance, almost all villages have box hedges in the cottage gardens.

The north-west corner of Berkshire might be a hundred miles from the rest of the county. It stretches from the Vale of the White Horse to the stripling Thames. Its capital is Faringdon. It abounds in elm trees. The older buildings are in golden grey limestone, of which the noblest is the huge tithe barn at Great Coxwell (fourteenth century) whose dark timber-supported interior is like a cathedral. From the Thames up the long slopes of the south banks are elm trees, and on the ridge—known locally as the Golden Ridge because of the rich people's houses thereon—are stately stone mansions in timbered parks.

Swan "Uppers" catching swans on the Thames near Windsor preparatory to marking the birds. All Thames swans belong to the King or the Dyers' and Vintners' Companies.

111

Ascot was laid out as a race-course in 1711 by order of Queen Anne. The June meeting is the most. fashionable in the racing calendar. The principal events are the Ascot Gold Cup and the Royal Hunt Cup

Coleshill (seventeenth century, Faringdon House, Buckland and Buscot (all eighteenth century) are the best. Turn your eyes south from this ridge on a moonlit autumn night and look over the Vale. You will see the elm tops of that rich dairy district, looking like tree-clad islands in a vast silver lake, and beyond them, like cliffs, the distant outline of the north Berkshire downs. This outline is broken here and there by grass ramparts of Iron Age, Roman and Saxon times—Uffington camp, Letcombe Castle, Scutchamore Knob—when the Ridgeway along the top of the downs was the only track across this part of England.

### Villages of Another World

Ascend from the Vale of the White Horse, the greensand to these high chalk downs. Already in the lovely villages directly below them you are in another world, like Sussex at the back of Brighton. Probably the finest downland scene in Berkshire, after White Horse Hill, is above Streatley, where the Thames cuts through a high chalk ravine. But once on the western Berkshire downs near Lambourn, where the singular early classic shape of Ashdown House stands lonely among its devastated plantations, you are in the airy height of velvety turf and the Lambourn racing stables.

The trainers' establishments stretch all along the downs to the east, as far as atomic Harwell. "The Druid," that close observer of English scenery and best of all writers on racing and livestock, described it superbly a century ago: "Once at the summit, and the downs seem to stretch away for miles in one vast, brown, rippling surface, with no sound to break their stillness, except the bleatings of the Hampshires, as they answer their newly born lambs; and the bullock language of the white-smocked ploughmen. The Vale of the White Horse, so dear to Tom Brown's heart, furnishes a delightful sunny panorama rich with trees and water behind us. In front is a strip of tableland flanked on one side by a woodland dell, where the fox lies curled at the mouth of his earth, careless of the hunting horn and hound; while on the other is Compton Bottom, with its patches of stunted bushes and undergrowth, and peopled with countless generations of 'merry brown and straight-backed hares.'"

South of the downs is the third type of Berkshire scenery, the Kennet valley, flat meadow-land planted with poplars and willows. On the slopes above it are wide commons of bracken and heather, silver birch and oak, so very recently cut up into military and prisoner of war camps.

112

# BERKSHIRE

And above the commons rise chalk downs, to the north those we have just left, to the south Inkpen Beacon and the Hampshire downs. "The Kennet swift, for silver eels renowned," Pope called it. But the fishing is not what it was, not even in the Kennet and Avon Canal which runs many-locked, all down the valley to Reading beside the little river.

And south of Reading is a fourth type of scene, the vale of the "Loddon slow, with verdant alders crowned." Pictures, almost over-lovely, like a Birket Foster water colour, have been left of this district before the red tongues of Reading licked it out of shape. They are to be found in *Our Village* (1819) by Mary Russell Mitford, who was generally describing what was then Three Mile Cross, near Swallowfield. Here were the lanes she loved "winding between small enclosures of pastoral land on one side, and the grounds of the great house, with their picturesque paling and rich plantations on the other; the depth and undulation of the wild cart track giving a singularly romantic and secluded air to the whole scene, whilst occasionally the ivied pollards and shining holly bushes of the hedgerow mingle with the laurels and cedars and fine old firs of the park, forming, even in mid-winter, a green arch overhead, and contrasting vividly with a little sparkling stream which runs gurgling along by the side of the pathway." Few such lanes remain in these parts.

## Country of Orchards

Two more, the fifth and sixth types of Berkshire scenery, may be more briefly dismissed. East of the Loddon is the coniferous and sandy district of Bagshot Heath already described. Between Abingdon and Wallingford is a flat fruit-growing district, with some attractive half-timbered villages,

Abingdon, ancient market town, which was already prominent in the eighth century, has clothing, carpet and agricultural industries. It houses many of the workers from the Harwell research station.

in particular Blewbury, where Kenneth Grahame lived, and East Hagbourne.

Penultimately, Royal Windsor stands on its own. William the Conqueror's castle has been altered and improved beyond recognition. Its extreme beauty, so wonderful when seen from the Great Western main line over the flat Thames valley, with storm clouds behind and a gold, after-storm sun on it, is almost entirely due to the genius of Sir Jeffrey Wyatville. He started altering the outline of the castle in 1824, inspired by George IV, a great patron of arts. Far the best medieval building in the castle—and in the county—is St. George's Chapel. The present building was started by Edward IV and finished by Henry VII. King's College Chapel, Cambridge, St. Mary Redcliffe, Bristol, St. George's Chapel, Windsor, are the three greatest late Gothic buildings in the country. And it is hard to say which of these lace-like forests of glass and stone is the loveliest. Away into what remains of Berkshire stretch the oaks and elms of Windsor Great Park, where here and there the fanciful Georgian houses of Royal relations appear between the trees. The steep hill-town is full of Georgian houses, but the outskirts of Windsor are singularly squalid.

Finally, there is the Berkshire river scenery upstream from here, and half of this is shared with Buckinghamshire and Oxfordshire on the northern bank. The

flowery gardens of lock-keepers and wide willow-bordered meadows, chalk cliffs, more willowy meadows, the parks of great houses, the Edwardian houses on the banks of the stream itself, with their white wooden balconies and turrets, Maidenhead, home of half-dead night-clubs and business-men's hide-outs, Sonning and Wargrave and Cookham with their week-end houses and so on, through Reading to the reaches by Streatley and to Wallingford's lovely noble semi-classic steeple. The beauty of the Thames south of Oxford is more often for the lover of rowing and punting or out-board engines and more for the lover of love. When the river was fashionable, when every young guardsman had his punt and every mother with a marriageable daughter hired a river-side house at Maidenhead, J. Ashby Sterry wrote his river rhymes which caught an atmosphere that still lingers among the houseboats:

We toiled in June all down to Bray,
And yarns we spun for Mab and May;
O, who would think such girls as they
    Would turn out swindles?
But *now* we toil and spin for jack
And in the evening we get back
    To Skindle's.

And I prefer to get back to the old Berkshire in the west and north and to the little Thames which passes on its Oxfordshire bank the grey-walled Kelmscott Manor of William Morris.

*Training Racehorses on the Berkshire Downs*

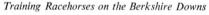

*Mayflower Barn, Jordans*

# BUCKINGHAMSHIRE

### By MARTIN HALLIWELL

PROMINENT on the county arms of Bucking-hamshire is a swan, and there is something about this bird—contemplative, enigmatic, withdrawn into itself yet masking hidden fires beneath its serene exterior—which gives a clue to the quality of the county and its slow evolution through the centuries, the peace and calm of its inhabitants, un-ruffled except at moments of unbearable strain, and then erupting into demonstra-tions of sturdy individualism surprising in their intensity and whole-heartedness. It is in fighting mood, indeed, that the swan is depicted on the county arms. Buckingham-shire is a small county, in some ways a backwater, yet the men and women who have lived there have affected English history to a degree disproportionate to their numbers. Let us take a look first at the small corner of the earth in which they live.

The shire of Buckingham was constituted during the ninth cen-tury, after the expulsion of the Danes. As might be expected in a part of England as wild as the Chilterns then were, the King's

advisers had little detailed knowledge of their task, and the grouping of the hundreds in the county is entirely arbitrary, with little natural unity between different areas. Buckingham-shire to-day is most conveniently to be thought of in four separate regions, each of which will require some detailed description before we can understand the psychology of the people. I do not wish to load this short chapter with population figures, rainfall statistics or geological details; but it is necessary to get a grip of the widely varying nature of the country and towns included thus arbitrarily in this county's boundaries, to think geographically for a moment, before we can arrive at a true picture of the people of Buckinghamshire against their home background.

Think first of the Thames valley —of the north bank from just west of Staines to just east of Henley, for this is the first section that concerns us. Colnbrook, Slough, Eton, Taplow and Marlow are the principal towns situated in the flat and fertile country whose closeness to London and excellent

*Badge of Buckinghamshire*

# BUCKINGHAMSHIRE

JORDANS MEETING HOUSE

STOKE POGES CHURCH

CLIVEDEN HOUSE

NORTHAMPTONSHIRE

OXFORDSHIRE

BEDFORDSHIRE

OLNEY

Railway Works
Cowpers Summerhouse

NEWPORT
PAGNELL

WOLVERTON

STONY
STRATFORD

FENNY
STRATFORD

Stowe School

BUCKINGHAM

BLETCHLEY

Bow Brickhill Church

WINSLOW

Stewkley Church

North Marston Church
Bucks

Wing
Church

AKEMAN ST.

Windmill at Brill

Ivinghoe
Beacon

R. THAME

CANAL

BRILL

The Forge
Dinton

CANAL

AYLESBURY

WENDOVER

CHILTERN HILLS

WEST WYCOMBE

PRINCES
RISBORO

Chequers

Chesham
Church

CHESHAM

BRADENHAM

HUGHENDEN

Amersham

The Market

West Wycombe

PENN

Fingest
Church

HIGH
WYCOMBE

The Guildhall

CHALFONT
ST. GILES

FINGEST

BEACONSFIELD

GERRARDS CROSS

MARLOW

CLIVEDEN

Burnham Beeches

DENHAM

Denham Film Studios

RIVER THAMES

TAPLOW

STOKE POGES

SLOUGH

ETON

MIDDLESEX

R. COLNE

BERKSHIRE

BLAKE

ETON COLLEGE –
Lupton's
Tower

N

W

E

S

Miles

0        5        10

the county. The earliest remains so far found within the county are palæolithic, and there is evidence that nearly all the races which successively invaded England from the continent — Celts, Britons, Romans, Saxons, Danes and Normans— swept across Buckinghamshire and left traces of their presence. Of those mentioned, Danes and Normans left fewest traces, the latter merely superimposing a new landed aristocracy on top of the old Saxon lords, with little effect on the life of the ordinary man in the county. The fair-haired Saxon type, then, is possibly the predominating type, if any type can be said to predominate at all; but we must add that this holds good for north Buckingham-

spirit of innovation and adventure unexpected in such placid surroundings, which makes Buckinghamshire more important in English history than some of its neighbouring counties. The characteristic is sufficiently marked to be worth noting, even before we look at some of the famous men who as individuals have brought renown to the county. The lines in G. K. Chesterton's poem *The Secret People*

It may be we are meant to mark with our riot and our rest
God's scorn for all men governing . . .

speak well enough for the men of Buckinghamshire and their determination not to be put upon, particularly in religious

Seen against a fine setting of trees the bridge and church at Marlow present a view characteristic of this section of the Thames. Marlow is a boating centre.

shire only—in many places, especially in the Chilterns, you can distinguish dark Celtic survivals as well. In fact, it is more realistic to write down the men of the county—as, by and large, of England herself—as of mixed and indeterminable parentage—mongrels, if you like—than to look for a typical Buckinghamshire man.

But though I cannot find a distinctive type, I can point out how the inhabitants of Buckinghamshire have throughout their written history collectively given repeated proof of a sturdy independence and a

matters. I like to believe that Magna Carta, the inalienable charter of all our civil liberties, was signed (June 15, 1215) by King John within the county boundaries, as it may well have been if, as many authorities hold, the document was executed on Charter Island, and not in the meadow of Runnymede, which, of course, is on the Surrey side of the river. Later, the Lollard movement, the earliest stirring of British religious nonconformity, instituted by John Wyclif in the fourteenth century, but even more influential after his death, was widely supported by the Buckinghamshire land-owners and their followers, many of whom were burnt at the stake for the cause. Wyclif himself had held the living of Ludgershall in the county, though he worked mainly from Oxford; but it must have been through the villages of Bucking-hamshire that his message of asceticism and strict adherence to the Christianity of the Bible first spread south-east towards London on the lips of his travelling friars.

### Civil War Battle

In the struggles between the King and the people of England which led up to the Civil War, Buckinghamshire men were again to the fore on the Roundhead side, and it was a Buckinghamshire squire, John Hampden, of whom I shall say more later, who helped to bring matters to a head. In 1642 one of the first battles of the Civil War was a few miles north of Aylesbury; here the Roundhead headquarters were first set up; Charles I's headquarters were later at Buckingham, and throughout the war the county was much fought over.

In the seventeenth century George Fox, the Leicestershire shoemaker's apprentice, found in the county some of the earliest and most devoted members of his Society of Friends (nicknamed Quakers from Fox's stern injunction to an erring magistrate to "*quake* before the Lord"). Some of the oldest Quaker meeting-houses are in this county, including the world-famous house at Jordans, where the grave of William Penn, founder and "first proprietor" of the state of Pennsylvania, is much visited by Americans. The county can show many fine chapels, specimens of local builders' work—a genuine folk art which we may later come to admire as we admire the village churches to-day. Of the latter, too, the county has many fine examples. The Eccentric Period church of the Dashwood family at West Wycombe is celebrated.

I mentioned John Hampden, and should like him to be thought of as the typical Buckinghamshire man, bred in the county on the proverbially excellent "Buckingham-shire bread and beef." He became squire of Great Hampden near Wendover in 1620 soon after his marriage. It was in respect of

a property at Stoke Mandeville, just south of Aylesbury, that in 1635 he endeared himself to countless Englishmen of his own and later generations by refusing to pay what he considered an unjustifiable imposition—twenty shillings of "ship money," an out-of-date defence levy which Charles I wished to revive and enforce. He continued to play a leading part in all the disputes, legal and parliamentary, which followed, and after the start of the Civil War commanded a Buckinghamshire battalion of the Parliamentary army. Wounded at the battle of Chalgrove Field in 1643, he died at Thame and was brought home for burial to Hampden, where his family continued to live for many years.

Next after Hampden must be mentioned the two poets of the county: William Cowper (1731–1800), whose association with Olney has already been mentioned, and Thomas Gray (1716–1771), who was educated at Eton, returned frequently in after life to his mother's house at Stoke Poges, and in the churchyard there wrote his famous *Elegy*, celebrating for all time the simplicity and the pathos of ordinary life in an English village. Other poets—Milton (who wrote *Lycidas* and *L'Allegro* among the Thames-side meadows near Colnbrook), Waller and Shelley—have had brief associations with the county, but Cowper and Gray must be àccounted its principal men of letters, together with the eccentric Thomas Love Peacock, who wrote his best known satires, *Headlong Hall* and *Nightmare Abbey*, at Marlow between 1815 and 1820, the latter being probably inspired by the gloomy bat-ridden fastnesses of nearby Medmenham Abbey.

### Distinguished Immigrants

Apart from William Penn, whose claim to a Buckinghamshire ancestry is doubtful, the county can claim few other natives of more than local distinction, though the roll of distinguished immigrants to the county who owned property there and refreshed themselves in its sleepy countryside for their work in London is a long one. It includes Burke (1729–1797), who lived the last twenty years of his life at Gregories, near Beaconsfield; Benjamin Disraeli, Lord

Hedged lanes and elm trees combine to give distinction to this countryside near Chalfont St. Giles where the Chiltern Hills fall to the valley of the Thames.

123

Beaconsfield (1804–1881), whose father purchased the manor house at Bradenham which Disraeli describes in his novel *Endymion*, and who later moved to the neighbouring village of Hughenden, where he is buried; the historian Grote (1794–1871), who wrote most of his *History of Greece* near Farnham Royal; the two Herschels, Sir William (1738–1822) and his son Sir John (1792–1871), pioneers of astronomy—it was near Slough that the elder Herschel erected his revolutionary forty-foot reflecting telescope for the study of the stars, parts of which are still preserved to-day; W. H. Smith, the newsagent, created first Viscount Hambleden; Lord Dawson of Penn, royal physician; and, since 1918, the successive Prime Ministers of the day, each of whom is enabled by the generosity of the late Lord Lee of Fareham to use as his private country house the mansion of Chequers, tucked away near Monks Risborough in one of the loveliest folds of the Chilterns. Buckinghamshire can claim her influence, too, during the .vital formative years of adolescence, on all the pupils of her famous public schools—Eton and Stowe for boys, and Wycombe Abbey for girls—and on the hundreds of Royal Air Force men who begin their service careers at Halton, near Wendover.

I cannot leave this catalogue of Buckinghamshire characters without a tribute to one whom I should call the most enterprising of them all—Master John Shorne, saintly thirteenth-century rector of North Marston near Winslow, who is said by his exceptional piety to have successfully imprisoned the Devil in a boot, out of which he would pop his head when required by the rector to do so. How long the Devil stayed there we are not told, but the incident gave rise to our modern toy the Jack-in-a-Box, and several inns in the neighbourhood are still called "The Boot."

Such is our county, its physical appearance, its leading employments, its past history and its outstanding individuals—matters for the man born and bred in the county to contemplate with pride and affection. The old order changeth, the fundamental unity of the county—for geographical reasons, as we saw, never very marked—has already been impaired, and will be still further impaired, by an ever-growing London just over the border. But those newcomers or part-time residents who settle in the county and abandon themselves to its charm will find just the same things to be proud of, and one day to love: good food and drink, an air of sober prosperity in towns, in the country a hundred secret beauty spots of their own discovery in addition to those already famous, fat cattle and land in good heart throughout the Vale of Aylesbury, the glory of winter sunsets seen from a ridge of the Chilterns, beechwoods golden in autumn and the tenderest of greens in the spring, and after dark the nightingale.

*Ivinghoe Beacon*

*Magdalen Tower and Bridge, Oxford*

# OXFORDSHIRE

### By S. P. B. MAIS

GEOLOGY largely determines not only the face of the landscape and the main industries of a county, but also the character of its people. It is evident that Derbyshire people share many of the characteristics of their native limestone and gritstone. In the same way Oxfordshire people owe much of their individual character to the Cotswold Hills and the valleys formed by the rivers which spring from them.

Their dialect is an odd mixture of Midland and Southern tongues, as befits a county that forms the link between the south and the industrial heart of England.

With Berkshire, from which it is separated by the winding course of the Thames, Oxfordshire forms a rough rectangle lying midway between the Severn and Thames estuaries and equidistant from the Midlands and the south coast. Its extreme length from Banbury in the north to Caversham in the south is something over forty miles. Between the chalk of the Chiltern escarpment in the south-east and the limestone of

*Arms of City of Oxford*

the Cotswolds in the north-west the greater part of the county is a plain formed of two bands, the clay and the greensand. On the latter lies the city of Oxford, centrally placed where the roads from Southampton to the north and from London to South Wales intersect. This position complicates its traffic problems, but makes it obvious why the Pressed Steel Company and Morris Motors chose it in preference to, say, Coventry.

Oxford is one of the most easily accessible of all English cities both by road and rail. It is therefore easy to understand why its narrow streets are always congested and its population numbers over two-fifths of the entire county. Nearly half its male workers are, in fact, immigrants. Indeed, its fame so far overshadows the rest of the county that few tourists know anything of Oxfordshire beyond the boundaries set by the Oxford city walls. While Oxford is not Oxfordshire, it is so important in the county's life that any description of the latter must begin with

125

the former. This proud city of towers and spires with its exquisite college gardens, had its beginnings long before the foundation of the university. In the cathedral lie the remains of a king's daughter, St. Frideswide, who founded a nunnery at Osney and died as long ago as A.D. 720.

It was not until the twelfth century that scholars sought sanctuary here and the oldest colleges, about the seniority of which there is considerable dispute, came into existence in the thirteenth century.

University College may perhaps be the oldest though there is no foundation for the claim that it dates from the days of Alfred the Great. All that we know is that University College, Balliol, Merton and St. Edmund Hall were all in existence before 1270. Exeter, Oriel, Queen's and New College followed in the fourteenth century, Lincoln, All Souls and Magdalen in the fifteenth, Brasenose, Corpus, Christ Church, St. John's, Trinity and Jesus in the sixteenth, Wadham and Pembroke in the seventeenth, Worcester and Hertford in the eighteenth and Keble in the nineteenth.

Towards the end of the last century the growing freedom of women showed itself in the foundation of the first women's college, Lady Margaret Hall, in 1878. In the fifteen years which followed three more women's colleges, Somerville, St. Hugh's and St. Hilda's, came into being.

Christ Church is the largest, richest and noblest college, Magdalen the most beautiful, and Merton (Mob Quad) architecturally the oldest. The gardens of St. John's, Worcester, New College and Wadham are outstanding in natural beauty, an exquisite medley of smooth lawns, herbaceous borders and splendid trees. World famous, and an integral part of the university, is the Bodleian Library founded in 1603.

Oxford during term-time is very different from Oxford during vacations. The terms, however, are short, consisting only of eight weeks each, and during the Long Vacation, which begins in the middle of June and ends in mid-October, the colleges, though open to the public, are tenanted only by summer schools and conferences and lack the swarming youthful life that gives each its character.

The revenue of the colleges comes partly from property, and, in consequence, their financial status varies considerably. St.

**The Butter Cross at Witney, a market town on the Windrush. It is famous for the manufacture of blankets from wool provided by Cotswold sheep.**

**Blenheim Palace was built at Woodstock as a gift of the nation to the first Duke of Marlborough for his victory over the French and Bavarians at Blenheim in 1704.**

John's owns the larger part of north Oxford which is now the main residential area, and its wealth is inevitably great. The total revenue of Christ Church has been computed to be about £500,000 a year.

The actual tuition fees of the university are very low. It is the college dues for board and lodging that used to make university life impossible for those unable to afford £200-£300 a year. To-day, owing to State bursaries and Government grants, about seventy-five per cent of the undergraduates pay no fees at all. In other words, post-war Oxford is a poor man's university. Moreover a number of students do not now go there direct from school but after completion of their National Service, a factor tending to raise the average age of undergraduates. In consequence, in this post-war undergraduate population, there is far less irresponsibility and far more concentration on work than there used to be. Nevertheless, a sport and recreational activities still play a large part in the undergraduate's life, for the value of an Oxford education lies as much in the human contacts that are

there made as in the lectures listened to and the books read. Incidentally, lectures are now so overcrowded and books so hard to get that it is difficult for the undergraduate to cope with his work.

There are innumerable societies and clubs to cater for all tastes, and it is in these societies—notably the Union—that the young man learns to find his feet in debate and social intercourse. Many a future statesman has been introduced to politics and oratory at meetings of the Union.

Discipline in the town is preserved by a proctor (a don) who, accompanied by two bull-dogs (college servants in bowler hats and gym shoes), prowls about to see that undergraduates wear gowns after nine o'clock at night and are in college by midnight. Only Christ Church men are privileged to be out until 12.20 a.m. To be absent after this hour is an offence that incurs severe penalties. An undergraduate may be sent down (expelled) for absence.

All colleges are under the direction of a principal, but he is only known as a principal at Brasenose, Hertford, Jesus and St.

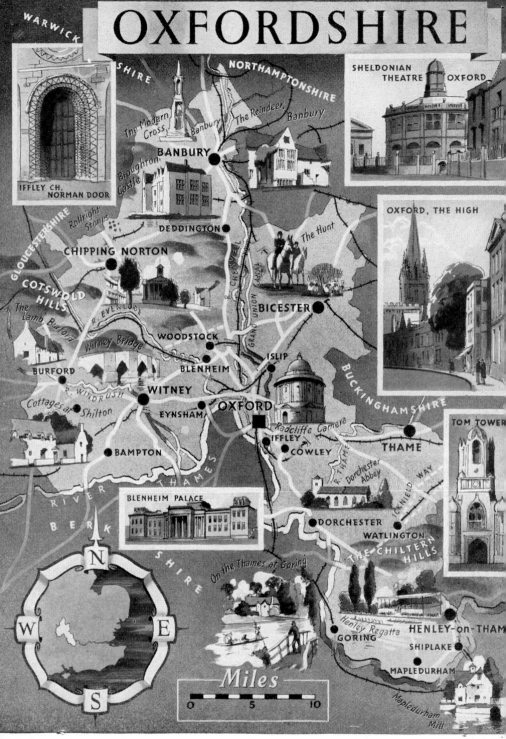

# OXFORDSHIRE

IFFLEY CH. NORMAN DOOR

SHELDONIAN THEATRE OXFORD

OXFORD, THE HIGH

TOM TOWER

WARWICKSHIRE

NORTHAMPTONSHIRE

The Modern Cross

Banbury    The Reindeer, Banbury

BANBURY

Broughton Castle

DEDDINGTON

GLOUCESTERSHIRE

Rollright Stones

CHIPPING NORTON

COTSWOLD HILLS

The Lamb, Burford

R. EVENLODE

The Hunt

BICESTER

WOODSTOCK

Witney Bridge

BURFORD

BLENHEIM

ISLIP

R. WINDRUSH

WITNEY

Cottages at Shilton

EYNSHAM

OXFORD

Radcliffe Camera

IFFLEY

COWLEY

THAME

BAMPTON

BUCKINGHAMSHIRE

R. THAME

Dorchester Abbey

ICKNIELD WAY

BLENHEIM PALACE

RIVER THAMES

BERKSHIRE

DORCHESTER

WATLINGTON

THE CHILTERN HILLS

On the Thames at Goring

Henley Regatta

HENLEY-on-THAMES

GORING

SHIPLAKE

MAPLEDURHAM

Mapledurham Mill

N

W        E

S

Miles

0        5        10

Edmund Hall; All Souls, Keble, Merton, New College and Wadham are controlled by a warden; Balliol, Pembroke and University College by a master; Corpus, Magdalen, St. John's and Trinity by a president; Exeter and Lincoln by a rector; Oriel, Queen's and Worcester by a provost and Christ Church by a dean who is also the dean of the diocese because Christ Church is also the cathedral.

### Links with Schools

The layman is apt to find these titles confusing. It is worth remembering, too, that New College is never abbreviated to "New" and that Christ Church is usually known as "the House." Some colleges have a close link with particular schools, others with particular counties. Most Winchester boys go to New College, because both belong to the same foundation; most Etonians to Magdalen, most Westminster men to Christ Church. Queen's caters specially for men from the north, Westmorland and Cumberland in particular, Jesus for Welshmen, Exeter for west country men and so on. All Souls, founded to commemorate the men who fell at Agincourt, has no undergraduates. It contains only fellows, all of whom have earned that honour by passing a stiff examination.

The list of famous men educated at the university is far too lengthy to enumerate. Christ Church alone produced William Penn, John Wesley, John Locke, Sir Philip Sidney, Lewis Carroll, John Ruskin, W. E. Gladstone and Edward VII, besides five Prime Ministers of the nineteenth century. The poet Shelley was for one term at University College, but Cambridge, for some occult reason, has reared a far greater number of major English poets than has Oxford.

### Expanding Modern City

The colleges, for the most part, stand very close together within the confines of the old city walls. But modern Oxford has splayed out in every direction, for two or three miles along the Woodstock and Banbury Roads and over the adjoining heights of Cumnor, Headington and Boar's Hill. The main growth has, however, been at Cowley,

where stand the vast factories erected by the organization of which Lord Nuffield is the head. Lord Nuffield has given large sums towards the establishment of a medical school and founded Nuffield College for the promotion of research work in industrial relationships, besides other large benefactions.

Cowley is now large enough and important enough to be a self-contained entity, but the Cowley workers still rely on the city for their main entertainment and shopping. Oxford has recently been called the Latin quarter of Cowley.

Oxford also contains a very large cattle market, but this has been overshadowed by Banbury, which has recently become with Reading the best cattle market south of the Tweed with a turnover of well over a million pounds a year.

This brings me to Oxfordshire's second claim to fame, farming.

### Wealth from Wool

In the Middle Ages Cotswold wool was one of the chief sources of revenue in the country and from their profits the Cotswold wool merchants built a series of magnificent Perpendicular churches and splendid stone manor houses, of which Chastleton is perhaps the outstanding example.

Indeed, within a radius of ten miles of Burford, the one-time centre of the wool industry, but now known chiefly as a retreat for retired professional and service men and an attraction for tourists, you will find more fascinating villages than in any other area of similar size in Great Britain. This fascination is partly due to the fact that the houses and churches were built in a period when stone masons were supreme craftsmen, when men had a feeling for style and harmony that is now lost, and partly to the nature of the local stone which weathers to the colour of honey: as a result the buildings look as if they had been saturated for centuries with sunshine. The medieval masons took an especial pride in decoration, so that the chimneys are twisted into spirals, the tall church towers surmounted by delicate battlements, the windows stone-mullioned, and the porches decorated with heraldic devices. In addition, most of the farms and manor

**"A medley of timbered thatched cottages"—a view of Clifton Hampden, one of the many lovely Thames-side villages between the Gloucestershire and Buckinghamshire borders.**

houses are provided with a stone dove-cot and a stone-roofed tithe barn.

The beauty of the Cotswold villages is enhanced by the crystal clear trout-streams that ripple past the cottage doors. The valleys of the Evenlode, Windrush, Cherwell and Thames are also enriched by the tall swaying poplars and squat pollarded willows which line the water's edge.

This is a gracious, serene landscape that has inspired many poets and novelists, among whom Matthew Arnold and Compton Mackenzie are notable.

But this land not only looks good. It is fertile and still brings considerable profit to farmers in spite of the enclosure of the Cotswolds, the decay of craftsmanship and the eclipse of the Cotswold and Oxford Down sheep.

Money in farming to-day lies in dairy herds, so it is not surprising to find that the Cotswold sheep are giving way to herds of Ayrshires and Friesians. The Oxfordshire farmers are unusually intelligent, up to date in their methods and are hard workers. It is notable that one of the best books written on modern farming comes from Oxfordshire. It is called *The Farming Ladder* and its author is a farmer, George Henderson of Enstone. The Oxfordshire farms are

not large compared with the Wiltshire farms, but they are compact, orderly, and usually give one the sense of serene well-being.

As a hunting county, Oxfordshire is famous, whether for the hedged country of the Bicester or the upland stone wall country of the Heythrop, Cotswold or Vale of the White Horse (Bathurst), normally referred to as the V.W.H.

But farmers are less active in the hunting field now that their responsibility is greater, the big landowners are fast disappearing, the country houses and parks, when derequisitioned, were often found to have been seriously damaged by the occupying troops, and it is unlikely that Oxford undergraduates will be able to support the local hunts as they used to do. In spite of these facts, the popularity of hunting is increasing rather than decreasing. But the huntsmen are different. Hunting, once the sport of kings, has become the pursuit of the many, and the Cotswolds, as you can see from a cursory glance at Lionel Edwardes' spirited sketches, make an ideally open country for a gallop.

In the old days almost every shop in the main street of Bicester contained a stable, but war has changed the attitude of the

Bicester people. They now entertain some fifteen thousand employees of the enormous Army Ordnance Depot and strongly approve of the proposal to establish light industries in their neighbourhood designed to increase five-fold the population of the town. These changes would inevitably entail a lessening of interest in and facilities for hunting.

Other Oxfordshire market towns take the opposite view, setting their faces strongly against any radical change in their pre-war occupations. Witney, for example, having won a world-wide fame for blanket-making, is content, and probably wise, to maintain its reputation in that one direction. The quality of these blankets is said to owe its special excellence at least in part to the waters of the Windrush with which they are bleached.

Witney also possesses a flourishing and up-to-date market of which it is very proud. This is a matter of some importance, because the post-war tendency is to concentrate on a few big markets, like that at Banbury, and let the smaller ones, like that of Bicester, die out. Perhaps the Bicester people do not mind as they have their eye on industrial development.

Small country towns like Chipping Norton, Charlbury and Woodstock are increasing in prosperity; they are also becoming more self-contained, concentrating on the development of some single industry, such as glove-making, in addition to providing a shopping centre and market for the surrounding villages.

Indeed the merits of Oxfordshire, as opposed to the city of Oxford, have never been sufficiently recognized by visitors. Not only is it easily accessible by road from the Midlands, south and north, but there is much to attract the sightseer over and above its undulating wolds, its many fascinating little tree-fringed rivers and its enchanting stone villages. For the lover of antiquities there are, three miles north-west of Chipping Norton, the famous Rollright Stones, consisting of a large circle of seventy-seven stones, with a solitary larger stone resembling a cobra's head and known as the King's Stone standing one hundred yards to the

**A characteristic of many Oxfordshire towns are broad streets, wide enough to allow the holding of markets. Thame, shown below, serves an agricultural area extending into Buckinghamshire.**

A corner of Christ Church, "the largest, richest and noblest college" in Oxford.

north and a smaller group of four upright stones four hundred yards to the east known as the Whispering Knights. As to their origin and purpose, we can only speculate; they still remain four thousand years after their erection, mysterious and feared by some local people.

The Priory at Minster Lovell is said to be the scene of the Mistletoe Bough tragedy when a young bride, playing hide-and-seek with her husband, was found dead in a heavy chest, the lid of which was too strong for her to lift when she tried to get out.

At Godstow, on the banks of the Thames, stand the ruins of the Abbey over which reigned the fair Rosamund, mistress of Henry II.

Oxfordshire is so rich in rivers and water-meadows that the visitor will get a better sense of the county's unique atmosphere and gain a better notion of its historic past and vigorous present by wandering along its river banks than by any other means.

As he follows the upper reaches of the stripling Thames, he will find himself in a sequestered land with Kelmscott as its centre. In the grey Elizabethan manor house that stands just half a mile from the stream, lived that great reformer and poet, William Morris, whose designs in glass, fabrics, sculpture and woodwork did so much to raise the artistic standard of English homes in the Victorian age. The Kelmscott Press will long be remembered for its efforts to extend artistry in design to typography and the printing of books.

### The Rose Revived

Just below is the ancient bridge of Radcot and beyond is that of Newbridge (where a battle was fought in the Civil War). An inn still stands at either end of this bridge, one of which rejoices in the attractive name of The Rose Revived. Both these bridges were old in the fourteenth century.

At Bablockhythe, where there has been a ferry for at least seven hundred years, we recapture memories of *The Scholar-Gipsy* celebrated so nobly in verse by Matthew Arnold, and then the river winds round the foot of Wytham Woods to Godstow. On reaching Folly Bridge the Thames changes its character and becomes wide and deep enough to enable steamers to ply all the way to London.

It is on this reach of the river, between Folly Bridge and Iffley, that the university holds its bumping races, where college eights, starting one behind the other, endeavour to bump the boat in front in races for the headship of the river. In the Lent term these races, on fixed seats, are called Torpids, in the Summer term, on sliding seats, Eights. Eights Week is Oxford's gala week of the year; it is usually wet.

### Riverside Villages

Below Iffley, where is one of the finest Norman churches in the country, the river winds its way past Radley College, one of the most renowned of rowing schools, past Nuneham Courtenay, the seat of Lord Harcourt, by way of Abingdon to Clifton Hampden, a medley of timbered thatched cottages with a tiny church perched like a citadel on a steep rock overlooking a grand sweep of the river, where tall poplars tower above the bridge that leads to the Barley Mow inn which figures so amusingly in *Three Men in a Boat*.

Just beyond is the quiet hamlet of Burcot, the home of John Masefield, the Poet Laureate, and above stand the twin hills known as the Wittenham Clumps, the lower of which is the site of an Iron Age camp.

Villages crowded thickly on or near the river banks hereabouts, notably Dorchester, whose noble church stands on the site of a Saxon cathedral built in the early part of the seventh century, and Benson, where King Offa of Mercia won a battle against the West Saxons in 777.

To-day this is a land of aeroplanes and motor-cars, houseboats and canoes, with well-frequented and picturesque riverside hotels, notably those at Shillingford and Moulsford. The Thames here cuts its way through a gap in the chalk downs with the Chilterns rising gently to the east and the smooth Berkshire Downs to the west.

North and South Stoke still preserve their rural atmosphere, but at Goring the river becomes more congested owing to the proximity of the railway and Reading.

But the beauty of the hanging woods and the smooth lawns that run down to the

The hamlet of Westwell near Burford is an example of the beauty of the Cotswold villages. Oxfordshire has many such villages in the valleys of the Evenlode, Windrush, Cherwell and Thames.

water's edge enhances the charm of the river, and Mapledurham would still be recognized with its great cedars, elm avenue and yew hedge by its one-time frequenter, Alexander Pope, who stayed here as the guest of Theresa and Martha Blount. Lower down again at Stanton Harcourt, Pope, in a quiet tower, translated the *Iliad*.

And so by way of Shiplake, with its memories of another poet, Lord Tennyson, the Oxfordshire Thames reaches its end and fitting climax at Henley, the scene year after year of successes by Oxford oarsmen at its world-famous regatta. The fine wide stretch of the river, known as the Fair Mile, is bordered by broad grassy margins below avenues of towering elms. Nowhere is the Thames lovelier than at the spot where it leaves Oxfordshire.

But the Thames is only one of the shire's attractive water-ways. The Cherwell threads its quiet way right through the heart of the country from Cropredy in the north to Oxford, where it joins the Thames.

At Cropredy the curfew has been rung at eight o'clock each evening continuously since 1512, and on Cropredy Bridge, which

was built in early medieval times, was fought one of the most bitter skirmishes of the Civil War, reminders of which occur all up and down the county. A few miles away stands Broughton castle, the finest in Oxfordshire. The home of Lord Saye and Sele, it combines early fourteenth and late fifteenth century styles.

The Cherwell River trails by the side of the railway all the way from Banbury to Oxford, now on this side, now on that, deserting it at Hampton Gay, which has a picturesque ruined manor house, to flirt with Islip, the birthplace of Edward the Confessor, before becoming the happy retreat of undergraduates lying at ease in punts moored up under the willows below Marston Ferry.

And as you thread your way through the heart of the county along this quiet stream, you will pass through a land of rich pasture excellent for fattening cattle, much arable on which barley yields a good harvest, but you will rarely see a flock of sheep.

Even more enchanting is the valley of the Evenlode, which runs into the county just south of Warren Hastings' house at

Daylesford and winds its way near the Wychwood villages of Milton, Shipton and Ascott, under the lee of the great Forest of Wychwood, which in medieval times was the hunting ground of kings, and close to the walls of the vast park of Blenheim, where stands the palatial monument to the great Duke of Marlborough.

Woodstock itself is a typical pleasant Oxfordshire village built of Cotswold stone, but Blenheim Palace, covering three of the two thousand five hundred acres of parkland in the estate, is a monstrous and overwhelming pile of masonry. It cost £500,000 to build and took twenty years to complete. The beautiful park in which it stands does, however, compensate for the unlovely building.

Perhaps most loved of all the Oxfordshire waters that feed the Thames is the Windrush, which enters the county just west of Burford, and flows past the enchanting hamlets of Widford, Swinbrook, Asthall and Minster Lovell to join the Thames at Newbridge.

It is a narrow water, reedy and often iris-fringed. It was the setting for that idyllic romance of Compton Mackenzie, *Guy and Pauline*. If you want to understand the lure of this bird-haunted water, you cannot do better than re-read that story in which we follow the moods of the river through the year.

There are other smaller but scarcely less happy streams, like the Glyme and Dorne, that will take you past the three Bartons and the fine stone houses of Sandford St. Martin. There is also the wider and better known Thame to take you close to the battle-field of Chalgrove, where John Hampden was mortally wounded and through the town (which takes its name from the river) where Hampden died. Thame possesses the exceptionally wide street that you find in all Oxfordshire market towns; it is wide enough to hold markets without disrupting the traffic. Thame is a place of quiet dignity, with the usual ancient grammar school, church, park and inns, one of which, the Spreadeagle, gained a high reputation under the ægis of that remarkable innkeeper, John Fothergill. Thame Park of three hundred acres was enclosed in Saxon days.

With our eyes on the glory of the Cotswold uplands and rich river valleys, we are

**A view of the Reach during Henley regatta, founded in 1839 and now the most fashionable boating event on the Thames. Famous trophies include the Grand Challenge Cup and the Diamond Sculls.**

apt to overlook the scarcely less remarkable charms of south Oxfordshire, where we come into the wooded greensand country and climb up over the ancient Icknield Way to the beech-crowned Chilterns. Here among the secluded gorse-covered commons and deep-wooded dells are a succession of quiet little hamlets and villages among which Watlington and Ewelme may be taken as typical, witnesses to the lack of change that the centuries have brought in this fair land. Ewelme was intended for a model village built by Chaucer's granddaughter, the Duchess of Suffolk, and her red brick almshouses have continued to perform their Christian function uninterruptedly for over five hundred years. In the church stands the magnificent alabaster tomb of the duchess, probably the most ornate monument in the kingdom. To-day Ewelme carries on a profitable trade in its watercress beds which enhance the loveliness of an exceptionally lovely village.

Here we are indeed in the south country with no trace of Midland influence either in speech or in architecture.

There remains one area of the county which bears no resemblance to the stone wall uplands, the low-lying water-meadows or the wooded Chilterns.

This is the great belt of marshland known as Otmoor that lies just to the north-east of Oxford. Over this commonland the moorland villages of Oddington and Charlton formerly had the right to graze their cattle and sheep, but as it is only partly drained by the sluggish River Ray it became a morass. When, however, in 1830 the authorities decided to enclose this waste land the moormen attacked the workmen employed on the drains. A less spirited age has put up no opposition (or perhaps less demonstrative opposition) against the acquisition of the moor by the R.A.F. as a bombing area.

But if you can no longer cross this eerie, bird-haunted marsh, you can and should visit the villages on its fringe, notably Charlton-on-Otmoor, where you will see one of the most delicately carved oak rood screens in England, with the original crimson paintings on the panels. Unfortunately, the Morris dances on May Day—still carried on after five hundred years at Bampton —have been allowed to lapse.

I hope I have shown that wherever you go in Oxfordshire you will find some fresh point of interest, some interesting link with the past, considerable industrial activity in the present, a lively, intelligent and soft-spoken people, who keep, by virtue of their geographical position, in touch both with the ancient seat of learning and the modern world of commerce and mechanized farming.

*Rollright Stones near Chipping Norton*

*Salisbury Cathedral from the River Avon*

# WILTSHIRE

By DAVID G. PECK

THAT great lover of the south country, Hilaire Belloc, once urged that "chalk should somewhere be warmly hymned and praised by every man who belongs to the south of England, for," he said, "it is the meaning of that good land." Indeed it is, and of no county more than Wiltshire, for the chalk substratum underlies three-fifths of it, and has endowed the county not only with its characteristic appearance, but also with much of its history and way of life. Here it is not a matter of a limb of chalk, of a mighty hill wave, as in Surrey or Sussex, but of a bulky upland mass, a whole sea of chalk. This great mass is split, if not entirely separated, by the wedge-shaped vale of Pewsey running and narrowing from west to east, pointing a finger at the pinnacle of Inkpen and its Beacon, which, rising to nine hundred and sixty feet in Walbury Hill, stands guard over the Hampshire and Berkshire borders.

The Vale, however, is never wide enough to constitute a real break in the chalk country. But when

the chalk ceases, as it does with some abruptness towards the northern and western borders of the county, another Wiltshire is disclosed, different in looks, characteristics and, if we are able to believe some judges, in the temperament of its folk. To this other Wiltshire we shall come in due course.

The chalk, the essential Wiltshire, makes a dry upland country of bare rolling hills and flying cloud-shadows. Little grows here but turf which is natural sheep-grazing and where sheep have, indeed, fed from a time beyond our history, keeping the grass, in the days of the great flocks, like a lawn with their teeth, and producing lilliputian varieties of plant and flower by their close nibbling. The thorn and the juniper are the only native trees, but the beech on its importation proved to be a lover of chalk, and nowadays it is impossible to think of the downs without imagining their great clumps of beech riding the swells.

To some minds this is a bleak country, empty and monotonous, where the rain can be pitiless and where, statistics report, it is some-times as cold as on the north-east coast. The eighteenth century, which so reduced the terrors of travelling as to fill the country

*Arms of Wiltshire*

137

# WILTSHIRE

GLOUCESTERSHIRE

THE WHITE HORSE, WESTBURY

THE AVENUE, SAVERNAKE FOREST

Market Cross, Castle Coombe

The Manor House, Gt. Chalfield

Westbury Church

Mere Church

CRICKLADE

St. Sampsons Cricklade

MALMESBURY

The Cross, Malmesbury

WOOTTON BASSETT

SWINDON

Railway Work Swindon

BERKSHIRE

CASTLE COOMBE

AVON

CANAL

Hackpen Hill

MARLBOROUGH DOWNS

Marlborough House

CHIPPENHAM

CALNE

RIDGE WAY

CORSHAM

AVEBURY

MARLBOROUGH

Savernake Forest

LACOCK

In Lacock Village

Silbury Hill

CANAL

MELKSHAM

BRADFORD ON AVON

DEVIZES

VALE OF PEWSEY

PEWSEY

TROWBRIDGE

WAY

UPAVON

Sidbury Hill

EDINGTON

RIDGE

LUDGERSHALL

WESTBURY

SALISBURY

WARMINSTER

HEYTESBURY

Stonehenge

PLAIN

AMESBURY

R. BOURNE

Salisbury Cathedral

MERE

Mere Church

R. WYLE

DINTON

WILTON

TISBURY

R. NADDER

SALISBURY

Witham House

AVON

DOWNTON

High St. Gate Salisbury

CRANBORNE CHASE

Miles

0    5    10

N

W    E

S

SOMERSET

DORSET

HAMPSHIRE

with tourists, had some uncomplimentary things to say about Wiltshire. One such traveller considered the views "naked," while the Rev. Mr. Gilpin, who invented the word "picturesque," roundly declared that "the chalk spoils everything," and Marlborough Down he thought a "vast dreary scene."

### Search for the Remote

The world of a hundred to two hundred years ago was a more cosy age, and its travellers recoiled from the forbidding "vastness" of the Plain, a description surprising perhaps to the modern motorist, who skims over it in an hour or so. Tastes have changed. The twentieth century, emerging from its urban hives, shows a tendency to like its earth "undecorated." Moors, mountains and rocky coasts have now more attraction than the farmlands of work-a-day rural England. Our search for the remote, at any rate in Wiltshire, has, however, been largely forestalled. For long Salisbury Plain has echoed to booms and bangs of an army in training or at exercise: the hideous "tin towns" of the military have become a feature of the district, and during the last war ever larger areas of the county were taken over. In these areas the green carpet of the Plain was gashed by the tracks of tanks or festooned with barbed wire and the litter of broken things which are the inevitable accompaniment of the modern exercise of the profession of arms, even in defence of freedom.

### Indifferent to Praise or Criticism

Where the army has left it alone, there is a spaciousness about this high country, with only the clouds and the winds of God above it, which is indifferent to man's praise or criticism, and which enfolds his foolish mimic strife in its silence. It is a country which yields little to the casual traveller or the superficial glance. Its virtue is to introduce men to elemental things; it inspires meditation rather than appreciation. From his youth in its hills, Richard Jefferies drew enough of the raw materials of contemplation to last him his lifetime of writing. The spirit is invaded rather than the eye charmed by this quality, which

is, perhaps, why even the children of the downland become consciously aware of their affection chiefly when their souls are starved in exile. Edward Wyndham Tennant, overwhelmed by spring-time in Flanders fields, found

> all my soul was dancing. . . .
> Dancing with a measured step from wrecked and shattered towns
> Away . . . upon the Downs.

Men such as Edward W. Tennant, Alfred Williams, Richard Jefferies and W. H. Hudson spoke not only for themselves: they spoke for all the men of the Wiltshire Downs who are dumb, but who nevertheless share their feelings.

### Harmony of Vale and Downland

Yet the impression of Wiltshire as nothing but a vast downland is far from accurate. The well-wooded Wiltshire valleys, and that subtle integration of vale and downland into a living harmony wrought by Nature and the generations of men, are too often missed by the hurrying traveller. Cobbett, that shrewd Englishman with one eye on beauty and the other on usefulness, brought out a true picture of the Wiltshire scene in his *Rural Ride* of the Wiltshire Avon:—

A most beautiful sight it was! Villages, hamlets, large farms, fields, meadows, orchards and very fine timber trees scattered all over the valley. The shape of the thing is this: on each side *downs* very lofty and steep in some places, but each *out-side* of the valley are downs. From the edge of the downs begin capital *arable fields* generally of very great dimensions, and in some places, running a mile or two back into little *cross valleys* formed by hills of downs. After the corn fields come *meadows* on each side down to the *brook* or *river*. The farm houses, mansions, villages and hamlets are generally situated in that part of the arable land which comes nearest to the meadow. . . . I delight in this sort of country.

This "shape" is repeated all round the edges of the downs and in the riverless vale of Pewsey as well as in the river valleys. The valleys give to the chalk a rich diversity without breaking its homogeneity. In the Marlborough Downs the shining Kennet, in the Plain its five rivers—the Ebble, Nadder, Wylye, Bourne and Avon—carve their beauty through the high chalk. All bear their train of villages, each of a similar type, yet all of infinite variety. Each has its measure of downland, arable, wood and pasture, for every English village was originally in large measure a self-supporting economic unit.

In Wiltshire, save for the few upland villages such as Imber in the south and Aldbourne in the north, the position and shape of villages are determined by the conformation of the chalk and the need for water. Where the water leaves the chalk, forced out by some less porous material below, there are the villages. So we find them round the escarpments of the Downs or following the river valleys. Of the valley villages Enford-on-Avon stands for them all. The clear chalk stream runs under the bridge where I am resting on a May morning; around me lies the village, and the cuckoo's monotonous call comes to me across the flower-strewn meadows.

### Streams in the Streets

The five rivers of the Plain all run to Salisbury, "vulgarly," as an old traveller notes, "called the sink of the Plain." Vulgarly indeed of this city standing in its green cup amidst its bright waters. These once ran in its very streets, as old Speed pictures them in the inset in his map of Wiltshire and as Leland tells: "Al the streates in New Saresbyri hath little stream-lettes and arms derivyd of Avon that runneth through them." The rivers have vanished from "al the streates," but they still run through and around Salisbury, "a red-brick and red-tiled town," as W. H. Hudson wrote, "set lower on that circumscribed space whose soft brilliant green is in lovely contrast with the pale hue of the downs beyond."

It was in 1219 that Richard Poore, the then Bishop of Salisbury, removed from Old Sarum, that most ancient of British towns, and set up on the banks of the Avon to build a new city round the new cathedral which shelters in a bend of the river. He planned well, and even our own times have not yet succeeded in spoiling the fine, straight run of streets north and south from market square and Close. Salisbury is a fair city, yet she is also a bustling market town with a variety of industries. Above all, she is a regional capital, drawing in her country children for business and pleasure, and held in wide affection. Salisbury is big enough to attract the best into her region: not so big as to drain its vitality.

### Salisbury Cathedral

The heart of Salisbury is the cathedral, "standing upon its sweep of lawn—a silent beatitude." It was consecrated before Henry III in the year 1258, and Christopher Wren said of it in 1668, ". . . it may be justly accounted one of the finest patterns of the architecture of the age in which it was built." But of the Close, the cathedral and spire I will not be tempted to write. "There are in England other cathedrals, there is no other Salisbury Close." So declares a gracious Wiltshire lady, Edith Olivier, and all who count themselves of Wiltshire share that same contented, proprietary satisfaction which she expresses. The spire, too, soaring more than four hundred feet above the meads of Avon, must be seen, for its beauty cannot be fully conveyed in the terms of any other art. Constable failed magnificently to put it into paint; others have failed less magnificently to put it into words. Never the same, it puts on glory or austerity at will. I remember it near against frosty stars, or riding the blue and white gustiness of a March sky; and, again, far off from the Downs south of the Nadder, a finger of light.

### Relics of Human History

Yet Salisbury is very young by Wiltshire standards. Few people who live in the chalk country can be very far from some strange relic of human history. These confront even the traveller upon the main through roads, for if he makes for Exeter he will pass Stonehenge, or if for Bath he will pass Silbury Hill, whence a short detour brings him to Avebury, a temple earlier than Stonehenge, and more impressive in scope, if not in workmanship. Around him everywhere are the grave mounds of a race long

Looking west over Salisbury Plain from Normanton Down, near Amesbury.

Longleat, near Warminster, seat of the Marquess of Bath, is among the most famous Elizabethan houses in England. It was completed about 1580, and stands on the site of an Augustinian priory.

vanished, while the "earthworks," the hill-top "camps," frown down upon him from the high places.

These "antiquities" had brought many visitors to Wiltshire even before John Aubrey escorted Charles II up Silbury or Pepys visited Old Sarum at nightfall—"prodigious," he declared it, "so as to fright me to be in it alone and at that time of night."

Some of these visitors are learned savants piecing together a remote past from flints, pottery shards, ornaments and the bones of animals and men. Man's most modern inventions are employed to discover his oldest secrets. Aeroplanes have been used to detect from the air traces and clues invisible from the ground. So the site of Woodhenge—the wooden counterpart of Stonehenge—was revealed, the post-holes still affecting the growth of the wheat.

Others may be amateur explorers of the ancient roads which remain indelible on the hill-tops. Of these, the Ridgeway, coming in from Berkshire and following the high arc of the Marlborough Downs to link with the other "green roads" of the Plain, was once the great arterial way. To-day, silent and untravelled, the Ridgeway is perhaps the oldest road in the world.

No other county has anything like the array of such relics of this lost age as are found in Wiltshire, and if any should wonder why this should be so, the answer is, briefly, the chalk. The relics are the works of men who came to England when the chalk

hills gave the only foothold to human habitation. Below were forests and swamps; but upon the dry chalk hills which grew no more than a thin scrub, primitive man found his simple tools adequate to the task of establishing his homesteads. Here he kept his cattle and grew his grain, shaped his pottery and wove his cloth, here he traded with strangers who travelled the hill roads, and worshipped whatever gods impelled him to the enormous tasks of Avebury and Stonehenge. Around him he buried his dead with ceremony in the mounds we call barrows. And the chalk, by its nature, preserved his works.

A long time they lived in Wiltshire, the race of stone-tool users, ultimately giving place to men of the Bronze Age, whose time passed placidly away like a summer afternoon of long ago yet lasting a thousand years. They, in turn, were supplanted by other invaders, Iron Age Celts whom the Romans found and fought. But this ancient civilization, longer in time than our own, has bequeathed nothing living to the life of Wiltshire. Yet something intangible and imponderable may have come down from them to us. A generation or so ago Wiltshire folk talked with pleasing familiarity of "the old people"; and here and there you will still find a countryman whose imagination has been caught and held by the ancient story of the forgotten past and who is the repository of lore and legend.

Wiltshire history is very largely pre-history. For though this high ground

142

remained a strategic, and therefore disputed territory among the invaders who followed the Roman withdrawal from these islands, seeing many bloody battles in the Ages we call Dark, witnessing Alfred's defeat of the Danes, yet its later story is in "the rural works of dear domestic peace." Farming has made the life of Wiltshire, and still does. This means that to-day the Wiltshire working life is in essence very much the same as the life of any other predominantly rural county.

It was not always so. For centuries Wiltshire had a highly distinctive manner of farming which produced a well-defined character in Wiltshire life. "The sheepfold must be the sheet anchor of its husbandry," declared the Board of Agriculture's Report on Wiltshire a hundred and fifty years ago. So it had been, and so it then was. The sight of great flocks spreading the Plain—for sheep were the backbone of old-style Wiltshire farming—apparently tickled the Arcadian fancy of gentlemen from London. Wiltshire, however, did not grow sheep to improve the landscape, but to dung the arable, to which the sheep were subsidiary. "Corn and sheep" were as much part of each other as the downland and vale into which they dovetailed.

The doom of "corn and sheep" was prepared in far-off lands. The grain and mutton of the New World—"cheap food" which suited England's economic assumptions when she was the "workshop of the world"—knocked the bottom out of arable farming. A few disastrous harvests did the rest, and Wiltshire arable, even in the fertile vale of Pewsey, the very centre of Wiltshire high farming, tumbled down to pasture.

Yet English farming is pertinacious and resilient. Modern inventions came to the aid of Wiltshire. If sheep declined to a quarter of their previous numbers, cattle more than doubled. Piped water, wire (and now electric) fencing made possible this transformation, while the urban milk market kept farming alive. This was the period of "Down Corn, up Horn," representing the farmers' response to the purely commercial basis of our national economy. This policy profoundly affected life in the corn areas, of which Wiltshire was one, altering their farming and appearance and reducing their population. (Incidentally, a hundred acres of grazing maintains only fifteen people *per annum* compared with the hundred and fifty who can be maintained by the same area of arable.) This "Up Horn" policy meant that, for commercial reasons, we had ceased to be anything like self-supporting. Wiltshire escaped the worst ravages of "depression" by turning over

Castle Coombe, an old and picturesque village and a great attraction for tourists, was once a centre of the Wiltshire cloth industry. Merchants gathered round the old market cross to sell their wares.

to milk production, assisted by foreign feeding stuffs—that is, by trying to do what every other county was doing, and so ceasing to be herself. To-day, while five-sixths of the county is farmed, a large part of the area is permanent pasture. War-time ploughing was, however, considerable.

Regret there must be at the passing of the old-style farming; for the end of the great flocks (even if Wiltshire-bred Hamp-shire downers still go to Europe, Australia and the Americas); for the silent sheep-bells and the departure from the scene of that traditional Wiltshire figure, "the shepherd of Salisbury Plain." Strands of wire and the growing roughness of down-land freed from the sheep's "lawn mowing" are no compensation to the eye. At the moment it is almost impossible to write of a distinctly *Wiltshire* farming. Modern tech-niques are ubiquitous, and destroy local characteristics. Factory-made machinery replaces the old local instruments made by craftsmen from local material and accord-ing to local needs and tradition. Yet survival is the main thing. To-day, at least, the corn

has come back in some measure, and the tractor plough and "artificials" have enabled the modern Wiltshire farmer to crop high land without the aid of the sheep's "golden hoof." There is some concern over a too ready use of "artificials" and a too wide-spread ploughing of the thin soils of the high lands. But I, for one, hope corn will stay in Wiltshire, for it belongs here, and I see the cornfield as Jefferies saw it, "a triumph of culture." Beauty will come again as the corn has come, not only as Nature's gift, but as the testament of those who love their place and can count upon their livelihood.

The "works of domestic peace" have pro-duced history enough. The enclosures of a hundred and fifty years ago fell with particular severity on Wiltshire. The peasant with some stake in the country became the landless labourer, the victim of the overthrow of the old subsistence economy and the wild scramble for profits. Incredible poverty and vicious poor laws eventually produced the Last Peasants' Revolt of 1830. Conducted for the most part

**On Oak Apple Day the villagers of Wishford, on the edge of Salisbury Plain, take part in the Grovely Oak ceremony. By means of it they assert their right to gather dry wood in Grovely Wood.**

Sheep being driven through Savernake Forest, former hunting ground of Henry II, and one of the few forests which can still justify its title. Many new trees have been planted there in recent years.

with restraint and dignity, it was, none the less, suppressed with "catastrophic vengeance." No fewer than one hundred and fifty-four men and boys were sent away for transportation.

To-day the rural worker is unrecognizably better off than he was then, but he is restless as his grandfather was not. He is less local in character, too. That dialect which refined ears in the past found "more grating even than that of their neighbours in Somerset" and "prevailing" even among the gentry, has largely disappeared. He is less and less "of" his place, and he dreams of urban migration for his children, if not for himself. How is this "drift from the country" to be arrested? How is that feeling of "belonging" to a place to be restored? Only, I am convinced, by "abolishing" the labourer, restoring to him something of his patrimony in England's soil, and giving back to him some measure of direct ownership and so of responsibility. Only so shall we rediscover local pride and local patriotism.

Wiltshire folk, incidentally, are supposed to be stupid, and they may, indeed, be a thought more taciturn and abrupt than their neighbours. But I doubt the stupidity, the legend of which derives from such stories as the moonrakers of Bishop Cannings

pond, the essence and prototype of all Wiltshire stories. They replied to the stranger who asked what they thought they were doing with their hay-rakes in the dewpond: "Zomebody bin and lost a cheese, and us be a-raking of un out o' thic thur pond." But the stranger was an excise man, who in due course was flattered by the roars of laughter which greeted his story at The Bear in Devizes, his audience knowing better than he that the Cannings dew-pond was a recognized dumping-ground for smuggled liquor. The modern Wiltshireman is perhaps less rough and blunt than his forefathers: he is no less shrewd.

Marlborough Down is the northern limit of the chalk. It is a country much like the Plain, though the passage through it of the Bath road has left a legacy of fine inns from the days when the quality sped down it in the "machines" to take the fashionable waters, together with a sprinkling of petrol pumps from more modern days. To the south-east, too, there is a distinctive landmark—the ancient forest of Savernake. Few travellers along the Bath road which cuts its northern fringe recognize that the forest is new as well as old. Here at least extensive felling has been followed by extensive planting—and planting with an

145

Stonehenge, the most famous pre-historic monument in England, is thought to date from the Bronze Age and to have had significance in religious ceremonies of the times. The stones of which it is built are believed to have been brought from the Marlborough Downs and Pembrokeshire.

eye to the characteristic look of the place. The heart of this region is the old town of Marlborough, with its memories of spacious coaching days (to which its noble High Street bears ample witness), its great public school, its celebrated market and the Five Alls Inn.

From the northern ramparts of the Downs we look out over the edge of the chalk country and its light soil upon a fat, flat land. Beeches have given place to elms, big arable fields to small grazing meadows, the grey-green of the chalk grass to deeper and more luxuriant tones. This is the dairy-country of Wiltshire, watered by the stripling reaches of the Upper Thames, the southern beginning of the great midland plain of England, over which the eye is stretched even to the smoke of Birmingham. Its Wiltshire portion is unlike the rest of Wiltshire—as literally unlike as chalk is to cheese. Here they traditionally make this last substance, along with butter, in their dairy-farms. A pleasant but not distinguished countryside is this, on the edge of which incongruously sits that slice of industrialism we call Swindon. Swindon is not a beautiful town. It was planned rather than allowed to grow—and to contrast it with the gracious market town of Devizes

or the Stone towns of the Bristol Avon is to realize that all planning is not good. The chalk has forced the main line of the Western Region Railway to run to the northward, though a branch follows the Pewsey Vale, and so the chalk may perhaps be blamed for the vast railway workshops that have grown up in the town of Swindon. Yet Swindon is not wholly indifferent to the ideals of modern town-planning and the need of proper restraint towards and harmony with its own countryside. Its town plan, if implemented, will be a model.

In the people of this country north and west of the chalk John Aubrey detected a great difference of temperament. There are to-day no such discernible differences between the people of the Wiltshire high and low lands. But, though they are distinctive countrysides, they have a symbol of unity. This is the pig—the large white variety of which made Wiltshire bacon the best in the world. Reared on the milk wastes remaining after butter and cheese-making, fattened on corn from the arable lands, there was once no pig like him. Chippenham and Calne, west of the chalk, still support bacon-curing—one of the oldest surviving regional industries in Wiltshire. Yet it is doubtful whether the

Wiltshire bacon of to-day is very much different from any other.

Farther west still, in a land watered by the Bristol Avon, lies yet another Wiltshire—a region somewhat apart and with a very distinctive character; for here are little towns of stone sprung from the great Bath stone quarries beneath them. A golden stone this, breeding its generations of craftsmen as the downland bred its shepherds. Perhaps the most interesting example of their works, both old and new, is to be found in Corsham Church, where there are two stone screens, both of excellent workmanship, both of local stone, one of the twentieth, the other of the fifteenth century. Yet these stone towns were once linked to Wiltshire by the sheep, for they were the homes of the West of England woollen industry before it was killed by the Industrial Revolution. But now the woollen industries are dead, and replaced by others less local in character, which might as well be anywhere else. The cloth trade still survives at Trowbridge and Chippenham, but these two, like Malmesbury, Bradford-on-Avon and Melksham, are now chiefly agricultural centres where malting and flour-milling offer minor competition to cattle and cheese markets.

Quarrying of the fine, white local stone is still extensive, the main centre being Bradford-on-Avon.

Yet there are new regional industries in Wiltshire which are really part of its characteristic life—for example, the milk factories at Chippenham, Salisbury and Wootton Bassett. In the growth of such rural and regional industries as these lies hope for the future.

Generations ago the countryside was full of industry—the industry of the craftsman. It was drained into the new urban areas by the Industrial Revolution and the factory system. One local industry, carpet-making, has survived, and still flourishes in the town of Wilton, the third oldest borough in England, the ancient capital and the town from which the county derives its name.

Electricity and modern transport have given industry a new mobility and made possible its dispersal, with a consequent possibility of the restoration of variety of occupation to the countryside. Country industries must, however, not merely be *in*, they must be *of* the countryside. Wiltshire possesses a good example of a modern regional factory in the Devizes flax factory, where real skill is fostered in the revival of a

**Silbury Hill, in the Kennet Valley near Avebury, is an artificially built mound of chalk 135 feet high, and 552 feet across. It is probably of about the same age as Stonehenge, and may have been used as a burial mound. Its pre-Roman origin is proved by its being skirted by a Roman road.**

once-dead industry, now again in living relationship with its region.

Wiltshire is rich in noble manors, if poor in castles. Only the ruins of Wardour Castle, near Tisbury, are of any significance. For, after the wars with the Danes were ended, Wiltshire settled down to a period of peacefulness probably unrivalled by any other English county—until the military, jealous perhaps of so much calm, took it for their own in their mimic wars. Even the ruins of Wardour are less prized than is the fine manor of that name that stands nearby. Of other manors, I can only mention, besides Wilton House, which Inigo Jones partly rebuilt in the late seventeenth century, and where Sir Philip Sidney wrote his *Arcadia* and William Shakespeare acted his plays before James I, the Elizabethan house of Longleat, near Warminster, with its vast park of trees, Littlecote Park, mentioned by Sir Walter Scott in his poem *Rokeby*, Stourhead, near Zeals on the Somerset border, famous for its beautiful gardens, Corsham Court on the Bath Road, once part of the dowry of the early English queens, and Fonthill Abbey, built by William Beckford the younger, which is not, as its name implies, a religious foundation.

Of such foundations in Wiltshire, those at Malmesbury, Wilton and Amesbury are pre-Norman. Amesbury was once a leading town of the ancient Kingdom of Wessex; here in the year 932, the parliament or witenagemot of that kingdom met. Most celebrated of monastic houses, however, is Lacock Abbey, not far from Chippenham. Part of the thirteenth-century buildings and the fifteenth-century cloisters still survives.

In this account of Wiltshire I have deplored the passing of that regionalism which gave distinct character to the life and work of particular places, though these did not necessarily conform to county boundaries. To-day, although the richness of that local, characteristic work and life has largely disappeared before the onrush of modern scientific and "progressive" industrialism, there are signs of a reviving sense of the importance of regions. Throughout the countryside Women's Institutes and Young Farmers' Clubs are doing something to revitalize interest in, knowledge of and pride in one's own place. And they are only two symptoms of a returning mood. Even if, then, the old Wiltshire is disappearing, there may be hope that it will express itself in new forms and new ways of life realizing anew its own essential nature, and remaining "fertile and plentiful of all things . . . pleasant and delightsome," as old Camden found it so many years ago.

*Village Cross, Lacock*

*Devil's Chimney, near Cheltenham*

# GLOUCESTERSHIRE

## By ROBERT BRYAN

These high wild hills and rough uneven
ways
Draw out our miles and make them
wearisome.

Thus Shakespeare's Richard II, describing,
not, as you might think, the mountain
country of Snowdonia or the steep ascents
of the Yorkshire Fells, but the Cotswold
country of Gloucestershire.

To one who has stayed and walked in the
Cotswolds, Richard's description must
seem singularly inapt. There are steep
ascents, certainly—the climb, for instance,
up from the Stroud Valley to the lovely expanse of Minchinhampton Common; there
are plenty of footpaths where the need is for
stout shoes. But the prevailing impression
of the Cotswolds is of a rolling, pleasant,
smiling land, unique not for its sav-
agery but for the beauty of its grey,
stone-built farm and manor houses,
its low stone walls in place of
hedge or paling, its remoteness still
from the threat of urbanization. I
have yet to find a walker in the
Cotswolds who found the miles
"drawn out" or "wearisome."

*Arms of Gloucestershire*

It is the Cotswolds of which most people
think when the word Gloucestershire is
mentioned. This range of grassy uplands,
running south-west from the Midlands to
the Bristol Channel, is the geographical
heart and centre of the county, even as in
days gone by it was the chief source of its
prosperity and wealth. But it would be a
mistake to overstress this single feature of
Gloucestershire. The county has many
other facets.

Gloucestershire has more neighbours than
any other county except Northamptonshire. To the west it stretches out to the
Welsh Marches, where it borders Monmouthshire and Herefordshire. To the
south it touches Wessex, where it meets
with Somerset and Wiltshire. Northwards
it has, as Midland neighbours,
Worcestershire and Warwickshire.
To the east are Oxfordshire and,
for a few contiguous miles, Berkshire, outpost of the Home Counties.

Geographically the county, like
Cæsar's Gaul, can be divided
into three parts. To the east, the

149

Cotswolds; to the west, the Forest of Dean; and down the centre, the country of the River Severn, the vales of Berkeley and Gloucester. To the east, the pastoral areas of sheep-rearing; to the west, the minefields; in the vales, the great orchards which are one of the glories, and sources of material profit as well, of the West Country.

### Busy Inland Port

Centrally situated in the county, on the lower reaches of the Severn, is Gloucester, the capital, a cathedral city, old in tradition and dignity, oddly wedded to the paraphernalia—the docks and wharves and merchant seamen—of a still busy inland port. A small distance to the northwards is the large residential town of Cheltenham Spa—once for a brief period, in the heyday of George III, the Mecca of the world of fashion, but now the abode for the most part of the elderly and pensioned. And at the south-western corner of the county, on the Somersetshire border, eight miles up the River Avon from the Bristol Channel, lies the ancient port, busy manufacturing town and modern university centre of Bristol.

These are Gloucestershire's three main urban centres. Certainly they must take an important place in any description of the county, as must the mining villages of the Forest of Dean. None the less, Gloucestershire is predominantly rural, an area of pasture land or orchard, dotted with small and peaceful country and market towns. More than three-quarters of the total area (1,254 square miles) of the county is under cultivation, most of it permanent grass. Sheep-farming no longer brings Gloucestershire the prosperity it afforded her in the Middle Ages and early Tudor times, but it is still probably the county's clearest distinguishing mark.

There are some English counties—Cornwall is a notable example—which have histories of their own, sharp and distinct. Gloucestershire is not to be reckoned among them. Rather has it partaken through the centuries of the main stream of the nation's events.

In Roman days the great Fosse Way ran straight from south to north across the Cotswold Hills. Its course is followed today by a metalled trunk road passing through the old market town of Cirencester, with its fine church tower and famous Perpendicular porch. But Gloucestershire bears many traces of far earlier inhabitants. The Cotswold country abounds in burial-grounds whose flint arrow-heads date them as belonging to the Later Stone Age. The Nailsworth area abounds in these "barrows," often known locally as "tumps." Among the best known is Hetty Pegler's Tump at Uley. Equally common in the Cotswolds are the great rectangular earthworks and camps, whose shape shows them to have been also pre-Roman in origin, and which were probably unsuccessfully defended when the Romans, advancing from the coast, established one of their earliest permanent settlements at Corinium (the modern Cirencester).

But it was over a thousand years later that Gloucestershire made its bow as an English county. It is first mentioned as such in the *Anglo-Saxon Chronicle* in 1016. From this century date the castles of Bristol and Gloucester, built by William the Conqueror in part to ward off the plundering expeditions of the Welsh, in part to hold down the conquered English. Bristol Castle became the chief stronghold of the party of the Empress Matilda against her cousin Stephen in the civil war that followed the death of Henry I. One chronicle, indeed, refers to this struggle, which in fact raged over most of England, as the Bristol War.

### Independent Bristol

Bristol was the scene, two hundred years later, of probably the first example of a struggle between the middle classes and the king. The townspeople of this already busy trading port objected to the payment of certain dues to the king's constable, and rioted in protest. The king countered by depriving Bristol of its civil liberties. Open rebellion followed, and for three years the Bristol citizens maintained an independent republic within the English kingdom, withstanding the onslaught of an army of twenty thousand sent against them.

Bristol was to declare against the king once more, in the Civil War. One of the

# GLOUCESTERSHIRE

STANTON

WORCESTERSHIRE

WARWICKSHIRE

CHIPPING CAMPDEN

R. AVON

STANTON

MORETON IN THE MARSH

Tewkesbury Abbey

at Chipping Campden

The Cross, Stow on the Wold

TEWKESBURY

STOW ON THE WOLD

DEERHURST

WINCHCOMB
Cleeve Hill

UPPER & LOWER SLAUGHTER

DYMOCK

Timbered
Tower,
Upleadon

The Pump Room,
Cheltenham

CHELTENHAM

BOURTON ON THE WATER

NEWENT

UPLEADON

HEREFORDSHIRE

GLOUCESTER

NORTHLEACH

RUARDEAN

WESTBURY ON SEVERN

The Porch,
Northleach

W O L D S

R. WINDRUSH

BIBURY

COLEFORD

NEWNHAM

Robt. Raikes House,
Gloucester

CIRENCESTER

OXFORDSHIRE

Forest of Dean

LYDNEY

STROUD

CANAL

Source of
R. Thames

FAIRFORD

SHARPNESS

NAILSWORTH

MINCHINHAMPTON

R. THAMES

14th Cent. Cross,
Lydney

BERKELEY

TETBURY

BRISTOL DOCKS

WOTTON UNDER EDGE

The Market Place, Tetbury

FOSSE

THORNBURY

The Cross Hands Inn,
Chipping S.

BERKELEY CASTLE

CHIPPING SODBURY

University Tower
Bristol

ONMOUTH

WILTSHIRE

N

BRISTOL

R. AVON

Miles

0     5     10

W       E

ton
ispension
Bridge
Bristol

S O M E R S E T

S

**Guiting Power, on the upper waters of the Windrush, is typical of the multitudinous small Cotswold villages, "self contained, little touched by the outside world."**

chief victories of the Royalists was the capture of the city after the battle of Roundway Down in 1643. But Gloucester, the county's capital, held fast for Parliament, withstanding a murderous three months' siege. Had it fallen, a great belt of the West Country would have been assured to the king, for Worcester and Shrewsbury, as well as Bristol, were already in his hands. Its relief was followed by the recapture of Bristol, and may be regarded as a turning point of the war.

In the intervening centuries the county had prospered. The later Middle Ages and Tudor times saw the heyday of Gloucestershire's wool trade, and, so long as it throve, so did the ports of Bristol and Gloucester flourish and expand. A later development was the growth of the broadcloth industry in the Stroud Valley. And all the time iron was being worked from the rich deposits of the Forest of Dean.

In the sixteenth and seventeenth centuries Gloucestershire wool was yielding pride of place to the produce of the Yorkshire Dales. And Bristol, in particular, suffered a corresponding decline. But the conquest and exploitation of the West Indies brought to the city a revival of prosperity which has persisted ever since. Bristol became the great entry port for the sugar, the bananas and other tropical produce which the West Indies now provided. At about the same time there was added the bulk of the new tobacco trade which was developing with the North American continent. Later, cocoa and chocolate from the West African colonies were added to Bristol's wealth. To-day the port handles nearly ten million pounds worth of goods a year, and her docks can cope with all but the very largest vessels afloat.

The men of Somerset can rightly claim a share in Bristol's fame. For part of the city lies across the River Avon, which forms the border between the two counties. But Gloucester is all Gloucestershire's own. Here, in the Middle Ages, parliament was often summoned when the king was on a progress through the West Country. Here in the fifteenth century the Commons successfully demanded and secured against Henry IV the right to freedom of debate. Here a succession of Earls of Gloucester schemed in semi-independence through Plantagenet, Lancastrian and Yorkist times till the most notorious of them all, Richard, the hunchback, murderer king, fell on the field of Bosworth. Here, too, was the birth-place of the Perpendicular style of Gothic architecture. The fourteenth-century choir of Gloucester Cathedral is the first example of this style in England, just as the cloisters contain the first experiment in the design of roof vaulting known as fan tracery.

Another Gloucestershire town which forms part of English history is Tewkes-bury. On the banks of the Warwickshire Avon, at its confluence with the Severn, stands the lovely red stone abbey, an almost unblemished specimen of Norman architecture. At Tewkesbury the House of Lancaster met in 1471 final defeat at the hands of the Yorkists. Tewkesbury, too, is, by tradition, the home of the best mustard in the kingdom. "He is a good wit," says Falstaff of Prince Hal's boon companion Poins. "Hang him, baboon; his wit is as thick as Tewkesbury mustard."

Through the pattern of Gloucestershire's story run, too, the names of great families prominent from the Middle Ages. The Beauforts (descended from John of Gaunt) at Great Badminton, where the stabling is the most extensive in the country; the Berkeleys, owners of Berkeley Castle, which since the days of William the Con-queror has looked frowning out across the wide waters of the Severn towards the Welsh Marches; the Bathursts, who have lived in and owned great estates for centuries round Cirencester. And among famous men Gloucestershire can claim a share in John Cabot, who beat Columbus to it in discovering the continent of North America; Whitbread, who made Bristol a centre of the Methodist faith; Simon de Montfort, who owned estates in Gloucestershire, and, in more modern times, the greatest cricketing personality the world has ever known, Dr. W. G. Grace. Gloucestershire's cricketing history is a story in itself. I have no space for it here. I cannot forbear to mention, however, that apart from the Grand Old Man of English cricket the county has produced Walter Hammond.

So much for Gloucestershire's past. To-day the county displays within its borders almost every facet of the national life. No area in the country can better serve as a cross section of modern England, can more thoroughly illustrate the multifarious activities of the British people.

In the wide uplands and green valleys of the Cotswold country you will find English domestic rural life at its most peaceful and serene. Through these valleys flow the little

Gloucester is a busy inland port. Its docks, part of which is seen below, provide an outlet for the products of the county and the Midlands; the chief imports are grain and timber.

Chipping Campden, once the centre of the Cotswold woollen industry.

154

tributaries of the Thames—the Windrush, the Coln, the Evenlode—names as lovely as the countryside through which the streams meander. And in these uplands—one of England's great watersheds—rises the Thames itself.

## Cotswold Life

Walk through this country on a fine spring or summer evening, and you will be surrounded by a scene of utter peace. For miles around there is no sign of movement save for the grazing sheep or cattle. You may be tempted, indeed, to conclude that this is the peace of a land whence activity has drained away. But you would be wrong so to conclude. It is the peace of unhurried labour. There is plenty doing in the Cotswolds, but it is done without fuss or intolerance of any kind, to the background of years and centuries in which men and women have won their living from the land, unharried by urban incursions of any kind. It is said that the inhabitants of the Cotswold country town of Painswick hold the English record for longevity. If so, it must surely be because their surroundings enable them to live their lives at an even pace, and to live it thoroughly and whole.

The centres of Cotswold life are the multitudinous small villages—six or more of them perhaps within a three-mile radius. Some of these are no more than a dozen houses grouped round a church many sizes too big for them. All of them are focal points for the local activities. The life of the village is the be-all and end-all of the inhabitants. It is a land of small communities, self-contained, little touched by the outside world, indifferent though friendly to the tourist traffic that will pass through them on a fine week-end.

## Architectural Paradise

These villagers live in a paradise of domestic architecture. Man-made as well as natural beauty surrounds them. Many of the small manor houses which abound in the district date from Elizabethan days, and the more modern houses are built, for the most part, on the same architectural plan. All are constructed from the warm grey local Cotswold stone—a stone which weathers rapidly and gives, even to quite modern buildings, the pleasing impression of ripe old age.

This special Cotswold asset is shown to perfection in the little town of Bibury in the Coln Valley. Not all of Bibury's houses are old, but all look old, and the architecture is of a piece. If its special glories are the old mill and the row of tiny almshouse cottages preserved by the National Trust, it is the general homogeneity of the town which gives it a unique place in the English landscape.

The Cotswolds stretch northwards to the boundaries of Worcestershire and Warwickshire. At their north-eastern end is the town of Moreton-in-the-Marsh, an important stage in Roman days on the great Fosse Way. Nearby is the most startling architectural feature in all Gloucestershire, the great house of Sezincote. Here, in the middle of English parkland, is a formal Japanese garden, complete with temple, surrounding a replica, perfect in every detail down to the zenana quarters, of an eighteenth-century Indian noble's palace.

## The County Town

Moving west out of the Cotswold country, you come to the city of Gloucester and the town of Cheltenham, the busy administrative centre and the tranquil residential spa. In Gloucester the affairs of the county are administered from the City Hall, and of the diocese from the Cathedral Close. The English county and cathedral town has an atmosphere all its own. Here town and country seem to mingle, the influence of the latter barring the way to ugly industrialization. Gloucester is the scene of considerable industrial activity. There are engineering works and foundries and slate yards. There is the still busy river port, connected with the deep waters of the Severn estuary by the Gloucester Ship Canal. But somehow these seem anachronisms, disturbing but not pervading influences in the life of a city still dominated by its cathedral spire, its streets and houses still rich in the traditions of the past.

Gloucester is the home, every third year, of the famous Three Choirs Festival, when the choirs of Gloucester, Worcester and

155

Hereford Cathedrals unite to give an example of massed choral singing unrivalled in England, and probably anywhere else in the world. This Festival dates from 1724.

Cheltenham is different. Its charm and atmosphere are solely residential. Its Regency crescents and squares, its wide, tree-lined promenades, tell of accumulated wealth disbursed in the autumn of life. Its comfortable hotels, its hideous, glass-domed Winter Garden, its wealthy-looking shops, denote a population whose active days are over. The young in Cheltenham are to be found only in the famous boys' and girls' colleges, and in the week of steeplechasing when the Cheltenham Gold Cup is run!

The neighbourhood of Cheltenham witnessed, some time after Sir Walter Raleigh's great discovery, the first, and only serious attempt to grow tobacco commercially in England. The revenue authorities objected violently, sending a party of horsemen out from Gloucester to destroy the crop. Post-war attempts have also failed (fortunately, as some smokers think) to disturb the supremacy of the Virginia product.

### Fine Panorama

Six miles from Cheltenham is the great western spur of the Cotswolds known as Cleeve Hill. Here can be seen one of the finest panoramas in all England. Right and left are other Cotswold spurs. In front the land dips sharply and steeply to the wide-flowing Severn. Across the river lie water meadows and orchards, and in the far

ABOVE: **The Church of St. Mary Redcliffe, Bristol, a fine example of late Gothic architecture.** BELOW: **Clifton Suspension Bridge which joins Gloucestershire and Somerset.**

distance rise the blue and jagged outlines of the Malvern Hills.

Descent into the Severn Valley—into the two Vales of Berkeley and Gloucester—brings a complete change of scenery. Here is the southernmost extension of the great orchard lands of Worcestershire, a land of pears and apples—famous for the brew of pear cider known as perry—ablaze in early spring with white and pinkish blossom. It is a land, too, whose loam soil yields a rich pasturage for shorthorn cattle; the land of the double Gloucester cheese. Gone are the Cotswold stone walls and manor houses. Hedges and fences, and mellow brick buildings take their place.

### Forest of Dean

But the Severn Valley here is narrow in width. And as, from the Vale of Berkeley, you cross the river westwards, there is another abrupt scenic change. The land rises sheer from the river bank to the plateau of the Forest of Dean, which stretches to the borders of Monmouthshire and the banks of the River Wye.

Unlike Hampshire's New Forest and most of the other "forest" areas of England, the Forest of Dean retains in large measure its primeval aspect. It is an area of dense woodland and great trees, of small streams and scanty communications, a land where beauty and ugliness go hand in hand.

For the Forest of Dean is not only a forest. It is a mining area as well. Deep in the forest the mining villages are buried. One moment the vista is of sylvan beauty.

ABOVE: The tower of Bristol University, founded in 1909 to replace the old University College. BELOW: A view of Stanton, a village between Cheltenham and Chipping Campden.

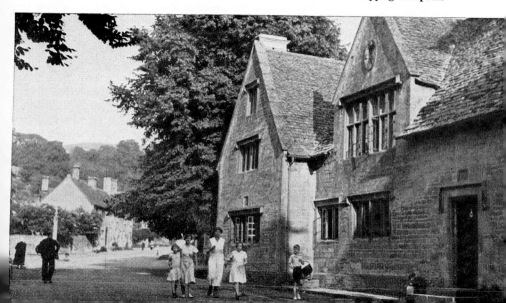

Turn the corner, and the gaunt outline of the pithead, with squat cottages surrounding it, meets your eye.

It is an area of small mines, which yield high-grade coal but, through high working costs, make even in good times small profits, and in other times no profits at all. The shadow of a depressed area hangs over the Forest. The inhabitants of the mining villages are socialists to a man, many of them bitter from many years on the borderline of poverty.

It is hard to believe that Cannop, the largest of these mining communities, and Cotswold Bibury are in the same county. In every aspect they are worlds apart. But just

old associations—such is the amalgam which is modern Bristol. Only London can claim an equal or greater diversity. Among provincial cities Bristol can fairly claim to be unique.

As a trading centre Bristol is the headquarters of the tobacco, cocoa and chocolate trades. Industrially, the aeroplane works in the suburb of Filton have made the neighbourhood a key centre of the aircraft and aero-engine industries.

The air is Bristol's new development. The sea is her old stand-by. She has as old a seaport history as London, an older one by far than her modern rivals, Liverpool, Glasgow and Southampton. The great

A view of Gloucester from the River Severn. The cathedral, mostly of the Norman period, was originally the church of a Benedictine monastery, and is notable for its cloisters.

as the Cotswold country is unique in England, so is the combination of ancient forest and industrial toil and unparalleled ugliness.

There is something of everything in Gloucestershire. Sweeping uplands and alluvial vales, cathedral city and famous spa, small market towns showing domestic architecture at its best, mining villages, England's two finest rivers, tributary trout streams and the abode of salmon on the River Wye. And, lastly, there is the great industrial city of Bristol.

A major port, a great industrial district, an important university centre, a city rich in

docks at Avonmouth and Portishead (the latter in Somerset), joined to Bristol by rail and by eight miles of the finest motor road in the country, keep her relatively as important in the shipping world as she was when the Cabots sailed from Bristol in the ship *Matthew* in search of the "Island of Brazil," and found North America instead; or when, a century ago, the *Great Western*, one of the first steamships to cross the Atlantic under steam alone, started down the Bristol Channel.

On the high ground to the north of the River Avon lie the fine modern buildings of

Every Boxing Day the villagers of Marshfield perform an 800 years old mumming play, the origins of which have been forgotten. The players are led round the village by the town crier.

Bristol's University, its tower dominating the lower part of the city, presided over for seventeen years by Mr. Churchill as Chancellor. Here Britain's greatest war leader bestowed honorary degrees on the chief British and American military commanders in the struggle against Nazism. Nearby are the two Clifton Colleges, one for boys and one for girls.

In the city's centre considerable damage was sustained from air bombing. In the midst of the biggest shopping and traffic districts, close to the modern railway termini, once stood the Dutch House, which

"One moment the vista is of sylvan beauty. Turn the corner and the gaunt outline of the pithead, with squat cottages surrounding it, meets your eye."—A coalmine in the Forest of Dean.

tradition relates was brought over piece by piece from Amsterdam in the reign of William of Orange. Near by was St. Peter's Hospital, erected at the close of the Middle Ages, about 1500. Only a memory now remains of these lovely links with the past. But the old and the new are still to be found in close juxtaposition. Bristol has modern cinemas. It possesses also in its Theatre Royal the oldest playhouse in England. Built in 1766, it numbered for a while among its audiences the smart world of the day who, in search for new watering-places, made Clifton, with its medicinal springs, a fashionable resort.

Bristol is no longer a glass of fashion. But it remains one of England's great meeting-places. It is pre-eminently the junction of the Midlands and the West Country, the point of contact for Plymouth and Birmingham, for the men of Cornwall and the citizens of the Black Country. Halt, late at night, in the echoing station of Temple Meads, and you feel you are on the borderland not only of two counties, but of two separate countries.

Pause for a week-end, and there is plenty for you to see in Bristol. The deep wooded cleft in the landscape formed by the Avon Gorge; the high-flung, slender Clifton Suspension Bridge—Brunel's masterpiece; the manifold activities of a busy city proud alike in its history and in the scars of many recent bombings.

Bristol is not Gloucestershire. Nor is Gloucestershire dominated by Bristol. No part of the county, indeed, can lay claim to represent the whole. Its charm is no more solely the peaceful Cotswolds than its significance is the grim background to the Forest of Dean. There is no space to mention in detail all its features, but market towns such as Fairford or Winchcombe must be noticed alongside Bibury and Painswick. In Gothic churches and ancient monuments the county abounds.

Famous cricketers, great explorers, families whose roots go back deep into the Middle Ages; Shallow and Silence, the county justices of Shakespeare's imagination in their Gloucestershire orchard, the fashionables who flocked to Clifton or Cheltenham, the aircraft workers who stood steady under the rain of German bombs; the Cotswold pastures and the orchards of the vales, the broadening Severn and the infant Thames—all these are part of Gloucestershire. They are part of England, too. They could not belong to any other country in the world.

*Gateway of Stanway House, near Cheltenham.*

*Village Green, Finchingfield*

# ESSEX

### By C. HENRY WARREN

THE INDICATIVE fact about Essex is that it is, and long has been, predominantly agricultural. I am well aware that more than half its population lives and works in the London fringe, but this is no more Essex than New York is America. There was a time when East and West Ham were as authentically Essex as Dunmow itself, and Forest Gate was one of the entrances to the Forest. Rainham, too, was a village; and in a county famous for its country mansions, Wanstead once possessed the greatest and most famous of them all. But these are now part of the "Great Wen" where Essex is irretrievably lost in a maze of slums and factories, small industries and the no-man's-land of suburbia. I am well aware, too, that quite an appreciable proportion of the rest of the population of Essex lives in its seaside resorts: Frinton, Dovercourt and Walton-on-the-Naze—fashionable watering-places all three, whose long stretches of sandy beach are a children's paradise; Clacton,

*Arms of Essex*

that every north Essex villager tries to visit at least once every summer to get his taste of salt sea air; and Southend, that other and even more popular resort, with its mile-and-a-quarter pier, its abundant and noisy amusements, and its deserved reputation as the Cockney's Blackpool. But neither the London fringe nor the seaside resorts are Essex in anything but name.

The authentic Essex lies mainly inland. You must look for it in the Rodings—those sprawling parishes of corn and willows where (so it is said) the wheat berries grow so big they have to be dragged from the ear by horses; in the stretch of country between Chelmsford and Colchester, where the fruit is made into some of our finest jams; and, perhaps most of all, in the whole of the north-west corner, where the pleasant undulations are a source of surprise to those who had always supposed that Essex was flat and uninteresting, and where the thatch-and-plaster cottages and the beautiful farmsteads nestle so comfortably in the fields of roots and corn. These regions are the true heart of Essex, and agriculture is the be-all (if not quite the end-all) of each one of them.

F

161

(E.N.C.)

North-west Essex has many lovely small towns and villages which retain their ancient thatched cottages and country atmosphere. An example is Wendens Ambo, shown here, near Saffron Walden.

Pride of landscape does not necessarily depend on hills and dales and heather-painted moorlands. A man-made landscape, of well-tilled fields and well-drained meadows, of tended hedges and pruned orchards, is, to the seeing eye, just as appealing. And Essex is almost entirely a man-made landscape. "God made the country," said the poet Cowper, a little recklessly, perhaps, "and man made the town." It is not true, anyway, of Essex. There, whoever made the town, man certainly made the country. The point is that it requires a more calculated approach properly to appreciate the cultivated landscape than it does the wild: it requires, in fact, some understanding of stock and crop, of husbandry, and of the arts and crafts of the agricultural life in general. But nobody can hope to get the best out of Essex who is not prepared to make this effort. It is, however, an effort well worth the making.

Not that Essex had not once as wild a landscape as any in the kingdom. Epping Forest is nearly all that remains to-day of a forest (which did not necessarily mean all trees) covering the whole of the county. It was called the Forest of Essex, and its sixty-six thousand acres extended from Bow almost to Cambridge, in the north, and thence, eastwards, to Colchester. Forest Gate was one of its gateways; and such place-names as Rayleigh, Hadleigh and the like are reminders of one-time "leys," or clearings in the forest. But Epping's deer now hide as deep as they can get in "the Londoners' Playground," and Epping's oaks are mostly to be found among the structural beams of Essex cottages and farm-houses. But the transition from wild to cultivated was intensive. Enclosure, in Essex, was almost entirely direct from the forest, which may possibly account for the large number of villages in the county, since good farming inevitably increased the population.

In agricultural matters, therefore, Essex has had the lead all along, however backward she may have been in certain other directions. Near as she is to London, for instance, she has remained, prior to the popularity of the motor-car, as inaccessible as if she had been on the other side of the island; and even now she is isolated by inadequate means of communication. Forbidding indeed is the way into Essex out of

162

London, whose East End (whether you go by rail or road) is a dragon that has hitherto guarded her from the spoiling hand of the tripper and the week-ender and has helped to keep her rural scene intact. For it is one of the astonishing things about Essex that, of all but the most isolated counties, she, so near London, should, in this industrialized and mechanized century, have remained the most rural in mind and habit, a place where dialect is still (in spite of the schools) a common speech and where the countryside is often as uncontaminated as anywhere in the land. She is thus a county of violent contrasts: of teeming industrial centres such as Dagenham and rustic villages such as the Easters, both Good and High, of ports like Harwich and Tilbury, astir with traffic to and from the Continent, and quiet, little yacht-building villages like Tollesbury and Burnham. It is an old Essex saying, "the worse for the rider, the better for the bider," but it still has a certain applicability. Indeed, in most of the amenities of the civilized life Essex is astonishingly lacking—it was never strange, yesterday, to come upon old men and women who had not been in a train, much less to London. But if Essex has been obstinately unprogressive in her pursuit of the civilized life, she has been progressive enough in her pursuit of the Good Life.

Some of our most famous agriculturists have been associated with the county. The sixteenth-century Thomas Tusser, whose *Five Hundred Points of Good Husbandry* helped generations of farmers by telling them, in such homespun verse as even they might commit to memory, how to order their affairs for the betterment both of their land and of their pockets, was born at Rivenhall and sometime lived at Fairstead, not far away. Himself a failure at farming, he nevertheless taught others how to succeed, and nigh four hundred years have not minimized the pertinence of many of his points. Another, who failed at the practice but succeeded at the theory, was Arthur Young, secretary, under Sir Arthur Sinclair, to the first Board of Agriculture. He, too, though born over the border, had close associations with Essex and farmed, even if unsuccessfully, Sampford Hall, not far from Tusser's birthplace. Farther towards the coast, and a little nearer our own time, Alderman Mecchi, at his Tiptree farm, made agricultural history with his methods of manure irrigation.

Such men were masters of farming in the days of pre-mechanized agriculture; and it

**Southend-on-Sea has earned the title of the "Cockney's Blackpool." This view of its beach at holiday time makes it difficult to believe it was once an Essex fishing village. The pier is a mile and a quarter long.**

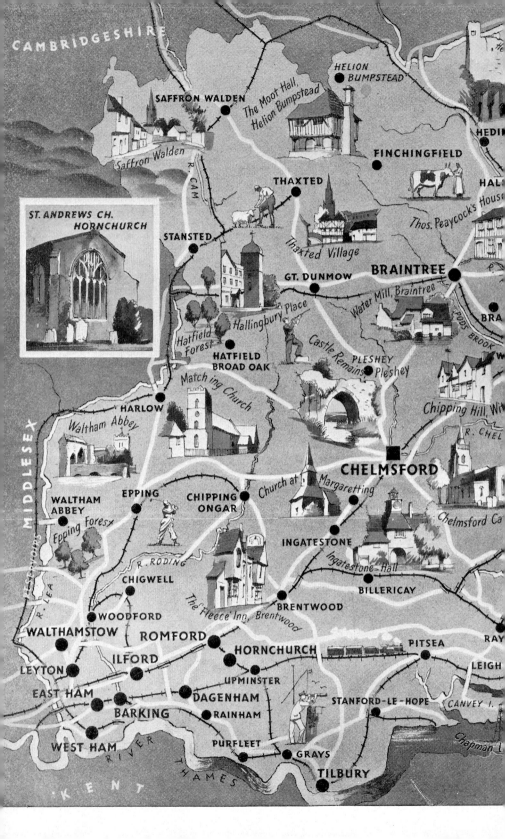

CAMBRIDGESHIRE

HELION BUMPSTEAD

SAFFRON WALDEN

The Moot Hall, Helion Bumpstead

FINCHINGFIELD

HEDI

HAL

R. CAM

Saffron Walden

THAXTED

Thos. Peaycock's House

ST. ANDREWS CH. HORNCHURCH

STANSTED

Thaxted Village

BRAINTREE

GT. DUNMOW

Water Mill, Braintree

BRA

PODS BROOK

Hallingbury Place

Castle Remains

PLESHEY Pleshey

W

Hatfield Forest

HATFIELD BROAD OAK

Chipping Hill, Wi

Matching Church

R. CHEL

HARLOW

Waltham Abbey

CHELMSFORD

WALTHAM ABBEY

EPPING

CHIPPING ONGAR

Church at Margaretting

Chelmsford Ca

MIDDLESEX

Epping Forest

INGATESTONE

Ingatestone Hall

R. RODING

BILLERICAY

CHIGWELL

The Fleece Inn, Brentwood

BRENTWOOD

R. LEA

WOODFORD

WALTHAMSTOW

ROMFORD

PITSEA

RAY

LEYTON

ILFORD

HORNCHURCH

LEIGH

UPMINSTER

EAST HAM

DAGENHAM

STANFORD-LE-HOPE

CANVEY I.

BARKING

RAINHAM

WEST HAM

PURFLEET

GRAYS

Chapman L

RIVER THAMES

TILBURY

KENT

# ESSEX

SUFFOLK

R. STOUR

Flemish Houses, Dedham

DEDHAM

The Cork Lightship

R. COLNE

MANNINGTREE

DOVERCOURT

HARWICH

COLCHESTER

Tidal Mill, St. Osyth

THE NAZE

THORPE-LE-SOKEN

GESHALL

15th Century Houses, Colchester

RESERVOIR

WIVENHOE

FRINTON

WALTON ON-THE-NAZE

y Towers

BRIGHTLINGSEA

ST. OSYTH

MERSEA I.

CLACTON

**TILBURY DOCKS**

DON

BLACKWATER

St. Peter's Chapel, 7th. Cent.

SOUTHMINSTER

**THE KEEP, COLCHESTER CASTLE**

**THE ROYAL EAGLE OFF SOUTHEND PIER**

UCH

BURNHAM ON CROUCH

OCHFORD

"Nice day for a sail"

FOULNESS I.

N

HEND

SHOEBURYNESS

The Mouse Lightship

The Nore Lightship

W

E

**DUTCH HOUSE CANVEY I.**

S

## Miles

0          5          10

Saffron Walden, so called after the saffron which used to be grown locally.

166

is only natural, now that the tractor has revolutionized all arable husbandry, that the late Henry Ford, who perhaps more than any other man helped to popularize its use on the land, should have elected to farm in Essex, for at Dagenham are the huge works of the Ford Motor Company.

### Craftsmen Inventors

But good husbandry is the result of the efforts of the farm-hand as well as of the farmer, and many an Essex labourer—and rural craftsman—has contributed some agricultural improvement which, if at first local in its application and evolved out of local needs, became soon of wider importance. Thus, it was an Essex millwright who invented one of the first successful threshing-mills, whilst an Essex blacksmith contributed an early swing-plough, a horse-rake and a hand-mill for grinding corn. Such things deserve emphasis, not only because they indicate the pioneering part which the county has played in the national farming, but also because they illustrate how close in Essex is the bond between man and the land. Farming is in the Essex man's blood. Is there any other county, for example, quite so prolific in those agricultural rhymes and tags which every labourer can quote so pat upon the occasion? Many of them, naturally, are concerned with corn. "Sow wheat in the slop, heavy at top." "Wheat always lies best between wet sheets"—and so on. And if it is not corn, then it is probably manure, as might be expected in a county where muck-carting is (or was) used quite as frequently as the local fair-day as a convenient date by which to recall events, big or small.

### Fertile Clay

In Essex, in fact, the land governs all—and land, in this case, means clay. No man knows Essex who knows it only in summer, when the golden corn is ripening under the broad, blue skies. He must know it in winter also, when the rains have converted the fields into a sea of mud. "Blood and sand," the natives call it, dragging their laden boots across the sugar-beet fields. But if clay makes for hard work, it also makes for rich returns. Essex clay is sheer

fertility: in it the rains are stored up—even when the surface is baked as hard and dry as stone—for the corn to feed upon, whose roots go as deep as the stalk is tall. So the nature of the land dictates the nature of the crops, and the crops the landscape—and often, in the case of Essex, the houses punctuating that landscape. For wheat yields straw, as well as flour; and how would Essex look without its thatched cottages and barns?

To the uninitiated, straw would seem of all materials the most intractable; yet how pliant and adaptable it becomes in the hands of a man from the corn-belt! Thatch is but one of the uses to which he puts it— thatch that keeps a house warm in winter and cool in summer. See how, with a minimum of tools, he smooths it into place, to take the running rain, and doubles it at the ridge, where the fall of water is heaviest, and gives it a strengthening pattern at the eaves, where it will be most vulnerable to the winds.

### Made from Straw

But a thatched roof is by no means all an Essex man can make with straw. In many of the churches, at Harvest Thanksgiving, a dexterously woven corn dolly (or neck) may be seen hanging from the chancel screen— relic of the days when these fanciful toys, whose origins are lost in pagan antiquity, were everywhere made out of the last sheaf. In these mechanized days the art is dying out, but there are not many villages in the north-west corner of the county where somebody does not still practise it, or can be coaxed into doing so with the promise of a pint of beer.

Once upon a time, too, it was an Essex custom to weave button-holes out of straw. And it is not accidental that, of all the districts where straw-plait was made, Essex contributed the largest share. In other counties the cottage women made lace, but in Essex they made straw-plait; and with their nimble fingers they earned as much, in their spare time, as their men-folk did by working all week in the fields. The plait, of numerous and lovely patterns, was wound in scores (twenty yards), and so carried to the nearest dealer, who, in turn, took it off

167

to Dunstable, or Luton, where it was made into straw hats. One of the last of the straw-plaiters still lives in Finchingfield, and can even now be persuaded to show her skill; but, for the rest, it is a country craft that has gone the way of all the others. Indeed, this ingenuity with straw may soon disappear altogether, when decreasing hand labour induces an even greater mechanization in the fields.

Complementary to corn, in the Essex crop rotation, are roots, and of these the most outstanding (and incidentally the one that demands most in the cultivation and the harvesting) is sugar-beet. What the turnip was in the days of "Turnip Townshend"—the days of stock in the yards and muck in the fields—sugar-beet is to-day. It is no exaggeration to say, in fact, that the sugar-beet industry, though it dates no farther back than 1925, has changed the face of Essex. Especially is this so in winter. Then, from October on into January, the harvested roots are piled by the roadside, where they wait for the lorries to come and take them away. All roads then lead to Felstead, whose odorous factory can be whiffed on the breeze miles away. With the wind biting their faces and the frost numbing their fingers, the men harvest this valuable crop, whose waste products, tops and pulp, are as useful in feeding the cattle as the sugar itself is in feeding us. But work in the sugar-beet fields begins in early spring, when singling brings the women out to earn a wage comparable with what they will earn later in the year at pea-picking; and it goes on all through the summer, for there are few crops today which require more attention, or which are more important to the nation's economy.

### Unusual Crops

In earlier times, however, there were many Essex crops that demanded an amount of attention (and hand-labour at that) which would not be considered practical now. One such crop, almost peculiar to the county, was saffron, grown for culinary, dyeing and medicinal purposes. This curious crop was first introduced into Essex in the reign of Edward III, when Sir Thomas Smith, a London merchant, grew it in his fields at Walden, now Saffron Wal-

**Brightlingsea Creek is typical of the marshlands and mudflats which form the estuaries of the Rivers Blackwater, Crouch and Colne, and where farming and fishing are equally important.**

**Fishing boats at Leigh-on-Sea. This old fishing village has now been absorbed in the borough of Southend and principally caters for visitors. It is also a popular yachting centre.**

den. To collect and dry the stigmas, which alone were of use, must have been a tedious business. Nevertheless, when the saffron fields were converted (like so much of England's arable) into sheep-walks, the discontent of the saffron-pickers contributed in no small measure to the unrest that finally boiled up into the rebellion led by Robert Kett and his brother William in the summer of 1549.

### Curious Harvest

Another Essex crop, involving an even more tedious cultivation and harvesting, was the triple one of coriander, carraway and teazle. The coriander, being an annual, was the first to be harvested; next year the carraway and teazle both yielded a crop; but the teazle continued for at least another year. The coriander and carraway were threshed out on the field, by flails, and the teazles, after being bound in bunches, or gleans, and secured to a staff, were taken off to the cloth manufacturers, who used them in raising the knap. Teazles may still be seen growing round the headlands of the fields to remind us of the day when they constituted one of Essex's most profitable and curious crops.

In a countryside where corn has always played so prominent a part in agriculture it is not surprising that the many customs associated with it should have persisted longer than perhaps anywhere else. The chances are that a Fordson draws the last load into the rickyard to-day, but, for all that, it will often be decorated, as in former times, with a few green boughs snatched from the nearest hedge. And if there is no hallooing, no singing, and not much drinking in the modern harvest-field, somebody is certain to keep the old traditions alive by making the comment (as the last sheaf is pitched on to the wagon) without which no Essex in-gathering would ever be quite complete. "That's the one we've been looking for all harvest," he will say. As for "horkey," which is the local name for harvest home, this, too, survived in Essex longer than in most places. Some sort of a successor there is to-day, wherein the farmers of the parish unite to give a feast to all who have helped with the harvest; but, either because harvest is not so strenuous a

The village church of Stock, near Chelmsford. The belfry tower is a particularly fine example of the timber work which distinguishes church architecture of Essex.

business with self-binders and combine-harvesters as it was with scythe and sickle, or because the countryman, even in Essex, is growing too self-conscious for such festivals, there is certainly something lacking that was present in the convivial "horkeys" of which our fathers tell.

### Scythe, Sickle and Flail

The scythe, the sickle and the flail (or "frail," as it is invariably called)—these should surely be incorporated in the county arms, for on their use much of the prosperity of Essex has always rested until now. If the scythe is still used for opening the fields for the reaper-binder, the sickle and the flail are now hardly to be seen outside museums and private collections. It is true that one may occasionally come upon some old upland farmer using a flail to thresh out a few beans, but the stick-and-a-half (as it was called) is now for the most part only a memory of the times when, for ten shillings a week, the Essex labourer sweated in the barns all winter and counted himself lucky so to be doing.

And if the flail and sickle of arable Essex rest now in museums, the cheese-press of Essex pastures rests in farm-house attics. Yet there was a time when Essex cheeses, especially from the Dengie marshes, were talked of far and wide. The poet, John Skelton, talked of them for one; and so did John Norden, who said they were "wondered at for their massiveness and thickness." Those huge cheeses, however, are now forgotten; and the dairies where they were made, along with butter, of which Hilman said it had "a smell and flavour beyond anything to be met elsewhere," no longer rattle with the clang of pails and pans. But the rich, grazing lands down by the estuaries still produce their milk, and as far inland as Hatfield Peverel passengers on the N.E. Railway may see the collecting stations of Lord Rayleigh's famous dairies.

Corn and roots are her chief products today, but Essex is still entitled to at least some of the praise for that other plenty which John Norden bestowed on her three and a half centuries ago. She is, he said, "moste fat, frutefull, and full of profitable thinges, exceding anie other shire for the general comodeties and the plentie. ... She seemeth to me to deserve the title of the englishe Goshen, the fattest of the lande: comparable to Palestina, that flowed with milke and hunnye...." Corn and roots; milk—if no cheese; and to these must be added, of her "plentie," fruit and jams, sweet peas and, of course, roses. To see her flowers, one should make the journey from

Witham, through Kelvedon, to Coggeshall, home of some of her best-known seedsmen. Away from the road, on either side, like a stretched banner, blaze the gay plots of the nurserymen. But indeed Essex excels in flowers everywhere, as much in cottage gardens, where lilies and roses line the cobbled paths up to the doors, as in the walled and spacious gardens of those Tudor noblemen who loved to escape here from the ardours of court life.

In her smaller market towns, such as Thaxted and Dunmow and Halstead, the talk in the street is more often than not of stock and crop, whilst her market-towns such as Chelmsford and Saffron Walden are hardly less rural in character, so much are they the centre of the countryside they serve. Only in the London fringe is the temper really urban and the occupation predominantly industrial. In stressing the fact that Essex is farming first, last and all the time, I would not minimize, however, her considerable small town industries. Agricultural implements, as might be expected, figure among these, especially at Maldon; also cattle cake, foodstuffs and fertilizers. Beer, too, in a county famous for the quantities once consumed in the harvest-field (though it was home-brewed then),

should not be forgotten. But the most characteristic industry is that of cloth, the first great prosperity of which, in Elizabeth's reign, is owed to the refugees from Flanders who settled here and at once improved upon the old coarse English cloths.

### Cloth Trade

Colchester became the headquarters of these honest, well-behaved and most industrious Flemings, who established there the famous Bay and Say trade—the new drapery, as it was called. Coggeshall, where a fine cloth known as Coxall's Whites was produced, and where the noble home of one of the most outstandingly wealthy of all cloth-merchants (John Peaycock) still attests to his prosperity and to his excellent taste, was another centre of the cloth trade; as also were Halstead and Braintree, nearby. Braintree later gained some prominence as a silk-producing town, under the guidance of George Courtauld, the Huguenot refugee who first launched the venture in 1798 and whose family name is still associated in the town with the same thriving trade, as it is, also, at Halstead.

In the end, however, it is to farming, whether of arable or pasture, that the tale of Essex must always return. This is even true,

**Epping Forest, lying between the valleys of the Roding and Lea, has been a popular resort for Londoners since 1882, when it became public property.**

to a considerable extent, of her wide marsh-lands and mud-flats—those mazy estuaries of Blackwater and Crouch where the plough shares with the boat the chief attention of the inhabitants and where cows and yachts seem equally in occupation. There are some people, I know, for whom this strange landscape of mud and grass and sky holds no attraction; but there are others—and by no means all sportsmen, for whom these tidal channels and oozy, bird-haunted marshes have their special appeal—who find therein a delight no other scenery can quite afford. It is enchanted land, full of the smell of the sea and yet without a sight of it anywhere, lonely and haunted by the ghosts of old-time smug-glers (and, down by Maldon, of Saxons who fought with invading Vikings here in one of England's most famous battles), a place where the rotting hulks of small craft lie up-ended in the mud and where yachts wait at anchor in their strange berths for the rising tide. It is enchanted at all times, but never so much as at sunset, when the mud is transformed to colours of unimagined beauty and when the hammers in the yacht-building sheds are still and the wan-derer along the lonely sea-wall has only the gull and the wind for company. Away to the north, on the distant horizon, lies Mersea, whose oyster-beds have been prized for centuries, whilst to the south lies the islet of Osea, whose only farmer must wait on the tides before he can transport his produce across to the mainland.

And what, to conclude, is the charac-teristic feature of the sons of Essex? How shall they be known from other agricul-tural countrymen elsewhere in the king-dom? Essex is a land of heavy clay and clear, open skies; and here, I believe, lies the key to the Essex character. The bright sky above and the pitiless mud beneath—it is compounded of the very qualities of these. Who, like the Essex labourer, wades so deep in clayey mud to go about his daily business? And who, like him, has the wide-open sky for such constant company? From the one, perhaps, he derives that in-tense realism which has made him, all down history, among the first to fight for his common rights as a wage-earner; and from the other that blend of natural awe and superstition which has caused his county to be numbered among the last strongholds of witchcraft and even to-day (though London lies just over the low rim of his hills) a place where old customs and old words and old rural usages die hard. The clay may tend to make him somewhat dour and crass and obstinate; but, redeeming this, he has the open sky to give him more than the com-mon touch of poetry. Emphatically he does not wear his heart on his sleeve—but per-haps it is the more trusty heart for that.

*Audley End, Saffron Walden*

*Willy Lott's Cottage, Flatford Mill*

# SUFFOLK

## By R. H. MOTTRAM

SUFFOLK is the second main component after Norfolk of the little-known, well-preserved and relatively unspoilt and happy portion of England known as East Anglia. Let us be quite clear at the outset. This is purely accidental. The Suffolk man, who is, of course, by a slight majority, a Suffolk woman, is in no degree inferior to, or behind, his Norfolk compatriot, with whom he shares most of his environment, geographical and climatic, linguistic and historic. In some ways he has prouder boasts to make than his neighbour dare venture. Yet the fact remains, and we cannot escape it, that East Anglia, as a district, is composed of Norfolk with its one million three hundred thousand acres and its half-million population, small parts of Essex, and Suffolk of nine hundred and fifty thousand acres and four hundred thousand people at the census of 1931. Nor is this a mere barrage of figures, with which, we know, anything can be proved. It is a real Suffolk quality. Norfolk is remote from the

*Arms of East Suffolk*

main stream of modern material life that runs from London to the north, and is, or was until yesterday, mechanized to buy food by exporting manufactures. In many essentials, Norfolk ought to be a thousand, not a hundred miles from London. Suffolk, even nearer to the metropolis, is farther away. We shall see why. There are villages in it, like Ufford, that belong to the Middle Ages. Lavenham is the ghost of a medieval town. If Shakespeare descended to it to-morrow, and turned his back to the little railway, he would find nothing unfamiliar in the street frontages of Lavenham. There are places in Suffolk at which, if you broke your leg, cycling or walking, or if your car ran out of petrol, you might be many hours before anyone discovered you. It is no accident that Mary Tudor took refuge here when her throne was threatened, or that the shy, sensitive Edward Fitzgerald, poet and translator of Omar Khayyam's *Ruba'iyát*, wrapped himself in the atmosphere, as if insulating himself for the work which he knew was to be his. It is the sort of place in which you expect to find opposition to change. And all this has its direct bearing upon the life of the man of Suffolk. Let me hasten to make amends to the

173

Suffolk man. In many ways his county is among the most famous of the forty English shires (incidentally it is one of the twelve of them that are not "shires," and thereby hangs a tale). If Norfolk has Sandringham, Suffolk has Newmarket, and what could be more royal than that? If Elveden and Euston (which gives its name to Euston Road and Station) are not quite so famous as Holkham and Blickling, they are very famous. Even industrially, Suffolk is well up in the running. Ipswich has at least four industrial units that are larger than any Norfolk or Norwich possess.

But all that is nothing. The great characteristic of Suffolk life is that of East Anglia. Because change has been relatively slow and limited, human existence is relatively happy, although the figures of wages paid may not be high. The ancient and even the modern industries are well distributed, and mixed with a rich and abundant agriculture. It has its cultural, and above all its recreational balance. Nowhere is game preserving nearer being an industry. It has only half the length of coastline that Norfolk can boast, but it has plenty of fishing, and a considerable port at Ipswich. And nowhere did the nineteenth-century rush to change the whole aspect of life, by the sudden irruption of new industry, leave Suffolk any of those devastated areas that were for so many years the grief and danger of twentieth-century England.

What, then, is the determining character of Suffolk that makes it different from Norfolk and its southern Essex margin? The answer is a simple and natural one. For reasons mainly arising from ancient water-borne communications, the chief centres of population in Suffolk, ancient markets or modern towns, are all on its verges. Mid-Suffolk is a low tableland taken up with its own not unprosperous agriculture, but even today without any main road or rail crossing it from east to west. Ipswich is in the south-eastern corner of the county, Lowestoft at the extreme north-eastern. The rich Stour valley is on the southern border, Bury and Newmarket are in the west. There is nothing comparable to the Yarmouth-Norwich-Dereham-

For most of its course of fifty miles the River Waveney forms the boundary between Suffolk and Norfolk. Below is a view of Waveney Marshes near Herringfleet.

When the Suffolk wool trade flourished Kersey became famous for the manufacture of the fabric to which it gave its name. Today it is known for its architectural beauty.

Lynn highway and rail, linking all Norfolk. So much so that Suffolk is divided into two administrative authorities, East Suffolk and West Suffolk County Councils. The latter centres on Bury St. Edmunds, and you have only to look at the streets of that delightful town, or talk to its inhabitants, to know why. There are only seventeen thousand of the latter, but they feel that they adequately balance the hundred thousand in Ipswich. Ridiculous? Not a bit. Try to get from Framlingham to Bury by road, or to go to Laxfield by train, and you will see. All mid-Suffolk depends on itself, can feed itself, never had any great river or trackway, nor needed one. In the eastern division the rivers make deepish water for sea-going ships or local trade. Lowestoft and Ipswich can, and do, take ships of considerable tonnages. The Stour, the Ore, the Alde and the Deben only lead now to little, half-forgotten ports like Woodbridge and Orford, while Aldeburgh, Southwold and Felixstowe are today far better known as holiday resorts than as harbours.

Where, then, do Suffolk people live? The answer is, very roughly, a hundred thousand in Ipswich, about forty-two thousand in heavily bombed Lowestoft, twenty thousand in Bury St. Edmunds—that is just on half the total. The rest are to be found in towns of less than ten thousand population, along the road from Beccles, through Halesworth, Wickham Market, Saxmundham, and Woodbridge, with a pocket of industry (agricultural machinery, etc.) at Leiston. Or at Eye and Debenham and Framlingham, with another pocket at Stowmarket. Or at Lavenham and Clare, Sudbury and Long Melford and Hadleigh, and the five hundred rural parishes.

We must give these last pride of place. There are still thirty thousand agricultural workers in them, cultivating half a million acres of arable—just about half the area of the county—which declined by only about ten per cent. during the bitter 'thirties. I am not clear how completely are included some thousands of fishermen at Lowestoft, with its large modern fleet of fishing vessels, and in the longshore villages with their distinctive type of smelt boat.

Let us begin, then, with the agricultural and sea worker, who is, in the general

175

Drifters in harbour at Lowestoft, centre of Suffolk's fisheries.

estimate, the typical Suffolk man, rather than those engaged in industry. The minutely detailed examination of the Land Utilization Survey can discern nine separate farming districts. For a more general survey it is perhaps sufficient to say that in the extreme south-west, and over the whole of the centre of Suffolk, the soil is very fertile, if drained and worked intensively. Around this central district are grouped highly distinctive variations. In the extreme north-west corner the county boundary includes a portion of the Cambridgeshire fenland—flat, alluvial soil around Lakenheath and Mildenhall, of very high fertility, and largely occupied by specialized farming of unmistakable type. Settlements are few and new, reflecting the late and gradual conquest of uninhabited marsh.

### Breckland Forestry

In complete contrast, to the east of this, from Brandon down to Bury St. Edmunds, runs Suffolk's share of Breckland—the sandy waste of light, intermittent cultivation, of which Norfolk has slightly the larger share. Not unnaturally, this has long been the site of some of Suffolk's largest and most historic sporting estates, such as Elveden and Euston. One hopes that some day our escape from want may be so reasonably certain that this use of the thin soil, friable to the point of being carried off in clouds by the wind, may be devoted, not to the arduous production of essential crops, in which it has done splendid service, but to the two interlocking uses for which it is pre-eminently fitted—game preserving and forestry. In this latter, or newer employ, forty thousand acres have been taken since the early nineteen-twenties, and ten thousand planted, mainly, of course, with conifers, but also with a sprinkling of deciduous trees, which we may hope, as the passing of generations completely changes the nature of the district, it may be possible to increase.

There is, of course, another side to this picture. However beneficent afforestation may be, it does nothing to restore the sometime denser, if never very dense, population, and it tends to obliterate the

ancient character of the land. Probably most people who hear of the Suffolk Breckland at all, hear of the family of Brandon flint-knappers, carrying on their prehistoric trade in the heart of what must have been, many tens of thousands of years ago, the great industrial district of our half-human ancestors. Nor does progress, good or bad, stop there. We may never use flint again, except where some competent amateur wishes to have walls or buildings of local material. The next feature to disappear is the characteristic rabbit, dear to rabbit-lovers, the staple meat of the poorer countryman. Rabbits and forestry cannot exist side by side. True, the man who works for the Forestry Commission has his permanent job with a holding of his own, the life is healthy, interesting for those who like it, and is undoubtedly helping to create a national asset. But it is a radical and permanent change.

It is not the only one. If present political tendencies continue, the great sporting estates may change out of all knowledge. Is this a good or a bad thing? Can they be replaced as centres of employment by new industries, new services, such as transport or recreational centres? It all comes home to one vividly, if one visits pleasant, and to-day prosperous little Brandon, with its fishing inn and its timber yards. Here was a town so rich that it could, in the Middle Ages, afford to divert the river, to build a bridge, while the ancient wooden wheels of the staunches or single-sill locks testify to the sometime thriving prosperity of the water-borne trade. One is always sorry to see means of livelihood go out of use. May new and better ones be found for the Suffolk man of Breckland.

### Newmarket

In an odd pocket, at the extreme west of the county, stands the great racing town, historic Newmarket, "the topmost, breeziest and best" ever since Charles II's day. Here are about ten thousand acres "dominated by the race-horse," as the Land Utilization Survey acutely remarks. Grassland (paddocks and gallops in plain English) take up forty per cent. of the area, and

*Badge of West Suffolk*

"To enter Bury St. Edmunds appears at first sight to be taking a journey back through the ages." This view of Angel Hill shows the massive Abbey gateway and wall, remnants of the once magnificent Benedictine Abbey. It was at one time the largest Abbey Church in England.

the typical man of the district is the saturnine "lad," who may be sixty or more, but who dresses as sixteen, and never loses his air of possessing, in some inaccessible portion of his head, all the wisdom about all the winners. Like his great-uncle, the "post boy," of whom it is said in Dickens that no one had ever seen a dead one, it is impossible to imagine a "stable lad" of the Newmarket type ever following the course of nature. We wonder why, knowing so much, like the conjuror, he does not make his fortune and retire. Perhaps he does, for, retired, he would be unrecognizable. He is a luxury, of course, and could not be justified by economic theory. Is that why we hope he never will need this, and that we may be able to afford him? For he is a fundamental figure of the Suffolk, nay, of the English scene. He has a code regarding those creatures who are so much more human than many a human being, he has even some illicit allegiance to the goddess of chance. No, we must afford him, or forfeit being the people we hope we are.

On the southern border of the county, never far from the River Stour, which forms it, lies a strip of heavier land, and, incidentally, a belt of little old towns once

forming an industrial district comparable, until the eighteenth century, in position in the national economy, with that which parts of the West Riding hold to-day. Haverhill and Clare, Lavenham and Sudbury, Hadleigh and Long Melford. You can tell what they were by the splendour of the churches the rich wool merchants built, by the houses hardly less so, by the fame of Kersey. How many women who used to buy Kerseymere material reflected that it is named after a little village near Hadleigh? How many think that Clare is the original barony of the Duke of Clarence?

### Air of Well Being

Of course, the days of Suffolk's woollen industry are all that is long, long gone, and what lingers will hardly be regarded as industry by a big modern combine. Yet in those places still hovers an air of well-being that is not opulence, but which must be the envy of many a depressed area, that grew to sudden riches a hundred years ago. There is still something in pleasant surroundings; agriculture may be in a state of chronic depression, but it never goes right out, as does many an industry. A farmer can always eat his materials and live in his establishment,

178

the clear sky and fresh air are still there, and a market is always a market, even when it is not an "exchange" and cannot deal in futures. The population has dwindled, and is still declining, the Stour has silted up and is no longer navigable, but how can you obliterate a district that produced Gainsborough and Constable and laid the civilized world under a debt?

### Coastal Region

In the same way, the small various western districts are balanced by various eastern seaboard ones. In the extreme north-east, the virtual island of Lothingland, north of Lowestoft, and almost enclosed by Norfolk, is of a lighter soil, and governed by its proximity to Yarmouth and Lowestoft. South of Lowestoft, a belt of light soil, often called the Sandlings, stretches all down the coast to a depth of some six or eight miles. It is split up, in all directions, as we have seen, by deep estuaries, some effective to-day for sea-going tonnage, some little, old, and half-silted up, like those of the Alde, or

Ore, and Deben, and those in which navigation has ceased, like the Minsmere and the Blyth. The Beccles–Ipswich road and rail roughly mark the limit of this distinctive district, with its sheep-walks and afforestation, its muddy creeks and little rivers, its sand and its salt air.

All the rest of Suffolk country, from the Cambridgeshire border to Lowestoft, from Breckland to Ipswich, is the great main Suffolk tableland of boulder clay covered with mixed farms of moderate size, one to three hundred acres, sixty per cent. arable. The necessities of working and draining makes for deep ditches instead of hedges, roads of causeway type leading irregularly from one village to another. The streams are small, railways remote, cottages mainly of colour-washed plaster, often with traces of the Essex "pargetting" or stamped patterns upon it, roofed with tiles, and surrounded with flowers. A fair proportion of large estates still ensure a sufficiency of woodland, and the graceful cricket-bat willow is perhaps quite as representative

Eye is a small town on the central Suffolk tableland. The church of St. Peter and St. Paul, seen below, is celebrated for its magnificent tower, decorated with local flint. The town also possesses a grammar school, founded in 1566, and the town hall was once used as a corn exchange.

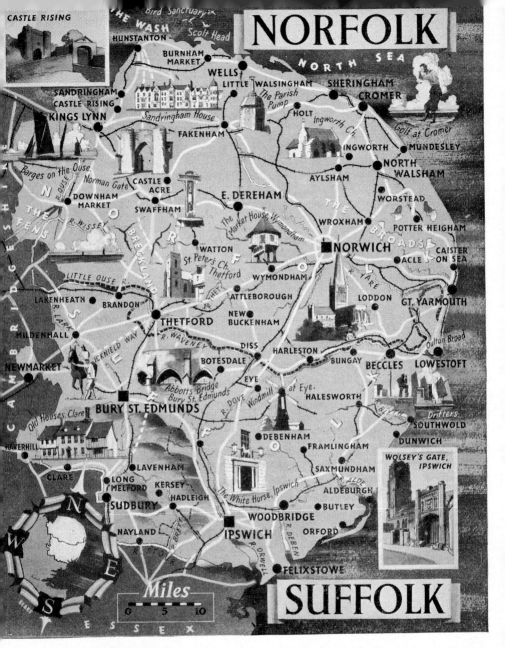

as any of the abundant hedgerow and small plantation timber.

Such is the country in which the Suffolk countryman lives his life much as he has always lived it. The bus takes him into the larger town more than the rail ever did; he has some access to radio; his housing, education, and other services look after him at least as much as the local landlord used to, if in a different manner. He is gradually leaving the soil, and it will be interesting to see if this process will be reversed in an England which may be obliged to grow its own food to a larger extent than ever before.

Now, the other half of the inhabitants of Suffolk—those engaged in industry—live on its borders—in Bury, Lowestoft and Ipswich. Let us take Lowestoft first, because it is a port at the extremity of the county. It is strongly divided into north and south by the partly artificial works of its harbour, and outlet from the big Broad at Oulton just inland of it. The old town was on the high land on the northern side, where the steep High Street still holds one or two seventeenth- and eighteenth-century houses, near the modern town hall, and ends in the pretty park at Sparrows Nest. It is on the steep "scores" of this district, descending to Lowestoft Ness—the most easterly point of our island—that the china-clay pocket made possible the brief Lowestoft china industry, now only a collector's memory.

The South town, to which you proceed by the swing bridge, is entirely Victorian in its slightly aristocratic character. The harbour needs constant attention to keep it free of sand.

The town has a certain amount of industry, much of it connected with the fishing fleet, for Lowestoft is one of the most important fishing ports in England. Indeed, Lowestoft, which was a hamlet in 1086, owes its origins to its fisheries, but the industry caused much ill-will for centuries with the naval port of Yarmouth.

It has had a remarkable growth during the past seventy years as a watering-place. Despite the brutal bombing to which it was subjected during the last war, Lowestoft has quite regained its pre-war popularity as a holiday resort.

### Medieval Memories

In complete contrast, let us turn to a town little more than a third of the size Lowestoft ought to be. To enter Bury St. Edmunds appears at first sight to be undertaking a journey back through the ages. The railway station is reminiscent of the days when the London road ran through the town. But as we approach the centre we find older and older buildings, until, at Angel Hill, we see one whole side of the town, bounded by the gigantic wall of the monastery, second in the kingdom only to Glastonbury, and now laid out as a public park, within its exterior walls and gates that have survived. The market-place, opposite,

contains Moyses' Hall, now a museum, but sometime the typical stronghouse of a Jewish financier of the thirteenth century. Woolhall Street and the Athenæum complete the varied but always imposing picture, showing what medieval commerce and culture of the eighteenth century were.

### Bury's Famous Citizens

It would be difficult to say which is the more famous of Bury's citizens. Mr. Pickwick (you can see the wall of the house over which he was hoisted at the instigation of Jingle) is perhaps better known than Abbot Samson, who ruled the great monastery, and both are more heard of than Milner-Gibson-Cullum, who gave his fine library to the town. Under such a weight of past glories it is highly creditable to the inhabitants that their market has so brisk and modern an appearance, and that their sugar-beet refinery and maltings are so prosperous. The place has also a certain air, as the result of the nearness of Newmarket and some large country seats. It

**The Ancient House, built in 1567, stands in the Buttermarket at Ipswich. It is a perfect example of Elizabethan domestic architecture.**

is the county town of the administrative county of West Suffolk.

So finally we come to Ipswich, in which nearly a third of the people of Suffolk live. It has been a port for ten centuries, and still has a fair water-borne trade. It shared at one time the weaving industry of East Anglia, but this is now superseded by at least four very large heavy engineering establishments. Again, just to the north of it are considerable artificial manure establishments. More engineering workshops and a sausage factory help to fill up the western suburb.

In fact, there is some little mystery about Ipswich which meets the visitor in its brisk, busy streets. Just as Suffolk plays a second fiddle to Norfolk, so it seems remarkable that Ipswich, with its larger individual industrial units, and its excellent shopping facilities, should not have outgrown Norwich long ago. But it has not. There is no big central cattle or provision market, the main buildings, ancient and modern, in spite of a gateway that perhaps Wolsey knew and a magnificently housed folk museum, somehow provide no really spectacular vista. No castle or cathedral dominates the skyline, and it is difficult to get a single striking view of the town and estuary from any one spot—as, for example, one sees Norwich from Mousehold. It has a small number of exceptionally graceful church towers, and some interesting ancient buildings have been retained. Its demolition of gaol, town wall, and slums has been as drastic as its re-housing scheme has been extensive. It has had an oddly contentious political history. At intervals its character has been predominantly conservative, and its representation distinguished. But, in contrast, it was for some years represented by the late Sylvester Horne, a great Congregationalist Minister of a generation ago. In more modern times it has returned one of the more marked figures on the Labour side of the House as its representative. It is the home of typical old brewing and banking families of Quaker origin. But whatever its past may have been, there can be no doubt as to the impression made on the visitor coming from Norwich. He will find Ipswich much, much more than forty miles nearer to London, in speech and activity, the scale of enterprise and the scope of its commitments. It could hardly have done more if Wolsey had remained to see it prosper.

*Wool Hall, Lavenham*

*Sailing on the Broads*

# NORFOLK

By R. H. MOTTRAM

NORFOLK * is the fourth largest county in England, if you count Yorkshire and Lincolnshire as only one county each, although they contain several administrations. Norfolk is one administration, and on that score ranks, after Devon, as the largest single county council area. It is the easternmost county of England. True, most geographers measure the breadth of England from Lowestoft Ness which is just in Suffolk, but the difference between this point and Yarmouth in miles is negligible. The northern half of the county boundary is drawn by the beaches of the North Sea, the remainder by the Rivers Little Ouse (flowing west) and Waveney (flowing east) whose sources are parted only by the width of the road that leads from South Lopham into Suffolk. The Welney completes the circle.

Norfolk is, therefore, virtually an island, a gravelly hump or moraine left as the prehistoric Rhine delta developed into the North Sea. But its distinctive physical character derives from separa-

*Arms of Norfolk*

tion from the remainder of England by the Great Fen. Even to-day there is only one land bridge into the Midlands. It is on Newmarket Heath far down in Suffolk. A comparatively modern road through Ely and the Fens leads to Peterborough; the older ones were far less direct. This isolation has been exaggerated, ever since mid-nineteenth century, by the fact that Norfolk is a hundred miles from the nearest coal-mine. Yet Norwich is easily the largest of the old county capitals. I recite these physical facts first because they lead up to something more important. It may be objected that all towns and many villages in Norfolk have electricity from the Grid, that electrical machinery is made in Norwich, that modern air transport cares nothing, and modern road transport very little, for the Fens, and that thus the ancient remoteness from the centres of national life will shortly disappear, especially as two successive generations have been all over the world in the fighting services.

Perhaps, perhaps not; the objection raises an interesting question of sociological development which will not be finally decided for some years. It leads, moreover, directly to the purpose of this chapter which is to say what Norfolk people are really like. At the

* For map of Norfolk, see page 180.

1951 census there were half a million of them, one hundred and twenty-two thousand living in Norwich, fifty-one thousand in Yarmouth and twenty-six thousand in King's Lynn. There are no other towns of more than ten thousand inhabitants, and these three have certainly not increased in war-time. As near as one can discover, Norwich has now not much more than one hundred thousand plus some thousands in the surrounding country parishes. Lynn still has probably twenty-five thousand people and Yarmouth about forty thousand. It was largely evacuated in 1940, and I only pray it may recover all it lost as a watering-place, a minor industrial centre and above all, a fishing station.

### Holidays and Herrings

This recovery may not all depend on the repair of war damage. Yarmouth used to be one of the Meccas of the less fortunate East End or Lancashire holiday-maker, who would come for a week (with a gold sovereign in his pocket) or for a week-end, direct from Manchester. He now has more money and wider ideas, owns perhaps a small car or motor-cycle combination, or lives on a bus route.

The herring fishery was so important that trainloads of women workers came from northern Scotland every October to carry out the packing operations, while the drifters were tied up four deep along the quay. Will all or some of that come back?

Again, Lynn docks have seen some vicissitudes. Will they grow more or less active? Finally, will Norwich retain its heavily-bombed clothing, light metal, constructional and milling works, and its boot and shoe trade? Will it retain its place as the second corn and cattle market in the country after London, and the administrative and transport centre of Norfolk and a good deal beyond, a cultural tourist centre, the largest town for a hundred miles? This, of course, depends partly on physical events, but far more on the perpetuation of the highly independent, freedom-loving and industrious character of the people. If they want to live in Norfolk, they will see to it that their old industries allow them to do so or that they find new ones that will. We shall see, when we come to consider the case of Norwich, how tendencies, such as mechanization, which have drawn people away from the land for nearly a century, may in another stage draw them back.

There are some one million three hundred thousand acres of land in Norfolk of which over the last half-century there has been a slight decrease, owing to the fact that erosion has been greater than accretion. No great industrial revolution has changed the face of the countryside as in the Midlands and North. Outside the towns, nine hundred and eighty thousand acres are occupied by crops and grass, a decrease since 1890 of one hundred thousand acres, which has been surrendered to spreading towns and rough grazing. The agricultural industry is carried on by nearly thirty-eight thousand workers, almost exactly the same number as in 1831, though there were five thousand more in 1928, and ten thousand more in the 1950's. To-day the crews of the Yarmouth herring drifters, and the sparse longshore fishermen of the coast villages should be added, as a good many of both sorts do a job on the land to fill up slack time.

### Typical Farms

In general, the Norfolk farm, standing in one of the five hundred odd Norfolk parishes will run from one hundred to three hundred acres, getting larger as we go west and north, though the Fen in the extreme west, over the Ouse, provides peculiarities. This latter is really Lincolnshire country with small intensively cultivated smallholdings, concerned with fruit and flowers to a larger extent than is found in Norfolk proper, and dependent for its fertility upon drainage. Its centre is Wisbech, in the Ely division of Cambridgeshire. The more typical Norfolk land will generally be two-thirds arable, held on lease, rent payable half-yearly. Great changes have recently been made, such as mechanization, involving larger fields and perhaps larger holdings, the decrease of sheep and horses, the increase in dairy farming, highly scientific poultry rearing and sugar-beet cultivation over a large acreage.

The county can be roughly divided into seven districts. A strict survey, such as

Horning Ferry is familiar to many who sail on the Broads. Horning village lies on the River Bure between Wroxham and Acle, the chief cruising centres on the Broads.

185

Years ago the village of Blakeney, in north-west Norfolk, grew rich through the wool trade it carried on. Though the trade has now declined, many sheep are still pastured on the neighbouring marshes.

the Land Utilization Survey, can make a dozen but, for the general reader, there are essentially seven different parts in which Norfolk countrymen live.

The Norfolk Broads, in the north-east, lie mainly along the course of the Bure. There reed thatching and fruit-growing flourish.

### The Broads

Mixed up with the farming of the land between the Broads and the fishing of the coastal villages is a tourist trade which, if it spoils the countryside, is nevertheless financially very important for several summer weeks. I leave Yarmouth for separate treatment, but the coast from its suburbs northward to Mundesley, where high cliffs begin, only just divides the Broads from the sea, and looks like becoming a continuous chain of holiday camps. The inland water cruising centres are Acle and Wroxham, but Stalham on its Broad is the typical town of the district. Even here change is constant, and the motor cruiser tends to drive out the picturesque but skill-demanding "one-design," a type of small cutter, and the converted wherry or erstwhile cargo sailing-boat.

Broadland is a triangle, bounded by the sea on the north-east, the River Yare on the

south, and a low ridge from Norwich to Mundesley on the north-west. Once you mount this you are in the second part, north Norfolk.

North Norfolk is an undulating, well-wooded district, with parks like Blickling and Gunton and Felbrigg, stretching as far as Sheringham on the coast. Here again there is a belt of tourist traffic in the small towns (Cromer is the largest) and crab-fishing villages.

North Walsham has the Paston Grammar School and Holt has Gresham's. Aylsham is a pleasant market town. The Norfolk man is here concerned with mixed farming and fruit growing, and his wife is generally more than willing to let rooms, especially if she lives near the coast.

South-west of the Norwich-Holt road and north-west of the Norwich-London road is mid-Norfolk, covering the higher reaches of the Yare. The centre of the district is the thriving market town of East Dereham; on its southern limit are Wymondham and Attleborough and on its northern limit Reepham. The mixed farms are remarkable for turkey rearing, and the two first-mentioned towns have vigorous industrial elements whose factory hooters sound odd, and whose crowds of cycling operatives look

186

strange against the rural background. At Wymondham they are employed at two large brush factories, and at Attleborough at a cider works. There is no tourist traffic here, and estates are small.

Very different is north-west Norfolk, roughly a rectangle north of the Dereham–Swaffham road, west of that from Dereham to Holt, bounded north and west by the sea. Here, on the "good sands," are larger estates, Holkham, Houghton, Raynham and, above all, the King's modern country house, at Sandringham. Here they grow the finest barley in the world. It is great sporting country with fox- and staghounds and coursing and vast coverts. The two coasts are low-lying with tidal harbours at Wells and Blakeney, and a considerable tourist trade centring on Hunstanton where there are low cliffs. But the tourists here are richer people who can afford to yacht and fish and shoot. Blakeney Point and Scolt Head are bird sanctuaries. Here, too, there are visitors; there are fewer smallholdings, but there is or was a shell-fish trade on the tidal sands. King's Lynn is the shopping town, but Fakenham has a good deal of importance on the other side of the region. A peculiar feature is the carrstone, a soft local sandstone used for building. Lynn is an interesting example of resistance to economic adversity, a very ancient port of Hanseatic and whaling tradition, whose docks were modernized just when it became cheaper to send goods by rail and later by road. But it maintains its position as an industrial and communication centre, has a pleasant appearance and strongly marked local character, and may have a future.

### District of Breckland

South of this, from Swaffham to Thetford, from the banks of the Ouse to beyond the London road lies Breckland, the fifth section of the country, an irregular but fairly consistent block of some one hundred and seventy square miles of land which has never been good enough for continuous cultivation. It has produced rabbits in such numbers as to constitute an industry. It once had very large sporting estates, but they are now being reduced by taxation and social conditions. It may well have a future under afforestation, aerodromes or other highly modern, intensely organized uses. It can never support a large population by agriculture. The towns, Swaffham and Thetford, lie at its extremities, and its

**Scots girls packing herrings at Great Yarmouth. Its fine sands also make Yarmouth a popular holiday resort, particularly with East Enders from London and cotton workers from Lancashire.**

powdery heaths and meres that vary in extent with the saturation of the soil have interest as repositories of prehistoric culture and wild life. Migrant birds and rare creatures haunt its loneliness. It already has an educational and recreational value. The strip of fen along its western border really goes, in spite of sharp differences, with the Norfolk Fenland west of the Ouse already mentioned.

East of the Norwich-Kenninghall-Lopham road and between the Rivers Yare and Waveney lies south Norfolk with its distinctive Suffolk-type coloured plaster and thatched cottages, its beanfields and poultry. Its markets are Diss and Harleston, both on the Waveney; the former has some industry. There are no very large estates and farms are not large.

With the Fenland this makes the seven districts of agricultural, fishing, tourist and sporting Norfolk. In these districts live and work the forty thousand agricultural workers and fishermen, together with some twenty-five thousand other persons, gentry, clergy, professional and official, transport, shopkeeping and other small town and village dwellers. Wages have increased many-fold in this century, but I suspect that house, food, fuel, grazing and other "allowances" are not so common as they were. But it was in Norfolk that the labourer first had a Union. He is a great poacher and sportsman, and the bus and the radio are changing him more than his cycle did.

Before I turn to the towns and their industries, I am going to insert the link between the Norfolk townsman and his country colleague, something which is the visible sign of their history, and makes one hesitate to pronounce on their future. If I said: "It is religion" you would scoff, and quite rightly. It is rather the outward appearance of the religious compromise of the seventeenth century, with all its social and political implications, which is still more visible in Norfolk than in most parts of Britain. In every village in Norfolk, in nearly every street in Norwich, there is a church or chapel. Yarmouth was dominated by the spire of St. Nicholas until the Germans knocked it down. King's Lynn still has its church of the same name.

This general characteristic of the landscape or townscape is as common to all Norfolk people as the climate, but it does not mean they are specially devout. It suggests three questions that are worth consideration: (a) how did this county and its towns have so much religious architecture

**Holkham Hall, near Wells, was the estate of "Coke of Norfolk," founder of modern agricultural practice. His land was poor and neglected but the many improvements in raising crops and stock-breeding which he introduced increased the rental of his estate ninefold during his lifetime.**

Before the development of mechanical power, windmills such as this one at Denver near Downham Market were used extensively in the flat lands of East Anglia for pumping water and grinding corn. Although few of these mills are still in use, they nevertheless add character to the countryside.

both Anglican and Dissenting? (*b*) why does it still loom larger than any industrial, transport or administrative erection? (*c*) does it help us to assess the probable immediate future of Norfolk, or is it merely accidental and likely to disappear?

The answer to (*a*) is the wool trade. Five hundred years ago sheep were not kept on inaccessible walks of the north country hills, but in Norfolk meadows, and Queen Philippa brought in Flemish weavers from Bruges and Ghent. It was because of the profits of this trade that you see pocket cathedrals in tiny obscure villages like Salle or Terrington, or little towns like Wymondham or Blakeney. The place called Worstead gave its name to worsted yarn. Cistercian monks fostered sheep breeding, and that is why there was more Church land in Norfolk than elsewhere. But men who weave get together, begin to think, to argue and, it may be, to rebel. By the seventeenth century the weaving had migrated to Norwich, and the dour "possessed" type of Puritan

189

The market cross at Wymondham. It was built in 1616, and was once the meeting place of merchants engaged in the wool trade.

was so strong here that Norfolk was completely within Cromwell's East Anglian Association. Indeed, King Charles' execution is said to have been decided upon in a flint-faced inn on Yarmouth quay.

When the extreme bitterness softened, it could be seen that these people had been building chapels, some quite beautiful which stand, almost literally in rows, in Norwich, and in tiny villages like Hapton, and small towns like Diss. This went on (with decreasing taste, in my opinion) well into the nineteenth century. This answers question (b) and explains why I give all this detail about the past. The average Norfolk person lives within sight of a church or chapel. These are still more numerous and bigger than any administrative, industrial, educational or transport building. This is true of Norfolk, and untrue of most of the Midlands and North, London or university towns. Why? Because Norfolk, especially Norwich, missed the great rebuilding and replanning that took place over half of England in the mid-nineteenth century. While everywhere, north

of the Trent and Avon, new towns were arising and the country was being honey-combed with mines and furnaces, the weaving left Norwich and Norfolk, and from the 1830s to 1860 Norwich starved, Lynn stagnated, and the country villages, while they had their own troubles, suffered no major revolution in their appearance. To-day the Dissenter will take off his hat to the Anglican dignitary, who will smile benignly on him; and there are no longer clericals and anti-clericals. This comparative mildness in the religious climate or, if you prefer it, contemporary indifference can be traced largely to the work of two great Englishmen. One was Wesley, the other was Bass (I use these names as typical of the influences they exercised). The poor Englishman of the 1840s caught up in a new state of affairs, could always pray, or get drunk. Often both in turns. So, provided with these safety valves he did not organize any formal rebellion. Something of what it meant can be read in Disraeli's Sybil.

You may ask what happened to make modern Norwich so large a city with so wide a range of industry. Lynn and Yarmouth we can understand, and the arable fields, pastures and markets were not affected by the industrial revolution. But what of Norwich? Thereby hangs a curious tale. There was, of course, no national or other public means of repairing the disaster of the 1830s to Norwich life, the sudden removal of the trade which had been its principal occupation since Plantagenet times. But various individuals either knew, or stumbled upon the fact, that a whole population of skilled weavers had certain powers in their fingers that did not reside in just any fingers.

### New Industries

An old-established ironmonger began to set people to weave wire netting. In the course of half a century this had branched out into large firms. The manufacture of boots and shoes was just beginning to be undertaken by small masters—"garret-masters" they were called in Norwich, because they hired the old weaving garrets with the long "weavers' lights" that were part of, or near, the ex-wool-merchants' mansions.

Here they gave out the materials and received the half-finished shoes which those who had been weavers began in their tenements, because weavers could do the "turn shoe" work, which involved early processes in which the footwear was sewn inside out, and turned. Larger firms undertook assembling and marketing, and before the 'forties were out, biggish concerns were beginning to make Norwich one of the centres of the footwear trades.

### Mustard and Confectionery

A little later, in the 'sixties, flour, starch and mustard milling were brought from the village under-shot watermill at Stoke Holy Cross, four miles south of Norwich, to a riverside site, just beyond the old south gates. About the same time a chemist began making mineral waters, then confectionery, finally Christmas crackers. Now all these things are packet goods; they can only be distributed in small, convenient parcels, boxes, tins or bottles. Here again the weavers' fingers could do the work of packing. Finally, at the end of the century there was founded a firm which electrified Norwich, and formed part of the Eastern Electricity Board. Such were some of the principal elements that built a new city amid the ruins of the old, through the inherited manual skill of a population whose trade had gone north.

Of course, we are obliged to simplify to see it clearly. For it was not so simple as all that. For one thing, all the weaving did not go. There were certain things that could still be done as well in Norwich as elsewhere, and one large silk firm remains. There have been small ones, too, until quite recently. And in the background were the market, the inevitable distributing trade and administration of a large district, which retained great prestige as a social centre, a musical festival, a local school of painting, literary and scientific associations that could only exist where a fairly wealthy and leisured middle class can support them, a famous medical centre, a Cathedral Close with its clergy and an ancient Grammar School. People as diverse as George Borrow, Sir Josiah Banks Hooker, Dr. Parr, Bishop Stanley, Dr. Lubbock, and in recent times, Sir Frederick Bateman, were either born or lived in Norwich.

Do such people make much difference to the life of the people? I think they do. Certainly the great doctors, clergy and schoolmasters do. But others do also, because there lingered in Norwich, through all the incidents of the nineteenth century, far more strongly than in many a larger town, the tradition, perhaps the necessity, if you were a professional man, of living in one of those magnificent Georgian mansions of which Norwich has so many to-day.

The poor neighbour who existed in one of the five hundred Norwich yards, squalid rookeries, generally contrived on what had been the garden or stables of the great house, looked up to the wealthy neighbour, and did not look in vain. This leads on to the fact that nineteenth-century Norwich produced the beginnings of two financial institutions of world-wide renown. One of them was the bank that the Quaker Gurneys founded, which again arose from the

**Old houses in Church Lane, Swaffham, a small market town situated on the edge of Breckland fifteen miles from King's Lynn.**

wool trade, but was too firmly established to die with it. Members of that remarkable family, of whom the most celebrated is still probably Elizabeth Fry, are yet to be seen in and around Norwich. When, in 1896, they amalgamated their bank with that of their relatives, Barclays of London, five out of the twenty directors of that great combine could be seen, for yet another thirty years, sitting in the old Bank "parlour" at Norwich every Saturday. What that has meant in philanthropy, before there were any public services to speak of, what it has meant in leadership, in credit, in the facility for new undertakings, would be difficult to assess.

The other is the equally world-famous Norwich Union Insurance. There had been attempts by groups of local merchants to found an insurance office as early as 1785, but the founder of the Norwich Union was Thomas Bignold, who did not devote himself entirely to insurance until 1807. He was succeeded by his son Samuel, who was knighted in 1853 for his public and political services. During five generations, extension, amalgamation and ramification have taken the name of the old city to the remote parts of the earth, and made it a familiar sight in the United States and the Dominions, the great ports of South America and the Far East.

### Norwich's Industries

To all these places have gone Norwich men, and from them has come something that must affect the lives of Norwich people. Of course, to-day, all the big bank and insurance offices have branches in Norwich, but the two above are local products of a century and a half's standing. Nor must we ever forget a whole quarter of the town, built, employed and watched over by the industrial genius and constant goodwill of three generations of Colmans.

Around these nuclei, major trades and financial institutions are grouped, the strong local newspaper with its evening counterpart, the distributing and transport trades, the building and timber organizations, one of which, at least, spreads out over the neighbouring counties. There are also, necessarily large, entirely local stores—it would be grossly unjust to call them shops—

some of which have stuck to their original line, drapery, grocery, stationery and printing; others have expanded into the general store type. With these must rank the establishment of the very strong local co-operative movement. I should say they maintain a fair balance one with another, and with the great international chain stores that have, of course, their branches here as elsewhere.

### Mixture of Town and Country

There still confronts me the very difficult task of leaving the reader with a fair and balanced idea of Norwich, a very big and still locally important town, flanked by Yarmouth and Lynn, the whole surrounded by the county with which they retain closer connexion than do most towns with their countryside. What is it like, this still largely homogeneous town and country mixture, with its slow rate of change, its old, still vital local conditions? How does Norwich stand against the background we have set up? Certainly like nothing in the nineteenth century industrial regions, or the counties surrounding London. Aberdeen is a possible comparison, but Devon is better, and there are churches and chapels, cider and grazing in common. Even so, Norwich is much larger and more central than Exeter, and Yarmouth, Lynn and Cromer are no match for Ilfracombe, Plymouth and Torquay. I think I must recall that in 1909, just before the twentieth century began to be catastrophic, a book called *Norwich, a Social Study*, by C. K. Hawkins of Toynbee Hall, was published. One paragraph I cannot resist quoting:

"As regards housing, it is clear that the standard in Norwich is a high one. . . . In respect to food, Norwich people eat less meat than in most industrial centres . . . on the other hand they consume more vegetables, especially potatoes, and flour in the shape of puddings. . . . Clothes are an important factor in the general environment which reacts upon character. Class for class, Norwich girls are better dressed, and in better taste, than similar girls in London."

This will not do for the county, of course, where war-time rationing has revealed the demand for meat. Norwich housing, too,

Norwich Cathedral originally a Norman building, was altered and added to up to the sixteenth century. The cloisters and the two cathedral gateways are notable architectural features.

has been revolutionized, but Norwich girls are still pretty, and many aristocratic families, when those words were written, still sought their ladies' maids in Anne Boleyn's county. Little did Hawkins think that his book was hardly in print before the chief citizen in Norwich was designated Lord Mayor, National Insurance revolutionized the economic status of the worker,

and that the ancient cavalry drill-ground became an airport.

To-day the citizen of Norwich can see more of his churches and chapels than ever he could. Norwich has been laid waste, many of its larger stores are gone, one railway station and many a familiar street. Before that, between the wars, nearly eight thousand houses had been built in half a dozen estates by municipal housing efforts; and since the War this work has been resumed, so that to-day there are over 14,000 dwellings on the estates.

The centre of the City has been rebuilt, to include a number of handsome new shops. In the older parts of Norwich, most of the war-damaged churches which were not irreparably destroyed have been rebuilt or repaired; and in the suburbs a number of new churches have arisen, the most notable architecturally perhaps being the Trinity Presbyterian Church on Unthank Road.

A revised development plan for the City was approved by the Government in 1955. It incorporates a new Central Library, a covered Swimming Pool, and the removal of the Cattle Market to a site on the south side of the City. The suburbs have extended so much that although the population of Norwich itself is slightly less than before the war, the total urban population is considerably greater.

As has been the case for many years, the largest trade here is the manufacture of boots and shoes. In 1955 this industry employed about four thousand six hundred men and four thousand seven hundred women over the age of fifteen. Some of the best-known brands of good footwear are the product of Norwich craftsmen.

Clothing, milling, brewing, last-making, the manufacture of precision tools, and body-building for cars and caravans are among the City's other industries; and a large firm of manufacturing chemists has recently opened a factory on the north side of the City.

How these many activities, old and new, will affect the structure of Norfolk life remains for the future to disclose; but it is an undeniable fact that, whether for good or ill, the spread of manufactories all over England has come to stay and must inevitably in the end influence the agricultural districts strongly. Yet this is not entirely a bad thing; for romance must give way to reality. Man's power over his environment is increasing so rapidly to-day that it is difficult to discern if in future it will be to his advantage to grow barley in Norfolk and to make shoes in its capital city. The Tower of St. Nicholas' Church is now standing again and plans for rebuilding the church itself are going forward; a challenge from the past to the present! But the present—the hard economic necessities of a small island with an ever-growing population—will surround the past, even if it does not for a long time submerge it. Herring must continue to be fished from Yarmouth. Holiday-makers will still seek the bracing air and freedom of the Norfolk coast. The spread of electricity, derived in due course from atomic power, will brighten every home.

In general, if we are now to be a food-producing rather than a manufacturing, shipping and exporting country, the future for Norfolk agriculture may be bright, while its distance from the coalfields may be less important than it was. That is a question which only time can answer.

*Castle Acre Priory, near Swaffham*

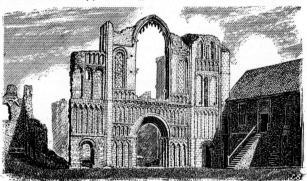

*Bridge over the Ouse, St. Ives*

# HUNTINGDONSHIRE

## By SIR WILLIAM BEACH THOMAS

THE Great North Road and, rather more accurately, the old Great Northern Railway, cut the little shire of Huntingdon* in halves along its longest axis, which is only thirty miles. What hosts of people have hurried through it without any notion of its character or the names and nature of its villages! Nevertheless, these birds of passage exert a definite influence on the social life that they hardly touch. The claim that transportation is civilization, a favourite thesis of Kipling's, is curiously illustrated by the annals, new and old, of several villages. One quaint example may be recorded. Soon after the Great North Road enters the county from the south, it passes through Buckden. Though this historic village never became a town, as was expected at several periods of its history, it was a very well-known place in the coaching days when it was a famous stage in the journey between London and York. When the railways robbed the roads of their eminence, and

the Great Northern Railway outpaced the Great North Road, Buckden fell back, and its famous inns lost much of their old prosperity and also something of their sense of rivalry. Happily, the whirligig of time does not cease to revolve. When the motor-car came to restore their busy life to the roads, it was found that Buckden, about sixty miles north of London, was a convenient rest for those who could escape from London after business hours on Friday; and so get a flying start for a longer expedition on Saturday. The two chief inns each kept a man by their entrances to catch the arriving motorists, as was made manifest to the world by the report of a stand-up fight in the street between the two propagandists. These very excellent inns, like many others, are now, we may hope, permanently restored to prosperity. The village itself is large and prosperous, but the long red wall and tower of the old palace of the bishops of Lincoln indicate that once upon

*Arms of Huntingdonshire*

* See map on page 206.

195

The tower of the church of St. Mary's at St. Neots, seen from across the river Ouse.

196

a time Buckden was no less prosperous than it is at the present time and certainly much more important.

When the motorists leave Buckden on Saturday morning for their extended journey, they see at the first crossroads, one of which leads to Huntingdon, a signpost with the pleasingly condensed legend "To the North." A little farther on, after passing through Alconbury, they are offered a telling illustration of the general structure of the shire, if they have eyes to see it. On their right, to the east, stretches a singularly spacious view over the fens, so-called, the flattest and now the most fertile land in England. The surface—hence the fertility —is sometimes of peat, sometimes of silt, underlaid by marl, which has proved ideal for fertilizing the alluvial or black soil overlaying it. The road itself is well kept up, and the land on its west side is agreeably undulating, moulded out of some of the toughest clay in England. It has not always had a good name among farmers, but it provides admirable bean and wheat land when well worked and drained.

### Good Land in Decay

This proviso indicates a serious social change in the shire. When the price of wheat fell to the neighbourhood of a guinea a quarter, acre after acre of good corn land was allowed to fall back to rough, often very rough, grass. I, personally, am very familiar with fields (giving excellent cover for partridges, hares, rabbits, moles and ants) which followed the course of the Garden of Eden after the Fall. They were choked by thorn and briar. The ditches were not cleaned, and so the water held up by the clay could not escape and the hedges spread into bits of woodland. Not a penny of profit came to the landlords, and the farmers had much ado to live. Farm buildings and fences fell into ruin. The clergy began to fear that their tithes would cease to be paid. Indeed, much of this part of the shire was well on the way to become prairie.

It is on authentic record that an M.F.H., standing as candidate for parliament, was heckled by an opponent, who finally called out, "And what is the chief industry where you come from?" He replied instantly "Fox 'untin' "—and was cheered to the echo. The impression which the heckler had tried to create was defeated by its own success. The hunt was indeed the only prosperous industry and was popular with all classes.

### Rural Depopulation

Now, for a part of the year the Fitzwilliam hunt made its headquarters at Great Gidding. Perhaps its most famous meet (Catworth guidepost, excepted) was Gidding windmill. Towards the end of the nineteenth century the mill, once very prosperous, fell into disuse and the village of Great Gidding ceased to deserve its attribute. It became little bigger than the more famous Little Gidding and Steeple Gidding. When I first knew Great Gidding and rode my pony to the meet, the population was about eight hundred. When I visited the place some forty years later it was about three hundred. The place reminded me of Galway on the west coast of Ireland and of Constantinople, of both of which the outskirts consist of houses that had been allowed to tumble into shapeless ruins. But the unsightly outskirts of Great Gidding have, I understand, been tidied up since last I visited the village.

No county in England suffered so dramatically as did Huntingdonshire from rural depopulation and loss of land value. The decline had probably been in progress for several hundred years, as indicated by the foundations of great houses, the avenues leading from nowhere to nowhere, the fishponds and moats, and the memorials in the huge churches, now standing over tiny hamlets often consisting of no more than a few ill-thatched cottages.

### Fall in Values

The fall in the value of properties is hard to believe. A good example is the fortune of the farm just below the parish church in Little Gidding. The farm in question, owned at one time by a squarson of an almost forgotten type, was bought in 1777 for £22 an acre. The purchaser spent at least as much as the price of the land on cottages and farmhouses and homesteads, which have proved solid enough to defy the attacks of time. In 1915, the farm with all these excellent buildings was sold for £12 an acre, a sum that would not pay for the houses alone. The end was not yet. A few years later, the farm with buildings was again sold at the rate of £4 10s. an acre. And this was good land, in a beautiful scene, very well treed with a running brook at the boundary, and little more than sixty miles from London. What had we done to England that such a place should be worth only about half as much as a houseless farm of indifferent quality land in thinly populated Australia?

The squarson, who owned a good deal of property in Huntingdonshire, was a glorious character. He came once to take duty at the next village to Steeple Gidding, dressed in a coat of unknown pattern, and thus explained its origin. "You see," he said, "I had to have a coat in which I could hunt on Saturday, do duty in Hamerton Church on Sunday and attend Peterboro' market on Monday!" With the rector he established on the glebe a sort of communal cow-pasture, which greatly assisted the more energetic members of the village. Common grazing, associated with private patches for haying, and the provision of funds for the purchase and insuring of milch cows have brought back some of the spirit of pre-enclosure days.

### Start of Revival

"*La terre qui meurt*" might have stood as title for a tale of this bit of England; but the land did not quite die and never will. It was near the point of extinction at the opening of the First World War; it was on the way to revival in and after the Second, though the old value has not yet returned. This fall in land values is most clearly reflected in the diminution of tithes. To-day, in consequence, one parson does duty in three parishes, each of which once owned its vicar or rector. At the very period when this clay land was going out of cultivation and losing population, the fenland east of the Great North Road was growing both more populous and more productive.

The shire is not famous for its landscape beauty, but those who have their home there

see in its spinneys and farms and hamlets and hedges an epitome of rural England. The hunting man who followed the hounds over a favourite line of country from, say, Buckworth Wood to Salome Wood and thence to Hamerton Grove through Gidding Gorse to the big wood of Aversley, will ask for nothing better. There is nothing within the shire that suggests the urban. Even its capital, Huntingdon, is less like a town in many regards than a village, and its neighbour, Godmanchester, though not very much smaller, is village pure and simple. However, both towns, in spite of the village atmosphere, are the proud possessors of mayors and corporations, thanks to the antiquity of their histories.

### An Ancient Bridge

Incidentally, these two little townships are joined by a causeway across marshy ground and a fourteenth century bridge of exceptional beauty across the Ouse. Passage to-day, of course, is free, but the bridge was at one time financed by special tolls; and it is recorded under date 1279, that these included "on every Jew and Jewess crossing the bridge on horseback one penny, on foot one halfpenny." The first bridge was almost wholly destroyed and the greater part of the present bridge was built in 1332.

One of the sins of our time is a disregard of our rivers. The Ouse (a word which, like Usk, and Wye, means water) is not poisoned like the Lea, the chief river of Hertfordshire, but its general management as a navigable water-way, which once extended from Bedford to the sea, has been grievously mismanaged in recent times, chiefly by neglect of the locks in the neighbourhood of Godmanchester. It has at times flooded seriously, with the result that the whole of that glorious plain known as the Port Holme, has been under water. Those who have suffered from floods along the lower reaches where the slow stream has difficulty in reaching the sea at the Wash, have been in constant conflict with those responsible for the upper reaches. An admirable scheme (by which all neighbours of the river from Bedfordshire to Cambridge through Huntingdon would have bene-

Haymaking by the old mill at Houghton, between Huntingdon and St. Ives. Now in use as a Youth Hostel, Houghton Mill, with its timber framing, figures amongst the best known of the many buildings of historical interest in the county.

fited) was worked out and put forward by the famous engineer Rennie, but no wholescale reformation was then put into effect. Happily, the Ouse Drainage Board has since carried out extensive alterations and the floods are now properly controlled.

However, at all times the Ouse at Huntingdon has remained a waterway of singular beauty. Some of the reed beds are as dense as forests. They are much enjoyed as roosting places by thousands of swallows and starlings; and nowhere perhaps are the deep swinging nests of the reed-warblers found in such numbers. The waters abound in coarse fish, such as perch, bream, tench and pike; and there is no good reason why salmon should not run up from the sea. It is put on record in the registers of the church at the beautiful village of Hamerton, lying on a brook which has a nine-mile course before it reaches the Ouse, that after a famous flood "a salmon a yard and an inch long was found stranded in Farmer Newton's meadow." I have seen the same little brook flood the village street and invade a number of the thatched cottages; and it is recorded that "low fevers"

were at one time frequent and severe. Happily, a thorough cleaning of the bed not so long ago put an end both to the flooding and the fevers, and the brook is more conspicuous for its absence in any dry summer than for its excesses in winter.

### Historic Hinchingbrooke

It is written in a standard and popular life of Cromwell that Hinchingbrooke, the lovely and historic house just west of Huntingdon, is situate on the Ouse. It is not, but the rich gardens run down to this brook, which at that point has almost the dimensions of a river. The house, which is of great charm, was founded on the site of a nunnery. It was bought from Sir Oliver Cromwell by Sir Sydney Montagu, whose descendants, the Earls of Sandwich, have adorned it not only within by famous pictures, largely on naval subjects, and without by as beautiful gardens as you could wish to see, but have enlarged and added to the structure with great architectural taste. It was famous in both the world wars as a hospital. After the last war it was made over by George Charles Montagu, the ninth earl of Sandwich, to his eldest son, Viscount Hinchingbrooke.

Its one rival in architectural charm is a Norman doorway of the old grammar school at Huntingdon, where Pepys and Oliver Cromwell were educated. The discovery of this relic and its subsequent restoration are in pleasing contrast with many acts of iconoclasm in the neighbourhood. Of late one of the loveliest old mills in England, in Godmanchester on a branch of the Ouse where it approaches the old Ermine Street, was of necessity pulled down by local authorities. The mill, with the junction of the two divisions of the river, the island (joined to a beautiful house by a willow-pattern bridge) and the little, almost Venice-like, boathouses set a flourish on as charming a corner of river scenery as could be found in any county.

### Course of the Ouse

This little county is dominated by the Ouse, which enters it at St. Neots, called after a monk whose relics were stolen from Cornwall and placed in a priory in the little town. From the picturesque old water-mill, converted into a paper-making factory about 1807, the river, once the third biggest in England, flows in a broad, slow stream through twenty-five miles of the county and touches some of the loveliest villages in England, first by the mill and lock at Offord, then at Brampton, past Pepys' farm. After ten miles it reaches first Godmanchester and then Huntingdon. The scene from the Huntingdon bridge drew almost ecstatic admiration from William Cobbett; and his tribute is still well deserved.

### Cobbett's Tribute

"The valleys terminate at the foot of rising ground, well set with trees, from which church spires raise their heads here and there. I think it would be very difficult to find a more delightful spot than this in the world. To my fancy (and everyone has his taste) the prospect from this bridge far surpasses that from Richmond Hill."

Houghton Mill, some three miles farther down-stream (now a youth hostel) is perhaps the best-known mill in England, and the village itself is one of the prettiest in the whole county. Two miles farther on past a lock and mill are twin villages, a mile and a half apart, which county patriots, not without good argument, claim to be among the loveliest in England.

Rising above the willow-pattern bridge at Godmanchester is the spire of St. Mary's church, one of the finest Gothic churches in the county. This corner of the town, with its placid waterways, old buildings and boathouses is in many respects reminiscent of Venice.

Certainly both Hemingford Grey and Hemingford Abbots, with the river, the churches and Elizabethan cottages and houses, may compete even with Finchingfield or Ewelme. The Norman manor house at Hemingford Grey is the oldest inhabited house in England.

At the seventeenth mile from St. Neots the river flows under a bridge that is very nearly unique, by reason of the old chapel still standing on its middle. The views, though lovely, are not to all tastes. It is written in a life of Laurence Sterne, who had his first curacy at St. Ives: "Thanks to the torpid influence of that Midland landscape, where church bell answers church bell across miles of fen, and the damp plain stretches unbroken as far as the towers of Ely humped against a glimmering sky ... the atmosphere of Sterne's charge was, doubtless, doubly soporific."

There is less interest in the next few miles, till the boundary of the shire is reached at Bluntisham and Earith, which have inspired both a remarkable book on local folk-lore (*Bluntisham-cum-Earith. Records of a Fen Parish*) and an account of birds in a rectory garden by E. A. Peake, once a well-known Oxford cricketer. Until the railway era, the two villages were important as a junction of two branches of the river, where was the first high ground, so described, reached by vessels in their passage upstream. To-day their wealth comes not from barge traffic but from their orchards. After it leaves its favourite county, the Ouse becomes a medley of canals that have altered its character and abbreviated its length.

### County Names

Many Huntingdonshire names are of particular interest. Thus it is written of the county: "It is remarkable that so small an area in the Midlands should include four such ancient names as Gidding, Yelling, Lymage and Wintringham suggesting that the original settlers were Angles." As to Earith: "We must have here and in Frith (Kent) a compound of Old English 'ear' and 'hyth' meaning perhaps 'muddy landing place'."

One other river, though smaller, less lovely and much less important, has great historic interest. The Nene flows reluctantly along the northern boundary of the county to much the same bourne as the Ouse and meets similar difficulties. It was famous for the monasteries on its banks, and these were the chief nurseries of the form of English that has survived and conquered in the making of our modern tongue.

The river Nene has become a household word among naturalists, partly because of the genius of Lord Lilford, who rivalled the Dukes of Bedford in his zeal for natural history and naturalization, and, more especially, for aviculture. Lilford, just over the county border, was one of the places where the little owl was naturalized and the species still flourishes excessively throughout the shire, as the grey squirrel does in Bedford and Hertford.

### Skating on the Fens

Huntingdon is a shire of little towns and little villages. To this generalization the only exception is its slender northern tip, where three counties join and where also a west-to-east Midland line crosses the North Eastern. Just south of this peak are to be found the best doorways into the fen country, especially in times of a bearing frost. (Now a bearing frost is a commoner experience in the fen region than anywhere in England, till the far north is reached.) One of these doorways is at Conington Castle, so-called, a castellated country house, successor of a medieval manor which stood about half a mile to the south. The house has been in possession of the family of Heathcote for two hundred years and more. One of them wrote and illustrated for private circulation a book on the fens in 1876 and reported a particular trip on the ice. He and his companions put on skates a quarter of a mile from the house and skated on and on till they reached the neighbourhood of Ely Cathedral, delighting in the exercise and the scene. "The scenery of the Fen rivers at all times beautiful, in the eyes of those who appreciate Dutch art, is peculiarly so in the winter. The mills, of various form and colour, are conspicuously placed on the banks. ... Boats, eel-trunks frozen up in the ice, slackers all closed up

Two miles beyond Houghton Mill stand the twin villages of Hemingford Abbots and Hemingford Grey. The latter, seen here, is claimed by many to rival in charm Finchingfield in Essex.

and useless, little gunning boats with their sprits lying on the bank, stacks of reed beside the river, groups of figures skating, some drawing sledges loaded with sedge—all these are objects of beauty and interest." I myself have made a similar expedition, which may still be undertaken by anyone with the requisite stamina and skill. We put on our skates a hundred yards from Holme station on the North Eastern Railway by the side of a dyke, and the freedom of the fens was open to us. Our roadways were two dykes known as the "Forty-foot" or the "Sixteen foot" and the old Nene, and we covered some thirty miles before returning to our starting point.

### Fifty-Mile Journey

A certain official of the Bedford Level Corporation gave a fascinating account of a fifty-mile journey in 1799. Ramsey offers another starting point and much archaeological interest. The demesnes of the Abbey ("where every monk lived like a gentleman") were granted to Sir Thomas Cromwell, and Sir Oliver lived there after leaving Hinchingbrooke.

Whittlesea Mere, which is near by, was the scene of the most dramatic and historically interesting event in English reclamation. I have spoken with those who saw the last drop of water flow away, when muddy acres were left entirely covered with fish, pike up to 20 lb. and perch to 6 lb. with hosts of other coarse fish. The making of the dyke and lodes there and thereabouts opened up pages of prehistoric history. The remnants of vast trees, oak and others, prove that the land was once a dry forest; but the bog oak was less interesting than the bones. Among these were identified the hippopotamus, rhinoceros, elephant, aboriginal cattle, deer of several species, wolf, beaver and, finally, under Whittlesea Mere itself, a grampus. A long, primeval boat scooped out of the trunk of an oak, was one of the treasures of Whittlesea. These draining operations have interest for the layman as well as for the archaelogist. Ramsey Abbey was enriched by the game and the fantastic number of eels (in which commodity rents were often paid). Now the whole district is rich in grain and sugar-beet; and many a labouring fenman has achieved independence and a certain degree of wealth. It should be put down to the enhancement of their fame, that fenmen on their pattens played bandy or shinny generations before the world learnt that ice hockey is one of the best of games.

The welfare of both farmers and labourers in the fertile eastern plain, stands, I fear, in sharp contrast to that of the men who live on the undulating clay-lands on the western side. Most of the farms there, too, are fertile, but they need hard continuous labour and mechanical aids. This necessity handicaps the small holder, and in many parishes, the cottages, though most picturesquely thatched, are very humble. However, labourers here and there rise to be small farmers, even on the toughest soil, as in the neighbourhood of Leighton (a living once given to George Herbert, who restored the fine church). Not too long ago to be remembered, you could see women sitting outside the cottage doors, with stout pillows on their knees, working hard at lace-making. Money earned in this excellent village industry, as straw-plaiting in Hertfordshire, formed the foundations of the labourer's capital. In few districts has the population consisted so exclusively of farmer, labourer and parson as in this one, for country houses are widely separated and industries hardly to be found. Even the little towns are few: Huntingdon, with Godmanchester, St. Neots, St. Ives, Ramsey and Kimbolton virtually complete the list, and their total population does not approach forty thousand.

### Few Historic Remains

While the fens have revealed vast treasures of very ancient history, the signs of more recent history about the county are, if the fine churches are excepted, curiously few. Even the rule of the monks from Ramsey and Sawtry and Hinchingbrooke has left few architectural relics. Even Castle Hill by the bridge between Huntingdon and Godmanchester carries no evidence of the fact

**The gateway of Ramsey Abbey is practically all that remains of the Benedictine monastery founded by Aylwyn in the year 969. It is a notable example of Perpendicular work.**

that the castle was destroyed in Norman times, and neither Dane nor Roman has left much evidence of their occupation of this key point in both attack and defence.

One libel upon the county that has appeared in several books of reference should be refuted. It is described as comparatively treeless. There is small excuse for this charge. The woods are peculiarly beautiful from Barnwell Wold to Monks Wood (a great haunt of entomologists as well as hunting folk); and trees are well distributed in hosts of spinneys and hedgerows. Nowhere perhaps does Milton's famous line:

Bosomed high in tufted trees

more insistently come to the mind's eye, as you look down from the tops of the pleasant undulations, on to the great towers and spires of the village churches.

### Land of Fine Churches

The churches and the surrounding trees, chiefly elms, are scarcely to be separated; and the churches are supreme. It has been written in a standard book on churches: "It is not too much to say that Huntingdon and Rutland, the two smallest counties in England, have the highest proportion of fine churches." The number of so-called broach spires is great. Spaldwick, Conington, Alconbury, Warboys and St. Neots and Buckden have special features. From the promi-

nence of the churches it has perhaps resulted that the clergy have done much for local annals. Cuthbert Bede, the pen name of a curate of Glatton, is known wherever students of folklore foregather, and he recorded local customs, superstitions, ceremonies and words at a crucial date. Most are disappearing or have disappeared, but you would still fail to persuade a surprisingly large number of farmers that pork and bacon would not suffer if the pig was killed at the waning moon.

### Wartime Scars

The county in general advances in prosperity and is remarkably free from defacement; but its landscape will take a long time to recover from the war. Owing to the flatness of the land, the smallness of the population, and in some degree to its central situation, it was selected as ideal for the airmen. No fewer than ten large aerodromes were built, and of all forms of building, concrete roads and foundations are the most tiresome to destroy and the least useful in peace time; and the Americans used it lavishly. Some of these wartime additions are likely to last only less long than the ridge and furrow so deeply patterned on hundreds of grass fields. Grass-covered earth may yet prove more enduring than stone.

*The Ouse at Hemingford Grey*

*Bridge of Sighs, Cambridge*

# CAMBRIDGESHIRE

By R. H. MOTTRAM

THOSE who, very properly, seek to know from the reports of the Land Utilization Survey how Cambridgeshire lives, will be confronted, in the one dealing with Cambridgeshire proper (that is, excluding the Isle of Ely) with Rupert Brooke's verse, which must be quoted:

God! I will pack, and take a train,
And get me to England once again!
For England's the one land, I know,
Where men with Splendid Hearts may go.
And Cambridgeshire, of all England,
The shire for Men who Understand.''

This is a good beginning, for, truth to tell, the county in question is by no means among the larger or more populous of all England, and is further reduced by its division into two jurisdictions, Cambridgeshire and the Isle of Ely, and still further by the fact that, perhaps partly from ancient sentiment, and partly from the nature of its soil, the centres of population on which its villages depend are nearly all just outside its

*Arms of Cambridgeshire*

boundaries. When you still further deduct the adventitious presence of a university which has nothing to do with the character of the soil, and is a possession of the English-speaking world and a good deal beyond that, it is remarkable that Cambridgeshire should have as much distinctive character as it has, and none could possibly grudge Rupert Brooke's generous tribute to the rather accidentally chosen site in which he spent his happy undergraduate days. In fact, the danger is, that any easy-going inquirer will find out a lot about King's College Chapel and Grantchester and Ely Cathedral, and other international, literary and archæological matters, and miss the real Cambridgeshire altogether.

Let us begin, therefore, with the ordinary school atlas. The double county you will find there depicted is a shire of England, in all some forty-five miles from north to south, just missing the Wash, on the shores of which Lincolnshire and Norfolk meet, and just losing

205

# HUNTINGDONSHIRE & CAMBRIDGESHIRE

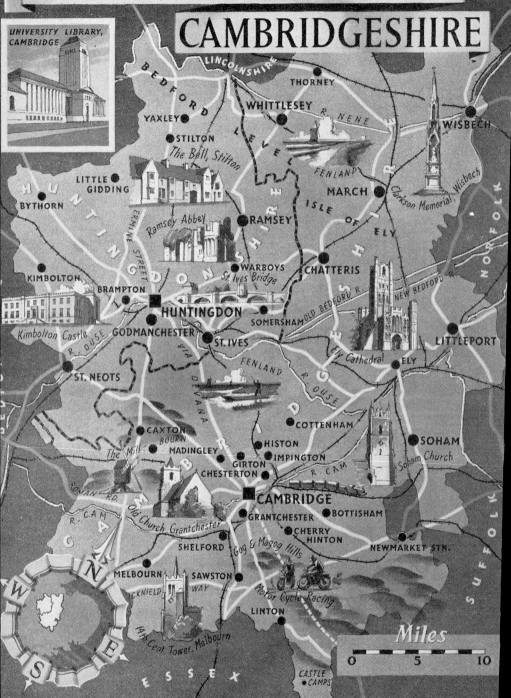

UNIVERSITY LIBRARY, CAMBRIDGE

BEDFORD LEVEL

LINCOLNSHIRE

THORNEY

WHITTLESEY

YAXLEY

R. NENE

WISBECH

STILTON

The Bell, Stilton

FENLAND

MARCH

Clarkson Memorial, Wisbech

LITTLE GIDDING

BYTHORN

ISLE OF ELY

Ramsey Abbey

RAMSEY

ERMINE STREET

WARBOYS

CHATTERIS

St Ives Bridge

KIMBOLTON

BRAMPTON

HUNTINGDON

NEW BEDFORD R.

OLD BEDFORD R.

NORFOLK

Kimbolton Castle

R. OUSE

GODMANCHESTER

ST. IVES

SOMERSHAM

Ely Cathedral

ELY

LITTLEPORT

ST. NEOTS

FENLAND

VIA DEVANA

R. OUSE

COTTENHAM

SOHAM

CAXTON

BOURN

The Mill

MADINGLEY

HISTON

IMPINGTON

Soham Church

GIRTON

CHESTERTON

ROMAN RD.

Old Church Grantchester

CAMBRIDGE

R. CAM

GRANTCHESTER

BOTTISHAM

R. CAM

CHERRY HINTON

SHELFORD

Gog & Magog Hills

NEWMARKET STN.

MELBOURN

SAWSTON

ICKNIELD WAY

Motor Cycle Racing

SUFFOLK

W N E S

14th Cent. Tower, Melbourn

LINTON

Miles

0    5    10

ESSEX

CASTLE CAMPS

206

Royston, at the southern extremity, to Hertfordshire. It is some twenty-five miles broad at its widest, from Newmarket Heath (the town is in Suffolk, but not the railway station) to just outside St. Neots, which is in Huntingdonshire. It is, therefore, very roughly, oblong. It is cut into two fairly equal parts by the course of the Great Ouse through Ely, which is a kind of minor capital of the northern half. The area of the whole is just over half a million acres (half the size of Norfolk) three hundred and thirteen thousand three hundred and ninety-two acres in the Cambridge part and two hundred and thirty-nine thousand nine hundred and fifty in the Ely part. The countryside is entirely agricultural. In the Cambridge area you can see some signs of cement works, but ninety per cent. of the land is under crops and grass. In the Ely part the proportion of agricultural land is lower, there are sixty thousand acres of wild fen, and immense artificial water-ways. We had better establish here and now the little-known fact that this, north Cambridgeshire, legally known as the Isle of Ely since the Norman Conquest, is the real fen. Cambridgeshire, where this Fen country really is, is a deeply interior part of England, with a belt fifty miles broad separating it from the North Sea. Norfolk and Suffolk have little part of it, and that only for administrative convenience. The Isle of Ely merges insensibly into southern Lincolnshire, the appearance, cultivation and climate of which it shares.

### Prehistoric Marsh

The Isle of Ely is quite unmistakable to anyone who has to cross it by road or rail. It is prehistoric marsh, which has been embanked and drained on various occasions dating from Roman times; a more vigorous effort was made under expert Dutch supervision in the seventeenth century, and later still—in the later nineteenth century. Wentworth Day (whose family has owned land in the district for centuries and whose essay on Lincolnshire appears later in this book), described in his *Farming Adventure* how his

*Arms of Isle of Ely*

mother, visiting cottages in what were even then inaccessible fastnesses, found conditions that might have seemed more natural in Asiatic Russia. It is maintained, as you see it, by power pumps and constant vigilance and expense.

### Ely's Prosperity

To-day the appearance, save for Ely Cathedral, Thorney Abbey and a few old-fashioned houses, is entirely modern and extremely prosperous. The farms and houses scattered along the immense artificial drains (the Bedford River is so long and straight that it is one of the stock means of demonstrating the roundness of the earth's surface) are all new. The population clusters in little Ely, perfect example of a cathedral town, which has more cathedral than town, and in the "islands" of Thorney, Whittlesey, March, Chatteris, Littleport, to which Wisbech and Soham really belong by nature, trade, appearance and communication. Only March and Wisbech exceed the ten thousand population mark. But I should say that the general level of prosperity, both for its wide distribution and lack of fluctuation, is easily the highest in all England, the Boston division of Lincolnshire excepted. Many fields are under highly specialized crops which run a great risk for the sake of great profits, as the climate is markedly Continental, being entirely different from that of East Anglia, only twenty miles away. The cold can be so extreme that the more celebrated skating events take place on the regulated waters of the drains, and very late and heavy frosts are always possible. But the general economy appears well able to stand up to it, and has completely forgotten and outgrown the loss of the ancient inland navigation that used to serve six counties. The district is not easy to describe; it is not spectacular. The best way to get an idea of it is to stop for a few hours in Wisbech, and look at the majestic range of merchant houses lining the Brinks, or in little Chatteris to observe the traffic. Or again, survey it all on a map which marks its mighty embankments as "twelve-foot drain," "sixteen-foot river," "Parson's Eau," and so on.

Plainly, such a place was once fever-haunted swamp, and I have heard the late W. G. Clarke describe how the great floods of 1849 drowned the vipers, of which many could be seen, he had been told, hanging in trees into which they had contrived to climb. To-day drinking water is still a matter for careful thought. I heard long and anxious discussions in 1940 as to the possible result of the water tower near March being hit by a German bomb.

The next most important industry is the railway. There are approximately one hundred and eighty-five miles of the L.N.E.R. in Cambridgeshire and the Isle of Ely, these being served by forty-three stations. The two marshalling yards at Whitemoor are amongst the biggest in this country.

The area administered from Cambridge lies south of that town and of the roads from it to Huntingdon and to Newmarket. It has much in common with the neighbouring parishes that happen to be in Hertfordshire or Bedford and nothing whatever in common with the Isle of Ely, or indeed with the basin of the Cam north of Cambridge. Anywhere around Melbourn and Linton you find farms of about two hundred acres, two-thirds under plough. The labourers live in picturesque thatched and plaster-faced or brick cottages, and intelligent preservation has done much, as might be expected in the orbit of university influence, to make agriculture look its best. Above all, the people of the region have the advantage of quite exceptional educational and cultural facilities in the Village Colleges.

This remarkable group of institutions, first mooted in 1925, was finally launched in 1930 when Sawston village school (seven miles south-east of Cambridge), rebuilt to form a college, was formally opened. The money needed was raised from many sources, largely voluntary. The original venture gave facilities for nine neighbouring villages, but since then several other village colleges have been opened, chiefly those at Bottisham, Linton, and Impington.

The curricula are both interesting and varied, ranging from craftsmen guild's work to lectures on current affairs. Recreational and sports facilities are extensive and, under the ægis of various societies connected with the colleges, visits are regularly paid by students to centres of occupational interest and educational value, such as cattle breeding stations and model farms.

A library, common room and games room are features of each college, which is controlled by a warden, supported by a

**Thatch and tile for roofing, plaster-faced and half-timbered walls contribute to the variety of building styles found in East Anglia. This Cambridgeshire village, Great Abington, is a typical example.**

**Many of the Colleges of Cambridge University back on to the Cam and the stretch of the river alongside their lawns is therefore named the "Backs." Here is seen Clare College, founded in 1326.**

freely elected council of the students. This sends a representative to the board of managers convened by the county authority. Nothing is given free, but costs are kept within the compass of the wage-earner's pocket. Sometimes premises have to be hired, but the only paid staff consists of the warden, adult organizer and caretaker. Much of the effort is voluntary, a rota of seventy women helping at Impington canteen, for instance. Linton has an organized bus service and celebrity concerts; transport for villages lying at some distance is general, and averages over forty persons per night. Such is part of the background of Young Cambridgeshire in the post-war era. Will it keep them on the land?

Westward, along the Bedfordshire border, the characteristic chalky soil is replaced by a much stiffer boulder clay, which presents many additional difficulties to the farmer and renders cultivation expensive and arduous. There is also a portion of similar distinctive soil in the extreme south-east of the county.

The typical Cambridgeshire countryman is a farmer or farm labourer, working on the normal type of mixed farm averaging about two hundred acres, cropped until the First World War on the Norfolk four-course system or variations of it. Even at that date a considerable progressive modification could be observed by the traveller moving north from, say, Melbourn. As soon as he passed Cambridge town he found himself descending from the chalky ridges, of which Gog Hill forms the best known, to flat alluvial marsh. As he progressed he found himself in an increasingly artificial landscape, where many of the fields were below the level of the water in the great dykes that are far more numerous than roads or railways. Farms were isolated, and built mainly on the "islands," those relics of the time when all this fertile land was swamp more impassable than the remote Highlands, joined by causeways running between deep wet ditches.

It is difficult to estimate how far the average farm worker drew any comfort from the loveliness of the towers of Ely Cathedral. One has the impression that the worker in this district was far worse off, less independent and able to stand up for him-

209

self than his brother in Norfolk. How far this rose from lack of the strong Scandinavian strain found in the districts nearer the coast, how far it resulted from the translation of marshmen living on the margin of civilization into farm workers, it would be hard to trace. It seems to the writer that a great change has taken place well within the last fifty years which has raised decisively the status of Cambridgeshire agricultural labour. This change, of course, is not peculiar to Cambridgeshire alone.

### Modern Agricultural Methods

All modern mechanical means have been in his favour. The intensive cultivation of relatively small holdings in the Isle of Ely and as far south as Soham, could only be made profitable with highly modern means of communication. As swift road haulage has been increasingly provided it must have a lot to do with the prosperity which is obvious here. Perhaps it only began in the mid-nineteenth century with the increasing demands for better food from swollen town populations. But it has certainly been advanced by the ultra-modern establishments of the great jam-producing firm at Histon, north of Cambridge, and the sugar-beet factory at Ely. This, however, does not explain Wisbech, which must be one of the richest places, for its size, in the kingdom. Nor, indeed, does any modern mechanical advance explain the presence of three ancient cathedrals—Ely, Peterboro' and Lincoln—all on the shores of the same fen, and the fact that Ely is one of the richer bishoprics. We are left with the fact that such places sheltered the arts of peace, and commanded the only means of transport for centuries. Wisbech has a castle, but the chief reason for its importance was the fact that it gave access to sea-going craft.

### Reclaiming the Fen

The great advance in drainage of the fen seems to have been made in the early half of the nineteenth century. A survey was made by Vancouver in 1794 and another made for the Royal Agricultural Society in 1846. From comparison of these two emerges the significant fact that, while in the portions of the county of older cultivation the progress of enclosure has not been unlike that of neighbouring counties, all the newly won land was enclosed as soon as it was drained.

We may, I think, take a reasonably bright view of the future of the agricultural worker in Cambridgeshire. All modern developments, any move towards greater facility of transport, or finance, every regulation of the townsman's diet, will help to improve the position of agricultural labour. Even the pockets of heavy and heartbreaking clay in the south-east and south-west of the county could be brought into useful cultivation by organized public effort. The seriousness of the food situation will almost certainly call this effort into being.

But what does the other half of the Cambridgeshire population do, which is not concerned with any sort of agriculture? The answer is that the two main industries of the chief town are the railway, already noted, and the university. It is no business of this chapter to trace the history of one of the most ancient and honourable seats of learning, but only to describe one of the means by which many of the inhabitants of the place in which at least half the people who live in Cambridgeshire proper, earn their living. Even those who do not, cannot go far from their doors, whatever their occupation, without being aware of such an institution in their midst.

### The University

It is best to approach the matter in this way, and to get rid at the outset of the idea that Cambridge owes its origin to the university. Trevelyan, who should know, states that the first colleges, or the nucleus of them, "inns," "halls," groups of scholars following some teacher with no discipline and small resources, came to Cambridge from Oxford, where they had just grown into recognizable units, as a "result of town and gown feuds of a more murderous kind than usual." The choice of Cambridge resulted from its being " a meeting-place of waterways and Roman Roads convenient for the North and East of England . . . just over fifty miles from London, which has no University." (Roman Roads were the only metalled roads outside towns until Stuart times) ". . . the first Colleges were started

St. John's College was founded in 1511 by Lady Margaret, Countess of Richmond and Derby, and mother of Henry VII. It succeeded the hospital of St. John which dated from 1135.

"Happy Knight" winning the 1946 race for the Two Thousand Guineas on the famous Newmarket Course. The racecourse itself falls just inside Cambridgeshire though the town of Newmarket is in Suffolk. Other classic races run here include the Cambridgeshire and the Cesarewitch.

... (Balliol, Oxford 1261, Peterhouse, Cambridge 1284, that is all the "seniority" Oxford enjoys) ... to provide food and maintenance for scholars." Paris and Padua also had many colleges "which have since disappeared with very few exceptions. .... But they never attained to the size, wealth and importance eventually reached by corresponding institutions in England ... until in Stuart times they devoured their mother the University."

The town to which the refugees from Oxford came was already a very considerable market, with its great Statutory Fair known as the Stourbridge Fair, which was held just outside its eastern gate. The nucleus of the town lay round about Magdalene Bridge, with the castle on the high land just to the west, and the Templars' circular church a few yards to the east.

Since the object of this account is not archæology, but chiefly explanation of the daily life of the man or woman who lives in this town of Cambridge, it is pertinent to ask, as would any intelligent inquirer:

"Why on earth is the nucleus of a fairly important provincial centre, a market town, (which, you tell us, has almost accidentally had this venerable university planted upon it five and a half centuries ago) at an extraordinary corner like this, where two in-

tolerably narrow main streets meet at an acute angle, one to the other, before a ridiculously narrow bridge?"

This, after all, is an everyday matter to Cambridge, and it illustrates a fact about the citizen that you cannot ignore. You may land from the most modern aircraft at the airfield on the Newmarket Road and be driven by high-speed car to the Senate House, or University Library, or some working modern establishment of a progressive university of world-wide fame, but your direct route lies round that awkward corner. Why? Because the easternmost of the two streets that form it is the Roman Road from Colchester to Chester. To-day it is called progressively Bridge Street, Sidney Street, and St. Andrew Street as it stretches south. The other, long the High Street of the medieval town, to-day St. John Street, Trinity Street, King's Parade, Trumpington Street, is the way to London by road. That is how the early trading and inland water centre of Cambridge (the bridge over the Cam, to-day Magdalene Bridge) happened to grow up, along a Roman Road, beneath a Saxon or Danish Castle on a mound just to the west of it (and to-day the county administration is still carried on there). If you are from overseas you may well say:

212

"How ridiculous. It would pay them a thousand times over to pull down St. John's College, and this old church of the Templars, double the bridge, and get some space to turn round in!"

Just so. When you have mastered the fact that no sum of money, no other prospect you could hold out, will induce the people of Cambridge to do as you so wisely instruct them, you will have begun to grasp the cardinal fact about the life of the average citizen of Cambridge. He has got something you cannot buy.

The thing he has got, and which began to take noticeable shape, so far as anyone can now tell, about 1380, transformed the then trading and transport town into the university town. The university did not become an effective corporate body until much later, indeed it only gradually became "present" at all. To-day it consists of seventeen Colleges, very loosely and tolerantly banded together with ample autonomy within the organization of the whole. Twelve of them lie along the ancient High Street (or Trumpington Street, King's Parade, Trinity Street, St. John's Street) and the River Cam. Only one of the twelve, Magdalene, stands on the left or west bank of the river, and two, Corpus Christi and Pembroke, to the east of the street. The others occupy, with their spacious and lovely courts and buildings, best seen from the "Backs" or back entrances on that same west bank (the choice prospect of which has been so desecrated by military camps and car parks during this latest war), the space which the older trading town used to fill. You can trace some of the old streets running from the market-place on what they call a "Hill" in Cambridge (meaning that it is not liable to floods), in Silver Street and the various lanes between the colleges.

Five more colleges are to be found along or beyond the other main street from Magdalene Bridge. Seven of the lot have dedications similar to colleges in Oxford. Otherwise they exhibit most of the utter variety and individuality with which they were dowered at their inception. The titles by which their heads are called, their numbers of students, their private non-state-provided funds, their specialities, if we may use such a word, all vary as much as anyone could contrive if he tried. Beyond their appearance, dominating the main streets and

This busy shipping scene at Wisbech shows that Cambridgeshire is not all colleges and crops. Wisbech is a flourishing town in the Isle of Ely with a large fruit-canning trade. The river Nene, on which the town stands, is connected with the central waterways of England by a canal system.

Looking east from The Gallery towards Ely Cathedral. The cathedral, begun in 1083, took over three hundred years to complete. Many styles of architecture are incorporated in the building.

214

*Great North Road at Stamford*

# LINCOLNSHIRE

By J. WENTWORTH DAY

LINCOLNSHIRE, that broad, bright land, which lies seventy-five miles long by forty-five miles wide, between the Humber and the Wash, its face to the bitter North Sea, its back to the mosses of Yorkshire and the wide fields of Nottinghamshire, Leicester and Rutland, is no place for weaklings in stature or for bad farmers. It has something of the bleak independence of Norfolk but more of the harsher, more northerly, characteristics of Yorkshire. It is half-way house between East Anglia and the north. And it stands as a buffer between the North Sea, whence came the Vikings and the Danish raiders, and the warmer, wetter Midlands.

So you have a county blended of the characteristics of north and east, but with little of the damp, dull Midlands to temper the edge of its North Sea individuality.

Eastern England has always stood with its face bold to the invader. When Harold fell at Senlac it was a man of Lincolnshire, Hereward the Wake, the Saxon lord

*Lincolnshire: Lindsey Arms*

of Brunne, which to-day is Bourne, who held out last and longest among the shining meres and reedy fens.

And when the king is crowned in London, one man alone in all the Empire, Dymoke of Scrivelsby, a Lincolnshire squire, has the right to ride into Westminster Hall on a charger, clad in a full suit of shining armour, and there cast down his clanging gauntlet upon the stone floor, and challenge any baron or knight in Christendom to mortal combat in defence of the King of England's right to his throne and crown. That Lincolnshire squire is, by right of ancestry, the King's Champion.

Thus Lincolnshire may write her claim to have bred the last defender of Saxon England and the present defender of the Queen's Majesty. On a gentler scroll she may write the names of Tennyson and John Wesley, of Cecil, the great Elizabethan "Lord of Burleigh," and Daniel Lambert who, since he weighed fifty-two stone eleven

217

pounds, was, I should guess, the fattest man of all time, and a hundred more of equal or lesser fame.

In the three divisions of Lindsey, Holland and Kesteven which form this, the second largest county in England, are represented most of the elements which make the natural wealth and beauty of England—farming, the best in the country; fishing, with the largest fishing port in Britain; iron and steel; manufacturing; forestry; sheep and the wool trade; innumerable country market towns and two famous horse fairs at Lincoln and Horncastle; watering-places, abbeys, castles, great mansions, Roman roads and ancient cities; great airfields; vast areas of reclaimed land with, to round off the picture, the Great North Road running across the southwest of the county like a skein of romance.

### Agricultural Eminence

It is a picture bold in scope, broad in outline, compounded of all things English, both old and new, nurtured in tradition and strong in modern endeavour.

Of its agriculture it may fairly be said that few counties equal Lincolnshire in up-to-date methods, large-scale units and output per acre, whilst none surpasses it. In potatoes, sugar-beet and bulbs it is pre-eminent.

Hand in hand with agriculture goes sea-fishing, and here, at Grimsby, the biggest fishing port in the country, are deep sea trawling fleets which cover the seas from the Dogger to the Barents Sea, from Iceland to Bear Island.

The development, in our lifetime, of the great iron and steel area round Scunthorpe has transformed that one-time sleepy little country town into a teeming industrial centre; whilst at Lincoln, Grantham, Louth, Gainsborough and Boston—that once silted-up port with a long and honourable record of seafaring history—are great factories which turn out agricultural machinery locomotives, pumping plants, steam rollers, motor-car parts, excavators and dredgers, pit winding gear, down to such lighter products as film studio fittings, farm fertilisers and ticket punches.

Many changes have taken place in the Lincolnshire scene in the last hundred years.

Grimsby, for example, was a small fishing port, a mere marshland village in 1847. To-day it has a population of ninety-seven thousand, one hundred and forty-one and a half acres of docks, a fleet of five hundred steam fishing vessels; an airport of one hundred and fifty-four acres, and an average annual landing of over two hundred thousand tons of fish.

Scunthorpe, which was a village forty years ago, is now a town of fifty thousand people.

These two examples of the change in the face of the land are completely dwarfed by the astounding change in the Lincolnshire fens where hundreds of thousands of acres of once impassable swamp and mere have, in little more than a century, been transformed into some of the richest and most highly farmed land in the world. Of that more in its place.

Lincolnshire is a county of three facets—the marsh, the wolds and the fen. Each is distinctive, each so dissimilar, that any one of the three districts might well belong to other counties. The marsh and the fen are both flat lands reclaimed from water—the first from the sea, the fen from fresh-water bogs. There the similarity ends. They produce different crops and their people gaze on different landscapes, live different lives.

But though the Lincolnshire scene may change, Lincolnshire people are much the same throughout the county. They speak the same slightly harsh, almost north country, tongue, share the same sardonic sense of humour, the same facility for making money—I have met no Lincolnshire farmer yet who is a poor man—and the same commercial realism.

### Character of the People

The characteristics of the Lincolnshire people are, in fine, like the characteristics of their county—uncompromising, dour in parts, ugly in patches, downright, and of a thorough-going English independence.

There is little that is soft about them, least of all about their women. The Lincolnshire mother would rather clout her offspring on the ear than kiss it! They believe in work and making money. Their humour is unsparing but seldom subtle. There is a take-it-or-

**Ploughing by tractor at Spalding. Lincolnshire farming is highly mechanised.**

# LINCOLNSHIRE

YORKSHIRE

RIVER HUMBER

NORTH

N
W E
S

Iron Ore Mines

BARTON UPON HUMBER

IMMINGHAM

New ANCHOLME

R. ANCHOLME

SCUNTHORPE

ISLE OF AXHOLME

R. TRENT

BRIGG

CAISTOR

GRIMSBY

CLEETHORPES

Donna Nook

GAINSBOROUGH

STREET

MARKET RASEN

THE WOLDS

The Mill Saltfleet

SALTFLEET

LOUTH

MABLETH

SUTTON ON S

R. BAIN

SOMERSBY

HORNCASTLE

Holiday Camp

Tennyson's Birthplace

The Old Hall, Gainsborough

LINCOLN

The Jews House, Lincoln

ERMINE STREET

R.A.F. Staff College

WOODHALL SPA

R. WITHAM

TATTERSHALL

SKEGNE

WAINFLEET

"The Angel," Grantham

at Cranwell

SLEAFORD

HECKINGTON

Tattershall Castle

BOSTON

THE WASH

King John lost the Crown

Boston Stump

R. GLEN

THE FENS

GRANTHAM

Isaac Newton at Woolsthorpe Manor

Bourne Abbey Church

BOURNE

St. Leonard's Priory

HOLLAND

SPALDING

R. WELLAND

NORFO

LINCOLN CATHEDRAL

Stamford

STAMFORD

CROWLAND

Crowland Bridge

Miles
0    5    10

LEICESTERSHIRE

NORTHAMPTONSHIRE

leave-it spirit of local pride, a box-your-ears defiance of people from other parts and a knock-down rivalry between town and town, village and village. All this was unkindly put in that old verse which some forgotten Lincoln versifier wrote of Boston:

Boston, Boston, Boston!
Thou hast nought to boast on
But a grand sluice and a high steeple
And a proud, conceited, ignorant people,
And a coast which souls get lost on.

In the cities and towns of Lincoln, Grantham, Gainsborough, Scunthorpe, Boston and Grimsby are such diverse industries as shipbuilding, engineering, blast furnaces, sugar-beet factories, seed-crushing mills, machinery workshops, breweries, maltings and brick-works. Some are among the first in the country in their own spheres.

But in the main, Lincolnshire is agricultural. Indeed, it claims to be the richest farming county in England.

Let us consider, then, the first facet of the rural scene—the marsh, that flat, rich, cattle-grazing belt of country, seven or eight miles wide, which fringes the coast from the Humber to the Wash. It is a sea-brisk country, protected from the ocean by marching ramparts of tawny sandhills, whose hairy crests are crowned with wiry marram grass, sea-holly and orange-berried buckthorn. Beyond them stretch miles upon miles of some of the most magnificent sands in England. This wide, wild and lonely sea-coast country which lies beneath "the wide-winged sunsets of the misty Marsh," is a land of wild geese and wheeling gulls; of terns, flashing in the summer tides; of grey, haunting clouds of curlew in the autumn mists; and of droves of seals who lie out on the sandbanks like huge slugs.

Inside the sea-walls the marsh itself is some of the richest grazing land in England, comparable to that pocket of agricultural gold, the warp-lands of Watchet in Somerset, or that ten thousand acre prairie of cattle marshes which lies between Acle and Great Yarmouth in Norfolk. You can feed cattle on the Lincolnshire Marsh country and fatten them for market on little else, so rich is the land, so fine the flush of the grass.

It has a touch of Holland, a sense of the flat polders, this long land which lies by the sea, dappled with black-and-white Friesian cattle and slow-moving Lincoln Reds.

Inland, the wolds, the second facet of the Lincolnshire scene, run in two great spines of upland from north to south. Huge fields are crowned by umber coloured clouds of massed woodlands. Old grey villages crouch in their hollows. Grey stone manor houses guard village greens where geese waddle by quick-running becks—for here the breath of the north country is felt and the brook becomes a beck, in spite of Tennyson's "brook." And from the crests of the wolds, rising to five hundred feet, you may look down to the long green belt of the marsh with its rim of blue sea and yellow sand, or standing on the marsh itself, alone with the cattle and the hares, with the herons fishing in the dykes, realize that besides her money-making industries Lincolnshire has a wealth of beauty all her own.

### "Pure Agricultural Gold"

The third facet of the Lincolnshire scene is the fen. To-day it is a vast prairie of the richest land in England, pure agricultural gold, the land of corn and potatoes, and of acres of brilliant bulbs.

The motorist who drives along its arrow-straight roads, by dyke-bordered, well-tilled fields and neat modern farmhouses, set amid all the evidence of a highly farmed countryside, and who is told that farmland there is worth from £100 to £300 an acre, should remember that the fen to-day is an utterly different countryside from the fen of a hundred or more years ago. The fenman of 1850 would not recognize his native fen to-day.

For all this land was once steaming bogs and shining meres, mile on mile of rustling reed beds and long snaky channels of water. The wildfowl rose on a thunder of wings and yellow-faced men walked on stilts, herding their great droves of geese upon lone, willowy isles.

Here, in the fen, were, until comparatively recent years, the greatest duck decoys in England, ponds from which radiated tapering

Lincolnshire:
Holland Arms

tunnels arched with netting, up which the gambolling antics of the little rusty-red decoy dogs, whom the fenmen called pipers, lured tens of thousands of ducks to their doom. There were no less than thirty-eight decoy ponds existing at one time in the Lincolnshire fen, mainly between Sleaford and Crowland, and from Wainfleet to Boston. If you drew a line from Sutton St. Mary's, near Crosskeys Wash, via Crowland, Market Deeping, Bourne, Falkingham, Sleaford, Tattershall, Spilsby and Wainfleet, to the sea at the latter place, you would enclose most of the Lincolnshire decoys, and many of the great fens in which they existed.

Some idea of the value of the duck decoys alone can be gained from the fact that no less than 13,180 wildfowl were caught in the Dowsby Decoy, near Falkingham, in six months alone, in the winter of 1765–6, whilst the enormous total of 95,836 duck (wild)

were taken in thirty-five seasons in the Ashby Decoy at Bottesford, near Brigg, between September 1833 and April 1868.

Beginning north, near Wainfleet, the principal fens, now drained and converted to farmlands, are the East and West Fens, to the east of which are the Friskney, Wainfleet and Wrangle Decoys. These fens are Wildmore Fen, Holland Fen (twenty-two thousand acres), the Kyme Fens, Sempringham Fen, Pinchbeck Fens, Bourne Fen, Deeping Fen (fifteen thousand acres), Cowbit and Whaplode Fens. In addition are the great fens of Gedney, Holbeach and Moulton, east of Spalding, lying between that town and the sea.

More fens stretched north-west from Tattershall to Lincoln, but they were drained at the end of the eighteenth century, when between twenty and thirty-five square miles of country were enclosed and brought under cultivation.

The motorist or farmer who visits the Lincolnshire fens to-day, and sees mile on mile of closely tilled, incredibly rich land, growing acres of potatoes, sugar-beet and brilliant splashes of flowers, should, as I have said, cast his mind back to little more than a hundred years ago, when much of this land was the wildest and most impenetrable in England, haunted, so the natives said, by witches and goblins and those "swart devils out of the marsh fen" who dragged St. Guthlac, the Saxon saint, out of his cell and thrashed and beat him "till he near died." His affliction was probably no worse than a bad attack of the ague, that fever of the fenlands, which lingered on as a malady to be countered by draughts of laudanum and poppy-head tea and pills of opium, drugs taken by the parents of old fenmen still living.

### Before the Fens were Drained

It is well to remember the importance of these fens, some of which, notably the East Fen, were not drained until 1867, for before drainage they were stocked in summer with immense numbers of horses, cattle, sheep and geese. One old fenman alone kept an average stock of two thousand old-brood geese.

During pre-drainage days in Wildmore Fen were bred thousands of horses of a

**The Boston "stump," the tower of St. Botolph's church, is a celebrated Lincolnshire landmark.**

The village of Woolsthorpe on the Lincolnshire–Leicestershire border. In the distance is Belvoir Castle, the seat of the Duke of Rutland, and the centre of a stretch of fine hunting country.

particular breed known as Wildmore Tits. These were not very large, usually grey, beautifully shaped and most active, and were said to be of Arabian descent. Undoubted relics of this breed and half-bred descendants can still be seen on many Lincolnshire farms. The Holland and Wildmore Fens were normally covered in water to a depth of from three to six feet for six months of the year, right up to 1810. So great a harvest of wildfowl and fish did they provide that carriers took immense quantities to the London markets, and when the enclosure of Holland Fen was proposed in 1768 a serious riot took place, troops were called out and many people injured. In other parts of the fen, the fenmen blew up the sluice gates of the new drainage works, blew great holes in the embankments, thus flooding thousands of acres that had been drained, and murdered the drainers and engineers with their duck-guns.

All this constitutes a unique chapter in the history of Lincolnshire, and in the history of England, and it forms a necessary background to a proper understanding of the life and wealth of the dwellers in the Lincolnshire fen to-day.

To-day, the main fact which governs the life of the agricultural people of Lincolnshire, is that the fens are completely drained, and, owing to their centuries of inundation, full of valuable humus, which is a reservoir of gold to the farmer.

Quite a large proportion of the fenland is silt as distinct from the marsh, which was formerly saltings, frequently overflowed by the sea. It is, on the whole, heavier land and therefore much more suitable for permanent pasture and cattle-raising. The wold country is largely from two hundred to three hundred and fifty feet above sea level, high and dry, much of it lying on limestone, and regarded for centuries as only fit for grazing sheep, growing barley or merely as unfenced and uncultivated open heathland. Much of the work of reclaiming the wold country was done following the wonderful example set by a bygone Earl of Yarborough, at Brocklesbury Park. He was to

223

This view of Lincoln shows the Cathedral begun in 1078. The fine high street leads through Stone-bow, an old building erected on the site of the south-gate of the Roman city, and climbs thereafter steeply up the hill. The Cathedral, one of the finest in England, is rivalled in all Europe only by Durham for the magnificence of its dominating position.

eighteenth century Lincolnshire what "Coke of Norfolk" was to East Anglia.

Let us begin with the fen. There, land is worth up to three hundred pounds an acre. There are few great houses, for the old landowners, naturally enough, did not choose to dwell among the malarial fens, although many of them took a leading part in draining the fens, and bringing them to a high state of cultivation.

Hence arises one of the interesting psychological changes in Lincolnshire. Where the old landed aristocracy has sold out, a new landed squirearchy of practical, working farmers has stepped in. Many of these farmers are the sons of small yeomen farmers. Some began life as agricultural labourers. To-day they and their sons own and farm estates ranging in size from ten thousand acres to thirty-two thousand acres. They are a new phenomenon in rural England, these wealthy farmers, whose skill is unequalled in the world.

### Wealthy Smallholders

Another phenomenon, also new, is the large number of fen smallholders, men owning from three acres to just under a hundred acres, who are proportionately rich, richer by far than many a prosperous London stockbroker or well-to-do business man. These fenland smallholders grow fruit, bulbs, tomatoes, asparagus, peas and potatoes—high priced crops on high priced land. They live in excessively ugly cottages and small farmhouses, built, for the most part, within the last eighty years, of that glaring white Cambridge brick, which, next to ferro-concrete, is civilization's worst gift to good architecture. These square, grim boxes, with their square windows, whose draped lace curtains hide unbelievable aspidistras and dreadful, shiny suites, bought from the mass production furniture factories of the East End, are hideous to the eye, cold in winter and hot in summer. They and their blue slate roofs have supplanted the old, thatch-and-plaster farmhouses and cottages of the fenmen who were grandfathers of the present occupants. They are set by the side of ruler-straight roads, which march like swords, dyke-bordered, through long, luminous fields which turn to plum-purple under the magnificent sunsets which over-arch this wide land at evening.

These straight roads were introduced under the general drainage scheme. They follow the old Roman plan of the Fosse Way, Icknield Way, Ermine Street and other Roman roads.

### Fenland Trees

Poplars and willows, with a few scattered elms, are the only trees. The oak is an alien. Here and there tall windmills still grind corn. An old, black draining mill, its skeleton arms bare of shutters, stands once in twenty square miles at a junction of shining dykes, a wind-beaten memorial of the hard days of the old fight against the fenland waters. Modern pumping-stations, square, brick and ugly, with tall shafts like factory chimneys, have taken over their work.

The smallholders and their wives work like horses. They are in the fields "all the hours that God sends," the men driving tractors, hoeing, ridging and ploughing. The women wear sun bonnets and are as much masters of field-work as their men. They make a lot of money quite often and they deserve it. I heard of one smallholder who cleared three hundred and fifty pounds profit from one acre of strawberries.

These fen farmers pay heavily in taxation for their skill and industry, though many continue to do extremely well in a small way in one pound note transactions.

The big farmers, who live in square, white-brick houses, usually called halls or granges, set in twenty or thirty acres of bright green fields with tall lines of marching elms about them and neat, overtrim, suburbanized gardens, stuffy with laurels, blazing with geraniums, these men pay on a heavy scale.

### New Farming Methods

Something of a farming revolution has recently happened on the high farms of Blankney, which are almost, but not quite, wold country. It is an object lesson to show what can be done on a great deal of the wold land. Until recent years the land was ploughed not more than from three to five inches deep. That was because the topsoil is shallow and the subsoil is chalk, lime and

H              225

gravel. So the farmers said there was no need to plough deeper since it would merely turn up the chalk and the gravel. They say the same to-day in many parts of Yorkshire, Dorset, Wiltshire and Hampshire, and parts of Oxfordshire.

But the fen practice of deep ploughing was brought to the skirts of the wold. It was ploughed from eighteen inches to two feet deep. This turned up the subsoil, mixed the lime, the chalk and the topsoil. It was then manured heavily and well with farmyard manure—none of your repeated dosing with artificials which add no humus—and grew fifteen and sixteen tons of potatoes to the acre. To-day tomatoes are grown by the ton on farms which a few years ago produced nothing but sheep and barley. And at Nocton is one of the greatest flax works in England. It is handling six hundred and fifty tons or more of flax a year and employs a hundred and eighty people, mainly girls. Lincolnshire flax is reckoned to be the best in England and Belfast merchants say that they would rather have it than any other.

There is a great future for Lincolnshire flax growing on the higher lands where there is a medium loam with a clay subsoil. Before the war seventy-five per cent of our flax came from Russia and the Baltic States, whilst Belgium produced the ultra-fine quality. Lincolnshire can compete with them all. This is no extravagant claim from a county which also claims to be the most important agricultural county in England. And that, since it produced corn, wool, potatoes, beef, mutton, tomatoes, fruit, flowers, pigs, a host of vegetables, together with valuable sea fisheries of which Grimsby, with its great fleet of deep sea trawlers is the queen, is a first claim to importance in an England that must live to an ever-increasing extent upon her own produce.

### Bulb Industry

In the fens, too, is the unique Lincolnshire industry of bulb growing with its acres of glowing colours which give the countryside the appearance—and the name—of Holland. The industry was started with bulbs imported from Vienna in the sixteenth century, although it did not grow to any great proportion until fifty years ago. Spalding,

with its Dutch-like wharves and old inns, is the capital of the trade, which represents some hundreds of thousands of pounds worth of business each season from its six hundred bulb farms employing several thousand workers. From March to May the very air is perfumed by flowers.

### Great Houses

But when I think of Lincolnshire, a county in which I have a far-distant affinity through that Roger Wentworth who, by his marriage with Margery, Lady Roos, in 1423, inherited the wide Despencer lands of Goxhill, I think not only of the flat and shining fens, the windy wolds with their beechwoods and sheep, or the marsh with its magnificent dawns and cattle-dappled miles, but of old mansions like the great and austere Blankney; Brocklesby in its ancient park; Gunby, whose lovely manor house, where Massingberds have lived since before 1400, is now covenanted to the National Trust; and, noblest of all, Tattershall Castle. That magnificent brick building, rising sheer from the flat country to a height of a hundred and twelve feet, with walls fifteen or more feet thick, is one of the most splendid and impressive buildings in this or any other county.

The great chambers, each of them thirty-eight feet by twenty-three and seventeen feet high, give on to the most beautiful vaultings and mouldings in the smaller rooms and galleries which, in the thickness of the walls, run round the big central rooms. The whole is contained in a double moat. The magnificent mantelpieces, which at one time were removed and later restored, show the coats of arms of the Cromwells, Tattershalls, d'Eyncourts, Marmions, Dribys, Bernaks and Cliftons.

This tremendous and impressive castle, which has no superior in England, stood empty and roofless for years, until the late Lord Curzon bought it, re-roofed it, restored much of its glory and then presented it to the nation. The enormous oak beams which carry the floors, each of them twenty-four feet long and eighteen inches square, were cut from trees in Lord Middleton's park at Wollaton in Nottinghamshire. To-day, after two hundred and fifty years' neglect, Tattershall is Lincolnshire's unique monument of the past.

There are many lesser manor houses, from Scrivelsby Court, where dwells the King's Champion, with his suits of shining armour and the gold drinking cup presented by George IV at his coronation in 1821, when the Champion last rode into Westminster Hall, to Tennyson's old home at Somersby; that charming little manor house at Silk Willoughby, the Old Hall at Gainsborough and the ruins of Great Goxhill Priory.

The ordinary citizen, who dwells in no manor house, nor has the entry to that close corporation of farmers, whose homes are so often notable in a solid English way, but finds such poor comfort as he can now contrive to do in an inn, will turn his mind to that superb and imposing hostelry the "Angel and Royal" at Grantham, where, they say, King John held his Court in 1213 —although the present house is of the fourteenth and fifteenth centuries—and to the "George" in the same town.

I like to think, too, of the "White Hart" hard under the shadow of the magnificent cathedral, lording it over the city, with its chimneys and roof-tops, from its high hill. Its cellars once equalled its collection of old clocks which chime their sober notes to the booming tones of Big Tom. Then, down the hill, at Lincoln, there is the "Saracen's Head" and at Sleaford, the "Bristol Arms," a sober-faced farmers' inn, looking on a busy street, its creeper-hung courtyard set out on sunny days with wooden tables and long benches, where men bargain in cattle and horses, potatoes and machinery.

## Machines for Farming

For Lincolnshire is a highly mechanized county. It is no pretty picture-book place of comfortable Dobbins and rumbling farm wains. Probably the biggest farm machinery repair shops in England are at Spalding, where the sons and grandsons of village blacksmiths work with the most modern tools and appliances. Grantham is the home of the world's largest makers of steam-rollers, and it builds also oil engines, loco-motives, pumps, boilers, cranes, concrete mixers, excavators and contractors' plant which go all over the world. Grantham has,

like many Lincolnshire towns, many small, mean, dull streets. That ubiquitous white brick has cast an architectural blight over half the county.

Nor can one pretend that Grimsby is beautiful. An unlovely town, which claims that it was a village in 2000 B.C., it has nothing like the charm of old Boston.

### Pageant of History

Lincoln itself is an ancient and noble city dating from dim Celtic times when it was Lindun—the fort by the pool. It is a city to capture the heart and enthral the eye, for here are a magnificent cathedral, a Norman castle, the oldest dwelling-houses in Europe, the only existing Roman arch still spanning a main road—the Newport Arch—and the only medieval bridge in the country which still bears houses upon its arches. It is an architectural pageant of English history.

The city stands superbly on a high lime-stone ridge looking east across the valley of the Witham to the wolds and west to the Vale of Trent. It is dominated by its lovely cathedral, standing three-towered on top of Steephill, two hundred and fifty feet above the lower town streets. Hence marched the Ninth Legion of Rome to meet death at the hands of Boadicea's tribesmen. Hence the knights of Stephen rode out to greet Queen Matilda. Here dwelt John of Gaunt as Constable of the Castle, which Cromwell stormed centuries later. And here, too, John Wesley preached in the castle yard. That is the mere fringe of the tale of Lincoln's history. The gaunt ruins of the Castle keep stand bare and forbidding with their memories.

As you come down Steephill from the castle, down a narrow street of ancient houses, on the left is Aaron, the Jew's House where, in the twelfth century, lived a famous Jewish money-lender who was the financier of the wool trade. Lower down the street is the Jew's House and Jew's Court, both relics of the same period. A magnificent Tudor archway, called the Stonebow, spans the street at the foot of Steephill. This arch embodies the Guildhall, which is approached by a fine oaken stair-case. It has a magnificent timber roof and contains a fourteenth-century Mote Bell,

**Ancaster is typical of the numerous villages that dot the rich agricultural south and west of Lincoln-**

which is still rung to summon the city council, and one of the only two fourteenth-century state swords still left in England.

Lincoln High Street spans the River Witham by way of the High Bridge, which, as I have said, is the only medieval bridge in existence with houses still upon it. The centre is pure twelfth century, whilst on the west side are timbered houses built about 1540. Here and hereabouts are many old houses, formerly inhabited by merchants and others in the wool trade, for Lincoln green cloth was woven in Lincoln long before the days of Robin Hood.

Lincoln is rich in old churches, two of which, St. Mary-le-Wigford and St. Peter-

**shire. Many of the buildings along the east coast are made of a local stone quarried at Ancaster.**

at-Gowts, have Saxon towers and much Early English work. The old hall of the medieval Guild of St. Mary, now called John of Gaunt's Stables, was built about 1150, and is an interesting and quite impressive specimen of the architecture of the time. A few traces still remain of the Old Palace, which is generally supposed to have been begun by Bishop Blowet in 1110, and views of great beauty can be seen from the ruins to-day.

Lincoln is indeed a city of charming views, old world corners and unexpected glimpses of the past.

Stamford is another town, dating from Roman days, rich in Norman remains, and so full to-day of antique beauty that to walk through it is, as someone once said, "like ransacking an old jewel case." Brasenose Gateway is a relic of the hall where "rebels" attempted to set up a rival university in the fourteenth century, whilst King Charles' Gateway in part of the old town wall, celebrates the king's escape in 1646. Browne's Hospital is a really lovely fifteenth century almshouse, with an exquisite chapel, whilst the old Bede House, another charity foundation, has a superb ceiling. Burghley House, Lord Exeter's magnificent seat, one of the best houses of its period in England, just across the river in Northamptonshire, is open to the public by courtesy of the owner.

I have never been able to regard Gainsborough as a town of any great architectural merit although the Old Hall is a good specimen of late fifteenth century work. But like Grantham, Gainsborough is too busy with industry to bother much about beauty. Boston, on the other hand, is a fascinating old town almost more Dutch in appearance than many towns in Holland.

Boston is the mother town of Boston, Massachusetts, and near it are two American outposts called Bunker's Hill and New York, a fact which reminds me that near Grimsby is the smallest London in the world—one house in a farmyard. But Bos-

ton was the premier port of England in the thirteenth century when it sent seventeen ships to the French wars of Edward III.

Gradually, however, during the seventeenth century the river silted up. Splendid old houses stood empty. The wharves were idle and the markets decayed. The corporation begged to be released from taxation, declaring that the town was "decayed and ruined." And so it was.

Later, from 1764 onwards, the river was deepened, ships tied up again at the quays and commerce flowed in from the sea once again. Boston to-day is a busy, bustling old seaport, a town which has married age with progress, commerce with beauty. In its old and windy streets, with their Flemish-looking houses, crow-stepped gables, magnificent doorways and medieval alleyways, the sea-winds seem to whisper of deep waters. The lordly church of St. Botolph's, which they call Boston Stump, gazes like a centurion over the town and across the salty, curdled miles of the Wash to the low cliffs of Hunstanton. Boston is one of the most fascinating towns in Lincolnshire.

It is, indeed, like most of Lincolnshire, a blending of old and new, of a sturdy Englishness which, whilst it wastes no hours and leaves no acres barren, maintains a respect for tradition. That is of the whole spirit of Lincolnshire.

*Tulip Fields at Spalding*

*Gold Hill, Shaftesbury*

# DORSET

### By H. J. MASSINGHAM

DORSET is the most diversified of all the counties of England, a kingdom, for its size, more various in its soils and styles of landscape than any other in the world. The reason, of course, lies in the complexity of its geological strata, a score of which crowd and jostle and tumble together along the littoral between Studland in the east and Lyme Regis in the west. They are so confusingly superimposed one upon another as to present a drama of change in headland, bay, cliff, stack, ledge, pinnacle and estuary unequalled by any other shore-line in Britain. Each one of these strata, epitomized in the paint-box of the coast-line, expresses its own distinctive landscape over the length and breadth of the county.

The resultant changes of scenery are rendered still more complicated by varieties within each geological formation. Thus the chalk of the backbone of Dorset, which runs from the Wiltshire border in the north-east as far as William Barnes's "sweet Be'minster" in the west, possesses quite a different

*Badge of Dorset*

aspect from the southern hook, curving inwards from the central massif. The latter forms part of the coastal belt and travels east parallel with the main range as far as, and in outcrops beyond, the Purbeck Hills in the south-east. The mid-Dorset chalk ridge is overlain with Tertiary beds that break up and enrich, with their woodlands and arable fields, the linear continuity and natural serenity of such bare chalk uplands as the Chaldon Downs, west of Lulworth Cove, and the hog's back of Ballard Down in the Isle of Purbeck. Still more striking in multiformity of character are the Dorset limestones. The long, narrow muscular ridges of the Purbeck Hills, the squat-snouted bulk of Portland, the oolite belt squeezed between chalk and lias, that thrusts up from the tawny cliffs of Burton Bradstock north-eastward into Somerset—you would never guess that all these landscapes belonged to the same family of limestones.

This constant or inconstant ringing of the changes from one type of country to another would be less spectacular than it actually is were it not for the fact that the variations are so frequently abrupt. The heathy topknot of Blackdown, topped by the obelisk

231

The Chesil Beach curving away to the left towards Abbotsbury. Portland harbour is on the right with Weymouth in the background. The beach is a wide strand of shingle fifteen miles long and separated from the mainland for most of its length by a strip of water.

of the Hardy Monument, is clapped down upon a particularly bold and massive chalk landscape; the soft sheltered combe of Encombe is a green enclosure of the black Kimmeridge clay inset among stark and embattled shapes of grey limestone; the liassic cliffs to be seen from the Cob at Lyme Regis frown like a fantasy of Hades, while the liassic and equally fantastic hills round Powerstock, a few miles to the east, are characters of comedy.

### Contrast of Scene

The individuality of these sudden contrasts may be felicitously appreciated (to give one instance out of many) from the great Iron Age fortress of Eggardon, with Beaminster Down, the most westerly promontory of the chalk escarpment that runs across southern England from distant Beachy Head. Look east from Eggardon and the great, calm folds and rotundities of downland melt into the horizon; look west, and a hotchpotch of ragged hills, intensely green and of the oddest and gayest contours, tumbles in wild inconsequence over into Devon.

The two prospects may be neighbours in space; but in differences of scenic value they are the Antipodes. Yet both are Dorset. It has been said that as Dorset approaches Wiltshire by Cranborne Chase in the northeast, Hampshire by the New Forest, Devon by Axminster and Somerset by Chard, so it half surrenders its identity to each in turn, the very instability of the succession of different scenes compromising its own individual meaning. I disagree. There are no such monarchs in east Devon as Pilsdon Pen and Lewesdon that lord it over the motley company of hills in west Dorset. In south-west Wiltshire there is no such assembly of hills as that by Shaftesbury and there is no prehistoric heath like Egdon even in the New Forest. Though all these features are richly differentiated, the face is Dorset's and Dorset's only.

Dorset was important to the Romans, as their roads and villas and Durnovaria, now Dorchester, reveal. All the Roman roads of Roman Britain led to Rome, and that sums up the economy of the Roman Empire. Theirs was an export economy and the

Romans regarded Wessex much as a speculator regards real estate. It was a field for exploitation, not a new home to be colonized. But because the Wessex of their military and financial invasion was to them Ultima Thule, we find evidence of continuity with previous cultures more deeply rooted in the native soil than the Roman ever was. Tesselated pavements and Samian pottery were purely Roman, as were the agricultural system of the *latifundia*, or factory farms, run on forced gang labour. But the roads, the garrison towns of Hod Hill and Durnovaria and the amphitheatre of Maumbury Rings (with seating accommodation for twelve thousand) at Dorchester, were nearly all adaptations of settlements and communications in existence centuries before the legionaries stormed the ramparts of Maiden Castle and massacred its defenders. This mixture of cultures was to be seen in the ancient villages of Cranborne Chase where the native Celtic arts were blended with the amenities and mass-produced refinements of the Romans in much the same way as the Dorset cottager to-day has a wireless set, a London newspaper and (if he is lucky) electric light.

### Remains of Ancient Cultures

The cultures that preceded and postdated the Romans have left far more evidence of their regional reality than have those of the Romans. Cranborne Chase, the heights along the Stour, and the plateau of the southern band of chalk are so prodigally strewn with tumuli of the Early Bronze Age and the earthworks and arable fields of its successor that the downland has been remoulded by them. Maiden Castle, first occupied as a fortress nearly four thousand years ago, and later as a market town, is probably the largest earthwork in the world; but the great camps of Eggardon, Rawlsbury, Chalbury, Flowers Barrow, Pilsdon, Badbury Rings and others, if not so large, are none the less most strikingly and impressively ancient. Tumuli of the Stone Age, bell barrows, bowl barrows, ring barrows are found everywhere; they are frequently to be seen in groups and sets like the bell barrows round Stonehenge. The Five Marys are such an assembly, gazing over the Chal-

# DORSET

THE GIANT, CERNE ABBAS

HARDY'S HOUSE,
MAX GATE, DORCHESTER

SHERBORNE

S O M E R S E T

R. AXE

Pilsdon Hill

Sherborne Abbey Church

B L A

DEVONSHIRE

R. CHAR

BEAMINSTER

The Mill, Maiden Newton

Old Gateway, Cerne Abbas

CERNE ABBAS

LYME REGIS

CHARMOUTH

POWERSTOCK

BRIDPORT

MAIDEN NEWTON

GODMAN

Lyme Bay

R. FROME

R. CERNE

THE GLOBE, SWANAGE

St. Catherine's Chapel, Abbotsbury

Maiden Castle

DORCHEST

BLACK DOWN

R. WEY

ABBOTSBURY

N

W        E

S

BLAKE-

CHESIL BEACH

WEYMOUTH

Weymouth Bay

Ringste

Portland Harbour

Miles

0          5          10

West Bay

PORTLAND

Shambles

E N G L I S H

Portland Bill

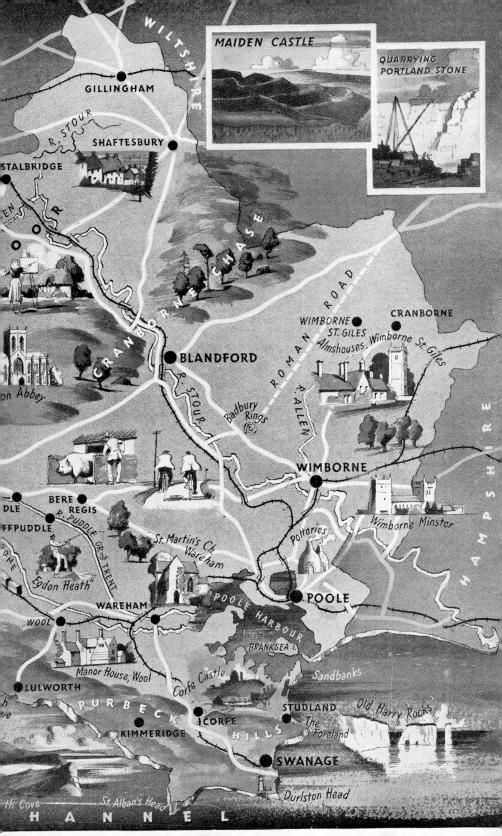

MAIDEN CASTLE

QUARRYING PORTLAND STONE

WILTSHIRE

GILLINGHAM

R. STOUR

SHAFTESBURY

STALBRIDGE

CRANBORNE CHASE

ROMAN ROAD

WIMBORNE
ST. GILES
Almshouses, Wimborne St. Giles

CRANBORNE

BLANDFORD

R. STOUR

R. ALLEN

Badbury
Rings

on Abbey

WIMBORNE

Wimborne Minster

HAMPSHIRE

BERE
REGIS

DLE

FFPUDDLE

R. PUDDLE OR TRENT

St. Martin's Ch.
Wareham

Potteries

"Egdon Heath"

WAREHAM

POOLE HARBOUR

POOLE

WOOL

BRANKSEA I.

Sandbanks

Manor House, Wool

Corfe Castle

LULWORTH

PURBECK

HILLS

STUDLAND
The
Foreland

Old Harry Rocks

KIMMERIDGE

CORFE

SWANAGE

th Cove    St. Alban's Head

Durlston Head

HANNEL

don Downs in perfect harmony with the chalk landscape.

In equal harmony is the Giant of Cerne Abbas. The legend goes that St. Augustine on his great mission was once driven with ignominy from Cerne by the worshippers of Giant Helith who with his club is outlined on the steep bare flank of Giant Hill. But he left his well behind him, cool and deep under its enormous limes, and the monks of the Benedictine monastery founded close by, left undefaced the rude pagan figure above the sacred building, practising a tolerance not followed by Victorian visitors six centuries later. I have no doubt that this monstrous image of fertility, symbolizing the perpetual cycle of death and renewal in nature, this native Hercules, was scored into the turf in the Early Iron Age about 500–200 B.C. by a branch of the same people as constructed the great ovals of Maiden Castle.

### Saxon Influence

The site of the village of Cerne Abbas itself, seen from the heights above it, is an enchantment. Around Beaminster also is a girdle of great bluffs, but the lie of the town is not so perfect as at Cerne Abbas because the latter lies almost but not quite in the centre of a flat valley floor (to have been quite in the middle would have been too formal) into which five other valleys converge, the long tongues of their promontories sinking into the tiny plain with what seems a ceremonious gesture. In the centre of the village rises the tower of the church. No wonder that such unconscious rightness of planning once made Cerne the capital of Dorset.

To the Saxons (who showed a similar feeling for rightness of planning) we owe the sites of the Dorset villages, the use of those local building materials in which the county is so rich and the system of winding roads and lanes connecting village with village and each village with the headlands of its open fields. In the jumble of the liassic hills of west Dorset, this system is so intricate that only the most Dorsetwise of travellers can avoid getting lost among the high-banked lanes. And, after they had burst through the Bokerly Dyke that lies like a great mythological serpent across the plateau of Cranborne Chase, the Saxons finally established along the rivers and streams the chief Dorset industry from the time of the stone circles onwards—agriculture.

For Dorset is first and last an agricultural county. The same may be said of many other counties in Britain. But none of these

**Lulworth Cove, the result of a remarkable formation of hills, is nearly half a mile across. It provides no anchorage for any large vessel but was an historic landing place for smugglers.**

Milton Abbas is one of the first model villages. It was built after 1771 to house the villagers from Milton which was demolished as being too near Lord Dorchester's home, Milton Abbey.

possesses so great a diversity of rock formations and so of soils as Dorset. The heavy clays of the Vale of Blackmore form a miniature wheat belt, similar to, if not so dry as, that of the eastern counties. The slopes of the downland are also propitious for corn, especially barley and rye, if planted in judicious moderation. But this is mainly a country for sheep, while the valleys of Frome, Stour and Brit are pre-eminent for dairying. But their water-meadows are also provided by nature for fattening both winter sheep and store cattle, a bounty recognized by the old husbandmen in the special evolution of the two breeds of sheep, Downs for the grass and hurdled Horns for the arable.

### Dorset Industries

Dorset also has ample marginal lands for rough grazing and breeding healthy stock and so enabling farmers to rear their own calves and lambs. West Dorset, the country of the lias, is particularly adapted to the all-round mixed husbandry of the small family farmer, oats and dredge corn for winter feed replacing the wheat and barley of the more easterly regions.

All the indigenous Dorset industries, even those of the rich woodlands, were conditioned by this agricultural primacy. The ports and sea-towns, such as Swanage, Poole, Weymouth, Bridport and Lyme Regis, have, until recent years, been markets between the sea and the land, the spinning-mills of Bridport, for instance, having made both rope for ships—and, indeed, rope for the hangman!—and linen from flax. Though they are now mainly "resorts" (Weymouth and Lyme Regis from the eighteenth century onwards, when they were popularized by George III), they were founded, and continued for centuries, as ports and markets. The inland towns like Wareham (once a port), Bere Regis, Blandford and Dorchester, were always market towns, serving and served by the neighbouring countryside, until modern times

237

Studland Bay, between Poole Harbour and Swanage, is one of Dorset's quiet resorts. The Foreland or Handfast Point, seen here, is the tip of the Purbeck Hills, source of the famous "marble."

disrupted this stable economy. Hardy's "Casterbridge" (Dorchester) is invariably pictured as essentially a market town, as it probably was before the Romans made it a temporary military station. Thus urban Dorset has been from prehistoric times to the opening of the twentieth century a natural development of agricultural Dorset, both of the sea and of the land.

The same regional principle has directed the Dorset industries, not only those organically concerned with agriculture like thatching, wheelwrighting, smithying, farriery, hurdling, basketry, carpentry, weaving, tanning, milling (Stour and Frome once had a mill to every mile) and the like, but those less obviously linked with food-production like quarrying, building and forestry. Forestry and agriculture are really inseparable because woodlands control water-supply to farmlands and from the woods came the raw material of countless farm implements and buildings, quite apart from

their value as shelter belts and for other agricultural uses. The great stone industries of Purbeck and Portland came into being to house an agricultural community and to build its churches, market towns, land-owning manors and self-supporting monasteries. The export of building stone beyond the county boundaries (though later it developed prodigiously, much of London owing its structure to Dorset) was always secondary to its usages in Dorset. Dorset became a builder's paradise for that very reason. It is not generally known that Portland Bill, Hardy's "Isle of Slingers," was up to the nineteenth century the habitation of an intensely localized community, which being self-subsistent was the home of many strange customs and distinctive practices. It even had its own currency.

Thus the history and meaning of Dorset have been largely regional. The richness of the resulting local culture speaks for itself; Thomas Hardy, William Barnes,

Forde Abbey, Sherborne Abbey, Athelhampton, Eggardon Camp, the Dorset sheep, Horns and Downs, the Frome meadows, the happy little farms of the lias, the flax mills, Dorset butter and the Dorset speech were all integral parts of it. Dorset only began to decay when its localized economy and way of life were supplanted by a very different economy imposed from without.

The Middle Ages and the Dorset men who followed, up to the time of the Industrial Revolution, extended and even intensified the Saxon example of intelligent regionalism by multiplying the local trades dependent upon agriculture. They virtually inaugurated the first of the great architectural periods whose long and renowned procession ended with the cheerful and generous Regency fashion found in Beaminster and Weymouth. It was in the thirteenth century that Purbeck "marble" first began to be widely carved in clusters of slender arches supporting nave arcades and chancels. The golden stone of Sherborne Abbey with the darker yellow stone of the Upper Lias area came into use throughout west Dorset; from the limestone quarried in the Isles of Purbeck and Portland were built the grey stone villages between Corfe Castle and Lulworth and again between Weymouth, Bridport and Dorchester. The richness of the soil and the superabundance of the natural deposits gave the buildings of medieval Dorset three types of roofing, the heavy slats of Purbeck stone in the east, the thatch of the Great Heath and of central Dorset—the Abbotsbury tithe barn is thatched to this very day—and the tiles of the clay valleys.

### Unique Church Roof

The interior of Bere Regis Church (where the D'Urbervilles were buried) happily illustrates how sensitively the medieval builders and their successors caught up the natural diversity of the Dorset scene. The hammerbeam roof is unique because the figures of the Twelve Apostles at the corbels are horizontal instead of vertical. These richly coloured wooden images of medieval characters, each one different and individual in expression as well as in colour and robing,

project life-size over the nave, while the huge bosses are in brilliant polychrome. The gazer upwards receives a vivid impression of the intense variety of medieval life, not in spite but because of its fidelity to the regional environment.

### Flax and Hemp

In the local building styles of cottage, farmhouse and the smaller manors there was very little change between the Middle Ages and the Industrial Revolution. Some think of flax-growing to-day in west Dorset as a great novelty. Actually it was probably grown by the megalith-builders four thousand years ago, and west Dorset is full of ancient buildings that once hummed with the processing and spinning of the fibre. In Bridport is a fine building lettered, "Joseph Grundry and Co., Manufacturers of Fishing Nets, Lines and Twines, Spinners and Doublers." That inscription reveals the essential purpose of the old rope-town, though the hemp-fields of the neighbourhood have gone. Dorset and Lincolnshire were once the paramount counties for the growing of hemp for rope-making. Teasel was another crop (in rotation with caraway and coriander for seed) once grown in west Dorset and Somerset. It was used for carding the wool of the two specific Dorset breeds, Dorset Downs and Dorset Horns, both of which sheep often lamb twice a year.

Few are the flocks of either to be seen to-day and along the southern coastal downs, ideal sheepwalks, none at all. The dirtiness and poverty of these fields, which are too dry for heavy stocking with cattle, reveal the consequences of the present attitude to sheep as "uneconomic." Red Devon cattle, still to be seen in west Dorset, belonged as much to Dorset as to Devon. There is a tradition that the monks of Abbotsbury, which is sub-tropical in climate, had vineyards along the terraced slopes of St. Catherine's Hill. How far back in time do the quarry-workings of Purbeck and Portland extend? Nobody knows: but their grim fastnesses are full of legend and the relics of old custom. Within living memory a Purbeck craftsman built the roof of Kingston Church. In the seventeenth century the Dorset Clubmen rose against

**The Manor House at Woolbridge, on the bank of the Frome between Lulworth and Wareham, was made famous by Thomas Hardy, as Wellbridge, home of *Tess of the D'Urbervilles*.**

both Roundhead and Cavalier, because their political quarrel was interfering with the proper tillage of the Dorset fields. The Tolpuddle Martyrs were transported in the nineteenth century as felons, when they tried to recover freedom for the men of those fields.

Dorset would be regarded as illustrious in any age for its manor houses. What gives them their special lustre is that they are as typically distinctive of Dorset as the humblest cottage. Their range is from late Gothic to late Georgian and the early Tudor manors in particular are of a domestic individuality that is regional rather than national. A regional style virtually has no periods; the passage of time enriches rather than tyrannizes over it. This truth is to be seen in the beauty of Athelhampton, Mapperton, Binghams Melcombe, Toller Fratrum, Sandford Orcas and others.

Regionalism always means continuity. "Arnold the freemason" built Cranborne Manor. So in the seventeenth and eighteenth centuries Blandford, which the itinerant Celia Fiennes called "a pretty neate Country town" in 1680 and Defoe, half a century later, classified as famous for "the finest Bonelace in England," was added to by its own architects, the Bastard family. They and their pupils and teachers had a hand in the making of many of the Dorset

manors. Even the great baroque and classical houses of a too dominant aristocracy, like Crichel and Kingston Lacy, retain many features of local building idiom, while the smallish manors like thatched Hammoon, Tess's Woolbridge, Purse Caundle and Wynford Eagle look like glorified farmhouses, sprung from their indigenous soil like the stone that built them.

Up to the eighteenth century ash-grey Purbeck and the golden Ham Hill stone from just over the Somerset border, built manors whose names were as pleasant to the ear as they were fair to the eye, and in that century Portland stone began to be used for facing. Local brick (in scanty use until the seventeenth century) built Dewlish, Kingston Maurward and others. Of the brick manors none has quite the soft warm texture of plum-coloured brick with stone dressings, nor the elegant and yet homely composition of John Tregonwell's seventeenth-century Anderson Manor, which was so grievously maltreated by troops stationed there during the war.

Forde Abbey in the Valley of the Axe, one of the earliest Cistercian houses in England, sumptuously embellished by Abbot Chard in 1528, with its Inigo Jones staircase and screen in the chapel and the marvellous tapestries woven from the Raphael cartoons, is one of the supreme

240

monuments of regional culture in England. It is fascinating for yet another reason. Much of the medieval portion is built of the traceried golden stone on which time confers so lovely a patina. But part of it is also eighteenth-century "neo-Gothick." Yet the sham Gothick of the Age of Reason is entirely compatible with the genuine Gothic of the Age of Faith, since a regional tradition in building binds together all the ages of craftsmanship, no matter what their innovations. It was the Industrial Revolution that blew into utter ruin the great building traditions of the English counties.

There is no county in England so haunted by the past as Dorset. Its influence is felt most at Cerne Abbas which is "rounded by a sleep." But most of Dorset has this dreamlike quality. This is not only because the past broods over it but because the present has contributed to it so little that is worth while. Its evidences are, however, manifest enough—"pre-fabs" on the Weymouth cliffs, "by-pass variegated" brick villas in the stone belts, a whole row of cottages in Winterbourne St. Martin once thatched and now roofed with corrugated iron, dumps of litter and barbed wire everywhere, turf scored by tank tracks and shell holes, erosion and reversion into wilderness on Egdon and in the Isle of Purbeck, suburban spillings out of Weymouth, Poole and Dorchester, total hillside fellings (so that sheet erosion is bound to follow) at Little Bredy and on the Weld estate at Lulworth. But except for the admirable Dorchester and Pitt-Rivers Museums (the latter at Cranborne Chase) and a very few other isolated instances, the modern age, unlike all previous ages from the Palæolithic onwards, has done literally nothing towards the enrichment of the great legacy which old Dorset bequeathed to us. The nineteenth century uglified the towns and persecuted the Dorset labourer. But it gave to Dorset Alfred Stevens, Thomas Hardy and William Barnes, the last two of whom distilled the essence of the Dorset past into literature.

So far from making the Dorset inheritance yet wealthier, the modern age has notably impoverished it, so that the Dorset of to-day is Dorset in decay. The cause of this decline can be put into a few words.

In every previous age with the partial exception of the Roman, Dorset lived on herself. Her agriculture was always self-supporting; her arts and crafts and industries developed organically out of the crops she grew and her natural resources. Her culture was a regional one. But from the Industrial Revolution onwards, the national economy has fostered manufactures at the expense of agriculture and the trades dependent upon it, and the growth of the modern system of urban centralization has gravely restricted self-government. These two developments have proved fatal to that self-sufficiency which has been the substance of the Dorset economy and the very soul of the Dorset culture. Nothing has been put in its place.

Artificial respiration, such as State subsidies, in time of war or threat of famine, followed by desertion and an enforced economic penury, inevitably depresses and destroys the activity of regional life. It is a nice point as to whether the interference or the subsequent neglect does the more harm. The one imposes purely urban valuations upon the community of the county, robs the land, disfigures the villages and the towns

**Six men of Tolpuddle were transported in 1834 for forming a combination of workers in which they administered "illegal oaths." These martyrs have become heroes of the Trade Union movement. This is their memorial.**

and only allows the remnants of the local trades to survive by imposing upon them from above alien and abstract concepts. The other is economic starvation. Yet for Dorset to become self-governing once more in administration, self-supporting on the farms and self-developing in the traditional industries is her one and only life-line.

There are signs of a re-awakening within the county. One of these concerns afforestation. Certain woodlands are being replanted at Wimborne St. Giles and Charborough Park in east Dorset, at Bryantspuddle, Affpuddle and Milton Abbas in central Dorset, at Fontmell Magna in the north and in the far west at Forde Abbey. The Forestry Commission is planting up the great heaths round Wareham. These recent developments in forestry mark a Dorset not only stirring on her own behalf but applying the principles of local ecology in the best interests of the county as a whole.

Another good hope for Dorset is the liveliness and freedom of the Young Farmers' Clubs. There are twenty-five of these in the county with a membership of over a thousand. They have resisted organization from without, make up full and interesting programmes for themselves and indeed run themselves with the county president acting as the link between one club and another. Another is the amount of re-thatching going on in various parts of the county. Dorset has a rich thatching tradition: the flowing curves over the eaves and the warm texture and colouring of the reed (red wheat straw) are a true Dorset idiom. But that it should be revived is a remarkable achievement when it is remembered not only that thatchers in the English counties are few and far between and nearly all old men, but that less than ten per cent of them have apprentices.

In the west, too, and particularly in the Vale of Marshwood and along the coastal area between Bridport and Lyme Regis, the yeoman and the small farmer continue to hold their own. These virile small farmers of the west are grand cultivators, as I know from personal experience when acting as judge in 1945 in a competition for the best flax-ricks. There is very little market-gardening in Dorset, and these men practise a mixed husbandry of corn and horn, reinforced by flax, cider orchards and a few hoggets when they can afford to keep them. Where there is a cluster of such men helping one another in neighbourly fashion, the countryside is less distressingly empty than elsewhere. Though cheese-making is all but extinct, some of them make a little butter, though nothing like so much as healthy farming demands.

So here and there Dorset is struggling out of her adversity. The pity of it is that she can never be her provincial self again, building upon her great past to serve the present and the future, until our century learns by bitter experience the folly of depressing the land for the sake of the city and of wasting a real in the pursuit of a fictitious wealth.

*Corfe Castle*

*Cheddar Gorge*

# SOMERSET

### By M. LOVETT TURNER

AN ANCIENT book is a lovable thing. Its mellow binding and hand-tooled monogram, its unhurried phrasing and careful choice of words all speak of leisure and the soft passing of time. So it is with Somerset. The mellow charm of its countryside, embossed with many an ancient building, has never been disputed. No one hurries, the rush and bustle of modern life are rarely encountered, and no pall of smoke dims the sun over its towns, or casts a gloom over the lives of its people. It merges almost unnoticeably with the surrounding counties, and yet retains its own characteristics.

Is there anywhere as rugged and unkempt as Cheddar, with its famous gorge nearly two miles long, and its caves, with pendants and columns of stalactites and stalagmites looking like jewels that bring the story of Aladdin to life as no pantomime producer could accomplish?

The highlands of Somerset roughly divide the county into three. The Mendip Hills (an area almost rivalling Manchester for

*Arms of Somerset*

rainfall), cross the county in the north from Frome to Weston-super-Mare; the Quantocks, giving renewed health and strength with every breeze that blows, are at the centre, while the Brendon Hills, in the west, lose themselves in the lovely, heather-painted heights of Exmoor.

Exmoor itself gives glimpses of prehistory in its herds of wild deer, and the frisky moorland ponies that roam amongst the monoliths and stone circles. The prehistoric bridge of Tarr Steps crosses the River Barle at Hawkridge—a name that speaks for itself. Dunkery Beacon gazes out across moor and to the sea from its height of seventeen hundred odd feet in a lordly and serene manner.

There are lowlands, too, in Somerset. The watery plain of Sedgemoor, and the fertile Vale of Taunton Deane, as well as innumerable combes and valleys where the corn grows plentifully in summer.

Somerset possesses few seaports of importance, though there are many lovely little bays made for holiday folk where, to borrow Jane Austen's words: "Fragments of rock among the sands make them the happiest spots for watching the flow of the tide, for sitting in unwearied contemplation."

243

Wrington, famous as the birthplace of the philosopher John Locke, lies at the foot of the Mendip Hills.

Nature has been kind to Somerset, and man has taken every advantage of her gifts. Even before the days when Caesar glibly spoke of the natives as those who for "the most part do not sow corn, but live on milk and flesh, and have their clothing of skins," the Somerset farmer was cultivating the land and sowing crops of grain. Men had built enormous hill-top forts and compact little villages on the slopes and in the marshes, and were trading with dark-skinned strangers from the Mediterranean, who voyaged there for the lead so plentiful in the district.

The settlers had little need to wander far afield—those early men who had fought their way across from the Continent—for Somerset provided them with all they needed. They were content to remain in their homes, even as they are to-day, for

244

**It is typical of the Somerset villages clustering round the Mendip, Quantock and Blackdown Hills.**

explorers and adventurers are rarely to be found amongst Somerset folk.

They are a peaceful race, though capable of fighting for their homes and possessions when the need arises. They held back the Saxons long after the rest of the country had fallen. The noble King Arthur fought many of his legendary battles on Somerset soil, notably at Badon Hill, near Bath, about the year A.D. 520. It was in Somerset, too, that King Alfred sought refuge after his defeat by the Danes in the year 878, when he fled to the Isle of Athelney, there to lay the plans for his subsequent victory at Ethandune and, incidentally, to burn the old woman's cakes.

All through history the men of Somerset have fought for freedom to cultivate their land and live in peace. It was not for the lust of war or plunder that they took

# SOMERSET

SELWORTHY

WESTON-SUPER-MARE, THE PAVILION

WELLS CATHEDRAL

MONTACUTE HOUSE

R. SEVERN

PORT

CLEVEDO

Flat Holm

Steep Holm

WESTON-SUPER-MARE

AXBRIDGE

R. AXE

BURNHAM-ON-SEA

BRIDGWATER BAY

Axbridge Ch.

CANAL

POLDET

NETHER STOWEY

BRIDGWATER

Bar

Sec

R. PARRETT

I. of ATHELNEY

LA

MUCH

SELWORTHY

MINEHEAD

WATCHET

QUANTOCK HILLS

PORLOCK

DUNSTER

DUNKERY BEACON

OARE

EXMOOR

Yarn Mkt. Dunster

R. EXE

VALE OF TAUNTON DEANE

R. TONE

MUCH

R. BARLE

BRENDON HILLS

Muchelney

DULVERTON

WIVELISCOMBE

TAUNTON

ILMINSTER

DEVONSHIRE

WELLINGTON

BLACKDOWN HILLS

## Miles

0     5     10

sides in the Civil War, but for their rights, guided by common sense. Why pay taxes to be spent goodness knows where or why? said they in their day.

Somerset raised an army of peasants to follow the ill-advised Duke of Monmouth to his death, not because they loved fighting, but because they thought that by so doing they would rid the country of religious tyranny. Is there a village in Somerset that did not, in sorrow, erect its war memorial to those who fought in the First World

246

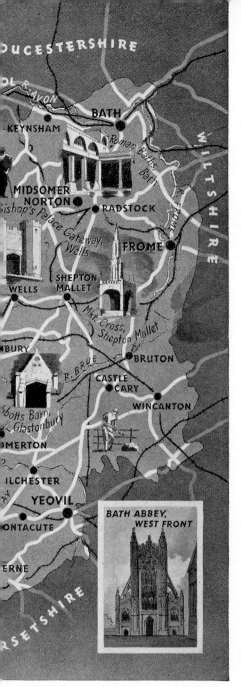

leaving their womenfolk to look after the London children evacuated to Somerset from Britain's front line of battle.

Perhaps it is a heritage from the far distant past that the distrust of strangers is such a marked characteristic of the Somerset man. With him his own folk always come first. There are villages where nearly everyone is related, and farms that have been in the same family for generations. Dunster Castle has changed hands only once since the Norman Conquest, and names mentioned in Domesday Book are still to be found in every district.

It is this patriarchal pride that also makes them dislike anything new. What was good enough for their fathers is good enough for them or, as the motto on the rood screen in Low Ham Church says, "My son, fear the Lord and the Kinge, and meddle not with them that are given to change."

### Old and New

Though rarely among the first to try an innovation, when it has been tested the Somerset farmer is ready to give it a grudging trial. I have seen most up-to-date machinery chugging its noisome way over a field, while in a neighbouring one a man was sowing grain from a basket slung round his neck in a truly Biblical manner. It is no strange sight to see a tractor relentlessly forcing its way through the rich, brown earth on one side of a field, while a team of horses gently ploughs the other. The Somerset farmer sees nothing incongruous in such things.

But the life of Somerset is not all lived in the fields. "Gurt" factories show a broken skyline and modern machinery hums with unholy music in towns and villages—though their products often have a country flavour. The works of a dairying firm at Chard Junction employ many men, and a malted-milk factory at Ilminster is rapidly becoming a small town in itself. The factory stands contemplating the River Isle, as if jealous of the anglers and kingfishers who, apparently, make the river-bank their homes.

Cheddar cheeses, of course, are made in Somerset. They seem to have shrunk somewhat since Camden spoke of their "pro-

War? I doubt it. Cheerfully and doggedly they went, these young men more used to the plough than the rifle, to fight for the land their fathers had tilled for centuries. Doggedly, too, though not so cheerfully, they went during these last black years,

digious size, needing more than one man's strength to set them on the table." Before the war, and its resulting cheese rationing, Cheddar cheese decidedly overwhelmed the visitor to this renowned beauty spot. Cheeses were everywhere; mixed with postcards and tourist trophies on stall and counter; sitting aloof in shops where they were the only commodity offered for sale; on café tea-tables and hotel menus, in manor and cottage; for no real meal was complete without a liberal helping of Cheddar cheese.

### Cheese for a Queen

It was on a certain day in 1839 that seven hundred and thirty-seven cows gave their best milk to be made into a special cheese which, when ripened, was to be given to Queen Victoria as a wedding gift from the people of Cheddar. It weighed ten hundredweight, was nine feet in circumference and twenty-two inches high; hardly a dainty dish to set before a queen!

But cheese is not the only product of Somerset. There is a bacon factory at Highbridge, and breweries at Shepton Mallet, Oakhill, Frome and Wiveliscombe. Cider-presses lurk unseen in almost every group of farm buildings. The hides of slaughtered cattle are made into gloves at Yeovil and in the cottages surrounding this busy, go-ahead town—for glove-making is still a rural industry, and cottagers fetch the skins in sacks, stitch them in their own homes, and return them ready to wear to the central factories.

Collars, too, can be partly made at home where collar factories flourish, as at Taunton and Ilminster. Slippers are made at Glastonbury, as everyone who appreciates comfort must know. Cloth mills are to be found at Frome and Wellington, greatly helping to solve clothing problems. Lace mills at Chard have been working for several generations. Market gardens at Petherton and Chard help to make Somerset gardens gay with delphiniums and roses, and paper is manufactured at Wookey, near the cave in which the River Axe makes such a charming twilight picture, and the Witch of Wookey sits in everlasting silence.

Even underground Nature has been bountiful. Coal is plentiful around Radstock, lead is mined in the Mendips, though not as abundantly as in the past. Many churches and buildings owe their beauty to the mellow weathering of the buff-coloured stone brought from the ancient

The market place at Somerton, which gave its name to the county. To-day it is a quiet country town but once it was the capital of Wessex. The market cross dates from the seventeenth century.

Exmoor Forest, thirty square miles in extent and famous in literature as the scene of Blackmore's *Lorna Doone*, is now mostly heather and grass. This picture shows the Weir Water Valley.

quarries on Ham Hill, and Bath is indebted to the clear light coloured oolite from its surrounding hills for much of its dignified charm.

With the exception of Bristol, half of which is claimed by Gloucestershire, the seaboard towns are not, apart from their holiday season, very important. Bridgwater manufactures bricks, and has roofed its houses with home-made tiles that are so beautiful that one is tempted to spend one's time star-gazing instead of looking where one is going. Bath bricks, ironically, are not made at Bath, but at Bridgwater, where slime batches, ingeniously placed at the side of the river, provide their substance.

### Retiring Factories

In spite of all these varying manufactures, factories do not detract from the charm of Somerset, or fill one's nostrils with smoke or grime. They seem decently retiring or gay with flowers and, if they happen to be near a stream or river, alive with water-hens, swans or ducks.

The most notable feature of Somerset is its stately buildings. Magnificent mansions, their walled gardens imprisoning the sun in order to ripen the peaches, stand in their own parklands. Churches, with many pinnacles pointing towards heaven from their towers, rise above clustering villages and streets filled with shops, each church worthy of special mention, and very beautiful. Castles and abbeys bring medieval life into reality. Manor houses speak of the good old days when the squire looked after his own estate. Many a cottage shows a picturesque exterior which, one is ashamed to say, often hides a dark and insanitary interior. Council houses, built in alien groups, form shocking modern contrasts with the old world towns or villages, but the Georgian houses still manage to hold their own even in the midst of busy towns. They stand unashamed on the very footpaths, showing a classical dignity never since achieved in domestic architecture.

Many of the Somerset towns are so old that legend alone can date their birth. To Bladud, the father of King Lear, is given the credit of having founded the city of Bath in thanksgiving for its hot springs having cured him and his pigs of leprosy. For that great necromancer king, as a youth, was afflicted with this dread disease

The remains of the Roman baths at Bath, discovered in 1755 and opened to the public towards the end of the last century. In the background is the tower of the Abbey begun in 1499.

and, in consequence, was forced to leave his father's court and earn his living as a swineherd.

The stones at Stanton Drew, if legend is to be believed, owe their existence to the Devil, who, disguised as a fiddler, played for a wedding party to dance long after the Sabbath had dawned. When daybreak came the Devil departed, leaving the wedding party petrified into the stones as we see them to-day.

Keynsham was the home of the Welsh saint, Keyna, who lived in a neighbouring wood and, most obligingly, turned all the snakes into stone—or ammonites, as geologists insist on calling them.

Wells owes both its name and place in ecclesiastical history to the springs still flowing in the grounds of the Bishop's Palace, for it was near a sacred well that King Ina, King of Wessex, was persuaded to build a church to be served by a body of secular canons.

King Ina also "founded a burgh" by the River Tone—hence the name Taunton. The castle he built was destroyed by his wife, Aethelburga, twelve years later, not from temper or wifely insubordination, but to prevent it from falling into the hands of their mutual enemy, Allrig, the rebel, who was then ravaging the western counties.

### Alfred and the Cakes

King Alfred is said to have fortified Burrow Mump, near Athelney, where, as already mentioned, he was so busy forming plans for the defeat of the Danes and the building of a British navy that he let the cakes burn, and earned a severe scolding from the housewife's bitter tongue.

Cadbury Castle has been identified with the Camelot of Malory's famous epic. On midsummer eve, it is said, Arthur's knights still ride round it, their horses shod with silver—a legend that must have been founded on fact, for Camden speaks of a silver horse-shoe having been found there in his day!

Chard takes its name from Cerdic, the roystering Saxon chieftain who fought his way from the little bay at Charmouth, on the Dorset coast, to Somerset, where, according to the *Anglo-Saxon Chronicle*,

"strive tho' he might, Cerdic could make no inroads into Somersetshire."

Glastonbury, the most sacred of all places in Somerset, was the sanctuary of St. Joseph of Arimathea. Here he built the first Christian church above ground on the spot where, according to another legend (perhaps not generally believed), our Lord Himself once lived in youthful contemplation.

### Legend of St. Joseph

Priddy, a little mining village noted for its sheep fair, is reputed to have been one of the places where Christ came with St. Joseph—a kinsman of His Mother—on his quest for metal. That St. Joseph was a metal merchant is undoubted, and that he came to the West Country in search of metals is probable, else why do the Cornish miners chant "St. Joseph was a tinman" when the molten tin flashes in the pan?

Priddy was then a thriving mining area, ringed around with smelting-furnaces. The Romans made good use of its metal, thoughtfully leaving, as evidence, a "pig" of ore with the date clearly inscribed.

The character of a race must rest, to a large extent, on its traditions. These may, at times, be hard to believe, but excavations, on the other hand, bring unmistakable evidence to the surface.

The existence of the lake villages of Glastonbury and Meare was proved by Dr. Arthur Bulleid and Mr. St. George Grey. They were flourishing before the Roman occupation. The Great Bath, at Bath, with its steps worn by the feet of Roman citizens, was discovered only in the eighteenth century. A prehistoric pit village was found on Ham Hill, not far from the small Roman amphitheatre, or cockpit, humorously called the Frying Pan.

### Roman Remains

There is a sacred well and Roman villa at Whitestaunton, near Chard, where a mining engineer must once have lived, for it is near a mine undoubtedly worked by this intrepid race.

The lately-discovered Roman pavement at Low Ham is perhaps one of the greatest treasures to be unearthed in Somerset. The

Minehead today is a watering-place and hunting resort on the edge of Exmoor. The old town, seen here, is built on the hillside; the new town lies below. Minehead was once a busy port.

flowing cloaks of the horsemen give a vivid picture of the winds that always seem to be touching gale force on Ham Hill. What Venus lacks in modesty and elegance is amply atoned for by her happy family gathering in another panel of this delightful mosaic work.

What the Danes destroyed in Somerset, the Normans rebuilt, often to be destroyed during the Civil War. Only a stone gateway now shows where a Norman castle stood at Bridgwater. Taunton Castle still cherishes its Norman Constable's Tower and outer gateway. A few remnants of the walls and towers are all that is left of Stoke Courcy Castle, built during the reign of Henry II.

The nave, transepts and choir of Wells Cathedral date from 1174, and the magnificent west front was completed in 1239. The Bishop's Palace nearby also dates from the eleventh century, though the greater part is of the thirteenth century. It is on the moat of this fortified palace that the swans ring a bell for their dinner, a habit taught to them by the daughter of Bishop Eden, nearly a hundred years ago. Habit dies hard in Somerset, even among birds!

Of the many churches that date from Norman times, few are of greater interest than the little church at Stoke-sub-Hamdon, with its strange mythical beasts welcoming the stranger from the tympanum on the north porch, and its richly carved chancel arch.

### Norman and Elizabethan Treasures

But it is at Glastonbury that one finds the perfect gem of Norman architecture. Built on the site of the first wattle-and-daub church that was destroyed by fire in 1184, St. Mary's Chapel is so beautiful, even in its ruined state, that one cannot grasp what its loveliness must have been. It was a king's greed that, at the time of the Dissolution, turned this mighty abbey into a quarry for the road menders. The abbey church, its severed arches still standing in mute appeal to heaven for vengeance, is strangely appealing—in spite of the car park nearly at its gates.

It is to the Elizabethans that Somerset owes the finest of her domestic buildings. Montacute House, perhaps the best known, was built at the end of the sixteenth century by John Thorpe for Sir Edward Phelips. It remained in his family until 1913, when the National Trust took it into its fatherly keeping. Typically Elizabethan, with prominent porch and enveloping side-wings, it overlooks a pleasure-garden where cedars and yew trees, balustrades, classical temples and garden houses form a fitting setting for so magnificent a mansion.

Barrington Court, though of an earlier date, is somewhat similar. The Queen Anne stables, built by one of the Strodes, have been converted into a charming dwelling-house, making an interesting contrast to the dignified court at its side.

Brympton D'Evercy had a new frontage built to the older portion by Inigo Jones about 1680. Newton Surmaville retains its old-world atmosphere in spite of the railway that tries to overlook the grounds. It is

The weir and tea gardens on the Avon at Bathampton, a well-known retreat for summer visitors. The Avon in its upper reaches is popular with fishermen, and river parties abound.

within a few minutes' walk from the centre of Yeovil, but remains a thing apart.

Clevedon Court was once the home of Arthur Hallam, to whose death we owe Tennyson's elegiac verses. Here Thackeray wrote parts of *Henry Esmond* and *Vanity Fair*.

Coker Court, near the birthplace of William Dampier, is a fifteenth-century building, modernized in Georgian days. Dampier was the unwitting cause of Daniel Defoe writing his immortal story of *Robinson Crusoe*, for Selkirk, whose adventures formed its foundation, quarrelled with him and left his ship, later to be marooned on the island of Juan Fernandez.

Mells, the deeds of which little Jack Horner successfully concealed in a plum pie during the snatch-and-grab process that went on during the Reformation, still belongs to the Horner family. These noble houses, and many more, testify to the greatness of the sons of Somerset, and the love they bore their home county.

While the squire and nobleman were building their mansions, the country people were enjoying life in their own way. Many of their festivals, even then many centuries old, are still enjoyed to-day. There are still a few villages with their maypoles stored away ready to be gaily decorated and beribboned when a festive occasion draws near.

The candle auction at Chedzoy dates from 1490. Every twenty-one years Church Acre, a field in the parish, is put up for auction. The bidder whose voice is raised at the moment the candle expires is the owner of the field for the next period. The same type of auction is held annually at Tatworth, near Chard, and the bidders are regaled with a hearty meal of bread and cheese and cider afterwards.

At Tatworth, too, a real harvest supper is given to the harvesters after the grain is safely gathered in. Parsons still perambulate their various parishes to bless the crops on Rogation Days, and at Buckland St. Mary the plough, duly cleaned and decorated with flowers, is brought to the gates of the church by two stalwart horses to receive a similar blessing.

Sheep fairs are held annually in nearly every market town, usually on the patronal festival of the church. Bridgwater has its annual jollification, when fireworks and bonfires cause havoc to shop windows, and sometimes fill the local hospital with casualties.

The Minehead hobby horse still prances round the town on May Day—one of the many survivals of those far-distant days when paganism reigned supreme. Horseshoes and, sometimes, a holed stone, hang in stable and shippon to keep the witches away, and country folk look to the phases of the moon before sowing their gardens.

Old customs die hard in Somerset, and long may it be so.

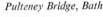

*Pulteney Bridge, Bath*

*Widecombe-in-the-Moor from Honeybag Tor*

# DEVON

### By JACK SIMMONS

DEVONSHIRE* ranks third among the counties of England in size: it is very little smaller than Lincolnshire. But whereas Yorkshire has for centuries been split up into three Ridings, and Lincolnshire into the Parts of Holland, Kesteven and Lindsey, Devonshire remains undivided—the largest single unit in English local government to-day. This unity is deceptive. For the county falls into three regions, each with some special characteristics of its own. In the past the life of each of them was to a large extent separate from that of its neigh-

---

* "Devonshire" or "Devon"? Except for certain special purposes, the two forms are interchangeable as nouns. Both are found in the *Anglo-Saxon Chronicle* (e.g. "Defenascir," "Defenun"), and the county historians use them indiscriminately. Neither is therefore to be preferred over the other. "North Devon" and "south Devon" are, however, obligatory. In general the adjective is "Devonshire," though "a Devon man" is familiar and perfectly correct.

bours; and even now the improvement in communications has certainly not broken down all the barriers between them or done away with their differences.

In the first place, there is the great division between north Devon and south Devon. This can be seen very simply in terms of physical geography. The general course of nearly all the main rivers of the county lies north and south. North Devon is therefore the region watered by the Taw and the Torridge, with their tributaries; south Devon is the country of the southerly rivers—Axe, Otter, Exe, Teign, Dart, Plym, Tavy, and Tamar. No precise dividing line can be drawn between north and south Devon, but roughly the division may be said to run from Lifton on the Cornish border up the valley of the little River Thrushel, round the north-western edge of Dartmoor, over the watershed at Copplestone, thence to Tiverton and so to the Blackdown Hills and Somerset.

South Devon, thus defined, includes Dartmoor. But the moor is very different from the surrounding country, in appearance, in history, in the life of its people. It forms the third of the county's main regions.

*Arms of Devon*

255

*North Devon.* To most English people north Devon means the coast: Lynmouth, Lynton and Ilfracombe, motor-coaches up and down precipitous hills, the quaintness of Clovelly, golf at Westward Ho! But that leaves four-fifths of north Devon out of account. What is it like as a whole?

### Wind-swept Grassland

To begin with, it is comparatively poor country. There are rich lands in the Taw–Torridge basin, and market-gardening round Ilfracombe; but on the whole north Devon is high, wind-swept grassland, with oats for its characteristic cereal crop—very different from the richer south and east, with their wheat and potatoes and apple-orchards.

The type of its villages, too, is distinctive. Very often they are dispersed, the church standing by itself or with only a few houses round it, the rest of the parish comprising scattered farms or separate hamlets. An example of this on the largest scale is Hartland, where the "borough" is two miles from the "church-town," the hamlet of Stoke with the great church, and the outlying farms are dotted all over the parish, which measures some four miles by six.

Again, the towns in north Devon bear a much less important relation to the countryside than they do in the south. They are fewer in number, and it is worth noticing that four of them showed a falling population between the last two censuses. Though this decline may be only temporary, the drop at Ilfracombe and Lynton was extremely sharp, amounting to more than twenty per cent in each case; and there was a similar trend, on a smaller scale, in the rural districts. Over most of England there is a steady drift away from the countryside and the small towns to the large centres of population; but here in north Devon it seems to be proceeding faster than elsewhere—certainly faster than in the rest of the county.

If most of the lesser towns in north Devon show some tendency to decline, Barnstaple fully maintains its position as the capital of the region. If you want to know what a traditional English market day is like, and that on a big scale, you should go to Barnstaple on a Friday. It has a large covered-in Victorian market-hall, where the goods for sale are displayed in great baskets called panniers. Early in the morning the town begins to fill with people from far and wide; countless buses jostle one another in the awkward streets; the place is brimming with activity. For this market is still a real commercial focus, one of the things that contribute most to the distinctive life of north Devon to-day. Exeter's radius as a shopping centre is large, and always growing, but Barnstaple market still holds its own.

Barnstaple has lost the great position it once held as a port, the herring fishery, the trade with Ireland and America remarked upon by Defoe. It has shared in the eclipse of the Devonshire woollen industry, and the pottery, which produces "Barum ware," has certainly not re-established it as an important centre of manufacture. To-day it is a market and residential town, subsisting mainly on retail trade and to a small extent on visitors in the summer.

### Huguenot Settlers

But it has a definite flavour of its own. One or two of the shops display curious names, of French origin, for a considerable number of Huguenots settled here at the end of the seventeenth century. (Sometimes these names have undergone strange alterations: "De Boursaquotte" was too much for the tongues and pens of Barnstaple people, who sensibly transformed it into "Buzzacott.") The Huguenots were kindly received in the town. That is not surprising, since Barnstaple, like the whole of north Devon, has always borne a strongly Puritan, Nonconformist character, which endures to this day. Chapels abound, not only in the town itself, but in villages and hamlets, even in isolation by the roadside, so that you might almost be in Cornwall or Wales. And, as usual, Nonconformity expresses itself politically in terms of Liberalism: the Barnstaple division returned a Liberal member to the last Parliament, and even in the *débâcle* of the party in 1945 the Liberal candidate stood second in the poll with more than 13,000 votes.

The Nonconformity and Liberalism of north Devon point perhaps to a greater de-

Old cottages at Branscombe, a tiny village between Sidmouth and Seaton.

(E.N.C.)

# BRISTOL CHANNEL

**LUNDY ISLAND**

ILFRACOMBE

LYNTON

COMBE MARTIN

*Morte Point*

17 miles

*Baggy Point*

BRAUNTON

**EXMOOR FOREST**

**WATERSMEET nr. LYNTO**

"Sharks Fins"

**BARNSTAPLE**

*Hartland Pt.*

CLOVELLY

BARNSTAPLE BAY

APPLEDORE

WESTWARD HO

**BIDEFORD**

SOUTH MOLTON

HARTLAND

GT. TORRINGTON

R. TAW

R. MOLE

CHULMLEIGH

Hartland Pt. Lighthouse

*Parish Ch. Barnstaple*

At Tiverton

HOLSWORTHY

R. TORRIDGE

HATHERLEIGH

R. TAW

CREDITON

RIVER TAMAR

OKEHAMPTON

*Moll's Coffee Hse. Exeter*

**EXE**

YES TOR

*Widecombe Ch.*

MORETONHAMPSTEAD

**DARTMOOR**

LYDFORD

MANATON

R. TEIGN

BRENTOR

BOVEY TRACEY

"BOWERMANS NOSE" MANATON

TAVISTOCK

WIDECOMBE IN THE MOOR

**TEIG**

PRINGETOWN *Prison*

ASHBURTON

**NEWTON ABBOT**

**FOREST**

HOLNE

BUCKFASTLEIGH

RIVER TAVY

TOTNES

R. DART

**PAI**

TOR

PLYMOUTH

DEVONPORT

PLYMPTON

*East Gate Totnes*

DARTMOUTH

BR

The Sound

KINGSBRIDGE

## Miles

BIGBURY BAY

*Slapton Ley*

START BAY

0    5    10

SALCOMBE

Start Pt.

*Eddystone Lighthouse*

*Bolt Hd. Prawle Pt.*

**ENG**

CORNWALL

# DEVON

EXETER CATHEDRAL

Toll House Honiton BLACKDOWN HILLS

R. OTTER

HONITON

Ashe House, Axminster    AXMINSTER

MARY

SEATON

SIDMOUTH

HARTLAND

DLEIGH
TERTON

HALL, TOTNES

PULPIT, HOLNE

TOR

N
W    E
S

ANNEL

gree of independence in its people than you will generally find farther south. This is partly the natural consequence of a poorer soil and a harder life. But it is also due to the relative absence of great estates, with the influence that landlords can exercise over the opinions of their tenants. North Devon has its own gentry, of course, and many of its families show a long history—Fortescue, Chichester, Bourchier, Coffin. There are delicious valleys and combes, perfect sites for an Elizabethan or Georgian house: I think of the Taw valley, with its long, sweeping curves and Tawstock Court at its mouth, or Weare Giffard in the narrower valley of the Torridge, or the astonishing peace of Hartland Abbey, only a mile back from the open Atlantic and the wicked coast. But, as a whole, north Devon is too windy and bare: the eighteenth-century landscape-gardener looked at it with horror as hopeless material for him to work upon. So it has remained, what it always was, pre-eminently a small farmer's country.

*South Devon.* If you drive from Barnstaple to Exeter, the last dozen miles of your journey lie through a country quite different from that farther north. You pass Crediton, ancient and sleepy, with its magnificent red sandstone church; then Newton St. Cyres, which has somehow managed to keep its pink cob-walled cottages, even though it lies all along the main road; and then a few minutes later you are in the valley of the Exe, over Cowley Bridge and into the outskirts of the city. Everywhere here you see mixed farming, fat cattle, timber trees, a park-like landscape: you are in the richest part of the county—the true "red Devon," in fact.

As you compare south Devon with north, more and more of these differences will strike you. Here in the south the villages are larger and more concentrated, like the villages of southern and eastern England. There are a great many more towns. Apart from the cities of Exeter and Plymouth and the string of holiday resorts on the coast from Seaton to Salcombe, the little market towns like Honiton, Tiverton and Kingsbridge are thriving places, often with some small light industry attached to them.

Something of their spirit was caught and preserved for ever by Trollope when he created the Devonshire town of "Baslehurst" in *Rachel Ray*. I have often wondered which of them he had in mind when he wrote it: Baslehurst may be a composite picture, a blending, say, of Totnes and Tiverton. It is one of his lesser novels, short, very quiet and gentle; but it provides a fascinating commentary on the close society of these little towns, their sectarian and political rivalries, the gossip, the huddled intimacy of their life. You can catch the same feeling still, walking about one of them on a market-day, or watching the religious activity of a Sunday morning, for things here are very slow to change—as slow as in the countryside, perhaps in some ways even slower. If these towns no longer return their own members to Parliament, most of them remain municipal boroughs. Their wool and serge industries have closed down, except at Buckfastleigh; but Tiverton keeps its big lace factory, and at Totnes they now bottle milk and cider. As for the people in the book—the weak, genteel Mrs. Ray, her censorious elder daughter Mrs. Prime, Mr. Tappitt, the small-town brewer—their descendants are living here still.

### South Devon Coast

It is hardly too much to say that south Devon nowadays is dominated by its coast. The south coast has always been much more important in relation to the interior than the north. For this, there are a number of reasons: the numerous valleys have made it more easily accessible; it is better provided with good harbours, in its estuaries and in Torbay, a splendid natural refuge from the south-westerly storms; the English Channel is a bigger highway of trade and war than the Bristol Channel ever was in its greatest days. In the past a good deal of the farm produce of south Devon went to the victualling of ships in harbour. Now it goes to the victualling of visitors, at Exeter and Plymouth, at Sidmouth, Exmouth, Torquay, Paignton. Of the old ports with their great history, only Plymouth is of real importance to-day, though it was exciting during the war to see some of the others coming to life again—French and English

naval ships side by side at Dartmouth, unaccustomed American voices in the streets of Salcombe.

But if it revived these little towns, the war also brought them danger and destruction. All of them were bombed, at one time or another. Dartmouth suffered severely—the famous Butter-walk was only just standing, its rich, decorated front horribly mauled; and as for Plymouth, it was one of the most heavily blasted towns in the country, comparable with Coventry and Hull. Nor was it only the coastal towns that were attacked. I well remember the shock I got when walking down to the village of Aveton Gifford on the road from Plymouth to Kingsbridge and coming upon its fine church (the best Early English building in Devonshire) bombed into ruins, the walls cracked, the tower fallen, grass growing over the uprooted grave-stones. The houses in the village, too, were much damaged; some of them utterly destroyed. One became used to sights like that in the great cities; but here in the open country—miles from a town, away from the sea—the spectacle was altogether more dreadful and strange. It reminded one grimly that south Devon was once again in the front line of England's defence, just as it had been against the Spaniards in the sixteenth century.

Now that we are back at peace, the life of south Devon has settled down into its old ways. Once more the trains are crowded with holiday-makers bound for Exmouth, Torquay, and Paignton, the hotels full, the townspeople out to make up for the lean war years. In these coastal resorts during the years to come we may expect to see mile added to mile of concrete promenade and —unless we are much more careful than we have been in the past—mean suburbs spreading out, eating their way relentlessly into the countryside. But beyond their reach things will go on as before, in the quiet places that tourists overlook: in tiny towns like Modbury and Bradninch and Ottery St. Mary, at Torbryan with its exquisite church, in the water-meadows of the Axe, under the great oaks in the park at Powderham.

*Dartmoor.* Dartmoor can be defined in several different ways. The Royal Forest of

These cobbled steps form part of the principal street, known as "Up-along," at Clovelly. A port in medieval times, it was still important in Elizabethan days. Now tourists and fishing keep it busy.

A panorama of the Devon cliffs and countryside round the fishing village of Beer. Years ago, before

the days of tourists, Beer's seclusion allowed its inhabitants to take part in large-scale smuggling.

A view of Torbay showing Torquay on the right and part of Paignton on the left. Semi-tropical plants flourish in the mild Torbay climate.

Dartmoor (which forms part of the Duchy of Cornwall) covers only the centre of the moorland: its outer edge is divided up into commons held by the inhabitants of the bordering villages. These villages have always been an integral part of Dartmoor, and the term should therefore be held to include them.

The moor is like nothing else in England —except its smaller counterpart in Cornwall, Bodmin Moor, and that shows some important differences. It is a great mass of solid granite, high, wind-swept, bleak. It affords pasture for cattle and ponies in summer, but agriculture is almost entirely confined to the shelter of the river valleys. On the other hand, Dartmoor is rich in minerals, which are hardly found elsewhere in Devon: they have made it from time immemorial an industrial area. That phrase "from time immemorial" is in this case literally true. We do not know when the tin on the moor was first worked, or by whom. The organization of the stannaries—that is to say, the mining districts of Devon and Cornwall—was already highly developed in the twelfth century, when its written records start. Nor was it only tin that was important. Copper and manganese used to be raised here, too. Most of this activity is now dying or dead, killed by the much greater supplies of these metals that have become available from other parts of the world; but you can still see the traces of tin-streaming and mining in many parts of the moor. And even now it has not lost its character as an industrial district. Dartmoor granite is still quarried, as it was for the building of London Bridge and Waterloo Bridge over a hundred years ago, and since 1834 china clay has been extensively worked in the south-west, particularly at Ugborough and Shaugh Prior.

But man has left his mark here in other ways as well: most obviously at Princetown, the one substantial settlement on the open moor. Its great prison was originally built to accommodate Frenchmen and Americans captured in the Napoleonic wars.

Since then it has been used for several purposes, and even at times altogether disused. It is surely, beyond competition, the grimmest building in England: one shudders to think that it once held nine thousand men. Princetown itself is as gloomy as you would expect. It caters, not very well, for tourists in summer, but its bleak position and the proximity of the gaol have effectively damped such spirit as it might have had. What a refreshing contrast to descend to one of the ancient stannary towns below the moor: to Tavistock, for instance, with its beautiful green stone houses, its memory of Drake and the great abbey and so many of the Russells.

A little industry, the business of the prison, some afforestation and agriculture in the sheltered places: these make up the life of the moor for nine months of the year. July brings the visitors, who have come to play almost the chief part in its economy,

264

many farmers having found that they yield quicker and surer profit than the land. By the end of September they are almost all gone, leaving the moor to withdraw once again into the storms and long mists of winter.

These, then, are the three regions of Devonshire, and some of the contrasts they present to one another. Nevertheless, they have many features in common: I have already pointed to a few of them. It is time to turn now to the character of the county as a whole.

Looking at the four south-western counties of England together, you will often find that Devonshire is linked more closely with Somerset than with its other neighbours Dorset and Cornwall. Devon and Somerset are bigger than the others; their agriculture has always been more prosperous; they were the greatest centre of the south-western woollen manufacture from the Middle Ages to the eighteenth century.

It is not always easy, but it is very important, to understand how rich Devonshire once was, until the woollen industry moved north, to be near the Yorkshire coalfield, a change that occurred less than two hundred years ago. In 1700 Exeter was indisputably the fourth city in England for wealth and trade; and as late as 1792 an acute political observer could remark of the county that "the extensiveness of its territory, the number of its inhabitants, and its weight of property, give it a capacity for the importance of a state equal to some of the American governments."

This past prosperity has left many marks upon the county to-day, upon its houses and towns and villages, upon the landscape itself. You get the sense of it immediately in such a church as St. Saviour's at Dartmouth, with its brasses and screen of the fifteenth century, its gorgeous Tudor pulpit, its great Jacobean gallery, where the cen-

265

Dartmoor, a granite tableland two hundred square miles in extent, was once thickly forested. Some of the sheep and wild ponies which pasture on it today are lost in its treacherous bogs.

turies are, as it were, piled in layers, one on top of another. Or look, again, at the lovely Georgian terraces of Exeter: those, that is, which escaped the German bombs.

The triple foundations of this wealth were the woollen industry, the shipping at the ports, and agriculture. By 1850, as we have seen, the first of these had decayed. The second also showed a marked decline in commercial importance, though this was largely compensated for by the great development of Plymouth as a naval base during the Napoleonic wars. Plymouth had

been a considerable town since its incorporation in the fifteenth century, but it ha become a great town (and ultimately a city only in the last hundred and fifty years. Yo can see the evidence of its rapid expansio still in the decent plain Regency houses— street after street of them—in Devonpor and Stonehouse, with churches and civi buildings to match. But Plymouth was, an is, primarily a naval port. Some ocea liners call there, but far fewer than at it rivals Southampton and Liverpool; and th same is true of its cargo shipping. In th respect the Devonshire ports have never recovered lost ground.

The county's agriculture, on the other hand, retained its full prosperity much longer, until the great depression of the 1870s. A steady fall in the acreage of arable land then set in, checked only in the war years. By 1907 the area under wheat was little more than a third of what it had been forty years earlier; by 1937 it had fallen lower still.

Yet though the ancient trades and the agriculture of Devonshire are slowly declining, they are not by any means dead. Small colliers still lie by the quay at Bideford; lace-making goes on in east Devon, even if Honiton is no longer its centre; cider-orchards cover many acres round Exeter and in the south—the county contains 8 per cent of the orchards of all England. You cannot understand the modern life of Devon without taking these things into account.

But what, you may ask, is coming to replace them? Or is the story simply one of a slow, almost imperceptible decay? Certainly not. During the past century and a half Devonshire has been going through an economic revolution, comparable in local importance to the far greater industrial revolution that has changed the whole life of the Midlands and the North. The Devonshire coast and Dartmoor have become one of the greatest holiday areas in England. The tourist industry has arrived, putting the county's economy on a new basis, raising it to perhaps a higher level of prosperity than it has ever reached before.

It began on the south coast at Sidmouth, Exmouth, and Torquay, which became watering-places early in the nineteenth century. Torquay was much the biggest of them, steadily developed by its wise, and lucky, owners. The result is a typical Victorian English town. It owes a great deal to its lovely site, but much also to good planning: the harbour with its fine quay and the Regency terraces behind it, the roads winding leisurely upwards, the handsome villas on Park Hill among their trees, the spire of Holy Trinity church precisely punctuating the landscape.

But Torquay, alas, is an exceptional town, and its outer edges are as dreary as those of any other. The general level of modern building in Devon is, I am afraid, more truly represented by its next-door neighbour, Paignton. Here the old village lay close under its fine red church and the bishop's palace, of which a wall and a tower

**Harvesting wheat on Shaldon Hill near Teignmouth. The rich soil of south Devon—the true "red Devon"—encourages the growing of wheat; the poorer north mainly produces oats.**

remain. It was a village still within living memory; but in the last fifty years it has expanded into a town of twenty-five thousand people. This development, as usual, has been very little controlled. Houses have sprawled into the countryside along the main roads towards Brixham and Totnes; they have joined up with Torquay, and threaten to engulf the village of Stoke Gabriel on its quiet creek of the Dart. All this development takes its origin from Paignton's popularity with holiday-makers.

The same problem appears, over and over again, on the coast, not only near the large towns, but at small places like Hope Cove in the south, Combe Martin and Instow in the north. It happens everywhere in England, this slow destruction of the countryside, and it is deplorable. But here in Devonshire it must in the long run prove suicidal, for the beauty of the landscape is the staple of the county's main industry. Happily, however, we may now be able to redeem some of the mistakes of the past. The Ministry of Town and Country Planning has adequate powers to prevent undesirable building, and they will be rendered much more effective if Dartmoor and some parts of the coast can be declared National Parks—though the prospects, at least as far as Dartmoor is concerned, get

gloomier every month. It is clear, in spite of all the protests that have been made, that the War Office intends to keep a tight hold on a large part of the moor, and on Braunton Burrows too.

After the last war the cities of Exeter and Plymouth faced a great opportunity, and in Exeter particularly the designed reconstruction of the shattered districts took in the importance of the city to the West Country. Here as elsewhere the plans were far in advance of the means for carrying them out. Exeter has been considerably rebuilt; while in Plymouth the rebuilding of the city has provided it with a fine modern commercial and shopping centre.

We need not be altogether pessimistic about the future. For even between the wars, while the worst attack was being made upon the English countryside, here in Devon there was some good building, to intelligent general designs. I am thinking, for instance, of the very pleasing estate just across the Exe at Tiverton. Let us have more of such houses, concentrated, not dispersed. Let us keep the coast free from further damage, if necessary by drastic restrictions, such as have been imposed with success at Clovelly. There is still time to do it now; in another twenty years it may be too late.

*Cliffs on the South Devon Coast.*

268

*Land's End*

# CORNWALL

By CLAUDE BERRY

IN THE most south-westerly of the counties of England there is still current and cherished an old saying that the Devil never ventured to cross the River Tamar from England into Cornwall for fear of being put into a Cornish pasty.

Now, although the Cornish housewife is avid of variety in the fare she provides, she is also extremely fastidious in her choice of ingredients for a pasty, her "national" dish; but let that pass. The point is that the Devil, in having selected the left bank of the Tamar as the south-western limits of his goings up and down the English land, may well have had in mind other considerations than the possibility of an ignominious end in the roaring oven of a Cornish kitchen.

Indeed, he may have been versed in precedents. For in thus neglecting Cornwall he was following the example of some quite notable representatives of human kind. In high summer nowadays, when Cornwall accommodates with great difficulty the hosts of

*Arms of Cornwall*

eager holiday-makers who come, chiefly, to explore her incomparable coast, it is odd to recall that for long centuries she was left almost completely to her own devices.

The Romans did not carry their great roads westwards beyond Exeter, and they merely infiltrated into Cornwall, the most highly mineralized portion of the land they had conquered, in order to ensure for themselves a supply of tin and antimony.

It was nearly four centuries after the arrival of the heathen English into Britain that they turned westwards to subdue the denizens of the narrow, tapering peninsula that thrusts out for some eighty miles into the restless Atlantic. The subjugation was no easy task, quite apart from the quality of the Cornish Celts as warriors of dash and fire. A contour map will show clearly that, before the invention of gunpowder at any rate, the conquest of Cornwall required ample time and overwhelming forces. And the English never wholly accomplished their purpose.

What they did, among other things, was to foster in the Cornish the long-prized legend of their semi-mystical Celtic champion, King Arthur, whose cult has ever since been associated with Tintagel

269

A popular waterway for yachtsmen, Helford River is a Cornish beauty spot well-loved by tourists for the charm of its scenery and the many delightful bays which are found on its shores.

and to a lesser degree with Camelford and Dozmare Pool; and to leave in the peninsula, except perhaps its extreme eastern portion, a heightened consciousness among the Cornish of their land and themselves, their language, traditions and customs, as being apart and distinct from England and the English. Not even yet has that sense of being "different" vanished from Cornwall.

Indeed, the Cornishman returning to his native county, has a feeling which is not fully shared by the sons and daughters of any other county of England on their homecoming. When he crosses the Tamar, by Brunel's superb viaduct between Plymouth and Saltash, or by the broad-beamed ferry to Torpoint, or by the road over a lovely fifteenth-century bridge which spans the river in its upper reaches, the Cornishman feels that he is doing more than pass from a neighbouring county into his own. To him, the crossing into Cornwall is one out of England into his "own dear country."

Not that there is, as the phrase is commonly understood, a Cornish nationalism. In every period, in fact, from the time of Queen Elizabeth onwards when England has been threatened from without, your Cornishman has proved himself as good an Englishman as the next. For one thing, Cornwall has been closely linked with the royal family since the fourteenth century, when the Black Prince was created Duke of Cornwall, a title ever since borne by the king's eldest son. But although there has been this special inducement to loyalty, Cornwall has not, through the intervening centuries, been uniformly quiescent. There were three risings in Tudor times, the last, in 1549, being occasioned by the issue of the first English Book of Common Prayer and the Act of Uniformity.

The Cornish, who had hitherto been allowed by a wise and benevolent Church to use their own Celtic language, with a certain amount of Latin, in their churches, had no liking for the new service. For one thing, only a few of them could speak or understand English. For another, they were then, and have been ever since, sticklers for "what do belong to be," and they did not like the new form of worship. It was, they said, "lyke a Christmas game." With a perfectly sincere profession of loyalty to the English crown, they yet protested that they must "utterly refuse this new Service." This protest many of them sealed with their blood in battle, while others who escaped death on the field perished on the gallows. Since the crushing of the Prayer Book Rebellion there has never been from Cornish people any serious opposition, manifest or latent, to conformity with the broad, general pattern of English life. There never will be now.

The Cornish, however, have retained, woven into that general pattern, one that is distinctively their own. Though the quick ear can detect the inverted commas in their tones, Cornish people still refer to the English as "foreigners." In their own county, and more especially the eastern portion, where place-names are Saxon more commonly than anywhere else, the Cornish have happily inter-mixed and inter-married with the English; but for the most part they have retained the qualities peculiar to, or usually found in, people of Celtic stock. The English Prayer Book, the fact that the Bible was never translated into Cornish, the lapsing of the old Cornish miracle plays, the new commercialism of Tudor times, and the new place assigned to Cornwall in the defence of the country before the war with Spain in which Cornish seamen played such a gallant part—all these contributed to the decay of the Cornish language. By the beginning of the eighteenth century nearly everybody in Cornwall could speak English, and not many could also speak Cornish, though the language lingered on in the west for many years. It has, indeed, never completely died out, and it cannot while Cornish place-names and surnames, some of them the most bewitching sounds in any language, endure. As a language of the people it is finished; but it must be recorded that many more Cornish people can speak and write their own language than could do so even twenty years ago.

In that period, too, there has been a revival of the ancient Gorsedd of the Cornish Bards—a picturesque and impressive ceremony among the hills and moors—and of such pagan rites as the Midsummer Eve bonfires, into which are tossed garlands of flowers, herbs and weeds. Immediately after the First World War there sprang into being all over the county Old Cornwall Societies, pledged to gather up and preserve the fragments that remained of Cornwall's past. Within a year of the conclusion of the Second World War these societies, mainly adult, were augmented by Young Cornwall Societies.

Why this pre-occupation with the past? The answer probably is that the Cornish have such a rich heritage. There are few areas, for example, of greater interest to the archæologist. Charles Henderson, first among Cornish scholars, once declared that there was scarcely an acre in the county which, to the skilled field worker, would not

**Kynance Cove, on the south-western tip of the Lizard peninsula, shows the famous Cornish coastal scenery at its best. Although it is difficult to reach it is thronged with visitors in the summer.**

# CORNWALL

ST. IVES

ST. MICHAELS MOUNT

MULLION COVE

ATLANTIC OCEAN

Kelsey Head

WHITESAND BAY
Longships Lightship
LAND'S END
Runnel Stone
Blake
ST. JUST
Market Place Penzance
ST. IVES
ST. IVES BAY
Godrevy
St. Agnes Head
PERRANPORTH
NEW
ST. AGNES
PENZANCE
NEWLYN
MOUSEHOLE
MARAZION
St. Michaels Mount
MOUNTS BAY
HAYLE
Boatbuilding at Hayle
CAMBORNE
REDRUTH
Truro Cathedral
TRURO
Trevithick's Cottage. Camborne
N
W
E
S
HELSTON
PORTHLEVEN
The Flora Dance, Helston
FALMOUTH
ST. MAWES
MULLION
HELFORD R.
FALMOUTH BAY
Landewednack Church
LANDEWEDNACK
Kynance Cove
The Manacles
St. Anthony's Lighthouse
Lizard Point

yield up some interesting relic of a bygone age. This is particularly true of the Land's End peninsula and the Bodmin Moor, where are grouped or scattered stone circles and massive dolmens, wind-swept barrows, hill-forts and cliff-castles, and re-

mains of villages of as long ago as three or four thousand years.

Among the sand-dunes of Perranporth is a little Celtic church of fifteen hundred years ago: it is the oratory of St. Piran. To-day its comelier walls are encased for pro-

LOOE from the Railway

MOUSEHOLE HARBOUR

BUDE BAY

WIDEMOUTH BAY

BUDE

STRATTON

Trevose Head

Pentire Point

BOSCASTLE

TINTAGEL

PADSTOW

Wadebridge

CAMELFORD

Boscastle Harbour

Newquay Sands

WADEBRIDGE

China Clay

BODMIN MOOR

LAUNCESTON

ST. COLUMBE MAJOR

BODMIN

The South Gate, Launceston

R. FOWEY

R. LYNHER

R. TAMAR

CORNWALL

DEVON

ST. AUSTELL

LOSTWITHIEL

LISKEARD

CALLINGTON

Polperro Harbour

Royal Albert Bdge, Saltash

FOWEY

ST. AUSTELL BAY

GISSEY

POLPERRO

LOOE

SALTASH

an Point

LOOE BAY

Miles

WHITESAND BAY

0      5      10

Rame Head

tection in concrete, though it is never likely again to be buried in the sand as it was for many centuries. St. Piran was one of over a hundred Celtic saints who came, in miraculous ways, by sea to Cornwall, where they gave their names to parishes, villages, churches and holy wells, and an origin to the saying that there are more saints in Cornwall than there are in heaven. A similar oratory is known to lie buried under the sand at Gwithian, across the bay from St. Ives. (This wild and rugged north coast of Cornwall has suffered much from blown sand—the introduction of marram grass at length kept it reasonably stable—and for years the priest who had charge of the chapel-of-ease of St. Enodoc, across the Camel Estuary from Padstow, had to reach the interior by descending a ladder through the roof.)

It is thanks largely to the Celtic saints of Cornwall that Christian worship has had there from Roman times an unbroken continuity of which England generally cannot boast. "If St. Augustine had come to Cornwall," Archbishop Benson once remarked, "he would not have had to have made his way through crowds of heathen people who wondered what he was come for; for here in Cornwall he would have found people to meet him with the full knowledge of the Gospel, worshipping here day after day, as well as from Sunday to Sunday." From that Age of the Saints have come down a hundred holy wells, the water of many of them even in recent times believed to have miraculous properties, including the cure of many of the ills that flesh is heir to. Then there are some three hundred Cornish crosses, the granite of some of them elaborately carved, and the largest, at Mylor, near Falmouth, seven feet in the ground and ten feet out of it.

### Celtic Legends

But as interesting a legacy as any from the Celtic saints is the store of legends accumulated during the centuries after their passing: of the dwarf, St. Neot, for example, standing on the base of the churchyard cross and throwing the key into the church door lock, which it then turned of its own accord; of the jovial Piran, patron saint of Cornish miners, stumbling over the sand-dunes from his experiments in tin smelting, with a head buzzing from over-much tippling; or of battles fought with slabs of Cornish granite as weapons, between neighbouring holy men, whose tempers were quick and whose lives were preserved only by Divine diversion of their lustily flung missiles.

To these legends of the saints must be added many more. Some of them, such as those relating to Tristan and Iseult and to King Arthur, which have been narrated by bards, poets and story-tellers, have now passed into the realms of immortal romance. And the Cornish have also a fascinating store of folk-lore, much of it peculiar to themselves.

Why should this be? There are doubtless several answers, and one almost certainly is that through the ages the Cornish have been chiefly a fishing and mining people. (Agriculture was shockingly neglected until, in late Tudor times, a temporary decline in mining "drave them to play the good husbandmen.") Than fishing and mining there are few occupations more fraught with many and great dangers.

### Dangerous Occupations

A tremendous storm suddenly sweeps the Cornish coast: a fishing fleet is destroyed and a fishing village bereft of most of its menfolk. There is a cloudburst over a tin mine and the water rushes down the main shafts so that scores of miners below perish by drowning. Or there is a fall of ground and miners are buried; or premature explosions rock the galleries underground—the safety-fuse had yet to be invented—and Death stalks through the acrid smoke. In a famous mining parish which, in the course of a century, had produced over ten million pounds' worth of copper, one out of every five miners met a violent death. And the remaining four were always threatened by a premature end from "miner's trouble," consumption or silicosis, which made theirs the shortest working-lives in British industry.

Leading such an arduous and insecure existence, is it so very strange that these old miners were prone to look to the Little People of their own imagining as allies in the dangerous struggle for survival? Even nowadays a Cornish miner, though he will sing as only a Cornish miner can, will never whistle at his work. Nor will he, in that dank underworld of his, make on the face of the rock at which he is working any sign resembling a cross. It may be nonsense—he will admit it—but deep in his heart the Little People, who must not be offended by these things, still have life, and he listens, when the roarings of the pneumatic drills

274

The picturesque harbour of St. Ives has given the fishing port a permanent artists' colony.

The foundation stone of Truro cathedral was laid in 1880 by the Prince of Wales. The design is in the Early English style. The city is on the Truro river, which enters the sea in Falmouth harbour.

have subsided, for the faint "knocking" that indicates the friendly, protective presence of the Little People, as his forebears, between the blows of their picks, listened long ago.

For mining, like fishing, goes back to the very beginnings of things in Cornwall. It was for tin that the dark-eyed strangers of the Mediterranean shores came to this peninsula, which they thus brought into contact with civilization before it reached the rest of England. Through the clay-slate surface of Cornwall ages ago, in the course of

terrific convulsions deep below, were erupted big "islands" of granite—the Cornish hills, the broken backbone of the county, having round their bases a variety of minerals: a little gold and silver; some lead, iron and zinc; cobalt, antimony and manganese; bismuth, tungsten and arsenic; and much tin and copper. Production of tin, which has taken the Cornish miner as deep as two thousand feet "below grass" and even far out under the sea, dominated the Cornish economy until the eighteenth

276

century. Then copper, hitherto so despised that field hedges were made of it, came into its own; and at one time in the last century Cornwall was producing the bulk of the world's supply. One in every five persons in the county was engaged in tin or copper mining, and fathers clambered up and down the hundreds of feet of ladders in the shafts with their sons on their shoulders: co-workers in an industry which, although it sometimes yielded fantastic profits, ill repaid the mass of working miners.

### Decline of Mining

In the most prosperous period of the industry there were over three hundred mines at work. Now there are only three: two producing tin and one wolfram, which is used for hardening steel. The explanation of the virtual extinction of the mining industry is not that Cornwall's abundance of minerals has been exhausted, but that tin and copper can be produced much more cheaply elsewhere. And so thousands of Cornish miners, whose forefathers were the world pioneers of deep mining, have gone reluctantly from their native towns and villages to all parts of the world, giving rise to the saying that wherever a hole has been dug in the ground in the quest for minerals, there a Cornishman will be found. Still active are the engineering and fuse-making industries of Camborne-Redruth, the largest town in Cornwall and one which shows how little men thought of planning and the graces in days when mining absorbed most of their time and energy. At Camborne, too, there is still a School of Mines which feeds Empire and other countries with first-class mining-engineers. And what else remains? Hundreds of mine-shafts, their stone walls now covered with bramble and grasses and wild flowers, and besides these, perched on lonely headlands, scattered over the heath-clad downs, or grouped at the foot of granite hills from Chapel Carn Brea in the far west to Caradon near the Devon border, scores of slowly crumbling engine-houses, from which almost every vestige of human activity has vanished.

Cornwall's other principal industry through the centuries has also fallen upon evil days; though it has vitality still and may yet, with wise fostering, flourish again. The decay of Cornish fishing is a story too long and complicated to be told here; but its beginnings can be ascribed to that time not so long ago when the pilchard suddenly changed its migratory course and came no longer to Cornish waters in its scores of millions. Pilchard fishing was the basis of a lucrative export trade to the Mediterranean countries, particularly Italy; and the home market in Cornwall—English "foreigners" have never given this tasty, nutritive little fish its due!—was steady and remunerative. Given a good pilchard season, the fisherfolk could rub along though all else failed. They have never recovered from the blow of that change in pilchard migration. Instability of markets and prices for other fish has also been a factor in the melancholy diminution of fishing-fleets, as has been the unwillingness of young Cornishmen of the coves and ports to follow their forebears into an industry in which so much is risked for returns so small and uncertain.

### Farming Methods

To the stranger from the fat, rolling plains of England, Cornwall's multiplicity of small farms and tiny fields, with their thick, stone hedges, is a source of wonder and surmise. But they are perfectly appropriate to a hilly county much of which is downland and moor with granite under the thin, acid soil, and great tracts of which, until comparatively recently, were laid waste—as, alas, was so much Cornish woodland!—in the quest and production of minerals. In all, a large acreage has been reclaimed for cultivation; but by degrees and in small pockets. So the county is one predominantly of smallholdings, there being three times as many farms of fifty acres and under as of a hundred acres and over. Thus confined, the farmer has had to put his land to the best advantage. He has done this by pasturing more cows to the acre than are found in any other county, and by rearing a pig population more numerous than elsewhere, at the same time maintaining large poultry flocks. The Second World War and its aftermath have sadly disrupted this economy, and the acreage under the plough has been more than doubled—a remarkable achievement by farmers many of whom felt they were flying directly in the face of providence by giving over to the plough land that was so clearly ordained for the pig, the hen and the cow.

The war seriously disturbed also the even and profitable course of the specialists in fruitful valleys of the south-running rivers and in those "golden acres" north and east of Mount's Bay from which England obtains her earliest spring flowers, new potatoes, and up to seventy thousand tons of broccoli each season. There is a normal export trade to England of about five thousand tons of Cornish blooms every year; but this, of course, dwindled to minute proportions as the war went on and from flowers the growers turned to vegetables. At one time during the war some three thousand acres in the Penzance district were laid down to new potatoes, which were followed by either broccoli or sugarbeet and cabbage. This three-crop production is made possible chiefly by the mild and equable climate and a humid soil, but another important factor is the liberal use of seaweed as manure. And Cornwall's extensive coast—the longest of any county—contributes in another way to the fertility of land between the hills and the sea, for the sea-sand of the north coast is immensely rich in carbonate of lime, and farmers for centuries have been legally free to take away as much as they require.

### China Clay Industry

How completely agriculture and horticulture have ousted mining from its old proud position may be deduced from the fact that for every person now engaged in mining there are thirty occupied on the land, almost a precise reversal of the position in the early and mid-nineteenth century. Just before that period, around the granite mass of Hensbarrow, north of St. Austell, a new industry had its beginnings. This was the china clay (*kaolin*) industry. The traveller by road or rail through mid-Cornwall must often have been puzzled by the enormous greyish-white pyramids of the district. The hills are composed of china clay waste, from which a special form of concrete block is now being manufactured for use in what is known as the Cornish Unit house, a most suitable prefabricated house for Cornwall. China clay itself is a carefully processed product of Cornwall's weathered granite, which is washed and baked and, ultimately emerging as a pure white powder, is used in an ever-increasing variety of articles, ranging from pottery and paper to textile fabrics and linoleum, cosmetics and toilet powders, and medical supplies. The industry in its best year produced nearly a million tons, much of which was exported to all parts of the world. In normal times, indeed, china clay comes second only to coal in bulk among British exports. The future—in which mechanization will play a much larger part than ever before—seems assured; for there are almost illimitable supplies of china clay still under the surface, and the deeper the pits go down the whiter and purer the clay becomes.

### Granite Quarries

Before the war some four thousand men and youths were employed in this industry based on the weathered granite—many more than were occupied in the quarrying of granite in its extremely durable form. Even so, the Cornish granite quarries north and east of Bodmin, the county town, and between Redruth and Penryn, comprise an important undertaking, the product of which has found its way to the streets, embankments, bridges and monuments of London, and as far distant as India and the Far East. It brings in annually about a million pounds. Much of the granite is of the lovely silver-grey that is seen at its best in such buildings as Truro Cathedral (the first cathedral built in England since the Reformation) and the County Museum and Art Gallery in the same city—which, though not the capital of Cornwall, is the nerve centre of its administration. The County Hall there is of another pleasing Cornish stone, a warm-coloured elvan found in dykes near the granite. Like most Cornish buildings, the hall is ideally roofed with native blue-grey slate, which is quarried at Delabole in north Cornwall. The quarry there has been worked for about four centuries, and it is now a mile in circumference and about a quarter of a mile deep. Some four hundred men and youths win and fashion Delabole slate which is still "the best to cover houses that is within this Region."

Work in the slate and china clay industries, though onerous, is healthy; but granite workers share the miner's liability to contract silicosis. For the prevention and cure of this disease medical science has been experimenting with a method tried out successfully in Canada: the inhalation of aluminium dust with which the men's changing-rooms are sprayed. Should every other source of aluminium fail, Cornwall could yet produce her own—from the very accommodating china clay; but although this was accomplished experimentally in the stress of war, it is not a normal commercial proposition.

In the past fifty years, and mainly during the past two or three decades, a new industry has grown in Cornwall. It is one upon which the Cornish, shaken and depressed by the decline in their traditional fishing and mining, and foreseeing "the end thereof as a bitter day," embarked with misgivings and reluctance. From the earliest times the Cornish have had a reputation for hospitality and courtesy, and the people of the peninsula have been delighted to find their county a potent source of attraction to "foreigners." But when it came to "making money out of the visitors," that was a different matter. Hitherto, in a variety of occupations in which individual skill and initiative were prime requirements, the Cornishman had retained the sturdy independence and the good manners of his forebears. Could he go on combining these when he began, as Sir Arthur Quiller-Couch put it, "to take pay for entertaining strangers." "Q" was not the only one who was troubled because it would be a hard reputation to keep.

Yet kept it has been, and in circumstances which "Q," fifty years ago, could not have foreseen, since it was chiefly between the two Great Wars of our time that the entertainment of strangers for pay established itself as a basic industry of Cornwall. Why do people from all over the country and farther afield flock in such great numbers to Cornwall every summer? Chiefly, of course, because of its incomparable coast, one hundred and eighty square miles of which—made up of the whole of The Lizard and Land's End peninsulas and a belt of the north Cornwall

**The Furry or Flora dance is one of the best-known of the old Cornish customs which have survived modern times. It takes place yearly on 8 May in Helston, and young and old may all take part.**

Polperro is as famous as a show place in Cornwall as Clovelly is in Devon. On the south coast, between Fowey and Looe, it attracts crowds of visitors every summer.

coast three miles deep from Padstow Bay to the Devon border—were once earmarked as a National Park. The selection was modest enough, for the Cornish coast is remarkably varied and presents some quite astonishing contrasts. In general, the north coast is more towering and majestic than the south, and cliffs from four to five hundred feet high are not uncommon there. They reach a climax of grandeur in the north-east, where they attain a height of seven hundred feet, about half the height of Brown Willy, the county's highest hill. These northern cliffs are the haunts of innumerable sea-birds and of such rare species as the Cornish chough, the buzzard, and (this family sadly reduced during the late war) the peregrine falcon. Deep down from the cliff tops one may sometimes see a grey seal disporting itself or floating, solemn and

shining, in the green water which fills a sanded gully; but the grey seal—not unjustly, it must be said—has been branded the enemy of fishermen and its numbers systematically reduced.

Along this north coast, except in a few sheltered places, there is scarcely a tree to be seen, and all the more welcome therefore are the cool, dark green of the tamarisk that fringes the bays and the grey-green of the marram grass among the sand-dunes— which, by their softness, provide such an element of welcome contrast when you come suddenly upon them from the majestic cliffs. There are only two harbours of any consequence in the north, neither of them a harbour of refuge such as a coast of this wildness and ill-repute in autumn and winter really needs. The harbour of St. Ives is small and exposed, and Padstow's, while

280

t is spacious, is all but choked with sand—the outcome, it is said, of a mermaid's curse.

The south coast has more and better harbours, and in Falmouth's has one of the finest land-locked harbours in the world. There are several memorable headlands along this coast, but although it lacks altogether the peculiar charm of the sand-dunes t is much softer, as a whole, than the north. Nearly all the Cornish rivers run south to the sea, so that there is along the south a succession of enchanting wooded valleys sheltered from the gales that sweep across the peninsula and dwarf the wild flowers and grasses of the north, causing the wild rose there to creep close to the ground and trimming the clumps of furze as though with an enormous razor. The south has a profusion of tropical and sub-tropical plants and shrubs, and at Falmouth bananas have been cultivated in the open. Presumably it is the mild climate of the sheltered and picturesque south, in particular, that has fostered the illusion during the past thirty years of Cornwall as England's Riviera. It is, of course, not a Riviera. By comparison with the rest of the country, Cornwall has warm winters and cool summers; in other words, its climate is remarkably equable, which the Riviera's is not. Moreover, even south Cornwall shares, though not so abundantly as north Cornwall, the exhilarating breezes of the Atlantic, compared with which the Mediterranean air, as "Q" once remarked, is as stale soda water to freshly poured champagne.

The coast is the chief glory of the county —where else is there a cove as beautiful as Kynance, near The Lizard; a stretch of cliffs as grand and impassive as the granite that confronts the sea near Land's End; or a bay as blue and gold and spacious as Perran's or Newquay's? But the wise stranger will not neglect the inland scene, a succession of hill and valley which has its own dramatic qualities and its own small delights: a village like Blisland, on the edge of the Bodmin Moor, or Mawgan-in-Pydar, deep in the lovely Vale of Lanherne; a shade-dappled, sun-spangled moorland stream rippling under a little fourteenth or fifteenth century bridge; a winding lane, topped with the bright fire of furze and flanked with tall fox-

gloves, and dropping suddenly to a valley where rare and varied ferns grace the hedgerows; or (that uncommon spectacle in Cornwall) an exquisite little church spire thrusting upwards from the familiar cluster of slate-grey roofs which, from a distance, are like one of Cornwall's also familiar pearl-grey mists enwrapping the feet of the hills.

If church spires are rare in Cornwall—though not so rare as the nightingale, which has only recently been authenticated among the county's three hundred different species of birds—so also are magnificent parish churches with richly ornamented towers. For the most part Cornish parish churches are long, low buildings with tall and simple western towers: the kind one would expect in a comparatively poor county and one that is so much exposed to stress of weather. The churches are mainly of the fifteenth century, though Norman work has been traced in more than half of them. Among their chief delights are the towers of St.

These disused mine-stacks at St. Day are typical of the Cornish inland scene. Bleak and gaunt, the buildings dot the landscape, half-ruined reminders of Cornwall's prosperous past.

Austell and Probus; the richly-coloured windows of St. Neot; the frescoes of St. Breage and Poughill; and some of the old bench-ends upon which the medieval craftsmen exercised their wit and devotion.

From their forebears the Cornish have inherited a love and a talent for singing, but they no longer use the dialect in talking as commonly as their grandsires did. The decline set in after the Education Act of 1870 and has been most marked since secondary education happily became available to large numbers of Cornish children. But the dialect—like many a peculiarly Cornish dish, with names like "star-gazy pie" and "figgy-obbin"—lingers resolutely in the country districts and fishing-coves: a dialect full of apt and memorable similes and racy and salty phrases.

Popular pastimes from the earliest days have survived. Hurling has now a firm hold only at St. Columb, where play with the silver-cased ball attracts large crowds every year. Wrestling in the Cornish style has at times lost its old place, but there has been a remarkable quickening of interest in it since the early part of the century, and in the aftermaths of both World Wars it acquired a new buoyancy. The Puritans and John Wesley and his followers doubtless expunged from the Cornish calendar many a joyous ritual and observance from the old times; but at Padstow the Hobby Horse, with its mingled grotesqueness and beauty and its unremarked fertility rite, still prances through the streets on May Day linking the little town with the ancient British settlement near the harbour mouth and a week later at Helston an altogether more decorous and elaborate festival brings together crowds from a wide area as in the days of the medieval fair, though even then the Flora (Furry) Dance must have been an ancient custom.

How long will these and many another old pastime and custom survive into the Atomic Age? And for how much longer will the Cornish people retain their individuality?—the character in which *naïveté* is mingled so charmingly with subtlety, sturdy common sense with native superstition, forthrightness with the oblique, enormous vitality and energy with the *mañana* of the Iberian peninsula whence their early ancestors came. Nobody can say, but it may safely be said that nowhere is a more determined resistance being offered to the featureless hosts of uniformity in the byways of life —and youth is flocking to this resistance movement.

In the end, perhaps, the sea will be the chief factor in preserving Cornwall's individuality, as it has been the dominating factor in her history. By many miles to the north and south it separates the county from the nearest land, and to the west stretch two or three thousand miles of rolling ocean. So the sea may, with its own savour and integrity, preserve Cornwall's also—and with them, Cornwall's magic.

*Cadgwith near Lizard Point*

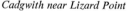

*Thoresby Hall near Ollerton*

# NOTTINGHAMSHIRE

By FRED KITCHEN

TWO MAIN facts stand out clearly in the shaping of Nottinghamshire's early social and economic development. The first is her position on the main routes from southern to northern England; the second, her great waterway, the River Trent. The shape of the county is an irregular oval, measuring just over fifty miles from north to south and twenty-seven miles at its greatest width. Two important roads run parallel across its entire length; the old North Road (to distinguish it from the more important Great North Road) traverses the western side of the county, starting at Rempstone in the south, passes through Nottingham, Mansfield and Worksop, and enters the West Riding of Yorkshire at the border village of Bawtry. The other, the Great North Road, traverses the eastern side; from Grantham in Lincolnshire it enters the county just below Balderton, crosses the ancient Fosse Way and passes through Newark, Tuxford and Retford, all famous post-towns in

*Arms of Nottinghamshire*

the coaching days, whence it bears north-west to Bawtry. Bawtry is the converging point of all roads from Nottinghamshire leading to the north because of the swampy, low-lying nature of the land in the extreme northern corner of the county; in the days before these "Carlands" were drained and reclaimed, Bawtry was the only point at which traffic might safely pass round the swamps into Yorkshire.

Bawtry, now a quiet township close to the borders of Nottinghamshire, Yorkshire and Lincolnshire, was, before the railway age, the focal point of all trade and commerce in the north Midlands. Strings of pack-horses brought to the wharf at Bawtry hosiery goods from Nottingham, lead from the Derbyshire mines, cutlery from the region of Sheffield; because of the bad condition of the roads before the Turnpike Trusts took them over, these goods were then loaded on to boats and carried by the River Idle to Stockwith on the Trent

283

# NOTTINGHAMSHIRE

YORKSHIRE

NOTTINGHAM CASTLE

WORKSOP PRIORY GATEWAY

THORESBY

"The Bell, Barnby Moor

WORKSOP

E. RETFORD

Railway Wks. E.Retford

Clumber Park

WELBECK ABBEY
The Dukeries

Thoresby Park

OLLERTON

TUXFORD

Collieries

RUFFORD ABBEY

Southwell Cathedral

CARLTON

MANSFIELD

SUTTON IN ASHFIELD

MARKET NEW

DERBYSHIRE

NEWSTEAD ABBEY

SHERWOOD FOREST

SOUTHWELL

NEWARK

HUCKNALL TORKARD

The Castle Gate, Nottingham

R. TRENT

LINCOL

THE "MAJOR" OAK SHERWOOD FOREST

NOTTINGHAM

WOLLATON HALL

FOSSE WAY

BINGHAM

CANAL

Colston Bassett Cross

GOTHAM

The Mill, Costock

COLSTON BASSETT

N

W

S

Miles

0    5    10

LEICESTERSHIRE

and from there to the Humber and the port of Hull. In the same way, from the fourteenth century onwards, water-carriage on the River Trent supplied a lucrative trade route from the south of the county, while a network of canals from the West Riding and from Chesterfield placed Nottinghamshire in a favourable position to take advantage of the later speed-up of the industry in the nineteenth century.

To many people who only know the county by report, the mention of Nottinghamshire calls up visions of pit chimneys, factories and a vast industrial area. While it is true that a flourishing industry covers the western regions, Nottinghamshire on the whole is still fundamentally a notable agricultural county.

### Geological Divisions

It is generally accepted by the inhabitants of the county that geologically one belongs to "the sand" or to "the clays," so sharply is the land divided between the Bunter sandstone of the west and the Keuper marl on the east, and it is interesting to note how completely these geological formations determine the social and economic structure of the county.

Thus, on the extreme west, a narrow strip of magnesium limestone forms a continuation of the Derbyshire hills. These constitute the only high ground in Nottinghamshire, the surface of which is elsewhere generally flat or undulating. On this western border, where it touches northeast Derbyshire, lies the Nottinghamshire coalfield and, farther north, the South Yorkshire coalfield, in the Doncaster area. In the nineteenth century Mansfield became the centre of a busy mining area, though long before that time Woolaton and Eastwood, near Nottingham, had been famous for "outcrop" on its "visible coalfield". During the present century the coal area has pushed eastward as far as Clipstone and Ollerton (places which lie above what geologists call the concealed coalfield). Northwards the collieries now extend to Harworth on the south Yorkshire border, thus converting a large area in south Yorkshire and north Nottinghamshire which, a few decades ago, was a purely

agricultural district, into a continuation of the coal area with its attendant industries.

The sinking of pits in a new coalfield naturally attracts mine workers from distant collieries. These immigrants are usually of two types, the majority enterprising, the minority unenterprising. The erection of a new pithead gear always brings together men with a greater diversity of language (most of it bad) than did the erection of the Tower of Babel. Even in the purely agricultural villages in the vicinity of the coalfield a new race of inhabitants came into being. In Nottinghamshire the native villager left his plough for the more lucrative employment in and around the mine, so that the farmer, to replace his staff, crossed the Trent to engage his men from the agricultural districts of Lincolnshire. Though nowadays the farm men in the western coal area may claim to be Nottinghamshire born, a surprisingly large number are descended from parents who hail from "beyond Trent." It would seem, then, that the colliery villages are composed of a heterogeneous population gathered from every county that has a coalfield; only large towns with long-established industries can claim to have a true-bred native population.

### Remains of a Royal Forest

By far the most interesting, though the least productive, of the geological divisions of the shire is the Bunter sandstone, which stretches from Nottingham in the south to Bawtry on the northern edge and embraces Sherwood Forest and the Dukeries. This sandy district was formerly forest land throughout its entire length; it was, moreover, a royal forest, greatly favoured by the Plantagenet kings. Though most of this forest land is now under very intense cultivation, enough of it remains to make this part of the county an ideal spot for the tourist and the romantic explorer into the realm of Robin Hood. Sherwood Forest to-day stretches from Nottingham to Worksop, including the country around Mansfield and covers some two hundred square miles of territory. It includes the greatest number of private parks and the stateliest oak trees to be found in any comparable area in England. That part of the area which is

Sherwood Forest, familiar to many people through the romantic legends of Robin Hood. It stretches from Nottingham to Worksop, extending over an area of two hundred square miles. Most of the land is disafforested and is now under cultivation.

usually referred to as the Dukeries got its name for the reason that, in the eighteenth century, four dukes had their residences in the neighbourhood.

Clumber, now taken over by the National Trust, was the beautiful residence of the Dukes of Newcastle from the eighteenth century until recent times.

At Thoresby lived the Duke of Kingston-upon-Hull, of whose noble family the best remembered name is that of the celebrated beauty and wit of the eighteenth century, Lady Mary Wortley Montague. One of the most beautiful of the Dukeries' many fine parks is undoubtedly Thoresby Park.

At Welbeck Abbey the Dukes of Portland have resided through seven successive generations, and, though public opinion may not, in general, favour dukes, it cannot be denied that agriculture in Nottinghamshire owes more to the Portland family than to any other single fact in the shire.

Formerly Worksop Manor was the seat of the Duke of Norfolk, being also associated with the famous Bess of Hardwick, Elizabeth Talbot, Countess of Shrewsbury. While on the subject of these ducal seats,

I should mention several other large estates, notably Rufford Abbey, long the seat of the Savile family, which came, by marriage, into the possession of the family of the Earl of Shrewsbury. There is also that fine old Augustinian house, Newstead Priory, in which Byron spent part of his childhood.

So, in this beautiful forest, the peer and peasant exist side by side, with not too much distinction nowadays between rank. But then, there never has been really, as this extract from an eighteenth century letter of a noble lord will show:—

" On Monday last I was very tolerably drunk by 5 o'clock, and though I went through a variety of ceremonies . . . supping and drinking with many companies . . . I walked home about 5 o'clock in the morning, having kept myself, in fact, continually drunk or elevated for eleven hours. I had a very good night's rest and was not at all the worse next day."

That letter might have been written by a peer or a miner.

The question may be asked why some counties have much larger private estates than others. The answer largely depends on how many abbeys and religious houses the county possessed at the time of the dissolution of the monasteries. Nottinghamshire was fairly rich in ecclesiastical lands and, when these passed to lay-lords, their estates were vastly increased though not often, unfortunately, to the benefit of the poor agricultural community.

As regards towns on the Bunter sandstone (that is, roughly, the western half of Nottinghamshire), the city of Nottingham is the most important. For many generations Nottingham has been the home of the stocking-frame weavers and the centre of the lace industry, though only a generation ago many of the surrounding villages worked stocking-frames as a home industry. The trend of modern requirements, along with the emancipation of women, has, however, changed Nottingham's staple industry. In place of lace and stockings, the demand now is for cycles, cigarettes and cosmetics. It also has considerable printing and chemical industries.

Situated on the Trent, which is spanned by a fine bridge, the town is known to cricket enthusiasts the world over. In Trent Bridge it possesses one of the finest county grounds in the country.

Nottingham Castle still lords it over the city. Built on an elevation of sandstone rock, honeycombed with caves, notably Mortimer Cave, the reputed hide-out of Roger Mortimer and Isabella, Queen of Edward II, the castle was acquired and rebuilt by the Corporation in the 1830s and is now an art gallery.

The shire, being mainly agricultural, claims few other towns of outstanding industrial importance, the only two on the western side being Mansfield and Worksop. Mansfield owes its rapid growth to the development of its coalfield and certain industries affiliated to coal and iron; but it maintains its ancient reputation as an agricultural market town. Close by is Mansfield Woodhouse, the reputed site of a Roman villa. North of Mansfield is Worksop, known as the Gateway to the Dukeries. Its chief industries are coal, timber and malt, though a generation ago chairmaking was a notable and a natural trade for this town near the forest. A clean, pleasant town, it makes an ideal starting-point for visitors to the Dukeries, being the nearest

**Trent Bridge and the church of St. Mary Magdalene at Newark seen from the canal. The waterway is an important transport route exploited by the brewing and malting industries and iron and brass foundries of Newark, which is both an agricultural and industrial centre.**

town within reach of Clumber, Welbeck and the forest around Edwinstowe.

Of the towns in the eastern (Keuper marl or clay) half of the shire, the first of any importance coming from the south is Newark-on-Trent. The centre of an agricultural district, it holds a key position on the Trent water-way and the Great North Road and has long been famous for its corn market and annual fairs. It owns an historic castle, notable as the place where King John ended his reign; and later as a stronghold in 1646 for the King's party during the Civil War. The castle is now in ruins, but is well worth a visit from travellers along the Great North Road. The surrounding district, and notably Carlton-on-Trent, also holds a high place in England for its fine breed of shire horses. Its main industries are connected with iron, brass, brewing and malting.

Travelling north we come to Tuxford, of no great importance nowadays, but with a pleasant, old-world look about it that reminds one of its importance as a post-town in the old coaching days.

A little to the north of Tuxford, still on the Great North Road, is Retford. Retford owes its chief importance to it position as the junction of the L.N.E.R. main line from London to York and the north and the line from Sheffield to Lincoln through Worksop. This latter line was originally called the Manchester, Sheffield and Lincolnshire Railway and the bucolic wit of the Nottinghamshire ploughmen was quick to interpret the initials M.S.L. on carriages and wagons as "mucky, slow and lazy." Retford is the centre for the Parliamentary division of Bassetlaw and, besides having a large agricultural market, i notable for its iron foundries, paper mill and rubber works.

### Agriculture and Stock Rearing

The district around these three eastern towns is purely agricultural, the soil, a rather heavy clay, being of similar nature to that found in the neighbouring county of Lincolnshire. Wheat is the main crop, with a fair acreage of beans, while of root crop sugar-beet has become of most importance since its introduction into this country at the beginning of this century.

On the sand land barley is the most suitable crop, with sheep as the main stock; while on the clay lands, which are too wet for sheep root crops for fattening cattle are the most suitable. As the clay has long been noted for its type of heavy horses, so has the forest sand been noted for its hunters and bloodstock. Followers of the Turf of a few years ago will be familiar with the old stables of Welbeck and of Worksop Manor. But Nottinghamshire has always been famous as a stock-rearing county whether of bloodstock, shires or cattle Another notable difference between the sand and clay agriculture is the size of farmholdings. In the forest regions the farms are usually large units from one hundred to five hundred acres, whilst the clay lands (apart from small holdings of around fifty acres) tend to run to a fairly level unit of about one hundred acres.

In the north around Walkeringham Misterton and Misson—what splendid

Newstead Abbey, near Nottingham, was founded in 1170. It was for long the seat of the Byrons, but was sold after the poet's death and now belongs to the city of Nottingham.

Laxton parish church and pound seen from the village green. The church, though largely rebuilt, contains some interesting monuments. The village lies three miles south-west of Tuxford.

names for a swamp!—and for a considerable stretch along the Trent, the soil is alluvial, river-sand or warp-land. This small area has been continuously improved and drained, from the seventeenth century onwards, and has been converted from a swampy wilderness to the most productive land in the shire. Periodically the land is irrigated by the silt from the river ("warped" is the native term) and newly warped

well-equipped and efficient Midland Agricultural College at Sutton-Bonnington in the south-west corner of the county. This college serves the counties of Nottingham, Leicester, Lincoln and Derby as a research station and a school for budding agriculturists in farming, both theoretical and practical.

Amongst Nottinghamshire's natural resources are limestone quarries, brick and

Reputed to have been a halting place of the Crusaders in the time of Richard the First, the inn, Ye Olde Trip to Jerusalem, is situated under the crag upon which Nottingham Castle rises.

land is particularly favourable for market garden produce, celery and root crops of every description.

Other breaks from the sand and clay occur in the Trent valley and on the Leicestershire border in the south of the county. Here the rich alluvial deposits make ideal feeding-grounds for dairy farming and stock raising.

No account of agriculture in this county would be complete without mention of the

tile works and gypsum quarries. Consequently the villages are built, fairly equally, of limestone and brick. In very old cottages plaster floors and ceilings of gypsum were the usual feature, though now floor-boards are the normal practice for bedrooms, an innovation welcomed by the stockinged feet of the village labourer. On the other hand, the native brick-and-tile cottage, which would look out of place in the grey landscape of hilly Derbyshire, merges well

Poppies and corn in high summer, a typical Nottinghamshire landscape scene. Four-fifths of the county is under cultivation, and crops can be harvested almost as early as those in the south.

with the red soil of Nottinghamshire and, when mellowed by age, is the essence of the charm for which the forest villages in the county are noted.

Nottinghamshire is not only famous for its industry; it has always held a high position in the realm of sport, notably cricket, while, as a hunting district, it has centuries of traditions behind it, from the killing of wolf, deer and badger, down to the present-

day killing of foxes. Though the chase is not so popular in the present age, the sight of pink-coated huntsmen, dappled hounds and lovely horses moving across the landscape supplies just sufficient pageantry to make hunting a pleasant and popular factor in the lives of the people. Because the miner does not hunt on horseback, it does not follow that blood sports are abhorrent to him. He, too, enjoys a chase, as is duly

The Council house and Long Row, Nottingham. This, the civic centre, opened in 1929, was traditionally the site of the market square. Today lawns and marble pavements replace the old cobbles.

recorded in the county's local weekly press, where the number of his "catch", "who caught him" and the cost are duly set out.

But the best known of the county's sporting activities is undoubtedly cricket. Here Nottinghamshire has always been well to the front, and many famous names in county cricket belong to natives of this county. Trent Bridge, the home of Nottinghamshire's cricket, is a famous field for county and international games.

Early in the nineteenth century we find the name of William Clark, founder of the Trent Bridge ground; following him comes a long list of doughty champions of the wicket, William Gunn and his two nephews, John and George, "Johnnie" Dixon, Tom Wass and so on until we reach the present.

Where does the county recruit its great players? From every colliery club in the shire; from every village and from every estate where there are workmen enough to form a team. Cricket is the only thing that matters in Nottinghamshire on a Saturday afternoon in summer, and not a boy in the forest glades but thinks of Trent Bridge as he shapes up at some young "Larwood" out to spin his bails.

Nottinghamshire possesses two famous football clubs, Notts County and Notts Forest, and football is a game followed by thousands; but when discussing the county's sporting prowess with the native folk, it is best for the stranger to stick to cricket.

Nottinghamshire Musical Festival and the many dramatic societies which flourish under the guardianship of the Nottinghamshire Rural Community Council demonstrate the county's interest in the fine arts. A remarkable feature of village life during the winter months is the number of choral and dramatic societies in existence, along with discussion groups. Moreover, the adult education movement is bringing much light into the traditional darkness of the winter-time Nottinghamshire village.

Though Nottinghamshire has not many literary lions, her few poets and writers have been men of merit. The best known, of course, is Byron, while of lesser merit was Kirke White, who was born in Nottingham. Of more recent celebrities, D. H. Lawrence was a native of Eastwood near Nottingham.

And so Nottinghamshire, from her vantage point on the main arteries that circulate the life-blood of trade and traffic through the kingdom, adds her quota with her miners, artisans, farmers, cricketers and poets (whether they be of the sand or the clays) to its overall flow.

*Major Oak, Sherwood Forest*

*Woodhouse Eaves*

# LEICESTERSHIRE

## By BERNARD NEWMAN

THE League of Nations ranked Leicester and Lille as the most prosperous cities in Europe. This ranking must have had some good basis, for prosperity is seldom achieved by accident.

Leicestershire is a remarkably compact and self-contained county. If it were suddenly cut off from the rest of the world, it could feed, clothe and house its people. Here is one of the keys to the county's well-being: its economy is varied, and is based upon essentials rather than upon luxuries. In its turn, this results from its geography and geology.

Leicestershire is the central county of England. Most parts of it are nearly a hundred miles from the nearest sea-coast—an unusual distinction in this small island. It enjoys a midland climate—indeed, the nearest approach to a continental climate which England knows. The effect of its distance from the sea is shown in its considerable range of temperatures: in summer it is often hotter than on the south coast by day, but its nights are much colder. This climate has affected the natural

resources of the county, and it is well known that climatic conditions have wide effects upon human character.

The central position of the county made it a vital centre of communications, even before the coming of the Romans, who built their town of Ratae (Leicester) at the junction of the Fosse Way and the Gartree Road. It is still so today: two of the main railways from the north to London, and many main roads, pass through Leicestershire, a fact which has banished the isolationist ideas that might have prevailed in a more detached county. Travellers passed through it continuously, bearing the news or trends of the day. Thus in Leicestershire today are to be found minds which are receptive rather than dynamic: but because of its continual contacts with the greater world outside, there has developed a slight inferiority complex, which often expresses itself in exaggerated self-criticism.

In older days Leicestershire was almost entirely agricultural: indeed, this condition prevailed until a century ago, when the fertile county

*Arms of Leicestershire*

293

still provided famous grazing grounds: and although considerable crops of grain and roots are grown today, Leicestershire sheep and cattle are still famous the world over. Indeed, the county can claim to be the nursery of the scientific breeding of animals. When the Leicestershire type of sheep was first bred, wool was as important as mutton, and the long wool of the sheep, nurtured on local pastures, led directly to the founding of one of Leicestershire's major industries.

## The Hosiery Industry

Even in the fourteenth century Leicester was an important centre of the woollen trade—which had begun in Norman times. On the invention of the stocking-frame four hundred years later, the local merchants saw the chance of developing a more lucrative trade. The long staple wool of the local sheep favoured the making of stockings and other hosiery. In 1792 it was estimated that forty per cent. of the population of Leicester was engaged in this trade; the number of stocking-frames in the whole of Britain in 1844 was forty-eight thousand four hundred and eighty-two, and of these twenty thousand eight hundred and sixty-one were in Leicestershire.

They were worked by hand and foot—some may still be seen in the villages. The introduction of steam power revolutionized the industry. Here, again, the local resources of the county were invaluable.

The Leicestershire coalfield, situated to the south and west of the Charnwood Forest, is small—only twenty square miles in extent—but its position makes it important. One pit is only eight miles from Leicester. Thus, in the vigorous days of the Industrial Revolution, the county had ample supplies of fuel, and was well able to maintain the rapid progress of the day. The old village industries merged into great factories, complete with the most modern machinery for making every kind of hosiery. Even American and Russian visitors have been amazed at the huge and efficient plants, which supply not only home needs but a large export market. Leicestershire hosiery is known and appreciated in every country in the world, for many firms have recognized the selling value of quality above mere cheapness in price.

The change in methods has imposed its effects upon the life of the people. Once a family worked a frame at home: then its women travelled into Leicester or some other manufacturing town to work in the factories. Ibstock, reputed to be the largest village in Britain, with a population of over six thousand had, until recently, only one tiny factory and a brickyard, but supplied a large labour force to the towns. Now, however, the decentralization process is in force, and gradually industries are being developed in the villages and small towns. Hinckley is an important hosiery centre, and factories are in full operation at Coalville, Shepshed, and adjacent places. Leicester's own industries have over-spilled into neighbouring villages like Syston, Blaby and Earl Shilton.

Today the wool of Leicestershire sheep would not supply more than a fraction of the industry's needs. Huge quantities are imported and processed before use. The range of products is now so wide that cotton and rayon goods are also extensively manufactured.

Another major industry also springs direct from the native soil. The extensive grazing grounds, their gentle slopes well-watered and protected from cold winds by abundant trees, provided sustenance for vast herds of cattle—even today dairy farming is a considerable industry, and London draws a proportion of its milk from the midland shire—which is also the home of Stilton cheese.

## Manufacture of Boots and Shoes

In older days the herds made available large numbers of hides. As a natural result, tanneries were established for the making of leather, and the boot and shoe industry attained some importance. Again, at first it was a local trade, but in the last century machinery was introduced, and today Leicester houses the largest boot factory in the world. The trade employs twenty-two thousand people, compared with hosiery's thirty-four thousand.

Industry breeds industry. Leicestershire people are independent, and like to be self-

A peaceful scene near the village of Groby, four and a half miles from Leicester. It is one of several centres at which granite is quarried for roadmaking, and it was here that Elizabeth Woodville lived before her marriage to Edward IV.

**High Street, Melton Mowbray.** This old town stands at the confluence of the rivers Eye and Wreak, fourteen miles from Leicester, and is noted for agricultural produce, cattle and pork pies.

supporting. Thus in the county there are now considerable engineering works, providing machinery for all local industries and exporting it abroad.

Some trades arise automatically from local resources. The ample deposits of clay encouraged the development of a considerable manufacture of bricks and sewer pipes. The hard rocks of the Charnwood Forest have been quarried for centuries: the streets of London are paved not with gold, but with Leicestershire granite.

This does not end the chronicle of Leicestershire occupations. Still more depend on local products, like the making of wicker baskets and chairs. Others have developed from local enterprise, and today Leicester manufactures range from typewriters to optical lenses.

One other product may be mentioned. In the seventeenth century Leicestershire was famous for the quality of its pigs—a contemporary writer attributes this to the vast quantity of beans grown and consumed. The numbers of pigs have now decreased, but their fame persists, and Melton Mowbray pork pies are still counted as a special delicacy. This town shares with Market Harborough a wide fame for agricultural products, but the latter centre is rapidly becoming a scene of industrial activity.

Thus the greater part of Leicestershire's industries have evolved from agriculture—which, in itself, is still a major industry. In normal times grazing is more important than grain production; it can be worked with fewer hands, and can compete more successfully than grain can with foreign products. Two-thirds of the area of the county is permanent grass. No house in Leicestershire is far away from the rich green meadows, with their luxuriant hedgerows and frequent spinneys.

Yet, although the overwhelming proportion of Leicestershire folk follow the occupations chronicled above, it is notable that to some people the county is merely the hunting shire. It is true that this sport has long been established. The county is a hunter's paradise. The numerous small woods and coverts provide natural breeding-grounds for the foxes. The gentle slopes of the hills, giving broad views; the undulating grass lands, with no precipitous descents, admirable for cross-country gallops; the frequent hedges, to add a spice of excitement; the absence of impassable rivers; the large areas dotted only with tiny villages—all these combined to attract hunting people. By local report, the lush Leicestershire grass was the dominant factor in earlier days, since cattle could be fattened in two years instead of in the normal three: they were sold in the autumn, leaving considerable districts free for the chase.

Today fox-hunting is gradually becoming a picturesque survival, for it is expensive, and the number of people who can afford it constantly diminishes. Yet most villages of the county know the thrill of a meet. Local people delight to follow the hunt—some on horseback, some, in these lazy days, by motor-car; schoolboys and other adventurers on foot.

Geographical conditions, then, have had marked effects upon local life—intensive in older days, considerable even now. What of history? A man can seldom escape from his traditional background.

The city of Leicester is much older than its county. It was a Celtic settlement long before the coming of the Romans. They, appreciating the importance of its central position, made it an administrative centre, then called Ratae. Later, Angles and Saxons occupied the land, and for a time Leicester was the centre of the kingdom of Mercia—and was the traditional home of King Lear. It fell to the Danes, who left many traces of their occupation—Leicester was one of their five principal Danish boroughs. The Norman impact in the area was only slight, and the basic strain of the local people is a fusion of early English and Danish.

Since this was the source of the modern English language, no sharply marked dialect is found in the county. There is a pronounced accent, especially on vowel sounds, tending towards that of Yorkshire, but there is little trace of those strong provincial dialects which are almost local languages. Where unusual phrases and expressions are encountered, they generally owe their origin to early English rather than purely local forms of speech.

It was not until the tenth century that history records the Midlands as divided into

The old, half-timbered grammar school at Market Harborough was founded in 1614. It stands in the Market Square, where it shares pride of place with the fine medieval church of St. Dionysius.

Charnwood Forest, near Ling Hill. Known as the "playground of Leicestershire," it is a rugged upland district covering some fifty square miles. It is now largely disafforested.

shires—a little later the Normans dubbed them *comtés*, or counties. The boundaries of Leicestershire have changed but little in a thousand years. Geographically they are well formed, for they follow over the greater part of their length the outlines of the basin of the River Soar, a tributary of the Trent. This, together with the gentle gradients of the countryside, permitting easy communications, encouraged the growth of that compact and balanced community to which I have already referred. It is interesting to note that, so far back as records have been kept, the population of the city of Leicester has almost always exactly equalled that of the rest of the county.

First effect of a people's history is on its culture. Apart from its churches, many of Leicestershire's buildings reflect the vicissitudes of the years. Once dwellings had to be designed for defence as well as for living, but most of the ancient castles of the county are now mere ruins. In later years, when

security was established, houses became places to live in, and many examples of every period remain, from the magnificent Belvoir Castle to humble cottages.

The county is not especially rich in historical buildings. In the capital itself survive the Newarke Gate, the old Town Hall where Shakespeare is reputed to have recited his verses to Queen Elizabeth, some ancient churches, and a few Roman remains. In the shire principal points of interest are Kirby Muxloe Castle, the ruins of a fifteenth-century castellated mansion; the old manor house at Peatling Parva; old houses at Thurcaston—one of which is claimed as the birth-place of Hugh Latimer; among the churches sentimental interest is highest at Lutterworth, with its associations with John Wycliffe; and of the ruins pride of place goes to the castle at Ashby-de-la-Zouch, made famous in Scott's *Ivanhoe*—though most of the "historical" events described therein are fictitious. A historical site of far greater importance is Market Bosworth, where the battle of 1485 changed the course of English history. A cairn of stones over a spring whence the ill-fated Richard III took his last drink is the only monumental reminder.

The essential feature of local architecture and design generally is practicability. Local materials have been used, ranging from brick to stone. Some cottages were built of blue slate from the old Swithland quarries—now so valuable that a man has been known to pay for his own funeral by selling his grandfather's tombstone.

Thus in Leicestershire there are few of the half-timbered houses encountered so picturesquely in the neighbouring shires. Modern building, especially, is of plain brick or concrete. A building is intended for service rather than ornament.

This plain, unvarnished utilitarian outlook is a combined legacy from both history and geography. Centuries of comparatively easy life, dependent upon hard work and the utilization of local resources, have bred a reasonably sturdy people, very practical in their outlook. The county boasts but few famous names among its sons—few artists and poets: but it has produced very large numbers of practical men, from George Fox, the founder of the Society of Friends, to Thomas Cook, the pioneer of organized popular travel.

Leicestershire has produced no Prime Ministers and very few conspicuous figures, but among the administrators, professional men, technicians and skilled workers who make up the solid body of the nation, her reputation is very high. Her sons are to be found in every corner of the world. Conditions at home have encouraged not a race of romantics, dreamers or philosophers, but a breed of enterprising people of solid worth.

This outlook is reflected in the business position. As has been mentioned, the county's industries have been founded upon essentials rather than luxuries—principal

**Standing in a wooded valley in Charnwood Forest are the ruins of Ulverscroft Priory, an Augustinian foundation of the twelfth century. They are in a remarkably good state of preservation.**

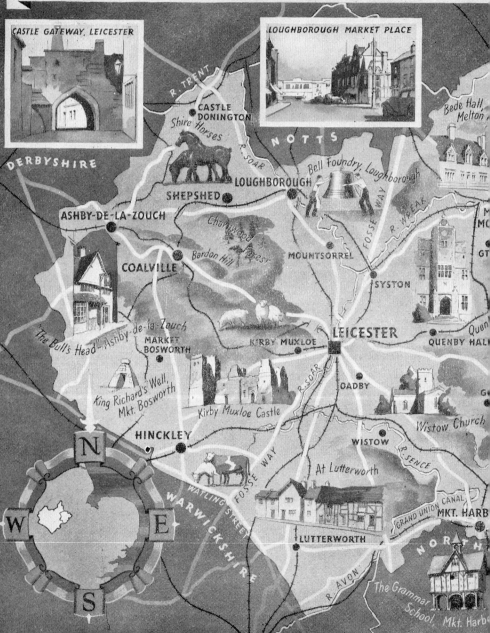

# LEICESTERSHIRE &

CASTLE GATEWAY, LEICESTER

LOUGHBOROUGH MARKET PLACE

R. TRENT

CASTLE DONINGTON

Shire Horses

DERBYSHIRE

NOTTS

R. SOAR

Bede Hall
Melton

Bell Foundry, Loughborough

LOUGHBOROUGH

SHEPSHED

ASHBY-DE-LA-ZOUCH

Charnwood Forest

FOSSE WAY

R. WREAK

MOUNTSORREL

Bardon Hill

COALVILLE

SYSTON

M
MO

GT

"The Bull's Head" Ashby-de-la-Zouch

MARKET
BOSWORTH

KIRBY MUXLOE

LEICESTER

QUENBY HALL

Quen

King Richard's Well,
Mkt. Bosworth

R. SOAR

OADBY

G

Kirby Muxloe Castle

Wistow Church

N

HINCKLEY

WISTOW

R. SENCE

At Lutterworth

W

E

WATLING STREET

FOSSE WAY

WARWICKSHIRE

GRAND UNION CANAL

MKT. HARB

NORTH

S

LUTTERWORTH

R. AVON

The Grammar
School, Mkt. Harbe

300

# RUTLAND

OAKHAM CASTLE

THE TOWER BLOCK, UPPINGHAM SCHOOL

Miles

0     5     10

products are food, hosiery, boots and building materials, which people *must* have even in bad times. Thus it has always avoided the worst effects of devastating slumps. A region dependent upon a single industry is always in a precarious position—in its most prosperous days it can be on the edge of disaster. Leicestershire's industries are so widespread that catastrophe could never be complete.

(The idea of a mixed economy, incidentally, also applies to agriculture. It is seldom that a Leicestershire farm is found specializing in a single crop. More usually it produces grain and roots, breeds cattle and sheep, and houses a dairy herd. Thus, if one section of agricultural produce fares badly, the others should relieve the situation.)

Although some of the Leicestershire factories are among the biggest in the world, the tendency is towards a large number of medium firms rather than one or two gigantic companies. This is the result of the industries growing out of local conditions. Factories were not planted by outside operators, but were built up and developed from very small local industries, directed by local men.

Their practical outlook, however, made the manufacturers realize that there are many problems which are common to them all so that research and technical education are as advanced as in any other part of the country. Loughborough Technical College, indeed, attracts students from every corner of the world. In the town are large engineering and hosiery works, and a world-famous bell-foundry; the war memorial here took an unusual form—a carillon rivalling those of the Low Countries in its range and quality. The fact that it provided a dignified memorial and at the same time an advertisement of Loughborough's skilled workmanship is perhaps another example of the practical outlook which is so characteristic of Leicestershire folk.

The experienced, practical man has confidence in his own ability. Managers are generally far-sighted and progressive, keen on modern adaptations, and alive to the value of adequate publicity. Workers can compare with their like the world over: hosiery operatives help to maintain the high

The church at Newtown Linford. This village, with its quaint slate and thatch cottages, stands in the Charnwood Forest and is typical of the many picturesque hamlets in the north-west of the county.

quality of their products, and the output of the Leicestershire miner is the highest in Britain. This confidence in trade and occupation is in strange contrast with the self-criticism to which reference has been made, and which is a Leicestershire failing. No one likes a boaster, but a man who constantly decries himself may gradually sink to the standards of which he speaks. Local pride can be a valuable asset. Because of its

central position, and of its small size and population, Leicestershire has seldom had a proper appreciation of its own worth.

Due to its comparative prosperity, Leicestershire has known fewer economic disturbances than any comparable county. This, again, is due to local conditions. Reference has been made to the high output of the Leicestershire miner, who is not merely a good worker, but is more contented than most of his kind. The explanation may lie in his wider interests. There is no such thing as the colliery village, so common farther north, where the miners are virtually segregated from all their fellows. The one-class community is dangerous to morale: it breeds introspection and a short-sighted outlook. If the pit is doing badly, the entire village is involved in the disaster.

In Leicestershire a miner may live between a farm worker and a hosiery operative: his viewpoint is broadened: he sees that his is not the only job which matters in the world. This makes him not only a better worker, but a better citizen. And his mine manager also lives in his village, shares his life and his problems, and is readily approachable. This mingling of the population in all classes and occupations is one of Leicestershire's assets.

The Leicestershire towns are not distinctive, but fit into the general pattern of our time: especially, they are practical—and clean. The older features of the county are best seen in the rural districts—in the little market towns, when the farmers gather, or on the great days of a cattle show or an annual fair. Similarly, in studying its education, attention should be given not only to modern technical colleges but to the ancient grammar schools dotted about the county.

Too many foreign visitors come to London and think that they have seen England. It is just as big a mistake to visit Leicester and imagine that one knows Leicestershire.

Physically Leicestershire is not especially distinguished. Its wide valleys and undulating countryside are relieved scenically only by Charnwood Forest—now, alas, denuded of most of its trees. Once, the geologists say, this was a range of great mountains rising from a midland sea. Now the hills are a mere nine hundred feet high, but their fern-clad crests are a welcome playground for the local people.

There is little of the picturesque about Leicestershire, but a solid simplicity and a green freshness of great appeal. It has often been called the fortunate county, but this does not imply any lucky dispensation. Nature has been reasonably bountiful, but the local inhabitants have not wasted their sustenance. They have worked in co-operation with Nature, a sure road to prosperity and happiness. As might be expected by their geographical position, they share the faults and virtues of north and south, east and west. They have some of the stolidity of Yorkshire, but with it a touch of volatility. They rouse easily, but their enthusiasm can fail. They are not brilliant, but exploit what gifts they have.

*Church Street, Lutterworth*

Since ancient times the lords of the manor at Oakham have had the right to demand a horse-shoe from every peer of the realm first setting foot in the town. This remarkable collection which includes horse-shoes given by George VI and his Queen, today lines the walls of the Assize Court.

*Ram Jam Inn, Great North Road*

# RUTLAND

### By J. WENTWORTH DAY

"I AM THE only person I have ever known who has been to Rutland. I admit that I have known men who have passed through Rutland in search of a fox, but I have never met a man who has deliberately set out to go to Rutland; and I do not suppose you have."

Those words are not mine. They were written by my old friend, H. V. Morton, the man who put the heart of England into golden prose. And he is right enough. Do you know a man who has ever set out to go to Rutland? I do not. But if an American were to ask me to show him the heart of England, the England that has its roots struck deep and strong in Saxon history, the England of thatched cottages, with white-washed walls, of stone manor houses with mullioned windows, of great deer parks where the deer pass like dappled shadows under the forest oaks, the piece of England that gives its title to a duke, where a village called Ketton annually pays a few shillings to provide the Queen with leggings, that taxes every visit-

*Badge of Rutland*

ing peer, prince or king and makes him pay a horseshoe: then, I repeat, if my American wanted to see such an humbly rich slice of England, rich in cattle, houses, customs and fields of corn, I should say: "Go to Rutland."

That is a long paragraph to spend on a small county. Rutland is only seventeen miles long and about seventeen miles broad. It has only two towns, Oakham and Uppingham, and neither of them is big enough to be a municipal borough. Think of it—a county without a single mayor! But Oakham has something much more important than a mayor and corporation. It has the remains of a splendid Norman castle in whose Great Hall they hold the Assizes twice a year (although no one ever commits any crimes in Rutland!), and hang up on the walls the most astounding collection of horse-shoes in the world. Some are small and some are big. The biggest are beaten out of strips of metal seven feet long.

The reason for this display is that by ancient custom, so ancient that no one quite knows when it started, every peer, prince, king and queen who passes through Oakham must pay a tax of a horse-shoe. If he does not pay the people of the town have the right to take one from his horse.

This pleasant pastoral scene near the village of Whitwell, between Oakham and Empingham, gives a good impression of the fine, open hunting country for which Rutland is renowned.

And as fox-hunting is, with farming and a little stone-quarrying, the principal industry of Rutland, quite a lot of peers, princes and kings have passed through Oakham on horseback in search of a fox. George IV gave a solid bronze horse-shoe which stands seven feet high and cost £50. Queen Elizabeth gave an enormous shoe. Queen Victoria, Queen Alexandra, Edward VII, Edward VIII, George VI and Elizabeth the Queen Mother have all added their horse-shoes to this unique display.

The custom began, they say, when Walkelyn de Ferriere, Master of the Horse to the Conqueror, held Oakham Castle. He was the ancestor of the present Earl Ferrers, and it may be that, having been in charge of the farriers who had to keep the battle horses and pack animals of the Conqueror's army well shod, he knew the value of a free supply of good horse-shoes.

But there is more to the credit of Rutland than horse-shoes. It is small, but rich. Rich in the pastoral scenery of hill and vale, of great woodlands and broad shining valleys, of villages, nearly all of them small, nearly all built of stone or with thatched roofs and plastered walls, villages which crouch in friendly company about their little churches, their cosy manor houses, their greens, their ponds and waddling ducks.

It is rich in cattle, for this is a cattle-grazing country, and rich, too, in corn. There are no factory chimneys to stain the bright air and that I account, indeed, as a great richness. There are only three main roads, the Great North Road, the Kettering to Nottingham road, and the Birmingham-Great Yarmouth Trunk Road, to bring the stink of petrol and the unholy haste of motor-cars into this county which has lived for centuries to the sound of the galloping feet of horses and the slow tread of fat cattle. And that, again, I account a richness.

But there is a little left of an ancient British track-way which they call Horn

306

Lane, and there is a maze of other quiet lanes and country roads, edged by hedgerow oaks and wild honeysuckle, where you need move to one side for no one but the harvest wagons with their clouds of attendant finches, the farmer on his way to market or the fox-hunter, of the early morning, hacking to the meet.

Unkind wags have said that Rutland takes its name from the bad state of its rutted roads, of which Richard Parkinson wrote in 1808:

"The ruts are so deep that the traveller must keep the wheels of the vehicle in the ruts, by which both he and his horse are thrown and tost about in the most horrid manner imaginable."

Arthur Young says in his famous *Tours* of the Rutland roads:

"Some of them had ruts four feet deep by measure, and into these ruts huge stones were dropped to enable wagons to pass at all; and these, in their turn, broke their axles by the horrible jolting, so that within eighteen miles I saw three wagons lying in this condition."

### How Rutland Got Its Name

Rutland took its name from none of these slanders. The Saxons, who made it neither a county nor a shire, called it Roteland, or the Red Land, because no less than twenty-four thousand one hundred and seventy-eight acres out of ninety-seven thousand and seventy-three acres are red land. That is why they call Rutland men "Raddle Men" to this day. Rutland is, in fact, the solitary example of an old Mercian division of England which has outlived the West Saxon redistribution of the country into shires.

This tiny county of softly blended woodland, cornfields, brooks and villages, contains a great part of the old Royal Forest of Leighfield, many of whose mighty oaks are still to be seen in Beaumont Chase and Burley, Exton and Normanton Parks.

There were, before the war, and I devoutly hope still are, herds of deer in the great park at Exton where lives the Earl of Gainsborough and in the park at Nor-

manton where the Earl of Ancaster lived before the fine mansion was demolished. That other great mansion, Burley-on-the-Hill, was formerly the seat of the Finch family, a mighty house, commanding a great stretch of country. The north front is no less than one hundred and ninety-six feet long, with a great Doric colonnade which consists of sixty-four single columns. It is an imposing but not a lovely house, but the park, which is six miles round and extends to just over one thousand acres, is one of the loveliest stretches of scenery in the whole county, magnificent with lakes and woods.

### Rutland History

There are ruins of a beautiful old Elizabethan mansion called Exton Old Hall, which has grand gables and beautiful chimneys, and of another early Tudor house called Tolethorpe Hall which was built in 1493 or thereabouts, although even that is not as old as the old manor house at Ryhall, which was once the home of Hugh le Despenser and was first built in the thirteenth century. Alas, the ancient house is now cut in half between two owners and one end serves as the village ale-house, which again, I think, would astonish my American, but is all part of the woof and pattern of this shy, small county.

Nearly every village has its little manor house of local stone, with high-pitched gables and mullioned windows, many of which are now farmhouses.

Perhaps this general air of quiet, pastoral prosperity and old feudal history has given the people of Rutland that happy simplicity of nature, that essential calm philosophy, which makes them the pleasant, friendly, rather shy people that they are. They have none of the uncouth roughness of the Staffordshire folk, the suspicious independence of the Norfolk people, or the hard rural commercialism of the Lincolnshire farmers. They are essentially village people, living in a part of England which you might, at first sight, take to be all one rather sleepy, patriarchal, benevolent sort of feudal dukedom.

But the Duke of Rutland does not own Rutland; indeed, today he has little more than historical association with it. In

307

The market town of Uppingham is chiefly notable for its grammar school, on left of picture. Founded in 1584, it was raised from obscurity to its present high status by Edward Thring, its headmaster from 1853 to 1887.

Edward the Confessor's time the monks of Westminster did, however, own the whole of Rutland and that is why the town of Oakham is still divided into separate jurisdiction of the "Lord's Hold" and the "Dean's Hold," and a triennial court is still held in the latter under the authority of the Dean of Westminster. The near-by manor at Barleythorpe, which belonged to Lord Lonsdale until its recent sale, has the unique distinction of dating from the time of Edward the Confessor.

Thomas Cromwell and the Harrington family, which flourished in the county for six hundred years, both owned the manor and castle of Oakham. George Villiers, Duke of Buckingham, also held it and lived there in prodigal splendour. The Finchs of Burley-on-the-Hill, who have given great lawyers to the State, were until recently Lords of the Manor of Oakham.

Only one battle has been fought on Rutland soil—that was at the place known as Bloody Oak where, on March 12, 1470, no less than ten thousand men were killed in the clash between the Royalist army of Edward IV and the Lincolnshire levies of the House of Warwick. In Rutland they call it the Battle of Losecoat Field, since the survivors of that bloody massacre flung away their coats in order to run the faster from the havoc of the King's artillery.

The only other warlike event was a short, sharp siege during the Civil War by forces under Lord Grey, of Henry Noel (ancestor of the present Earl of Gainsborough) in his house at North Luffenham. Noel held out for twenty-four hours with two hundred of his Rutland friends and neighbours against a besieging force of thirteen hundred men. Noel was for the King, but when the Roundheads set fire to his stables, barns and cornstacks and started to burn his cottagers out of their homes, he surrendered, to save further bloodshed and was put in prison, where he died. This is the sort of small neighbourly battle which is as much as you would expect of a county that has hardly

ever produced a criminal, although Sir Everard Digby, who was one of the Gunpowder Plot conspirators, had an estate at Stoke Dry. But the plot to blow up Parliament was not hatched there.

Even the Danes failed to get to Rutland. That is why you do not find a single Danish place-name in the whole county, though plenty of ancient British names. The Rutland dialect is much like that of Cambridgeshire, but they have odd words of their own which I have never come across in Cambridgeshire such as "doted" (decayed); "to boom" (to help); "cade" (tame); "stoven out" (swollen).

There are only fifty churches in the whole of Rutland, forty-five of them are ancient and it is said that no two of them are alike. Of these, the most notable architecturally are the churches in the tiny villages of Bur-

ley and Braunston: but the most celebrated is that at Langham where, every year, on the first Sunday after June 29 the church is strewn with newly-mown hay.

There is only one brewery, but there are excellent stone quarries which go back to a very early date at Ketton, Casterton and Clipsham. Ketton stone, which has been quarried for four hundred years, was used to build St. Dunstan's Church in Fleet Street, the Law Courts, and that wonderful three-hundred-year-old Customs House at King's Lynn. It has been used to repair the Tower of London, York Minster and Exeter Cathedral and many churches in Norfolk, Suffolk and Leicestershire are built of it. Nowadays they are excavating iron-stone at Cottesmore and Market Overton.

A hundred years ago, Oakham, which today lives on farming and fox-hunting and goes to sleep in the afternoon, had a considerable wool trade and there were weavers in many Rutland villages. But although Rutland still breeds a good many sheep, it is a butchers' and breeders' county and not a land of weavers. Rutland used to graze two hundred and eighty-six cattle and nine hundred and twenty-nine sheep to every thousand acres devoted to them, and, indeed, before the war, no less than fifty-four thousand six hundred and eighty-six acres, or more than half the county, was down to permanent grass. Much of that was broken up during the recent war and put down to corn, but the Rutland graziers are anxious for a quick return to permanent grass.

Rutland has always been a good barley-growing area, particularly on the limestone spine of wold which runs through the eastern part of the county from Lincolnshire.

The church at Cottesmore, with its graceful Gothic tower and spire, compares with several churches of note within the county. The village is known to sportsmen as the home of the Cottesmore Hunt.

Only about one hundred acres in the whole county are under orchards and much less than one hundred acres are devoted to small fruit, such as strawberries, raspberries and currants.

Despite its relatively diminutive size Rutland did not escape the eye of the Air Ministry during the last war and aerodromes built at Cottesmore and North Luffenham brought a crowd of young and roisterous invaders, first in R.A.F. blue and later in the dark khaki of the U.S. Army Air Force. The ancient streets and hostelries of Oakham and Uppingham echoed with technical slang of airmen and the varying accents of the English-speaking nations from New Zealand, Texas and the Scottish Highlands. For the boys of the famous public school in Uppingham this was both a momentous and joyous invasion. For the county as a whole, it was undoubtedly valuable. The invaders carried with them a gusty wind from the greater world, a wind that did something to blow away the cobwebs of the somewhat sleepy

parochialism in which the people of the county were too thickly draped.

Rutland has its fair proportion of famous people. William the Lion, who became King of Scotland in 1165, held the Manor of Exton and Robert the Bruce succeeded him in it. Elizabeth, Queen of Bohemia (the Queen of Hearts), spent her early childhood at Exton and the great avenue there is still known as the Queen of Bohemia's Ride. The grandson of Edward III, Edward Plantagenet, who was "smothered to death" at the Battle of Agincourt, was created Earl of Rutland in 1389. The present Dukedom of Rutland was conferred on John Manners in 1703. The Finch family, members of which have been Speakers of the House of Commons, Lords Keeper of the Seal, Recorder of London, Attorney-General and Lord Chancellor, as well as holding other offices of state, have always kept Rutland to the forefront in Parliament. Simon de Langham, Archbishop of Canterbury in 1366, was born at Langham in the county and Jeremy Taylor, the well-known divine,

310

who accompanied Charles I through most of the Civil War and was presented with his royal master's watch and some jewels before the King's execution, was Rector of Uppingham from 1638 to 1642.

Rutland has had only one poet, John Banton, but it has given three Lords Mayor to London, including Sir Gilbert Heathcote, ancestor of Lord Ancaster, who was one of the founders of the Bank of England.

The oddest of all Rutland characters was Sir Jeffrey Hudson, the astounding dwarf, whose history reads like a mad opera. His father was a drover of Oakham where he was employed by the Duke of Buckingham. Jeffrey was born in 1619 and was never more than a foot and a half high until he reached the age of thirty, after which he gradually grew up to three and a half feet in height. He was served up in a cold pie at Court before King Charles and Queen Henrietta, was knighted by the King, sent to France on Court business, captured by a pirate, fought a famous battle with a turkey cock, about which the Poet Laureate of the day wrote a poem, was again captured by a Turkish pirate, was sold as a slave, escaped and returned to England. He became a Captain of Horse in Charles I's army and took part in a charge with Prince Rupert at Newbury where the Roundheads forced both the Prince and the midget knight to flee at full gallop. Queen Henrietta took him to France, and there he fought a duel with Mr. Crofts, a member of the Queen's Household. Crofts took a large water squirt to the duelling place with which to "snuff out his opponent," but Hudson, who was mounted on a pony, turned up with a pistol and shot Crofts dead. He was forced to fly and was later arrested on suspicion of being involved in the Popish Plot. He died in 1682 at the age of sixty-three. His tiny waistcoat of blue satin and his little breeches and stockings, also in blue satin, are in the Ashmolean Museum at Oxford.

It is surely appropriate, that Rutland, the tiniest county, should have produced the tiniest courtier, the smallest captain of cavalry and the most minute duellist on record.

Of course, many modern Americans know Rutland well; as I said, they invaded it effectively during the last war. But if a stranger from the States were to go to Rutland he would, I think, still agree with H. V. Morton—"In all England is there anything quite so Old English as a county town where the fox is the chief industry, where they thatch the main street, tax peers, go to sleep in the afternoon, burn wood, never see chars-à-bancs or factory smoke, never, as far as I can find out, murder each other, and where the girls, when you ask them a question, look down at the floor and go red round the ears?"

*Butter Cross, Oakham*

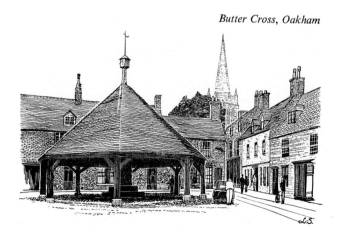

311

Badby, two and a half miles from Daventry, is one of the many unspoilt villages which lie scattered about the uplands. The church and village, seen above, are typical of a county which is famed for the variety and excellence of its parish churches.

*Market Square, Brackley*

# NORTHAMPTONSHIRE

### By W. H. OWENS

SPLENDID churches and stately homes set in a background of undulating farmlands have made Northamptonshire traditionally the county of "spires and squires." Richer than most in its heritage of medieval architecture, this somewhat narrow strip of country lies for the most part in the broad limestone belt across the centre of England. Nowhere, perhaps, has the wealth of the soil been used to more lasting advantage over so long a period, for the Northamptonshire churches can show the most varied examples of every English style from Saxon to late Tudor. Towers and slender broach spires dominate the landscapes everywhere, rising as beacons to direct the stranger to some rare village or gracious town built of the same pleasing stone. In the heart of this historic countryside are the ancestral homes of such old families as the Spencers, the Comptons, the Montagus and the Treshams who have contributed illustrious pages to our island story.

*Arms of Northamptonshire*

Most people, however, will primarily associate Northampton and its shire with the ancient footwear industry that has made its name famous in many parts of the world. In very recent times the manufacture of steel from the vast ironstone beds at Corby has added appreciably to the county's industrial wealth and importance. Yet Northamptonshire has contrived somehow to remain more pastoral than almost any other part of the industrialized Midlands; perhaps because its own manufacturing centres are confined in area and, while as progressive as any, have not sprawled too far. Apart from Corby, Peterborough and one or two lesser places, most development has taken place chiefly in the triangle of towns formed by Northampton, Wellingborough and Kettering.

But outside these towns and some of the larger villages concerned with leather and shoe-making, rural life goes on in its own quiet way much the same as for generations past,

313

and the well-kept farms show signs of healthy progress and solid worth. Northamptonshire owes its prosperity very largely to stock-raising and agriculture; the extensive grasslands, which attracted the yeomen graziers to the uplands and valleys centuries ago, comprise some of the best pasturage in England, and the well-watered and extremely fertile soil, formed by the rich marl of limestones and clays, is cultivated on the largest scale. Such a large area of the county has been brought under cultivation that almost the only waste lands are the worked-out quarry pits which scar the surface here and there.

### Centre of England

By reason of its geographical position, Northamptonshire is well served by roads and railways. Ever since the Romans made the Watling Street and Ermine Street, founding important settlements at Towcester and Castor, all through traffic from London to the north has passed this way. Yet in spite of its accessibility, the county is probably as little known outside its chief towns as it was in the heyday of the Irish mail coaches. Many motorists go speeding across it day by day; how few of them leave the highways to explore.

If they did so they would certainly find much worth seeing, and of its wonderful old churches, mansion homes and historical sites there will be more to say in due course. Meanwhile, let us take a glance at the pattern of the landscape itself.

While Northamptonshire is the plain, homely England of the farmlands—the real England—with nothing in the way of unusual or distinguished scenery, it is not without variety. No fewer than nine other counties adjoin its borders and each lends to it something of its own character. The remote south-western corner is essentially part of the Cotswold belt; several of its villages are true Cotswold type. Examples are Aynho, terraced on its rocky hill overlooking the Midland Plain, and Evenley with trim cottages set round a green under shady elms. Yet could any other English shire offer greater contrast than that presented by these cosy hill villages, on the one hand, and the vast flat spaces of the reclaimed fen at the opposite corner of the county, on the other?

But between these extremes are found the landscapes that are most characteristic of Northamptonshire. Stretching away north to the Leicestershire and Rutland borders and covering a third or more of the whole county, are the breezy stone-walled uplands whose gentle curves and flattened summits Horace Walpole must have had in mind when he wrote of the "dumpling hills of Northamptonshire." This is fine, open countryside giving exhilarating views though, except in the west, the land seldom rises much above five hundred feet and is frequently broken by long valleys chequered with woods and cultivated pastures. Scattered about these uplands are a host of unspoiled villages, some of the best in the county, like Moreton Pinkney, Badby, Ashby St. Ledgers and, at the northern edge in the hunting country, Rockingham with its venerable castle and unforgettable street of stone houses above the Welland valley.

The highest ground is near the Warwickshire border and contains two great watersheds, the first centred about Naseby and the second about Arbury Hill to the south of Daventry; from these hills are distributed the county's chief rivers—the Nene and the Welland, the Tove, which joins the Ouse below Towcester, and the little Ise. This last is a delightful stream that meanders pleasantly through the wold past Naseby battlefield before turning south at Geddington to feed the Nene at Wellingborough.

### Meadowlands of the Nene

The long Nene valley, extending sixty miles across the county to Peterborough, has a distinct character of its own. Here is a countryside of broad smiling meadowlands, golden in summertime, and most attractive where the river divides the rich agricultural districts around Oundle. This, the fairest of all the towns of Northamptonshire, is a place of fine stone houses and comfortable inns which are the regular meeting places of the local farmers every market-day.

Ever since the Anglo-Saxons drove along its banks to establish the town of North

314

# NORTHAMPTONSHIRE

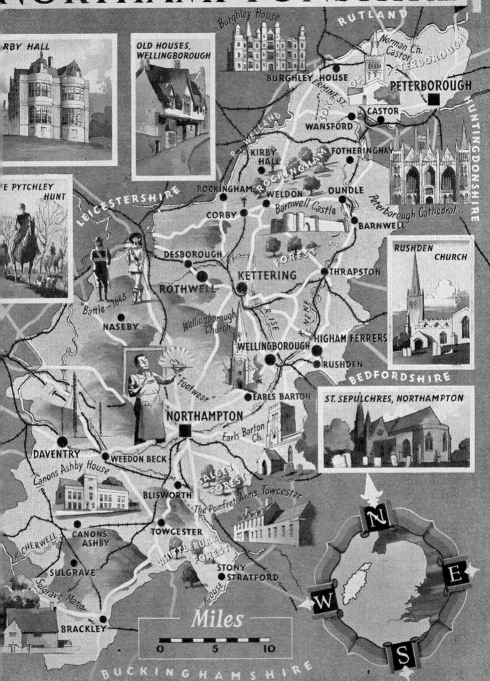

RBY HALL

OLD HOUSES, WELLINGBOROUGH

Burghley House

RUTLAND

Norman Ch. Castor

PETERBOROUGH

BURGHLEY HOUSE

CASTOR

ERMINE ST.

SOKE OF PETERBOROUGH

WANSFORD

HUNTINGDONSHIRE

R. WELLAND

KIRBY HALL

FOTHERINGHAY

Peterborough Cathedral

THE PYTCHLEY HUNT

ROCKINGHAM

WELDON

OUNDLE

LEICESTERSHIRE

ROCKINGHAM

CORBY

Barnwell Castle

BARNWELL

FOREST

DESBOROUGH

KETTERING

THRAPSTON

RUSHDEN CHURCH

ROTHWELL

"Battle - 1645"

NASEBY

Wellingborough Church

R. NENE

RISE

WELLINGBOROUGH

HIGHAM FERRERS

RUSHDEN

"Footwear"

BEDFORDSHIRE

EARLS BARTON

ST. SEPULCHRES, NORTHAMPTON

NORTHAMPTON

Earls Barton Ch.

DAVENTRY

WEEDON BECK

Canons Ashby House

SALCEY FOREST

N

BLISWORTH

The Pomfret Arms, Towcester

W

E

CANONS ASHBY

TOWCESTER

R. CHERWELL

WHITTLEBURY FOREST

STONY STRATFORD

SULGRAVE

Sulgrave Manor

R. OUSE

W

BRACKLEY

## Miles

0    5    10

S

BUCKINGHAMSHIRE

315

ampton in the sixth century, this great waterway has influenced the life and development of the county almost as much as the roads which cut across it. The success of the Nene navigation scheme, undertaken in recent years, has finally conquered the menace of winter flooding in this valley and provided the industrial centres with a canalized transit route direct to the Wash and East Coast ports. And now Northampton has visions of becoming a port itself with a new proposal to widen and deepen the river along the whole of its navigable length so that fairly large sea-going vessels can use it.

Northampton today is a busy, go-ahead town with many and varied industries; too busy, perhaps, to be over-concerned with its vivid historical memories. But shoe-making is still the chief source of its prosperity, as it was throughout the Middle Ages when its craftsmen were already widely renowned for their skill. Over a thousand years ago Alfred the Great came here to organize the first community of shoe-makers so that his soldiers might go about their difficult tasks well shod. At that time there were dense forests around and

stretching far beyond Northampton—the surviving remains are Salcey and Yardley Chase, between the Nene and the Ouse, and the scattered remains of Rockingham Forest to the north and east. From the bark of the abundant oak trees was obtained the necessary tanning liquor to treat the hides readily supplied from the herds of the grasslands. Throughout the centuries English soldiers have marched victoriously to battle in Northampton-made boots, thanks to the enterprise of King Alfred.

Nowadays, the footwear industry is still traditionally carried on by large and small firms in many towns and villages, though the chief centres outside Northampton itself are at Kettering, Wellingborough and Rushden.

### Centre of Politics

In Norman and Plantagenet times Northampton was a lively centre of the political life of England where the kings and the barons held their councils in the towns scattered throughout the forests which gave them sport. In the almost vanished Norman castle, residence of William Rufus and his successors, Henry I assembled Parliament

**The ruins of Barnwell Castle, dating from the time of the Conqueror, are today a show place with elegant lawns and lily ponds. The Norman gateway alone remains of this once famous stronghold.**

Castle Ashby, seat of the Marquis of Northampton, is an Elizabethan mansion with additions by Inigo Jones. It is renowned for its magnificent architecture, its fine gardens and its great park.

the year 1131 and the Barons swore fealty to his daughter Matilda (the Empress Maud). During the subsequent two centuries many other English Parliaments sat in the great castle hall, the scene of King John's meeting with the Barons before Magna Carta and the trial of Thomas à Becket. The Wars of the Roses were also centred on Northampton Castle where, in 1460, Henry VI was made prisoner after the Lancastrians had suffered a crushing defeat at the hands of the Earl of Warwick's forces. In Northampton's famous round church of St. Sepulchre we recall that the town was a gathering place of the Crusaders after their return from the Holy Land. This church was built by Simon de Senlis, first Earl of Northampton, who took part in the first Crusade and died in France while on his way home from another.

### Fotheringhay Castle

Further along the Nene, near Oundle, is the site of Fotheringhay Castle, birth-place of Richard III, but chiefly associated with the tragic end of the unlucky Mary Stuart. Within the walls of this castle she ended her eighteen years of imprisonment at the age of forty-four, meeting her fate on the scaffold erected in the banqueting hall by order of Queen Elizabeth, who signed the royal death warrant. Tradition has it that this castle, where so many kings and queens

kept state, was dismantled by James I to wipe out the bitter memory of his mother's death. But of this we have no definite historical record. Of the other ancient castles, only Rockingham and Barnwell survive, both of them having been converted into manors and lived in continuously since Norman times.

Close to Rockingham and just south of the Rutland border are some of the chief quarrying districts, where an industry begun in Roman times has been carried on right up to the present day. The Barnack quarries were once among the richest and most famous in England, providing exceptionally fine building stone, known as Barnack rag, for the building of Peterborough Cathedral, Ramsey Abbey, in neighbouring Huntingdon, and scores of churches not only in Northamptonshire itself but all over the eastern counties. Some of the older university buildings in Cambridge are built of it and we can find it even as far afield as Rochester in Kent. It is hardly surprising that the Barnack quarries were worked out before the end of the fifteenth century, when they were superseded by those at Gretton, Weldon and elsewhere.

At Collyweston a local slate industry is maintained by craftsmen who still work in the simple ways of their ancestors, keeping up a tradition of many centuries. Yellowish-white in colour, this thick slate is to be seen on the roofs of churches, farms and cottages everywhere. It is extracted in blocks of convenient size to be split and trimmed with hand tools in the old-fashioned way.

Yet another source of mineral wealth is ironstone. Great development followed the word Soke comes from the Anglo-Saxon "soc" meaning a place privileged to hold a court of law, and in medieval times the district came under the jurisdiction of the Abbot of Peterborough. Since the dissolution of the monasteries the area has been reduced by about half, but it still retains its

Northamptonshire is well provided with transport facilities, and is easily accessible. There are however, many lovely villages off the beaten track, such as Grafton Underwood, seen above.

discovery of the ironfield at Corby—one of the biggest in Europe—and has transformed the one-time village into a grimy steel-town. Corby's famous fair, held once every twenty years since it received its charter from Queen Elizabeth, was last held in 1947.

Where Northamptonshire merges into the fen country is that narrow neck of land containing the Soke of Peterborough. This own magistrates who are nominated by *Custos Rotulorum*, the Marquis of Exeter of Burghley House.

Much might be written of Peterboroug Cathedral, one of the finest Norman monu ments in all Europe. It grew from the orig inal abbey founded there by Saxulf in th seventh century and destroyed by the ruth less, invading Danes. But I will confine my self to the glory of its west front, that co

Despite the industrial prosperity and bustle which have come to the manufacturing centres, most of Northamptonshire is fundamentally tranquil and pastoral, as this view of Syresham emphasizes.

summation of the Early English style which gave William Morris inspiration for lines in *The Earthly Paradise*.

I who have seen
So many lands, and midst such marvels been,
Can see above the green and unburnt fen
The little houses of an English town,
Cross-timbered, thatched with fen reeds coarse and brown,
And high o'er these, three gables great and fair,
That slender rods of columns do appear,
Over the minster doors, and imagery
Of kings and flowers no summer field doth see,
Wrought in these gables.

The three arches with their delicate columns, surmounted by the richly decorated gables, towers and pinnacles are as inspiring a work in stone as is to be found anywhere in these islands. "The noblest conception of the old Greek translated into the speech of Christendom," as someone has aptly described it.

The wealth of church architecture for which Northamptonshire is noted is a vast subject on its own. Touching on it very briefly: there are the famous Saxon churches of Earls Barton, Brigstock, Barnack and Brixworth, the most interesting of their type in England; Norman work is found in great variety all over the county,

The village of Clipston, close to the Leicestershire border, retains, despite its station on the L.M.S., much of its old-world charm. It gives a picture of rural England which is still representative today.

**Although the Soke of Peterborough is a separate administrative county, it falls geographically within Northamptonshire. Its fine cathedral, seen above, is notable for its magnificent west front.**

Peterborough Cathedral giving a complete expression, but notable examples being the parish churches of Maxey and Castor on the edge of the fens. Of fourteenth-century church building an unrivalled example is at Higham Ferrers, whose lovely soaring spire is a landmark for miles in the Nene valley: the western doorway with its marvellous scrolls ranks as the richest specimen of medieval craftsmanship in the county. The church of St. Peter at Oundle, with one of the tallest spires, shows Perpendicular and Decorated work of the highest merit,

and a very beautiful five-lights lancet window of Early English style.

A striking feature of the Northamptonshire churches, of course, is their spires, and about two-thirds of them are the broached type. Nowhere can they be seen to better advantage than against the wide open skies of the fens, particularly when silhouetted in the twilight of a frosty winter's afternoon.

While there are very few castles in the county, there is a great number of beautiful old houses. Two of the finest of them,

# NORTHAMPTONSHIRE

Castle Ashby and Althorp Park, stand a few miles east and west of Northampton. Castle Ashby, seat of the Marquis of Northampton, has been associated with the Compton family since the time of Henry VIII, and is renowned for its gardens and parkland extending into Yardley Chase. Althorp Park is the ancestral home of the Spencers who were once great wool merchants of Northamptonshire. The mansion is a splendid example of the Renaissance period and in the last three centuries many kings and queens have been entertained on a lavish scale there. Althorp was the centre of English social life in the days when proud Robert Spencer, second Earl of Sutherland, held the office of confidential secretary to James II. When John Evelyn visited the place he found it "perfect from cellar to garret."

Burghley House, outside Stamford on the Lincolnshire border, ranks as the largest and the most ornate of late Elizabethan mansions. John Thorpe, who also designed Kirby Hall near Rockingham, built this palatial home for Queen Elizabeth's Lord Burghley, founder of the Cecils, whose tombs fill the neighbouring church. Few of England's homes can reveal such treasures inside and we read how Horace Walpole, coming to Burghley for the first time about 1720 was "filled with admiration and reverence" by the grandeur of the place and the magnificent works of art, which still adorn its spacious galleries today. Kirby Hall, with its arcaded front by Inigo Jones, has been rescued from its derelict state, in which it stood for over a century, by the Office of Works, and its gardens restored to their former beauty. Other splendid homes within the county include Boughton House, home of the Montagus, and Drayton House, both not far from Kettering. Rushton Hall of the famous Treshams has five centuries of history, the present mansion being a perfect example of Elizabethan and Jacobean work, with fine chimneys and gables rising above the solid square walls. Holdenby, near Northampton, has a place in history, though only the gateways now survive of the original house of Sir Christopher Hatton in which Charles I was staying at the time of his capture by Cornet Joyce.

The discovery of ironstone at Corby resulted in the development of one of the largest ironfields in the world, and transformed what was once a small country village into a flourishing industrial centre.

The church at Evenley, a charming village on the Ouse close to the Buckinghamshire border.

Among the smaller manors of Northamptonshire none is so well known as Sulgrave, near the Oxfordshire border. It was Lawrence Washington, three times mayor of Northampton, who bought Sulgrave, part of an ancient priory, from Henry VIII at the Dissolution. There the family lived until about 1610 when, their fortunes having declined, they moved to Little Brington. John Washington, grandson of the original owner of Sulgrave, emigrated to America some forty years later to escape persecution by the Puritans and it was his great-grandson who became the first President of the United States. In 1914 the manor house was purchased by public subscription raised on both sides of the Atlantic to celebrate the century of peace between the two great English-speaking nations.

Along the main roads passing through Northamptonshire is many an interesting inn which came into prominence during the coaching days. Towcester was an important stopping-place of the Holyhead coach and here stands the "Saracen's Head," the well-known inn which Dickens so often visited and which he introduced into *Pickwick Papers*. Known for some time as the "Pomfret Arms," it has now reverted to its former name. Dean Swift frequently put up at the "Talbot" on his journeys to and from Ireland, and the chair in which he always sat is now preserved as a literary relic in the town hall. At Wansford on the Great North Road is the old "Haycock" whose sign was once one of the sights of the county. This showed an old fellow named Barnabee who, as the story goes, once came to Wansford while a plague was raging in the town. Fearing to enter any house, he slept the night on a haycock beside the river bank and was carried off downstream by a sudden flood while he was asleep. The "Talbot" at Oundle, a seventeenth-century stone-built house, is said to have been erected with materials from Fotheringhay Castle nearby. A former landlord used to persuade his guests that the very fine Jacobean staircase inside was none other than the one down which Mary Stuart walked to her execution.

While it can be admitted that Northamptonshire is unexciting in its scenic interest, it is still truly representative of England. Its colourful history and associations rival those of many a larger shire; its wealth of varied architecture surpasses that of most. And those lovely old churches and mansions, which blend so happily with the serene landscapes to delight the eye everywhere, serve to emphasize the long traditions of craftsmanship in which this county and its people can justifiably take pride. Even today something of the same eager spirit which went to the building of such masterpieces as Peterborough Cathedral or Castle Ashby may be found in the skilled craftsmen in the factories and workshops of that famous industry which maintains a direct link with the Northamptonshire of King Alfred's day.

*Sulgrave Manor*

323

*Felmersham near Bedford*

*Elstow Moot Hall*

# BEDFORDSHIRE

## By J. WENTWORTH DAY

IF A MAN were to ask me to show him an English county which typified the life and growth of modern England, I should take him to Bedfordshire. To Bedfordshire, because it lies near to the territorial heart of England. It is crossed by great roads which are arteries of England, its farms and market gardens grow corn and vegetables which help to feed the capital of England, its great houses have sheltered great leaders, its cottages have bred great Englishmen, and, today, its industries are among the best in that modern and industrial England which is striving to shake off the grim inheritance of those "dark satanic mills" of Victorian industrialists.

To the traveller on the Great North Road, who sees acre after acre of market gardens, and smells the horrid putrescence of dead cabbages, Bedfordshire seems, at first, a dull county, dull and flat. And if he goes to Luton, whose population has leapt by fifty thousand in the last hundred years or so, or to Bedford,

*Bedfordshire. County Seal*

which has spread itself with ever-reaching tentacles of mediocre little villas and prim little streets, he will say that the towns, like the county, are mediocre, workaday and standardized.

You might say the same thing with the same truth of almost any small or medium-sized English provincial town which has spread its skirts in the last eighty years. We have little to be proud of in our minor domestic architecture built during that period. Much of it is grim, grey and ugly. The snub-nosed little bow windows, slate roofs, pocket-handkerchief front gardens and parallelograms of terrace streets, do nothing to enhance the beauty and less to advance the native culture of a country whose older architecture blends the beauty and brains of the craftsmen and masons of nine hundred years of history.

But not Bedford or Luton or Dunstable or any lesser Bedfordshire town is alone to be derided for this creeping paralysis of ugly houses and grim streets, a paralysis

325

# BEDFORDSHIRE

LUTON TO...

BEDFORD SCHOOL

NORTHAMPTONSHIRE

FARNDISH

13th Cent. Doorway, Farndish

SHELTON

The Mill, Keysoe

SHARNBROOK

HARROLD

KEYSOE

17th Cent. Mkt. House, Harrold

R. OUSE

OAKLEY

Bunyan's Statue, Bedford

The Dovecot, Willington

EATON SOCON

Basket Making

KEMPSTON

■ BEDFORD

ROXTON

WILLINGTON

R. OUSE

Aspley House

ELSTOW

CARDINGTON

ASPLEY GUISE

SANDY

WOBURN

OLD WARDEN

POTTON

The Cross, Leighton Buzzard

Bunyan's Cottage, Elstow

AMPTHILL

BIGGLESWADE

SUTTON

CLOPHILL

BUCKINGHAMSHIRE

LEIGHTON BUZZARD

Toddington Church

SHEFFORD

Abbey Ruins, Old Warden

Packhorse Bdge., Sutton

WATLING ST.

TODDINGTON

BARTON IN THE CLAY

ICKNIELD WAY

DUNSTABLE

"Gliding"

ARLESEY

VAUXHALL MOTOR WORKS, LUTON

Open Air Zoo

Dunstable Downs

LUTON Hats

WHIPSNADE

HERTFORDSHIRE

R. LEA

HERTFORDSHIRE

HUNTINGDONSHIRE

Miles

0     5     10

326

arising largely from local apathy which is indifferent to the ravages of the speculative builder and unconcerned by the absence of plan or beauty in council building estates. Too seldom has the genius of a Lutyens raised a ripple of distinction or beauty in this grey tide of grey bricks and grey slates.

But go into the villages and the small market towns of Bedfordshire. See the houses, old and gracious, built of lath and plaster, sleepy under deep thatch, their walls washed in warm pinks and yellows or in bright, welcoming white. Walk by the reedy edges of the slow, unhurried Great Ouse, the fourth longest river in England, since it is a hundred and fifty-six miles in length, the river of great pike and grey-plumed herons, of moorhens pattering on sedgy islands and reed warblers swinging like mice amid the reeds, the river that waters thousands of acres of fat-cattle pastures where herds of Friesians and Red Polls, Shorthorns and Lincolns move in comfortable majesty.

See the fields of beans and barley, of tawny wheat and purple swedes that run up to gentle skylines over which blown rooks and wailing plovers cut their frescoes, and you will see a part of the peace and the heart of the England that is not of alien, grey slate or little, grim streets.

Run over your tongue the names of villages, Aspley Guise, Marston Mortaine, Houghton Conquest, Woburn, Cockayne Hatley, Eaton Socon and Higham Gobion, and you have a roll of echoes from Norman England.

### County's Great Sons

There is not, however, much martial history about this peaceful county of farms and great woods and flat market gardens. There are no trumpet notes of great battles nor clash of arms ringing down the corridors of history. The Wars of the Roses left scarcely a mark. The Civil War, for all that Cromwell was a neighbour and Montagu a near-by feudal lord, brought little bloodshed to Bedfordshire. Its great men have, for the most part, been men of high performance in the service of the State, men like the Russells who, from their great houses at Woburn, Ampthill and Oakley, have filled almost every office of peace from the premiership of England to Acting-Viceroy of India, and innumerable embassies abroad and lesser posts in politics and the armed forces. To Francis Russell, Fourth Earl of Bedford, and William, the First Duke, England owes one of her greatest agricultural boons—the drainage of the fens.

Those early Russells, with their neighbouring squires, and a few rich merchants who put up funds, performed the colossal task of reclaiming from feverish swamp and shining meres more than a quarter of a million acres of the Great Fen, which drowned half Cambridgeshire and much of Lincolnshire, Bedfordshire, Huntingdon, and Norfolk. It was a huge undertaking, which, if it were carried out today by any government department, would cost millions of money and years of endeavour. Today some of the richest farmlands in Bedfordshire are the quiet but visible monument to that great work, initiated by Bedfordshire men in Carolean days and carried on doggedly, with ever-increasing improvements for more than two centuries.

### Home of John Bunyan

If this great work owes its inception to a Bedfordshire earl, sitting in the panelled quiet of his library, England owes no less a debt, an embellishment as great, to John Bunyan, the tinker who turned soldier, but was at heart a dreamer, a poet and a preacher. He was born near Harrowden in the parish of Elstow in 1628 and spent twelve years in Bedford Jail from 1660 to 1672, during which time he dreamed and schemed his immortal *Pilgrim's Progress*.

Thomas Tompion, the father of English watch-makers, was a notable product of Bedfordshire earth, but there, indeed, you may end the roll of great names, for I will not admit as native products either Samuel Butler, who was merely a resident in the county for a few years, John Howard, the prison reformer, who lived at Cardington, or the long list of parsons, from Dr. Donne downwards, who made their names.

Bedfordshire has its share of great houses, though most are of a heavy, classical magnificence, a magnificence born of the Grand Tour and not sprung in kind, Elizabethan

A Bedfordshire farm near Studham
on the Hertfordshire border

Gathering chrysanthemums beside the sixteenth century dove-cote at Willington. The village lies about four and a half miles to the east of Bedford.

warmth from English soil. Woburn is a great house, one of the greatest in England, and its park, which is some ten or twelve miles round, contains the largest private collection of deer in Europe, with every other sort of rare, exotic bird and animal that will flourish in our climate.

I would not choose to live in that vast mansion of Woburn Abbey, which, for all its wealth of pictures and books, of fine furniture and state rooms, is too magnificent, too overpowering. It and its park, its shining lakes and massed woods, its neat, well-cared-for villages—for there are no better landlords in England than the Russells—is a fit home for a duke, but it is no squire's house, nor even the comfortable hall of a rural peer. It is a palace.

About it lie thousands of acres of prosperous farms and immense woods. The lands rise to five hundred feet or more, and that is mountainous country in this flat, unpretentious county of Bedfordshire. They are beautified by the landscape gardening, the forestry and the farming of generations of landowners whose hearts and money

have been sunk in the betterment of the soil and the improvement of the conditions of the people who live on it. For that reason you may regard Woburn as one of the most outstanding agricultural estates in all England. Its record is a record of good. Thanks to the vast possessions of the Duke of Bedford and the careful investments of generations of forebears who town-planned in Bloomsbury as nobly as they country-planned in Bedfordshire, it remains, despite the economic blizzards of two great wars, a noble and intact estate. The present duke lives in a house nearby.

Other great houses of Bedfordshire have suffered worse, for Haynes, the old seat, first, of the Newdigates, and then of the Earls Granville, which stands in a great park of eight hundred acres, was sold in 1914, the estate cut up and the timber cut down. Most of the house was modernized and rebuilt about 1800. Wrest Park, a great classical mansion, whose lands had been in possession of the de Greys from 1330 to 1918, was also sold when the last of his line, the late Lord Lucas, was lost in an aeroplane. Melchbourne, the seat of Lord St. John of Bletso, whose family obtained it from the Russells in 1608, is a large red and yellow brick house built in 1741 and floridly restored in 1877. It, too, has recently been up for sale. But Ampthill House, which was built in 1694, still stands in its ancient park, full of those witch-like, stagheaded oaks condemned by Queen Elizabeth as being too ancient and hollow to make into good warships, even in her day. Southill Park, modernized for a Whitbread in 1795, is a fine classical house, full of good pictures and furniture, and still maintained in a style which only well-breeched dukes and long-established brewers can afford.

Scattered over the county are plenty of small manor houses of Elizabethan and Jacobean times, many of which were turned into farm-houses in the early eighteenth century when men's minds were obsessed by the flamboyant vanities of their new Palladian and Doric mansions. It seems likely now, that, in Bedfordshire, as in other counties, the sardonic wheels of Fate, grinding their owners under remorseless taxation, may bring back a revival of affection for the smaller, more domestic, more truly English village manor house, whilst the great porticoed Pentonvilles, born of Whiggery, may well become either lunatic asylums or houses for inebriates or those of criminal mentality.

Ickwell Bury, recently destroyed by fire, was a truly beautiful manor house well worth seeing, but there is still good seventeenth-century work at Brogborough Park farm, the Tofte at Sharnbrook, Sharnbrook Grange, Colworth House, Aspley Guise, and many other places, whilst at Hinwick are two excellent eighteenth-century houses, the principal one of which was built by Richard Orlebar in 1710. As a pretty compliment to his wife, Diana, he ornamented the south front with a large bas-relief of the goddess Diana, seated in a chariot and attended by her hounds. There are still Orlebars living in the house, and the family gave us, in Air Commodore A. H. Orlebar, one of the pioneers of high-speed aviation.

Then there are the Houghton Ruins, hard by Houghton Conquest, which are supposed to have given John Bunyan his original idea of the House Beautiful. The house was built by the Countess of Pembroke soon after 1615, after the plan of a palace in ancient Rome, but it was unroofed in 1794, and has been a ruin ever since.

When I think of Bedfordshire, I see a series of pictures. And the first is of two sober figures walking. . . .

" Now their way lay just upon the bank of a River; here, therefore they walked with great delight, for the water was pleasant and enlivening to their weary spirits: besides on the banks of this River were green Trees, and on either side a meadow; and it was green all the year long."

You may be sure that when John Bunyan wrote this passage in *Pilgrim's Progress*—

The fine Gothic church at Toddington, four and a half miles north of Dunstable.

whose reading to me is a duty, a solid, pedestrian duty, and no pleasure, for he was a dull though righteous fellow—he was thinking of the Bedfordshire Ouse. The Ouse that runs through green meadows, overhung with tall elms, rimmed with reeds and osiers, with weir and lock and ancient water-mill, sitting, weed-grown, upon its peaceful bank, with towers and spires of village churches half hidden among cloudy elms and willows that turn like silver in the sun, and tall poplars that whisper on the quietest day of no wind.

I think of the river at Oakley, where we fished in youthful days and stayed in that house of the Russells, with its Chinese Chippendale wallpaper, its bouncing black retrievers and after-dinner talk of embassies and rajahs, of the Czarist glories of pre-1914 St. Petersburg and the splendours of the India of the Moguls. And I think of the same river at Turvey, and at Eaton Socon, flowing through the same sort of peaceful pastures, under the same autumn golden elms. I think of Eaton Socon with its ancient, cheerful inn, the inn that knew the coaches and ringing horns in the gay days of the Great North Road, when there were highwaymen lurking at Norman Cross, and Kisby's Hut was a hovel high on the dun heath, and if you went east to Cambridge there were corpses swinging in chains on Caxton Gibbet, and ravens beating the wastes.

I think of gay shooting parties, for this is a great county of the pheasant and the partridge and the attendant fox, slinking out of the woodside like a red shadow. There are mallard, and teal, and widgeon, up the river in winter, and redshank ringing their bells on the wet green meadows of spring. Sometimes the wild grey geese go over when the river "washes" flood out, swollen with winter rain. And then, some faint echo of the old vanished fen comes back to the valleys of Bedfordshire, the flat lands by the river that once were all swamp and spreading waters.

I think, too, of Dunstable, high on its chalk downs, looking into the blue, misty Vale of Aylesbury. Dunstable, where in the eager days before the 1939 war, when Germany was a cloud on men's hearts, we flew gliders. I can see still the schoolboy faces, the eyes of adventure, the young men arriving in smelly little sports cars, anxious to risk their necks and pit their brains in the study of air currents, to follow in the flight of a bird.

For Bedfordshire is high in the history of the air. Was it not that great gaunt hangar at Cardington which saw much of the birth— and the prelude to the tragic death—of

**Ickwell ranks high in the list of pretty Bedfordshire villages. The beautiful manor house of Ickwell Bury, nearby, was gutted by fire and only the old stable and pigeon house are left.**

Final of the Junior Eights at the 83rd Bedford Regatta. In the background can be seen the old town bridge and the fourteenth century church of St. Paul's.

British airships? The memory of the R.100 and R.101, the echo of that ghastly crash in pouring rain on a French hill above Beauvais when some of the best brains in British aviation died in the flames, will always be heavy in Bedfordshire memories. The United States Eighth Air Force operated in the recent war on droning wings from Bedfordshire airfields, hidden among cornlands and behind great woods, and Bedfordshire skies were thunderous by night and glittering by day with high armadas that dealt their savage blows at the pagan heart of Germany.

I think of the little lacemakers, toiling with strained eyes and worn fingers in tiny villages, at Bedfordshire point, torchon and maltese, precisely as their forebears toiled minutely when Catherine of Aragon from her prison palace at Ampthill introduced this ancient art whilst she lay waiting for sentence of divorce from Henry VIII. That is why in some of those villages along the Buckinghamshire border they still call St. Catherine's Day the "Feast Day of the Lacemakers," and eat "Cattern's Cakes," a dim inherited memory of the sad queen who taught their ancestors their dying art.

I think, too, of Luton, its narrow streets and streams of hurrying workers on bicycles,

men and women who work at the straw-hat trade, in that little town which has been the metropolis of their industry since 1764. It and its subsidiaries are still a flourishing business, though many hundreds are now employed in the manufacture of motorcars, which has led to a great expansion in the size of the town during the present century.

There are great engineering works in Bedford itself, and that, for all its featureless suburbs, is no bad town when you get to the heart of it. It has a fine school founded in 1552, and endowed by Sir William Harper who was Lord Mayor of London in 1561. He gave it more than thirteen acres of "meadowland" in the parish of St. Andrew's, Holborn, land which is now thick with streets and houses between Southampton Row and Gray's Inn Road. Sir William bought it for £180 and today its revenues are worth £20,000 a year. The school has grown until today its name is known throughout the world, and Bedford itself thereby has something of the atmosphere and characteristics of a smaller university.

This old town of Bedford was a Saxon town and stronghold. The Danes captured it and held it, were thrown out by Edward the Elder, but returned again in 915 and were routed with great slaughter. Ninety-five years later they burnt the town. The Normans had a strong castle there, and there is still a high mound behind the Swan Hotel to mark where the great keep once stood. There have been sieges of Bedford since then, but the bloodshed ended when Henry III hung William de Breauté, defender of the castle, in 1224; since when it has known peace save for that brief incursion of Prince Rupert and his cavaliers when they captured the town in 1642.

To-day Bedford is clean, brisk and mainly modern. Even the Bunyan Meeting House was rebuilt in 1849, and its magnificent bronze doors given by Francis, Ninth Duke of Bedford, date only from 1876.

Sharnbrook, Shefford and Sandy are large villages or small towns, as your fancy pictures them, and each has that air of agricultural prosperity, the panorama of well-farmed fields and tidy woods, the glimpses of mansions in pleasant parks, the memories of Roman camps and roads. At Chicksands, near Shefford, is the old house of Chicksands Priory, standing in a large park and formerly owned by the Osborns, who have been lords of the Manor ever since old Peter Osborn was Lord Treasurer's Remembrancer of the Exchequer and Keeper of the Privy Purse to Edward VI. He was imprisoned in Queen Mary's reign, but under Queen Elizabeth rose in the esteem of Lord Burleigh, and became a High Commissioner for Ecclesiastical Affairs.

And there, in an outspread map of neat and progressive towns, with their modern and unobtrusive industries; of old villages and straight Roman roads that knew the tramping legions and the dusty coaches; of villages that lived by milking stool and plough; of market gardens that send their strings of lorries thundering through the night to London; and of great houses sitting in ancient parks, some, alas, now forlorn and cast on lean days, you have a picture of this unobtrusive English county through which, placid and peaceful, winds the broad and reedy Ouse, the river that is alike the backbone and the wealthgiver of these flat lands and the gentle hills which flow down from empty skylines.

*Sharpenhoe Hill*

334

*Anne Hathaway's Cottage, Shottery*

# WARWICKSHIRE

By HENRY CHANDLER

"WARWICK, near Stratford-on-Avon." That was the legend I saw in a popular magazine recently beneath a picture of Warwickshire's county town, and I can think of nothing that more neatly summarizes the woefully mistaken attitude of most people towards one of England's most beautiful counties.

The reason is that most people think of Warwickshire as first and foremost the land of Shakespeare: his memory has, as it were, stolen the limelight from most of the other attractions the county has to offer, and there are many. Stratford-on-Avon and Shakespeare's country closely surrounding it are but a small part of the county's total area, yet it is to this part that tourists come from all corners of the world to do homage to the "Bard of Avon." Actors, students, Americans and other sightseers come by the hundred thousand every year, yet despite this annual invasion from without, the great bulk of Warwickshire remains comparatively unexplored. Yet nowhere in England is finer woodland scenery to be found,

and few counties are more steeped in history and romance of England's turbulent past.

The geographical centre of England certainly lies within the county, but the exact spot seems to be in dispute, for at the village of Meriden, five miles from Coventry on the road to Birmingham, there are the remains of a cross which was erected to mark the supposed centre, whilst at Leamington Spa the "Midland Oak," claims the same distinction!

Warwickshire is a medium-sized county, neither too large to be intimate nor small enough to be cramped. It covers an area of almost nine hundred square miles spread over which live rather more than a million and a half people. The industrial northwest, as one would expect, absorbs most of the population. Birmingham, second only to London amongst English cities, alone houses just over a million people, whilst the other industrial towns—the chief of which are Coventry, Rugby, Nuneaton, Solihull and Sutton Coldfield—absorb approximately a further five hundred thousand.

*Arms of Warwickshire*

335

There are, therefore, only about a hundred thousand people spread throughout the country areas, yet at the time of writing some five-sixths of the county are devoted to farming, about two-thirds of this for permanent pasture. Fortunately, the county's large and highly organized industries are extremely centralized and, as a result, encroach less than most industries do upon the large areas of unspoiled country that Warwickshire has to offer.

### Geological Make-up

The county is blessed with rich soil and a mild climate, and these two factors together have encouraged extensive dairy farming and market gardening. The main grain crops are wheat and oats, and there are excellent orchards. Nor, as we shall see, is Warwickshire lacking in mineral resources. It is, in fact, a county admirably balanced from a social and an economic point of view.

Geologists tell us that the physical structure of Warwickshire is simple, but the language they use to describe it makes it sound most complicated. However, we should briefly consider the lie and composition of the land, for from it we can learn quite a lot about the grouping of industry, of its natural resources, and even about such matters as changes in scenery and in the architectural styles of buildings throughout the county.

The Avon, which flows through Warwickshire from north-east to south-west, divides the county into two unequal parts, that area on the north-west of the river being the larger. Most of this latter is composed of triassic marls and sandstones, the main sandstone belt running from Kenilworth, through Coventry, to Atherstone, near the north-eastern border. Along this border, too, runs a narrow strip of the coal measures. It extends from Nuneaton, through Atherstone, to Tamworth, and although comparatively small, is extremely productive of high-quality coal. This is Warwickshire's share of the Black Country, a land of collieries, forges, ironfields and canals, where belching chimneys darken the land and begrime what few trees and hedge-

Less than two miles from Warwick, on the Avon, is Guy's Cliffe, formerly the seat of Lord Algernon Percy. The legendary hermit, Guy of Warwick, is said to have lived here in a cave after his pilgrimage to the Holy Land. The lovely old mill seen below faces the mansion.

Within the borders of Warwickshire are villages which rank among the loveliest in England. A few miles beyond Stratford, to the west, is Exhall, mentioned in an old rhyme, quoted on page 341, as one of the meeting places of Shakespeare and his friends.

rows remain. Tacked on to the eastern end of the coal belt is a valuable vein of Hartshill quartzite which is extensively quarried.

The southern and the smaller of the two divisions into which the Avon divides the county consists mainly of lias limestone. Evidence of this foundation is reflected in the architecture of this area; the villages possess many of the Cotswold characteristics and provide welcome relief from the brighter-hued buildings found on the other side of the river. Here, too, where the northern spurs of the Cotswolds fringe the county's southern border, the land is highest, rising to eight hundred and twenty-six feet in Edgehill, with Brailes and Kineton on either side. These hills command magnificent views over the central plain where the silver ribbon of the Avon flows in leisurely way past Warwick and Stratford-on-Avon through some of the finest sylvan scenery in Britain. Camden called the country south of the river the Feldon or open country, as opposed to the north, or Woodland, where the remnants of the great forest of Arden, which at one time covered most of the district, still justify the county's title of Leafy Warwick.

Warwickshire is not particularly rich in prehistoric remains, doubtless because Arden covered so much of its area for so long. There are, however, remnants of ancient earthworks at Beausale camp, Nadbury camp and Oldbury camp. Saxon remains, too, are sparse, but fragments are found along the old Roman Fosse Way which enters the county at Halford, on the Worcestershire border, and runs across it in a straight line from south-west to north-east. A Saxon cemetery of the fifth or sixth century was discovered in 1924 at Bidford, near Stratford-on-Avon. The famous Watling Street forms the county's north-eastern boundary from a point near Rugby to Atherstone.

### Historic Associations of Warwick

Warwick, the county town, stands roughly in the centre of the county on the Avon, amidst glorious typically English scenery. It still retains much evidence of life in the Middle Ages despite the fact that it was ravaged by fire in 1694. Its old east and west gates, dating from the twelfth century, still stand, although very little of the ancient walls remains. Its many half-timbered Tudor houses are without equal in England. Here there is an air of quiet, unhurried life. Here the townsfolk go about their business as they have done for hundreds of years

337

past, and it is difficult to imagine, as one watches the barges gliding silently down the Grand Union Canal, which skirts the town to the north, that Birmingham is only twenty miles away.

## Warwick Castle

Warwick is a very ancient town. It arose around the great mound which Ethelflaeda, Lady of the Mercians and eldest daughter of Alfred the Great, fortified in the year 914. Its crowning glory is its magnificent castle (dominating a site of great natural beauty) whose walls rise sheer from the rock that forms the north bank of the Avon. If you go in by the gatehouse to the central courtyard, you will see Ethelflaeda's mount, with Cæsar's and Guy's towers opposite. What history these walls must have witnessed! Here came John Giffard when he captured the castle for Simon de Montfort during his struggle with Henry III: here Warwick the Kingmaker kept Edward IV his prisoner in 1469. The castle contains many beautifully panelled rooms and a fine collection of furniture and pictures. The armour is regarded as one of the finest collections in existence.

Outside, in the town, is St. Mary's Church, distinguished by its lofty tower through the base of which the roadway runs. But perhaps the most interesting building is Lord Leycester's Hospital. It was originally a guildhouse, but was turned into an almshouse in 1571 for persons maimed in the wars of those times. Today it still serves a similar purpose.

## Memorial to the Past

The countryside around Warwick is rich in associations with the past. Only two miles away is Guy's Cliffe, in the grounds of which is the cave where lived that legendary hermit Guy of Warwick after his pilgrimage to the Holy Land. The chapel of St. Mary Magdalene, founded to his memory by Richard Beauchamp, Earl of Warwick, who died in 1491, contains a mutilated statue of the hermit.

About midway between Warwick and Coventry lies the pleasant little town of Kenilworth with its castle, immortalized in Sir Walter Scott's novel. Few castles in England can boast of such extensive remains; none can claim a finer or more picturesque setting. John of Gaunt built the Strong Tower, the Banqueting Hall and the White Hall, and later additions were made by Robert Dudley, Earl of Leicester, upon whom, in 1562, the castle was conferred by Queen Elizabeth. On the road from Warwick to Kenilworth is Black Low Hill, on which a cross marks the spot where Piers Gaveston, favourite of Edward II, was executed after his trial in the great hall of Warwick Castle.

Two miles to the east of Warwick, where the Leam joins the Avon, is Leamington Spa. It belonged in early times to the priory of Kenilworth, and although its mineral springs were known in the Middle Ages, it was not until 1786, when the baths were erected, that any extensive use was made of them. Today Leamington is a dignified, sometimes pompous residential town catering for the usual colony of well-off and not-so-well-off retired hypochondriacs and invalids that are always found in such spas.

## Birthplace of Shakespeare

Foremost of Warwickshire's show places is, of course, Stratford-on-Avon, only nine miles from Leamington. Had it not been for Shakespeare, it would probably be just a fine old market town nestling in the leafy beauty of the Avon valley, unspoiled by a constant influx of tourists and sightseers.

Stratford arose around a monastery as far back as the year 691, but it was not until 1553 that it was incorporated as a town. Eleven years later, on April 23, 1564, William Shakespeare was born.

It was through the agency of David Garrick, towards the end of the eighteenth century, that the poet's memory was first honoured in his native town, but another hundred years were to pass before Charles Flower founded the Memorial Theatre and the Stratford Festivals which each year commemorate the poet's birth. The present theatre, the architectural merits of which are much in dispute, was opened to the public in 1932, and replaced the original building which was destroyed by fire in 1926. Whatever the merits or demerits of the new building, few people would suggest that it is

Fosse Way near Eatington,
south-east of Stratford

Victoria Square, Birmingham, showing New Street. This is the oldest street of modern Birmingham and includes among its notable buildings King Edward's schools, the Theatre Royal and the Exchange. The first performance of Mendelssohn's "Elijah" was given in the town hall, seen on the left.

not a great improvement upon the original —a frightful eyesore. The buildings occupy a magnificent and commanding site on the banks of the Avon close to the famous Clopton Bridge. They contain, besides the theatre, a library, picture gallery and conference hall.

As one would expect, most of Stratford's notable buildings have associations with the poet. His supposed birth-place in Henley Street was purchased for the nation in 1874; New Place, where he died in 1616—strangely enough on the anniversary of his birth—was destroyed by fire, but the site was purchased by public subscription in 1861. He is buried in the cruciform parish church of Holy Trinity beside Anne Hathaway, his wife.

In addition to its Shakespearean relics and memorials, Stratford possesses the fine old guild chapel, dating from about 1450, as well as a notable guildhall and the beautiful Elizabethan Harvard House once owned by the parents of John Harvard, founder of the famous American university which bears his name.

The countryside around Stratford, like the town itself, is rich in Shakespearean associations. At Shottery, just a mile away, is the exquisite thatched cottage in which Anne Hathaway was born. It was purchased for the nation in 1892.

Charlecote Park, where Shakespeare was said to have shot a deer, an act which brought him before Sir Thomas Lucy, high sheriff of the county, is near-by. It is now the property of the National Trust. In later years Shakespeare commemorated this event by caricaturing Sir Thomas as Mr. Justice Shallow in *Henry IV* and *The Merry Wives of Windsor*, but he was tactful enough to place Mr. Justice Shallow's house in Gloucestershire lest Sir Thomas be affronted.

The traditional eight villages around Stratford, where Shakespeare used to make merry with his friends, are mentioned in an old rhyme, attributed to the poet, although the first two mentioned are actually just over the county boundary in Worcestershire.

> Piping Petworth, dancing Marston,
> Haunted Hillborough, hungry Grafton,
> Dodging Exhall, papist Wixford,
> Beggarly Broom and drunken Bidford.

It would be a hopeless task to try to catalogue all the lovely little villages in this area. There are far too many of them, and each one seems to have some special charm of its own that distinguishes it from its neighbour. The walker will discover these villages for himself, and what country this is for walking! Dunchurch, near Rugby on the main London–Coventry road, is famous for its beautiful avenue of trees, planted in 1921 as a memorial to the 29th Division, which was billeted in the neighbourhood before embarking for Gallipoli in 1915. Would that there were more memorials of this kind. The Lion Inn is a reputed meeting-place of the Gunpowder Plot conspirators. Meriden, between Coventry and Birmingham, claims to be the centre of England, as already mentioned. Besides its old cross it has an obelisk which commemorates cyclists who fell in the First World War. Here, in the park of Packington Hall, the Woodmen of Arden, an ancient society of archers, keep alive their curious old customs each year.

Between Rugby and Coventry is Knightlow Cross, noted for its hundred moot. This is still held every year on St. Martin's Day (November 11), and at dawn the representatives of the eighteen parishes in the hundred meet the steward of the Lord of the Manor, the Duke of Buccleuch, round the hollow stone at the top of Knightlow Hill into which the dues are cast. These dues range from one penny to two shillings, and defaulters are liable to a fine of twenty shillings for every penny and "a white bull with red ears and a red nose." The duke provides hot rum and milk and his health is drunk at the conclusion of this ceremony.

There are one or two excellent examples of domestic and monastic architecture in or close to the Avon valley. Foremost of these are Wroxall Abbey and Baddesley Clinton Hall, both to the west of Kenilworth. They date from the twelfth and fifteenth centuries respectively. On the Avon, about two miles east of Kenilworth is the great mansion of Stoneleigh Abbey, the seat of Lord Leigh. It dates from the early part of the eighteenth century and is built in the Classic style, but portions of the twelfth century Cistercian monastery, founded by Henry II, survive.

In the Feldon country on the other side of the river the countryside takes on quite a different appearance. The land here is more hilly and, as I have said already, the architecture has much in common with that of Worcestershire, owing to the use of the local limestone.

The showplace of the Feldon is Compton Wynyates, the seat of the Marquess of Northampton. In Elizabethan maps it is

**A corner of Warwick looking towards the parish church of St. Mary. The roadway runs through the base of the church's battlemented tower.**

marked as Compton-in-ye-Hole, and the old name has a peculiar aptness lacking in the new, for it lies in a hollow between Edgehill and Long Compton, literally in a hole. The great house is picturesque beyond description—a beautiful mixture of stone and half-timber. Built by William Compton, who was knighted in the Battle of the Spurs, it was originally moated and is perhaps the finest example of Tudor domestic architecture in existence. The house was taken by the Parliamentarians in 1646, and the adjacent church, destroyed by them, was restored in 1663.

### Forgotten Towns

Here in the Feldon we are very close to the past, and one cannot help feeling a little sad when one recalls that some of the places, now little more than hamlets, were once foremost amongst the towns of England. Take Brailes, for example, one of the forgotten towns of England. Valued in the "Domesday Book" at more than a score of Birminghams, it was in those distant days second only to Warwick. It was a great centre of the wool trade, and even today, although there are few sheep to be seen on the surrounding hills, it retains something of the grandeur of the sheep-farming days. The church and the George Inn face one another in the main street. The inn is the older by fifty years, and here were housed the workmen who built the church in the great heyday of wool. The church is now far beyond the needs of the parish, but it is a notable example of the Decorated style, comparable with anything to be found in the county. In Brailes today you might be living in an England of five hundred years ago, and were it not for the intruding motor-cars, or perhaps an aeroplane overhead, Elizabethan broadcloth would look more appropriate than modern clothes.

Not far away the leaning tower of Barcheston Church marks all that is left of what was once the most famous tapestry town in England. There is only a farm, a cottage and a rectory there now, but Sheldon tapestries are still the most sought after of English fabrics.

The old village of Kineton is chiefly interesting because of its associations with the battle of Edgehill, the first important action in the Civil War, which was fought on a near-by ridge on October 23, 1642.

It is strange to note that just as the Feldon country has declined in importance with the

**The castle is Warwick's crowning glory. Built upon the rock which forms the north bank of the Avon, it dominates a site of great natural beauty. Parts of it date from the twelfth century.**

The estate of Compton Wynyates, eight miles south of Kineton, has been in the ownership of the Compton family for over seven hundred years. The house was built between 1450 and 1523.

passage of time, so has the Woodland developed and progressed. Today all Warwickshire's large modern towns and cities are north of the Avon where, of course, the great bulk of her mineral wealth lies.

Foremost in size of all these is, of course, Birmingham. Like tentacles, the arms of this straggling city stretch out and threaten the surrounding countryside. They reach out beyond Redditch, in Worcestershire, threaten Henley-in-Arden, and roughly follow the course of the river Alne towards Beausale and Wroxall Abbey. Along all the main roads there is the usual unsightly ribbon development; modern villas, petrol-filling stations and roadhouses now stand where quick hedges once grew, and the sound of motor-car engines has replaced the more leisurely plod of horses' hooves. Concrete highways and back gardens cover much of what was once the good cattle land of Arden. Yet even here, in the fields between the main roads, the old holders of the land still wage a relentless but losing fight with the ruthless advance of bricks and mortar.

Cobbett contemptuously called Birmingham the "Wen" to summarize all that he found distasteful, yet for all its unpopular-ity with the true countryman it has brought wealth and prosperity to the county, and within an incredibly short space of time has risen from an obscure Puritan settlement to proud place of second amongst English cities. As the chief centre of the hardware trade of the world it has more than fifteen hundred distinct trades within its boundaries, ranging from the manufacture of small arms and explosives to railway wagons, machine tools, rubber goods and chemicals; to mention only a few.

### The Great Cities

The city is built on a red sandstone site between the valleys of the Rea and Tame, with its suburbs extending over the borders into Staffordshire and Worcestershire. It looks down upon the central plain from heights varying from two to six hundred feet, and its position nearly at the centre of England makes it a railway junction of the first importance.

Most of the old buildings in the centre of the city disappeared in the great clearance of slum and insanitary property, begun in 1875, and nearly all the buildings are, in consequence, of comparatively recent construction. Nevertheless, even today, and despite aerial bombardment, Birmingham

Rugby School, the home of Rugby football, was founded in 1567 by Lawrence Sheriff, a native of the town. Thomas Arnold, its headmaster from 1828 to 1842, raised the school to a high position.

is still cursed with some of the most fearsome slums in Britain.

The Town Hall, Art Gallery, Theatre Royal, Exchange and most of the finest buildings, are to be found in the central thoroughfares of New Street, Corporation Street and Colmore. The university grew out of Queen's College, founded as a school of medicine in 1828, and later moved to Edgbaston, where its buildings now stand.

Birmingham, like Coventry, is the seat of a bishop, and its chief magistrate has been a lord mayor since 1896. Its fine cathedral, originally St. Philip's Church, is built in the Palladian style and its stained-glass windows by Burne-Jones are admired by many. The city's mother church, St. Martin's, was the only parish church until 1715.

The city has acquired some valuable breathing spaces on the near-by Lickey Hills, of which about a square mile has been presented to the public by members of the Cadbury family. Sutton Park is a fine stretch of wild heath close to Birmingham, but it actually belongs to the adjoining borough of Sutton Coldfield.

The well-known chocolate factory of Bournville, built by George Cadbury, although actually in Worcestershire, is included in Greater Birmingham. It was built on garden city lines in 1895.

Coventry, second of Warwickshire's cities, is of very old foundation. It grew up around the Benedictine monastery founded by Leofric, Earl of Mercia, in 1043, and in the fourteenth century ranked fourth in commercial importance in England. Originally it was surrounded by a wall pierced by twelve gates, but the walls were razed by Charles II, and only two of the gates remain.

Coventry had experienced the ravages of war long before the German bombers introduced the word "Coventrated" into the English vocabulary. In the Wars of the Roses it declared for the Lancastrians, whilst Warwick supported the Yorkists, and during the Civil War it was besieged after the fateful battle of Edgehill.

Coventry has grown since Peeping Tom bored a hole in his shutter to watch Lady Godiva ride by. Up until the close of the

344

seventeenth century, it was a centre of the cloth industry, and later it became noted for ribbons, watches and sewing-machines. To-day it is a great industrial city populated by some of the most skilled artisans and workers in the country, whose productions range from aeroplanes and motor-cars to artificial silk and all kinds of electrical apparatus.

Even before the heavy air raids of November, 1940, wiped out most of it, the central area with its narrow medieval streets had become quite unable to cope with the heavy volume of modern traffic, and the city's architect had already prepared a plan for rebuilding this area. The plan envisaged a wide ring road round the central area on to which all through traffic could be diverted. The area enclosed within this road was to have been rebuilt without disturbing the numerous fine historical monuments that fell within it. However, the devastation wrought by the raids has facilitated the carrying out of this plan, and the Mayor's first remark on seeing the damage was "we have always wanted a site for a new civic centre, and now we have it." But the destruction of so much that was lovely and irreplaceable, so many cherished links with history, particularly the fine cathedral church of St. Michael, was a fearful price to pay for the chance to erect a new and more spacious city centre. A great new Cathedral is rising on the ashes of the old.

Standing on the Avon to the east of Coventry is Rugby. From the train as you approach the town you will see the tall wireless masts of Hillmorton which connect Britain by beam radio with the farthest ends of the earth. Rugby is a substantial market town and hunting centre, and besides being one of the chief railway junctions of England, it houses two great electrical works. The famous school, immortalized in *Tom Brown's Schooldays*, is also the home of Rugby football, for it was here, in 1823, that W. W. Ellis astonished his schoolfellows by grabbing the ball and running with it towards his opponents' goal.

These, then, are some of the towns and villages within the borders of this lovely English county. The picture is incomplete, for it would take a whole book to sing all its praises and give the reader anything like a comprehensive view of Warwickshire's many-sided activities.

But no sketch, however short, would be complete without at least some attempt to describe the Warwickshire man.

What is really meant by the Warwickshire man? Is it the million and a half men and women who live and work in the great

The Woodmen of Arden, an ancient society of archers, hold their ward-mote each year in the lovely park of Packington Hall at Meriden, where they keep alive their curious old customs.

# WORCESTERSHIRE

SHROPSHIRE

DUD

FOREST OF WYRE

R. STOUR

STOURBRIDGE

TENBURY

BEWDLEY

KIDDERMINSTER

HALESOW

ABBERLEY HILLS

CLENT HILLS

KYRE MAGNA

EASTHAM

STOCKTON ON TEME

STOURPORT ON SEVERN

LICKEY HILLS

HARTLEBURY

House at Ombersley

BROMSGROVE

SHRAWLEY

ABBEY GATE, EVESHAM

OMBERSLEY

STOKE PRIOR

CAN

RE

MARTLEY

Elgar's Birthplace, Broadheath

DROITWICH

R. TEME

R. SEVERN

BROADHEATH

ASTWOOD BANK

WORCESTER

WORCESTER CATHEDRAL

POWICK

Pershore Abbey

GRAFTON FLYFORD

MALVERN HILLS

The Bell Tower, Evesham

GT MALVERN

Powick Bridge

ALCE

LITTLE MALVERN

PERSHORE

R.

UPTON UPON SEVERN

Priory Ch., Little Malvern

VALE OF

EVESHAM

HEREFORDSHIRE

BREDON HILL

Battle of Evesham 1265

The Beacon Tower, Broadway

BECKFORD

BROADWAY

SHAKESPEARE MEMORIAL THEATRE, STRATFORD

GLOUCESTERSH

WORCESTERSH

WORC

N

E

S

W

Miles

0     5     10

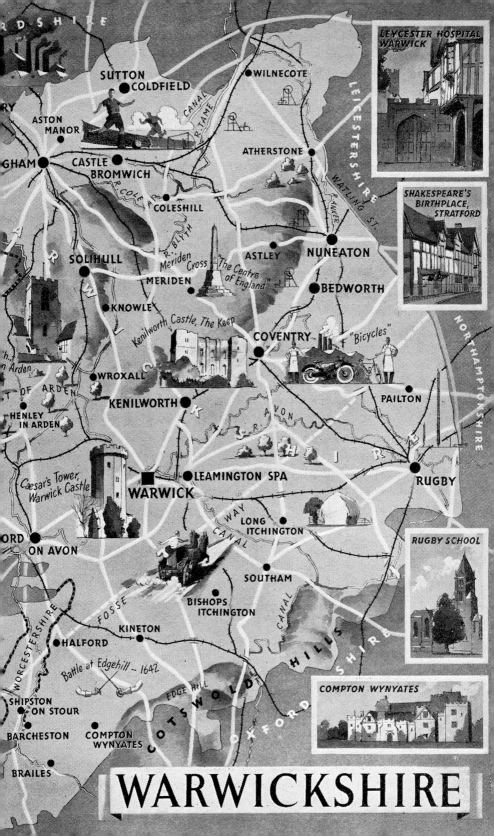

LEYCESTER HOSPITAL WARWICK

SHAKESPEARE'S BIRTHPLACE, STRATFORD

RUGBY SCHOOL

COMPTON WYNYATES

SUTTON COLDFIELD

WILNECOTE

ASTON MANOR

ATHERSTONE

GHAM

CASTLE BROMWICH

COLESHILL

SOLIHULL

Meriden Cross

ASTLEY

NUNEATON

MERIDEN

"The Centre of England"

BEDWORTH

KNOWLE

Kenilworth Castle, The Keep

COVENTRY

"Bicycles"

WROXALL

KENILWORTH

PAILTON

HENLEY IN ARDEN

Caesar's Tower, Warwick Castle

LEAMINGTON SPA

RUGBY

WARWICK

LONG ITCHINGTON

ORD ON AVON

CANAL

WAY

SOUTHAM

BISHOPS ITCHINGTON

FOSSE

KINETON

HALFORD

Battle at Edgehill – 1642

EDGE HILL

SHIPSTON ON STOUR

BARCHESTON

COMPTON WYNYATES

BRAILES

COTSWOLD HILLS

OXFORDSHIRE

WORCESTERSHIRE

LEICESTERSHIRE

WATLING ST.

NORTHAMPTONSHIRE

R. TAME

CANAL

R. COLE

R. BLYTH

R. ANKER

R. AVON

# WARWICKSHIRE

cities or the hundred thousand minority spread over the country areas? To me it is in the countryside that the true soul of Warwickshire is to be found, for there you will find the product of a thousand years of evolution amid the Woodland and the Feldon.

Warwickshire countrymen are solid, un-emotional folk, men of a dozen skills, whose mixed farming allows little development of that specialization that prevents a man from turning a hand to any other job than his own. You will often find a couple of hundred acres farmed by a farmer, his wife, two sons and, perhaps, a hired man. Yet, despite the endless work this entails, they will take a pride in their hedging and ditching, and their ricks will always be well and neatly thatched with a skill that has been handed down from father to son for countless generations.

They are quiet, reserved men, not easy to understand, and if they rarely open their hearts, you will, sooner or later, catch them unawares and be surprised at the depth and sincerity of their friendship. They are hospitable people, too, but above all they are great traditionalists. Representatives of the old craftsmen, they still defy the machine; hurdle-making is still a considerable art in many areas, and only the fierce drive of competition has forced many of them against their will to employ the "new-fangled" tractor instead of the horse.

These men of Warwickshire are fiercely devoted to their county. Loftily intolerant of "foreigners" who trespass on its soil they are equally averse to crossing the borders of their native land into the "heathen" areas that lie beyond.

What else could one expect from men whose names were known in the land at the time of the Norman Conquest; whose land was their father's and their father's fathers? These Warwickshire countrymen live very close to nature; the land is their whole life, and, like the land they till so lovingiy, they can be cruel as well as kind but they are always honest, industrious and straightforward.

In the large towns and cities a new race of Warwickshire men has grown up, a race who have forsaken the quiet and dignity of labour on the land for the hurry and bustle of the machine age in the cities. Many of these men are Warwickshire's adopted sons, for her industry has absorbed thousands who were persuaded to leave their age-old callings: and it is still in clamour to satisfy its ever-growing needs. And if the two races, the Warwickshire countryman and the polyglot machine minder, do not mix too readily, and if the countryman is a little suspicious of the town-dweller, they both have the same goal before them and march forward hand in hand to the greater honour and prosperity of the beautiful county in which they live.

*Mill Street, Warwick*

348

*Cropthorne near Evesham*

# WORCESTERSHIRE

## By ROBERT BRYAN

"A LAND rich in corn, productive of fruit in some parts by the sole favour of nature, in others by the art of cultivation, enticing even the lazy to industry by the prospect of a hundredfold return; you may see the highway clothed with trees that produce apples, not by the grafter's hand but by the nature of the ground itself, for the earth, of its own account, rears them up to fruit, and that excellent in flavour and appearance, many of which wither not within the year, nor before the new crops are produced to supply their place."

The writer is the twelfth-century chronicler, William of Malmesbury. The county he describes is Worcestershire.

"Productive of fruit"—what struck the chronicler over eight hundred years ago, still remains the abiding impression alike of those who know Worcestershire by experience or only by repute. The Pershore plum, the Worcester apple, the blossom in the gardens of the Vale of Evesham —these still are the most famous

*Badge of Worcestershire*

of Worcestershire's products. Worcestershire means to most of us the orchard land of western England, soft in landscape, rich in soil, mild in climate, a gentle land through which the broad Severn gently flows.

But it is dangerous to generalize. Is Worcestershire all soft in landscape? On its western borders rise the steep, jagged Malvern Hills. Is it all orchard and pasture? The smoky chimney stacks of Stourbridge and Dudley in the north of the county give the immediate lie to any such idea.

Worcestershire is, in fact, part of the West country, of the Welsh Marches, and of the Midlands. Its life is as powerfully affected by industrial Staffordshire and Warwickshire, as by rural Oxfordshire and pastoral Gloucestershire. It stretches in the west to the eastern slopes of the Welsh mountains, and in the Middle Ages derived much of its prosperity from entrepôt trade carried on with the Principality. It is a small county to hold so

349

Looking towards the Malvern Hills from Bringsty Common, close to the Herefordshire border. Although Worcestershire nowhere exceeds forty miles in length or breadth and has an area of under 700 square miles, it contains an amazing diversity of scenery.

much diversity. Nowhere is it forty miles in length or breadth. It totals only six hundred and eighty-seven square miles. And for so small an area it has many neighbours. Gloucestershire, Herefordshire, Shropshire, Staffordshire and Warwickshire—all have common borders with Worcestershire.

Lastly, its population, too, bids fair to outrun its size. In the county's southern half the inhabitants may still be sparsely, rurally scattered, but in the industrial north they have, in the past hundred years, rapidly increased, and the threat of an urban sprawl menaces today much of the Severn valley.

350

# WORCESTERSHIRE

Worcestershire's early history is the history of the city now called Worcester, but known to the Romans as Wigorna Castra (the warrior's abode). Here from very early pre-Christian days there was a ford across the River Severn which then flowed between dense forests. The Romans established some sort of settlement—an outpost against the fierce, unconquered Celts of the Welsh Marches. But the place did not grow, it never reached the status of a Roman town. Nor was this part ever seriously colonized in Roman days. There is an analogy with the territories in India across the Indus over which the British exercised for long only fitful and purely defensive jurisdiction.

Presently Christianity came to England. In the seventh century the see of Worcester was established, with its jurisdiction corresponding closely to the present area of the county. Thenceforth, though it was not until the early Middle Ages that it became the capital of a county, Worcester grew steadily in importance.

At first the importance was purely ecclesiastical. The ford across the Severn was the chief highway for Christian missionaries penetrating into heathen Wales. A succession of notable bishops in Saxon times raised the town's status. And Bishop Oswald in the ninth century founded there the first great Benedictine monastery in England.

It was the first of many monastic establishments which left their mark on Worcestershire. The Franciscans and Dominicans came to Worcester itself. The Benedictines settled at Evesham and at Malvern. The Cluniacs came to Dudley, and, later, the Austin Friars to Droitwich.

Hence it came about that at the end of the Middle Ages Worcestershire was perhaps the greatest stronghold of monasticism in the country. It followed that the suppression of the monasteries by Henry VIII caused a great upheaval in the county. There were widespread changes in the land ownership, and the new merchant class that was then coming to power and position reaped the benefit.

It followed also that Worcestershire was strong for the Roman Catholic faith.

Among the staunchest of the Catholic families were the Winters and the Habingtons. It was at Huddington Court, home of the Winters, that, with the aid of Robert Catesby, the Gunpowder Plot was planned. It was to Huddington Court that the conspirators fled after the plot's unmasking. And it was there that Winter gave himself up to his pursuers while Catesby and Habington made a further brief escape.

One other result of the establishment of monastic houses in Worcestershire must be mentioned. Today the county includes a number of enclaves in neighbouring shires. Parts of Worcestershire are entirely surrounded by Gloucestershire. The Dudley area is enclosed on all sides by Staffordshire. These areas were, in the Middle Ages, monastically owned. Thus Broadway was owned by monks of Pershore. The power of the monasteries was then so great that they could persuade, in fact almost force, the civil authorities to draw the county boundaries so as to include their lands.

**King's Norton, a suburb of Birmingham. In the south of the city, it was, with Northfield, a separate urban district prior to 1912.**

In the Middle Ages and in Tudor times Worcester prospered commercially. From very early days glove-making has been a staple industry. In the thirteenth century records there is mention of a Glove-makers Street. The Glovers Guild was incorporated in 1497. In the reign of Elizabeth Worcester was the chief centre in the country of the clothing trade. In the north of the county the town of Bewdley was enjoying a similar prosperity. Being a river port on the Severn, it carried on a valuable entrepôt trade. It was the emporium, for example, for Welsh flannel goods. It was the stage where groceries, regularly brought into the country at Bristol, were unloaded for transportation both to Wales and Lancashire. And on its own account it manufactured, with considerable profit, combs and sailors' caps.

As time went on the importance of Bewdley declined. Worcester, too, lost its pre-eminence in the clothing trade. But in the eighteenth century the development of the Worcester porcelain industry gave to the city a new interest and a prosperity that have proved lasting. In 1751 the Worcester Royal Porcelain Works was founded by Dr. John Wall. Dr. Wall was by profession a physician. He was, in fact, the prime mover in starting the practice of hydropathy at Malvern. Research into porcelain manufacture was for him a side line only, a hobby. But the sideline was encouraged and financially backed by the Hanoverian Party of the city. They wanted to be behind a new manufacture in Worcester so that their voting strength might be increased. Dr. Wall with his new process in which, for the first time, soapstone was used in the product, gave them their opportunity, and today Worcester porcelain is prized and valued all over the world.

There were before the dawn of the nineteenth century a number of local industries, such as scythe-making, scattered rurally over Worcestershire. In particular many cottagers were engaged in the manufacture of nails in the local nail forges. But for the most part the county was a backwater of England. Even its orchards and hopfields could not, in popular estimation, rival those of Kent with their far greater proximity to London. It was Kent that was known as the Garden of England. It is only in the last hundred years that

The fourteenth century Edgar Tower, entrance to the Cathedral close at Worcester. In the vicinity are the picturesque ruins of the Guesten Hall which afforded shelter to the visitors to the Benedictine Priory with which the Cathedral was connected.

Pershore, in the valley of the Avon, was one of the greatest of several religious houses that were founded in early Norman times. The old bridge seen above is no longer in use, a modern structure having been built alongside. The town is noted for its horse and cattle fairs.

coal beneath the grass has made of half of Worcestershire an important industrial centre, and that the saline springs of Droitwich and the water and air of Malvern have given to the county two of England's leading spas.

Worcestershire before the Industrial Revolution was a homogeneous county of river, meadow and orchard, with hills on each flank. Worcestershire today is an area of great contrasts in a small space. In his poem *Bredon Hill*, A. E. Housman tells how

> Here of a Sunday morning
> My love and I would lie
> And see the coloured counties
> And hear the larks so high
> About us in the sky.

An idyllic rural scene. But no one has rhapsodized or could conceivably rhapsodize about winter-time in Dudley or Halesowen, where smoke and grime surround the blackened rows of squalid and uniform buildings, and factory life with all its harsh insistence is the unending rule.

Today it is from Bredon—a northwestern outpost of the Cotswolds—or better still, from the top of Broadway Beacon, that you look out over all that is lovely in Worcestershire. The view from the latter is so extensive that it includes the spires of Coventry and Warwick to the north as well as the Wrekin in Shropshire and May Hill in Monmouthshire, far across the Severn and the Wye. But in the comparative foreground lies southern Worcestershire, bounded in the distance by the Malvern Hills shimmering on a fine spring morning with the blossom of plum, apple and pear, rich with the green of water meadows and of spreading trees.

Broadway itself is old and quaint—perhaps too self-consciously quaint—but an unfailing draw for tourists from the United States. It is one long, wide street, lined with stone-built houses of the sixteenth century, possessing in the "Lygon Arms" one of the famous inns of England, where Charles I once stayed during the Civil War and where now guests are assured of modern comforts in an ancient setting. But though Broadway is in the administrative county of Worcester, it belongs to Cotswold Gloucestershire, by which it is surrounded. So, too, does Bredon to the

M

(E.N.C.)

The ferry across the river Avon at Fladbury, three miles north-west of Evesham. The village, in common with its near neighbour Cropthorne, is noted for its beautiful old church.

south, where you will find Norman work in the parish church. You must move farther west, down from the Cotswold heights, before you come to the real Worcestershire.

Worcester, the county town and cathedral city, proud in its civic motto "The Faithful City," lies on the River Severn. It is more industrialized than is Gloucester, being a nearly equal blend of old and new. But the tempo is leisurely and serene; the old has still not yielded pride of place.

### "The Faithful City"

The motto "The Faithful City" was earned in the Civil War. The county was staunchly and solidly Royalist. Worcester was indeed the first city in the land to declare for the King. Throughout the following years, until the King's final defeat at Naseby, the Parliamentary forces could gain no established footing in the county. Then for five years the gentlemen of Worcester had to nurse their Royalist pride in resentful silence. But in 1651 there came what seemed a second chance. Charles I was dead, but his son was march-

ing south from Scotland with a gathering force. He reached Worcester, halted there, made his headquarters in the building now known as King Charles' House in Friar Street. Worcester rejoiced.

But Cromwell, with a greatly superior force, was advancing from the south. On the night before battle, the Duke of Hamilton entertained the young King in the Great Hall of the Commandery (which visitors are shown today). The next day the Royalists were routed. Hamilton died in the Hall where the previous night he had been host, both his legs "broken short off" by a cannon ball. But through the devotion of Worcester citizens the King made a perilous, but successful escape. And on his restoration to the throne he granted permission to those citizens to use on their civic coat of arms the inscription "The Faithful City."

Worcester Cathedral delights the eye by virtue of its situation, rising from the green banks of a placid reach of the Severn River. It contains within its walls a whole history of medieval architecture. The apsidal crypt, one of four in England, is early Norman work. Elsewhere, in the choir and the nave, there are examples of the early English and Decorated early Perpendicular Gothic styles. Later Perpendicular work can also be seen. All through the Middle Ages, in fact, the cathedral was building. But viewed from the outside it does not today give an impression of age. For to preserve the structure, a complete restoration had to be undertaken in the last century, from 1857 to 1874.

In Friar Street can be seen a long row of the old, half-timbered, black and white houses in which Worcestershire abounds and which are one of the county's distinguishing architectural features. In the centre of the city stands the Guildhall, with a façade unexcelled as an example of the style of the reign of Queen Anne. The windows of the Commandery are famous for their fifteenth-century glass.

But in the realm of the arts, Worcester is today chiefly distinguished, more even than for its china, as one of the three homes of the Three Choirs Festival. The beauty of the singing in the annual event, when the choirs of Worcester, Hereford and Gloucester join together to render the sacred music of the world's great composers, has been, since the year 1724, a unique feature of England's national life.

South of Worcester the Severn flows on to its junction at the border of Gloucestershire, near Tewkesbury, with the Avon. It flows through orchard lands and through hopfields, too. For Worcestershire is still the hop-garden of the West of England, and the Hop Market in Worcester city does a thriving trade. In this district you can see Croome Court, home of the Earl of Coventry, with the gardens which were laid out by the famous "Capability" Brown, and the village of Strensham, birth-place of the seventeenth century Samuel Butler, the author of *Hudibras*.

The village of Daylesford, formerly in Worcestershire, but transferred to Gloucestershire in 1931, was the ancient home of the Hastings family.

### Legend of Evesham.

In the south-eastern corner of the county, on the banks of the Avon, lies the old town of Evesham. This town gained its name in Saxon days from the legendary incident of the swineherd and the angels. Eoves was the swineherd's name. Angels appeared to him as he was tending pigs.

**The Malvern hills from below Bromsberrow. The range rises on the western borders of the county and extends for about nine miles north and south, giving views across six counties.**

Attracted by the story, the Bishop of Worcester visited the place. He saw the angels, too. In gratitude to God he founded an abbey on the spot, called after the swine-herd Eovesham.

West of Worcester the rich, alluvial land, watered by the Severn's tributary, the Stour, continues right up to the foot of the Malverns. You can see them from Worcester, rising sharp and sheer, hazy blue in the summer light, this short, surprising, narrow range, that once, geologists say, was a peninsula between two estuaries of the sea.

The plutonic rocks out of which the Malvern Hills are largely formed, and which

Typical of the orchard land of western England is this view of fruit trees in blossom at Evesham.

left cairns, barrows and beacons in abundance. And the invalid—the sufferer from gout and rheumatism—can gain relief or even cure from Malvern's famous waters.

On the slopes and summits of these hills lie the seven Malverns, forming today, with Great Malvern as their centre, a prosperous and growing holiday and residential resort. But a hundred years ago the Malverns were almost unknown. Great Malvern itself was no more than a small village. Then, in 1860, the first hydropathic establishment was opened. They are comparative newcomers to the ranks of English Spas, but they are today as famous as any.

With its mild, yet bracing air, its spacious lawns and gardens, its comfortable hotels, Great Malvern, "that wonderfully clean and tidy town" has much to offer the old and ailing. There are donkey chaises, too, to convey them along the steep paths which wind through Malvern Castle, affording almost alpine views. From the Worcestershire Beacon they can behold a view which embraces fifteen counties. Here there has been erected a toposcope—an instrument enabling you to read off on a map the panorama before you—as a memorial to the reign of Queen Victoria. And for the Malverns "Victorian" is the right epithet. The neighbourhood has links with a far remoter past. Warwick, the Kingmaker, for example, was granted by the Crown the right of ownership over Malvern Chase. In the Priory Church at Great Malvern is a west window which was the gift of King Richard III. And it was "on a May morning on Malvern Hills" that the poet Langland had his "Vision of Piers Plowman." But the Malverns grew to prosperity in Victoria's later days, and there is much that is Victorian in the atmosphere still.

Worcestershire possesses another famous Spa. Some twelve miles north of Worcester lies Droitwich. And like the Malverns, Droitwich owes its present fame to a nineteenth-century discovery. Droitwich has salt springs whose saline content is ten to twelve times that of the ocean. In the Droitwich baths it is impossible *not* to

have been so changed by earth movements as to make their origin sometimes very doubtful, have long been a happy hunting ground for geologists. Parts of the Malverns are owned by the National Trust. The antiquary is happy, too, for before the Romans came, these hills were the stronghold of the British tribe, the Silures, who

357

Broadway, whose beauty has given it a national reputation, belongs in character to Gloucestershire. Among its grey Cotswold stone buildings are some seventeenth century houses.

float. But until 1832 nothing medicinal was done about them. In that year there was a serious outbreak of cholera. Owing to the shortage of fresh water, brine baths were used for the sick. The effect was magical. The mortality rate among the cholera patients began to drop at once. Droitwich's value as a health resort had been established.

Droitwich is a northern outpost of rural Worcestershire. Industrialization is still a little way off. A few miles farther north lies Bromsgrove, southern outpost of the Black Country. In Bromsgrove's High Street you can see Tudor half-timbered houses, reminders of the olden days. But you can see factory chimneys, too, and breathe factory smoke. Bromsgrove has become a manufacturing town.

And to the north a drab, discouraging tale unfolds. You have reached, on the one hand, the suburbs of Birmingham; on

the other lies the land of coal, ironstone and clay deposits on which have arisen the industries of such towns as Stourbridge and Dudley.

At Stourbridge, where there are rich deposits of fine clay, glass-making has been carried on since the sixteenth century. The industry was first established by Hungarian refugees in the reign of Elizabeth. The manufacture of spades, scythes and anvils followed from the intensive working of the neighbourhood ironstone fields in the last century. Between Stourbridge and Smethwick, just outside the county boundary, which possesses some of the biggest ironworks in the country, the land is densely populated, the countryside disappearing before the onward march of little streets and big factories, of tram and train and bus. Near-by is Halesowen, where men and women labour to make edge tools and rivets, and farther north is Dudley, where heavy industry has been based on the rich seams of coal, and deposits of iron and limestone.

Kidderminster has a different *métier*, and a longer manufacturing history than its neighbours. This town, dusty and un-beautiful in appearance, has none the less brought beauty to countless homes. It was the home, in the eighteenth century, first of the Wilton and then of the Brussels carpet. Earlier still it was a centre for the manufacture of woollen cloth, the industry being granted protection in the reign of Henry VII. The fame of Kidderminster carpets rests on the brilliancy and dur-ability of their colours, achieved through the peculiar qualities of the water of the River Stour, on which the town stands.

Last of Worcestershire's industrial centres is the town of Redditch, where in the 1800's the manufacture of fish-hooks gave profitable occupation, but where now the bicycle industry reigns supreme.

From all this industrial belt the beauties of the countryside have vanished. It is vain to wish them back. But in a far north-west corner of the county we come again on a rural scene full of the nostalgic charm of a statelier, more leisured past. Here, on the banks of the Severn, in the countryside known as the Wyre Forest, stands Bewdley. The town is a backwater today, known only to the general public as the birthplace of a twentieth-century Prime Minister. Gone from its quayside are the bustling activities which made it once a leading river-port. But the big houses of the old-time merchants still line the river bank in reminder that formerly prosperity and architectural beauty went hand in hand.

**Worcestershire has several of these unusual church towers of black and white half-timbered construction. This one is at Pirton, between Worcester and Evesham.**

In a county of contrasts nothing is more startling than the juxtaposition of old and new in the town of Dudley. Here part of the old medieval castle still stands, showing traces of the early decorated style of Gothic architecture, calling to mind the days of baronial wars and a feudal way of life. All around are the smoking chimneys of modern industrial society, whilst fumes rise from the limekilns, and at night the ruined castle is lit up by the red flames from the blast furnaces.

Dudley gave its name to the earldom bestowed on the family of Ward, long and still prominent in Worcestershire life. But for many years the chief family seats were Witley Court, a vast mansion in the florid Palladian style, and Himley Hall, more typical of English domestic architecture, in Staffordshire. Other great Worcestershire houses include Madresfield, in the country between Worcester and Malvern and now the home of the Earl Beauchamp, and Hagley Park where the Lytteltons have lived since the sixteenth century, and the gardens of which excited the admiration of the fastidious Horace Walpole. Families like the Lytteltons and the Lygons belong to a side of Worcestershire which is exemplified, also, by the county's cricket team, with its long tradition of amateur prowess upheld by cricketing families like the Fosters and the country-house atmosphere of the Worcester cricket ground. Here, on a fine summer day, you are far removed from the stresses and strains of urban England—as distant as when you listen in the cathedral to the soaring voices of the Three Choirs Festival—or as the men and women who gather plums and apples in the orchards round Evesham and Pershore.

This is the Worcester which the lover of English rural tradition must cherish. This is the Worcestershire that will always draw the holidaymaker who seeks for beauty. There is an obligation on all of us to see that urban encroachments do not further spoil the scene.

But the potential wealth that in northern Worcestershire lies under the ground cannot, and should not, be ignored. The Black Country is a fact, and a fact which, however destructive it may have been of natural beauty, has contributed powerfully to Britain's greatness, and, in recent days, to her survival against the enemy. The men and women and the industrial resources of Worcestershire's manufacturing centres proved themselves potent weapons of victory.

Disraeli once wrote of England being divided into two nations. He had in mind the contrast between rich and poor. Worcestershire today exemplifies the danger of a different cleavage, between our urban and rural populations. The county is a borderland. It is a land where orchard and factory meet, where the stark and the gentle mingle, where beauty and ugliness are neighbours. It is of the utmost importance that somehow they should go hand in hand.

*Worcester Cathedral*

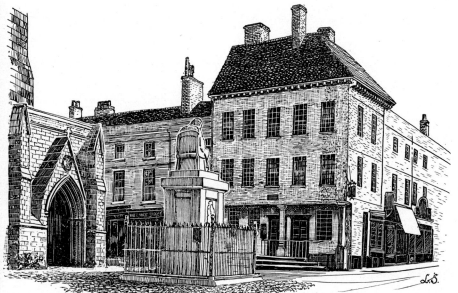

# STAFFORDSHIRE

### By GILLIAN PRICE

To MANY people Staffordshire means the county of the Potteries and the Black Country with their smoking kilns and furnaces. Into these two small areas, which have contributed so much to the wealth of the country, are crowded over a million people or nearly three-quarters of Staffordshire's inhabitants. Seventh in population of the English counties, Staffordshire is only fifteenth in size. Industry is the pre-occupation of modern Staffordshire, whether it be coal, china, beer or hardware. Outside the industrial areas the county is sparsely populated though not lacking in its share of natural beauties.

A broad undulating plain forms the centre of the county. It is the countryside of the dairy farmer for whose products there is a heavy demand in the industrial districts. Over half the county is given to pasturage. In the centre of this delightful country with its villages and lanes, the characteristic heritage

of rural England, is Stafford, the county town on the River Sow, which joins the River Trent a few miles to the east. This, too, is the country of the big estates and houses.

In the north of the plain are situated the Potteries, where a quarter of a million people live in a space nine miles by three, an industrial area of a kind in which Staffordshire has no rival in the whole of the British Isles.

The character of the north of the county is completely different. Here the southern ends of the Peak District overlap into Staffordshire from neighbouring Derbyshire. Both these counties share the beauties of Dovedale. The valley of the Dove is justly claimed to be one of the loveliest and least spoiled parts of England, and is now, happily, largely in the hands of the National Trust. The Dove, which forms the county boundary, flows in a deep valley, with domed and tree-

*Arms of Staffordshire*

361

# STAFFORDSHIRE

LEEK

HARECASTLE TUNNEL,
NR. TUNSTALL

LICHFIELD
CATHEDRAL

CHESHIRE

AUDLEY

BIDDULPH

KIDSGROVE

Rudyard Lake

TUNSTALL

NEWCASTLE
UNDER LYME

BURSLEM

HANLEY

LEEK

LONGNC

STOKE-ON-TRENT

THE PENNINES

R. MANIFOLD

LONGTON

CHEADLE

ECCLESHALL

STONE

R. SOW

R. TRENT

CANAL

Stone

DERBYSHIRE

Izaak Walton's Cottage
Nr. Stafford

■ STAFFORD

WORTHINGTONS
BREWERY,
BURTON-ON-TRENT

CANAL

UTTOXETER

R. BLITHE

R. DOVE

SHROPSHIRE

St. Peter's Church
Wolverhampton

Needwood Forest

RUGELEY

TUTBURY

Cannock Chase

CANNOCK

R. TRENT

CANAL

BURTON-
ON-TRENT

WOLVERHAMPTON

BILSTON

WILLENHALL

LICHFIELD

HIMLEY

WATLING STREET

N

COSELEY

WALSALL

Samuel Johnson's House
Lichfield

W

TIPTON

WEDNESBURY

ROWLEY REGIS

WEST BROMWICH

TAMWORTH

E

SMETHWICK

WARWICKSHIRE

S

Himley Hall

Miles

0      5      10

WORCESTERSHIRE

less limestone hills along its banks. Nestling in the shelter of the hills are picturesque hamlets and delightful places where Nature has hardly been touched by man. The waters of the Dove hold a great attraction for fishermen, as Izaak Walton, a native of Stafford and the author of the *Compleat Angler*, bears witness for all time.

At the foot of the Pennine Chain, which separates the upper waters of the Dove from the rest of Staffordshire, lie the Weaver Hills and moorlands round the silk town of Leek, known as the capital of the moors. The moors form a rough, dreary tract of country where the snows of winter lie long and where the grouse, lapwing and curlew make their homeland.

South of Stafford, the plain is divided by the high land of Cannock Chase, thirty thousand acres of gorse, heather and fir, from the edge of which can be had some magnificent views over the Trent valley. Cannock Chase, at one time a royal hunting preserve, is now known chiefly for its rich coalfield, one of the four in the county, the other three being in the Potteries, to the east at Cheadle and in the Black Country.

South of Cannock Chase the ground falls away to the Black Country round Wolverhampton and Walsall, an agglomeration of industrial towns and villages running over into Warwickshire.

The River Severn pays a brief visit to the western edge of the county at Over Areley, but Staffordshire's own river is the Trent, which flows from its source in the northern moorlands near Biddulph in a great arc through Stoke, along the north side of Cannock Chase, and then turns north-east to leave by way of Burton, near which the Dove flows in from the north-west. Once out of Staffordshire the Trent leaves the smoke and dirt of an industrial region to become one of England's loveliest rivers.

The Trent flows through a valley composed chiefly of sandstone and marls, the latter containing veins of gypsum and bands of limestone. It is the gypsum in the water that has given Burton beers the quality that has made them famous. Because of its close association with the brewing trade, water is always referred to as "liquor" by the people of Burton.

Brewing appears to have started at Burton Abbey soon after it was founded by Wulfric Spott, Earl of Mercia, in 1002. The office of cellarer was an ancient and important one in connexion with monastic institutions. It is recorded that in 1295 the Abbey granted Matilda de Shovenhale, a resident of Burton, two gallons of beer daily for herself and seven for her man.

The modern industry, which did not, however, begin to take its present shape until the first decade of the eighteenth century, produces a number of the most famous of English brews. Today the town is sometimes called the "Mecca of ruin," a title which does not appear to weigh too heavily on the consciences of its citizens, who seem to display as genial an air as is to be found anywhere. Everywhere in Burton there is a suffocatingly heavy smell of malt from the town's twenty breweries.

### Brewing and Pottery

Burton's hops come from Herefordshire and its barley from Norfolk. In the making of beer "liquor" at a high temperature is added to the malt through a process known as sparging, the resulting mixture joining the hops in a battery of coppers to form wort, the name given to unfermented beer. Of the two methods employed in fermentation the more celebrated is the Burton Union System developed locally from the original system used by the monks. After fermentation has begun the wort is drained into a number of casks each having a copper swan neck in the bung-hole. As

Gardens at Alton Towers near Cheadle, a popular resort for people of the industrial towns.

A view of Hanley, one of the "Five Towns." This photograph shows about 50 kilns; altogether several thousand go to make up the 300 potteries in the area. Few pictures could better illustrate the growth of unplanned industry with workers' cottages crowded in between the factories.

fermentation proceeds the yeast works its way through the swan neck into a trough. This method is rarely used outside Burton. In the other method, known as the skimming system, the whole of the fermentation is carried out in one vessel. The yeast rises to the top of the beer to form miniature snowlike mountains to be skimmed off down a slide as surplus yeast. This

yeast eventually finds its way into our bread and our cakes.

Even more famous, perhaps, than Burton beer is Staffordshire pottery—a term which covers earthenware, china and porcelain. The Potteries and their products are world-famous.

The industry, comprising some three hundred potteries, is concentrated in the "Five

Towns." Stoke, Hanley, Burslem, Fenton, Longton and Tunstall form a string of densely populated centres sprawling into one another on both sides of the River Trent. In literature they have been made famous in the novels of Arnold Bennett, himself a native of Hanley. Stoke is the nucleus of these towns which, since their incorporation into one municipality, have been known collectively as Stoke-on-Trent. It was made a city in 1925.

Like most other industries, the pottery industry owed its origin and development in Staffordshire to the proximity of its raw materials—principally an abundance of red clay which is suitable for the coarser kinds of pottery. Fine china clay for delicate work has to be imported from Cornwall. Coal, too, is found locally in abundance, which, used for firing the products, confirmed the location of the industry during its eighteenth-century expansion.

**This view of the hamlet of Stanshope, between the Manifold Valley and Dovedale, is in strong contrast to that on the opposite page. The sparsely populated farmlands, and the beauties of Dovedale, are a world apart from the concentrated industry of the Black Country.**

Today the "Five Towns" are dominated by the bottle-shaped necks of the thousands of kilns and ovens which go to make up the three hundred potteries. Crowded in between the kilns are row upon row of small houses in which the pottery workers live. It is a smoke-laden, grimy area, though nowhere far from the open country.

Present conditions are the result of the development of the past two centuries, but pottery is in no sense a new Staffordshire industry. From the earliest times of pot-making Burslem, which stood near the old city of Chesterton, was known to the Romans. In 1680 Palmer, a potter, discovered the art of salt-glazing from the accidental boiling over of a pot of salt-liquor. Eight years later two Dutchmen named Elers came to England, and between Burslem and Chesterton they sought and found a vein of red clay of a quality which enabled them to make wares as good as the red porcelain of the East. In a later generation, Thomas Whieldon, already known for his marbled wares (made from mixing clays of different colours) and tortoiseshell (with mottled glaze) wares, took Josiah

Wedgwood, himself the son of a Burslem potter, as his junior partner into his factory at Fenton, where together they revolutionized the industry and gave British china a distinction which it had never before achieved. To Wedgwood we owe black basalt and jasper ware, the latter with a variety of colours and often decorated with white cameo reliefs. Wedgwood founded a firm which is still famous in the Potteries.

In Campbell Place, the main street of Stoke and named after Colin Campbell, three times its mayor, is Spode's pottery works, founded by a contemporary and scarcely less famous potter than Wedgwood. It is a tradition among present members of the firm that only the original Mr. Spode knew exactly how much bone should be mixed with the clay to make the china which they claim is superior to all other makes. In former days the china was painted by artists of the Royal Academy, the raw products being carried back and forth between Stoke and London on horseback to be alternately fired and painted. Spode's, noted for the delicacy of their wares, still

**A view of Dovedale, more than 6,000 acres of which have been preserved through the efforts of the National Trust. The river forms the boundary between Staffordshire (on the left) and Derbyshire.**

**Tamworth Castle from across the Tame. Tamworth is an ancient market town of considerable local importance serving an area of Staffordshire and Warwickshire.**

produce exquisite figures and birds and dinner and tea-sets with patterns ranging from their well-known China rose to painted chrysanthemums.

Newcastle-under-Lyme, which is not one of the "Five Towns" though it adjoins Stoke as closely as any of the five, might well be a country town miles from an industrial area, though it has textile and paper factories. Tunstall has a chemical industry in addition to pottery.

The development of industries in Staffordshire has cost the county many of its trees. Charcoal from the forests and local ironstone fed the furnaces, until, at the end of the seventeenth century, coal and coke from the coalfields of Cheadle and Wolverhampton began to be used for the smelting of iron, an innovation which became the basis of iron and steel-making processes throughout the world. In Staffordshire the legacy of the Industrial Revolution to which this contributed, has been the Black Country, a fitting name for the great industrial area between Wolverhampton and Birmingham.

Through many of the Black Country towns have histories going back to the Middle Ages and some to Saxon times, most of their past has now been swallowed up in the growth of the last two centuries, yet the area was famous for its products long before that time. So concentrated is industry and population that, like the pottery towns, the Black Country takes on the appearance of one vast city—a city of smoking furnaces mixed with crowded and dingy houses for the three-quarters of a million people who earn their livelihood by making almost everything in iron and steel. The Black Country is not a pleasant place to live in: it has sacrificed beauty and tradition in achieving a leading position in the country's industrial life.

It was at Smethwick that James Watt set up his first steam engine which worked for one hundred and fifteen years. Locks and keys are made at Wolverhampton, Wednesfield and Willenhall, saddlery and nails at Walsall, anchors at Tipton, chains at Cradley, boilers and steelwork for railways at Wednesbury, and hardware of all kinds throughout the district. World famous is the firm at Smethwick which employs thousands in the manufacture of window frames. One of its notable orders was for the

367

The village of Codsall, four miles north-west of Wolverhampton, is well known for the cultivation of flowers and fruit. Above is seen a field of Russell lupins in full bloom.

window frames for the liners *Queen Mary* and *Queen Elizabeth*.

Though industry dominates Staffordshire, the industrial areas are small and are surrounded by country as pleasant as any in the Midlands. Lichfield is a surprise. Despite its location on the north-east border of the Black Country, it remains a quiet cathedral town to which industry has come only in the present century. Its chief claim to fame is as the birthplace of Dr. Johnson, who spent his early life there and often revisited it, though he became a Londoner by adoption and taste. Nevertheless, he claimed that the purest English was spoken in Lichfield, a claim which did not convince Boswell. Now Johnson's statue sits in the market-place, with its back towards that of Boswell, facing the house where Johnson was born, and the "Three Crowns" where they both stayed together. Johnson left Lichfield with David Garrick, who was to achieve fame on the stage; together they sought fortune in London.

The little town of Uttoxeter, on the Derbyshire border, has its Johnson story. In the market-place is a picture of the great man exposing his head to the rain, which, he said, was in penance for the sin of pride when as a youth he refused to help his father at a stall. This old country market town (pronounced "Uxeter") was once part of the duchy of Lancaster.

Lichfield grew up round its cathedral, a triple-spired Gothic building, one of the most beautiful in the country, founded by St. Chad in the seventh century. In 1553 Lichfield was made the chief town of the county with its own sheriff who, as required by the ancient charter, tours the city bounds on horseback on important occasions.

The shrine of St. Chad was a favourite place of pilgrimage in the Middle Ages. Bishop Roger de Clinton founded St. John's Hospital for the benefit of the pilgrims. He also fortified the cathedral close, but not enough to prevent the Parliamentarians from damaging the cathedral during the civil war. In the cathedral close the town crier still cries the hours of the night.

Tamworth, south-west of Lichfield, is another old market town, for which the famous Sir Robert Peel was member of Parliament for a large part of his political career. Tamworth Castle dates back to Saxon times and now houses a museum; its grounds are national property.

### Superstitions of the Black Country

Because of her small rivers, immense forests and remoteness from the sea, Staffordshire was a backward county until the development of her coalfields. Superstitions and customs from those pre-industrial days still survive in many parts. Among the Black Country colliers superstition used to prevent (and, perhaps, has done so recently) their working in the pits on New Year's Eve or Day, nor on those days would their wives carry fire from one room to another nor give anyone a light, prohibitions deriving, it is thought, from the fire-worshipping practices of the ancient Druids.

In some parts of the county the Clogg Almanac, a means of reckoning the days of the year introduced by the Danes, is still in use. It consists of an oak box with three months marked in notches on each of its four sides. Saints' days have a symbol for the saint, attached to the notch. To celebrate the feasts of the saints the fairs came into existence. They were called wakes (and most Staffordshire people still use the name) because there were watch services or vigils of the feast or dedication which lasted a whole week.

In near-by Uttoxeter lives a family of Blores, originally gypsies, recently ruled over by a matriarch of ninety. Every year they perform a mummers show for the benefit of the surrounding farms.

### Legends of Robin Hood

At Abbots Bromley, said to be founded by gypsies, in September the Horn Dance is performed by twelve people representing Robin Hood, Maid Marian, a jester, a boy with a bow and arrow, two musicians and six men wearing reindeer horns. The dance commemorates certain rights acquired in Needwood Forest, once the hunting ground of John of Gaunt. Robin Hood, according to one of the many legends about him, was born at Loxeley, and it is said that a roving life led him to Tutbury, where he married a shepherdess because he was charmed by her skill in shooting a buck. Years later at Tutbury, Mary Queen of Scots was imprisoned in John of Gaunt's castle, which Cromwell in the next century left a ruined shell.

Architecturally, Staffordshire has many buildings of interest. Inside the church of St. Chad in Stafford, the county town, there has been little change since Norman days. The chancel arch is notable for its five orders of moulding, and the aisles for the forty-eight weirdly carved heads. The Priory Church at Tutbury is also an interesting example of Norman work. Over the doorway there is a picture of a boar hunt. In Stafford's busy Greengate Street is the famous High House, with sturdy gables and timbered sides, four stories high. In old Lichfield Street, Wolverhampton, are half-timbered houses, and one at the corner of John Street has very rare nogging with which the interstices of the timbers are filled. The collegiate church of St. Peter in Wolverhampton was founded in 996 by Wulfruma, a Saxon princess from whom the town derives its name.

East of Stafford is the country of big houses and estates. Pillaton Hall, near Penkridge, the family seat of the Littletons, is a battlemented and moated house in red brick and stone. Its staircase, each tread of which is a solid block of oak, is one of the very few of its kind in England.

Moseley Old Hall at Bushberry is a fine specimen of a timbered house. It was here that Charles II, drying his stockings in a room over the porch, saw Cromwell's troops approaching and had to hide in a secret chamber in the wall, which remains to this day. Near Sandon is the five-hundred-acre park home of the Earls of Harrowby. Wolseley Hall at Colwich was granted to the family by King Edgar in return for their services in destroying the wolves which in Saxon days infested the countryside.

Outside Leek Church, in the north of the county, is an ancient Gothic cross. Associated with it is the tradition that the shaft sinks imperceptibly lower into the ground every year. As local doggerel puts it:—

When the churchyard cross shall disappear,
Leek town will not last another year.

At Stone, between Stoke and Stafford, Wulf, King of Mercia, after incessant wars, reverted to paganism and murdered his two sons because they clung to Christianity. Overcome by remorse, Wulf pleaded for forgiveness before St. Chad, who instructe him to stamp out idolatry in his kingdom Queen Ermilda founded a priory on th site of the murders, in memory of her son All that is left of the old building is th cellar of the Priory House and part of th ancient walls.

Staffordshire is a county of contrast—th sparsely populated farmlands with the villages and market towns, and the beautie of Dovedale are a world apart from th concentrated industry of the Black Countr On one side are the Staffordshire men of th farms, on the other, the great majority wh labour in the factories which have mad Staffordshire's products famous in th country and all over the world. There ma be in the soaring spires of Lichfield symbol of hope that by their perfec symmetry they may in some measure aton for the grey ugliness of the Black Countr with its untidy slag heaps, pit-head windin gear, smoking chimneys, grimy factorie and innumerable squalid slums; for th miles of suburban dreariness; for the dra lives of the people in country which ha given away its natural beauty to mak England rich.

*The Village Cross at Ilam*

ous. Even the Normans found them turbulent neighbours, and grim keeps, the ruins of which can be found here and there amongst the hills, remain as mute witnesses to the way in which William of Normandy dealt with the problem which the Romans had shirked.

Derbyshire is old in a way in which softer counties are not. Warwickshire and Gloucester have their stately Elizabethan mansions, and so, indeed, has Derbyshire, but the real affinity of the countryside seems to be with a remoter, ruder age. Civilizations have come and passed, but they have not changed or tamed the wild moorlands, and the stone circles and ancient cromlechs which are to be found in the county are somehow more in tune with it, and with the descendants, still living in Derbyshire, of the men who built them. Only in Wiltshire and sometimes on Dartmoor in Devon does one still feel today this closeness to a prehistoric past.

Derbyshire people are tough; they were tough a thousand years ago, before the Normans came, and the witness to this toughness remains today in an ancient court, still legal and still in active jurisdiction: the Barmoot Court. This is a court concerned entirely with lead-mining interests, and goes right back to early Saxon times; what is more, it is the oldest survival of trial by jury in the Anglo-Saxon world. Long before Magna Carta was sealed at Runnymede, the Barmoot Court of the Hundred of the High Peak, or the Grand Barmoot Court of the Wapentake of Wirksworth, were meeting and discharging their legal functions, as they have met ever since and are meeting today. No lead may be mined

This typical Derbyshire village is Ashford on the Wye, two miles from Bakewell. Marble is quarried locally. Here the countryside is less rugged than in the Peak District, a few miles to the north.

373

without their permission, and from their jurisdiction there is no appeal save by way of certiorari. Through the changing conditions of the turbulent history of these islands, the men of Derbyshire have clung to this immemorial right, the right of determining their own disputes, and of trial before a jury of their peers. Here is sufficient evidence of character, of a toughness of fibre, of a resistance to outside dictatorship; these are the qualities of the men and women of Derbyshire of today.

### Uplands and Lowlands

If the people of Derbyshire are hard, so in the northern end, at least, is the county. Here is no easy living, no generous return from an over-fertile soil. For the most part the limestone or gritstone hills are barely covered with a thin few inches of earth, from which the northern farmer wrings his reluctant crops. For the most part this end of the county is given up to pasture, little fields which on the hill-sides encroach upon the heather of the higher moors. And everywhere the little fields and crofts are surrounded by the characteristic dry stone walls of the county, evidence of hundreds of thousands of man hours of patient work in the past. As the road drops from the northern to the southern end of the county, the stone walls give place to hedges, the soil deepens, more of the land is under the plough, and orchards and flower gardens begin to take on the appearance of the southern counties.

It is a mistake to imagine that the whole of the northern end of the county of Derbyshire is given over to bleak uplands and heather and gorse-covered moors. It is true that this area is called the High Peak, and it rises to Kinder Scout, two thousand and eighty-eight feet above sea level, but the flat tableland of heather and peat moss is intersected by innumerable cloughs, where the little moorland streams run down to join the Wye or the Derwent. Many of these are very beautiful, reminiscent of Highland

**Looking across the Wye at Bakewell. The fine octagonal spire, seen in the background, belongs to the old cruciform church of All Saints, mentioned in Domesday Book.**

The market town of Ashbourne. Notable is its traditional Shrove Tuesday football match played between the "uppers" and "downers," so named after the location of their homes.

glens, and as remote and as unspoiled as anything to be found in England. On the southern side of Kinder they open out into the lovely valleys of Edale and Hope, and many of the little streams have now been caught in the series of reservoirs, the last of which has recently submerged the villages of Derwent and Ashopton. These reservoirs form beautiful sheets of water in the midst of high bare hills, the shapes of which will soon be changed when the tens of thousands of trees, planted on their sides by the local water board, grow to maturity. The country lying north, east, and west of the Derwent reservoirs is still untamed, much of it preserved for shooting, and the haunt at weekends of many hundreds of ramblers who follow the wild tracks over Bleaklow or Kinder itself. Since 1951 the Peak District has been made into a National Park and from here will begin the projected Pennine Way which will open to the hardy walker a route over dale and hill, untouched by the motorist for a hundred and fifty miles, from Edale to the Scottish border.

But impressive and remote as are Kinder Scout and Bleaklow, it is still more im-pressive to stand upon some such hill-top as Win Hill, rising above the Hope Valley, or on Mam Tor, the site of an age-old British camp, looking down on the Norman keep of Peveril, and to look round at the hills, fold after fold, running away to the remote horizon. This is the real country of the Peak, foothills of the Pennines, last stronghold of the Celtic Brigantes, many of whose descendants, with their short stature and characteristically shaped heads, still farm the moorland acres.

### Roman Remains

Though the Romans passed this region by on their two great main roads to the north, they ventured into the hills in their search for lead. On the moor behind Tideswell pigs of lead have been found, stamped with Roman inscriptions, dropped by some careless hand, to be found nearly two thousand years later. The Romans built their little fort at Anavio, where the River Noe winds round a precipitous knoll not far from Hope, in order to protect their lead-mining industry. But this fort, a rectangular stone building the foundations of which

375

Derby, a modern industrial centre on the edge of a coalfield, is by far the largest town in the county. It possessed the first silk mill in England, but is now concerned chiefly with engineering.

still remain buried under the turf, was designed also for another purpose. These rare Roman roads, leading across the hills from east to west, were strategic as well as commercial; they linked the road running north to Eboracum, our York of today, with that other road which ran northward over the causeway between the marshes, through Stockport and Manchester. It was important to Roman strategy that an army marching up one of them should be able to give support to an army on the other, and so these roads were laboriously built across the hills, the rungs in a strategic ladder.

By the year 400 or soon afterwards the Romans had gone from Derbyshire, and indeed from Britain, but they left behind them in the High Peak the shafts which they had sunk in their search for lead; for hundreds of years lead mining remained the chief and almost the only industry of this area. On the hillsides of north Derbyshire white glistening heaps of spar mark the course of the veins of ore, and until about a hundred years ago these remote little villages were alive with a mining population. Then Spanish lead, cheapened by the high percentage of silver which it contained—

the small amount of silver in Derbyshire lead did not pay for its extraction—killed the Derbyshire lead-mining industry; now everywhere the shafts are deserted and the workings flooded, dangerous alike to man and beast. More than one unwary hiker has come by injury or death through falling down the open shafts of the old lead mines.

This northern end of the county is rich in little towns and villages of historic interest. Buxton, the spa of Blue Waters of today, is the Aquae of the Roman occupation, and Glossop, at the northern end of the Snake road over Kinder, was the Roman fort of Melandra; also there is Eyam, the heroic plague village, where three hundred years ago nearly four hundred villagers, led by their devout vicar, Mompesson, voluntarily cut themselves off from their neighbours, so that the infection should not spread. Whole families were wiped out by the terrible plague, the germs of which had come from London in a bale of clothes, and the living buried the dead in hastily dug graves in the fields. As the danger of infection made it inadvisable to assemble in the little village church, the dwindling congregation met

376

Sunday by Sunday in a little valley running southwards from the village; here from a rocky arch, the vicar upheld and strengthened his people, and today, on the last Sunday in August of every year, the villagers go again to Cucklet Church, the name by which the valley with its pulpit rock is now known, to keep alive the memory of the heroism of their forefathers. Before the plague subsided, five out of every six had died; only thirty-five living souls heard the bells which rang out as hope changed to certainty; none had broken the vow of voluntary isolation. Their reward was an incontaminated countryside; as a result of their selfless behaviour, no other village in the High Peak caught the infection.

In the High Peak is Peveril Castle, Scott's *Peveril of the Peak*, and surely one of the most romantic and forbidding of the Norman strongholds in the country. Under the very shadow of Kinder Scout, and built on the edge of the sheer gorge above Peak Cavern, Peveril is calculated to inspire sensations of awe in the most frivolous; in the days of feudal England it must have been a fortress of great strength. Even the ruined tower, which alone remains, has an air of menace, which the fact that one may inspect it for a small charge does nothing to dispel.

Peveril Castle owes much to its situation above the grim entrance to Peak Cavern, itself one of the wonders of Derbyshire. But this is no ordinary cave. Beneath the overhanging cliff on which Peveril Castle stands is a great cavern, like some mighty barbaric chamber, in which for generations the men of Castleton have lived and worked. For here, in this natural factory in the living rock, was one of the strangest workshops in the country, a workshop in which for hundreds of years, and up to the beginning of the present century, a primitive rope-walk turned out hundreds of fathoms of hand-made rope. Here was woven the rope to rig the ships which broke the Armada, and who shall say for how many centuries before that English seamen handled Castleton-made rope?

All limestone country has such caverns, but there is nowhere in the country where so many underground caverns and old workings, natural and artificial, can be explored as at Castleton. From here comes

This desolate country, which lies on the Derbyshire–Yorkshire border, is part of the moorland stretch that extends past Chatsworth House as far south as Matlock.

the famous Blue John, a very beautiful purple variety of fluor spar, much used for ornaments and personal decoration. Castleton is not the whole of the Peak, but it is a fitting introduction to some realization of what the Peak of Derbyshire once was.

With its wild moors, its tumbling trout streams, once fished by Izaak Walton, and its rich historical associations, the High Peak of Derbyshire is a little oasis in the heart of industrial England. The great manufacturing cities of the north, Manchester, Sheffield, Derby, Halifax, Leeds, Stoke-on-Trent, Nottingham, and their lesser satellites ring it round, but it remains inviolate, defying modern industrialization, and since 1951 has been protected as a National Park.

To go south from the Peak is to drop into a different countryside, peopled by a different race, given to different pursuits, inspired by different ways of thought. South and to the east of Matlock the county is more richly agricultural, where it is not given over to coal mining and iron smelting. The hills are lower and softer in out-

line, there is no heather, and south of Matlock itself nothing of the outcrop rock so characteristic of the northern end of the county. Derby itself is like so many other great industrial cities, with huge railway and motor works, a cathedral and a bishop, but no adequate theatre or obvious appreciation of the Arts. It does not, however, sprawl in the way that Manchester sprawls. It is surrounded by a pleasant countryside into which its 140,000 inhabitants can and do escape at the week-ends. To the west is pleasant undulating country leading to Ashbourne and the beautiful valleys of the Dove and the Manifold. These are probably amongst the loveliest valleys in the whole country and, like the Peak itself, are surely destined to be a National Park; a great deal of the land has been acquired by the National Trust, and year by year more of this beautiful and unspoiled countryside is being conveyed to the Trust by men and women of wealth and vision. Actually, of course, these valleys are on the very edge of Derbyshire. The Dove forms

**On the upper waters of Dovedale "among the loveliest valleys in the whole country." Izaak Walton fished in these waters. Dovedale is largely National Trust property.**

In the village of Stony Middleton, near Bakewell.   It is known for its warm spring baths.

the county boundary and the Manifold valley is actually in Staffordshire. But they belong to the same natural geographical unit, and it means very little to the tourist in search of natural beauty whether he has one foot over a County Council's arbitrary boundary or not.

Slightly to the east and running north from Derby is the belt of the coal-seam through such places as Clay Cross and Chesterfield, to Sheffield and beyond. This is technically a black area, but even here, in between the pit-heads, the country can still be beautiful. The huddled mining villages are without charm, but it is possible between them to stand with your feet deep in heather and look down on to the shaft-heads in the valley. A countryside of contrasts which even man has not been able entirely to spoil.

The real Derbyshire is older, far older than man's attempt to spoil it. Its rich maturity is represented by such lovely links with the past as Haddon Hall, the perfect example of a great Elizabethan residence; but its real past lies beyond recorded history. For us it is evident in the survivals of pagan customs which still live amongst the villages, far from the railways and the great north-south traffic routes. Here every year, during the summer months, the wells are still dressed with flowers and ceremonially blessed by the local priest, hardly aware that he is performing an age-old ceremony in direct and often unbroken succession from some remote Druid who blessed these same wells thousands of years ago. The memory of old dances still lingers in spite of this machine and machine-made age, country dances of an intricate pattern found nowhere else, and soon perhaps not even to be found here. Castleton, oldest of villages, has its Garland Day, but not one of the inhabitants could tell you anything of its remote pagan origin; Wormhill has its legend of a remote gigantic serpent, handed down from the days of myths and heroes. On the moors, half-hidden by the heather, are stone circles of unknown date and unimaginable rites, on the hill-tops are the burial mounds of Celts and Saxons and of the little questing men of the megalithic invasion, unnumbered centuries ago. They wandered over these hills, moving always westward towards the setting sun, man's immemorial instinctive migratory direction, but they left their traces: a flint instrument, a scratched bone, a half-baked shard for us to find. Here is a county with a past, a present, and a future, with an industrial area and with an unspoiled and, with its rugged physical features, unspoilable countryside on its doorstep; with a wealth of wild flowers almost under the reek of its factory chimneys, but most of all with the high places of the Peak, the heather and the gorse, the high clouds, and the lonely calling of the lapwing and the curlew. In its variety and its beauty this is one of the loveliest counties in England.

*Haddon Hall*

*Alderley Edge*

# CHESHIRE

### By I. O. EVANS

CHESHIRE IS in several respects a border-line
county, belonging to one group of conditions, but touched by the character of another. Thoroughly English, it interlocks
along its western boundary with Wales.
Largely agricultural, it overlaps one of
Britain's foremost industrial areas. In great
part a compact inland region, with a gently
undulating and well-cultivated surface, it
thrusts out two extensions to east and west:
the one climbs the bleak slope of the "backbone of England," the other is a peninsula,
whose coast though short is extremely important.

The very name of its county town,
Chester, recalls its history, being derived
from the Latin word *castra*, "a military
camp." Cheshire has indeed been a
battle-ground contested by many
armies, by the Ancient Britons, the
Romans, the English of Northumbria and of Wessex, the Danes, the
forces of Alfred and of Canute. Its
subjugation by William the
Conqueror did not bring it peace,
nor it was still exposed to raids

*Arms of Cheshire*

by the Welsh. It figured in the Wars of
the Roses and in the Civil War, and was
crossed by the Highland invaders who carried Bonnie Prince Charlie's flag southward
in the Jacobite Rebellion of 1745.

These conflicts introduced many racial
strains into the county's population and
varieties into its speech. In its west some
Welsh is spoken, and, near Chester, Welsh
words may commonly be heard in everyday
English. In its north is heard more than a
touch of the characteristic Lancashire dialect, and in its south, of the gentler Staffordshire accent. On the whole the language
of Cheshire has more in common with that
of the north of England than with that of
the south.

Here, as elsewhere, accent gives a clue to
character. Generally, the people of Cheshire
have that hard-headed practical-minded-
ness which one associates with the northern English. This characteristic is most
strongly developed in the county's
industrial fringe along the Lancashire boundary; it is less marked in
the south and east; and in the west
it is modified by a touch of Celtic
poetry and mysticism.

The countryside which fosters
this varied population is no less
varied, being itself the product

of widely varying rocks. These range from beds older than the coal-measures, yielding the petrified remains of creatures long vanished from the earth, to the sands deposited on the beach by the waves now breaking on the shore. The dominating tint underlying the green of meadow and forest is that of a reddish soil, lighter than that formed by the Old Red Sandstone of South Wales, but contrasting strongly with the more familiar brown that is usually found in England.

### Land of Foaming Streams

The county's eastern extension, jutting out like a horn between Derby and Lancashire, consists of moorland hills fringed with rock edges. Its foaming streams, dammed in the valleys below, give several towns their water supply. Thence westward to the sea a series of irregular hills and plateaux are separated by pleasant valleys. Here the cultivated lands are varied by "forests," woods alternating with open commons, by level tracts along the rivers and by patches of marsh.

This countryside is, however, the work of Nature, not left to itself, but deliberately moulded by man. Delamere Forest, a tract of glorious woodland which might easily appear altogether "natural," is, indeed, the result of human handiwork: part of the Crown Lands, it was deliberately planted to provide the raw material for shipbuilding in the days of the old "wooden walls." Many of the finest vistas were designed by landscape gardeners as manor-house parks. Of the many stretches of water, the most attractive were formed by artificially damming the streams to produce ornamental lakes; the less picturesque are an unforeseen by-product of the salt industry.

The fertile reddish earth produces rich grass, variegated by an abundance of flowers. The moorlands on the eastern hills are purple with heather; here, too, grow cranberries and bilberries. Furze gilds the heathlands farther west, and the hedgerows are white with may and pink with roses. The woods are pungent with the scent of wild garlic. The county's native plants are, moreover, diversified with those of foreign origin, sprung from seeds which have

been accidentally brought in cargoes of ballast from overseas.

The feathered life of Cheshire ranges from the game-birds of the moorlands to the sea birds of the coasts and river-mouths. There are few birds of prey to reduce their numbers, these having been destroyed by the sportsmen to whom they form rivals. Nightingales are seldom found so far north, and the tunes of the other songsters may be interrupted by the harsh cry of the corn crake or the dull boom of the bittern.

The county's animal life is also varied, from the commonplace rabbit to the rarer mountain hare and the red deer. Strayed seals, and even whales, have occasionally been stranded on its shores. The famous white cattle, once wild, have now been domesticated for the sake of their milk. Unsophisticated visitors have, however, been surprised by the absence of that no less famous animal, the Cheshire Cat!

The different parts of Cheshire vary somewhat in climate. It is much warmer in the west than in the east, and more rain around its boundaries than towards its centre. As in Lancashire to its north, the heights of the Pennine Chain trap the rain-laden west winds and make them deposit their moisture. This produces a damp atmosphere very favourable to cotton-spinning.

### The Industrial North

The industrial region in the north of the county forms part of the great Lancashire cotton area, and shares its general character. Here are thriving manufacturing towns with their great mills, their towering factory chimneys vomiting clouds of smoke, the hustle and their clangorous din. Here the owners pride themselves on being hardheaded business men, and are disdainful of what they regard as the "soft" Southerner. This attitude spreads among the armies of workers and helps to build the mill tradition. Hard toil, in which complicated machines are tended by deft fingers, is mitigated by a caustic humour and by an unsentimental kind-heartedness.

An intricate network of railway lines links the manufacturing towns with one another and with the outside world. It is only natural that not far from the main factory

*Mauretania*, one of the largest ships yet built in England, on the stocks at Cammell Laird's yard at Birkenhead. Shipbuilding is the town's greatest industry.

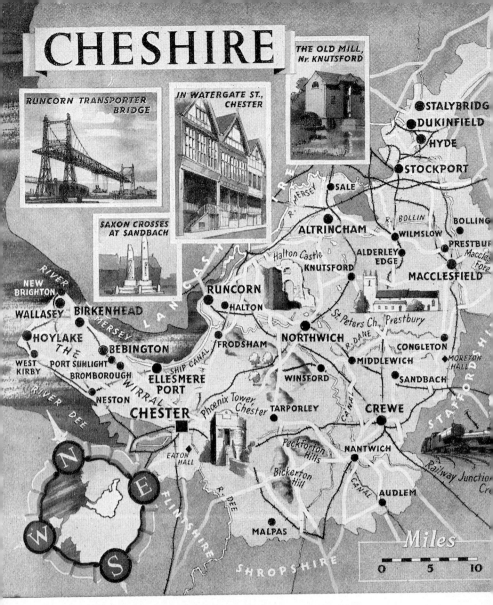

# CHESHIRE

THE OLD MILL, Nr. KNUTSFORD

RUNCORN TRANSPORTER BRIDGE

IN WATERGATE ST., CHESTER

SAXON CROSSES AT SANDBACH

STALYBRIDG
DUKINFIELD
HYDE
STOCKPORT
SALE
R. MERSEY
ALTRINCHAM
R. BOLLIN
WILMSLOW
BOLLIN
ALDERLEY EDGE
PRESTBUF
Maccle
Fore
KNUTSFORD
Halton Castle
MACCLESFIELD
NEW BRIGHTON
RIVER
RUNCORN
HALTON
St. Peters Ch., Prestbury
WALLASEY
R. DANE
HOYLAKE
FRODSHAM
NORTHWICH
CONGLETON
BEBINGTON
MIDDLEWICH
MORETON HALL
WEST KIRBY
PORT SUNLIGHT
SHIP CANAL
BROMBOROUGH
ELLESMERE PORT
WINSFORD
SANDBACH
NESTON
WIRRAL
Phoenix Tower Chester
TARPORLEY
CREWE
CHESTER
Peckforton Hills
NANTWICH
EATON HALL
Bickerton Hill
Railway Junction
Cr
R. DEE
AUDLEM
N
W
E
S
MALPAS
SHROPSHIRE
Miles
0    5    10
LANCASHIRE
MERSEY
RIVER DEE
FLINTSHIRE
STAFFORDSHIRE

zone Cheshire should include one of England's greatest railway centres. Crewe is both an important junction and an immense railroad workshop. It employs thousands of hands and demands the utmost technical skill in an industry which, though little over a century old, has already developed its own splendid tradition of efficient devotion to the public service.

The towns are, moreover, linked by a network of water-ways. It was indeed in Cheshire that the construction of canals first developed as a specialized branch engineering. Here is what is almost a uniqu feat of engineering, the Anderton hydraul barge-lift. Here, too, is one of the most remarkable means of communication, devise expressly to serve the cotton industry, th Manchester Ship Canal.

In spite of its name, and its purpose linking Manchester to the sea, the Sh Canal runs for the greater part of its lengt through Cheshire. It employs its own arm of highly specialist workers whose task strangely combine the most up-to-date techniques with the ancient traditions of the sea and the inland water-ways. The careful engineer, working to his schedules, co-operates with the mariner as the huge lock-gates open to admit the far-travelled ship. The countryside along the canal is enlivened by the sight of the passing vessels, stirring the hearts of the landsmen and especially of their children with thoughts of distant lands and of adventures on the sea.

The Canal emerges into the estuary of the Mersey, a stretch of water almost completely land-locked, the banks of which are lined with shipbuilding yards and other engineering establishments. Here, again, the industries of Cheshire are united with those of Lancashire, physically by a fleet of steam ferries and by a tunnel linking Birkenhead and Liverpool, and commercially by the Mersey Docks and Harbour Board

Work in a shipbuilding town, such as Birkenhead, has two aspects. The industry is a branch of engineering and, indeed, of applied science. Its wonderful machine-tools, the products of exact knowledge, and handled with consummate dexterity, wrest its raw materials to its own purposes. Here Man is in control.

But shipbuilding was in existence long before modern engineering; its tradition is age-old. Though using technical devices based on centuries of experience, it deals with incalculable forces, the weather and the sea. It cannot wrest these to do their own purposes; on the other hand, it serves them. Man may still be in control, but it is a control resembling not that of the blacksmith over the heated iron, but that of a skilled rider over a nervous, spirited, temperamental horse.

In shipbuilding the engineer's matter-of-fact outlook is thus tinged with the unfailing romance of the sea. The metal in the stamping-mills is to become part of a ship, to voyage into the unknown, to face unforeseeable perils, to trade with distant lands. A sense of achievement and of mystery reaches

There are few ancient buildings in Cheshire's industrial centres, but in the old towns such as Chester, Sandbach and Nantwich they still remain. These half-timbered cottages are near Plumley, a village off the beaten track between Northwich and Knutsford.

its climax as, in accordance with immemorial custom, the bottle smashes against the bows and, amidst a tumult of cheers and the scream of the sirens, the newly launched hull glides down the slip-way into the sea.

Cheshire has its own industries besides those which it shares with Lancashire. Macclesfield, farther south, is noted for its silk. Wool has ceased to be an important local industry, but the hat and the leather trades flourish; indeed, near Nantwich, the footpaths are paved with leather scrap. Soap is made at Port Sunlight and Winsford, jam at Stockport and margarine at Godley; at several places brewing is carried on. Port Sunlight is celebrated as a model village and industrial centre; it represents a social experiment of no mean importance.

Cheshire has, moreover, its own characteristic occupation: its salt was valued by the Romans and perhaps even by the Ancient Britons. Buried beneath its soil are masses of rock-salt, which are either mined much as coal is mined (though more easily), or are dissolved out by pumping water through their midst and later evaporating the brine. Thus are obtained not only vast quantities of table-salt but also a variety of other substances, the raw material of a flourishing chemical industry.

The salt-workings have had remarkable effects on the landscape, the ground subsiding as the materials on which it rested were dissolved from beneath it. In the towns the houses are supported by wooden rafts or by layers of brickwork, and are braced by rods holding large metallic plates against the outer walls. In the country the subsidences have filled with water and become vast ponds called flashes, which persist in spite of the masses of waste material dumped into them. The water of some of these artificial ponds is strangely discoloured and steams continuously because of the effluent allowed to flow into it from the chemical works near-by.

The Mersey is a water-way as well as a shipbuilding centre, and is a traffic route from the ports upon its banks to the outer world. It has made Birkenhead with its immense docks the most important town in Cheshire. Its approaches are, however,

**Peckforton castle, near Tarporley, stands on the finely wooded sandstone ridge of the Peckforton hills. The ruins of the more famous Beeston castle lies about three quarters of a mile farther north.**

Canals, from great waterways to small channels like this one at Chester, are important in Cheshire's commercial life. This "Bridge of Sighs" joins the church of Little St. John with the old city gaol.

navigable with difficulty because of narrow channels and shifting sandbanks, so that its shores have to be lined with lighthouses and brightly coloured buoys.

Here, as elsewhere, the sea is not only a means of transport but a source of food. Along the coasts of the Wirral—the north-western peninsula of Cheshire, between the Dee estuary and the Mersey—fishing is carried on. Deep-sea trawlers set out from Hoylake to seek for plaice and sole along the coasts of Lancashire and North Wales, or even as far as the Isle of Man. Smaller craft ply with trawl or rod-and-line in the shallower waters nearer inshore. Some of these waters are forbidden to them, how-ever; they are marine nurseries where fish are protected from destruction and allowed to grow to maturity undisturbed.

Trawl-nets sweep the sea-floor. Tram-mels, three-fold nets placed in the Dee, trap the fish brought down by its flow. Smaller

nets wielded by human arms capture the shrimp and prawn. Rakes similarly wielded scratch for cockles in the inter-tidal sands. But fishing off the Wirral has its perils other than those of wind and tide, for included in the catch may be a small but noxious fish, the lesser weaver with its poisonous spines.

The fisher-folk of the Wirral are, like those of other parts of Britain, a sturdy race, habituated to toil and danger, weather-beaten and with the look in the eyes of those accustomed to gaze at distant hori-zons. They are used to dealing with that in-constant element, the sea, in all its changing moods. They are equally ready to take the summer visitor for a pleasure sail or to man the lifeboat when the winter gale threatens to hurl some hapless ship upon the shore.

Though in recent years the Wirral has been much built over, it is the beginning of a stretch of fertile agricultural land which extends as far as the moors on the Pennine slopes. Over half of this land is, however, devoted not to corn-growing but to permanent pasture, chiefly used for cattle-rearing. Its purpose is the production of milk, most to be consumed in the local industrial towns or even in London, but some to be made into butter or cheese. Cheshire cheese has long had a well-deserved renown.

Even the land on which corn and other foodstuffs are grown is largely subservient to cattle-rearing. Wide areas are under grass, intended to be used as hay. The predominant corn is not wheat but oats, cultivated not so much for its grain as for its straw. The predominant vegetables are mangolds and other cattle-foods. Such human foodstuffs as potatoes are also grown, however, and Cheshire is noted for its damsons and other cultivated fruits.

### Trials of the Farmer

While having much in common with corn-growing, dairy-farming has its own special features. The farmers and herdsmen are brought into contact with wild nature and have to carry on their work in spite of all the vagaries of the climate. The rhythm of their life is, however, different; the dominant period of their years is not the harvest but the calving season. The farmer at harvest-time has to work from dawn to sundown or even in the moonlight getting in the ripened crops. The task of the dairy-farmer is less incessant, but no less exacting, for his cows may bring forth their young at any hour of the day or night, and in the most inclement weather, and he must be ready to face any complications. The exacting toil of his farm may suddenly call not merely for skill and experience, but for sympathetic gentleness with a suffering animal.

Part of the woodlands, with their undergrowth which affords a dense cover, are preserved for game. These and the parks also include some well-grown forest trees, of which the beeches are especially fine. Willows are grown in the marshes, giving the raw material for one of Cheshire's minor industries, that of basket-making.

In addition to providing food for town and country alike, and a livelihood for the farm-worker, the countryside of Cheshire affords a much-needed outlet to the folk of the industrial towns. Birkenhead has indeed won the name of "Liverpool's Bedroom," for as well as being a manufacturing town in its own right, it serves as a suburb of that greater Lancashire city. Work in the factories is necessarily monotonous and wearying, stimulating in the hands an eagerness for a complete change of surroundings. Some seek excitement in such pleasure resorts as the aptly named New Brighton, a suburb of Wallasey. Others prefer the peace of the open country, the pleasant meadows and woodlands or the wildness of the Pennine Moors.

Some of the highways of Cheshire follow the Roman roads or the more ancient British track-ways; a few are associated with the names of famous highwaymen. To-day they are busier than the Roman engineers could have imagined, and carry wares valuable beyond the wildest dreams of Dick Turpin. They link London with the northern industrial towns and with Scotland and North Wales, and even, by way of Holyhead, with Ireland.

They carry a heavy business traffic of men and merchandise; and also, at week-ends and in the holidays, a heavy pleasure traffic. Then the host of workers pour out in car or on cycle or on foot, to seek in the open air a happiness not to be met with in the towns. This traffic has called into being a number of places of lodging and refreshment, from the luxury hotel to the humble wayside café, the Youth Hostel and camp site. One Youth Hostel, on the edge of Delamere Forest, rejoices, appropriately, in the romantic name of Fox Howl!

### Ancient Chester

Cheshire, moreover, attracts an endless stream of visitors to its cities of ancient renown. Foremost of these is its capital Chester, with its splendid buildings and historic associations. It is unique in having a complete circuit of city walls, affording splendid views of the distant Welsh mountains and across the Dee. It is also unique in its famous "rows," the second storeys of which are set back behind a pavement running over the first-storey shops below. It contains many Roman remains and a

Farm labourers' cottages in the village of Eaton, nine miles north-west of Crewe.

Gawsworth church, near Macclesfield. The church contains monuments to the Fytton family, one of whom has been claimed to be Shakespeare's "Dark Lady of the Sonnets."

cathedral, among the treasures of which is a cutting from the Glastonbury thorn. Its quiet streets and old-world rows are lively with the footsteps and the voices of the sightseers.

Even the industrial towns, some of which are of ancient foundation, have their features of interest. The strangest of these is, perhaps, the brine-baths of Nantwich, once a salt centre. Here the waters are extraordinarily buoyant and are valued for their medicinal qualities. Other industrial towns of note are Stockport and Runcorn. The latter is also a Mersey-side port connected with Lancashire by a transporter bridge. It is here, too, that the Manchester Ship Canal enters the estuary.

Cheshire also possesses its non-industrialized market towns, and a number of pleasant country villages. Audlem owns an interesting open-air market shed; near Bunbury are the magnificent ruins of Beeston Castle; Grappenhall still shows its old village stocks. Knutsford, Tarporley and Congleton also merit a reference as small but characteristic and charming market towns.

The county's varied antiquities attract both serious students of ancient times and more casual sightseers. There are several prehistoric stone circles, of which the best known is the Bridestones on the Stafford-shire border near Buglawton. There are also British camps on the hill-tops. In Sandbach market-place stand several interesting Christian crosses, and at Upton, in the Wirral, was found a stone marked with that strange Scandinavian lettering, the Runes. Mow Cop, National Trust property standing on an outlier of the Peak, is partly in Cheshire and partly in Staffordshire: it is crowned with a tower and some ruined walls.

Cheshire, then, though one of the smaller English counties, includes a great variety of occupations and of conditions of life. These range from the fishers of the Wirral Coast to the gamekeepers of the Pennine Moors and the rangers of Delamere Forest, from the half-naked workers in the foundry and the miners in the salt-workings to the cattle-drover and the farmer. Its industries range from the vast shipbuilding yards along the Mersey and the huge cotton factories in the north to the basket-maker's shop by the side of the marsh. Its attractions range from the rows and walls of Chester to the cheerful sideshows of New Brighton beach and the scenic beauties of its countryside. Despite these varieties of occupation the essential backbone of its populace is still the farm-hand who has spent all his life, and found his happiness, on its fertile reddish soil.

*Moreton Old Hall*

The Feathers Hotel at Ludlow. Built in the early sixteenth century, it is elaborately carved and is one of the finest examples of black-and-white timbered architecture in England.

*Severn Bridge at Bridgnorth*

# SHROPSHIRE

### By PHILIP CLEAVE

IF YOU look at a map of Shropshire you will see a large county, divided into two nearly equal parts by the curving Severn. The northern part is gently rolling country, watered by the Perry and the Tern, flowing to the Severn, while in the south a network of streams whose names are softly musical, Corve, Onny and Clun, thread their way among the hills to join the Teme, itself ultimately a tributary of the Severn. On the map these Shropshire hills are grouped like the fingers of a shattered hand. If we imagine the wrist at Ludlow, then the Clee Hills in the east form the thumb; the fingers are Wenlock Edge, the Stretton Hills, the Long Mynd and the Stiperstones.

Towards the western boundary of the shire the place-names change abruptly from such pure Anglo-Saxon sounds as Newcastle, or Acton, or Whittington to such names as Bettws y Crwyn, Pentre or Llynclys. Yet this is England! The wavering line of language demarcation coincides broadly with Offa's Dyke, that eighth-century

*Arms of Shropshire*

bulwark constructed to protect the kingdom of Mercia from the marauding Welsh. Through the troubled centuries which followed, the Dyke, later reinforced by the castles of the Marcher Lords, fulfilled its task of keeping the invaders at bay. In this history is the clue to one aspect of Shropshire. It is a border county, and its people have much of the character we should expect of a border people: independence, vigour, toughness of fibre and a strong sense of kinship one with another, shown here, for example, in the well-known Shropshire toast, "All friends round the Wrekin."

It is perhaps symbolic of this tough, independent spirit that the first *representative* English Parliament should have met in Shropshire, summoned at Acton Burnell by Edward I in 1283. Throughout English history kings have found it expedient to make concessions to border nobles and their followers. Their sturdy independence, combined with fine fighting qualities, made them, for all their usefulness, more than a little dangerous as subjects. Such men, therefore, were best conciliated.

When the days of strife gave place to more tranquil times, the factors which had characterized Shropshire as a border county,

393

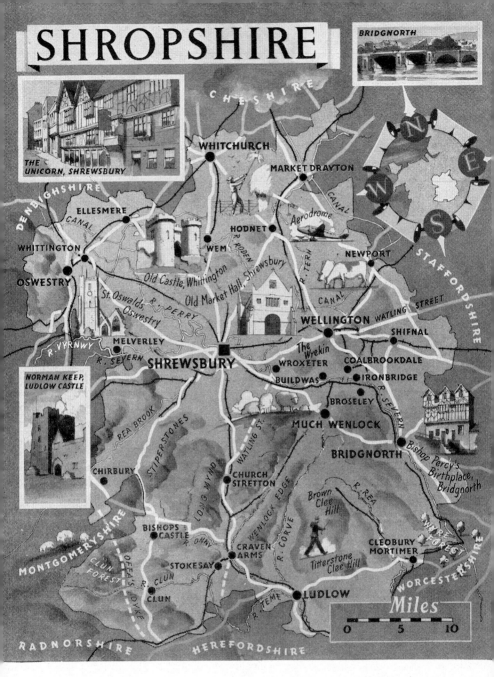

# SHROPSHIRE

BRIDGNORTH

THE UNICORN, SHREWSBURY

CHESHIRE

WHITCHURCH

MARKET DRAYTON

Aerodrome

DENBIGHSHIRE

ELLESMERE CANAL

HODNET

WEM

R. RODEN

NEWPORT

WHITTINGTON

Old Castle, Whittington

STAFFORDSHIRE

OSWESTRY

St. Oswalds Oswestry

R. PERRY

Old Market Hall, Shrewsbury

R. TERN

CANAL

WELLINGTON

WATLING STREET

SHIFNAL

R. VYRNWY

MELVERLEY

R. SEVERN

SHREWSBURY

The Wrekin

WROXETER

COALBROOKDALE

NORMAN KEEP, LUDLOW CASTLE

REA BROOK

BUILDWAS

IRONBRIDGE

R. SEVERN

BROSELEY

Bishop Percy's Birthplace, Bridgnorth

MUCH WENLOCK

STIPERSTONES

WATLING ST.

BRIDGNORTH

CHIRBURY

LONG MYND

CHURCH STRETTON

WENLOCK EDGE

Brown Clee Hill

R. REA

BISHOPS CASTLE

R. ONNY

CRAVEN ARMS

R. CORVE

CLEOBURY MORTIMER

MONTGOMERYSHIRE

CLUN FOREST

OFFA'S DYKE

STOKESAY

R. CLUN

Titterstone Clee Hill

WYRE FOREST

CLUN

R. TEME

LUDLOW

WORCESTERSHIRE

Miles

0      5      10

RADNORSHIRE

HEREFORDSHIRE

removed from the main stream of English life and lying under the wild hills of Wales, largely preserved it from the industrial development of the Midland counties. It remains mainly rural to this day; happy in its isolation, it is truly "the country for easy livers" of A. E. Housman's eulogy.

What better testimony could there be to this "easy living" than that great Shropshire figure Thomas Parr, celebrated as "Old Parr"? This worthy, born under the shadow of the Breidden Hills in 1483, lived until 1635 and might almost be living still had he not, at the invitation of Charles I left his quiet Shropshire and journeyed to London, there to be fêted and made much of! This change of air and scene was his undoing: he died, it is said, as a result of the banqueting, and was buried in Westminster Abbey.

Old Parr's cottage, of timber and thatch, is but one example of the homely dwellings of this quiet, comfortable land which later history has largely passed by. Many of them show at its finest that great glory of English domestic architecture, the black and white timber-and-plaster style. Whether in the rich merchants' houses in Ludlow, the town houses of the country gentry in Shrewsbury, many a farmhouse or wayside inn, or the justly famous Pitchford Hall, most beautiful of all, there is the same impression of comfort and well-being. This impression is found equally in buildings of later architectural styles, the manors and great houses of Condover and Benthall, Shipton and Wilderhope and Acton Scott. Incidentally, the Verderer's House at Upper Millichope, among the holts of Wenlock Edge, has claims to be regarded as among the oldest houses in the kingdom.

Shropshire is, in short, a land of homes. It is and has long been a land of yeomen farmers and country squires. What men were these easy-living squires, who put on no self-denying ordinance even when they went to worship! In Stokesay church is a superb squire's pew, with canopy and high screens of wood, to shield his lordship's slumbers from the gaze of the vulgar. This example is even surpassed by the pew, complete with fireplace and red curtains, in Hopton Cangeford church.

### Sheep and Cattle

In its essentials, life has changed but little in the country districts. In the south-west the wide moorlands of Clun Forest still provide pasture for, and give their name to, one of the hardiest and finest breeds of sheep. In these qualities it rivals even its neighbours, the renowned Kerry Hill breed of the Radnor and Montgomeryshire borders. Here, where the plovers wheel and cry, and brown trout streams twist towards the Teme, the old drovers' roads still traverse the uplands. Scattered here and there

are to be found series of earthen walls, usually about four feet high (originally topped by hurdles) and connected by gateways. They are the great cattle-sorting pounds, where the beasts were once inspected, sorted and exchanged. In them, too, the hill-cattle bound for the flat lands of England were shod with iron to protect their feet on the harder English roads. Today, the pounds are no longer used: they remain, decaying memorials of a style of farming that is unlikely to return.

High up on the moor, one thousand and four hundred feet or so, lies the hamlet of Bettws y Crwyn, meaning the Prayer House of the Fleeces. It contains but two cottages, the rectory and the church, in which you can read, painted on the pew-ends, the names of the lonely sheep farms whose shepherds and flockmasters still worship there every Sunday.

### Defence Against the Welsh

Hereabouts are some of the finest portions of Offa's Dyke still to be seen. This great defensive work, stretching a hundred and forty miles from the Dee near Chester to the Severn at Chepstow, is thought to have been built round about A.D. 765–792. Originally, it was an earthwork about twelve feet high whose defensive value was enhanced by a ditch seven feet deep in front of it. Certainly its makers built well, for in many parts it survives in all the impressiveness of its original dimensions. It is doubtful, however, whether it was ever a continuous work; here and there are gaps where defensive use was probably made of the dense forests, at that time so thick as to be virtually impenetrable. In the Middle Ages the law ran that any Welshman found east of the Dyke should, for a first offence, lose his right hand; for a second, his head. The enactment was harsh: it certainly proved effective in drawing a clear line of demarcation between the English on the east and the Welsh on the west. We find, for example, in close proximity a farm on the English side called Springhill and one on the side towards Wales named Bryndrinog. With the ending of inter-racial strife, the Dyke lost its *raison d'être*. Today Hughes, Jones and Davies are common surnames on both

The Castle and Dinham Bridge at Ludlow seen from across the Teme. Ludlow is the business and social centre of an agricultural district.

sides, and there are hybrid place-names like Llanvair Waterdine or Maesbrook.

The little River Clun flows down through a charming valley system wherein lie the famous Clun villages. The old jingle which ran:

> Clunton and Clunbury,
> Clungunford and Clun,
> Are the quietest places
> Under the sun

is no less true today. The focal point of all this countryside is its railhead, Craven Arms, a meeting-place, too, of important roads. Though only a tiny market town, its sheep fairs are among the largest in England. Its chief distinction, however, is Stokesay Castle, a moated and crenellated mansion of the thirteenth century, with a lovely detached Elizabethan gatehouse. The adjacent church suffered severely in the Civil War, but this merely material damage was a small thing compared with the horror enacted at Hopton Castle, a few miles away, where the Roundhead garrison, surrendering at discretion, were butchered to a man.

Northwards from Clun Forest is a striking district of two great ridges of hills, the Long Mynd and the Stiperstones. The Mynd is about ten miles in length and from three to four in breadth. Its summit is a broad, heathery tableland rising to nearly one thousand and seven hundred feet, crossed by two ancient trackways, and giving wide views over the south part of the county and across to the Welsh mountains. At one time the annual whinberry crop was of great local value, as was the rearing of wild ponies for the coal-mines. Both have now declined.

It is difficult for a stranger to realize the wildness and isolation of this district, especially in the depths of winter. Years ago, the last fair before Christmas held at Church Stretton became known as Deadman's Fair, for the reason that homeward-bound revellers sometimes perished in attempting to cross the hills. In January 1865, the Rev. Donald Carr, rector of Woolstaston, after taking service at Ratlinghope* was overtaken by a blizzard when making

his way over the Mynd in deep snow. Although his knowledge of the terrain was unrivalled, he wandered about for nearly twenty-four hours and, snowblind and exhausted, only reached safety after his parishioners had given up all hope of his survival.

On the eastern side of the Long Mynd, where the little spa of Church Stretton caters modestly for an increasing number of summer visitors, the range is cut into by steep-sided and highly picturesque ravines, locally called "batches," where mountain

* Pronounced "Ratchup."

396

streams foam beneath purple rocks jutting out from the precipitous slopes. On its western side the Mynd is not so steep, but steep enough to provide excellent facilities for the modern sport of gliding.

Still farther west, across the green valley of the East Onny, rises the ridge of the Stiperstones, heather-dark, with a spine of jagged rocks along its crest like the backbone of some prehistoric monster. Many legends connect the Devil with this wild, lost countryside. The association is not inappropriate: with its self-contained, lead-mining community, its few, lonely farms, and its fantastic rock formations—such as the detached Nipstone—it has about it a primitive, almost prehistoric, quality. It is claimed that the mines have been worked for lead since Roman times.

Some distance to the north-west are two more hill masses, the Long Mountain and the Breidden Hills, which mark Shropshire's boundary with Welsh Montgomeryshire. Farther north again lies the historic market town of Oswestry. A strategic stronghold in Border days, it is now busied with a

The Cardingmill Valley in the Long Mynd between Ratlinghope and Church Stretton.

wide variety of industries of which railway works are the chief.

The northern part of Shropshire is sometimes spoken of as a plain. Actually it is rolling country, with a few abrupt heights, such as the Wrekin and Haughmond Hill, rising boldly from the general level. That it is flat would be quickly denied by anyone who has toiled up and down the hilly streets of Whitchurch or walked through lovely Hawkstone Park. It has considerable variety. There is its "Lake District" of seven principal meres clustering about the ancient town of Ellesmere, and innumerable smaller ones besides. There are bogs where you may see peat being cut. For a countryside where there is so much agricultural activity it is comparatively well wooded. Rich clover fields pasture cattle, barley and oats are widely grown, and the proximity of the towns of the Black Country and the Potteries provides a ready market for dairy produce and for root crops. Of late, a new crop, the sugar-beet, has created a new industry and there are now a number of sugar refineries dealing with the local product on the spot. Newport, Wem and Hodnet are modest little market towns, whilst Market Drayton is something more, its cattle fairs being celebrated. Local cheeses, made notably at Whitchurch, have a high reputation.

The Wrekin has so far had bare mention; its significance for all Shropshire men—at once a symbol of home and a rallying cry—deserves some notice. From most points over all north and central Shropshire and over much of neighbouring Staffordshire, its whalebacked ridge, clothed in rich woodlands, is clearly to be seen. To those within its shadow it is more than a mere physical feature; rather is it a presence, the presiding genius of the shire.

## Shropshire's Black Country

East of this noble landmark, and of the busy market and manufacturing town of Wellington, lies Shropshire's little Black Country. In shape it is like a tongue thrust out from Staffordshire, a mere westward prolongation of the Cannock Chase industrial area. Oakengates, with coal and ironstone mines, is its centre. On a sunny day the landscape, much of it levelled slag heap,

positively glitters with the myriad of tiny metallic particles in the soil. Yet the kindly nature of Shropshire seems to have tempered the worst rigours of industrialism.

Although restricted in its impact to a small area the Industrial Revolution came early to this shire. The Severn Gorge, cutting cleanly through the coal measures, provided a ready-made open mine shaft, rendered doubly attractive to the early exploiters by the pockets of ironstone that are to be found in the cliffs. By 1709 Abraham Darby had set up ironworking at Coalbrookdale, and today the well-sited buildings with the neat and seemly workers' dwellings of the Coalbrookdale Company, the whole set in the green depths of a leafy gorge, form one of the pleasantest examples of "paternalism in industry." The single-arch bridge at Ironbridge, dating from 1779, is a famed piece of fine local craftsmanship.

### Local Industries

A mile away, at Broseley, are brick and tile works, though its ancient chain-making industry—a true craft still—is now carried on at Shifnal. In recent years, to meet the needs of the National Grid scheme, a huge electrical power station, towering over the ruined Cistercian abbey not far away, has been erected at Buildwas.

The most picturesque ornament of this dramatic gorge of the Severn is Bridgnorth. A town of many fine old buildings, it is built on two levels, at the top and bottom of the cliff, the two parts being connected by rocky stepped passages. Carpet weaving, malting and brewing are among its occupations.

Picturesqueness and a commanding position above the Severn are also attributes of Shrewsbury, the county town, which has given its name to the shire. Here the river makes a great bow within which stands the town. Its ancient walls crown the bluff; the only vulnerable place, at the neck of the loop, is guarded by the castle. So sited it became, inevitably, a stronghold and the gateway to Wales. Readily provisioned and reinforced from the east over the English Bridge, it commanded the crossing to the west, where the Welsh Bridge now stands.

This position still determines its importance. Standing at the crossing of the Holyhead road and that running from South Wales to the north and served by a web of railway lines, it is the centre of the administration, trade and social life of the county. The general atmosphere reminds one of a university town—understandably, for Shrewsbury School is famous and can boast many distinguished pupils, Sir Philip Sidney and Charles Darwin among them. Conspicuous are the many tall spires; quaint courts and alleyways with half-timbered shops and houses abound. The solid Georgian houses in the professional quarter do nothing to impair the unity of a town which is, architecturally, remarkably harmonious. The "King's Head" is one of the best of the old inns: only the very ingenuous will be impressed by the "Crown," a choice example of Brewers' Tudor. Shrewsbury folk do business in streets with such delightful names as Mardol, Dogpole or Wyle Cop, and take their ease in The Quarry, a charming riverside park, which is noted for its great avenues of lime trees.

To walk through its streets is to feel part of a story rich in past events and which is still unrolling, for this is a town which would seem never to have lost touch with its past. As Pengwern, it was the capital of the old Welsh kingdom of Powys. Offa, the powerful king of Mercia, carved much of his kingdom out of the territories of Powys and in turn made Shrewsbury his capital. In later times Roger de Montgomery, founder also of Ludlow Castle, built the Norman stronghold whose massive drum towers and gatehouses still dominate the town. His interests were not confined to the arts of war: he founded here a Benedictine monastery in 1083. It is the western portion of the old monastic church which to-day, under the name of the Abbey Church of St Peter and St Paul, serves Shrewsbury.

At Wroxeter, a few miles to the east, where the Watling Street crossed the Severn, are the extensive remains of the Roman city of Uriconium. Formerly the capital of the Cornovii, it became in its heyday the third city of Roman Britain in point of size. Alas for the transience of civic greatness! Complete oblivion overtook the city: indeed, the fact of its existence was scarcely known when in 1858 the first excavations revealed a great system of baths and the remains of the adjacent Basilica. Further digging at various subsequent dates has brought to light a line of column bases which must have formed part of the 400-feet-long frontage of the Forum. Most striking discovery of all was the broken

**The old market town of Bridgnorth is divided in two by the Severn. This part, built up a hill, is called the "High Town." Among its old buildings is the Grammar School, founded in the sixteenth century. It is the birthplace of Bishop Percy, the eighteenth century scholar.**

To Shropshire men the Wrekin, rising abruptly to a height of 1,335 feet, is a symbol of home. It is situated about two and a half miles south of Wellington, and its unmistakable whalebacked ridge can be seen from a wide area of north and central Shropshire and Staffordshire.

inscription recording its erection in honour of the Emperor Hadrian in A.D. 130. Many more precious relics are displayed in a museum on the site, and yet others in Shrewsbury Museum. St Andrews Church nearby, which shows much work of both Saxon and Norman times, is entered through a gateway supported by Roman pillars.

Running southwards from Shrewsbury is the main road to Hereford, Newport, and South Wales, with the long chain of the Stretton Hills fringing its eastern side. Fine timber stands in the vales at their feet, whilst in the secluded upland valleys and over the broad slopes wild ponies roam. The principal height, Caer Caradoc, is crowned by a camp, one of three places in Shropshire traditionally the scene of Caractacus' last stand against the Romans. Whether this claim be justified or not the

stone quarries on Hoar Edge, not far away, are said to date back to Roman times.

From these hills one looks south-east across the broad stretch of Ape Dale, a chequer of meadow and cornland, to the bold escarpment of Wenlock Edge. The long, limestone scar, remarkably regular in height and shaggy with hanging woods, is supported in rear by a parallel range of more shapely heights. It stretches away north-east for eighteen miles from Craven Arms to Much Wenlock, the latter a medieval market town with a ruined priory and a superb half-timbered guildhall.

Beyond Wenlock Edge there spreads the wide Corve Dale, bounded in its turn by the twin Clee Hills, of which Brown Clee, one thousand seven hundred and ninety-two feet, is the highest in the county. Capped with basalt, which yields first-class road metal, they are scarred by extensive quar-

401

The River Severn near the village of Buildwas, between Much and Little Wenlock. The river here divides the southern hills from the rolling plain to the north.

ries. The product, the famous *dhu* stone, is conveyed by aerial ropeway and light railway to Ludlow and Cleobury Mortimer for dispatch to all parts of the country.

Nestling on the slopes above Corve Dale are the celebrated Clee villages, of which Clee St. Margaret and Stoke St. Milborough are perhaps the prettiest. But the most beautiful object in the Clees is the perfect little Norman chapel standing in a field at Heath.

In the far south-east corner of the county, running over into adjacent Worcestershire, is Wyre Forest, formerly a royal hunting preserve. Verderers and huntsmen are long gone, replaced by the charcoal burners who cut the coppices and burn the sapling wood in the forest clearings.

Where the Corve joins the Teme is Ludlow, a veritable museum of old buildings, and, as C. E. M. Joad has described it, "with Bath the loveliest town in the country." In the twelfth century it was a walled town with seven gates: of these that which spans Broad Street is the only one now remaining. The Norman castle, founded by Roger de Montgomery, has a story which rings with the names of kings and queens and the warlike captains of the troubled March. Ludlow's custodian dispensed rough and summary justice throughout the Border land, the castle being long the seat of the Lord President of the Court of the Marches. Until after the Civil War it ranked as one of the chief strongholds of England.

The ruins are impressive in their massive strength. The Mortimer and Pendover Towers are famous, but must yield in beauty to the finely proportioned Norman round church, mere shell though it remains. In one of the rooms Samuel Butler wrote *Hudibras*, and Milton's *Comus* had its first performance in the Great Hall. Its huge extent and superb position are best appreciated from Whitcliffe, a path which runs above the bank of the Teme, where it curves between the two graceful bridges.

The ornate parish church of St. Lawrence, the many comfortable town houses and inns, all testify to the prosperity of medieval Ludlow in the days of its woollen trade.

Ludlow today pursues all the activities of an agricultural market town and also caters for great numbers of visitors.

It would almost seem as if the beauty and romance of Shropshire had drawn writers and artists to her. Milton has already been mentioned, and Samuel Butler, the author of *Hudibras*. Hazlitt spent his youth at Wem, and the south-west hill lands inspired some of David Cox's happiest landscapes: Housman practically adopted the county. The typical Shropshire lad, however, is at once more naïve and more robust than the wistful figure Housman portrays. The pessimism, the introspection, are a literary licence we gladly forgive the poet.

Among her own distinguished sons Shropshire numbers Robert Clive, Charles Darwin, William Langland the fourteenth-century poet, William Wycherley—one hesitates to mention Mary Webb in such company! Her novels have at least this merit: they make us aware of those overtones of mystery, tenuous and elusive emanations of a countryside where every hill has its camp, earthwork or ring fort, where Rome lives still in causeway and city, and where tumuli, stone circles and gaunt border castles stand everywhere.

Shropshire is indeed a land of richly varied interest, with a people whose easy, natural mode of living largely preserves them from the spiritual *malaise* which afflicts the town dweller in our urban civilization.

*Haughmond Abbey near Shrewsbury*

*Looking north over the Wye valley
from Symond's Yat, south of Ross*

*Ross-on-Wye*

# HEREFORDSHIRE

By I. O. EVANS

HEREFORDSHIRE is today one of the most peaceful counties in Britain. No manufacturing town fills its air with tumult and smoke; no minerals hidden within its rocks tempt the miners to turn its quiet hills into a clangorous hive of industry. No sea washes its boundaries, making the ground quiver with the thunder of its waves and threatening to overwhelm the shore at storm or high tide; no great rivers disturb its tranquillity with the rattle of loading cargoes and the hiss of steam. No crowded holiday resorts, or over-publicized beauty spots, attract hordes of visitors. The railways which traverse its country are comparatively few and lead to no great centre of population; hardly disturbed by an occasional passing train, the cattle graze on its green pastures, the product of its fertile red soil.

Yet this peaceful land was once the scene of war. Its very name, according to some authorities,

*Arms of Herefordshire*

speaks of its militant past: the Saxon words *here-ford* meant "the ford of the army." The remains of a great earthwork, a rampart flanked on the west by a ditch, runs through the county from north to south; this is Offa's Dyke, constructed centuries ago as a bulwark against attacks by the wild mountain tribes.

The south-western boundary of Hereford overlaps the fringes of a tract of highland country so sombre as to have earned the name of the Black Mountains. Some part of its eastern boundary runs along the crest of the Malvern Hills, crowned by another defensive earthwork, an ancient British camp. Between the two ranges lies an expanse of undulating country, varied by groups of minor hills, and broken by level tracts bordering the streams. Here, too, are prehistoric earthworks, chief of them Croft Ambrey, a huge encampment; here are the vestiges of Roman garrison towns such as

Herefordshire's quiet market towns and villages have retained many ancient buildings, particularly in the half-timbered style. Of the villages Weobley is among the most famous.

Kenchester (Magna) and Weston-under-Penyard (Ariconium); here, picturesque in their ruin, are the shattered remains of the Norman castles built by the stern Marcher Lords. Best known of these are Richard's Castle and Wigmore, guarding the northern border; Clifford, north-east of Hay; and Goodrich, on the Wye near Ross.

### Ancient Border Battles

The struggles in these parts were, however, no mere straightforward battle between the Normanized English east of Offa's Dyke and the Welsh to its west. South of Hereford city is a district once known as Archenfield; this, though east of the Dyke, was almost entirely inhabited by the Welsh. They kept their own language and laws; they were separately represented in the Shire Mote, the medieval equivalent of the County Council; they treasured their own customs. Yet they were on the most unhappy terms with the unsubdued Welsh of the mountains, who probably regarded them as despicable collaborationists and quislings; they prided themselves on always fighting in the van when the English sent a punitive expedition into the mountains and forming the rearguard during its return. It was in these wars that the use of the long-

bow was perfected, that weapon which was to change the history of the English by bringing them victory on the fields of Creçy and Agincourt. Not until the reign of Henry VIII was the region pacified, its peace soon to be shattered once again by the Civil War.

These ancient struggles are not as irrelevant as they might seem to the county's modern life. They have left their mark not only on the landscape in the form of ruined castles and hill-top earthworks and Offa's Dyke. They have left it in the place-names, many of which—especially in what was once Archenfield—are wholly or partly Welsh: such names as Llangarren and Llandinabo and Llangrove. Indeed, an alternative derivation of Hereford—the study of place-names is unfortunately not yet an exact science—is simply Henffordd, from the Welsh for "the Old Road."

Above all, the struggles, and the racial intermixtures which they produced, gave the present-day population of the county its distinctive character. Unlike its southern neighbour, Monmouthshire, Hereford is English, not merely in law, but in the speech and feelings of its people. Yet it undoubtedly contains a goodly proportion of Welsh blood, which expresses itself most obviously in accent, but no less certainly in character and outlook.

The Herefordshire dialect is that variety of English, sometimes called South Saxon, which may be heard in various forms almost everywhere in the southern parts of rural England. It is a pleasant speech, free from the comparative harshness of the north or the stridency of the Londoner. Yet in Herefordshire it is modified by the characteristic Welsh accent, that tendency to develop a musical lilt, to end each sentence with an upward inflection and to modify the usual English word-order. A number of Welsh words are still retained, especially those relating to the features of the landscape and the routine of the farm. A brook may be called a *prill* and a mound a *tump*; a ploughshare may be spoken of as a *suck*, while miscellaneous belongings and odds-and-ends may be summed up as *gwethil*.

The character of the Herefordshire people shows a parallel with their accent. They are a pleasant folk, without the dourness sometimes found in the North of England or the cheerful volubility of the Cockney. To the Welsh strain in their blood they owe a quick wit, a love of poetry and imagination. From Hereford comes the pithy saying that two classes of people cannot mind their own business—those who have no business and those who have no minds!

Though the people who live on it are a blend of two distinct races, the soil of Herefordshire is almost uniform throughout. The Wye, which enters the west of the county from Wales, flows between limestone cliffs; the Malvern Hills are built of intensely hard rocks, formed ages ago by an uprush of molten mineral from the depths of the earth; the northern hills consist of shale. These marginal areas excepted, however, the county is almost completely underlain by rocks whose colour and age have earned them the name of the Old Red Sandstone.

### Fertile Red Soil

From these rocks comes the dark red soil which is a distinguishing feature of Herefordshire, reminiscent of the red soil of Devon, but noticeably darker in hue. It is extremely fertile; untouched by human hand it generates plant life in luxuriant variety; artificially cultivated, it is readily transformed into rich pasture-lands, or-

**The county is watered by the River Wye and its tributaries, the Lugg, Arrow, Monnow and Frome. This picture shows the Arrow at Eardisland near Leominster.**

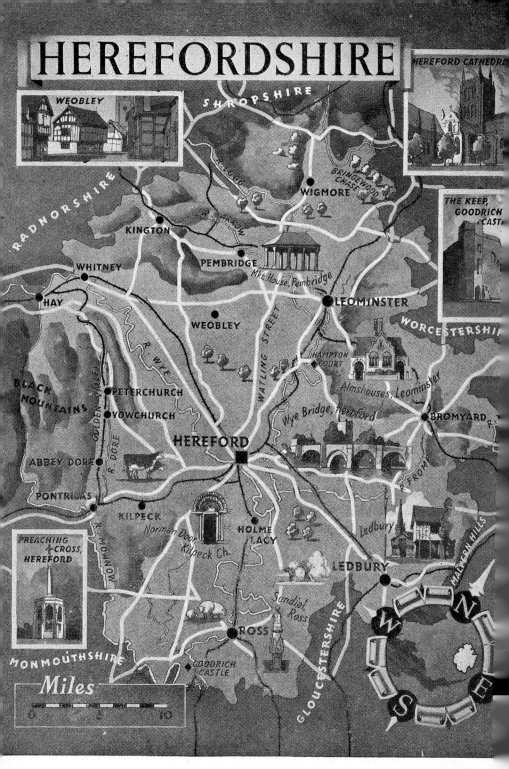

# HEREFORDSHIRE

HEREFORD CATHEDRAL

WEOBLEY

THE KEEP, GOODRICH CAST

SHROPSHIRE

RADNORSHIRE

R. LUGG

WIGMORE

BRINGEWOOD CHASE

KINGTON

R. ARROW

PEMBRIDGE

Mkt. House, Pembridge

LEOMINSTER

WHITNEY

WORCESTERSHIRE

HAY

WEOBLEY

WATLING STREET

HAMPTON COURT

Almshouses, Leominster

R. WYE

BLACK MOUNTAINS

PETERCHURCH

GOLDEN VALLEY

VOWCHURCH

Wye Bridge, Hereford

BROMYARD

R. FROME

R. DORE

ABBEY DORE

HEREFORD

PONTRILAS

R. MONNOW

KILPECK

Norman Door, Kilpeck Ch.

HOLME LACY

Ledbury

MALVERN HILLS

PREACHING CROSS, HEREFORD

LEDBURY

Sundial Ross

ROSS

GLOUCESTERSHIRE

MONMOUTHSHIRE

GOODRICH CASTLE

N W S E

Miles

0     5     10

408

chards, hop-gardens and cornfields, for which the county has justly earned such a high reputation.

In summer, the Golden Valley in the south-west of the county is bright with fox-gloves: south of the Malvern Hills the wild roses bloom. Spring flowers of many varieties are found everywhere in pro-fusion, with dense masses of fern. The Herefordshire woodlands show a fanciful analogy to the human population, for they consist largely of those two most charac-teristic English trees, the oak and the elm; but out of the oak grows the plant esteemed as sacred by the Druids of old-time Wales—the mistletoe.

Many of the Herefordshire hills are indeed well wooded almost to their crests. A stretch of unenclosed park-land, Bringe-wood Chase, near Ludlow, is the home of the fallow-deer, elsewhere almost un-known in Britain. The county also possesses otters and badgers, foxes, weasels and stoats in abundance, as well as a delightful variety of birds.

### Famous Breed of Cattle

Over half its surface is in pasture, grazed by herds of the famous Hereford breed of cattle. These animals, like the soil from which springs the grass that nourishes them, attract attention by their dark red colour; their faces and chests are, however, white, and their horns might be described as having a waxen look. Though they are beef and not dairy cattle, they are almost the only breed favoured in the county.

Herefordshire at one time also produced a noted breed of Ryeland sheep, their wool so valuable that it was known as "Lemster (Leominster) ore." These, however, have been so crossed with other strains as to have been almost completely absorbed. The grazing lands of the county are also cropped by a fair number of horses. Not all the farm land of the county is down for pasture, however: there are many acres devoted to the cultivation of barley, oats, wheat and other millable crops.

The prevailing occupation of Hereford-shire is thus agriculture, and its predomina-ting dwelling is the farm. Many of the older farm-houses, like the manor-houses of the squires, are built in the half-timbered style, sometimes known as black-and-white, a style which is indeed another characteristic of the county: the roofs, when not thatched, used to be formed of thin stone flags. A smaller, but very picturesque, feature of its scenery is the dove-cotes, for which also the county is noted.

In this part of the country agriculture is facilitated not only by the fertility of the soil, but by the equable weather. The mild air is free from extremes of cold in winter or heat in summer; the rainfall is moderate, the barrier of Welsh mountains to the west robbing the Atlantic winds of much of their moisture and breaking their force.

### An Exacting Life

However favourable soil and weather may be, farm life is, in the nature of things, none the less exacting. Its seasonal work demands unflagging labour guided by an experience and aptitude derived from a centuries-old tradition. There are the fields to till and sow, the harvest to reap, the animals to tend; there are the vagaries of the weather to cope with, for good as it is it cannot be expected to be perfect. There is the waywardness to contend with not only of nature, but of man, for here, as elsewhere in England, agriculture suffers needless dis-couragements in time of peace; only in war and in times of national emergency is it realized as vital to the national life.

Herefordshire is specially famed for two products of the soil, neither of which is of general occurrence elsewhere. One is the hop: with the adjoining county of Worces-ter, Herefordshire forms Britain's second hop-growing district. The eastern parts of its landscape are pleasantly diversified by the serried rows of the twining hops and the cowled shapes of the oast-houses.

### Hop-pickers from the Midlands

Wherever hops are grown, their picking in the autumn demands the services of an immense body of semi-skilled labour. Just as armies of Londoners go hopping in Kent, so at this season workers from the Midland industrial towns migrate to the Worcester and Hereford hop-fields. They travel in their hundreds by train or road,

Hereford is famous for its cattle which are thought to be descended from the country's original native species. They were formerly bred for the plough but are today famous for the meat they yield.

intent on supplementing their regular income by strenuous work while at the same time enjoying a holiday among informal surroundings in the open air.

Here, as in Kent, the hoppers from the towns bring into the Herefordshire hop-growing districts a liveliness lacking in the pasture-lands farther west; they give the country-folk among whom they stay a touch of the town-dweller's outlook and leave them less unsophisticated and more worldly-wise. In return the hopper, we may hope, benefits from his acquaintance, brief though it is, with rural life.

### Land of Apples

It is a coincidence that the county which challenges Kent's monopoly of hops, the raw material of beer, should also contest the pre-eminence of Devon as the home of cider! But so it is; cider apples were cultivated in Herefordshire as long ago as the seventeenth century. The diarist, John Evelyn, then described the county as "one continuous orchard," and Thomas Fuller, a chronicler of English affairs, claimed that it deserved better than any German dukedom to have the title of Pomerania, the "land of apples."

The county's orchards are still flourishing, and they bear a fruit which though not specially palatable either raw or cooked is eminently suited for cider-making. Whether the brew of Herefordshire be superior to that of Devon is a hotly disputed question which would perplex a connoisseur. Another less famous drink is almost a monopoly of Herefordshire. That is perry, a pleasant beverage somewhat akin to cider which is, however, made not from apples but from pears.

On some farms cider and perry are still prepared in traditional fashion: the fruit is crushed by a great roller propelled by a horse or in a press worked by hand labour. The juice, stored in casks, soon ferments into a heady brew very welcome for quenching the thirst of a farm-worker on a hot

410

summer's day or for celebrating a harvest-home.

The drink thus prepared is, however, not sufficiently standardized to be acceptable to commerce. For trade purposes the cider is mass produced by crushing thousands of tons of apples in vats holding tens of thousands of gallons. The fruit is sorted and blended carefully, and the standards of cleanliness are as high as in an up-to-date dairy farm.

This production of cider from local apples, perry from local pears, and beer from local hops, forms the nearest approach to manufactures which Hereford can show. The county also brews malt vinegar in smaller quantities, and carries on the usual rural industries of tanning bark from the local oaks, quarrying the local rocks and making bricks from the local clay.

Compared with the rest of England the county seems sparsely inhabited. This is not because extensive areas are unoccupied—they are not—but because it possesses few large towns. Its very county town, Hereford, cannot be called large, and its other towns, such as Ross and Ledbury and Leominster, are quite small. But why, indeed, should they be large? They are not homes of industry, but market towns and administrative centres for a rural countryside.

Small though they are, however, they are very charming, with their mansions and their half-timbered houses. Though Hereford Castle was long since "slighted," the splendid cathedral still stands, its ancient episcopal palace at its side. Here and in the smaller towns and villages are many churches renowned among lovers of architecture.

### Small Town Life

Towns as small as those of Hereford have all the disadvantages which come of localized interests; the inhabitants of such places are frequently accused of a narrow parochialism and of an undue interest in one another's business. On the other hand, their citizens lack the bleak impersonality of the Londoners and the people of the great manufacturing centres, in which, by country standards, nobody seems to feel or care about even their next-door neighbours. Certainly the smaller towns have the undeniable advantages of fresh air untainted by city smoke, of water fresh from the hills

**The Wye at Ross.** The English philanthropist John Kyrle, commonly known as the Man of Ross, is buried in the thirteenth-century parish church of St. Mary, seen in the background.

Every third year the choirs of Hereford, Worcester and Gloucester hold their festival in Hereford Cathedral. The cathedral, the earliest part of which dates from Norman times, contains a fourteenth century map of the world, and the chained library of 1440 books includes some printed by Caxton.

and of speedy access to the woods and fields of the countryside.

The special charms of Herefordshire have long been known. Thomas Fuller, already quoted, remarked that, though not limited to one letter of the alphabet, the county excelled in "the four W's," as he called its wood, wheat, wool and water. (Later cynics, of course, raised the number to six by adding wine and women!)

### Fishing on the Wye

One advantage of the absence of factories is that there is nothing to pollute the Herefordshire rivers. From the Welsh mountains they flow to join the sea, here meandering slowly in graceful curves across the plains, there rushing tumultuously between the cliffs and among the jagged boulders. Not even the largest of them, the Wye, is navigable for any distance, but many of them form reaches admirably suited for bathing, boating or angling.

Their clear waters abound in fish. The Wye is a famous salmon river, and also contains, as do the smaller streams, grayling, perch and trout. These are captured not only by the amateur equipped with the latest improvements in rod and line and bait, but by the professional fisherfolk using one of the oldest and most primitive of river craft.

This is the coracle, which one might expect to have vanished with the Ancient Britons. On the Wye, and on other Welsh and borderland rivers, it is still in habitual use much as it was described by Julius Cæsar. It consists of a lath framework, cleverly worked into oval shape, and covered with a canvas skin. In inexperienced hands it is tricky and unstable, but the local enthusiasts are skilled in its use.

### Adventurous Journey

Though there is no through traffic for larger craft, the deeper channels of the Wye are busy in summer with rowing-boats. Some adventurous sportsmen try to traverse almost its whole length from the mountains to the sea, dragging their frail craft over the shallows or even bodily carrying them. They cross the county by sixty miles of

412

pleasant water-way, passing through Hereford city, the town of Ross, and long stretches of an attractive countryside in which the villages mostly lie some distance from the river banks.

Though lacking in stereotyped tourist centres, Herefordshire has much to attract the discerning: its cathedral and churches, its ruined castles, its prehistoric remains, its manor-houses and farms and dove-cotes, its quiet market towns, its woods and rivers, its hopfields and orchards and meadowlands. Objects of interest are as plentiful here as scenes of beauty, and in Hereford cathedral is housed a unique treasure, a medieval map of the world. It is no wonder that lovers of the countryside delight to visit this pleasant tranquil land.

Constructed with a view to the needs not of holiday crowds, but of local traffic, several railway lines traverse the county. Of its excellent high roads, some are modern, some date back to the Romans; it is plentifully supplied with by-ways, lanes, and paths. Along the main roads and round the stations building develops, and here the

countryfolk are brought more into touch than elsewhere with modern affairs.

The visitors are catered for not only in the ordinary hotels and guest-houses but in the farmers' or villagers' spare rooms. There are, moreover, Youth Hostels and sites for camp and caravan. Such amenities are, of course, most plentiful in the towns, near the waters in which angling is permissible, and round the scenic delights which have earned a reputation.

Herefordshire is neither a pleasure-resort, delightful though its scenery is, nor an industrial centre, though it has its traditional occupations. It produces what is more essential than either amusement or manufactured articles: food and drink. Its fertile lands grow the corn from which comes bread and nurture the cattle from which comes meat; its hopfields and its orchards provide two of the staple drinks of these islands, cider and beer. It is the home of stalwart countrymen and of dwellers in towns small enough to give a sense of community, the descendants of two once-warring peoples now united in peace.

*Church Lane, Ledbury*

413

Chepstow Castle from the River Wye, which here forms the boundary between Monmouth and Gloucester. The walls and gates of this old town have been almost completely preserved.

*River Wye at Llandogo*

# MONMOUTHSHIRE

## By I. O. EVANS

THE COUNTY of Monmouth is a debatable
land, neither completely part of England
nor of Wales. Legally English, and not
one of the twelve Welsh counties, it has
none the less so much in common with them
that the words "and Monmouthshire" are
almost invariably added to the laws affecting Wales.

Were these islands as politically divided
as the Continent, this anomalous position
might have given rise to wars, both nations
having a plausible claim to the county and
seeking a "strategic frontier" along its
rivers! Though its early history was stormy
enough, however, its inhabitants, Welsh
and English alike, have long lived peace-
fully together.

Monmouth is a pleasant land. It possesses
a "black country" in the north-west, the
tip of the Glamorganshire coalfield. Centring around Ebbw Vale,
this "black" area embraces one-
fifth of the county's total area and
houses and employs about two-
thirds of its people. Another fifth of
the population live and work in
Newport, Monmouthshire's one

flourishing seaport. Apart from some small
semi-industrialized towns, the remainder
of the county, from the plains which border
the Severn to the tree-clad hills along
the Wye and the slopes of the Black
mountains in the north, mostly consists
of rich agricultural country. In the east it
is interspersed with tracts of woodland or
common, outlying portions of Gloucestershire's Forest of Dean.

Monmouth might well be called a county
of rivers. Its southern coast is washed by
the mighty flood of the Severn; on the east
its boundary is the cliff-shadowed Wye;
and on the west the River Rhymney
separates it from Glamorgan—and thus
from legal Wales. Through its heart flows
another lovely river, the Usk, and parts of
its northern boundary also run along tributaries of Usk and Wye. It is from
the River Monnow, which joins
the Wye at Monmouth, that the
county takes its name.

Its varied landscape teems with
plant and animal life. Along the
Wye valley the dark green of the
yew contrasts with the lighter hues

*Monmouthshire County Seal*

of the oak and ash. The woods and meadows that border the river are luxuriant with many varieties of wild flower and fern. The otter makes its home in the valleys and the fox and badger in the rocks. Sea and shore birds abound along the Severn, including the sandpiper, plover, gull and duck; the heron survives in the valley of the Usk; the buzzard and peregrine falcon have been seen in the hills. The butterflies of the county are much sought after by naturalists, and the Wye and Usk are equally renowned by fishermen for their salmon and trout.

## Racial Blends

Several racial strains mingle in the people of Monmouthshire. Both in Gwent and in Gwynllwg, as the eastern and western parts of the county were called, lived more or less peaceably two distinct races of Welsh—the Ancient Britons of our history books. The earlier of these, the Iberians, were short and dark, somewhat resembling the peoples of Spain; later arrived another people, the tall, fair, blue-eyed Celts. The Roman occupation, temporary though it was, introduced alien blood. With the coming of the English, and later of the Normans, this fair county became the scene of many a fierce battle, many a plundering raid and punitive expedition.

Pacified by the Lords Marcher with their strong castles, the county was further disturbed by later dynastic and civil wars. Meanwhile, as we have seen, it had been legally absorbed into England, Welsh though it was in sentiment and mixed though it was in blood. Local tradition still remembers the "old unhappy far-off things and battles long ago" of its turbulent past.

This racial blend has, of course, had its effect upon the speech of the people. The Usk acts almost as a language frontier. To its east the predominant tongue is English; to its west Welsh is in fairly general use, though even here many of the younger people speak only English. Yet the division is not hard and fast: English is commonly spoken with the lilting Welsh accent; and very few and elderly are the people who reply *"Dim Saesneg"* ("no

Saxon") when addressed in the English tongue. Welsh, as a language in everyday use, is, so to speak, retreating westwards towards the Glamorganshire frontier.

A strip of southern Monmouthshire lies on the direct route not only to South Wales, with its coalfield and populous cities, but also, by way of Fishguard, to the south of Ireland. Here the land is level and is traversed by a main line of railway and a network of roads. The junctions and the towns and villages along the highways have to cater for armies of travellers and transport workers, breaking their journey between London and the west. This part of the county is accordingly more lively and less tranquil, more sophisticated and less old-world than the undisturbed agricultural regions.

The most densely populated region of Monmouthshire, as we have seen, is in its industrialized north-west, with such manufacturing towns as Pontypool, Tredegar and Abertillery. Though always spoken of as a coalfield, this area also produces many other minerals. It was indeed first worked— in the fifteenth century, near Pontypool— for iron, which was at that time smelted by charcoal.

## Development of the Coalfields

When the development of the steam-engine enabled the deeper coal-seams to be worked, those of South Wales were found to yield a fuel consisting largely of carbon. Not adapted for domestic use, this steam coal was admirably suited for industrial work, for heating boilers and for iron-smelting. It became famous throughout the world, and produced ruinous results on wide areas of lovely mountain scenery. Coal and iron are wrested from the hills by human labour and complicated machinery, and the slopes and valleys are submerged under wide-spreading industrial towns. Street after street of functional dwellings are broken by mines and factories, above which hang lowering clouds of dust and smoke; the general effect is dreary in the extreme.

These coalfield towns house a sturdy population whose tradition is mining, who face a lifetime of toil as steadfastly as they

# MONMOUTHSHIRE

LLANTHONY PRIORY

LLANTHONY

NOCKSHIRE

N W E S

HEREFORDSHIRE

SUGAR LOAF

SKIRRID FAWR

R. MONNOW

BLACK MTS.

ABERGAVENNY

AR

EBBW VALE

BLAENAVON

St. Mary's Church, Abergavenny

R. TROTHY

MONMOUTH

MNEY

COITY MT.

ABERTILLERY

ABERSYCHAN

The Gate Tower, Raglan Castle

R. USK

RAGLAN

BEDWELLTY

R. SIRHOWY

PONTYPOOL

USK

Tintern Abbey

R. WYE

GLOUCESTERSHIRE

ABERCARN

PANTEG

Roman Amphitheatre, Caerleon

TINTERN PARVA

DWAS

CANAL

WENTWOOD

RISCA

CANAL

FOREST

R. EBBW

CAERLEON

Newport Cathedral, (St. Woollos's Ch.)

CHEPSTOW

ANSHIRE

R. RHYMNEY

NEWPORT

Chepstow Castle

R. SEVERN

RUMNEY

## Miles

0      5      10

MONNOW BRIDGE, MONMOUTH

o

417

(E.N.C.)

Monmouthshire's "black country" occupies one-fifth of the county's area and houses two-thirds of its population. Its centre is the coal-producing district of Ebbw Vale, seen above.

face the inevitable dangers of underground explosion and falling rock. Trade Unionism flourishes here, and the miners of Monmouthshire and South Wales are always ready to co-operate with their fellows in the other coalfields of Britain. Yet their Welsh descent gives them their special characteristics; they are more romantic and less matter-of-fact than the miners of England; they are especially famed for their choirs and their love of song.

Although situated in the Welsh Marches and employing armies of Welshmen, the industry is almost entirely controlled by "Saxons." The old landowners were not much inclined to develop their estates, and the mines were opened and are still largely run by "foreigners" from the industrial areas of England and Scotland. A touch of racial bitterness thus lends an added tang to the intermittent industrial disputes.

Monmouthshire is indeed exceptional in Trade Union history in that here the

workers literally took up arms in the struggle for their rights. Chartism, generally, was an orderly movement, but here, in 1839, Unionist strikers staged what might be called an attempt at revolution. Large bodies of Chartists, armed with pistols and blunderbusses as well as with more primitive weapons, advanced into Newport and opened fire on an hotel where their comrades were imprisoned. The Riot Act was read, the soldiers opened fire, and the Chartists were dispersed, leaving their dead and wounded lying in the square; their leaders were sentenced to transportation. The memory of this episode may still linger when the miners go out on strike.

The influence of the mining industry extends beyond the area it covers, to people whom it does not employ. The slime from the workings floats down the stream and kills the fish, the smoke and the dust drift over the hills and fill the cottages with grime. Cracks appear in the hill-sides and

418

threaten to develop into destructive land-slides. The farm-hand realizes that he need not remain on the land; he knows that he can hope to find work in the towns, and this gives him a bargaining advantage in wage-disputes.

The north-western hills of Monmouth, rising as they do in some parts to almost 2,000 feet, influence the climate. They give the western half of the county a somewhat heavier rainfall than the east, and make its northern half colder than the south. As one would expect, the hills are snow-capped—perhaps even snow-bound—when the flats along the Severn are clear. These climatic differences have obvious effects on the everyday life of the country people and the outlines of the farms, which are modified by the nature of the rocks below the soil.

The most fertile land in the county is found in the southern levels—the country-folk call them Moors. These were formed from the rich silt brought down by the Severn and deposited when its swift current was checked by the sea. Yet "what the sea gives it takes back again," and the coast has to be dyked against the floods caused when the rain-fed river meets an adverse spring tide—floods which farther up the estuary become the famous Severn Bore. The Romans fortified the coast with an earthen embankment twenty miles long; it has now been replaced by stone in some places.

The flatness of this part of the county greatly facilitates long-distance communications, by rail, road or canal. It is, however, a great hindrance to the cross-country movements of the farmworkers, for the Moors have to be drained by wide ditches called "reens," opening into the Severn by sluices known as "gouts." These ditches may be crossed—if the traveller be sufficiently skilful and energetic—by the aid of a long vaulting-pole called a "powt."

It is in the south that corn-growing is chiefly practised; in the northern parts of

The outlying hills of the Black Mountains provide a magnificent setting to Abergavenny. The Sugar Loaf mountain, seen below in the background, is a famous landmark.

Miners' cottages at the village of Pantywain, in the coalfield area. Narrow streets such as this a
typical of those found in the industrial north-west corner of the county.

e county cattle-rearing predominates. ne influence of the Welsh rural tradition :eps the farms small; many are family fairs, and few employ more than one bourer, whereas farms in the neighbour- g counties of Hereford and Gloucester :ed several. In times of great pressure, for ample at harvest-time, several neighbour- g farmers may co-operate.

### Rotation of Crops

On most of the farms rotation of crops practised, on what is known as the four- :ld system. The year after it has yielded s harvest of wheat, a field will be planted ith root-crops. The next year it will be )wn with barley, and the third with clover; len in the fourth year it will be ready for nother crop of wheat. By keeping differ- nt parts of his land in the various stages of ie cycle, the farmer can spread the work ver the year. This method also has great gricultural advantages: it enables the plant- )od to be reached at different levels nderground; it economizes manure, checks lant diseases and insect pests, and avoids ny risk of exhausting the soil and turning iis fertile land into a miniature "dust- owl."

The higher wages paid in the mining alleys may have hastened a process which i Monmouthshire has become almost eneral. Animal-tending needs less man- ower than corn-growing: did not Sir homas More complain centuries ago that, y causing unemployment among farm- orkers, "sheep were eating men"? What- ver the cause, in much of the country the rown of ploughed earth and the gold of ie ripened corn are much less evident in )ring and autumn than the green of the astures—or they were until the war.

### Cattle and Sheep

The cattle favoured in Monmouth are 1ose named from the adjacent county—the amous Herefordshires; these are reared ot for their milk, but for their flesh. For airy purposes the shorter-horned breeds are referred, one or two perhaps on the lonelier irms for the benefit of the family, herds 1 the neighbourhood of the towns. The heep are similarly raised for mutton rather than wool, and for this purpose the smaller breeds are in favour.

Welsh traditions also keep the villages in the west smaller than those in the east, the farms being scattered convenient to their fields instead of being grouped together. Historians explain this as due to the differences in national organization: the unit, so to speak, of Welsh life was not as in England—the village—but the tribe or group of families. However caused, the difference is certainly marked and gives the countryside west of the Usk the appearance of a scattered population.

The older farm-houses are not built of brick, but of the local limestone, roofed with slabs of stone or thatch. Unlike the dwellings in the town, which are mostly faced with rough-cast, they are white-washed or colour-washed in yellow or pink. This gives them a cheerful and attractive appearance, well harmonizing with the landscape from the stones of which their walls have been hewn.

Monmouthshire is not particularly rich in pre-historic or Saxon remains. There are, it is true, a few cromlechs and isolated stone circles, but compared with other counties such relics are scarce.

### Milestones in History

The important Roman road—Via Julia— crosses the county, and along it are to be found remains of Roman camps. Caerleon and Caerwent are the most noteworthy. The former, near Newport, was the capital of Britannia Secunda (Wales) and one of the traditional capitals of King Arthur. Its legends are preserved in Tennyson's *Idylls of the King*. The amphitheatre, its chief remaining relic, is national property. Caerwent, though somewhat smaller, was built on similar lines. The county also con-tains the remains of some twenty-five castles, remainders of the Marches war-fare, but these are mostly ruins. Raglan is perhaps the finest, but White Castle, Skenfrith, and Usk are also outstanding.

Chepstow, near the mouth of the Wye, is an ancient town, now partly modernized. It possesses the ruins of a castle, which for-merly dominated the river, and an attractive road-bridge; an efficient but ugly tubular

**Llanover parish church, on the River Usk. Sheep farms dot the hillsides of the beautiful Usk Valley and wheatfields flourish in the fertile soil. The Usk and Wye are famous for salmon and trout.**

railway bridge also spans the river at this point. Though its sea-trade has declined, it still ranks as a minor port, and shipbuilding is still an important industry.

The largest, most populous, most flourishing, and most highly industrialized of Monmouthshire towns—it is also the centre of local government—is not the county town, but Newport. Standing about four miles up river on the Usk, this is one of the greatest ports of the South Wales industrial area, challenging the supremacy of Cardiff and Swansea. Its vast docks and marshalling yards enable the coal and iron and tinplate to be shipped all over the world. Its coal-hoists empty complete truck loads of fuel into the waiting holds. Its gigantic transporter bridge, supported high above the river by twin metal-work towers, sus-

pends from its runways a large car, which crosses the water level with the land, and unites the two banks without hindering the river traffic.

Some of the county's smaller industries function in its river valleys, to the great detriment of their beauty. Gaps are quarried in the cliffs; a rusty effluent gives a name to Redbrook; gaunt bridges deface the landscape at Tintern, Chepstow and Usk.

These valleys are nevertheless so beautiful as to draw crowds of visitors from far away. The most famous sight of Monmouthshire is ruined Tintern Abbey, magnificently placed beside the Wye stream and between the tree-clad slopes on either side once a year the full moon may be seen framed in the circular window at the end of the roofless aisle. It was built about 1131 by a group of Cistercian monks from Waverley, in Surrey, but little now remains of the original monastery, as it was almost entirely rebuilt between 1269 and 1325.

Canoes traverse the surface of the Wye, and anglers seek its salmon. In the lower reaches of the stream rods and lines give place to nets, and the amateur fisher to the professional. Several ingenious devices are employed. "Tuck" nets and "draft" nets, hauled by boats, seek to capture the fish in bulk. The "lave" net scoops them out, the "stop" net entraps them, one by one. In the Severn estuary long tapering baskets, called "putchers," are used; the unwary salmon that enters one of these is unable to escape.

To cater for the canoers and anglers, and for the host of sightseers, the Wye Valley has developed a flourishing tourist industry. Tea-shops, garages, car-parks, guest houses, sprawl grotesquely across the countryside. Inns and road-side pull-ups are found everywhere, and many farms and cottages accommodate paying guests. There are several Youth Hostels, and the white tents of the campers gleam in the meadows where the canoes are drawn up high and dry above the water's edge.

In winter, however, the Lower Wye is subject to heavy floods, very destructive to property and endangering the lives of the dwellers in picturesque Tintern. It is a tidal river and is swept under favourable conditions by a tidal wave similar to, although on a much smaller scale than, the famous Severn Bore.

Here, and in the county's other beauty-spots, the villagers are not so isolated as in its less-frequented areas, are more in touch through their visitors with the outside world. The holiday-makers help them not only financially but by overcoming that loneliness and narrowness of outlook which are among the drawbacks of rural existence. In return the visiting townsfolk learn something of the tranquillity and wisdom which come from life upon the land.

In its west, Monmouthshire is a grim workshop where, in toil and peril, the stalwart miners wrest coal from the depths of the earth. In its east it is a scenic holiday resort much frequented by pleasure-seekers and lovers of beauty. To its south its coast is fringed with the nets of the fisher-folk. For the most part it is a pasture-land for herds of cattle and flocks of sheep. In it meet and blend the finest traditions of its two races: neither completely part of England nor of Wales, it combines the best features of both.

*Monmouth, the county town*

Kettlewell, near Skipton, is a convenient starting point for excursions into Upper Wharfedale which unfolds from the north-west of the county and provides some of the loveliest scenery in Yorkshire

*York Minster from the city walls*

# YORKSHIRE

By HARRY J. SCOTT

LEGEND has it that a man of York once stood upon Lendal Bridge and gazing at the Ouse beneath exclaimed, "How wonderful that this river took it into its head to flow through so fine a town." He might have spoken similarly at Richmond, on the Swale, at Ripon, on the Ure, at Knaresborough, on the Nidd, at Ilkley, on the Wharfe, and at Skipton, close by, if not exactly on, the Aire. He might even have said it of Doncaster, on the Don. For there is no other system of rivers in the whole of Great Britain comparable with this great gathering of tributaries by the Ouse and the Humber, tributaries which are each rivers in their own right, bearing on their banks cities and towns of no mean fame and flowing through some of the wildest and grandest and loveliest country in England.

Like the fingers of a giant hand outspread this system drains the Pennines. The Swale and the Ure give birth to the Ouse, reinforced by the Nidd, Wharfe, Aire, Calder and Don. The Rye and Derwent are the outstretched thumb. And in their grasp they contain most—

*Yorkshire: North Riding Arms*

but not quite all—of Yorkshire's life and industry.

This river system, and the physical nature of the country which gives rise to it, bestows upon Yorkshire a remarkable diversity. Within it there is every sort of watercourse from fierce mountain torrent to broad trout stream, from dawdling sylvan river to a spacious smooth estuary. In general, the scenery is powerful rather than charming, yet the diversity remains and there are stretches of gentle plain and wooded parkland as well as vast tracts of rolling moors and harsh fells. As a consequence of this river-born diversity of scene there is a diversity of occupation, of outlook and of character among those who live and work in the county.

In the north and west are the dalesmen, who wring their hard living from the Pennine fells and valleys; in the lower lands of the Aire and Calder are the woolmen converting the fleeces, home and imported, into clothing; and farther south upon and around the Don are the men of coal and iron in the black country of Yorkshire. Where the Ouse basin forms the palm of the outstretched hand of rivers are the plainsmen of the vales of Mowbray and York growing their corn and raising cattle in the fertile flat land

425

and to the east of them, on the tableland of moors which give birth to Rye and Derwent, are the moorland men settled traditionally on their heather-enclosed holdings with their turf fires and simple existence where odd superstitions still linger in this twentieth century. Only the men of the low, rolling wold country and the men of the coast owe no tribute to the river system of Yorkshire, but they, too, have their own characteristics and contribute in their own way to the diversity of the county.

### Administrative Divisions

These "natural" divisions do not exactly correspond with the three divisions into which Yorkshire is split for administrative purposes. The latter are known as North Riding—an area which includes the Cleveland Hills and the Moors, the city of York, Middlesbrough (by far the largest town), and Scarborough; West Riding—covering the great industrial areas of south Yorkshire, the chief centres being Leeds, Sheffield, Bradford, Halifax, Huddersfield, Barnsley and Wakefield; and East Riding—stretching south from York to the Humber

and covering the Wold, with its main centre at Hull.

Let us start, then, from the hard, grim, desolate fell-lands of the north-west where the Pennines form a mighty watershed, and where the dale country of the Swale and Ure produces the dour, weatherbeaten dalesfolk of the lonely farmsteads and grey, stone villages, whose world is made up of sheep and walls, cloud-capped fells and curlew-haunted hills, whose blunt talk is of tups and ewes, sheep sales and wool prices. The clatter of tiny hooves on cobbled streets is familiar music in every village and the yearly routine follows an age-old pattern of lambing and dipping and shearing that is little changed from monastic times, when the great Abbeys of Fountains and Jervaulx owned vast tracts of land and many thousands of sheep, and where the first Wensleydale cheeses were made from the rich milk of ewes which were fed on the nourishing limestone herbage.

Today, the cheese is made not in farm kitchens, but in factories, and from the milk of cows rather than of ewes. But it has its source in the same limestone grass. Cows'

**The Yorkshire dales are distinctive: there is one glory of Swaledale, another of Wensleydale, and yet another of Wharfedale. This view of Bolton Bridge is typical of the Wharfedale scenery.**

In Upper Swaledale is the remote village of Muker, sheltering under the lee of the Pennines at the foot of the Buttertubs Pass. Many names given by the Norsemen survive in this dale country.

milk is collected each day from hundreds of little farmsteads scattered up and down the dales. Sheep's wool is gathered in each autumn from the communal clippings which follow the annual round-up of the sheep which graze the year round on the high fells.

Each dale has its distinctive quality. There is one glory of Swaledale, and another glory of Wensleydale, and quite a different glory of Wharfedale. The upper reaches of the Aire and the vale of the Nidd have each their special charm, and as one descends from the higher lands and the more desolate fells they become softer in outline. The woodlands creep up the fell sides and wrap themselves along the river banks, but still the land's chief interest is sheep. This is the dale country of Yorkshire whose most characteristic sight is a shepherd setting out with his dog to round up the sheep from the fells which enclose the dales.

It is a world to itself—or was until the bus and motor-car began to penetrate to its fastnesses and link it with the larger community. "You can see all t'world from t'top o' Shunnor Fell," a shepherd once said and

there are some living today who have not travelled beyond the boundaries of that world.

The sleepy little market towns of Hawes and Leyburn, Grassington and Skipton, Settle and Pateley Bridge, were each the metropolis of the local countryside, springing into a wide-awake life on the weekly market day, serving as exchange and mart, courthouse and parliament, and then sinking into slumber again as the day ended.

Motor transport on the roads and mechanization on the land are already transforming this life of the dales. New ideas in agriculture are spreading here faster than in most areas, largely as a result of agricultural demands during the war. The influx of new methods introduced by wealthy industrialists from the West Riding who have taken up farming in the dales is also having its effect. Yet the dales have a way of assimilating the new and incorporating it into themselves, just as their ancient fells have seen many changes and yet remain changeless.

It is in this dale country that you will find places which retain the centuries-old names bestowed by the Norse ancestors of the present dalesmen, Shunnor Fell, Maiden Castle,

427

# YORKSHIRE

REDCAR

ESTON  GU

MIDDLESBRO

THORNABY-ON-T

DURHAM

RIVER TEES

HAMBLETON HILLS

LUNE MOOR

WESTMORLAND

NORTH

RICHMOND

NORTHALLERTON

Byland

THIRSK

CATTERICK CAMP

ROGAN'S SEAT

SWALEDALE

R. SWALE

LEYBURN

R. URE

Ripon Cathedral

R  RID

EAS

PENNINES

HAWES

BUCKDEN PIKE

MASHAM

RIPON

FOUNTAINS ABBEY

BOROUGH

R.

SEDBERGH

R. RIBBLE

WHARFEDALE

GT. WHERNSIDE

PATELEY BRIDGE

R. NIDD

RIPLEY

KNARESE

WEST

WHERNSIDE

INGLEBOROUGH

PEN Y GHENT

R. WHARFE

GRASSINGTON

Ilkley Church

HARROG

LANCASHIRE

INGLETON

SETTLE

BOLTON ABBEY

R. WHAR

HARF

HO

R  RID

SKIPTON

Skipton Castle

ILKLEY

## STONE WALLS IN THE DALES

Market Place, Settle

KEIGHLEY

R. AIRE

LE

SHIPLEY

PUDS

BINGLEY

BRADFORD

N

R. HODDER

HAWORTH

DEWSBURY

DERBYSHIRE

HALIFAX

R. CALDER

WAKE

BRIGHOUSE

## FOUNTAINS ABBEY

TODMORDEN

HUDDE

PE

HOLMFIRTH

## RICHMOND CASTLE

DERBYSHIRE

BEGGARS BRIDGE, GLAISDALE

STAITHES

THE WHARFE VALLEY

MARKET CROSS & STOCKS, RIPLEY

KNARESBOROUGH

NORTH SEA

WHITBY
ROBIN HOOD'S BAY
Whitby Abbey
DALE
ESK
THLAND
OORS
RSIDE
G
SLEY
Whitby Abbey
SCARBOROUGH
FILEY
PICKERING
R. DERWENT
Scarborough
BRIDLINGTON
Flamborough Head
Collecting Eggs
Bridlington Bay
MALTON
E A S T
GT. DRIFFIELD
R. HULL
HORNSEA
BEVERLEY
Stairway - Beverley Minster
R I D I N G
WITHERNSEA
YORK
Boatham Bar, York
MARKET WEIGHTON
KINGSTON UPON HULL
Spurn Head
STER
R. OUSE
Shipbuilding at Goole
R. HUMBER
Drifters at Hull
SELBY
GOOLE
Dutch R.
EFORD
LINCOLNSHIRE
ONTEFRACT
THORNE
N
E
W
S
dge, Wakefield
R. DON
DONCASTER
ISLEY
MEXBOROUGH
ROTHERHAM
IELD
OTTINGHAMSHIRE

Miles

0     10     20

The village of Rievaulx, famous for the ruins of its abbey, stands on the River Rye near Helmsley, in the North Riding. The abbey, founded in 1130 by the Cistercians, is in a good state of preservation.

Crackpot Hall, Buttertubs Pass, Muker, Kisdon and Keld. The old dialects linger, varying between dale and dale, and the old customs like "hirings," when farm workers find new jobs twice a year, continue in the little towns of Settle and Skipton even though the need of them has gone. And the dalesman himself alters little; he still remains a sturdy independent character, blunt of speech, hard at driving a bargain, but at heart generous and friendly.

To the south-east of this dale country, the Rivers Aire and Calder with the latter's tributary, the Colne, hold the woollen industry of Yorkshire's West Riding. It all began as long ago as the fourteenth century and even before, when the trade was drawn from Suffolk and Gloucestershire. The raw wool was at hand on the monastic lands of the dales. The many becks and rivers provided power and soft water for scouring the wool, and later the near-by coalfields offered further sources of power. At first the spinning and weaving were done at home on hand looms in houses such as those which still remain, with their rows of stone-mullioned windows in and around Huddersfield and Halifax. Enterprising men made up the wool into cloth, which they took to market on pony-back. Others turned the cloth into clothes, which found a ready market at Leeds and Bradford and later led to the establishment of great clothing industries there. Daniel Defoe records how he saw cloth drying on "tenters" round almost every house in Halifax, and the old prayer, "From Hull, Halifax and Hell, good Lord deliver us," reminds us of the severe laws against felons in districts where so much valuable property was left readily accessible.

It is worthy of note that in the one hundred and twenty miles between Hexham and Leek there are only three road routes across the Pennines below the one thousand-feet level. The northern road runs behind the Roman wall along the Tyne valley, the southern route is from Manchester through Rochdale and Todmorden, and the middle

Yorkshire:
West Riding Arms

money in their pockets, most of the industrial giants are still very warm-hearted.

And beneath an exterior dourness, so, too, are the woolmen of the mills. They have their gaieties and their outbursts—they still sing and play in the band, as well as being the stalwarts of Yorkshire cricket and football. In the streets of their towns, too, particularly at night, you will find how they have tried to overcome the drabness of the moorland stone from which their shops and houses have been carved. Gay lights, bright shops, glaring trams and buses, and often illuminations for special occasions—as if Brighouse or Holmfirth or Huddersfield were trying to rival the gay night life of Paris or Vienna.

The woolmen are fiercely contesting a suggestion that the official centre of their industry should be moved southwards. The research centre of the industry is Leeds. The trading centre is, by tradition, Bradford. Where, then, is the sense of an official centre elsewhere? So say the woolmen strong in their loyalty to their county and the liking for that part of Yorkshire where wool becomes cloth.

Where Aire and Calder join stands Castleford, and from that junction southwards

Yorkshire slides suddenly into a grimmer blackness, the blackness of coal and iron, of soot-grimed walls and gaunt pit-tops, of giant furnaces and smoking chimneys. Here the great industrial towns of Sheffield, Doncaster, Barnsley and Rotherham pollute the countryside with smoke and soot. An ancient rhyme says

Castleford maids must needs be fair
For they wash in Calder and rinse in Aire

but she would be a sadly misguided maid who tried the recipe today. There was a time when this was one of the loveliest stretches in England, with woods and parklands, fine houses and trout-filled rivers. Robin Hood and his merry men often slipped over the border and found it a hiding-place and a hunting ground when the Sheriff of Nottingham became too persistent. Robin Hood's Well stands on the road between Pontefract and Doncaster. Fishlake is hard by the River Don near Thorne. Ancient historic names, like Burgh Wallis and Hooton Pagnell, Ferrybridge, Wentworth and Conisborough, roll back the centuries and recall days of pageantry and splendour. Doncaster was, still further back, the Roman *Danum*,

**The village of Bramham, near Tadcaster, gives its name to the Bramham Moor Hunt, seen below. It was the scene of a battle, in 1408, at which the Earl of Northumberland was defeated by Henry IV.**

Near the village of Malham, in the West Riding, is Malham Tarn, an upland lake through which the River Aire flows. Nearby are Malham Cove and Gordale Scar, two great amphitheatres of rock.

and the tramp of the legions was doubtless a familiar sound as the military link was maintained along the great highway between north and south.

It is still possible here and there to catch a glimpse of this past—the imposing façade of Wentworth Woodhouse, the deep peace of the old forest of Barnsdale near Campsall, ancient farmsteads still surviving in view of pit-tops at Badsworth and Wentbridge, the noble circular keep of Conisborough Castle. But they are only glimpses. Perhaps it may all come back some day when all the subsidences due to mine workings have settled and when modern methods of getting coal and utilizing it eliminate smoke and dust or keep these under control. That time is not yet.

It was the discovery of coal and all that followed inevitably upon that discovery which altered the fair face of this part of Yorkshire and gave it a haggard look. The first coalfields were in the western area around Barnsley, for here the precious mineral was nearest the surface, but it spread south to Sheffield, north almost to the doorsteps of Leeds and east to Doncaster. The memory of ancient glories faded or was begrimed. Hordes of little streets of back-to-back houses, each exactly like its neighbour, row upon row, soon clustered near every pit-wheel, the grass and parklands were submerged by spoil heaps and colliery plant, the heart went out of the land literally and symbolically.

A new and different Yorkshire grew upon rather than out of the old in this segment round the Rivers Don and Dearne. In the place of farm hands, estate workers and rural tradesmen, came a great invasion of grim-faced colliers from other parts of England, the old villages were expanded and in-

435

Bridlington Quay, in Bridlington Bay, is the port for the old town of Bridlington, lying one mile inland. One of the most secure harbours on the east coast, it has fine sands and promenades and is a popular holiday resort.

creased by new building and in the end the new swamped the old. Where pheasant and partridge had once called and the bark of the fox had stirred the hunting gentry, there was the clatter of shunting coal trains and the whirr of pit-wheels. The land gave up its valuable treasure, but it exacted a heavy price.

Yet all is not lost even though the smoke and dust continue, and the mining community puts up a brave fight against the perpetual grimness of things. What strikes a visitor to Barnsley or Hickleton or Brodsworth or any other of the south Yorkshire mining towns and villages is the decorative effect of brightly scoured door-steps and window-sills, the pride taken in allotments, the enthusiasm of the miner for his whippets or his pigeons, and the pageantry of the annual miners' union procession with its array of flags and bands. For this the whole community turns out and indulges in an orgy of speech-making, tea in the miners' hall and general festivities. The miners' gala is the great day of the year as was once the country fair.

Because of the nature of his work the miner has a strong sense of neighbourliness with his fellows, side by side with an isolationism as regards the outside world. The mining community of south Yorkshire is tightly knit, keeping itself to itself, absorbed in the hard task of living. Gradually it is evolving improved social amenities, pithead baths, colliery institutes, parks, libraries and public institutions. In towns like Barnsley it is developing a civic pride, which may in time win the battle against drabness and grime. It is erecting what might almost be called garden cities, like the Woodlands near Doncaster. Some of the scars, however, are healing.

Yet even so it remains strangely aloof even from that other centre of blackness a little farther south which is concentrated around Rotherham and Sheffield where the men of steel and iron hold sway. Perhaps it is because the cutlers of Sheffield are of an older tradition—there was a Cutlers' Company with its own hall in 1638—and there are Little Masters still maintaining their specialized crafts side by side with the great concerns, as their predecessors did two centuries ago. This community grew up in the wooded country of Hallamshire around the Don and its little tributaries because of the

436

beds of iron ore, fire-clay and ganister, grit-stone for grinding and water power.

This area of industrial Yorkshire has still an immense future before it, because it has proved adaptable to modern methods and new technical ideas. The evolution of stain-less steel, the development of unsuspected uses for processed metal, the enterprise of the technicians may mean tremendous ad-vances yet to be associated with the name of Sheffield. Here, if anywhere, the magic of Aladdin is being sought to find new uses for old metals.

To understand the significance of the great Plain of York which, lying between the vast rigid block of the Pennines and the tableland of the moors of the north-east, divides Yorkshire into two halves, it is

A typical stretch of the Yorkshire coastline between Whitby and Staithes, in the North Riding. The sands extend from Whitby, seen in the distance, as far as Sandsend, in the foreground.

necessary to glance back for a moment to the Ice Age in what has been termed "our geological yesterday" when the mighty ice-flows from the north poured down upon Yorkshire. One vast sheet of ice flowed from the Scottish mountains, choking the Irish Sea and submerging the peaks of the Isle of Man, and found an escape through the Eden valley where it was reinforced by glaciers from the Lake District. It pressed across the Pennines where is now Stainmore and flowed down the valley of the Tees.

At the same time the North Sea was similarly choked by ice from the Scandinavian glaciers and pressed back against the ice flow from the west, closing the way out for the ice from Stainmore. Thus under the double stress of the flow from the Pennines and the counter-thrust from the North Sea a great sheet of ice was diverted as one gigantic glacier down the vales of Mowbray and York and so into the valley of the Trent.

But that is not the end of the story. As time passed and the ice melted and retreated it left in its wake a great swamp or morass

stretching ultimately from near Northallerton to south Yorkshire, a morass which existed in many places until the eighteenth century and lingers today in Askham Bog, Strensall Common, Skipworth Common and Thorne Waste. This extensive swamp was an almost impenetrable barrier between the highlands on either side of it and for long divided the halves of Yorkshire. It was crossed only at two places where the re-treating glacier had left high ridges of clay and gravel across the morass—what the geologists term moraines. Both of these are conspicuous today, one traversing the Vale of York from Stamford Bridge through Escrick to the Wharfe at Ulleskelf, the other from the same starting-point to Tadcaster. These higher ridges became causeways above the swamp level, being linked eventually with the Aire Gap already referred to, and acting as trade routes and cultural arteries between one half of the county and the other.

Today the extensive Plain of York is, largely as a result of its earlier ice visitation, among the most fertile in Yorkshire and the most prosperous. Where the dalesman talks of sheep and walls the plainsman talks of corn and cows and with justification. These low flat lands have a rich soil, a mild climate and a rainfall half that of the sodden fells to the west. The drained swamp-land has become highly prized as pasture and arable.

As you look down on this fertile plain from Sutton Bank on the Hambleton Hills or across it from the tower of York Minster (that venerable and most venerated of all buildings in Yorkshire), you have a picture of a very different Yorkshire from the rest, a picture to confound the Southerner whose notion of the county is a hotch-potch of gritty hills, mill chimneys and pit-head gear. Here are woodlands and mansions in fair parks, exquisite little church spires and towers, prosperous market towns like Thirsk and Ripon and Boroughbridge with their butter crosses, Georgian houses and coaching inns, cathedral cities like York itself and Ripon and older ecclesiastical foundations like Byland Abbey, Newburgh Priory and Kirkham Abbey and on its fringe the lovely Fountains Abbey, set in magnificent parkland. As a background to all this are the farms and nursery gardens, the stables of the horse breeders and trainers, the little rural industries and the annual country fairs.

The Great North Road runs north and south through the length of the Plain, and an atmosphere of coaching days still lingers round the towns along its course. Legends of highwaymen are still told of its heaths and inns. For a spell, in the railway days, grass grew in the streets of some of those towns and even on the Great North Road itself, but the motor car has brought a new activity and a new prosperity. The old inns are now often road-houses, the stables have become garages, village greens are parking grounds, and lorry drivers' all-night cafés are sprinkled along its edges.

But the Plain itself remains a fat land, watered by the Ouse, and offering vistas more frequently associated with the southern half of England. The ancient city of York in its midst, redolent of history and tradition, keeps a fatherly and ecclesiastical

Leeds, now slightly ahead of Sheffield, is the largest Yorkshire city. It stands in a rich coalfield area and has numerous industries. The Civic Hall, seen below, was opened by King George V in 1933.

eye upon its people and as the Ouse gathers its tribute from nearly all the rivers of Yorkshire so York, as the seat of the episcopal ruler of the north, gathers reverence from all the county.

As the Pennine fells form a mighty mass to the west of the York Plain so the high land to the east, the moorland area of Yorkshire, forms a clear natural division with its own special features and well-defined boundaries. It is a broad tableland which rises to no greater height than one thousand five hundred feet above the sea and stretches from the Vale of Pickering and the Plain of York to Cleveland and the Tees estuary. To the east the tableland runs close up to the coast, terminating in the noble sea cliffs which stretch from Saltburn to Scarborough. Within these boundaries there are between three hundred and four hundred square miles of land, practically all heather-clad, the home of the moorland folk.

It is a sparsely populated area, for these moorland heights do not offer fat livings. The scattered farmsteads have a long family tradition behind them, and in some of them the sweet-smelling peat and turf fires have never been out for a century or more and the tools and implements in use are almost archaic. It is a hard unending struggle to wring a living from these moors, where communications are still difficult and visitors rare save in the few summer months. The struggle has produced a race apart, with its own speech and customs, its folklore and superstitions, and its odd survivals from a previous age, like the annual Plough Stots dance at Goathland which celebrates the day on which the plough was put into the ground after the Deluge.

The smithy at Hawes, a small market town in the North Riding. The way of life in the dale country was essentially self-contained until the development of mechanized transport which linked small communities with the larger towns and cities.

Harvesting at the foot of the Hambleton Hills, near Stokesley, in the North Riding. The hills in this area are notable for their magnificent cliff scenery, and amongst the highest peaks are Black Hambleton, 1257 feet, and Arden Moor, 1289 feet.

Famous hunting-packs can be found in this country, the Sinnington, Goathland, Bilsdale and Staintondale among them, which have their origins far back in history and which have produced a host of famous sporting characters. So closely, indeed, is hunting linked with the life of the area that up to quite recently local hunt fixtures were given out among the Sunday notices in many churches. Cleveland horses are noted and horses and hounds form the staple of talk in village inns and at the weekly markets.

This is the coloured corner of Yorkshire where the artist can be lavish with his palette. The roads are red, the bracken-covered slopes deep green or gold, according to the season, the miles of heather a sea of purple in autumn, and even the rocks and shales vary from bright red to a lustrous blue. The farmsteads and houses are colourful, too, and over all is the patina of a mellow age, for modernity has in general not entered here. Indeed, more than in any other part of Yorkshire superstition lingers here, with ancient ways and speech that remains unaltered.

An old shepherd summed it up when he said, "There be things as never change. Things 'as been done and said syne men lived on the moor that be done and said still the same. There's customs that'll never die as long as the Hand of Glory's among us." And he explained that the Hand of Glory was "the hand of a 'ooman burned for a witch that is a safeguard agen devils, small-pox, misfortune and death. But it only acts for the innercent." Stories of witches and goblins and familiar spirits still linger, though, for the most part, these supernatural folk appear to be a friendly or at worst a provocative company.

One of the familiar spirits of Farndale in the centre of these moors was known locally as Hob o' th' Hurst who played many demonic tricks on a moorland farmer. To rid himself of the spirit he decided to remove to another farm. He procured his place and set off with his furniture and implements. On the way he met an acquaintance who remarked in the obvious manner of a friend, "Ah see thoo's flittin'." A deep voice came from the recesses of the milk churn on the cart, "Ay, we's flittin'." Whereupon the troubled farmer turned his cart about. "Ey, if thoo's theer too," said he, "we may as well gan yam agean" (go home again).

### Life of the Moorland People

There are no large towns on these moors and the largest villages house no more than a few hundred families. Contact with the larger world tends to find outlet on the one side with the little towns of Yarm, Thirsk, Helmsley, Kirby Moorside and Pickering on the fringe of the Plain of York and on the other with the coast towns and villages of Redcar and Staithes, Whitby and Scarborough. Here and there modernity seeks to creep in, but only on the fringes, and even that is steadily assimilated into the ancient simple life of the moorland folk.

The older towns of Yorkshire, like York and Richmond and Ripon, are full of history and in them thought inevitably turns to the past. But the coastal towns—with a few exceptions—are cities of the future rather than of the past. Their history, though notable, is the least part of them, and having a less glorious past to trade upon it is to the future that they look.

Like all Britain's North Sea coast, the long line which runs between Spurn Head in the south and Redcar in the north had its historic moments. The Norsemen landed on this coast. There were Roman signal stations along it. Henry of Hereford (later Henry IV) made Hull his port of entry. Queen Henrietta Maria landed at Bridlington with weapons bought by the sale of the Crown Jewels of England to fight the Parliamentarians—it required five hundred carts to carry all her impedimenta to York.

Whitby's famous Abbey marks the early years of monasticism in England and gave us in the person of Caedmon, a stable servant at the monastery, the first of our great English poets. Whitby itself was once the fourth port of England. Scarborough Castle played its part in the Parliamentary War.

Despite all that and much more the Yorkshire coastline is today less a line of history than a vast playground for the rest of the county. To this magic pleasure-ground, almost all of which from Tees mouth to Humber estuary is easily accessible, come the majority of the families of Yorkshire for their annual holiday—the woolmen, the steel workers, the men of the pits and the tradesmen and office workers. Once quiet sleepy little fishing villages and towns have in the past century awakened to a new fame and glory and a new ugliness. Old crafts and trades have vanished or have been called upon to give a new allegiance to the crowds which flock to the sands and cliffs and spas. Former lordly mansions are popular hotels or holiday centres. Here each summer is spent much of the money accumulated during the year in the old and new industries of the rest of Yorkshire. The hand of modernity, sometimes in garish form, has this strip of Yorkshire in a strong grasp. Yet even so the old and mellowed can sometimes be seen between the fingers.

### Blending of Ancient and Modern

In Scarborough old and new are wonderfully mixed. It has cinemas, motor-boats, speed-boats, sailing-boats and a Spa where iron and magnesia waters are disguised with fruit juices, a gabled stone house where King Richard III once stayed, an ancient smuggling inn which boasts a ghost, and also on show a giant tunny fish or a baby seal caught in the bay. Even the museum displays side by side with early British urns and skeletons pieces of shell fired at the town by the German warships during the First World War.

Every town and village along the Yorkshire coast has, beside its more popular holiday streets, its old and quaint, yet colourful clusters of cottages, the homes still of successors of the men who built them, a distinctive race of men owing less

Aysgarth Lower Falls, pictured at Aysgarth. The village itself stands on the River Ure, which is here spanned by a bridge dating from the sixteenth century. The two waterfalls, above and below the bridge, are together known as the Aysgarth Force.

443

allegiance to Yorkshire than to the sea whence comes their livelihood. They are often dour, close-lipped and close-fisted, still a little suspicious of strangers save as customers for their fish or patrons of their boats, superstitious and rough. Yet they show skill and bravery, and there are innumerable stories of stirring journeys in their little cobbles or in the lifeboat to assist the crews of unlucky ships caught in the terrific storm waters along the coast.

When the holiday-makers depart at the end of the summer these men return to their ancient craft, no longer what it once was yet still important, and go out with their nets and their lobster and crab pots into the grim seas.

Outside of Hull, Yorkshire has no great port, but as the third largest port in Britain Hull, or more correctly Kingston-upon-Hull, acts as the ever-open gateway from the county to the world. Yorkshire's products of coal and steel and wool and a thousand other things besides, pass through Hull on their way to the ships, where in the course of trade they are exchanged for an inward flow of goods which, in the form of pit-props, go to the Don valley, as feeding-stuffs to the isolated farms of the dales, as iron ore to Hallamshire and as raw wool to the towns of Aire and Calder. The people of Hull are a cosmopolitan company, in Yorkshire yet for the most part not of it. They are, nevertheless, a vital link between the rich full life of the county and the larger world.

Spurn Head is Yorkshire's Land's End, a sandy, pebbly spit of land with the North Sea on one side and on the other, a mere three hundred yards away, the Humber estuary. Yet Spurn Head will one day have vanished like Ravenspur, Somert, Penisthorpe and a score of other places which have been swallowed up by the sea in the course of centuries. Something like seven feet of Yorkshire coastline along a strip nearly thirty-five miles long from Spurn to Bridlington are being eaten away by the sea each year—a depth of well over a mile since William the Conqueror landed. Farm folk have seen fields disappear in their own lifetime. House-owners have watched their homes slip inch by inch into the sea. There is an insistent call for national action to stop this steady erosion to which each tide remorselessly contributes. Yet perhaps after all Yorkshire is extensive enough to spare an annual tribute to the sea. It can still boast 3,890,990 acres, or more acres than there are letters in the Bible.

*Byland Abbey*

*Albert Square, Manchester*

# LANCASHIRE

(*Excluding Furness*)

## By JOHN WARDLE

MY THEME is Lancashire without Furness. With Furness goes Lancashire's share of Lakeland and, consequently, some may think, all of the county that has retained its natural beauty without blemish. This view must be challenged. Although industrial Lancashire measures little more than thirty-five miles from north to south and twenty-five from east to west, there is much more than mill and foundry, mine and murk within its irregular area. Someone has called it "Continental" Lancashire, thus distinguishing it from Furness across Morecambe Bay and at the same time implying its variety of features, people and products. And yet this compartment of England, now so renowned, was late by comparison with other English counties in achieving its identity, but, for all its slow emergence as an entity, it soon acquired a quasi-autonomous character that was ratified by the grant of palatinate status, conferring upon it, amongst other things, the right to hold certain special courts.

For long after the Romans had left Britain, however, the north-western part of this country was to all intents and purposes a waste. In the "Domesday Book" itself there is no mention of Lancashire. All the land between the Ribble and the Mersey is in that book included in Cheshire, and the land to the north of the Ribble in Yorkshire. Just when the county of Lancashire, in the shape we know it today, came into existence it is difficult to determine. Though the Pipe Rolls of 1168 refer to a county of Lancaster, that indicated merely the north of present Lancashire. True, the rest had broken away from Cheshire, but it had become a separate territorial division, "'twixt Ribble and Mersey." When the fusion did take place, "Lancastershire" and not "Lancashire" was the first title and, in the time of Henry VIII, Leland, the antiquarian, was still using it.

Certainly the form "Lancastershire" does

*Arms of Lancashire*

serve to show how the whole county has evolved from the Roman fortification that once stood on the hill above the Lune near its estuary—Lone caster, or Lune-castrum. Here, perhaps, is the moment to say something of the city of Lancaster and ensure for the county town the priority that is its due.

445

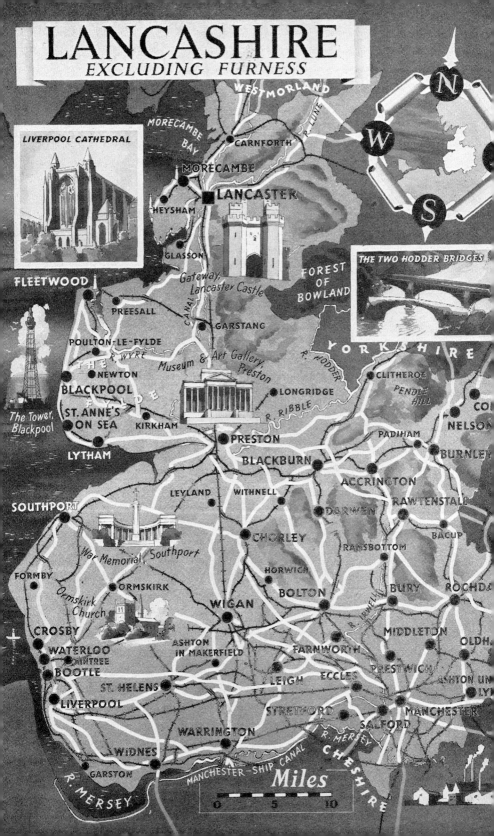

# LANCASHIRE
## EXCLUDING FURNESS

*LIVERPOOL CATHEDRAL*

*THE TWO HODDER BRIDGES*

WESTMORLAND

N
W
S

MORECAMBE BAY

CARNFORTH

MORECAMBE

LANCASTER

HEYSHAM

GLASSON

Gateway, Lancaster Castle

FOREST OF BOWLAND

FLEETWOOD

The Tower, Blackpool

PREESALL

POULTON-LE-FYLDE

R. WYRE

NEWTON

BLACKPOOL

ST. ANNE'S ON SEA

LYTHAM

CANAL

GARSTANG

Museum & Art Gallery Preston

R. HODDER

YORKSHIRE

CLITHEROE

PENDLE HILL

LONGRIDGE

R. RIBBLE

PADIHAM

COL

NELSON

BURNLEY

KIRKHAM

PRESTON

BLACKBURN

ACCRINGTON

LEYLAND

WITHNELL

DARWEN

RAWTENSTALL

BACUP

SOUTHPORT

War Memorial Southport

CHORLEY

RAMSBOTTOM

HORWICH

BURY

ROCHD

FORMBY

ORMSKIRK

Ormskirk Church

WIGAN

BOLTON

MIDDLETON

OLDH.

CROSBY

ASHTON IN MAKERFIELD

FARNWORTH

R. IRWELL

PRESTWICH

ASHTON UN

WATERLOO

AINTREE

BOOTLE

ST. HELENS

LEIGH

ECCLES

MANCHESTER

LIVERPOOL

STRETFORD

SALFORD

WARRINGTON

WIDNES

R. MERSEY

GARSTON

MANCHESTER-SHIP CANAL

CHESHIRE

R. MERSEY

## Miles

0     5     10

Lancaster has ceased to be the hub of the county, but it is, nevertheless, representative of the county as a whole. It has a large share in the county's typical industries, is intimately concerned with its agricultural output and is near to the sea, thus symbolizing the maritime character of Lancashire. It also epitomizes county history although the only obvious witnesses to its long past are the castle and the church of St. Mary. The town itself, except in odd corners, shows few remains of distant centuries. Visual evidence of its cotton spinning, cabinet making and linoleum manufacture is far more assertive; and, five miles along the Lune at Glasson Dock, ships of six hundred tons can berth. Engineering and railway wagon building are other industries. The inhabitants of Lancaster probably think as seldom about the castle and St. Mary's Church as do Londoners about the Tower and the Abbey or, if they remember them a little more often than that, it is only because the curiosity of visitors about their town is apt to come to their notice more frequently than the interest of the tourist in London does to the Londoner. The tourist is more conspicuous in Lancaster and something must be done to impress him. This urge to impress is true of Lancashire generally. Indeed, in some towns the degree of interest shown in the stranger is positively embarrassing. In Oldham, for example, he is a marked man. The interest is entirely benevolent but, if he likes to find his way about unassisted, let him be wary how he glances up at street names. Otherwise someone is bound to ask him where he wants to go and will probably insist on taking him all the way there.

### History of Lancaster Castle

But this trip to Oldham is a digression. We were making for Lancaster Castle. Of this castle the Saxon foundations still remain. More than that, the tower at its south-western corner is said to have been built in the time of Hadrian. As for the rest, most of it was built under the supervision of that forgotten Norman baron, Roger de Poictou, the virtual founder of Lancashire and consequently the first of its "lads," despite his Norman blood. The Assize courts are now held there and, in the seventeenth century, the castle saw the trials immortalized by Harrison Ainsworth, of the wretched Lancashire "witches." At Lancaster they were hanged, though Mother Demdike escaped that fate by dying before her trial.

The deep-rooted superstitions of Lancashire are illustrated by these notorious trials, but it has to be remembered that witchcraft in the seventeenth century, with a monarch and other eminent people writing sober treatises upon it, was a serious issue. More typical of Lancashire superstition was the belief in "boggarts," spirits sometimes just hideous and malevolent, at others imbued with a kind of slapstick mischief in the manner of the poltergeist. Lancashire's superstitions are today nearly all forgotten in the necessity of concentrating on earning a livelihood.

### Agriculture versus Industry

To see Lancashire in perspective both physically and economically, one must consider the east and south separately from the west and north. Until the time of the Industrial Revolution, that mixed blessing, or slightly mitigated curse, Lancashire was predominantly rural. Mechanical occupations, in so far as they existed, were domestic. In the richer farming districts there was little need to manufacture more than was required by the family itself or its neighbours, but in the bleaker areas, where only a meagre living could be wrung from the soil, some means of augmenting that livelihood had to be found. Not only did the bleak slopes of the Pennines force the inhabitants to look for an activity that would eke out a too bare livelihood; they also provided the conditions in which such an activity could be followed— humidity of atmosphere due to ample rainfall and abundance of streams with considerable power of fall. When spinning and weaving of imported cotton came to be undertaken, here were the conditions required both to obviate breakages of thread and to supply power when the factory system was introduced. When water power was supplanted by steam, new factories were built in these east and south-east Lancashire villages. The villages rapidly enlarged into towns through the feverish building of mills and of houses for the incoming hordes of country folk turned operatives. Thus we find today that the east and south of the county is largely industrial though, in the extreme south, fine wheat crops are produced.

What of the west? The Pennines, we have seen, compensated for scanty agricultural resources by providing the conditions in which the textile industry could thrive. Conversely, the west, much of it lacking those conditions (the average rainfall of the Lancashire plain is no more than that of some southern counties), discouraged the factory pioneers from attempts at development in its territory. As, however, along with agriculture, coal-mining had for centuries been a feature of its life, a cumulative spoiling of certain areas went on through the mounting of slag-heaps. Apart from the mining areas and a few such centres as St. Helens—famous for its glass—the Lancashire plain is green and unspoiled, as soon as one has escaped from the ribbon-developed property flanking some of its roads.

### Cultivation of Crops

There is a high density of population, too, if one remembers it is not always human beings only that are counted. Poultry has its census, also, and the poultry population of Lancashire—most of it concentrated in that part of the western plain called the Fylde—is greater than that of any other English county. Potatoes, too, are grown in great quantity and those from the Southport district are noted for their excellence. Their pedigree dates from the eighteenth century, in the early part of which a ship wrecked at Southport scattered its cargo of potatoes on what was then beach, but is now boulevard. The planting of these spoils of the sea constituted, though not the earliest, certainly one of the most successful, experiments in potato-growing in England. Tomatoes, a comparatively modern crop and, of course, under glass, occupy whole acres between Preston and Lancaster. Before the transi-

tion to motor transport had reached its present stage, there was also much breeding of sturdy dray-horses in the Fylde, chiefly for use in Liverpool.

Running through part of the West Lancashire plain is the River Wyre and, on the southern bank of its estuary, stands Fleetwood. The grain-elevator by its docks is a landmark for miles, but it is not by grain alone that Fleetwood lives. Its steam trawlers bring in vast catches of fish from as far away as Iceland. Fleetwood is a thriving holiday resort, too; though it does not possess so overwhelming a variety of "attractions" as its neighbour Blackpool, it offers considerable opportunity for turning leisure into strenuous exertion. It is still a port for steamer services to the Isle of Man.

### Playground of Lancashire

Blackpool is not only Lancashire on holiday but a representative part of Britain on holiday into the bargain, and October is usually out before the town is again comparatively deserted. It all began about 1750, by which time the black pool of peaty water, which is known to have existed, had probably disappeared. A few clay cottages were all that gave it identity, but Ethart Whiteside, having found that the woman he had married was the only person about the place who knew anything about cookery, thought he might as well turn the discovery to financial profit. He turned one of the larger cottages into a house of entertainment. All provisions had to be brought from the old market town of Poulton, then the metropolis of the Fylde, over roads so foul that even packhorses found them an adventure. They did not, however, deter strolling players from paying occasional visits, though this was a "date" that they can scarcely have reached by strolling. Their entertainments were the precursors of the Tower circus, the fun fair, the theatres and the cinemas and dance halls of today.

There was another pool that gave its name to a famous Lancashire centre, but the bird from which the pool itself took its name has so far baffled all attempts by ornithologists to identify it. It perches,

A network of canals connects Lancashire's manufacturing towns with the county's commercial centre of Manchester. The canal seen here is at Wigan, an ancient town which is the centre of Lancashire's coal industry and important in the cotton trade.

nevertheless, in imaginative effigy above the Liver building, with the Mersey and most of Liverpool spread out below it.

They say in Wigan that King John "planted" Liverpool. They wish it to be understood that Liverpool, although it had got its charter thirty-nine years earlier, is a parvenu compared with Wigan, which had been a town for centuries when King John, seeing the great possibilities of a port in the land that lay about a creek at the mouth of the Mersey, bargained for it with Henry

The Liverpool–Manchester arterial road, an example of the modernity of Lancashire's communications. Today it is no less important than was the Liverpool–Manchester railway a century ago.

Fitzwarine and attracted settlers to it by issuing, in 1207, letters patent conferring upon the place a status equal to that of "any free borough upon the sea." Liverpool did not, however, acquire much of a status until the seventeenth century had nearly reached its close. Then its participation in the slave trade made its fortune. In 1807, when the traffic was abolished, Liverpool had been transporting annually some fifty thousand slaves from West African ports to America and the West Indies where they were exchanged for cotton, sugar and rum.

Even after Liverpool had ceased to traffic in slaves, it continued to receive the product of their labour. Bales of cotton were unloaded at its docks long before the Negro workers on American plantations received their freedom.

Cotton is, of course, only a part, though a large one, of the story. Liverpool now

nks second among the ports of Britain (it
is thirty-four miles of quays). The huge
ladstone Dock (Gladstone was born in
verpool) is one of ninety that stretch for
ven miles along the Lancashire bank of
e Mersey.

## Achievements in Architecture

In the city of Liverpool, before the hand
war was laid upon it, architects had
hieved the magnificent. Every city has its
rdid aspects, but the nineteenth century
d done its best. How good that best
uld be is illustrated by the colonnaded
. George's Hall, built to the design of
arvey Lonsdale Elmes, who was only
enty-six when the foundation stone was
d in 1838. The oldest public building in
verpool, the Town Hall, belongs to the
ghteenth century though its dome was
ded in the nineteenth. The Walker Art
allery is the finest in the provinces. Its
hibits range from thirteenth century
lian works to those of Picasso. As
chitecture, the Liver building is not
garded seriously, but it has its own
gnity and is an impressive feature in the
award façade.

The two greatest glories of Liverpool's
chitecture are, however, still in the
ture, though one, the Anglican cathedral,
also visibly and beautifully in the present.
e other, the Catholic cathedral, has begun
rise in a quarter that has hitherto been
ved from drabness only by the presence
' the university. When completed, this
nception of Sir Edwin Lutyens will be
nger than any other cathedral in England
d will have a dome even greater than St.
ter's in Rome.

Liverpool again showed faith in the
eas of youth when Sir Giles Gilbert
cott's design for the Anglican cathedral
as accepted. He was then twenty-one.
he foundation stone was laid in 1904.
ow in red sandstone the fabric, rising
om St. James's Mount, crowns the city.
asically it is Gothic, but it conforms to no
an but its own highly individual one,
nsisting of choir, nave, double transepts
d what is called the central space. This
st is the lower portion of the cathedral
wer and stretches the full width of the

building. An octagonal chapter-house is
built at the north-east corner and, at the
south-east, is the lady chapel, which was
the first part of the cathedral to be consecrated. In the great nave of the cathedral
itself not a single pillar is reared. The
tower now has its full height of three
hundred and eight feet above floor level,
and is roofed with copper. In the tower will
be hung a peal of twelve bells that will be
the heaviest in the world.

The cathedral is in the high background
of the panorama towards which the incoming liners steam. The ancient little
church of St. Nicholas used to greet them in
the foreground, but war has altered that.
The Liver building escaped destruction,
but the domed Customs House was one
of the first casualties. Miles of dockside
property were razed or gutted, obliterated
shopping areas became temporary car
parks, the Walker Art Gallery and the
Public Library were severely damaged and
twenty-five thousand books were destroyed
in the latter. St. George's Hall itself might
have perished, but prompt action ex-
tinguished its blazing roof. China Town,
once full of Oriental immigrants, is no
more, and at Bootle most of the workers'
houses were destroyed. This sad list says
nothing of what happened at Birkenhead
and elsewhere on the Cheshire bank of the
Mersey.

## The Mersey Tunnel

Birkenhead must, however, be brought
into the story for one thing—the Mersey
Tunnel. We have stared at scars long
enough, and may lower our gaze to this
marvel of engineering and architecture
below land and water. Not that the architecture is all beneath the surface. There are
six ventilating stations, with towers ranging
in height from ninety-three to two hundred
and ten feet. It was in the face of much
opposition that the tunnel was made and
not before the alternative of bridging the
Mersey had been more than once considered. There had been a railway tunnel
between Liverpool and Birkenhead ever
since 1885, but, despite the growing in-
adequacy of the ferry service to deal with
road vehicles, it was December 1925

before everything was ready for the Princess Royal (then Princess Mary) to switch on the pneumatic drills. Nine years later, the tunnel was opened by King George V. It is not the longest under-river tunnel in the world, being little over two miles in length, but its wall-to-wall breadth of forty-four feet makes it the widest. It can take four thousand vehicles per hour and has a control room where intelligence of everything happening within the tunnel is received and all necessary action taken, from adjustment of ventilation to the telephoning of instructions to patrols or the signalling of messages to drivers.

If you journey from Liverpool to Manchester by rail, you travel over a classic track, for the first of all British passenger railway routes was opened between Manchester and Liverpool in 1830. On that line Stephenson's world-famous locomotive, "Rocket," passed its test.

The famous Ship Canal was cut through the plain in defiance of as much opposition as that encountered by the advocates of the Mersey Tunnel, but, when the Canal was opened in 1894, Manchester became virtually a seaport town. The canal is thirty-five and a half miles long and can take ships up to fifteen thousand tons. At the Man-

chester end there are eight docks coveri one hundred and twenty acres, and tv hundred and eighty-six acres more quays. The biggest dock is over half mile long. Industry has taken root alo the canal. The seventy miles of deep wa frontage have been the attraction. Barton the Bridgewater Canal passes abo the Ship Canal by means of an aquedu that can swing clear to allow the passa of ocean-going ships. The Bridgewa Canal is a monument to the enterprise the third Duke of Bridgewater and t resourcefulness of James Brindley, engineer. It conveyed coal from the Duk pits at Worsley to Manchester twenty-fi years before the steam engine was ready f Manchester's use.

Like Liverpool, Manchester, and pa ticularly its docks, shows the scars terrible air raids. In the city itself most the havoc was wrought in one hea attack just before Christmas 1940. T Royal Exchange, the Free Trade H (home of the Hallé Orchestra as well as memorial to the anti-Corn Laws campai of Cobden and Bright) and square miles business property were all gutted on th night. Manchester, Salford and, even mc so, Liverpool, bore the brunt of the blitz

**The village of Downham is widely known in Lancashire for its beauty. Far from factories and min it lies in unspoilt country on the Yorkshire border near Clitheroe and the Ribble Valley.**

ycoller, near Colne, with its packhorse bridge, is known to readers of Charlotte Brontë's *Jane Eyre* as the home of Jane's lover, Edward Rochester. The Brontës lived nearby at Haworth.

r Lancashire. Elsewhere in the county the ids were haphazard. But for Manchester d Salford the 1940 raid succeeded where ecades of social reformers had failed. removed acres of evil slums, though at avy cost to the unfortunate inhabitants.

Manchester appears to have resolved to d the remaining squalor, of which there far too much in workaday Lancashire. Bolton or Warrington, for example, ne soon comes upon it. Manchester, owever, has published its plans for a etter future. They are thorough and enghtened. This is characteristic. It may seem aradoxical that an appreciation of the rts, and consequently beauty, has long een manifest in Manchester, a city which n an average first glance, apart from a few nodern features such as the town hall xtensions and the public library, is about s ugly as the less morbid can imagine. et love of art and scholarship have gone and in hand with its money-making. The ohn Rylands Library, wedged among uildings in Deansgate, is one of the finest n the world. It is especially rich in ancient manuscripts. As architecture it is one of the best examples of perpetuated Gothic. Firebombs destroyed its closest neighbour in 1940, but left the library untouched. Manchester was the first of the provincial cities, outside Oxford and Cambridge, to build a university. De Quincey was only one of the famous men educated at its Grammar School, but appears to have been the only one who ran away from it. The *Manchester Guardian* guards far more than Manchester, standing everywhere for fearless, but balanced journalism. Miss Horniman's brilliant players at the Gaiety Theatre were the pioneers of the modern repertory theatre in Britain. The Hallé Orchestra now gives performances all over the north and sometimes visits London and the Continent.

Manchester's past is not seen in its streets without close observation. In front of the cathedral stands the statue of Oliver Cromwell in commemoration of the time when his forces held Manchester against the Royalists massed on the other bank of the Irwell in Salford, Lancashire's third

453

city. Close to the cathedral, but hidden by its own outer walls and the fire-gaunt shell of the original Grammar School, is Manchester's most historic building, Chetham's Hospital and Library. Here the seventeenth century has been kept alive, not by the building itself, which is older, but by the costume its boys still wear.

Manchester's trades and manufactures are legion. It is still the cotton metropolis, but it is now the buying and selling of cotton that is its business. Spinning, weaving, bleaching and printing have been delegated to the satellite towns. Even in these there exist, side by side with cotton and rayon, at least forty-two other industries of international importance. Among the oldest of all is coal-mining and, besides those ancillary to the textile industry, such as the manufacture of mill machinery, there is the construction of locomotives, cars, aeroplanes and general engineering of every kind. Paper making, soap manufacture and chemical industries may be added. Many of the new and lighter industries have also come to stay. The situation of the textile industry is a transitional one. What little can be said of it will be better saved for a later paragraph.

### Lancashire Cricket

Let us take our farewell of Manchester at Old Trafford, even though it means returning towards the Ship Canal. This famous cricket ground is a battlefield for a war of the Roses that is far more the concern of modern Lancashire than are "old unhappy far-off things and battles long ago." Old Trafford recruits its players from the amateur teams of small Lancashire townships, such as Westhoughton, which bred the Tyldesleys.

It is time to speak of these smaller towns (though some of them are huge enough) that specialize in producing the textiles that Manchester markets. They all have a variety of other activities that are anything but sidelines. Bury has its paper, Bolton a lot of things, including leather, Preston an unrealized significance as a port. They share, too, Lancashire's inheritance of ugliness already mentioned, but some, like Oldham and again Bolton, are fortunate in

being near to wide moorland. Others, li Accrington or Haslingden, in spite of joyless appearance, have at least a certa dignified solidity through the prevalence the local stone used in their buildings. A have some odd areas or, perhaps, no mo than corners, of beauty. Chorley, indee right at its centre, has the graceful Astl Hall in a green setting. Maligned Wiga has wooded dells close at hand.

### Expansion of Cotton Industry

The sudden expansion in Lancashi cotton spinning and weaving that occurre in the eighteenth century was due to tl inventive genius of Lancashire men. T 1738 both processes were effected by han but when John Kay, of Bury, devised tl flying shuttle, he at once supplied a gre impetus to weaving, and spinners we unable to cope with weavers' deman until, in 1766, a Blackburn man, Jam Hargreaves, evolved the spinning jenn Then came a barber, Richard Arkwrigh of Preston and later of Bolton, who, by more complicated device, the roller, accele ated spinning still further. Finally, Samu Crompton, of Bolton, constructed h famous "mule," so called because combined the principles of Hargreaves an Arkwright. This, together with the arriv of steam power, sent Lancashire's yar output soaring, but Crompton reaped littl financial benefit.

Though all processes of the industry ar carried on in some textile towns, it i usual for concentration to be placed on on or the other of them. Bolton and Oldhar are spinning towns, Bolton for the fine and Oldham for the coarser counts. Black burn, on the other hand, is essentially weaving centre, and so is Preston. Roch dale, famous as the birth-place of th Co-operative movement, specializes in fin counts, but has also a considerable woolle industry.

The transitional stage of Lancashire' textile industry is reflected in the intensiv plans for its reorganisation. Recruitin drives for labour are in progress, but toda labour has a much wider field of choice tha ever before. So far as hours of work are con cerned, there has been great improvemen

Blackpool beach and Tower

since the bad old days when, every morning at 6 o'clock, each Lancashire town echoed to the thunder of innumerable wooden clogs slapping on cobbles as the mill operatives trooped to work: but working conditions are still not uniformly good. The more progressive firms in pre-war years had excellent welfare services and this policy is now being adopted more generally. There are still operatives of the older generation who, after a lifetime of midday meals taken in the wheelgate (*i.e.* the way between the wheels), despise the canteen. Others resort to the handy alternative of the fish-and-chip shop. For many families the fish-and-chip shop has for years provided also the evening meal. Textile processes absorb so much female labour that it is usual for women to remain in employment after marriage. Children if too young to attend school, must be left with relations during the day and, after work is over, the meal that can be most quickly obtained is the most popular; hence the abundance of fish-and-chip shops. The care of the very young children of employees may become in future the responsibility of the mill management.

456

The Liver building (seen centre) is an impressive feature of the Liverpool waterfront. On the right are the domed Docks offices.

have weathered bad times before and are at their best in a dour fight for existence.

Lancashire has another product, very much for export. Rochdale is as proud of its Gracie Fields as of the Co-operative movement. It is through Gracie, both the George Formbys, Douglas Wakefield and all their contemporaries and predecessors, that the entire world knows something of Lancashire character. Our comedians are not the least of our ambassadors.

The Lancashire character is not so obvious in street, mill, office and farm as it is upon the music-hall stage. Modernity has done much to mitigate its sharper or more distinctive features. They are, however, still recognizable if one observes closely enough, whether in local bigwig, shop assistant, school-teacher, doctor, spinner or humble tackler. The tackler provides an illustration of Lancashire humour. For some reason he is regarded as a well-meaning creature hampered by inferior intelligence and is the object of amused contempt softened by affection. Lancashire as a whole has accepted him as the typical bungler. Consequently a whole literature—or rather, lore—of tackler stories brightens Lancashire existence.

Besides cricket and football, sport in all its forms from pigeon-flying to trout fishing is almost a matter of life and death to us. And, however coarse canal-side fishing may be, it seems to breed a fine patience. Bowls is played so intensively that from the air the grimiest town must appear to be dotted with spots of brilliant green. The miner still races the whippets he bred before the greyhound chased the hare at Waterloo and even longer before its electric quarry was switched into flight.

Fine things are grouped under an ugly name—culture. Lancashire knows much about them and is learning more. For formal education there are two universities, the public schools of Rossall, Stonyhurst and Merchant Taylors', the Manchester Grammar School and many other fine

during the hours that the mothers are at work. There is much reason to believe that the textile industry's future is hopeful, though opinions vary as to how far ahead its best times may be. So far as cotton is concerned, certainly the position as portrayed by the latest figures of the Board of Trade is not a happy one. Not only are there far fewer mules working than in 1950 or 1951, but far fewer operatives are employed, and the output of cotton (though not of rayons, etc.) is barely three-quarters of what the industry produced in the earlier post-war years. But the Lancashire manufacturers

The large quantity of coal available in south-east Lancashire has been an important factor in the county's great industrial development. The coalmine seen here is typical of the landscape in this area

schools and vocational colleges. But another kind of education is everywhere evident, a growing appreciation of art, music and the theatre and active participation in all three. Not only in Liverpool and Manchester, but in smaller centres, these matters are becoming a part of the life of the people and not merely the obsessions of a few devoted groups. Clubs fostered by the Arts Council are becoming typical Lancashire institutions alike in industrial and rural areas. The membership of the Arts Club at Haslingden, a town of seventeen thousand people, is already a thousand. It is a pity that Dunsop Bridge, near the Trough of Bowland, happens to be just a matter of yards over the Yorkshire boundary, for, with a mere handful of two

hundred inhabitants, keen members maintain an arts club in vigorous life.

Though it is by this dart into Yorkshire that we have escaped from the industrial region, we shall still be well clear of it as we walk back the little way that separates us from Lancashire. In the pass called the Trough of Bowland we are still on the border, but whether we walk south-east towards Clitheroe or north-west towards Lancaster, nothing of an industrial kind will obtrude itself for miles. To the north-west Lancaster would show the first concentration of it and, after that, there would only be Carnforth with its iron-smelting works. The rest is fell country, at its best when the heather is in bloom, descending northwards to the River Lune and westward

458

as far as the plains of the Fylde, which we have already visited.

This chapter must end in an advance towards the heart of a county in which it has left so much unexplored, but it will not go far enough south to run into the smoke again. Here on these uplands, as we begin the descent to Clitheroe, we may try to remember some of the men and women not hitherto mentioned whose fame, either because of their work for the county or their birth in it, is also Lancashire's. Charlotte de la Trémouille, wife of the seventh Earl of Derby, remembered for her heroic defence of Lathom House against the Parliamentarians, only to lose her husband to the headsman's axe at Bolton; George Fox, the Quaker, Sir Robert Peel, John Morley and (of all surprises) David Lloyd George, who was born at Manchester. For scientists, Dalton and Joule; for art, George Romney and Turner ("The Crook of Lune"); for good citizenship, Richard Owen; for journalism at its noblest, C. P. Scott; for enlightened commerce, William Hesketh Lever, first Viscount Leverhulme; for music, William Walton and Alan Rawsthorne; for the theatre, Robert Donat and Stanley Houghton. The list would be long: but here is Clitheroe. Its Norman keep on a limestone rock is only a ruin, interesting mainly because it is the smallest in England. Old Pendle towers above the town. Not far away is the village of Downham, which is to Lancashire what Broadway is to the Midlands. In the fifteenth-century tower of Downham's church hang three bells from Whalley Abbey.

And Whalley, in the vale of Calder, had better be the last of our Lancashire scenes or we shall be in Blackburn again. Because of its abbey and its church, Whalley belongs to the past, but it lies on the fringe of modernity. In spite of even its gravest misdemeanours, there are signs that modernity has at last some faculty, however incipient, for self-criticism. When its infiltration of Whalley has become occupation, perhaps it will have learned how to occupy gracefully. Meanwhile Cistercian ruins possess the scene with a grace that the feeblest imagination can recognize. The road south from the Abbey conforms to past and present, going first beneath a centuries-old arch and later under the railway.

*St. George's Hall, Liverpool*

Close to the famous Langdale Pikes, Chapel Stile, with farms and houses dating from the seven‑
teenth century, is familiar to many visitors who make the village a starting point for Loughrigg Tar‑

*Bowland Bridge*

# WESTMORLAND

### By KATHARINE CHORLEY

'PLANE PILOT'S view, flying over the long axis of south and east Westmorland from the Lancashire border north-west of Carnforth towards Appleby, would reveal a stretch of English country waved into grey and green hills and valleys in the south and moulded into sterner fells of heather and tussocky grass towards the east where the Pennines enclose the uppermost waters of the Eden. He would receive an impression of endless interlacing grey stone walls climbing the hillsides to mix with an occasional limestone outcrop on their tops and girdling the fields of a mixed farming economy on the lower levels. He would see sappy pastures where cattle and a few sheep are munching contentedly and in spring meadows of lush hay-grass and ploughland stencilled with the brilliant green of young oats or the quieter colour of some root crop. He would notice the grey solid farmhouses and outbuildings with hard-bitten elms beside them and a spray of damson blossom, the grey villages lying snug in folds and hollows, the country houses standing quiet and sturdy in their parkland. But he would observe none of the familiar signs of large-scale industry, tall chimneys, the canopies of smoke and the huddle of factories.

For Westmorland is a country of isolated farms and villages joined by winding grey-walled roads. The population of the whole county of five hundred thousand acres is only some sixty thousand. The towns are but four in number: Windermere and Bowness, Kirkby Stephen, Appleby and Kendal. Windermere and Bowness belong to the Lake District, dealt with in a separate chapter. Kirkby Stephen is scarcely more than a courtesy town though it has an ancient Grammar School and holds a market; there remain Appleby in the north-east and Kendal in the south.

*Arms of Westmorland*

Appleby, the smallest county town in England, has only a couple of thousand inhabitants. When you drive down from the Pennines along its streets about which the young Eden curls so as almost to encircle the town, you pass along a thoroughfare which

461

many people affirm is one of the loveliest main streets that can be found in any
country town. Closed by the castle at one
end and the church at the other, you feel at
once that air of sleepy casual activity which
pervades all little towns which live on partly
because they are centres for country men's
buying and selling and partly because they
are vestigial survivors of an economy now
long extinct but which once gave them purpose and energy. Appleby's heyday was,
indeed, long ago. In 1388, the Scots, in one
of their more daring border raids, burned
the town—the account of the destruction
and the difficulty of identifying the ruined
streets afterwards reads like the report of a
blitz—and Appleby seems never properly to
have recovered her prosperity, which must
once have been considerable since she was
one of the twenty principal towns of the
kingdom which sent burgesses to the Parliament of Edward I. The right to return two
members to Westminster remained until the
town was disfranchised in 1832.

Today, no one in Appleby makes anything in a factory, but the old Grammar
School, which has educated an astonishi
succession of bishops, still flourishes. T
town fills up on market days and to remi
it of its former dignity, one of His Majesty
judges on circuit proceeds twice a year in
the little courthouse escorted by his Sherif
Guard of javelin men, for Appleby is still
Assize town.

By every present fact of economic acti
ity and intellectual life, Kendal has a far b
ter claim than Appleby to be the coun
town of Westmorland. With a population
twenty thousand, it is the only town of a
size in the county. It has a museum,
excellent library, a large and flourishi
Grammar School, a Girl's High Scho
Kendal people run concerts and a music
festival of more than local note, a debati
society and a lively political life divided b
tween predominant conservatives and
knot of energetic radicals and socialists.

The woollen industry for which Kend
has been chiefly famous had its send-off
the time of Edward I who is said to ha
granted letters patent for the manufactu
of wool to a Flemish weaver, one Jol

**A gallop for a buyer at Appleby Horse Fair. Although long past its heyday, Appleby still has the a
of activity common to all little towns which serve the countryman as centres for buying and sellin**

A view of the village of Underbarrow, three miles west of Kendal. Nearly all the farm buildings in the area are set amongst damson orchards, the fruit from which is marketed in Kendal.

Kemp. The cheaper weaves were left to their natural colour, but the better cloth was dyed green by immersion first in a solution of yellow saw-wort and then in blue woad. The cloth was used throughout the length and breadth of England; Shakespeare refers to Kendal green as we should talk of Lancashire cottons or Harris tweed. But it was a coarse cloth, because the wiry fleece of the fell sheep does not admit of fine working up, and, as dress became better all through the country, Kendal cloth came to be used for horse-cloths, rugs, linseys, dusters and so forth. A grand tweed was also manufactured, a tweed which for wear and pattern could rival any Scottish production, but for no very clear reason this industry declined and the last tweed mill was closed down about 1931.

Today Kendal is the headquarters of a great insurance company; it has engineering works and breweries and an assortment of small manufactures, such as carpetmaking, woollens, tobacco-milling, brush-making. There are paper mills at Burneside, a mile or two outside the town, but the most important manufacture, the industry which has taken the place of Kendal green in national celebrity, is bootmaking.

Kendal cattle-market is known far afield. Buyers come from Yorkshire for bullocks and cows and take them off to be fattened in Lincolnshire and the Midlands for slaughtering.

Visitors from the south sometimes dismiss Kendal as a surly town. Its old and heavy buildings of grey stone can certainly look pretty dour under a lowering sky and the Kent flowing under its fine bridges chill and forbidding. But when a sparkle of sun glints over the town, Kendal lights up; the gleam and shadow play over the solid Georgian

banks and on the smart stone façade of the new County Hall and about the lovely stone-work of the old parish church in its corner by the river. If you lean over the parapet and watch the sunlight on the steady flow of the water, you think of the fishermen who are casting for salmon a few miles upstream, or even of those long dead fishermen who caught salmon in the Kent in days when they were so plentiful that Kendal apprentices won a clause in their articles which for-bade their masters to feed them on salmon more than three (or was it four?) times a week.

The direction from which one approaches a town matters very much to one's impression of its character. Pater has a description of the approach to Chartres across the corn-land of La Beauce in which he likens the cathedral soaring above the surrounding plain to a ship for ever a-sail in the distance. Few English towns have such a fine

employs more than one or two labourers. Thus it is essentially a peasant economy and peasants are seldom romantics and idealists. Westmorland farmers use and respect their dogs as a good company officer uses and respects his N.C.Os, but they never spoil them. They love and abide by their land as they love and abide by their families with a tenacious and tough affection, but they do not romanticize either. Intellectuals from an urban civilization may romanticize the farmer's life by contrast with the life of the factory or the office, but the men and women who, in fact, give their lives to serving the land are realists, and the harder the climate against which they have to protect their stock and raise their crops the less likely they are to look at their lives through tinted spectacles.

### Agricultural Produce

South Westmorland is certainly a difficult and capricious farmer's climate. A single night of May frost in the Winster and Lyth valleys, and how often it comes, may sear the creamy sprays of damson blossom which gleam around every group of farm buildings like foam breaking on big rocks. There is always a doubt as to whether there will be a damson crop in late September to take to Kendal market, and when, as sometimes happens, the crop is extra heavy, the glut will make it scarcely worth the picking for a few pence a pound. Apples and pears are gnarled except in sheltered nooks. Raspberries and gooseberries grow well in the damp gardens and most farmers have a few, but they are not kitchen gardeners, and vegetables are rare; they prefer tinned peas. But sometimes they make an excellent cheese, soft and crumbly and a little sour, and they cure hams, smoky and rich with spices, as they do also in the county of Cumberland. The weather is always of keen concern to the Westmorland man. You come up from the south and it is the first topic of discussion, nor is it a mere conventional opening gambit for a conversation. "We've had no

pleasant approach as Kendal from the railway; it appears as a grey mountain town seen through a translucent haze of smoke and lying safe in the lap of hills whose flanks are washed by the thin golden sunshine of the north.

The people of south Westmorland are apt to be hard-bitten, hard-fisted and hardmouthed. Farms are small or medium-sized compared with the acreages of Midland or East Anglian farms and a farmer seldom

# CUMBERLAND, FURNE

**THE LANGDALE PIKES**

**NAPES NEEDLE**

**L.M.S. DOCK, BARROW**

SOLWAY FIRTH

WORKINGTON MARYPORT

Ivon Shipb

WHITEHAVEN Coal

COCKERMOUTH R. DERWENT

EGREMONT LOWESWATER

C U M B

ENNERDALE WATER BASSENTHWAITE

SEASCALE CRUMMOCK WATER

GOSFORTH GRISEDALE PIKE 2595 BASSENT

PILLAR FELL 2927 BUTTERMERE

RAVENGLASS WASTWATER KESWICK

The Screes GT. GABLE 2950 SADI

R. ESK DERWENTWATER

BOOT GT. END 2984 THIRLMERE

DEVOKE WATER SCAFELL PIKE 3210

BOWFELL 2960 HELVELLYN 3118

BLACK COMBE LANGDALE PIKES 2403

OLD MAN 2635 GRASMERE ULLSWA

BROUGHTON CONISTON Grasmere HIGH ST. (ROM

MILLOM PATTERDALE

CONISTON WATER RYDAL

HAWKSHEAD HIGH ST. 2663 HAWES WATER

BARROW DALTON AMBLESIDE

FURNESS ESTHWAITE WATER

ISLAND ULVERSTON WINDERMERE

WALNEY FURNESS ABBEY WINDERMERE BOWNESS

Pier NEWBY BRIDGE W E S T M O

MORECAMBE BAY CARTMEL KENDAL

GRANGE R. KENT

ARNSIDE TEBAY R. LUNE

MILNTHORPE Limestone Quarry

BURTON

KIRKBY LONSDALE

L A N C A S H I R E

# WESTMORLAND

## INCLUDING THE LAKES

NOTE: The dotted line defining the area of the LAKE DISTRICT is based approximately on the recommendations contained in the Command Paper "National Parks in England & Wales" by John Dower

GT. GABLE

BOWNESS

R. ESK

WIGTON

LONGTOWN

HADRIAN'S

R. EDEN

CARLISLE

Lanercost Priory

BEWCASTLE

SIGHTY CRAG 1702

WALL

CALDEW

John Peel"

...le Cathedral

WETHERAL

LANERCOST PRIORY

BRAMPTON

R. IRTHING

NORTHUMBERLAND

Bridge, Penrith

Wrestlers

COLD FELL 2039

WASTWATER, The Screes

KIRKOSWALD

C H A I N

PENRITH

R. SOUTH-TYNE

E A M O N T

ALSTON

KENDAL

CROSS FELL 2930

P E N N I N E

APPLEBY

YORKSHIRE

Market Cross, Brough

W

N

BROUGH

S

E

ASHNESS BRIDGE

— BLAKE —

## Miles

0    5    10

**The ruins of the twelfth century castle at Brough. This castle, like those at Appleby and Brougham, was built by the Normans on the route from the north as a bastion against the Border raids.**

rain for a month. There's nowt growing." That means the ley grass will be light and no good for hay. Or later in the year: "They didn't get yon hay in Sunday an' now look at that," and he cocks his head towards Morecambe Bay, where indigo bulging clouds are trundling in from Ireland. Or, maybe you come in late August to see the fields of oats which swung so bravely in the wind in June laid in bleak patches, a mottled mass of grey-green and dim yellow.

### Castles and Manors

Livestock are more dependable, but the south Westmorland farmer does not graze sheep on the scale that the dalesmen of the Lake District, who have the open fells, can manage. His main reliance is on his stock-breeding and dairying. Surplus milk is collected every day and taken to Milnthorpe, where it is processed into liquid tinned milk.

Perhaps because south Westmorland is a hilly country and farms are isolated, and perhaps because the people are, like their confrères in Cumberland and Furness, des-

cendants of a virile and self-reliant race, the squire-parson-tenant relationship is not conspicuous.

There are a fair number of big manor houses with old traditions in the county, and along the ancient, and once the only, route from the north into the heart of England, up the Eden valley and over the pass of Stainmoor, stand the ruins of three castles built for strategic purposes by the Norman conquerors who were subduing this land at the beginning of the twelfth century. Brough and Brougham are deserted, and Appleby alone has been adapted to meet modern requirements.

Lowther Castle, a great mass of building on the site of an old hall, is relatively modern. But Lowthers have held the land since 1315 and in the eighteenth and nineteenth centuries increased their possessions to an almost fabulous extent in both Westmorland and Cumberland. Thirty-seven livings in the diocese of Carlisle were in their presentation and before the Reform Bill they could rely on returning nine of their own men to Parliament. Today these vast estates are in commission and the Lonsdale legend is embodied by the former Earl of Lonsdale who was, before his death, the great Westmorland figure, and, indeed, the great national figure of the sporting world. Everyone who remembers the Grasmere Sports before the First World War carries a picture in his mind of Lonsdale pomp and circumstance. Early in the day, you would see the Lonsdale *cortège* proceeding down the pass of Dunmail Raise, the splendid horses drawing a succession of canary yellow coaches in which rode the Lonsdale house-party headed by the old Earl with his stocky figure and blunt red face, his cigar and grey topper, his yellow waistcoat and grey morning coat with the large bright button-hole. Yellow is the Lonsdale livery colour and in Cumberland and Westmorland to this day Conservatives wear yellow on election day instead of the traditional Tory blue.

In the southern section of the county, Kendal Castle, where Catherine Parr was born, is a ruin, but Stricklands have held Sizergh Castle, a little farther down the Kent, since the time of King John. Sizergh and Levens Hall near-by are both fine examples of the English talent for continuity. The old grim Norman matrices have been transmuted down the centuries into finely mannered homes with pointed gables and deep mullioned windows. Levens has a Dutch garden of some celebrity.

### Traditional Sports

But the typical manor house of Westmorland is fairly small, often little more than a prosperous farmhouse. Most still carry the sign of the history of their turbulent past when moss-troopers rode up the Eden into the fertile Westmorland valleys to burn and pillage. The ruined peel tower still stands up alongside the dwelling-house. It was a stan-

**Meet of the Oxenholme foxhounds at the village of Hutton Bridge End. The country in this area, although undulating, is reasonably open and provides good gallops between the coverts.**

dard item in the specification of every medieval manor, a round strong tower into which cattle could be driven and where the family and servants could take refuge when news came that the Scots were out raiding.

The hard and savage schooling of border warfare which was the lot of south Westmorland people throughout the Middle Ages accounts perhaps for some of their hard and tough characteristics today. Their traditional sports, for instance, are the sports of a tough-minded race. Bull-baiting was forbidden by law in 1835 when at the height of its popularity. Cock-fighting was an even more popular entertainment and was carried on far into the nineteenth century. Indeed, it was said that until the war, if you knew where to go on some lonely bit of moorland of a Sunday morning, you might still find a surreptitious main in progress.

Hound trails, guide-races and, above all, wrestling, are favourite sports. In south Westmorland farms you may often see a dark leather belt with brass fittings nailed to the wall, the trophy of some bygone bout when the farmer, as a young man, threw his opponent in the ring at Grasmere or Pooley Bridge, and Westmorland men are good footballers.

The isolation of life for the women has been broken down in part by the bus services and in part by the network of Women's Institutes in the villages where they can meet and gossip over some co-operative undertaking. The men meet at markets and fairs. Brough Hill fair has been famous for generations throughout the north of England. Bampton is the meeting place for shepherds who gather there to identify and claim sheep which may have strayed on to another man's "heaf." They meet, too, at the hound-trails and the sheep-dog trials, though the latter are more a feature of the Lake District fell-farmer's life. None the less, in the entries for the competitions at Threlkeld or Rydal, you often see the names of a man and dog from one of the valleys which run up into the Pennines.

South Westmorland has been well served in literature. What Hardy did for Dorset, Constance Holme has done for her own county. For she is Westmorland born and bred and has lived all her life in her county boundaries. When you have read *The Splendid Fairing*, *The Lonely Plough* and *Crump Folk Going Home*, you will know what to expect of south Westmorland people. You will recognize and salute the humanity below the gnarled exteriors. They are like their own gnarled apples whose flesh is marred sometimes by a streak of canker, but is mostly sound and full of savour.

*The main street, Appleby*

470

*Town Hall, Carlisle*

# CUMBERLAND

*(Including Furness)*

### By KATHARINE CHORLEY

ON THE map Cumberland makes a rough rectangle with one long diagonal running north-east from Millom on the Irish Sea to the head of Liddesdale, nearly half-way along the Scottish border, and the other running north-west from the junction of the county with Westmorland and Yorkshire near Penrith to the head of the Solway Firth. The Lake District hills are on the southern baseline of the rectangle and thrust a blunt-headed wedge deep into the county area, thus dividing it into three well-defined sections. North of the mountains, the Cumberland plain spreads up to the Border hills, west of them, the coastal low-lands run out to the Irish Sea, and east of them the splendid vale of the Eden, held between the Lakeland fells and the central wall of the Pennines, broadens steadily towards the north.

These map divisions come vividly to life in the characters and occupations of Cumberland's people. In some parts of England the character and development of

a community is settled by a far-away geography. In Devon and Cornwall, for example, they learned to breed a strain of daring seamen who developed little sleepy fishing villages into busy ports because the riches of America were waiting to be won from the Spaniards. The great water-way of the Mersey was welded into Lancashire life like a new artery when the mills of the Pennine towns were hungry for the products of the cotton-fields of Virginia. But Cumberland has been influenced and moulded by her own immediate geography, and it is this which gives to Cumberland a certain excitement of interest all her own, through the interplay of differing social forces depending on the contrast of physical environment. The farmer from Liddesdale is a Lowland Scot by temperament and tradition, but since the exit from his valley is on to the Cumbrian plain, his economic affiliations are with Cumberland. The coal miner and the iron-ore miner from Whitehaven and Millom and the engineer

*Badge of Cumberland*

471

from Workington, have problems to solve and a way of life which are alien and unknown to the agriculturist of the Eden valley and the townsman of the market centre of Penrith. The large mixed farms of the northern plain have little work in common with the farming practice of the dalesmen from the fringes of the Lake District fells. Finally, there is Carlisle. Each of these four areas requires separate treatment.

### Fertility of Eden Valley

(1) The Eden River is the richest salmon stream in the north, and the Eden valley is rich and prosperous farming country. Protected by the Lake District hills, the land enjoys a drier climate than do the Westmorland valleys farther to the east. On sunny days, viewed from the high road which leads over the Pennines from Alston with its lead mines, it has the proud mien of a " wide and spacious champaign." It is a valley where the people tend to cluster in villages rather than scatter in isolated farms. This community grouping may be a survival of the Scottish variant of the "three fields" system of communal farming, whereby the land was divided into three equal parts, and strips or holdings were farmed according to a prescribed routine. Scottish variants are common in Cumberland. Or it may be the result of its wild history, since, throughout the Middle Ages, it was the route whereby the Scottish borderers rode south when engaged upon one of their intermittent raids. As in Westmorland a ruined peel tower still stands beside most of the ancient houses of any importance. (It is a small stone keep or stronghold into which the local inhabitants could retire with their flocks and more valuable possessions when Scottish raiders came over the border.)

Holdings tend to be fairly small, mostly from fifty to a hundred acres, except in cases where the farmer has the right to graze sheep after the Lake District fashion on some wide unenclosed area of fell. A curious social effect of these relatively small holdings is the tendency for the hired labourer—most farms only require one or at most two hired men—to live in as a

single man. Thus, when he wants to marry he may have to find not only a home, bu often also a new job. At Whitsuntide and Martinmas, the hiring fairs, when men are engaged for the half-year, are still held though their popularity is diminishing in favour of the more prosaic method o newspaper advertisement.

Since the early thirties of this century the economics of agriculture, which in the Eden valley used to centre round the breeding of livestock, have shifted toward dairy farming. Cattle breeding is still of great importance and there are many pedigree herds, Penrith district, for example being notable for shorthorns, but milk production is catching up. A generation ago, milk for export to other parts of England was produced only in the larger farms. It was sent chiefly to Tyneside Later, a depot was built at Appleby and drew thirty thousand gallons a day from the Eden farms for the consumption of Londoners. This outside contact with the remote villages in the little lateral dales running up into the Pennines and the Lakeland fells drew these secluded holdings into the general pattern of English economic life. This is, indeed, a good example of the modern interplay between city and country which is called forth by economic needs but which should express a deeper meaning, the sense of solidarity and co-operation between country and town, their pride in one another's skill and achievements, their willingness to work towards a mutual sharing of interests.

### Dairy Farming

The danger of dairy farming is, of course, the temptation to spoil the pattern of a good mixed agriculture, but in a valley like the Eden oats and grasses and roots must in any event be grown for feeding to stock. And from the farmer's financial point of view dairy farming is a great stabilizer. He gets his milk cheque regularly every month from the Milk Marketing Board and knows the amount beforehand. There is less waste of time and uncertain bargaining at cattle markets and fairs, no nagging fear that a bad harvest will drain away the income from corn—for wheat

The harbour and town of Whitehaven, seen from the Loop Road. Formerly a busy port and centre of the county's coal and iron industry, it has now been superseded in importance by Workington.

ripens here too uncertainly to make a good standard crop—and no holding of a wool-clip perhaps for two or three years in the hope of a rise in price.

Yet sheep farming in the Eden valley is still important, for the side valleys run up into hills on either hand where sheep can be grazed on the open fell. The flocks are mostly crosses from the black-faced fell breeds and Lazonby is a notable centre for the sale of cross-bred sheep, whose buyers come from all parts of the country.

Horses are also bred along the Eden, mainly big, heavy Scottish Clydesdales. You may see them pacing down the roads to some agricultural show with their manes and tails combed and plaited and their coats sleek and shining.

Most Edenside farmers own cars and come to Penrith on market day; it is the centre, too, for the fell farmers from the eastern dales of the Lake District. No fewer than six of the big banks have branches in Penrith. In a town which has no large industry of its own this is a sure proof of the healthiness of the countryside on which it depends.

(2) To drive from Penrith in a couple of hours through Keswick and Cockermouth into the coastal area is to take a journey whose end at Workington or Whitehaven or far down the coast at Millom gives

473

contact with a totally different way of life. West Cumberland is industrial, and since its traditional industries are the direct result of its own natural riches and resources, they have a kind of organic unity with their environment. But new industries are coming and have already come to relieve the fears of Cumbrians, for at Calder Hall and Windscale the first large atomic power plant in the world has now been opened.

### Industries of West Cumberland

The established West Cumberland industries, like those of Furness, are old. The iron-ore mines which feed the modern blast furnaces of Millom once fed the little bloomeries (early foundries where the rough iron was hammered into pigs) in Ennerdale and Wasdale. With the introduction of a technique for smelting with coal instead of charcoal, Cumberland's iron industries expanded steadily. By 1885, the small Cumberland area held second place in all the iron-working districts of Great Britain. The coal-mines around Whitehaven and Workington were opened in the first half of the seventeenth century by Lowthers and Curwens, and under the ægis of these two families grew steadily throughout the eighteenth century.

Ireland was largely supplied with Cumberland coal shipped from Whitehaven. The local iron smelting was for technical reasons done with coke from Durham, and it is only in the last couple of generations that Cumberland coal-mining and Cumberland iron-working have interlocked. Shipping from Whitehaven is now no longer of much consequence and the big solid quays and jetties are deserted, Workington being now the main centre both for industry and shipping. The great iron and steel works support the port whose docks must be well manned for the discharging of cargoes of ore and the loading of cargoes of rails and steel billets.

Maryport, to the north, with a fine harbour, has little or no ocean trade and suffered pitiably from unemployment in the inter-war years. There was, however, a small coastwise traffic and some fishing, and during the season the herring fleets

from the south of Scotland would put into Maryport and spread across the docks, row upon row of handsome drifters.

So West Cumberland is, in effect, divided between the iron-worker, the ore-miner and the collier. But stretches of agricultural land run up to the foot of the mountains and the industrial towns are small by Lancashire or Yorkshire standards. The mining villages still wear a country look and parts of the coastline are still unspoilt and beautiful for long miles on end.

The coal-miners, perhaps, set the atmosphere for West Cumberland more than the other types of worker. They tend to group in colonies round each mine and combine with their job of getting coal the outlook and activities of the countryman. They will work a garden, keep hens, a cow or a few pigs; they will net rabbits or be away poaching at night for the sheer love of adventure.

As with other Cumbrians, wrestling is their traditional sport, but the popularity of wrestling is decreasing and an ardent enthusiasm for Rugby (Northern Union) football is taking its place. Hound trials are as popular with the miner as they are with the fell-farmer of the Lake District valleys.

### Recreation in the Collieries

Colliery villages have one leisure outlet and activity which is all their own. Year after year each village holds a carnival and for weeks beforehand the women prepare, putting all their thought and skill and devotion into turning out the most beautiful show that they can conceive and execute. The carnival queens are throned on a horse-drawn coal lorry, which has been scrubbed and painted and then decorated with flowers and tinsel. Queens and retainers are all in fancy dress, and after the parade there are sports for the children and competing troops of girls dance in the open on a special stage made up of planks resting on beer barrels. On carnival day one can still see English villages able and enthusiastic to entertain themselves as they did in the times when the May Queen was crowned, not as a half literary survival but from the very heart of the village life

In these ways the colliers spend their leisure. Underground everything is rush, grab, sweat and rush again, for piece-work admits of no let-up. Yet below the grab and greed, there is a generous solidarity, which comes to the surface whenever a fellow collier is in need. Men will run at the double to an injured comrade and carry him back, perhaps three miles from the coal-face, never reckoning either danger or cost. I am not suggesting that these characteristics are confined to the West Cumbrian colliers, but they are typical of the Cumberland character as a whole—a strange amalgam of hardfistedness and generosity, of tenderness and a harsh, smouldering vitality.

During and since the last war, the features of West Cumberland have altered. Some, at any rate, of the great plants which were set up for the production of war material have been turned to peace-time uses and many new light industries are springing up; the coal-mines in which the latest American machinery has been installed are perhaps the most highly mechanized in the country. It is unlikely that West Cumbrians will feel again the forlorn bitterness of the inter-war years, when the area became a despairing pocket of industrial depression. The problem for the future may rather be to combine industrial expansion with care for the character and more gracious uses of their coastline and their hinterland, the Lake District fells and valleys. West Cumbrians are so placed geographically that a special trust is laid upon them; and schemes which involve the violation of some long stretch of sandy beach or of some quiet and untouched Lakeland dale must be weighed against the craving of thousands of workers from the gloomy sprawling cities of Lancashire and Yorkshire and the Midlands to spend their holidays in untarnished air and among lovely surroundings.

The flood of workers streaming into West Cumberland from other parts of England

**Looking across the Solway Firth from Silloth towards the hills of Kirkcudbrightshire. The mountain seen in the background is Criffel, a well-known landmark 1866 feet high.**

during the war has gone some way to break down the West Cumbrians' community sense of aloofness and to modify their traditional social habits. For six years they have worked and lived with men and women of differing industrial traditions and with different social concepts, and from them have derived new ideas and notions of behaviour. Perhaps this will make it easier for them to realize that their problems are not being thrust to one side, but that, on the contrary, they have been pulled out of their isolation as Cumbrians and pushed into the wider community of Englishmen.

### The Northern Lowlands

(3) The northern lowlands of Cumberland are fine farming country studded with market towns which are not only centres for their surrounding districts but have each, as a rule, a speciality which draws buyers from much farther afield. Cockermouth and Wigton markets handle each of them more than sixty thousand animals a year. Wigton has in addition a three-days' horse fair in November where the heavy Clydesdales, which are bred in these parts, change hands. Longtown, near the Scottish border, is notable as a market where wool clips are sold in June after the shearing. Aspatria is smaller, but has a cheese factory which absorbs the milk from several hundred farms.

Along the Solway sand-dunes, turves are cut for bowling-greens and tennis courts, turves which have helped to make English lawns famous throughout Europe. The "hoggs," yearling sheep from the high fell farms, are sent to the Solway mosses to spend their first winter in milder conditions, gaining strength for their subsequent life on the open fells. Farming on the lowlands is well mixed, wheat and barley can be grown with fair success. Indeed, before the great agricultural depression of the 1870's Cumberland might have been classed as a wheat-producing county, since flour as well as coal was exported from Whitehaven. Today oats take up a big percentage of the total arable land, although roots and grasses grow well. But by and large this broad northern area is a cattle country and dairying or stock-breeding and fattening are the main occupations of most farms. Hereabouts many farms are large, running to three or four hundred acres, and with well-found houses and byres and barns and work for half a dozen or more labourers. The peasant outlook on life, which is characteristic of small holdings, is transcended among these tenants, who are sometimes the owners of broad acres.

(4) In spite of local or specialized markets, all Cumberland north of the Lakeland hills turns towards Carlisle as its metropolis. In its old streets, with their solid buildings of red sandstone, you may meet the men from the English slopes of the Cheviots and the men from the northern valleys of the Lake District fells. Alongside and in contrast to the broad Cumbrian of the dales, with its roots deep back in the old Norse speech, you may hear the singing consonants and sharper vowels of Lowland Scots. Indeed, Carlisle often evokes a mild sense of foreignness. Although its history is that of a bastion city between England and the warlike Scots it is not quite an English town. A flavour of Scotland pervades it, as, indeed, a flavour of Scotland enters into many of the habits of life and speech of North Cumbrians.

### History of Carlisle

The great castle, whose walls of sandstone have weathered to a hue and texture which reminds one of the trunks of old Scotch firs, is a reminder of border warfare. Queen Mary's Walk is also a reminder of the time when the unfortunate Mary Queen of Scots was imprisoned in the castle after her defeat at Langside. The cathedral, also built of red sandstone, is as rich in border history. It was here that they took the Papal Legate to anathematize Robert the Bruce and "with candels light and causing the bels to be roong they accursed in terrible wise the usurper of the crowne of Scotland."

Today Carlisle is a flourishing industrial city as well as a county market and metropolis. The Cumberland tweed, blended of Cheviot and Herdwick wool, is woven here. There are manufactures of carpets and various fabrics, including the admirable "sundour" material; there are flour mills

The massive keep seen above is all that remains of the original stronghold of Dacre Castle, near Penrith. The square tower, with its large corner turrets, was built in the fourteenth century. The castle was for long a seat of the great family of Dacre.

and a famous biscuit factory. Carlisle is one of the principal railway junctions in Britain and a Carlisle engineering firm is said to manufacture the biggest crane in the world.

Despite this industrial background, the city is still chiefly important as the largest livestock market in England. It is noteworthy, too, for the fact that it was the scene of the first experiment in State ownership of breweries, inns and public-houses. The experiment dates from the end of the 1914–18 war when the high level of workers' wages resulted in serious street drunkenness, and State control was introduced in an effort to abate the nuisance. Today State ownership is a well-established system and a proved success.

For many centuries Carlisle was a fortress city. Scottish armies besieged and sometimes sacked it; English armies set out from Carlisle to subdue the Scots. Roman armies used it as a base for Hadrian's Wall. And the rich plain around and the border hills beyond were always the scene of savage warfare. Until the middle of the thirteenth century, disputes had arisen over

the ownership of Westmorland and Cumberland which had formed part of the ancient kingdom of Strathclyde and had never been incorporated in the Norman conquest. For two or three centuries afterwards tracts of Cumberland were still known as "debatable lands," and a tussle of ownership went on by means of raids and forays. In these conditions, a fierce border race was bred clustering round the great names on either side, Graemes for the Scots, Howards and Dacres for the English. It was a Dacre who led the Cumberland men at Flodden and who built the defensive castles of Askerton and Drumburgh and part of Naworth. Every Cumbrian held his land on condition of military service against the Scots.

Peace came to the border only when the crowns of Scotland and England were united under James VI and I in 1603. But the fierce memories linger in the ruins of the old peel towers which were attached to many farms and to every "hall." Sturdy and square, not too tall so as to avoid notice from afar, and with an enclosure for cattle, they afforded a safe retreat for the owner and his stock when the Scots were out. Yet today they stand as heartening reminders that quarrels can be settled and then forgotten in a fresh start of friendship between two proud peoples.

## "Island" of Furness

A brief introductory note to this chapter stated that the Lake District was being dealt with in a separate chapter in this book. That part of the district which falls within Cumberland is therefore not covered here. On the other hand, Cumberland is contiguous with that "island" of Lancashire known as Furness, which both in its way of life and its background resembles Cumberland far more than it does its administrative parent. For these reasons it has been decided to deal with it in this chapter; but part of the Lake District also lies within Furness and we are not concerned with that part here.

If you stand on the railway bridge at Hest Bank just north of Lancaster and look across the sands of Morecambe Bay, you will see the pale beautiful fells of Furness crowning the farther shore, the delicacy of their colour and outlines emphasized against the brown and golden waste of the great bay. A sense of remoteness touches that view. And, indeed, it is only when we apply for a road licence, pay our telephone bill or otherwise fill in some county form, that we who have homes in Furness recall with an odd little shock that we belong to an administrative area which includes manufacturing towns in the bleak Pennine valleys south-east and east of Manchester.

## The Palatine Court

But though we are cut off from the south by our geography and share our culture and economy with the dalesmen of the Lake District and the iron-workers of West Cumberland, our history joined us centuries ago to the great County Palatine. And we share the right of every Lancashire man and woman to its unique surviving privileges. We can take our disputes in equity to the Palatine Court and need not go, like the rest of England, to the High Court of Chancery in London, and we can drink the King's health in our own privileged fashion, referring to him by his local title of Duke of Lancaster. A planner would have thrown us in with West Cumberland, but feudal kings were not influenced by the concepts of planning, and in any case when Henry I joined Furness to Lancashire and made the whole over to his nephew Stephen, Cumberland scarcely counted as a part of the England which acknowledged the Norman conquests. And so Furness remains one of those anomalies which exasperate the tidy-minded and yet in their own peculiar way lend richness and variety to the texture of English life.

## Topography of Furness

It is a little triangular enclave fitted in between the Duddon valley and the northern shore of Morecambe Bay with the southern arm of the triangle extended across the hills to Windermere and then up the Brathay and the Wrynose Pass to meet the Duddon arm at the Three Shire Stone which marks the junction of the three Lake District counties.

Until the Furness railway was built about the middle of the last century, the only direct access from the south was by the oversands route across Morecambe Bay, a romantic approach with a spice of danger to flavour it. At high tide, twelve feet of water might be washing over the spot where the coach had halted a few hours earlier, while the " guide " prospected for the day's correct fording place over the River Kent. The road from Lancaster took to the sands at Hest Bank and regained terra firma at Kent's Bank on the farther shore. The general course—the details varied considerably even from day to day owing to the vagaries of currents—is marked on all the old maps and also on the modern ordnance sheet. From Kent's Bank there was an extension over the lovely Cartmel peninsula and then across the sands of the Leven and Crake estuary to the town of Ulverston. This was the more dangerous section; and the registers of Cartmel Priory Church are sprinkled with entries recording losses on the sands going back to the sixteenth century. But the route was regularly used long before that, for in 1325 the Abbot of Furness asked King Edward II to extend his jurisdiction to take in Leven Sands which were so dangerous and yet so much used that numbers of travellers (on one occasion sixteen) had been swept away by the on-coming sea. The petition was granted, and the abbot promptly established a chapel on a little island half-way across the estuary where monks prayed throughout the twenty-four hours for the welfare of voyagers. They also paid a regular guide to conduct travellers across.

It is twenty-one miles by the oversands route from Lancaster to Ulverston, and the greater part of the way lies over that odd sea-floor of superfine sandy mud, now slimy and hard like greased boards, now with every ripple of the outgoing water imprinted on it, now quaking and shivering ominously under a footstep; and always showing blue-black and menacing when-ever its dull brown surface is grazed. It is not surprising that, when for centuries direct access could only be achieved by so arduous a road, Furness built up a character and a seclusion of its own, a character and a seclusion which still distinguish it in spite of the spill-over of tourists from the more popular eastern and northern valleys of the Lake District, in spite of the charming and modest northern Bournemouth which has grown up at Grange-over-Sands where the sheltering hills and the mild sea-winter foster shrubs and plants more appropriate to southern climes, in spite of the great shipyards and engineering works at Barrow and the iron-ore mines about Dalton.

The mines and the iron and steel works and the shipyards have grown out of a way of life which was traditional in Furness. The Romans and possibly the Celts before them worked the mines and smelted the ore. But the foundations of the modern industries were laid in the Middle Ages

**Crocuses in bloom at Field Broughton, near Cartmel. Although Furness shares the diverse beauty of the Lake District, of which it forms a part, it is administratively part of Lancashire.**

The priory gateway at Cartmel in Furness. The monastery was destroyed during the Dissolution, but the cruciform church which survived is one of the finest in Lancashire.

480

when Furness was under the influence of the Cistercians of Furness Abbey.

The remains of this Abbey are the pride of Furness. Founded in 1127, the monastery, under a succession of able abbots, became one of the richest and most influential of the ecclesiastical centres in England in the Middle Ages. The rich endowments of the foundation multiplied and prospered, for the monks were not only energetic clearers of forest country and enlightened farmers and shepherds, they were also merchants and industrialists. Their ships sailed from Barrow with cargoes of wool for Flanders. They worked the iron-ore mines at Dalton and Orgrave and Martin and Plumpton. They managed the charcoal burning on the fringes of the hills and in the valleys and the little bloomeries nearby, to which the ore was transported for smelting. The years after the Dissolution were hard ones for Furness, because there was scarcely a valley which had not contributed in some way to the monks' iron industry. But prosperity returned with the reorganization of the industry in the seventeenth century and was maintained and increased. Exports of ore from Barrow amounted to some fifty thousand tons a year in the middle of the nineteenth century, yet Barrow itself was still a village. Its rapid growth came in the second half of the century when a company was founded to make steel by the new Bessemer process and the great shipyards were built, where naval vessels of iron and steel were constructed. Submarine building is a speciality.

### Traditional Way of Life

It is perhaps because the modern industries of Furness have grown in this way out of a traditional local way of life that there has been little clash between them and the life of the villages and countryside and the old town of Ulverston with its big market hall and its long sloping square. Barrow has never superseded Ulverston as a centre and rendezvous for the country people. Farmers from miles around send their sons to Ulverston Grammar School and their produce to Ulverston market.

If the industrial plan of life which the people of Furness follow today was sketched out for them by the monks in medieval times, their farming plan of life was laid down even earlier by Norse invaders. The Norsemen probably came over from Viking colonies in the Isle of Man towards the beginning of the tenth century. They nosed their boats up the estuaries of the Leven and the Duddon and the Crake and made settlements wherever they spotted a piece of land suitable for clearing and cultivation.

### Invasion of the Norsemen

Gradually, however, through the course of decades and even centuries, they pushed on inland, taking in more wild land up the valleys and sending their thralls on ahead to find and squat on summer pasturages. W. G. Collingwood has traced the process with fascinating clarity by reference to the place-names which they have left behind them, and he has given it life and romance in his novel *Thorstein of the Mere*. It is not so long ago that Coniston Lake was known as Thurston Water—Thorstein's Lake. The present name, taken from the village at its head, is a corruption of the Norse Konungs—king. Coniston was owned by Stephen of Blois who became King of England in 1135. No doubt he put a bailiff in to manage these lands, and the farm would be named after the king by men of pure Viking descent who must still have spoken the old language. Up the Leven valley there is Haverthwaite, the cleared field of oats, and Finsthwaite, Finn's field. In these parts, too, there is a Grizedale, the valley of the swine, which today will be remembered for long enough by more than one famous German general who has looked out from behind his barbed wire on to a landscape of meadow and wooded hillside, where the wild cherries star the slopes and there are little stone-built farmsteads whose aspect can hardly have changed in the centuries since some Norse farmer, perhaps the Hrolf of Rusland a little farther down the dale, kept his pigs rooting among the scrub oaks. Over the hill and a little to the north one Hauk made his summer pasturage beside the pleasant shores of Esthwaite water, hence Hawkshead, "Hauk's saetr." You can play this rather enthralling game with any of the Furness valleys working up from the coast, and with the Cumberland valleys, too, but if you love Furness you know that you are doing more than play a game, you are explaining the character and customs of your own neighbours in terms of their history.

The big-boned, fair-skinned farmer with firm eyes, who is dousing the pasture below your house with Government lime, holds land that has been farmed by men of Norse blood for a thousand years. It may be that today he is suffering from a selfish and ignorant landlord who will not give him the financial backing to keep up his fences and his land-drains and his byres. He is an able farmer and could almost certainly find the cash himself if he wanted to do the land-lord's job—but he is still of the same type as his forebears who struggled against the application of feudal methods of land tenure so effectively that they evolved a system of their own which made them virtually independent freeholders, paying only certain fixed and known services to their lords, and protected against eviction so that farms were passed down through one family as of right. His milking methods are primitive and would drive a modern, scientific farmer to despair, yet we drink his milk in preference to the tested liquid from a herd a few miles away because he is our neighbour. He and his wife will acclaim the day when the grid extends a line which

they can tap, but they are hardfisted and much as they want electricity, they will not put their hands in their pockets if they can help it, and will curse surlily if anyone should suggest that a bit more money might be paid in order to bury a line here and there where posts and wires slash a wide and lovely prospect. They tend to dislike tourists and never give their hearts to strangers. Their friendship, even when it comes, retains a quality of reserve; the proof that you have it lies in actions rather than in words. When you are accepted things will be done for you and nothing said. You will find some late January day, when the whole countryside is under a mantle of snow, that the plough has been driven up your lane in order to clear a passage for your snow-bound car. You will find that you are put wise about other neighbours. Jimmie Arnison of Blackbeck, for instance, is one for lifting things; never leave a tool about because Jimmie passes your way on his road to work. That warning means that you have been sized up and can be relied on to understand about Jimmie's little weakness and without complaining to authority. No doubt law and order and confidence cannot be built up in this way in great communities which have to treat their members impersonally; it is the way of little communities whose members trust and protect each other in spite of bickering and close their ranks against an outside world. It is our way in Furness.

*Furness Abbey*

*Derwentwater and Skiddaw from Lodore*

# THE LAKES

### By LORD JUSTICE BIRKETT

*respect of this chapter and this chapter lone a departure has been made from the treatment of England on the basis of counties, lsewhere strictly adhered to. The reason that, as Lord Justice Birkett points out in is article, the Lakes form an area of natural eauty which is a single unity and which mperatively demands national administra- on as a National Park. It was, accordingly, greed when the book was planned that the akes should be treated as a whole. More- ver, Lord Justice Birkett had in mind to ngage support for a widespread agitation to irn the whole of the 700 square miles of the ake District into a National Park, which ould be done under the powers possessed ῳ the Minister of Town and Country Plan- ing. After some years this aim was achieved nd became law in May, 1951. Large parts f the principal beauty spots in the Lake district are owned or administered by the ʲational Trust.*

HE ENGLISH Lake District is very small nd very lovely. Therein lies the secret of s power over the minds and imaginations f men. It has a long and fascinating history for those that can read it, going back to the earliest days when the mountains were first made, and the Lakes were first fashioned. Now it has become a great national sanctuary, the mountain sanctuary of England. But it was not always beautiful as it is today. For centuries the great peaks loomed over scenes of terrible desolation, over dark and gloomy forests, swamps and wild vegetation, and unrelieved and monotonous moorland. It took nearly a thousand years of man's ceaseless activity to make the Lake District the incomparable thing of beauty it is today. But since the eighteenth century, when the Lakes first became widely known through the coming of adventurous visitors, it is the natural beauty of the district which has given it life and fame, that beauty which arises from the harmonious blending of the works of Nature and of Man, in a very much deeper meaning than the old Yorkshire- man ever intended when he first said, "*In t'Lake District there's nowt but scenery.*"

To recognize that important truth in any consideration of the Lake District in modern times is the highest duty of all those who care for it, and who desire its preservation. For because it is so small and lovely it is the more susceptible to injury. Consider that the highest mountain is

483

only some three thousand feet, yet where else in the world can be found such noble and inspiring effects of sheer height? Where else is the work of Nature and of Man so perfectly united as in the cultivated dale-heads that thrust themselves right into the very majesty of the mountains? Where else is Beauty so satisfying and so complete as in the little tarns set among the lonely hills?

This is the theme of all the writers since the middle of the eighteenth century. This, they said, is the Lake District, there is none like it; and with that they were well content.

Today the emphasis must be placed elsewhere, for the beauty of the Lake District is now threatened as never before. The activities of man grow apace, and in his desire to enjoy more fully and more easily the splendours that surround him, he is in danger of destroying the thing he loves. Farming, afforestation, building, quarrying, road-making, the impounding of water, the damming of lakes, the creation of reservoirs, the erection of factories, the taking of land for military purposes, the use of motor-buses and speed-boats, the provision of holiday facilities—all these must be considered in the light of the supreme need to preserve the beauty of the district.

### Heart of Lakeland

Though it is the pride of three counties—Lancashire, Cumberland and Westmorland—the essential part of the Lake District lies within a circle not more than thirty miles across. This is not to depreciate the beauty or the value of the surrounding fringe described in other chapters of this book. The villages and towns of Lakeland Lancashire outside this small circle have a charm and distinction of their own not easily to be surpassed, and the same holds true of Cumberland and Westmorland.

Nevertheless, the essential part of Lakeland proper is very small. From the summit of Helvellyn on a clear day you may see almost the whole of it, certainly the great peaks, most of the Lakes, with Scotland, the Pennines, and the Irish Sea filling up the distance.

This is perhaps the best-loved spot in the British Isles, and in consequence has been described and praised in the most lyrical language by thousands of loving an[d] enthusiastic pens, good, bad and very ba[d].

In the engaging preface to *Eöthen*, King[s]lake said that he had endeavoured to dis[-]card from his book all valuable matte[r] derived from the works of others. But i[n] the case of the Lake District almost every[-]thing said must almost inevitably savour o[f] repetition. Yet no repetition can stale th[e] truth that within this small circle of thirt[y] miles there are to be found the richest an[d] the most varied treasures.

### National Heritage

Here are the mountains with the nob[le] names that fill the mind with a kind of so[ng] —Skiddaw, Helvellyn, Saddleback (wit[h] its lovelier and older name of Blencathra[)], Scawfell, Great Gable, the Old Man o[f] Coniston, Langdale Pikes, Fairfield, Bow[-] fell, High Street, and a score of others— and here are the lakes that have become par[t] of the national heritage with their equall[y] lovely names—Windermere, Ullswate[r] Derwentwater, Bassenthwaite, Conisto[n] Water, Grasmere, Rydal, Buttermer[e] Crummock, Ennerdale, Wastwater, Thir[l]mere and the rest. Here are the hills an[d] fells, the lonely tarns, the great mountai[n] passes, the peaceful dales, the quiet farm[s] with their white-washed buildings, th[e] crags and the wooded slopes, the rivers an[d] the becks, the stone walls running up th[e] mountain sides, the wandering mountai[n] tracks, the rich green pastures, the litt[le] villages and the old-world towns, th[e] country churches and the hospitable inn[s] and, indeed, all that makes Lakeland th[e] joy and delight that it is.

For those who love statistics (and th[e] strange taste is not at all uncommon) th[e] lakes and the mountains have all bee[n] surveyed and measured and counted. [It] must always be considered as being in th[e] nature of a miracle that in this little circ[le] there are one hundred and eighty mountai[ns] all of which scale two thousand feet, an[d] eight of which aspire to three thousan[d;] fifteen considerable lakes from Windermer[e] to Brother's Water; and no less than twen[ty] mountain passes.

The great name of Wordsworth is now s[o] inseparably linked with the three Lak[e]

The Langdale Pikes, seen from Blea Tarn. These mountains, Harrison Stickle and Pike o' Stickle, stand at the head of the Great Langdale Valley and are respectively 2,403 and 2,323 feet in height.

counties that he is popularly supposed to have been the first discoverer of their beauties. In the fullest sense, of course, this is true, for he stands without a rival in sympathetic understanding, artistic feeling and inspired interpretation. But for many years before Wordsworth the writers had been busy. The local poets, like Richard Braithwaite in the seventeenth century, and Josiah Relph in the eighteenth, had little to say of the local scenery, though much of the local people.

It was not until the middle of the eighteenth century when, as Professor de Selincourt has said, "a feeling for the rugged and mysterious in Nature became a fashionable affectation," that the real surge of writing began; and what was then begun has never ceased. Since that date there is no aspect of Lakeland life that has not had its faithful chronicler. The story of the rocks and the Skiddaw slates has been told in the most learned treatises; every bird, migrant or native, has been catalogued; every moth and butterfly has been noted; every wild flower has been named and indexed; whilst farming, fishing, the rural

industries, fox-hunting, climbing, walking, sailing, shooting—all have found their faithful and devoted historians.

Most of the early writers were scrupulous to observe the county distinctions. The antiquarian, Father West, who published his *Antiquities of Furness* in 1774 and his *Guide to the Lakes* in 1778, referred to the rivalry which then existed between Derbyshire and Cumberland respecting Dovedale and Keswick, each county claiming a superiority in natural beauty.

And when Wordsworth first published his famous *Guide to the Lakes* in 1810, it is interesting to recall that he published it as an anonymous introduction to a volume of sketches entitled *Select Views in Cumberland, Westmoreland and Lancashire.* The *Select Views* have long ago vanished, for as Wordsworth said of them in a private letter, "They will please many who in all the arts are most taken in by what is worthless"; but the *Guide to the Lakes* remains not only as a piece of literature, but as the first and finest handbook to National Parks. Wordsworth was the first to see the Lake District as a whole without distinction of county

485

boundaries, and to see it as it had never been seen before.

He had, of course, supreme advantages. He was born in Cumberland, educated at the Elizabethan Grammar School at Hawkshead in Lancashire, where he carved his name on the desk which is still to be seen as clearly as the pictures of old Hawkshead which he has left in *The Prelude*, and lived the whole of his life, save for three years, in the solitudes of Westmorland.

Beyond all, he had the inward eye, united to the power of immortal expression. His book was written, as he tells us, with the purpose of saving the Lake District as he knew it from those who would destroy "the tranquil, the lovely and the perfect." It is full of the rarest insight; full of knowledge and of understanding; full, too, of the acute awareness of natural beauty and of its significance. And, lastly, it abounds in the most practical wisdom.

486

Looking down Borrowdale towards the peaks of (left to right) Glaramara, Great End, Scafell, Lingmell, Green Gable and Great Gable. The village in the foreground is Rosthwaite.

beauty of the Lake District had already begun, and, indeed, much earlier, Father West had spoken of the evils of litter in terms which sound like a pamphlet issued by the Friends of the Lake District.

But Wordsworth's conception of the Lake District as a sort of national property is now almost universally accepted as both desirable and necessary. In the fullest sense, of course, it is already a national possession; for with a sure instinct, most people think of the Lake District as one and indivisible, where county boundaries have little or no meaning. Today, dwellers in the south of England find it difficult to believe that any part of the Lake District is in Lancashire at all, and they have little if any idea of where the boundaries run, nor do they greatly wish to know. Lancashire for them means Widnes and Bolton and Oldham and St. Helens, not that stretch of country that lies between the Duddon and Windermere, the glory of the Furness Fells, or Coniston Water or Esthwaite, or Hawkshead or Coniston Old Man, or the lovely Rusland Valley with its unmatched views of the distant hills and its glorious and famous beeches, or all that stretch of country that lies between the Winster and Windermere known as Cartmel.

Westmorland is better known, for it is perhaps the truest Lake County of them all. It contains Helvellyn, and thousands of people who have never ascended its neighbour, Dollywaggon Pike and never will, yet because of Wordsworth and Scott seem to know the summit of Helvellyn very well. They both recorded in verse the moving story of the faithful dog that watched by the body of its dead master for three months by Striding Edge. These verses were made the standard recitations in schools, and the imagination of many a child has been stirred by Scott's picture of the devoted dog in that lone place keeping its vigil—

How long did'st thou think that his silence was slumber?
When the wind waved his garment how oft did thou start?

The proposal to make the Lake District a national park is comparatively new. It has arisen as a distinguishable and determinate part of the problem of controlling the use of land in these complex days, and is a late development in the history of the preservation of natural beauty, whose necessity and wisdom painful experience has shown. But, prophetically enough, it was Wordsworth who first conceived the idea. The fight to preserve the natural

Friar's Crag stands on the north-east edge of Derwentwater close to the town of Keswick, and is the property of the National Trust. A memorial to Ruskin has been set up on the promontory.

Westmorland also contains High Street, the Langdale Pikes, Fairfield, Wansfell Pike and Loughrigg Fell, and, among its lakes, Grasmere and Rydal Water to which thousands of Wordsworthian pilgrims come yearly, the lovely tarns Codale and Easedale, and the rivers, the Kent, the Brathay and the Rothay.

Cumberland contains the greatest peaks. It glories in Scafell and Skiddaw and Saddleback (all over 2,000 feet high), the lakes of Derwentwater and Bassenthwaite and Wastwater, and the vale of Borrowdale, which many hold to be the loveliest of all the vales of Lakeland.

### Fame of John Peel

Just as the poems of Wordsworth and Scott made Helvellyn a household word, so the name of John Peel brings Cumberland to every hearth.

It is one of life's little ironies that a man whose name is known wherever the English tongue is spoken should have been made famous by men whose names are almost forgotten. To have kept a pack of hounds for fifty-five years is a slender claim to immortality.

But the world has literally worn a path to the grave of John Peel in the little churchyard at Caldbeck under the shadow of Skiddaw. Some, it may be added, have even gone to Troutbeck under the mistaken impression that he was born and lived there. But it was a Wigton man named John Woodcock Graves who was sitting with John Peel one night recounting hunting days, when an old woman began to sing a child to sleep with the old lilting tune of "Bonnie Annie."

Graves immediately took pen and paper and composed on the spot—

"D'ye ken John Peel with his coat so gray?",

and remarked with some insight—"By Jove, Peel, you'll be sung when we're both run to earth."

And it was a Norwich man who had sung in Carlisle Cathedral for fifty years, one William Metcalfe, who fourteen years after the death of Peel in 1854, re-set the music of the old tune we sing today. Hence, it is to Graves and Metcalfe that the world is really indebted, and John Peel lives on because of them, and not otherwise.

All the Lake Counties are rich in literary associations, and the great names of Wordsworth, Coleridge, Southey, De Quincey, Hazlitt, Lamb, Shelley and many others are intertwined with this rich part of England.

It is perhaps natural that in such a region, so rich in history and association, the life of the local people should tend to be forgotten. Yet a very remarkable local life exists. The dalesmen of the Lake District are almost as unique as the Herdwick sheep they breed. They are for the most part Norse in origin or extraction, practically untouched by the Celtic or the Saxon, certainly unconquered by the Normans, and intensely proud of their geographical and economic distinction. The Rev. H. H. Symonds spoke for generations of visitors when he said—

. . . those who have known the dalesmen of Cumberland and Westmoreland in the warmth of actuality, and have admired the pride, the courtesy, the independence of their spirit and stock—a certain magnificence and largeness of heart, which the high places of the earth have bred in them, and to which the severity of wind and weather have grandly led them on.

The chapters of this book which deal with the counties of Cumberland and Westmorland have spoken of the life of the people in the towns and villages, their history, their occupations and pastimes, and the people of the Lake District proper exhibit the same sturdy qualities and follow the same pursuits.

### Local Industry

See them at Threlkeld at the sheep dog competitions, or at Grasmere in the guide's race or at the ploughing matches, and you will feel the strength of the local tradition, note the ways of thought and feeling, and hear the rough beauty of the local speech. All these qualities are displayed in what has come to be known as the tourist industry on which the life of Lakeland so much depends. Yet the real mainstay of the local life is still agriculture. The mountains of the Lake District are made still more attractive by the presence of the

Herdwick sheep, a local breed that can flourish and thrive even in the cold and rain and snow of the district. They are bred for their wool and their mutton, the wool, rich in fat, and the mutton rich in taste and flavour. They can survive under the snow-drifts for weeks, and when fully grown, can live all the year round without hay or artificial feeding. This breed of Herdwick sheep is strictly local; it is not found anywhere else, and is, in truth, a basic industry.

But when all is said and done, the appeal of the English Lake District is simply the appeal of one of man's deepest needs, the need of natural beauty.

When Wordsworth put forward his great claim for the preservation of the district he said that the Lake District must be protected from rash assault because

it was capable of satisfying the most intense cravings for the tranquil and the lovely and the perfect to which man, the noblest of her creatures, is subject.

The present Master of Trinity, Professor G. M. Trevelyan, in his advocacy of National Parks has followed where Wordsworth led. He said—

It is a question of spiritual values. Without vision the people perish, and without sight of the beauty of Nature the spiritual power of the British people will be atrophied. . . . By the side of Religion, by the side of Science, by the side of Poetry and Art stands Natural Beauty, not as a rival to these, but as the common inspirer and nourisher of them all, and with a secret of her own beside. . . .

### Preservation of Beauty

But in this modern age these wise and brave words seem to fall on deaf ears. In recent years the fight for the preservation of the Lake District has been carried on with great intensity, particularly by the organization known as The Friends of the Lake District. That work has always been hard and almost thankless, but latterly it has become heartbreaking.

The enemies of natural beauty are so many, and their methods are so various, that eternal vigilance is essential. A score of conflicting claims arise which must in

some manner be satisfied. The great cities need water; the country areas need electricity both for light and power; the demand is made for quarrying and mining; the cry arises for more timber; great motor roads are driven through the remote places; and in rural solitudes artillery ranges and bombing grounds are established.

These claims and demands make great inroads into our diminishing store of natural beauty, and it is surely a grave national weakness that in a matter of such high importance as the preservation of the countryside the battle should be left to a few private and public-spirited individuals.

### National Parks

All this emphasizes as nothing else can the imperative and urgent need for the Lake District to be made forthwith a National Park. The name is a little unfortunate because of the conflicting ideas the words evoke. But there is no thought of regimentation or of nationalizing the land in the ordinary acceptation of that term. An authoritative definition has now been given by Mr. John Dower in his masterly Report to the Ministry of Town and Country Planning in May of 1945.

A National Park may be defined as . . . an extensive area of beautiful and relatively wild country in which for the nation's benefit, and by appropriate national decision and action, (a) the characteristic landscape beauty is strictly preserved, (b) access and facilities for public open-air enjoyment are amply provided, (c) wild life and buildings and places of architectural and historic interest are suitably protected, while (d) established farming use is effectively maintained.

Obviously, the whole of the Lake District falls completely within this definition.

In National Parks planning requires a more direct and specialized form of control designed to achieve the essential purpose of preserving for all time areas of grand and noble landscape, these to be chosen and determined by a fixed and common standard. The first essential is that the planning must be in the hands of a National Parks Commission with adequate administrative and financial powers. Its relation

A peaceful scene in the Langdale Valley near the lovely waterfall of Dungeon Ghyll Force.

to local and central government must be carefully defined, but the decisive word must lie with the Commissioners who will consider all questions from the national point of view. The whole success of National Parks lies in the character and quality of the Commissioners, and the nature and extent of their powers.

For the essential requirements of the Commissioners' policy are all-embracing. The local life must be preserved in its full integrity, and this means that farming must be fostered and improved as the main traditional employment and the foundation of all the local economy and life. The traditional rural industries must also be continued and encouraged, and what has been called "the tourist industry" is not the least of these. A comprehensive road policy must be formulated and adapted to the needs of a National Park. All carriage roads must be classified by reference to their use, and to the needs of through and local traffic. Certain mountain trackways and fell routes must be closed to motor traffic, except for farm use, quarrying and other wayside occupations.

The daleheads, lake shores and fell sides must be protected against all building except for agricultural purposes, and, in particular, the building of special holiday accommodation must be permitted in the National Park only on sites previously agreed and specified. New residential building must be confined to the areas already developed, and the building of rural houses and farm buildings and cottages must be encouraged in suitable places and on suitable sites. The local fauna and flora must be preserved and protected by suitable bye-laws.

The trees of Lakeland—the oak, ash, beech, sycamore and other hardwood trees—all add to the beauty of the countryside, for the planting is discontinuous and the variety enhances the effect; but the Commissioners must prevent the austere beauty of the hills being murdered by regimented and monotonous conifer plantations. It is also of the highest importance that effective control be exercised over all statutory bodies, subject to the overriding power of Parliament; and that a recognized procedure of appeal shall be set up to investigate and decide all threatened encroachments by departments of government in whatever form they are made.

It is only by the exercise of wise control that the Lake District can be preserved in its natural beauty, the local economy continued, and the area made more fully accessible for open-air recreation and public enjoyment. Practical proposals always sound a little dull, and the details of the working machinery a little uninteresting. But the sustaining and inspiring purpose is the determination that this noble heritage of beauty shall survive to stimulate and give pleasure to future generations of men and women.

*Hawkshead Grammar School*

*Barnard Castle from the River Tees*

# DURHAM

By JOHN CHERRILL

THERE IS, perhaps, no county in England that so graphically shows the speed at which man can scarify the face of Nature as does Durham. A little more than one hundred and fifty years ago, where now stands Gateshead, stood a small cluster of cottages, very little more numerous and not much more imposing than the settlement which stood there two thousand years earlier. And just over a century ago the River Tyne at that point could be forded comfortably at low tide by a man on a horse.

For the Industrial Revolution came to County Durham with a rush, and in a matter of less than a century, altered beyond recognition the face of the land in large areas. It did more in the same time to change the way of life of Durham men and women than had the previous one thousand and five hundred years of recorded history added to unrecorded millennia.

The main effects of the Industrial Revolution in Durham are to be found chiefly in the hinterland behind the coastal plain and along the lower reaches of the three main rivers, the Tyne, the

*Badge of County Durham*

Tees and the Wear. And the reason for both the suddenness of the change and the change itself which the Revolution produced in the county is the fact that Durham possesses three things of first-class importance to the development of industry, namely, harbours, coal and iron. Moreover, the coal and iron are found in abundance in proximity to the harbours.

Durham shares the Tyneside with Northumberland, and Teeside with Yorkshire. Its coastline, about thirty-three miles long, is relatively low-lying, but rocky. There are, however, long stretches of beautiful sand and the caves at Black Hall and the Marsden Rocks themselves are justly celebrated. Since both Tyne and Tees are navigable for some distance, the harbours on this coast extend from Jarrow and South Shields in the Tyne itself through Sunderland, Seaham Harbour and West Hartlepool on the coast to Stockton, some way up the Tees. All of these are fine, deep-water ports adjacent to large coalfields. It is not to be wondered at, therefore, that the bulk of the coastal plain is largely industrialized and bears everywhere the terrible evidence of how man, in pursuit of wealth, has replaced the simple, green beauty of original nature by a sprawling maze of grey and

493

grimy buildings and polluted the air with belching smoke and dust.

Yet for all the distressing ugliness of places like Jarrow, Stockton and the other industrialized towns and the innumerable mining villages spread throughout the eastern part of the county, it is possible to find even there a strange mixture of industry and agriculture. Coal has been searched for and found at widely scattered points. In consequence, slag heaps from the mines, pit-head machinery and even factories dot a landscape that is otherwise agricultural. The casual traveller through Durham will often be surprised suddenly by a pithead shaft rearing its head above the trees in a valley otherwise untouched by man.

The works of man in the county are, fortunately, not all as depressing as those found in such places as Jarrow—there is Durham Cathedral, for instance. In the main, what man has done to destroy God's handiwork is confined to the eastern part. The farther one travels westwards, the higher one climbs, up into the moorlands, until one reaches a maximum height of two thousand four hundred and fifty-two feet above sea level in Burnhope Seat. Here one can survey a scene which, for mile after mile, rolls on over the bleak rugged hills

that we call the Pennines, a scene as unchanged today as it was when first these hills were formed millions of years ago. Here, too, life goes on much as it has done, ever since man first learnt to live in communities. Here you find the shepherd and the farmer, the latter chiefly pastoral but finding exercise for his skill in the growing of crops in the sheltered and fertile valleys of the hill-streams that are tributaries of the main rivers of the county.

For those who like high moorland scenery, England has nothing finer to offer. Upper Teesdale, with its keen, bracing winds, its driving mists, its great folds of rugged hill and sharp valley is every whit as beautiful as anything to be found in the Yorkshire moors. From the charming little town of Middleton in the south of the county, a gateway opens to wonderful walking country. This is no country for weaklings; those who tend to puff on the gentle slopes of the Sussex Downs, will find little comfort in tramping the rough, boulder-strewn, one thousand feet and more climbs in the western territories of County Durham.

What is true of Teesdale is also true of Weardale. The River Wear flows in its upper reaches roughly west to east through

The Durham coastline is low-lying but rocky, and possesses some fine stretches of beautiful sand. The caves at Black Hall and the Marsden Rocks, seen below, are justly celebrated.

the centre of the county. In its lower valley, just before it reaches the coastal plain, is to be found some of the best agricultural land in the county. It is to be hoped that the intelligent afforestation carried on along the banks in its upper reaches for the last few years will be extended.

## Industries of the North

In upper Weardale there are some dour survivals of the past. Here are old, stone-built villages like Westgate and St. John's Chapel; here, too, in the wild moors to the northward, you will find the broken remains of many a long-abandoned lead mine, for lead was once mined extensively in Durham. Most of the mines, however, have long ceased to be economically worth while, and the mining industry is now concentrated in coal and iron. There still exist, however, extensive salt mines, and limestone is a major export from the county.

At Stanhope, also in Weardale, they quarry the famous Frosterly marble, a stone that provides architectural ornamentation for as many buildings in the north of England as does Purbeck marble in the south.

The upper reaches of the Tyne are less wild than, and scarcely as beautiful as, the upper reaches of the Wear and the Tees. It is a larger, slower flowing river with a wider and less tortuous valley. From the hills, above Brampton, where it rises, westward to the sea, its overall fall is far less, and it has nothing to show comparable with the magnificence of the waterfalls of High Force and Cauldron Snout in upper Teesdale. None the less, the tributaries of its lower reaches offer some lovely scenery, for the streams have cut deep valleys in a land that appears to be broad and flat.

The Tyne valley has for centuries provided the main east and west route across the north of England, and today it carries the main Newcastle–Carlisle road and the railway that runs roughly parallel with it.

The principal north–south roads across the county follow the coastal plain. The Great North Road enters the county in the south by the bridge over the Tees at Darlington and leaves it again by the Tyne bridge at Gateshead. For much of its course

it follows "The Street," the famous Roman road that leads from York onwards to the north. Lateral communications in the southern part of the county are furnished chiefly by two roads that lead respectively up the valleys of the Tees and Wear to meet at the town of Alston, in Cumberland.

Despite the spread of industrialization, two-thirds of Durham is given over to farming, most of it to permanent pasture. In the river valleys the soil is generally fertile, and there is to be found most of the arable land. The farther one gets from the rivers the more the fertility of the soil declines until, in the bleak regions of the Pennines, there is nothing but waste moorland that barely suffices to support the hardiest of sheep. Sheep raising is still the staple employment of the farming community though there is some breeding of horses and shorthorn cattle, and nearer to the centres of population, considerable mixed farming and dairying.

Industry, however, and industry in its heaviest form, gives employment to the bulk of the Durham population. There has been a welcome growth of light engineering, but fundamentally, shipbuilding, iron and coal-mining and the manufacture of mining machinery provide the backbone of the county's economic resources. The contribution made to Britain's war effort by the worthies of Durham during six years of toil and sweat was magnificent. The work of these men, both by hand and by brain, did much to keep this country equipped with the sinews of war.

## Years of Depression

This fact is all the more surprising when it is remembered what a load of bitterness these same miners and shipbuilders carried with them, almost up to the outbreak of hostilities. No county in England was worse hit by the depression that began about 1930. Nobody who would understand Durham today can do so unless he understands exactly what those years of depression meant to the industrial areas. Let him read *The Town That Was Murdered* by the late Ellen Wilkinson and see what happened to Jarrow. Let him look at some of the reports, harrowing, heart-breaking documents that

The crowning glory of Durham is its cathedral. It stands on precipitous rock above the River Wear on a site surpassed for magnificence in the whole of Europe only by Lincoln and Ely.

were published from time to time, such as *Employment and the Depressed Areas* by H. Powys Greenwood. This luckless area, unplanned, unlovely, without character, form or civic integration, a sordid product of one of the meanest and most grasping ages in all history, nevertheless supported a population on whose labours a large part of the wealth of England had been founded. To it, in the 1930's came unparalleled economic catastrophe.

It is not my task here to describe in detail this awful disaster of recent history, but it has so seared the life of Durham that it cannot be altogether omitted. I must, therefore, give three instances of what the depression meant to this area.

"Witton Park and Woodside. Total population two thousand six hundred. Six hundred and seventy persons, or practically every soul available for work, is on the live register, and nearly half of them drawing neither Unemployment Benefit nor Transitional Payments" (*i.e.*, having outrun qualification for them by reason of long unemployment).

"Leesingthorn. Population six hundred odd. Annual cost of Transitional payments and Public Assistance nearly £10,000, ninety-eight per cent of those on the live register having ceased to be eligible for Unemployment Insurance pay."

"Butterknowle. Thirty-two per cent of the many unemployed have been out of work for more than five years."

These three villages were not special, they were typical of what was happening throughout the whole of Durham's industrial area during that time, and in remembering this story of appalling misfortune it is cause for wonder that ever again the Durham man was capable of honest work, or able to forget his bitterness.

After the end of the war Britain faced a more crying need for coal and ships and iron than she had ever done before. Durham was scheduled as a redevelopment area, and it is to be hoped that never again will

the county's industrial population face such economic distress as in the hungry '30s.

Although towns such as Gateshead, Sunderland and Stockton are far larger in area and population, the real heart of the county is to be found in the city from which it takes its name.

Durham stands on a loop in the River Wear at the top of a sharp escarpment. It is a proud and ancient city, presenting queer contrasts. Across the river, from the main part of the town, lie squalid, mean streets

496

and houses, in astonishing contrast to the august, almost smug respectability of that part of the city surrounding the castle and the cathedral. The quiet, Georgian squares around the cathedral have an old-world, smooth placidity straight out of the pages of a Trollope novel. Dominating the city is the cathedral, on a site surpassed for magnificence in the whole of Europe only by Lincoln and Ely. From its foot the tree-clad slope falls sheer to the Wear below. "Half Church of God, half castle 'gainst the Scot"

was how Sir Walter Scott described it, and it is true.

There is a massiveness in the beauty of its exterior viewed from any angle, and its interior shows us the finest Norman nave in the world, vast, yet in perfect proportion. The beautiful leaf tracery in the west window dates from 1346; the rose window at the eastern end, designed by Wyatt in the eighteenth century, is also very beautiful. The foundations go back to 1093, though the noble central tower was only completed in 1470, replacing an earlier tower that was destroyed by lightning.

The cathedral and with it the city owe their being, it is said, to the legend that surrounds St. Cuthbert. He was Bishop of Lindisfarne in the year 687 when he died, and his monks carried his body westward to escape the Norse pirates who were harrying the coast from year to year. One day they came to rest in the little hamlet of Dunholme where his bier became "as firmly fixed as if it were a mountain." Round the site they built an early church and from that early church sprang the magnificent cathedral we see today and the city that surrounds it.

### Thanksgiving Ceremonies

On the top of Magdalen Tower, Oxford, songs are sung to welcome in May mornings. Durham Cathedral is the only other place in Britain where such ceremonies are performed. Twice a year the choir ascends to the top of the tower and sings in commemoration of two events, both significant in British history. The first, on the 7th of May, recalls the battle of Neville's Cross in 1346, an event which was actually witnessed from that very tower. In that year the fearful monks stood gazing at the clash of a battle scarcely a mile away and burst into thanksgiving when they learnt that the Scots had been driven back and their king David taken prisoner. The second, on the 29th of May, is a thanksgiving for the restoration in 1660 of King Charles II to the Stuart throne.

Besides the cathedral, Durham has its famous castle, first built about 1072, by William the Conqueror to maintain his hold on the turbulent north, after he had put down the Northern Revolt. The original castle was practically rebuilt between 1153 and 1195 by Bishop Pudsey, and probably all that is left of the earlier building is the Crypt chapel. Today the castle buildings house the University of Durham. The two buildings, the castle and the cathedral, set each other off extremely well. They symbolize a combination of secular and ecclesiastical power, and in doing so remind us of the time when the city was the centre of the county palatine and a long line of warlike and able bishops of the church wielded almost regal powers. These exceptional powers were not, in fact, abolished until 1836.

No reference to Durham city, however short, can omit mention of the justly celebrated bridges over the river. Each spans the deep valley of the Wear. The oldest, Framwellgate, was first completed as early as 1100 and carried the postern gate of the castle, though this was demolished when the bridge was rebuilt at the end of the fourteenth century. The next oldest is Elvet Bridge, first built about 1230; here, too, was once a gate or turret guarding the approach to the castle. The bridge has several times been restored or enlarged. The third, Prebends Bridge, gives access to the cathedral from the west. It is a much later bridge, having been completed in 1777, but is possibly the finest of them all.

Durham is the complete cathedral and university city, and the life of its people is centred very largely in the affairs of one or the other. It maintains no industries, yet it stands in the centre of the county's industrial area, and within a radius of twenty miles of the cathedral are almost countless collieries. To the east, the land slopes down steadily to the coastal plain; to the north, the River Wear runs a tortuous course through a deep valley to enter the sea by Sunderland. This north-east corner of the county is one of the most forbidding areas in England. Three of the largest towns are Gateshead, South Shields and Sunderland with Jarrow, Hebburn and other linking points, such as Boldon, forming a practically continuous sprawl of factories, mines and dwellings.

### Home of Bede

In the middle of the noise and grime and smoke that is the essence of modern Jarrow one can find St. Paul's Church, built on the foundations of the original Benedictine monastery that dates back to A.D. 681. In this monastery, by the side of the sluggish Tyne, amid pastoral surroundings, the Venerable Bede spent most of his quiet life, and there he completed his translation into the Anglo-Saxon tongue of St. John's Gospel. One cannot imagine what his reactions

# NORTHUMBERLAND &
# DURHAM

RIANS WALL

BERWICK-ON-TWEED

NORHAM

R. TWEED

Holy I.

Farne Is.

BAMBURGH CASTLE

Norham Castle

R. TILL

BAMBURGH

FLODDEN
Battle 1513

CASTLE,
THE KEEP

WOOLER

CHILLINGHAM

THE CHEVIOT

PASSENGER COACH
STOCKTON – DARLINGTON
1826 RLY.

THE CHEVIOT HILLS

ALNWICK

Alnwick Castle

WARKWORTH

Coquet I.

Rothbury

ROTHBURY

FOREST

R. COQUET

CARTER FELL

OLD BRIDGE,
DURHAM

GIRDLE
FELL

R. REDE

ROTHBURY

ASHINGTON

EEL
FELL

OTTERBURN

Warkworth Castle

MORPETH

BLYTH

R. WANSBECK

BEDLINGTON

S
E
A

R. NORTH TYNE

BELLINGHAM

Shipbuilding

SEATON DELAVAL

WHITLEY BAY

DEVIL'S

CAUSEWAY

NTH. SHIELDS

TYNEMOUTH

Saxon Bishop's Chair,
Hexham

WALL

WALLSEND

STH. SHIELDS

NEWCASTLE

JARROW

HOUSESTEADS

CORBRIDGE

R. TYNE

HADRIANS

R. SOUTH TYNE

HEXHAM

Corbridge

BLAYDON

GATESHEAD

SUNDERLAND

HALTWHISTLE

STANLEY

HOUGHTON
LE SPRING

SEAHAM
HARBOUR

PIKE
RIGG

ALLENDALE

CONSETT

CHESTER
LE STREET

R. DERWENT

DURHAM

SHOTTON

STANHOPE

HARTLEPOOL

R. WEAR

SPENNYMOOR

TRIMDON

WEST
HARTLEPOOL

WOLSINGHAM

SEDGEFIELD

BILLINGHAM

Barnard Castle

BISHOP
AUCKLAND

MIDDLETON
IN TEESDALE

STOCKTON-ON-TEES

N

BARNARD
CASTLE

R. TEES

DARLINGTON

E

## Miles

0   5   10

S

YORKSHIRE

A corner of the harbour at Sunderland. The harbour and docks together occupy over two hundred acres and can accommodate all but the largest of vessels. Shipbuilding is a considerable industry.

would be were he able to re-visit his home today. In such industrial squalor it is astonishing to discover that parts of South Shields are really delightful; the town's parks are rightly famous, and the sands are comparable with any in the kingdom. Yet despite enchanting names most of the villages inland and along the coast are horrible products of a sordidly commercial age; Boldon, Silksworth, Easington, are typical of mining villages throughout the county. Even Chester-le-Street, once a famous Roman military station and an historical town, is now just a city of coal and iron. So, too, is Consett, away to the west, though within a mile or so of Consett, the well-wooded, steep valley of the River Derwent offers delightful scenery.

It is a change indeed to find in Bishop Auckland, south of Durham, a market town. Here is Auckland Castle standing in a great park and for centuries the palace of the mighty bishops of Durham. South and east of Bishop Auckland the industrial areas lead on to Hartlepool, Stockton and Darlington. Stockton, with its shipbuilding, its blast furnaces and its ironworks is today

a sheer product of the Industrial Revolution, though it was once a pleasant enough place. Darlington, though it, too, has its woollen mills, its engineering shops and its vast railway workshops, still breathes, in parts, the air of a market town, which, indeed, it still is.

Stockton and Darlington can claim to be the most celebrated towns of the Machine Age. To connect them was built, between 1822 and 1825, the very first passenger carrying railway in the world. The project was made possible largely through the energy and initiative of the great engineer, George Stephenson, who was born in 1781 at Wylam, just over the Tyne from Durham. It was he who built and designed the famous engine "Locomotion No. 1" which hauled the very first train on the opening day, September 27, 1825. Passengers at Darlington station may still see the "Locomotion" on the platform.

Just north of Stockton is Billingham, once a pretty village, but now a cluster of dingy houses crouching under the towering walls of huge factories where the innumerable chimneys spew forth clouds of smoke large enough and continuous enough to keep the whole area in a grimy half-light even on the brightest day.

It is a relief to turn one's back on all this wealth of industry and to travel westwards up the valley of the Tees which, in its higher reaches, is as beautiful as in its lower reaches it is sordid. Here, in the midst of delightful scenery, is the picturesque, old agricultural market town of Barnard Castle, dominated still by the Norman castle which was built by Bernard Baliol (an ancestor of John Baliol) between 1112 and 1132. From the top of the circular Norman keep built eighty feet above the river wide-flung and lovely views over the surrounding countryside are to be had. The old town, sheltering below, still keeps its ancient gates, Gallgate, Bridegate, Thorngate and Broadgates. The last also gives its name to a mysterious stone house, the oldest building in the town and dating, in parts, from the time of Richard II. Here Cromwell stayed the night after his victory at Marston Moor in 1644.

Today the town's associations are more literary and artistic. In the Bowes Museum, a florid, but magnificent building and an almost exact copy of the Tuileries, is to be found a collection of works of art unrivalled in England outside the London galleries. At the King's Head, Dickens and his collaborator "Phiz" stayed in 1838 and subsequently immortalized the inn and the town in the books *Nicholas Nickleby* and *Master Humphrey's Clock*. Scott, too, chose Barnard Castle as the setting for his *Rokeby*.

### Story of Raby Castle

North-east of Barnard Castle, just off the main road to Bishop Auckland lies Raby Castle in its vast park. Whether it is thought of as the traditional home of King Canute, as the great fortress of the proud house of Neville or as the princely residence of the Vane family, it remains one of the showplaces of England. A Saxon manor probably stood on the site, for it is mentioned in a deed of gift of King Canute to St. Cuthbert, dated 1030. Most of the castle as we know it today was built by the Nevilles, chiefly by Ralph, hero of the battle of Neville's Cross, and his son John between 1331 and 1389. Here was born Cicely, the

"Rose of Raby" wife of Richard of York and mother of Edward IV and Richard III. Here was planned the conspiracy that led to the Rising of the North in 1569, a rising that resulted in the exile of the Nevilles and the destruction of Barnard Castle.

Unlucky restorations have done something to destroy the original perfection of the main castle buildings, but the great Neville's gateway and the nine towers of the original structure, some dating from the eleventh century, still stand.

### History of Durham

The great castles of Durham are both numerous and famous. The chief of them, apart from Raby, are Brancepeth, another home of the Nevilles, Lambton, Lumley and Streatlam. All bear witness to the grim and bloody history of the county in the Middle Ages. Durham was border-land and a happy hunting-ground for Scottish raiders. It was, too, far remote from London and the south, and the great baronial families, following the principles practised by the Palatinate's Bishops, maintained viceregal state and for centuries were impatient of any interference with their power.

Luckily, those distant, warlike years have yielded to more peaceful times. If the prosperity of the county has been founded on coal and iron, and if in the making of his wealth man has destroyed much of the gaunt, bleak beauty of the original land, none the less, order has been brought where no order existed and the county has been opened up by modern means of communications.

The great bulk of the county's population is crowded into the industrial centres, but elsewhere is to be found today the typical, short, tough, sturdy Durham man who, like his forebears through generation after generation, wins a livelihood from the bleak limestone and granite hills. He speaks the Geordie tongue of the Tyneside, but he is in every way a great worker and a great adventurer. Toronto, Philadelphia and Washington are the names of cities famous throughout the world. They were founded in the United States and in Canada partly by Durham men, for all three are the names of Durham villages that were old at the time when the sites of their North American counterparts were unclaimed wilderness.

Washington itself, now a mining village, was originally known as Wessington, and the manor there was purchased by a certain William de Hertburn in 1180. His heirs naturally assumed the name of the estate, a name which gradually became corrupted into Washington. A branch of the family later moved to north Lancashire, and it was a certain Lawrence Washington of this branch who acquired Sulgrave Manor whence John Washington, the great-grand-father of the famous George Washington, emigrated to America in 1656.

The Washingtons might be taken as a symbol and a sample of Durham men, who have provided engineers, scientists, adventurers, administrators, many of whom have left a prominent mark on history. It is little known, for example, that William Would-have and Henry Greathead, the inventors of the lifeboat, were two natives of South Shields, though it might have been expected, in view of the fact that so much blood of Norse sea-rovers runs in Durham veins, and of the challenge offered to skill and inventiveness by the North Sea storms that beat upon the sandy coast. George Stephenson I have already mentioned, but I have no space in which even to catalogue the names of men whose work in spinning, in the chemical industry, in shipbuilding and in iron and coal-mining have initiated and then changed the basic principles of our industrial life.

I cannot forbear to mention, however, John Lambton, first Earl of Durham who died in 1840. The Lambtons of Lambton castle are an ancient family with uninterrupted possession of estates in the county going back to the twelfth century. John Lambton, a great Whig and a great reformer, was Governor-General of Canada in 1838 following the French Rebellion and his "Report on the Affairs of British North America" is still regarded as one of our greatest State papers and has been a guiding principle of British Colonial policy from that time onwards.

Durham is two counties, indissolubly mixed, but utterly different. The first is found in the solid materialism that lies beneath the smoke and grime of the Lower Teeside and Tyneside and the mining villages. I prefer to turn my back on it all and climb to that other Durham high up in the bleak moorlands or along the exquisite tree-clad ravine-like valleys, of the Lune Forest and the headstreams of the county's main rivers, a land where the noise of the riveter's hammer and the blast furnaces gives way to the scream of a hawk above the heather or the tinkling roar of a mountain torrent. This last is the real Durham as, dedicated to its service, is the real Durham man.

*High Force, Teesdale*

*Roman wall at Housesteads*

# NORTHUMBERLAND

## By ARTHUR BLENKINSOP

SEE Northumberland as the lion head of England—the lion itself stands erect on the ridge over the River Aln by the side of the great Percy Castle of Alnwick. This was the wild head of England, the border-land of ballad and story. And still it is buffeted. North and west lies Scotland, and the winds and rains drive unchecked over the bare border hills and the heather and bracken moors. Eastwards Northumberland lies open to the sea with gentle breezes in the summer, but biting rain-soaked storms in winter. But this savage head has a tamed throat in the Tyne, the main valley of the county. The valley is bounded to the west by high, open moorland, but travelling east towards the sea the valley widens through green fields and fruit trees at Hexham to the shipyards and factories of Newcastle and the river mouth.

This is the land where life was insecure and hard—the land of war and feud—until the union of the thrones of England and Scotland in 1603 brought the hope of peace, and the peel towers and castles

*Badge of Northumberland*

throughout the land began to fall into disuse.

In the days before the union the King's power in this border-land lay in the hands of the Wardens of the Marches and their Keepers. A wild and lawless country they had to cover. Their task was both to help defend the country against the attacks of the Scots and also to deal as fairly as might be with the murder and thieving that made passage through the country dangerous. In Redesdale and North Tynedale robbery was the only regular trade that could maintain the population on such barren land, and often enough, in the near-by parts of the county, common cause was made with the Scots of Liddesdale against the English, who were expected to keep guard night and day on the main tracks out of the Rede and North Tyne valleys. The Keeper of the Rede had his stronghold at Harbottle Castle, probably regarding the six miles from the Rede as being short distance enough after the brutal betrayal and murder of a former Keeper—Percy

503

Reed—who was brave enough to live in the Rede Valley itself. Two hundred years after the union the memory of this record was sufficiently clear to make it difficult for anyone coming from these valleys to be accepted into apprenticeship in Newcastle.

If these men of Redesdale and Tynedale had merely been murderers and thieves they would hardly have been remembered today; but they were also poets, and their ballads, handed down by word of mouth from generation to generation, have a haunting melancholy.

Many a ballad tells the story of the forays back and forward across the Scottish border that left no man's family or cattle secure.

They spairit neither man nor wife
Young or old of mankind that bore life
Like wilde wolfes in furiositie
Baith brint and slewe with greate crueltie.

One ballad tells of the raids into Northumberland, of Wat Armstrong and the outlaws from Liddesdale across the Border.

'Twas some time gane they took our naigs
And left us eke an empty byre,

I wad the deil had had their craigs,
And a' things in a bleize o' fire.

Wild and lawless, too, the condition of this county must have been when the Romans built their great barrier from east to west, though in still earlier times life was perhaps more settled, for the rounded-earth Mote Hills, near Elsdon, tell of the meetings and law-making of early Celtic peoples.

This frontier-land has changed very little in its outward appearance. The great arc of the border between Scotland and Northumberland from east to west lies for a short distance from Berwick and the coast along the wooded beauty of the Tweed, though even here the memories of old battles are strong—Flodden Field lies close by and there were many dead bodies swept down by the Tweed and the more gloomy Till—

Tweed says to Till
"What gars ye rin sae still?"
Till says to Tweed
"Though ye rin wi' speed
And I rin slaw
Whar ye droon ae man,
I droon twa!"

The village of Cambo, some twelve miles south-west of Rothbury. Nearby is the stately mansion of Wallington Hall, home of the Trevelyans, which was bequeathed to the nation in 1941.

Looking along Dere Street, the old Roman Road that runs north from Corbridge through Redesdale to the Tweed Valley. Redesdale itself forms one of the main routes between England and Scotland.

But soon the border-line crosses the Cheviot Hills and Bloodybush Edge, Windy Ghyl and Hanging Stones are around us. This Cheviot country, though lonely, with only an occasional sheep farm in the valleys, is not all desolation. The hills are rounded and grassy with a rare break of rock. Springy "green rides" circle round the shoulders of the hills with wide views of ever-receding hills, though in rain the curtain descends and the walker, staggering off the tracks, finds himself waist-high in wet bracken or sinking in bog without landmarks to guide him.

The border country flattens out to the west into the waves of an endless open sea of heather and bracken, wide-open country of unchecked solitude, with the curlew's plaint for company and the occasional whirr of grouse. These great heather moors sweep right across the upper reaches of the North Tyne, across the line of the Roman Wall and south, leaving the Scottish border and joining the boundary of Northumberland with Cumberland and Durham.

The whole of this belt of north and west Northumberland has been little changed through the centuries—it has not been desecrated either by the jerry-builder or by the spread of industry. But it has not been altogether left alone. The Air Ministry built steel towers on the moorland overlooking the village of Otterburn and the Rede Valley from the south, while to the north, sprawling over the site of that chivalrous bout between Douglas and Percy—the Battle of Otterburn—over Roman and ancient British remains and right across to the Coquet valley are War Office ranges which scar the moors with white roads.

The isolated farms are strong, stone-built—built to survive hard winters, set up within a protecting belt of wind-twisted trees. They are large sheep farms with cattle enough for their own use. Most of the buildings up in this country are of stone, though there are a few brick bungalows in the villages.

The sense of isolation has not been much affected by modern communications: the main roads and railways, one to the north and one to the west from Newcastle, roughly mark out the confines of the county, as a pair of dividers; one main

505

road alone cuts through the centre of the moorland to win its way across to Scotland. True, a branch single-track railway runs across from east to west, and the silence of the moors above Redesdale is broken twice a day by the noise of the engine's exhausting climb, a noise which scatters the moorland sheep from their feeding and sounds incongruous in such remote surroundings.

Although many Scots farmers have come over the border to settle in the Cheviot country, Charltons and Fenwicks, Armstrongs and Croziers, Halls and Robsons, still live around the Redesdale and Tynedale valleys as in the days of the ballads, but their farms give a kinder welcome today to the stranger; while their children go to the nearest village school by bus and often enough they follow through to the university, coming back with new ideas on farming and forestry.

### The Roman Wall

One west road out of Newcastle over to Cumberland keeps up in the hills to the north of the main Tyne valley, and follows the line of the Roman Wall itself. For many miles it is probably built upon the site of the Wall and for many more the Wall lies immediately to the side of the road. After crossing the North Tyne at Chollerford the road climbs steeply out of the sheltered wooded valley, with the Roman camp in the fields near the river, and on to the open moor. Ahead to the west lies for some miles the finest stretch of the Wall in a setting which has remained unchanged through the years. The Romans used every natural feature to give added strength to their barrier, and so the Wall sweeps along the crest of the wave of hillside gently sloping down to the road, but breaking in sharp rock to the north with lake and marsh at the foot. Standing on the Wall here with the Housesteads Camp close by you look out across the wild open moor with faithless tracks through the reeds and bracken. Those very bogs were often a sanctuary for the raiders who relied on their knowledge of the tracks to get away to safety. When, as often, the rain is blown across the wastes, strong in the face, the Roman legions—mixed contingents of men

recruited from all corners of Europe—seem very near.

The old man who used to act as guide at Housesteads Camp had about the broadest Northumbrian dialect I ever heard—the characteristic burr was very prominent. The dialect spoken in these hills and moor is much richer than its town cousin—Tyneside—which, like most town dialects, is harsh by comparison. There are said to be many links between Northumbrian dialect and the Scandinavian languages, and certainly the vowel sounds seem to be similar.

South and east of the wild hill and moor land border that forms a watershed in which the Northumbrian rivers find their source, the land flattens slowly towards the coastal plain. Here there is rich farm land with strongly built prosperous farms, small townships in size. Ploughed land alternates with meadow; the rivers wind through woodland and private parks with church and village marking the hillcrests. It is pleasant country.

Morpeth, Hexham and Alnwick are old stone-built market towns, but with all their present bustle they still have something left of the days when they were within reach of a border raid aimed at setting free a prisoner in the local jail or paying off a score for a hanging. Alnwick, the county town, dominated by the great castle of the Percys, is a symbol of the old power of the Dukes of Northumberland. Hexham twenty miles west of Newcastle, in the Tyne valley, and Morpeth, some fifteen miles north of Newcastle, are both market towns, but there the resemblance ends. Hexham, with its abbey, has something of the sleepy atmosphere of the cathedral town, added to the shopping centre for the shire. Morpeth stands more clearly on a commercial main road; there is no abbey and surround to provide an oasis of quiet in the noise of its main street. Though Morpeth is outside the Northumberland coalfield, the mines are not far away, and this is the miners' town as much as the farmers'. Above all, it is the centre for the Northumberland miners' annual gala in the summer when the streets are filled with the bands and processions from the Lodges.

View of Newcastle-upon-Tyne from Gateshead. The handsome Tyne Bridge, with its span of 531 feet, was opened by King George V in 1928. The older swing bridge is seen in the foreground.

The band contest is held in the morning after the teams have arrived from all the colliery villages, then, after the sandwiches, eaten by the side of the river, the banners form up and the procession moves across to the meeting-fields, where the platforms are set up and a good-humoured holiday-making crowd of miners and their families listen to their local and national speakers.

The coalfields are concentrated, with few exceptions, into a small pocket in the south-east of Northumberland, towards the coast and near Newcastle. Here the pit-heap and shaft stand out against the farm-land around. The single colliery row of stone-built cottages backing on to the pit-heap runs into the main street of shops. Farther along the road, new red-brick houses have been built by the council.

Life in these villages and small towns—the social life, the concerts and dances, and the leek shows, as well as administration—revolves round the pit and the miners' lodge. The miner's house welcomes all visitors—and there is no welcome like it, as many a south-country soldier stationed in a mining village during the war will tell. Year after year, these miners race their whippets, and set off their pigeons. Their football teams are watched by the talent

scouts from the big clubs of Tyneside and farther south: but there are also serious minds who will sit round the club-room discussing philosophy or international affairs.

The mines in this corner of the county come close to the coast, but even along this short stretch and through the popular sea-side resorts by the mouth of the Tyne, the Northumberland coastline has kept its natural beauties of cliff and great stretches of firm sand. Along this shore the old castles of Bamburgh, Dunstanburgh and Wark-worth still stand sentinel, reminding us of the grim past.

The seaside resorts, only a few minutes by electric train from Newcastle, are residential suburbs as well as holiday centres. In the summer the trains are packed with fathers and mothers with their children and their spades and pails. The boarding-houses are full throughout the school holidays, and year after year the same families come down. Some choose "the more select end" of the sands and leave for others the fun fairs and cinemas and shops and wide promenades. Though these beaches are the most popular, many a Tyneside family spends its summer holiday farther north at one of the many beautiful old fishing villages by the coast. Seahouses, twenty miles

507

Hexham stands on the Tyne, above Newcastle. Famous as the scene of the Yorkist victory over the Lancastrians in 1464, it is today an important link in the communications of the Tyne valley.

south of Berwick, has become a favourite spot for the week-ending business man, and modern bungalows line the dunes. Out to sea lie the Farnes, a collection of small rocky islands which form a famous preserve for sea birds that nest there in such crowds on every ledge that it would seem impossible for them to take wing. Seals bask on the rocks, and innumerable sea birds scream and fight over every worthwhile morsel on the sea's surface.

An old car has taken the place of the trap that used to take visitors across the sands at low tide to Holy Island a little farther north. This island boasts a small golf course—of more modern significance perhaps to the Newcastle business man than the ruins of the old priory which was St. Aidan's home when he set out to convert Northumbria to Christianity in 635. A short walk along the sands leads to Ida's Castle of Bamburgh which "from its tall rock looks grimly down," while a little to the south lie the ruins of Dunstanburgh and Warkworth Castles—Warkworth, described as the home of Harry Hotspur in Shakespeare's *King Henry IV*.

The throat of this lion head of Northumberland lies in Newcastle and the neighbouring Tyneside towns. Shipyards and factories line the river banks, but some breath of the old border air blows from the great open space of the Town Moor down the North Road and into the city itself. From the south there is no wind from open moor; the smoke rises from the factory chimneys; but there the river is crossed by five high- and low-level bridges from the Durham side. Tumbling up the river bank lies old Newcastle—castle, keep and cathedral—while a few of the old merchants' houses are on the river front wedged in amongst tall dark office blocks.

The town soon developed beyond the old walls, now lost amongst warehouses and the back entrances of modern stores, and the old gates merely serve to name the main streets.

The export of coal from this river was already well established by 1300, and there are many old staiths or landing stages along the banks. A number of old cottages of the early workers still remains, though submerged today in the narrow, mean streets

508

that a later industrial age brought together with factories and new shipyards to the town, streets lively or despondent as trade flourished or declined.

The depression and poverty of the years before the Second World War had a deep effect upon the people of Tyneside. "Canny" has always been the most common non-commital answer of the Tynesider to any inquiry. It is typical of his caution and lack of exuberance born of long hardship. It has cloaked a wiry, independent spirit that refuses to accept face values. His bitter experience of the mass unemployment in the inter-war years, turned his caution into deep and bitter cynicism.

The shopping streets of Newcastle—for this is both the administrative and commercial centre of the north—are full of the workers from shipyard, factory and mine. In the great crowd surging out of St. James's Park football ground after the Saturday match, the cloth cap and the miner are supreme.

And, whatever changes may come from the new industries now being established on Tyneside, however the features of Newcastle may change with all the new develop-

ments that are planned, this will remain the miners' city. "Weel may the keel row" and "Keep yor feet still, Geordie hinney" will forever compete with "Blaydon Races" as the local anthem.

The face of Northumberland has changed very little in the past hundred years and is unlikely to change much in the next; while the industrial pocket will strive vigorously by new developments to build up its prosperity and prevent the recurrence of slump and despair, the border country, outwardly at least, will not change. With the necessary restraints of wartime now removed more and more young people will learn to appreciate the joys of the open moor and hillside and will understand Professor Trevelyan (whose brother lives in the stately Wallington Hall, near Cambo) when he writes "In Northumberland alone both heaven and earth are seen; we walk all day on long ridges high enough to give far views of moor and valley, and the sense of solitude above the world below, yet so far distant from each other and of such equal height, that we can watch the low skirling clouds as they 'port o'er land and ocean without rest.'"

*Warkworth Castle*

509

# INDEX TO PLACE NAMES

*Figures in italics refer to illustrations*

# INDEX

511

# INDEX